CONFLICT IN MODERN JAPANESE HISTORY

THIS BOOK IS BASED ON A CONFERENCE SPONSORED BY THE JOINT COMMITTEE ON JAPANESE STUDIES OF THE AMERICAN COUNCIL OF LEARNED SOCIETIES AND THE SOCIAL SCIENCE RESEARCH COUNCIL.

CONFLICT IN MODERN JAPANESE HISTORY

THE NEGLECTED TRADITION

Edited by
TETSUO NAJITA *and*
J. VICTOR KOSCHMANN

PRINCETON UNIVERSITY PRESS

CONTRIBUTORS

James R. Bartholomew	The Ohio State University
Peter Duus	Stanford University
Harry Harootunian	University of Chicago
Hashimoto Mitsuru	Kōnan Women's College, Kobe
Thomas M. Huber	Duke University
J. Victor Koschmann	Cornell University
Byron K. Marshall	University of Minnesota
Tetsuo Najita	University of Chicago
Ron Napier	Data Resources, Inc., Lexington, Mass.
Oka Yoshitake	University of Tokyo, Emeritus
Shumpei Okamoto	Temple University
Bernard S. Silberman	University of Chicago
M. William Steele	International Christian University, Tokyo
Conrad Totman	Northwestern University
Stephen Vlastos	University of Iowa
Ann Waswo	Nissan Institute of Japanese Studies, Oxford
George Wilson	Indiana University

CONTENTS

PREFACE   ix

Introduction: A Synchronous Approach to the Study of Conflict in
Modern Japanese History
BY TETSUO NAJITA   3

PART I

Ideology as Conflict
BY HARRY HAROOTUNIAN   25
From Reformism to Transformism: Bakufu Policy, 1853–1868
BY CONRAD TOTMAN   62
Action as a Text: Ideology in the Tengu Insurrection
BY J. VICTOR KOSCHMANN   81
"Men of High Purpose" and the Politics of Direct Action, 1862–1864
BY THOMAS M. HUBER   107
The Rise and Fall of the Shōgitai: A Social Drama
BY M. WILLIAM STEELE   128
The Social Background of Peasant Uprisings in Tokugawa Japan
BY HASHIMOTO MITSURU   145
Yonaoshi in Aizu
BY STEPHEN VLASTOS   164
Pursuing the Millennium in the Meiji Restoration
BY GEORGE WILSON   176

PART II

Generational Conflict after the Russo-Japanese War
BY OKA YOSHITAKE   197
The Bureaucratic State in Japan: The Problem of Authority and
Legitimacy
BY BERNARD S. SILBERMAN   226
The Emperor and the Crowd: The Historical Significance of the Hibiya
Riot
BY SHUMPEI OKAMOTO   258
Growth and Conflict in Japanese Higher Education, 1905–1930
BY BYRON K. MARSHALL   276
Science, Bureaucracy, and Freedom in Meiji and Taishō Japan
BY JAMES R. BARTHOLOMEW   295
The Transformation of the Japanese Labor Market, 1894–1937
BY RON NAPIER   342
In Search of Equity: Japanese Tenant Unions in the 1920s
BY ANN WASWO   366

viii   CONTENTS

Liberal Intellectuals and Social Conflict in Taishō Japan
    BY PETER DUUS   412
Epilogue: Parts and Wholes
    BY J. VICTOR KOSCHMANN   441

INDEX   449

PREFACE

Conflictual events in modern Japan are familiar enough to historians. Peasant rebellions, insurrections, assassinations, suicide, urban riots, strikes, student uprisings, coups, and so on punctuate the historical landscape, and it is impossible to avoid them. Yet it is also true that we have not found effective ways to discover in them broad interpretive significance, and in this sense they remain strangely unfamiliar. They appear as aberrations in an otherwise orderly flow of events, rather than as somehow essential to the historical experience under view. Indeed, the difficulty has been in the lenses we use to view history. We have been accustomed to viewing human time as a consensual flow or movement, regulated by certain stylized relationships such as loyalty to the group or superiors in Japan, and moving along in a mainstream or on a central track. Although the metaphors vary, the basic idea is the same. History proceeds in a causal or purposeful sequence. Those parts that do not conform easily to that central flow are put aside as insignificant, as peripheral, or as evidence of ineffectualness.

While not denying the importance of consensuality in the history of any society, the authors in this volume have presented exercises that emphasize the obverse of consensus, which is dissent, secession, and conflict. The approaches taken only begin to scratch the surface of a complex and rich dimension of modern Japanese history. Also, the overall framework advanced, that conflicts in this history are clustered around discontinuous and synchronic systems of events, is provisional at best and will, no doubt, require additional discussion and refinement. It is our feeling, however, that in organizing the volume as we have, around an often neglected subject and with a specific framework in mind, we will have added new ways of comprehending the history of modern Japan.

Fully convinced that the subject matter could not be dealt with at a single conference, we carried out discussions at small preliminary workshops beginning in 1976 and 1977 in New York and Chicago under the auspices of the Joint Committee on Japanese Studies of the Social Science Research Council and the American Council of Learned Societies. Papers were circulated in advance and then discussed at great length at a conference held at Pajaro Dunes in Monterey, California, between July 9 and 14, 1978. Ronald Aqua contributed enormously to the arrangement and execution of this conference at Pajaro Dunes. We were also joined at various stages of the planning and discussion by Susan Hanley, William Hauser, Fred Notehelfer, Kenneth Pyle, and Irwin Scheiner.

In the editing of the revised manuscripts, the editors received generous assistance from Anne Walthall, Althea Nagai, and Dori Shoji.

We are especially indebted to Professor Oka Yoshitake, now Professor Emeritus of the Faculty of Law of Tokyo University, for consenting to have his essay translated for this volume. Presented at one of his last seminars at Tokyo University in 1963, the essay has stood the test of time as one of the most suggestive introductions to the problems of individuality (*kosei*) in early twentieth-century Japan.

TETSUO NAJITA
J. VICTOR KOSCHMANN

CONFLICT IN MODERN JAPANESE HISTORY

INTRODUCTION: A SYNCHRONOUS APPROACH TO THE STUDY OF CONFLICT IN MODERN JAPANESE HISTORY

Tetsuo Najita

Sometimes labeled an optimistic science, history, not unlike economics, can also be seen as a dismal one. These contrasting images of our craft were captured by Lévi-Strauss in two essays dealing with widely differing matters. Unlike some other sciences of society that were still in a state of confusion, he argued in one of these essays, history had carefully "resolved" the problems of principle and method by remaining faithful to its original modest, documentary, and functional methodology. Lévi-Strauss further noted that this modest approach could not always be used by anthropologists because of the very nature of their data, and so they adopted the "synchronic" mode of analysis, studying relationships between constituent elements without regard to previous evolution. He nonetheless agreed with Boas that much could be learned from the historical method, for in the end, "everything is history."[1]

Elsewhere, engaged in a polemic with Sartre, Lévi-Strauss presented a far less sanguine view of history. Historians had not always remained faithful to the modest aims of their craft and had claimed, dogmatically and ultimately dismally, a privileged place among the human sciences for their discipline. They claimed succession in time to be intellectually superior to distribution in space, "as if diachrony were to establish a kind of intelligibility not merely superior to synchrony, but above all

[1] Claude Lévi-Strauss, "Introduction: History and Anthropology," *Structural Anthropology* (New York: Basic Books, 1963), pp. 1-27.

more specifically human."[2] Refusing to admit that history is always partial and biased, historians had failed to see that through the use of abstract schema history has in fact been made to function as myth. As they reduced a wide variety of experiences according to such normative schemes, historians had simultaneously excluded an equally wide variety of others as being "abnormal," thus suppressing, as Florian Znaniecki effectively put it, "all the social energies which seem to act in a way contrary to the demands of the norm, and to ignore all the social energies not included in the sphere embraced by the norm."[3]

How this approach has affected the treatment of conflict in the modernization of Japan will become evident as this essay proceeds. The main theoretical point to be emphasized here is that in their claim to objectivity vis-à-vis factual materials, historians have tended to resist a basic truth about the discontinuous and ultimately chaotic character of the historical reality they confront. "When one proposes to write a history of the French Revolution," to cite Lévi-Strauss again, "one knows . . . that it cannot, simultaneously and under the same heading, be that of the Jacobin and that of the aristocrat . . . their respective totalizations . . . are equally true." And all these totalizations lead, logically, to chaos:

> Every corner of space conceals a multitude of individuals each of whom totalizes the trend of history in a manner which cannot be compared to the others; for any one of the individuals, each moment of time is inexhaustibly rich in physical and psychical incidents which all play their part in his totalization. Even history which claims to be universal is still only a juxtaposition of a few local histories within which (and between which) very much more is left out than put in. And it would be vain to hope that by increasing the number of collaborators and making research more intensive one would obtain a better result. Insofar as history aspires to meaning, it is doomed to select regions, periods, groups of men and individuals in these groups and to make them stand out, as discontinuous figures, against a continuity barely good enough to be used as a backdrop.[4]

As the nooks and crannies to be filled are innumerable, the self-assurance of historians is unwarranted. Important implications, however, issue from this cheerless vision. We can no longer proceed on the assumption that a fact possesses self-evident meaning from which pure

---

[2] Claude Lévi-Strauss, *The Savage Mind* (Chicago: University of Chicago Press, 1966), p. 256 and passim.

[3] Florian Znaniecki, *On Humanistic Sociology* (Chicago: University of Chicago Press, 1969), p. 60.

[4] Lévi-Strauss, *The Savage Mind*, pp. 257-258. See also Hayden White, "The Burden of History," *History and Theory*, 5:2 (1966), 134.

experience can be empirically extracted. As Znaniecki noted, "a fact by itself is already an abstraction; we isolate a certain limited aspect of the concrete process of becoming, rejecting, at least provisionally, all its indefinite complexity."[5] Nor by the same token are we justified in viewing a complex event as somehow "given," or a single or composite phenomenon such as the Meiji Restoration as a simply "political" event. Each moment must be seen as virtually inexhaustible in richness and complexity. Indeed, all the "totalizations" that go into making up an "event" point to the inevitable conclusion that events, as conventionally understood, do not take place.[6] By considering this bewildering possibility, however, historians gain a distance—a sobering one—from a history that presents itself already encased in abstract explanatory schema (such as the "modernization" of Japan). What is "given" is thus rendered provisionally unfamiliar, and the historian can appreciate once familiar events as new and challenging to his imagination.

With what sort of "methodological prepossession," then, might historians proceed to give meaning to historical experiences as they unfold in a field of acknowledged factual disorder? As data do not contain self-evident meaning, such a prepossession is obviously essential. In Frederic Jameson's persuasive phrase, "the methodological starting point does more than simply reveal, it actually creates, the object of study."[7]

Like practitioners of any other discipline in the human sciences, in other words, historians can no longer believe that they simply "document" the facts as they appear to show true experience. They are not exempt from the "common obligation" of defining a methodological orientation.[8]

The fundamental methodological dilemma of an historian, regardless of the area, country, or theme he studies, is the choice between a chronological and a synchronic perspective. History without a time sequence punctuated by dates is unthinkable. Chronology is the conventional coding device of historians, serving to help substantiate the causal unfolding or development of events over time. It is an approach that has been attractive as well to social scientists searching for a scheme of developmental causation that might support more powerful analytical formulations about an important perceived phenomenon. Increasingly, however, the tracing of chronological sequence has come under critical scrutiny. It is not necessary that one historical phase produce another. In the words of Siegfried Kracauer, "We are not justified in identifying history as a process

---

[5] Znaniecki, *On Humanistic Sociology*, p. 83.

[6] Lévi-Strauss, *The Savage Mind*, p. 258.

[7] Frederic Jameson, *The Prison House of Language* (Princeton: Princeton University Press, 1972), p. 14.

[8] Lévi-Strauss, *The Savage Mind*, p. 58; Znaniecki, *On Humanistic Sociology*, pp. 53-124.

in homogeneous chronological time. Actually history consists of events whose chronology tells us but little about their relationships and meanings."[9] A chronological series, in other words, represents a particular "totalization" from the perspective of the historian's construction rather than encompassing a homogeneous flow. The importance of certain points in time, rather than being part of history itself, is primarily a product of the historian's creation. An accepted result often serves to justify the claim of causal development. Hayden White criticized this approach and challenged historians in his landmark essay, "The Burden of History." "The Historian," he wrote, "serves no one well by constructing a specious continuity between the present world and that which preceded it. On the contrary, we require a history that will educate us to discontinuity more than ever before; for discontinuity, disruption, and chaos is our lot."[10]

Built into linearity is the temptation to present a coherent sequence along an historical time line, grouping data in isolation from the rest of the society in which those facts are located. A social fact loses its sociality; what Znaniecki called the "humanistic coefficient" of data is shrouded from view. "What appeared as an experienced truth," Lévi-Strauss observed, "first becomes confused and finally disappears altogether."[11]

The presumption that social data can be isolated, moreover, tends to be part of a particular view of organization. In structured human activity, it is reasoned, definitions of action and, hence the selection of participants, are normatively determined, and these rules are specific to that organization, in contrast to social life in the less formal "external" world. This formal method of delineation, however, conceals the important fact that these data are not actually isolated from the whole of social life, which is brought home most forcefully in situations of crisis and conflict. Znaniecki argued this point, observing that social analysis begins

> whenever external tendencies not harmonizing with the organized activities are introduced into the system, when the workmen in the factory start a strike or the soldiers of the army corps a mutiny. Then the isolation disappears; the system enters, through individuals who are its members, into relation with the whole complexity of social life. And this lack of real isolation, which characterizes a system of

[9] Quoted in Robert A. Nisbet, *Social Change and History* (London: Oxford University Press, 1969), p. 290.

[10] White, "The Burden of History," pp. 111-134, esp. p. 134.

[11] Lévi-Strauss, *The Savage Mind*, p. 254.

organized activity only at moments of crisis, is a permanent feature of all the artificial, abstractly formed groups of facts.[12]

For theoretical and practical reasons, it can be argued that data must be grouped into some sort of framework. This truism, however, does not undermine a theoretical point of real consequence, which is that such groupings of material must also assume the interlinkage of specialized data and the social whole. Functionally divided classes—samurai bureaucrats, peasants, or merchants—are still segments of a related social universe whose meaning is accessible. Bakufu, *han*, village, and market town were not self-enclosed entities without broader social significance. Each impinged on each other and contained that "humanistic coefficient" that the sciences of society must explore.

Historians often rely on a stylized conception of time. They assume a coincidence of time and history. The problem, however, is complex and requires some discrimination. Time is seen as moments in sequence, each having an influence on the next. Simultaneous time—an entire social world undergoing constant discontinuity, replacement, and change, or what we might call historical dynamic or actuality—is enormously more difficult to conceptualize than the conventional understanding of time as interlinked moments. Yet, it is this "actuality" of simultaneous experience that historians most wish to penetrate and analyze. In this sense, quite ironically, historians must disengage themselves from their identification with "time." Boris Eichenbaum's thought on the subject sheds light for us:

> The real task is not simple projection into the past, but rather that of understanding the historical actuality of an event, of determining its role in that development of historical energy which, in its very essence permanent, neither emerges nor disappears and for that very reason operates beyond time. A fact historically understood is one which has been withdrawn from time.[13]

Paradoxically, then, the historian's identification of history with linear time has tended to interfere with the aim of achieving historical understanding. It is when the event is withdrawn from time that one begins to perceive and comprehend with sensitivity its "historical actuality," and to perceive through it not so much its "uniqueness" as a causal factor but its affinity with general human experience.

We should also note that the concept of time as applied to historical studies has assumed a complexity in recent times that goes beyond conventional usage. Mircea Eliade, for example, has dealt with time not in

[12] Znaniecki, *On Humanistic Sociology*, p. 61.
[13] Quoted in Jameson, *Prison House*, p. 97.

terms of lineation but in terms of long, circular, conceptual, and religious leaps from a present back to primordial totality and then back. Time in this regard is not the linkage of the present with immediate antecedents, but an unmediated identification with an ancient moment that informs action in the present. There is also Victor Turner's idea of liminal time, often ritualized but sometimes not, in which vertical norms of structure are supplanted by egalitarian and communal moments. The dynamic motion of structure and nonstructure in his theoretical frame may be seen as moving forward in a "processual" manner. But this certainly is not "time" in the conventional chronological sense. An objection may be raised that these are basically religious concepts of time and, properly speaking, should not be a concern of historians. However, as one reviews recent histories—Japan's most assuredly—there is a great deal of agitation in and out of time sequences through acts of "reviving," "reidentifying," "revolving," and so on that we must come to grips with. Many of these turbulent manipulations of time are grounded in indigenously acclimated theories of action that permeate society, although through Western eyes they often appear as "traditional" or "fringe" activities, and thereby lose their relevance.[14]

The synchronous perspective cuts across linear time, and is thus "ahistorical." Its strength, as well as its weakness, is that it does not seek to uncover chronological sequence between phases of history, but rather emphasizes historical actualities as "discontinuous systems." The question asked is not what changes produced what sorts of consequences in a chain of events, but what might be the meaning of change throughout a social field at a particular moment. To achieve this end, diverse social, political, and intellectual experiences in various parts of society are framed as simultaneous occurrences. The approach pluralizes historical "events" into diverse parts and seeks through these complex clusterings to arrive at fresh interpretations. We may borrow from Clifford Geertz' language in his essay, "Thick Description," to explain our aim:

> In short, we need to look for systematic relationships among diverse phenomena, not for substantive identities among similar ones. And to do that with any effectiveness, we need to replace the "stratigraphic" conception of relations between the various aspects of human existence with a synthetic one.[15]

---

[14] See Mircea Eliade, *The Quest: History and Meaning in Religion* (Chicago: University of Chicago Press, 1969), and Victor Turner, *Dramas, Fields, and Metaphors* (Ithaca: Cornell University Press, 1975).

[15] Clifford Geertz, "Thick Description," *The Interpretations of Culture* (New York: Basic Books, 1973), p. 44.

For those of us searching for new interpretations of events that appear on familiar historical terrain, this synchronous perspective is attractive.

It appears, then, that the problems of principle and method have hardly been resolved in the study of history. In our specific area of concern, "stratigraphic" schemes have been dominant. We have had to admit in recent years that many of our previous generalizations have been misleading, much in the manner that Mary Wright admitted former errors in one of her last essays.[16] Writing about the Chinese Revolution of 1911 on its fiftieth anniversary, Wright conceded that she and her generation's depiction of China during that period was almost completely wrong. It had been treated erroneously as a history in which nothing much had happened. In our field, too, we have handled "hot" chronologies as if they were "cold."

In workshops over the past several years, it became apparent to us that the developmental scheme widely applied to the study of modern Japan neglects large portions of that history. In particular, we agreed that the characterization of Japan as a consensual society proceeding along an evolutionary course or, at times, deviating from it, was misleading. The dimension of conflict, dissent, and, in general, the turbulence that one sees over the course of that history was usually treated as an aberration of the true course. Individual voices of agony were seen as those of marginal figures, sure losers lacking demonstrable influence. Yet, as Victor Turner theorizes, in the "intellectual jungle" of conscious debate and disputation, these so-called losers and occupants of the fringe are frequently the "most articulate conscious voices of values." These liminal voices include poets, philosophers, dramatists, novelists, painters, prophets, peasant rebels, and shamans. A list from our field can be quickly drawn up, to include such figures as Ōshio Heihachirō, Kano Heihachirō, Maki Izumi, Yoshida Shōin, Kōtoku Shūsui, Natsume Sōseki, Akutagawa Ryūnosuke, and lesser known shamanistic figures and nameless peasants who were "possessed by spirits of change before changes become visible in public arenas." The list obviously could be expanded quite easily.[17]

Quite aside from voices in the margins and fringes, we have yet to grapple with the dimension of conflict as a central or core experience in modern Japanese history. Moments of crisis, as suggested earlier, link the world of organized activity with the wider world of consciousness, customs, and habits. Indeed, these disruptions and the discourse on them reveal a good deal more about a history than the normal flow of events. The dimension of conflict, then, presupposes a state of continuous jux-

---

[16] See Mary Clabaugh Wright's "Preface" and "Introduction" to *China in Revolution: The First Phase, 1900-1913* (New Haven: Yale University Press, 1968).
[17] See Turner, *Dramas, Fields, and Metaphors*, pp. 17-28.

taposition of harmony and disharmony. Conflict and harmony, dissension and consensus are melded together in the same coin. Individuals and groups question norms or challenge them for purposeful social ends. This becomes visible to the historian as a crisis. But underlying what is visible is the continuous state of tension in which the conflictual dimension is central. All complex and literate fields of human consciousness, the argument goes, are rent with dissension, agitation, and anxiety. This is a truism from which Japan is not exempt. Alain Touraine states the general point of view in this way:

> Society is always shot through with refusals, revolts, and conflicts; it is constantly being challenged and contestation is constantly being repressed, which is sufficient to indicate the inadequacy of all conceptions of society either as a machine made up of interdependent parts or as an ideological construction.[18]

In Touraine's view, it is precisely because conflict is a continuous actuality in society that history should not be carved into categories developing along a "general evolutionary line." To fragment society into convenient pieces is to lose sight of how society operates and undergoes change. Crises are not so much disturbances to an organic system evolving in a predetermined course as they are dramatic manifestations of a deeper and persistent dimension of conflict. Conflict is, for Touraine, part of a dialectic of social self-reflection and action, of a society consciously acting on itself and on the history it has received. In this respect it represents a society "apprehending its own capability of action," creating new understandings of how things should be in the unfolding dynamic that the Japanese often refer to as the *jisei* or *jōkyō*; it is part of what Touraine has termed "historicity" or "system of historical action": "the totality of debates that animate a society, the totality formed by the problems with which the collectivity is faced."[19]

Through these lenses we see a different sort of historical "event" than we have been accustomed to. An event is not simply political or institutional action, struggle among competing interests, factional rivalry, coup d'état, or assassination. It is not a "single" act or cause that intervenes in a linear series of events. It is a totality of challenges and contestations through which a society with its diverse layers and segments acts on itself, works on its own achievements, turns back upon itself, and thereby reveals the discrepancy—or the "non-coincidence"—between itself and its own rules of operation.

Given the drastic changes that Japan has undergone over the past cen-

---

[18] Alain Touraine, *The Self-Production of Society* (Chicago: University of Chicago Press, 1977), p. 59.

[19] Ibid., p. 73.

tury, it is hardly tenable to look at that history as though conflicts were peripheral, as though divisive and disruptive dissensions were unimportant missions that failed. However difficult, we also must see them as generative elements within a variety of historicities. There is, of course, no easy way to achieve this analytic aim, as the approach is all too new to us. In the least, however, this methodological perspective helps to shape our intellectual concerns into an historical problem worthy of interpretive discourse.

Provisionally, our workshops leave us with the view that conflicts in modern Japan did not occur as one confrontation after another in a linear series. They appear to us as belonging to discontinuous systems of historical action, identifiable in the main with two deep vertical lines basically disengaged from each other, even though they may be arranged chronologically. One of these conflictual "systems" is evident in the Bakumatsu-Meiji period, roughly between 1850 and 1880; the second occurs between 1900 and 1930, the late Meiji-Taishō era. The former system is anchored by an "event," the Meiji Restoration. The latter does not have such a convenient benchmark. Yet each represents a major conflictual "moment," not a smooth and secure transitional point in Japan's history, and for this reason each may be compared to the other as a system of events containing a coherent set of internal identities.

o

A reappraisal of the Meiji Restoration as a comprehensive "event" is long overdue. The really startling fact is that a volume of interpretive writings on this subject has yet to be published in a Western language. Compared with the vast literature dealing with other decisive conflicts—for example, peasant rebellions in China or communist movements in Europe—Western-language studies on the Meiji Restoration as a comprehensive event are virtually nonexistent. Conventionally viewed as a political occurrence, its relationship to society as a whole, or even to the peasantry, has been seen as tangential at best. Although widely recognized among Far Eastern studies as the pivotal event in modern Japanese history, as the first revolution in Asia, and as one of the great conflictual events in modern times, it still lacks a persuasive theoretical place in the literature of transformational events.

Most Western studies on the Restoration exemplify a highly restrictive view of revolutionary change. The tendency has been to refer to the Marxian model to show that the Restoration was not a revolution. Yet few revolutions fit into the Marxian definition. Indeed, many historians do not see the French Revolution itself as having invested all sectors of society with a consistent ideology, and they deny that the revolution was a "social" one, going on further to doubt that a clear class of enterprising capitalists labored to achieve a social revolution. What all this suggests is that we have tended to view the Meiji Restoration in relation to a specific definition of what constitutes a fundamental break in another country's history. We must reject this approach and move toward a problematic one that will offer alternatives to historical and social scientific investigation. We should look at diverse areas of society, examining free-floating intellectuals, marginal religious groups, peasants, merchants, and bureaucrats. What did the chaotic turbulence of late Tokugawa and early Meiji mean in terms of change in samurai, merchant, and peasant consciousness, and how does this effect our present understanding of the "Restoration"? Above all, what are the psychological and intellectual resonances and conceptual interconnections between seemingly diverse events of the period?

Present-day historians, unfortunately, have not interpreted these interconnections in terms of conflicts, turbulent debates, and contestations. Other than Harootunian, few have attempted to penetrate the "rage" of the actors of the period. Their chronologies have been cold. Japanese historians, such as Takekoshi Yosaburō and Fujita Shigeyoshi, writing closer to the events of the time, saw things quite differently. Takekoshi especially, in his widely read history, *Shin Nihon shi*,[20] characterizes late Tokugawa society in terms of pervasive psychological chaos and intellectual uncertainty verging on revolutionary anarchy. The roots, moreover, are to be found in diverse sources beginning in the late eighteenth century: in the rebellious thoughts and actions of Yamagata Daini, Fujii Umon, and Ōshio Heihachirō; in the radical perceptions on political economy of the so-called "eccentrics" such as Honda Toshiaki, Hayashi Shihei, and Kaiho Seiryō; in the experimentations of intellectuals such as Watanabe Kazan and Takano Chōei; in the recurring contestations between village peasants and their leaders; and, more generally, in the language of commoners as they appear in popular drama in which officialdom is treated with contempt and derision, as in the popular saying, "Samurai pick their teeth even though they cannot afford a meal" (*bushi wa kuwanedomo takayōji*). All of these themes, in Takekoshi's eyes, converged in the event known as the Meiji Restoration. This convergence led to the discovery of an ideal of a comprehensive social union, or *kokutai*, and the popular expectation of prosperity, opportunity, and well-being for all, a vision that Takekoshi personally incorporated into his plea for parliamentary democracy. Takekoshi had absolutely no difficulty in seeing the Restoration as a chaotic and conflictual

---

[20] Takekoshi Yosaburō, *Shin Nihon shi*, in *Meiji shi ronshū I* (Tokyo, 1965), pp. 3-225, esp. pp. 3-28. Fujita Shigeyoshi's *Bunmei tōzenshi* is *ibid.*, pp. 226-286. For fascinating related materials, see also Tsurumi Shunsuke, ed., *Nihon no hyakunen: 1, Go isshin no arashi* (Tokyo, 1964).

social event. He called it a revolution—*ishin kakumei, ranseiteki kakumei, anarukikaru reboryūshion.*

Takekoshi's account, which still provides refreshing reading after almost a hundred years, does reinforce some of the themes we have discussed in our workshops. We have found abrupt and major changes taking place in the meaning of language among aristocrats and commoners. Dissension and vehement debates were evident in virtually every domain, not in just the "heroic" or "activist" ones of western Japan. Political actors and thinkers, many still very young (that is, in their late teens and twenties), shaped contending ideologies out of the available political language and involved themselves in a common discourse. There was an awareness of the drastic risks involved and of the serious implications of thought and action for political structure and process on the part of both ultimate winners and losers. Whether loyalism was understood in terms of Satsuma and Chōshū or the bakufu, "politics" was neither disagreement over petty personal interests nor ancient animosities warmed over. Tokugawa politics fits Victor Turner's characterization: "Politics in arenas or elsewhere is not merely a game. It is also idealism, altruism, patriotism . . . , universalism, sacrifice of self-interest, and so on. . . . People will die for values that oppose their interests and promote interests that oppose their values."[21] It is Tokugawa politics in this complicated sense that can be documented in a variety of ways—as Totman, Steele, and Huber demonstrate—which leads us to suspect that the existing order did not simply fall without premeditation. It was more likely paralyzed and unhinged through conscious actions and inactions.

Perhaps of greater significance, these conflicts also came to represent the expectation that intellectual uncertainty and fear of chaos could be surmounted. They took on a purposefulness in reordering the groundwork and the vertical shape of political and social certitude. In such a dynamic actuality, conflict itself gained a legitimacy that it could not have had in conditions of political and ideological stability. Bakufu leaders intensely debated how to redefine and reorient policy. A new centralized structure was considered. Innovative factions emerged. Doubt and uncertainty spread among those in position to observe this debate. Among the activists outside of the bakufu there was growing disbelief that the existing government could rule. Strategies were steadily radicalized, leading to large-scale military insurrection. Civil wars, as in Mito and Chōshū, were indeed contests over the fate of the nation. In all of these engagements of conflictual action, there was an expectation

---

[21] Turner, *Dramas, Fields, and Metaphors,* p. 140.

that drastic changes would bring about an end to chaos and usher in a new era of stability and strength.

A less visible and often unreported drama occurred in the countryside. Even as the economy showed steady improvement through commercialization in the Bakumatsu years, difficult and painful transitions were underway. Famines in various pockets in the 1860s revived excrutiating memories of the Tenpō period in the 1830s. Peasants continued to live in a world of economic and psychological uncertainty. Moreover, the reliability of the village as a communal whole underwent discernible erosion as the village began to articulate itself in terms of separate interests. Lower strata, in particular, contested the wisdom of village leaders, and some left the village to take part in the politics of the wider arena. Subtle changes could be detected in the language and character of peasant dissent. The premise that those who rule ought to attend to the fixed and unchanging needs of the peasantry gave way to a more disputatious view that some within the village had new interests to promote and defend that were not necessarily congruent with the whole; interest, it was discovered, was not evenly distributed. Existing language was adapted and words were given new meaning to deal with legitimate dissent. In the case of Aizu, as Vlastos shows, the peasantry rose up to capture the entire domain during the Meiji Restoration in order to restore a world of moral harmony and economic well-being.

In country towns and in cities, there was vigorous entrepreneurial action in response to the events surrounding the Meiji Restoration. In the traditional sector of the economy, there was psychological uncertainty and dislocation. Innovative economic opportunities also presented themselves, and counter efforts were made to protect and minimize risk. Innovative entrepreneurial procedures appeared economically advantageous to some, leading to major risk taking. In this diffuse economic flow, both the affirmation of traditional methods and the acceptance of new procedures reflected conscious choice and the weighing of risks in a context in which advantages were not clearly mapped out. The fate of small producers and of large organizations such as Mitsui, Kōnoike, and Ōnogumi all bear close attention. It is unfortunate that this subject has not received the serious research attention in the West it deserves.

Overall, ideological patterns reinforced the above picture of dislocation and change. One detects a deepening sense of crisis as to how the whole of the national community was to be defined and held together politically and spiritually. Political economists such as Honda Toshiaki and Hayashi Shihei, and later the thinkers of Mito, notably Aizawa Seishisai and Fujita Tōkȯ, debated the issue. Religious movements that mushroomed in this era "seceded" from the center, as Harootunian argues, creating religious communities that might "restore" the communal wholeness of the people. Wilson also shows that there was here a broad and comprehensive ideological field of creative discontent, much broader than heretofore conceived.

Drastic acts of dissent, risk taking, and spiritual secession thus reverberated beyond narrow social compartments and social spheres. Common to these varying experiences was an awareness of a breakdown in the received social, political, and moral universes. An ideological language legitimating dissent evolved and became generally accessible. In varying dimensions, there was fear and excitement, a sense of disbelief over the general state of confusion, and an awareness that previous methods could not correct the disarray. All this was accompanied by a sense of expectation of new possibilities, a flowering of large and small visions based on an anticipation that unusual things were about to happen to bring about a renewal, and that, through action defined in a wide variety of ways, new achievements were indeed possible.

If we are to view the "event" called the Meiji Restoration in these terms, the political process commonly associated with it is but one part of the broader psycho-cultural field. The Meiji Restoration takes on meaning as a comprehensive social event. The aristocratic world of political "innovation" (the arena of *ishin*) and the peasant and commoner world of moral "renewal" (the sphere of *yonaoshi*) share a common historicity, a common historical "actuality." Both partake in the "making" of an event that reminds us less of a political coup than it does of Shimazaki Tōson's perception in which aspiration, expectation, conflict, achievement, disillusionment, and defeat all commingle in the Restoration. They are, in short, part of an event as an "epilogue" or "summary" in which, in Eichenbaum's words, "perspectives of the future are opened, or in which the subsequent destinies of the main characters are told."[22]

○

Early in the twentieth century, in what is known as the late Meiji-Taishō eras, conflicts once again erupted on the historical scene—in crowd actions in the street, organized union activities, individual competitions to succeed, and in published debates. These conflicts, which will be the subject of the second part of this volume, clearly belong to a new historical era, a system of events separate from the Bakumatsu period treated in the first part. In that earlier period, the declining efficiency of political structures may be seen as having generated conflict, with the "center" no longer holding the various parts together bureaucratically or ideo-

---

[22] Quoted in Jameson, *Prison House*, p. 75.

logically, thereby producing structural strains and wide-ranging disputes as to how things ought to be. Something quite different informs the character of conflict in the early decades of the twentieth century. For one thing, a powerful and irresistible "center," the Meiji constitutional system, had now been hammered into place. From the center, comprehensive structures extended outward and downward to all parts of the nation. National geographical spaces had been redrawn with new systemic grids, administrative, political, industrial, and educational structures that overlapped each other. As Bernard Silberman argues provocatively, the simultaneous expansion and fixing of these structures generated conflicts distinctive to the modern era. The lives of everyone were irrevocably altered by the new opportunites as well as by the coercive demands produced by these structures. Although they convey an image of symmetry and coherence regulated by rational processes and procedures, these structures, under closer scrutiny, also reveal fault lines, seams, cracks, or what have been referred to with regard to the economy as the "differential structure." Although the differential is often masked or muted through ideological or institutional devices, the fact remains that some make it and many do not—a condition that is endemic to the constitutional system itself. Critical questions about equity and justice inevitably arise.

A new discourse thus came into existence in post-industrial and post-constitutional Japan that in its basic character differed radically from the one articulated during the Restoration period, and that may be seen as the defining of a new system of action. Conflict was seen as a datum in everyday social and legal reality. At the micro level, expectation of achieving success and the fear of failure were viewed as constantly present in a new pluralized field of competition. At the macro level, dissension and consensus were seen as continually present along a broad range of organized conflicts. There was an awareness that the new constitutional arrangements had become a permanent fact; there was recognition that through organized, legally sanctioned means legitimate political and social goals might be achieved; there was a general, albeit diffuse, sense of "failed expectation" about the course of modern development after the Restoration, and the belief that within the new order improvements were possible and overdue. In short, it was felt, all of society should be involved in reflection and action within the formal system of law in order to create legitimate and permanent spaces for justifiable goals, thereby interpreting the contours of the legal order in such a way as to make them less constraining and more encompassing of society's wishes and expectations.

A good deal of the discussion was carried on in terms of the creative role of conflict in the Meiji Restoration, which remained deeply etched in Japanese social memory. Efforts were made throughout the early twentieth century to recover the significance of conflict, to realize again the idealized position it had held in that event. It would often be articulated with the phrases "Taishō *ishin*" and "Shōwa *ishin*," in which conflict and competitive struggle were seen not merely as endemic to history but as essential for the creation of a more just national community. As an operating premise for action, creative and competitive dissent had become a public matter, in contrast to the earlier period when this idea may be said to have been discovered and sanctioned.

Competitive movements of dissent were intertwined with this discourse. Beginning around the time of the Russo-Japanese War in 1905 and the Taishō political crisis of 1912-1913 and continuing beyond the 1930s, we see the proliferation of these simultaneously occurring conflicts. Urban crowds collected spontaneously, and, in the name of "imperial justice," which they claimed to understand more intimately than government leaders, rioted against corruption and attacked local police boxes as symbols of the extension of the state. Laborers engaged in dynamic competition for jobs, and unions struck for better wages and working conditions. Intellectuals organized a movement for manhood suffrage that gained wide attention; others formed socialist parties to lead protests against the establishment. Women rioted over the price of rice, requiring troops to bring order. University students protested bureaucratic interference in matters of curriculum. Novelists and journalists openly questioned the meaning of human "individuality" in the new bureaucratic order, and they hurled polemics against the leaders in government for their ineptness. In the countryside, tenants organized unions to assert their rights against landlords; villages articulated traditional ideas about the sacred community, asserted the prerogative of adjudicating local disputes, and resisted the penetration of the central bureaucracy. Between country and town, major demographic shifts were underway, generating considerable competitive activity in a fluid labor market. Even this partial list of items, some of which will be treated in detail in separate essays by Shumpei Okamoto, Ron Napier, and Ann Waswo, is sufficient to convince us that the constitutional order did not produce harmonious historical evolution. Far from it, what we see is a new kind of turbulence being spawned along a broad spectrum of interrelated events.

The administrative state was, indeed, a ubiquitous influence in all of these diverse conflicts. Finding established values inadequate for the reconstitution of a predictable structure of authority, the builders of the new state relied on formal rules to redefine and also create a new administrative system including the family, village, and community. These were no longer "natural" but "administrative" expressions. Yet the creation of formal rules did not produce order. Concerns as to what constituted just shares under those rules set in motion organized, competitive movements. New kinds of conflict were generated in an ongoing search for permanency within the new order. In short, far from eradicating conflict, formal rules stirred society into "apprehending its own capability of action," discovering the possibility of acting on itself through legally sanctioned means to create something new, and uncovering in the process the uncomfortable truth that the wishes of society are often not congruent with the aims of the state. It is this apprehension that generated further debate, competitive encounters, and conflicting modes of consciousness.

Bureaucratic leaders were acutely aware of this emerging pattern of conflicting relations within the constitutional order. Familiar with the language of Social Darwinism current in their day, they viewed conflict not as unnatural but as inevitable, and, to a significant degree, necessary for survival. The problem, in other words, was no longer to eradicate conflict but to regulate it so that it would not be destructive to the national well-being, as might occur with an anarchic and mindless war of all against all. As a result of these debates, bureaucratic leaders agreed that conflict must be consciously hedged in and circumscribed with impartial administrative instruments. To some young bureaucrats in the Home Ministry this also involved the drafting of innovative social reform legislation. Duus writes, however, that intellectual leaders did not share in the optimism for this engineering. They pointed to the very same bureaucratic elite as the source of conflict itself. Relying on bureaucratic instruments with an attitude of privileged arrogance, they had incurred the resentment of the mass of society, as evidenced by the numerous popular protest movements stirred up by anti-bureaucratic slogans. This broad disagreement between the bureaucratic and intellectual worlds was repeated in the more narrowly confined disputes within the academic establishment itself. As James Bartholomew and Byron Marshall show, the question of bureaucratic leadership and educational autonomy was hotly debated between leaders of the Ministry of Education and those of Tokyo University. And that same ministry found itself pitted against the scientific profession in similar disputes. How these differences were articulated and adjudicated form an important part in this history of higher learning in modern Japan.

Indeed, the theme of knowledge and its relationship to status, wealth, and power recurs continuously over this period. What is, after all, knowledge? Is it universal in some normative, scientific sense, or is it ultimately moral? Is it particular and functional in an ideological way, or is it something else, perhaps a community's faith in its immortality and its closeness to a natural order? Involved is the question of who controls knowledge. Who serves as the arbiter of what proper knowledge might be, and who determines content? All of these issues serve to highlight the importance of epistemological concerns that undergird the broad pluralistic field of competition and conflict. The search for knowledge—or enlightenment, as it was called by an earlier generation—produces its own politics of dissension and disagreement. Knowledge, once made accessible to the public, moreover, not only serves as a key to wealth and power but is also manipulable in other ways, such as in the organization of labor and tenant unions. In Waswo's analysis, we see tenants using new legal knowledge to form associations and hire special counsels to represent their case in court. The dramatic field of peasant rebellion that one sees in the late Tokugawa era had been reconstituted into a new system of action.

Some of the movements listed earlier suggest that the quest for knowledge in the early twentieth century was also imbued with a sense of failed expectation, a yearning for creativity. This can be seen in responses to the expansion of bureaucratic power. There was a sense, too, of psychic exhaustion among intellectuals. It was widely believed that during the Restoration and developments thereafter those in power should have shown a greater comprehension of the expectations of society. Things somehow ought to have been better. Whereas polity and society were previously thought to be ultimately harmonious, in the early twentieth century there was growing suspicion that in fact polity, society, and individuality were likely to be incongruous. A language of reflective dissent and psychic fatigue found expression in such eminent writers as Kunikida Doppo and Natsume Sōseki. Doppo pictured himself lying spread-eagled on the tatami floor, mindlessly staring at the ceiling. And Sōseki, reflecting on the modernization of Japan, did not see it as the actualization of human expectations in which modern man is happier than his ancient ancestors, but rather as a cruel exploitative march leading to total nervous exhaustion.[23]

Other well-known writers and commentators were equally concerned, as Oka Yoshitake writes in a classic essay on this subject translated for this volume. Some pointed their criticism at the ruling elites as the source of alienation and discontent. Others, especially those who had achieved success in business, politics, and journalism, identified the problem in the motivation of the new youth and its understanding of "individuality" or, as Oka discusses, *kosei*. Tokutomi Sohō, Kuroiwa Ruiko, Gotō Shimpei, and others, addressing themselves to the new audience of university students, wrote best-selling books of "instructions on proper conduct"—*shoseikun*—explaining how competitive in-

[23] Natsume Sōseki, "Gendai no kaika," *Sōseki zenshū* 21 (Tokyo, 1957).

dividuality could lead to the promotion of national well-being. The concerns of these men over the relationship between individuality, competition, struggle, and the general social good resonated throughout a society in which each diverse part sought an equitable place in the new order.

○

The Meiji Restoration is a composite of diverse and simultaneous transformations taking place throughout society. In the spheres of authority relations and commerce there was a search for wider, more enduring, and more accountable relationships and organizational forms. Social and economic structures were transformed throughout the countryside. The Meiji state, indeed, represented a transformation from one kind of political system to another. It rested on a new conception of political space and of a national political community; it also rested on a system of knowledge that had been reordered and reorganized even as the historically received language might outwardly appear the same. Previous organizations took on new meaning and were reformulated. In short, the term "Restoration" is simply a name we give to these various simultaneous constructions.

The early twentieth century represents a separate system of events. There was a reliance on formal law that contrasts with the earlier period. The legitimacy of the legal order was less at stake than the problem of interpreting its meaning so as to accommodate the concerns for individuality, community, and social equity that encompassed the entire citizenry. The wishes of society and the actions of administrative politics appeared to be out of step, requiring "restoration" and "rectification." The perceived discrepancy animated unfulfilled expectations and encouraged movements of dissent and criticism.

In both periods, conflicts and disturbances were not random events. In the earlier period, these disturbances, as suggested by Neil Smelser, "erupt when obsolescence of the old structure is apparent but before the mobilization of resources to overhaul this structure begins. These disturbances . . . bear a symbolic resemblance to the specific points of obsolescence; for these reasons social disturbances are not simply random outbursts."[24] Disturbances in the latter period were also not random outbursts. However, the informing theme then was not "obsolescence of the old structure" but the formulation and manipulation of new rules of organization and action. The object was to emulate the new permanency of the legal order. The concern was to broaden the

---

[24] Neil J. Smelser, *Social Change in the Industrial Revolution* (Chicago: University of Chicago Press, 1959), p. 4.

scope and confines of that order so as to accommodate and allow a legitimate place for certain expectations perceived as just.

By placing these two historical "events" side by side, I believe we can begin to compare them as discontinuous systems of historical action. Their large and small conflicts, tensions, ambivalences, and contestations occurring in diverse parts of society reveal resonances and linkages that suggest in each a set of debates that animated society, a "totality formed by the problems with which the collectivity is faced."

A final brief note concludes my comments. If we maintain that linear causation is beyond the historian's analytic grasp, so, too, it may be objected, is the integrative experience that informs diverse and simultaneous experiences in a vertically conceived moment. Each leads in its own way to a dismal encounter with factual chaos. There is no easy way out of this dilemma except to grasp one of the poles and attempt to tread on familiar ground as if it were unfamiliar. The synchronous perspective we have shared in this seminar is in this sense a provisional device through which we might begin to conceptualize a history by approaching more closely the experiences of those who lived through and made the events we write about. Although separated from that specific historical actuality of time and space, we begin to perceive general meaning in it. Certainly, as Lévi-Strauss suggests, neither the historian nor the reader of his work can live through the experiences being looked at and become a "native." Just as the Meiji Restoration of 1868 is not the same phenomenon for a samurai as it might be for an honorable peasant, so it would also differ for historians such as Norman or Beasley when they write about it. However, like the ethnographer, we as historians must, with "skill, precision, a sympathetic approach, and objectivity," seek "to enlarge a specific experience to the dimensions of a more general one, which thereby becomes accessible as *experience* to men of another country or another epoch." Or to cite White's challenge to all of us, "the burden of the historian in our time is to re-establish the dignity of historical studies on a basis that will make them consonant with the aims and purposes of the intellectual community at large."[25]

However dismal our science is sometimes said to be, we may still rejoice in these humanistic visions.

[25] Lévi-Strauss, *Structual Anthropology*, p. 17, and White, "The Burden of History," p. 124.

PART I

IDEOLOGY AS CONFLICT

Harry Harootunian

INTRODUCTION: THE PRODUCTION OF IDEOLOGY

> *The ideas of the ruling class are in every epoch the ruling ideas,*
> *i.e. the class that is the ruling material force of society, is at the*
> *same time its ruling intellectual force. The class which has the means*
> *of material production at its disposal, has control at the same time*
> *over the means of mental production, so that thereby, generally*
> *speaking, the ideas of those who lack the means of mental produc-*
> *tion are subject to it. . . . The individuals composing the ruling*
> *class possess among other things consciousness, and therefore think.*
> *Insofar, therefore, as they rule as a class and determine the extent*
> *and compass of an epoch, it is self-evident that they do this in its*
> *whole range, hence among other things rule also as thinkers, as*
> *producers of ideas, and regulate the production and distribution of*
> *the ideas of their age.*
>
> Karl Marx and Frederick Engels, *The German Ideology*
> (New York, 1970), p. 64

Participants in few epochs in history have shown more consistency and
resourcefulness in seeking to conceal conflict and the inevitable clash of
claims to power than Japanese of the Tokugawa era. Much of the rhetoric of politics was pressed into the discourse on morality and ethics in
an apparent effort to displace power and the possibility for conflict as a
subject of conscious intention or as an object for serious analysis. Indeed, Tokugawa Japan might best conform to what Michel Foucault
described as a case in which power must always be partially concealed
if it is to be effective. If we are to catch a glimpse of its contours it must
be "caught on the wing." Any cursory examination of political thought
in the seventeenth century will invariably disclose the rumor or hint of
the presence of power; yet it will also indicate the elaborate sublimations
to which writers resorted in order to shift the object of thought away
from consciousness. Thus conflict, which the seventeenth century identified with private conduct and thus the class consciousness of a warrior
class on the rise, was ultimately dissolved in the claims of public authority and the destruction of human desire as a form of human activity.

In fact, it was the purpose of discourse itself to exclude certain objects of interest by establishing what was appropriate. Until the seventeenth century it was the function of discourse to define the limits of what was appropriate and inappropriate. Yet these rules pertained not to political relationships but to social conduct.

To understand the course and character of conflict in Tokugawa Japan is to understand the displacements in the discursive field. For to have conceptualized conflict or indeed to have imagined its possibility requires not simply recourse to supposed changes in the material conditions of life. It requires that we grasp how power is concealed in discourse itself and the process by which new discourses find a space to occupy. The "eruptions" of new discourses are invariably accompanied by shifts in the structure of knowledge and its relationship to power (what is appropriate and inappropriate). Eighteenth-century Japan, for reasons too complex to enumerate here, was the setting of such a shift along the received epistemological fault line. If the eighteenth century experienced an epistemological crisis (Bachelard's idiom) of "geological" dimensions, its resolution also made possible a multiplicity of meanings and cultural ambiguity where none existed before. Indeed, the new orientations in discourse ultimately reorganized the possible ways knowledge itself might relate to power, though it was no doubt power that would determine who would know what. Thus changes occurred in crucial relationships between knower and known, signifier and signified, agent and act so as to permit a proliferation of claims regarding what was real, true. The break caused one mode of knowledge (and power relationships) to displace another; syntagm as a model of knowledge succeeded paradigm; human activity was substituted for nature; calculability, order, and measurement displaced principle; and difference was elevated over resemblance as the object of consciousness.

Subsequent events in the late eighteenth and early nineteenth centuries would show that life could never be the same again; a ruined intellectual landscape, which did not disappear until the Restoration, became merely another sedimentary layer of vanished possibilities while a new field was being envisaged. Yet the possibility of even envisaging new fields suggests the presence of simultaneous claims to knowing, to what can be known, who can know it, and the determination of the nature of reality itself. Here is the beginning of ideology, or surely its production. For, the production of ideology is inevitably rooted in the propensity of groups to make "authoritative" claims to know and to fix the boundaries between the real and the unreal. The forms of such claims are determined by the relationship between this mode of representation and the authorizing discourse. It is the discourse, the defined field of knowledge and utterances passing for "common sense," that will invariably serve as the reference for the effort to secure representation. Such acts are invariably political, despite elaborate concealments, and thus attest to the possibility of generating conflict over the right to know what is to be known. (One need only recall the recent emphasis by highly placed U.S. government officials on "the need to know" as if large numbers of the population were to be excluded from the act of knowing.)

We are all familiar with the Geertzian assertion that ideological systems represent cultural categories that must be decoded for the meanings they emit. Such a view goes a long way to sensitize us not simply to the symbolic freight ideologies convey, but more, to the ways cultural codes are combined and recombined to explain the world at the time they are produced. Geertz is quick to caution us against seeing ideology simply as an instance of strain and stress or even as a reflection of interest. Yet the analysis betrays his best intentions, and we learn that often ideology is nothing more. Where Geertz remains most loyal to the functionalist projection is in his indifference to how ideologies are produced; it is the conceit of ahistoricity.

The production of ideologies is invariably related to the forms of knowledge that can offer not just the sanction to claims that are being pressed but indeed the very modes of expressability—cognitive and verbal—that give shape to that which is being represented. It is not, as imagined by Geertz and proposed by a generation of sociologists, simply a matter of the indirect, or safety valve, effects (as if society were envisioned as a large plumbing unit) of the systemic strain that generates the ideological impulse. Such determinations only mark the conditions of its function, if one can even convincingly argue that such a model of a social system actually exists, and surely not its possibility for "eruption."

Ideologies call attention to epistemological strategies, to cognitive fields, and to the effort therefore to envisage the shape of reality that is to be represented; they call attention to what is to be known, by whom, and how it is to be known.

Indeed, it is precisely these conditions of production that give shape to the functions of ideology and raise the question of determinancy.[1] Here ideology is seen not simply as the presentation of the political and economic interest of a class. Rather, it might be viewed as the way in which individuals or groups actively live their roles within the social totality. Indeed, ideology often seeks to imagine the shape and content of the social totality when specific contradictions between structures are

[1] R. Coward and J. Ellis, *Language and Materialism* (London: Routledge and Kegan Paul, 1977), pp. 61-92; Louis Althusser, *Lenin and Philosophy* (London: Monthly Review Press, 1971), pp. 127-186, also *For Marx* (New York: New Left Books, 1977), pp. 89-128, 221-247.

overdetermined.[2] At these times the function of ideology is to reaffirm what is "natural," even though different from received expectations. Thus, it will function to participate in the construction of a subject (*shutai* in Japanese), whether it is an individual or social group, so that it can act. In this sense ideology is a practice of representation, and one that seeks to produce a specific articulation, that is, produce certain meanings and necessitate certain subjects as its support. Moreover, it is, according to Louis Althusser, a material force insofar as it constructs such subjects in specific social relationships.[3] The materiality of this force is affirmed by its investment in concrete institutions and organizational practices.

The production of ideological verisimilitude is effective to the extent that it appears "natural," as "the way things are."[4] *Kokugaku* (nativism) early defined Shintō as the way things are, yet at the same time called attention to the obvious fact that such a conclusion depended upon how the so-called whole was conceived. Here, ideology, through its relationship to an authenticating knowledge system that I will discuss later, appears as certain "natural ideals," a horizon, an ordinary way of thinking, as not only accepted but perceived precisely as the way things are, ought to be, and will always be. However, this does not preclude imagining a world in which social relationships would be structured in ways different from what has been considered appropriate. The difference is rarely noted or articulated, and the restructuring is invariably sanctioned by the appeal to what is appropriate or "natural." This restructuring of social relationships is apparently prompted by a sense that the "natural" has somehow been abandoned or neglected. The social whole must be envisaged anew if the "natural" is to be determined precisely.

In connection with the effort to apprehend the individual or group as a fixed subject, ideology also presupposes consistency and coherence among the origins of ideas and action: the sense of a unified being.

---

[2] Althusser, *Lenin and Philosophy*, pp. 89-221. There is a brief definition of the concept in the glossary of *For Marx*: "Freud used this term to describe (among other things) the representation of the dream-thoughts in images privileged by their condensation of a number of thoughts in a single image (condensation/*Verdichtung*), or by the transference of psychic energy from a particular potent thought to apparently trivial images (displacement/*Verschiebung-Verstellung*). Althusser uses the same term to describe the effects of the contradictions in each practice constituting the social formation on the social formation as a whole, and hence back on each practice and each contradiction, defining the pattern of dominance and subordination, antagonism and non-antagonism of the contradictions in the structure in dominance at any given historical moment. More precisely, the overdetermination of a contradiction is the reflection in it of its conditions of existence within the complex whole, in other words, its uneven development" (pp. 252-253).

[3] Althusser, *Lenin and Philosophy*, pp. 166ff.; Coward and Ellis, *Language and Materialism*.

[4] Luckacs has referred to this phenomenon as a form of reification.

Under such circumstances, the individual can occupy a plurality of conflicting subject positions, and be given a plurality of representations. Admittedly this may be truer of modern ideologies than of those found in earlier times, but we cannot deny the importance to ideological production of the consistent subject.

Thus ideology, for our purposes, consists of the practice of representation and the construction of a subject for such representation. Individuals or groups are virtually produced through its mediation, as are their orientations to social structures, so that they can act within them. The proposed materiality of ideology is manifest in its capacity to construct in specific social relations subjects who act in concrete institutions and organizations, such as the family, the state, education, religious brethern, the domain, and so on, and in practices such as work. This function in which the subject is fixed in order to represent itself in the world of objects is necessary to societies of whatever kind chiefly because the individual or group is not the center of the social totality. The social process has no real center, only that impugned by the ideological representation of a dominant class; it has no single motivating force in the sense that Renaissance humanism saw man as the center of the world, actually willing the events of his social organization.[5] Instead, society is composed of multiple contradictions in relationships of overdetermination so as to create the potential for ideological conflict in the general effort to determine what is natural for groups and individuals.

In Tokugawa Japan, the very terms by which different groups were brought into ideological focus raised the distinct possibility of conflict between the various claims to representation. This was especially true when the specific contradictions between social relationships could no longer be contained by the existing apparatus of the control mechanism, and when, in the effort to reestablish what was "common sense" through the practice of centering the subject, groups and individuals apprehended the social whole. The form assumed by such imagining depended entirely upon what the prevailing discourse on knowledge might permit. Yet it is worth suggesting that the relationship between ideological production and discourse is far from a simple matter of the appropriation of form. Rather, as I will try to show, it is part of the very conditions determining the impulse to ideologize.

Ideologies also produce meanings through signs, and "ideology" functions as the dimension of social experience in which these meanings and values are produced. But, it must be repeated, it is just as important to note who is controlling the very signs that seek to convey the meanings and ideas. Ideology's fundamental function is to stress "practical consciousness" as a form of "sensuous activity"; ideology demonstrates

[5] Coward and Ellis, *Language and Materialism*, p. 74.

that signification is part of a central social process. Thus ideologies disclose the epistemological impulse that gives them expression; they show the relationship between power and knowledge, and even those, like Engels, who saw ideology as instances of "false consciousness," were forced to admit that it represented motives hidden from true consciousness. A better description of the insinuation of power could not have been made. Yet because ideology functions as signification in a social process it reveals how those who have remained outside of the established or received discourse seek to gain entry.

Ideology can often disclose the manner in which a central discourse gives way to new efforts to establish meaning. In establishing their own discourse and right to signification (as against official discourse), a number of groups in late Tokugawa society effectively claimed freedom to act in conformity with their conception of the true and the real. By implication, these groups challenged the authority of society, whether it was vested in the shogunal arrangement of power or in the principles of propriety. Such an act represented a secession from the state at a time when the authorities were having trouble in meeting their own responsibilities and satisfying demands for "relief" and "order." In defining themselves, such groups acted to establish their significance and did so as the necessary precondition for declaring their autonomy from the Tokugawa control system. To speak of signification and meaning takes us back to knowledge itself. The epistemological revolution in the eighteenth century allowed men to apprehend what hitherto had been consigned to the status of either the anomalous or the marginal.

THE DISCOURSE ON ORIGINS

> For man, then, origin is by no means the beginning—a sort of dawn of history from which his ulterior acquisition would have accumulated. Origin, for man, is much more the way in which man in general, any man, articulates himself upon the already-begun of labour, life and language; it must be sought for in that fold where man in all simplicity applies his labour to a world that has been worked for thousands of years, lives in the freshness of his unique, recent, and precarious existence a life that has roots in the first organic formations and composes into sentences which have never before been spoken . . . words that are older than all memory.
>
> Michel Foucault, *The Order of Things*
> (New York, 1970), p. 330

Historians of thought have, too often, sought the easy way out. They have explored traces of an idea, isolating the object of study, and writing what Stephen Pepper has called a contextualist history. In severing the subject from a larger referential framework, they have precluded the possibility of making the connections that might exist in a larger field. For most historians, context is both the license and the code name for formalism. Such approaches lead to biographies, individual or group, but rarely do they lead to a broader study of the epistemological basis of individual ideas or schools of thought.[6]

I wish to show that conflict had been generated by a profound epistemological break in the eighteenth century and the subsequent effort to overcome it. Large numbers of people found that the way they might know and apprehend the world they encountered had been altered. If such a conception of a break is truly consistent, it would compel us to demonstrate the linkages between the meditations of eighteenth-century Confucianists (*keisei saimin, settchū-ha*), nativist political theology (*kokugaku*), discussions on national defense and the new Dutch learning (*rangaku*), revitalized faith sects, new religions, and, perhaps, the apocalyptic visions pledged to immediate possibilities (*yonaoshi, ee ja nai ka*).

At one level, all of these late Tokugawa movements or moments were manifestations of a single discourse that sought to overcome a specific discontent. Yet the perception of a discontent was sanctioned by and grounded in new epistemological possibilities unleashed by a host of eighteenth-century thinkers, beginning with Ogyū Sorai. The essential property of this intellectual shift was the notation of a break in the line; its path to resolution was marked by an attack on *ri* (or rational speculation), rejection of an optimistic monism, the recovery of human feeling and emotion (*ninjō*) from its hitherto anomalous status, the new relativity of morality, and the concern for genetic origins. The issue struck at the root metaphor of Neo-Confucianism itself which, in its effort to apprehend the world in a series of resemblances, could no longer account for "differences" as mere anomaly.

The new choice was to explain the world in a modality of contiguity, so as to accommodate the apparent differences among phenomena, not continuity, which had previously been made possible by a paradigmatic model of knowledge. Contiguity called forth the model of the syntagm, spatial relationships, and the categories of order, measurement, calculation, and discrimination. In a new discourse, in contrast to Neo-Confucianism, the world of appearances would be broken down into dualities, oppositions, or contiguous linkages such as cause and effect, agent and act, visible and invisible. Such concerns showed the destruction of the earlier kinship between the seen and the read, eye and ear; hereafter discourse would indicate that what was stated was distinct from what

---

[6] Gérard Mairet, *Le discours et l'historique* (Paris, 1974), pp. 35-76, for a brilliant analysis of the historian's discourse and the problem of history.

an utterance was really supposed to represent. Eighteenth-century Japanese confronted the prospect of a vast cultural transformation in which thoughtful men would seek to make sense of a world where the word could no longer be confidently identified with what it presumed to signify.

Activity consisted less in drawing things together—in setting thinkers out on a quest for everything that might reveal some sort of kinship, that would induce emulation, or indeed sympathy, promising a sense of sameness or a secretly shared nature—than in accounting for the relationship between apparently different things. Eighteenth-century writers turned their sights toward distinctions and discriminations in a general effort to establish the identities of things. No longer were connections and identities inevitable. Here, discrimination imposed upon comparison as its main method the recognition of the primacy of difference. This comparative technique was used increasingly by a variety of writers, from the most formal philosophic types to those anonymous scribes who drafted peasant petitions; comparison was often expressed in terms of management and calculability (*hakaru*) and the establishment of an orderly series of things. Measurement presupposed starting from a whole and dividing it into parts. Yet it was the parts themselves that observers were to equate with the whole; order, in its turn, established elements, the simplest that could be found, to arrange differences according to the smallest degrees. The consequences of this metonymic strategy (the term was not used by the Japanese) was to permit observers to make qualitative distinctions where previously, under the regime of a paradigmatic model of knowledge, it had been difficult to do so; it was expressed increasingly in distinctions between competence and incompetence, equality and inequality, past performances and present experience, and so on. Indeed, the concern for comparison itself became, in time, a function of the search for orderly series.

By resorting to what I have called a metonymic strategy, Japanese thinkers were able to establish part / whole relationships in an apprehension of the world in which one thing—the part—is reduced to another or is substituted for the whole. In this epistemological scheme, parts of presumed totalities functioned to construct a series of attributes (the whole) that could reveal the web of relationships that bound entities together. Metonymy promised to make sense of things that appeared to be different by relating them to each other in contiguity. Scholarship and action proceeded under the sanction of wholes made up of discrete parts. Ogyū Sorai's historicist declaration that the Way is too large for anybody to comprehend or indeed for humans to exhaust suggests the presupposition of a whole whose parts are adequate to it, just as his celebration of the little virtues (*toku*), the plurality of human dispositions, showed that each was as good as the next because each represented a part of the whole society. It is important to notice the priority of the parts. Of course, this disposition should not be taken to contradict the claims of qualitative differences that would inevitably show up in any constructed series of attributes. Both the epistemological context for the Mito emphasis on proper relationships with its considerations of talent and practicality, and also the sanction for radical declarations of equality among new religious groups in the late Tokugawa period, disclose the degree to which a hierarchy of quality still prevailed in thought and action.

The characteristic disciplines of this new epistemology—political economism, *kokugaku, Mitogaku,* and even *rangaku*—in fact were all distinguished by a strategy that sought to link things, or parts, into comprehensive series (in the shape of a syntagm) in order to constitute a whole. Moreover, this strategy prompted the organization of new religious groupings that saw themselves ideologically as parts substituting for the whole. Yet imagining what kind of whole such parts might form represented not simply a utopian withdrawal from the *bakuhan* conception of social order but, more importantly, the conscious promotion of conflict as a necessary step in the achievement of a newly constructed series. The power of this new epistemological program in metonymy was to reduce things to essential parts, to search out, as a consequence, the genetic origins of things. While this form of reduction to origins was a necessary condition of metonymy, genesis itself usually offered a powerful warrant for action in the present. Perhaps the most dramatic instances of this expressive mode were *kokugaku* and *Mitogaku* which, like Sorai's historicism (*kogaku*), appeared to be propelled by a restorationist impulse that many writers have interpreted as simply "romantic," quixotic, nostalgic, or conservative. None has identified its essential realism. It is in the nature of the metonymic mode to reduce things to origins (in order to retrieve essentials and tangible meanings), whether exemplified in the purely secularized search for wealth among political economists or the active programs of the new religions.[7] The effort was prompted either by an attempt to control the object of the genetic search or to justify the organization of a group as part of a new totality. In the crucial sciences concerned with language, labor, and life (history), the search for essences of the object of study was carried on in one or another of the parts of the totality under consideration; language went back to pure and tangible meaning (*kokugaku*), political economism and nativism both sought out the sources of political authority. The new

[7] See Kenneth Burke, *A Grammar of Motives* (Berkeley and Los Angeles: University of California Press, 1969), pp. 503-517.

religions, sharing with *kokugaku* the genetic explanation of a particularistic world, dramatized the importance of human activity as a repayment of the blessings given by some deity at the beginning. Ironically, more than most modes they stressed the centrality of the human achievement over mere natural propensities.[8]

The shift from paradigm to syntagm signaled what Foucault has identified as a shift from representation to a theory analyzing representation, from quantitative to qualitative evaluations.[9] In this instance, signs, as linguists in the eighteenth century such as Fujitani Nariakira argued, no longer resembled what they were presumed to signify, and language itself became a tool for analysis. Fujitani developed an elaborate theory of grammar composed of four parts, on the analogy of articles of dress. A language in this mode could be reduced to any one of its parts.[10] Yet, to describe language in this way, using the analogy of clothing, was to speak of the human subject itself. Ogyū Sorai and his successors reconceptualized the human being into an autonomous, active, and, indeed, willful agency, for whom the gift of language represented a form of social praxis if not ontology. Here, too, was the means for later ideologues to recenter as subject the particular social groups they wished to represent. This, in any case, Sorai recognized as the primacy of passion and the necessity of desire. The particular endowment of each human, what Sorai called the "little virtue," explained both the necessity of division that produced a plurality of naturally different *toku* (virtues), and the condition of sociality—the whole—which characterizes all human communities at any given moment.

Ogyū and his successors argued that whereas differences between hu-

---

[8] The concern for origins is a perfect example of the metonymic strategy. It is necessitated by projecting backward the contiguous links until the beginning or the most simple form in the series is reached. Yet it permits the act of substitution by shifting discussion from the present to the past as a condition of understanding the present. Late Tokugawa thinkers were virtually unanimous in their quest to retrace origins. One of the most interesting Tokugawa discussions is found in Shiba Kōkan's *Shunbarō hikki* in *Nihon zuihitsu taikei* (Tokyo, 1936), 1:459.

[9] Michel Foucault, *The Order of Things* (New York: Random House, 1970), pp. 46-76.

[10] The eighteenth-century linguist Fujitani Nariakira was perhaps the most original thinker among a group of brilliant students of language and philosophy. Motoori Norinaga was in communication with him, and others acknowledged his genius. Nariakira contemplated nothing less than a complete and comprehensive structural analysis of the Japanese language, which premature death cut short. Yet this impulse was prompted not simply by an interest in language per se but rather a recognition, shared by many in the eighteenth century, that the question dogging philosophy related to the representative status of language itself. In any event, Nariakira has never, as far as I know, been integrated into a general discussion of late Tokugawa thought; he has been the captive of professional linguists who, naturally enough, count him as one of the founders of modern linguistic science in Japan. See Tokieda Motoki, *Kokugogakushi* (Tokyo, 1970), pp. 118-126.

man beings constituted natural parts, at one level each equal to the other and thus standing in a part-to-whole relationship, they also represented different dispositions for the functioning of community at any given time in history.[11] The implications of this argument were far-reaching. Such a rearrangement in the way the individual parts interacted socially projected a new image of the social itself (the whole) as the product of differences, not resemblances; individual will, not the determination of moral history or nature, brought together the parts making up the totality. History was, in fact, another way of expressing how differences had been related to each other in order to create the human order.

Ogyū explicitly characterized the seemingly infinite possibilities, indeed the inexhaustability, of the Way. Operating from this proposition, his successors showed that experience was mere manifestation of the Way, which could never be known in its fullness. To argue in this manner was to call attention to the part / whole relationship that the new strategy surely promoted. Moreover, to celebrate the centrality of naturally different endowments that could not be changed by some morally transforming process was to argue for the human, inventive origins of social life and the primacy of human agency in the making of history. This was not history, but histories or, as *kokugakusha* announced, custom. As the little virtues always made up a social whole, histories aggregated to make up the Way, which stretched out beyond human comprehension. Tetsuo Najita, in this connection, has stated the following:

> No individual should surrender that virtue in terms of something other than what he is, and no prince should demand that sacrifice. The idea that one can transform the "self" according to an abstract "good," therefore, was a coercive and "legalistic" ethical idea, according to Ogyū. . . . The prince, clearly, was a "social prince" . . . *Kun wa gun nari*, meaning quite literally that the prince was synonymous with a group of people and with community itself.[12]

Indeed, Sorai's putative divided consciousness, manifested in the separation between public and private, was no division at all but merely an effort to relate private (the parts) to public in metonymy.[13]

---

[11] This particular argument owes much to Tetsuo Najita's formulations on Ogyū Sorai. See especially Najita, "Reconsidering Maruyama Masao's *Studies*," *The Japan Interpreter*, 11 (Spring 1976), 97-108.

[12] Ibid.

[13] See my "Maruyama's Achievement," *Journal of Asian Studies*, 36 (May 1977), 527-534. Readers familiar with Professor Maruyama's argument on the separation of public and private will note that I have argued conversely, using the model of a metonymic relationship, that no separation took place. Maruyama's argument rests on the bourgeois

Basically, Sorai and the later political economists revealed a shift in the axis of Neo-Confucian epistemology to a discourse that would permit the entry of new objects for analysis. It would make room for a new definition of humans as subjective (passionate), inventing, and indeed calculating animals capable of acting in their own interests. This new emphasis upon a subject who analyzed theories of representation, a knower who conferred signification, could easily slide into a radical skepticism or solipsism. It might become a rejection of rational speculation or a disbelief in all reasoned explanations in favor of faith, wonder, and mystification, as in *kokugaku* and the new religions. But disbelief served more as a goad to action, and later secession, than a merely resigned acceptance, as so many writers have argued.

Skepticism as a philosophic form may inhibit certain kinds of action, but it is also an invitation to faith and wonder, which suggests the possibility that groups of people who had been judged incapable of rational discourse could find new means for the validation of action. Indeed, the new epistemology cleared the way for action by its concentration on the creative and inventive capacity of humans to establish social order. The disposition to relate parts in a series back to an essential origin in order to identify a whole ultimately obliged writers to posit authenticating fictions and chimeras as first principles; thus the proliferation of archetypal heroes, half men, half gods: Sorai's *Sen-ō*, the *musubi no kami* of the *kokugakusha*, the various primal deities of the new religions (each had its own version of a first fable and a generating deity), the concern for *kokutai* among writers of the later Mito school, not to mention their emphasis on the timelessness of the Great Thanksgiving Ceremony (*daijōsai*), the identification of the *kotodama* among eighteenth-century linguists, and the selection by late-Tokugawa ideologues of Peter the Great, George Washington, and Napoleon as cultural heroes. What this kind of strategic return to essences seemed to offer was liberation from the specific structural forms of political enterprise. New sources lent a new content that would provide those new spaces with the political validation necessitated by the act of withdrawal and secession.

It is interesting to note the contrasting results of such a strategy in *Mitogaku* and *kokugaku*. Both proceeded from the same explanatory program: *kokugaku* selected the form of a cosmological history (as did so many of the new religions), whereas *Mitogaku* opted for a synthetic history, to demonstrate connectedness. For nativism, connectedness originated in the creation deities, whereas for Mito the source was the

___

division between state and civil society, even though writers like Ogyū used terms designating "public" (*ōyake*) and "private" (*watakushi*).

Sun Goddess Amaterasu. For *kokugaku* the parts were related to a whole, which was the national soil (*kunitsuchi*) created by the *musubi no kami* and represented by what one might call the "fugitive" tradition of Izumo, whereas in the latter case the parts were related to a whole symbolized in the idea of *kokutai* (which also authorized the identification of Mito *han* with the whole) and representing the orthodox tradition of an unbroken imperial lineage originating in Amaterasu. The former envisaged a world stressing horizontal relationships actualized in the tradition of village communitarianism, wholeness, and the identification of politics and religion; the latter a world more vertical than horizontal, and symbolized by the hierarchical imperial order, a division of responsibilities and loyalties, and also the identification of religion with politics. (The tension between timeless structure as represented in the *daijōsai* with its horizontal associations and the hierarchical arrangement of things that history unfailingly disclosed made the Mito solution the most acceptable and perhaps least radical of all in the late Tokugawa.) The major difference in this identification of religion and politics, which all the new religions and *yonaoshi* (world renewal) groups promoted, is that in the case of the Mito writers the mode of expressiveness was in public institutions (calling for vertical relationships), whereas the nativist program emphasized a private world of "hot relationships" unmediated by institutions. Yet underlying these and other programs was, of course, the primacy of human capacity, the identification of human disposition with the parts: language, work, or ritual literally bespoke not of nature but of other people in terms of some sense of shared purpose and connectedness—man as a subject creating or performing through some form of praxis in order to reproduce the conditions of community.

Promising to establish syntagmatic relationships in metonymy, the new cognitive mode shifted the grounds of discourse from nature to human will, and produced a knowing subject who sought to deal with differences comparatively, qualitatively, and reductively. Ultimately the new epistemological strategy created a new history. The substantive concerns of many of the disciplines of the new discourse and their identification of specific contemporary issues disclosed less a reflective relationship between materiality and its encodation in history than the way in which certain objects were either formed or given representation in the new terms of discourse. Thus the new disciplines saw in custom, commercial wealth, calculability, agricultural work, ritual, and the Japanese language evidence of quotidian differences that required explanation on grounds other than recourse to resemblance and similitude as projected by the Neo-Confucian mode. The reductive strategy and the subsequent concern for origins—how things related to each other in a constructed series—offered the prospect of controlling the very means by which things were represented. If, as in the earlier discursive mode, nature served merely as a text whose truths were there for decipherment, the new epistemology saw the world as problematic, as material for the construction of a number of "texts" that would merely "represent" things rather than be the things themselves. Yet, to say this is to suggest not simply the subjective character of knower and signifier but surely how writers and thinkers, in performing such acts as encoding "texts," could presume to control the very things and objects that they prepared for representation. In this pursuit, primacy was placed upon the comparative thrust that sought to measure things in terms of qualitative criteria, as illustrated best by Fujita Yūkoku's transmutation of *seimei* (rectification of names) into *meibunron* (the discrimination of duties), or celebrations of ability over mere loyalty (*jinzai*), the acquisition of an instrumental knowledge for quotidianal purposes (*jitsugaku*), and the equitable distribution of land and productivity, which both nativists and adherents of new religions expressed in the call for mutual assistance. Indeed these were the very principles by which thoughtful people could, at a later time, envisage the possibilities of revolutionary transformation. It was in this way that the discourse on origins became a discourse on power.

Epistemology and Cultural Forms

> *To leave empirical reality behind can only mean that the objects of the empirical world are to be understood as aspects of a totality, i.e., as aspects of a total social situation caught up in the process of social change. Thus the category of mediation is a lever with which to overcome the mere immediacy of the empirical world and as such it is not something (subjective) foisted on to the objects from outside. . . .* It is rather the manifestation of their authentic objective structure.
>
> Georg Lukács, *History and Class Consciousness*
> (Cambridge, Mass., 1971), p. 162

It would be wrong to infer from my abbreviated account of the eighteenth-century intellectual transformation that such activity remained locked in a set of idealistic transactions that remained safely immune from the conditions of "real" history. The new strategy revealed its historicity by forming a discourse that might offer representation to things that had not been hitherto included in official consciousness. That is, whereas epistemology might offer possibilities for new kinds of expressibility, history (or how people saw history) would mediate such efforts and give specificity to the forms that might otherwise have remained as just so many unrealized potentialities. The strategy obviously made possible, in discursive form, representative space for people to inhabit (and to act on) where none had existed before: the merchants and artisans in political economism, the new upper and middle peasantry in *kokugaku*, the "eccentrics" in *rangaku* (the true heroes of the different), the lower peasantry in the new religions and *yonaoshi* events, and the "able samurai" and the domain itself in *Mitogaku*. Yet such discursive possibilities meant also including new relationships where before they either had been excluded or consigned to the margins of established discourse. The resulting discourse established new rules for inclusion, new combinations of mechanisms, yet the forms by which inclusion was given specific expression indicated the mediations of contemporary history.

The dialectic between epistemology and new cultural forms disclosed the less apparent relationship between knowledge and power: representation determined the kinds of power relationships that, it was believed, should characterize society. The creation of new cultural forms in *kokugaku* and *Mitogaku*, and the praxis-oriented constituencies of the new religions, meant declaring the right to be represented, an act that in itself would run counter to the received discursive mode identified with the *bakuhan* order. The possibility of conflict is always present when a group is formed and specifies its right to gain discursive representation; in the late Tokugawa period history specified the lines that such conflict would follow.

The creation of new spaces apart from the *bakuhan* control system represented an effort to deal with "reality" more effectively rather than a challenging alternative to the Tokugawa order. Such spaces sanctioned the importance of difference and defined the prospect for possible conflict with established authority. The conditions of and boundaries for conflict and transformation were obviously established by difference, contiguity, part / whole relationships, horizontality, ability, equality, and human agency through intentional reproduction (praxis) rather than sameness, continuity, verticality, ascription, and people behaving as objects to be acted upon. Yet the impulse was prompted by contemporary history and the way it was apprehended by those who acted to provide themselves with self-definition. Events were interpreted in such a way as to offer specificity to new discursive claims. What the new cognitive system permitted, above all, was identification of the problem. Emphasis upon the centrality of daily affairs and their importance for reproducing the communal unit, aid and relief, mutual assistance, equality and distribution, and ability did not necessarily "reflect" conditions in the bakumatsu, as is usually supposed, so much as "interpret" facts in a certain modality. To "interpret," indeed to arrogate the right to do so, was to embark upon praxis itself.

In any case, it is the nature of the claims that interpretation yielded and how they interacted with contemporary history that I wish to explore in the remaining section of this paper. It is important to reveal the ways in which claims were formalized into specific action groups, and the subsequent shape of conflict produced by the new articulations. But the real relationship between epistemology and cultural forms, between knowledge and the determination of new power relationships, where action intersected with "history," was provided by the part / whole relationship. That is to say, the metonymical strategy, stressing part / whole relationships, sanctioned ideological efforts to substitute the part, especially the new group, for the whole. In the Bakumatsu period nobody would disagree that the whole was the object of serious engagement— thus the disparate calls for a "land of the gods": *shinshū, shinkoku, kokka*, or what have you. The real problem was to determine which parts would, in fact, constitute the whole; such a determination would permit the subsequent conclusion that the whole, whatever it might be, was reducible to that part, that the part and the whole stood in a relationship of spatial contiguity; thus the Mito emphasis upon the primacy of the domain sanctioned by the essentialist *kokutai*, the *kokugaku* concentration on the village authenticated by its relation to the primal deities (transmitted through tutelary gods), the declarations of new forms of community marking most of the new religions, and indeed even the *yonaoshi* (world renewal) groupings in their effort to give permanence to their conception of epiphany and the liminal moment.

The resultant form of activity constituted a secession from the central control system, a withdrawal into a new space, whether the autonomous village of rural *kokugakusha* or the communitarian communities of the new religions. The intention informing secession and withdrawal was not consciously seditious but represented an evaluation of the contemporary situation that concluded that the shogunal control system, which was identified with a conception of the whole, was increasingly less able to provide the services by which it had justified its arrogation of power. Indeed such acts serve to remind us of Marx's famous injunction in the opening of *The Eighteenth Brumaire of Louis Bonaparte*: "Men make their own history but they do not make it as they please. They do not make it under circumstances chosen by themselves but under circumstances directly encountered, given, and transmitted from the past."

Conflict was produced by the decision of new groups who, by finding representation, felt justified in constituting themselves as autonomous entities related to the whole in metonymy. Although the immediate impulse to secede might have been prompted by the interaction of epistemology and the evaluation of contemporary history, its major promise was, I believe, not simply to repudiate the *bakuhan* system, though this was surely one of its lasting results. Rather, the reason these various secessions from the center seemed so dangerous and ultimately constituted sources of conflict was the shared effort among many groups to lower the historical temperature; to achieve immunity from the erosions of contemporary change and to achieve a timeless, self-sufficient and, by definition, autonomous community; to freeze the liminal moment into what Claude Lévi-Strauss has called a "cold society." Indeed, the secessions, whether the Mito elevation of domainal integrity or the actual withdrawal from established society as observed among several of the new religions, were invariably marked by programs of self-sufficiency (*fukoku kyōhei*) among the *han*, or mutual assistance (*ai-tasuke*) among *kokugakusha* and the new religions, as if to show the way the center had "failed to hold." All, too, sought to balance the claims of a timeless order with the incursions of contemporary history and perceptible change. Nowhere was this more true than in the Mito effort to match the claims of *kokutai*, a timeless structure to which all forms are reduced (expressed by the antique ritual that calls attention to it—the *daijōsai*), with the intrusion of historical change (*jisei*).

One other observation might briefly be made. In the case of *kokugaku*, which appropriated nativist sentiment to reconstruct the autonomous group, and even in the *yonaoshi* thrust, we have signs of not simply class-layered withdrawal and the subsequent loss of control in the countryside; there are also, in the acts of secession and autonomization, realignments along horizontal and communitarian lines that promised freedom or at least distance from the external world of public power and political relationships. Here, too, knowledge shaped the character of politics, not just by representing new social constituencies in discourse, where before there had only been silence, but by determining how they were to be related to each other. Only in the Mito projection can we detect a departure from this shared disposition, or surely an ambiguity that, owing to the juxtaposition of race and status in *kokutai*, made its position less sharp than it might have been. In any event it is important to call attention to the communitarian associations of this secession from the control system, and the obvious potentiality for collision with the established claims of vertical public political arrangements. In the end, conflict in Tokugawa Japan was generated by considerations of power disguised by what Michel Foucault has called "a will to knowledge."

Invariably, every manifestation by which the new discourse sought its own rules of formation and discipline disclosed an accompanying and almost obligatory concern for the foundations of knowledge and learning. But the central question was always, knowledge and learning for whom? and for what purpose? This was surely the problem faced by a generation of writers and activists in Mito *han* (Fujita Yūkoku,

Aizawa Seishisai, Fujita Tōko, Toyoda Tenkō) who early sought a form of representation by enunciating a program of practical discipline and education. Learning was the means by which Mito writers were able to give definition and expression to a new conception of political space—the autonomous *han*. Yet it was precisely the conception of the *han*, now elevated to a new status, that promised to serve as substitute for *shinkoku*, an unspecified whole and one that validated the domain-centric vision of Mito writers. Like Sorai's "social prince," the *han* related to the realm in metonymy; knowledge and learning would serve the new political space because its articulation already bespoke withdrawal and secession. The condition of autonomy, now required by the elevated status of the *han*, demanded self-sufficiency, which, of course, knowledge and learning of a specific kind promised to satisfy. This line of argumentation was thoroughly worked out later in the 1850s and 1860s by people such as Yokoi Shōnan, Takasugi Shinsaku (notably in his conception of *kakkyo* and *dai kakkyo*), and even Ōkubo Toshimichi, who saw a reconstituted domain, economically sufficient and militarily prepared, as a sure substitute for the realm. The lines were drawn first in Mito.

Thus it was the elevation of the part—the domain in this instance—that marked Mito rhetoric as a conflict-producing ideology. Perception collided with epistemology; writers recognized in continuing peasant rebellion and domainal indebtedness the shape of a general malaise and a threat to received conceptions of order itself. But to promote the domain—the part—as a resolution to the problems of the whole was, in fact, a possibility, owing to the new cognitive mode and its corresponding strategy. The sanction for this domain-centered projection was provided by the larger effort to reduce the various parts of a series to essentiality—*kokutai*. The Mito discussion on *kokutai* is familiar enough, but it is, perhaps, important to note that whatever else it meant, it also represented, much as did the nativist appeal to the *kunitsuchi* and *musubi no kami* or the several invocations to primal deities among the new religions, an effort to reduce things to their origins in order to identify the whole that the part stands for. For Mito writers, *kokutai* represented the indissoluble link between status and loyal behavior (*chūkō no michi*) and the network of duties and designations. It was their purpose to show how these normative principles might be reimplemented in the domain; how, in fact, *kokutai* required the resuscitation of the domain along such essentialist lines.[14] To argue in this manner was to propose

[14] I have written on the Mito school in my *Toward Restoration* (Berkeley and Los Angeles: University of California Press, 1970), pp. 47-128. I have learned much from J. Victor Koschmann's Ph.D. dissertation, "Discourse in Action: Representational Politics in Mito in the Late Tokugawa Period" (Chicago, 1980); and Bitō Masahide's "Mitogaku no to-

that the domain, refashioned morally, could substitute for the whole. This is surely the meaning of Fujita Yūkoku's enunciation of the lines of vertical loyalty running from the emperor down through the lower orders. Here, in his youthful essay "Seimeiron," is one of the possible functions for his call for discrimination, itself a device validated by the new strategy.[15]

Much of this strategy, then, was deployed to apprehend the nature of contemporary events as they were encountered in Mito. Mito writers moved along a rather broad arc whose terminal points were marked by a profound distrust of the masses and a moral sense of benevolence toward their well-being: fear on the one hand, blackmail on the other. Among the recurring anxieties expressed in Mito writings, none seemed more urgent or frightening than the possibility of imminent mass disorder in the countryside and, by implication, the seeming incapacity of the Tokugawa bakufu to stem or even arrest the swelling tide.

The incidence of peasant disturbance was related to perceptions concerning the disabled status of the *han* itself. Mito writers regularly chorused the plaint that the shogunate had pursued policies deliberately designed to undermine the domain's strength and to increase its dependence upon the bakufu. A resolution of one, the declining status of the domain, was a guaranteed solution to the other. People can be ruled, Aizawa announced, only by recourse to the Way of loyalty and filial duty.[16] But behind this conviction was a low view of human nature and, of course, a rather dim estimate of the masses, whom Aizawa constantly referred to as "ignorant fools" (*shungu*).[17] The masses were ignorant and unpredictably disorderly because they were forever prevented from acquiring the niceties of virtue and, as all Mito writers agreed, were capable only of being led. If left to their own devices, they would, like children, pursue profit, pleasure, and personal luxury—so Mito writers "interpreted" the nature of contemporary outbursts and disturbances.[18] Because they were fearful of spirits and ghosts, the masses would be gradually led to embrace Christianity, "a cruelly unjust and shallow doctrine." Peasant disorder was invariably seen as an expression

---

kushitsu" in Imai Usaburō, Seya Yoshihiko, and Bitō Masahide, eds., *Mitogaku*, Nihon shisō taikei 53 (Tokyo, 1973).

[15] Fujita Yūkoku, "Seimeiron," in Imai, Seya and Bitō, eds., *Mitogaku*, pp. 10–14. Rectification led to a restructuring of relationships. It resulted in representing what before was merely taken for granted; discrimination now became the condition for determining demarcations that, previously, had been viewed as inscriptions of nature. In Yūkoku's reformulation the domain secured a central status in the arrangement of authority.

[16] Aizawa Seishisai, "Shinron," in ibid., pp. 53, 62, 65ff. This is, I believe, one of the main arguments in this text.

[17] Ibid., pp. 69, 104.

[18] Ibid., p. 76.

of private interest. To offset this threat of mass chaos, Mito writers called for benevolence, and reminded the leadership of its obligations to "love" and "revere" the people. Love and reverence translated into concrete measures that would dissipate the fears of the managerial class, whose members saw worse things to come, by ameliorating disorder in the countryside. Aizawa, despite his scarcely concealed contempt for "mean people," argued that "loving the people" required hard commitments from the leadership. He could also agree with Tokugawa Nariaki who, upon his succession to the lordship of Mito, announced that it was the primary purpose of the leadership to love and care for the people. "Virtue is the root, commodities the branch," he remarked; virtuous leaders could in no way "prevent themselves from bestowing blessings on the people."[19]

The issue Mito writers sought to dramatize was, of course, the question of control. The "good teachings" of etiquette and civilization were guarantees of permanent order; by equating the status ethic and its proper discrimination with "loving the people," Mito writers could argue that if the leadership "bestowed proper blessings on the people" (feeding and educating them) the realm would thus administer itself. Yet, if "good doctrine" was abandoned, the people would "avoid political laws as one avoids an enemy; their yearning will be like the yearning of a child for an affectionate mother."[20] When people are not under moral control, Fujita Tōko reported, always mindful of Ōshio's rebellion in Osaka in 1837, they resemble a "product which first putrifies and then gives way to worms and maggots. People who are heretical are similar to those who are ill. Men who ably govern the sick will first promote their health; men who expel heresy will first cultivate the Great Way."[21] Nariaki, arguing in a manner that later observers would echo, asserted that if the peasantry "bears a grudge or resents the upper class, it will not stand in awe of them." But more than rhetoric was needed to secure control. Control required providing assistance, which, for Nariaki, meant "tranquilizing Mito domain and giving assistance to the people; if we succeed in exhausting our intentions day and night in returning the blessings, we will be able to sympathize with all hearts." Indeed, the lord of Mito saw the times ripe for a "restoration of the domain (kokka o chūkō-shi)" and a "renovation of custom in order to be unified with others."[22] The purport of this statement of purpose was to prevent the fragmentation that was going on in the domain. The long peace had

[19] Quoted in Shibahara Takuji, Meiji Ishin no kenryoku kiban (Tokyo, 1965), pp. 125–126. Also Imai, Seya, and Bitō, eds., Mitogaku, pp. 211, 212.

[20] Aizawa, "Shinron," pp. 110, 139, 144, 154; also Shibahara, Meiji Ishin, p. 126.

[21] Takasu Yoshijirō, ed., Mitogaku taikei (Tokyo, 1943), 1:79, 87.

[22] Tokugawa Nariaki, "Kokushiden," in Imai, Seya and Bitō, eds., Mitogaku, p. 211.

slackened "custom" and "morality" and had introduced confusion into the order of designations and duties.

Nariaki, like Yūkoku and Aizawa, constantly employed a language that called attention to the basis (*moto*) as against the nonessential (*mina sono moto o wasurete shashi ni chōji*). The complaint was directed at all groups within the domain. The logical solution was to return to essentials. Specifically this meant reapplying to the domain itself the injunction of the Great Learning: "The basis of the realm is the family, the basis of the family is in moral discipline." Despite appeals for the tightening of moral relations, the domain was required to embark upon far-reaching reforms in "custom" and "military preparedness." "In a tranquil realm," Nariaki wrote in the *Kokushiden*, "we can never forget about rebellion . . . we have forgotten about the thick blessings which have been bestowed by peace today . . . and we have been concerned only with being well fed and well clad. . . . The samurai have become effeminate and resemble a body that contracts an illness after exposure to cold, windy, or hot weather. They (*shi*) are the idlers and wastrels (*yūmin*) among the four classes."[23]

Thus it was the special function of the domain to offer the only prospect for a genuine restoration (*chūkō*). Toyoda Tenkō composed an essay in 1833 along these lines and argued that "ancient man wrote, 'a restoration is always difficult to accomplish' but it must be even more difficult to do so today."[24] Yet, he believed, the times were propitious, and even though ancient sages had invariably linked the achievement of a restoration to the successful conclusion of a rebellion, Tenkō saw the recent decline of the domain as an equivalent occasion for embarking upon the difficult task. The argumentation for this "restoration" had been powerfully pursued earlier by Yūkoku, and more recently by Aizawa, who had claimed that the bakufu had willfully followed a policy of self-interest in which the "base is strengthened while the ends are weakened."[25] If the lords are permitted to play the role they have been assigned by the emperor, Yūkoku asserted, then they can return to "rectifying" the boundaries of their domains. What this meant for Mito writers was simply the elevation of the domain—a virtual reversal of the base / ends metaphor. The program for this "rectification" was provided by a practical education stressing ability and utility, for if learning actually served such purposes, then people could be encouraged to carry out productive enterprises beneficial to the domain.

Yūkoku advised in a letter that the lord must perform meritorious

---

[23] Ibid., p. 226.

[24] Toyoda Tenkō, in Imai, Seya and Bitō, eds., *Mitogaku*, p. 197.

[25] Fujita, "Seimeiron," pp. 10-14. The argument in the "Seimeiron" projects the domain to central importance. Also Aizawa, "Shinron," pp. 73, 78.

works everywhere; first, he must insure an adequate food supply and a strong military organization to discourage rebellion. But, much to his recorded despair, there were signs everywhere of "inadequate merit" and "private desire": "the administration of Mito today is based upon the division between the rich and the poor, separate [standards of] virtue and separate behavior." Indeed, Yūkoku protested, "All this has to be changed. For, if there were a great crisis, how could we adequately accept responsibility in the several sectors of society?" Yūkoku's proposal called for a reform leading to *fukoku kyōhei*, executed by an able and efficient administration. It should be noted, in this connection, that such a reform, or, as it was later called, restoration, would be secured only after a reorganization of the educational capacities of the domain and through stringent "measurement of what comes in and what goes out."[26]

The intellectual sanction for this new edifice as envisaged by the Mito writers was, as suggested above, a reductive strategy that identified the whole in a mystical body called *kokutai*. Elaboration for this sanction was provided by Aizawa Seishisai in his seminal essay, "Shinron" (1825). The idea of *kokutai* functioned at two levels: it represented the whole to which the parts (the domain) could relate in metonymy; it also served as the essential origin to which all things are reduced. This is surely what Mito writers meant when they advised "not to forget about the trunk" and "to return blessings to the origins." Indeed, what could seem more essential than the "body" of the realm—the *karada* of the *kuni*? Whereas the thrust of Aizawa's text was to explain the meaning of *kokutai* (for the domain), his purpose was to link this sense of the whole to the new political space represented by the "autonomous domain." His proposals for reform were unexceptional, echoing Yūkoku's earlier suggestions and Nariaki's later measures. But more than most, Aizawa saw the domain as a heavenly endowment that "serves as the bulwark of the divine land" (*toku wa mina shinshū hampei ni shite*).[27]

o

The importance of the Mito achievement was to signal a general secession from the central control system in order to resolve problems of contemporary disorder that the Tokugawa increasingly failed to engage. The result was, of course, to reconstitute the domain itself as a substitute for a whole whose shape was less important than the part that called attention to it. Mito writers gave forceful expression to the growing incidence of peasant disorder and the subsequent failure of officialdom

[26] Takasu, ed., *Mitogaku taikei*, 3:178.

[27] Aizawa Seishisai, "Tekii hen," in Takasu, ed., *Mitogaku taikei*, 2:358-359; also Aizawa, "Shinron," p. 153 where he calls for a unity of effort between bakufu and domains.

to provide security. Their assessment of the contemporary situation dramatized the decline of authority and the withdrawal of services that the Tokugawa had pledged to uphold. In the end, the solution, expressed in the "autonomous domain," was reformulated later by people such as Yokoi Shōnan, Takasugi Shinsaku, and activists in Satsuma. They erected the independent domain in opposition to the bakufu's threat to reconstitute the whole at the expense of dissolving the parts.

Just as Mito writers merged epistemology with their understanding of contemporary reality, to decide what was "real" and "appropriate" and justify a form of secession in the autonomous domain, so *kokugaku-sha*, operating under similar constraints but representing different social constituencies, advanced a theory of the self-sufficient village community as the part for the unenvisaged whole. Under the theoretical reformulation of Hirata Atsutane, who employed Motoori's strategy but altered its focus, *kokugaku* ultimately sought to represent the rural rich (upper and middle peasantry occupying positions of responsibility in village administrations) against the apparent inability of the control system to provide security against disorder and assistance to the general peasantry. The latter invariably struck first at the rural elites in their own effort to gain identification and dramatize their claims. Nativists of the Hirata persuasion also recognized the intimate relationship between knowledge and power. Hirata's appropriations from Motoori were transformed into a discipline of study—*yamatogokoro no gakumon*—whereas one of his later followers, Ōkuni Takamasa, reshaped these doctrines into what he called "basic studies" (*hongaku*).

Hirata's own activities as an itinerant teacher in the rural areas of eastern and northern Japan, and his constant insistence upon lecturing to groups whom he said did not have time to read and to study books, discloses the same kind of concern noted among the Mito writers. Ironically, Hirata's lectures of the 1820s (chiefly the *Tamadasuki* and *Ibuki oroshi*) were directed essentially to townsmen in Edo. But the townsmen to whom he lectured were different from the audiences who attended Motoori's schools in Kyoto. Hirata's audiences were recruited first from the denizens of Edo street life; the most identifiable element were the *yūmin*: idlers, wastrels, floaters, a kind of middle-class lumpenproletariat, refugees from the fugitive culture of the floating world. He took the same message to rural Japan after he left Edo in the late 1820s. What is important is his conviction that such groups required learning for self-identification, and thus some form of discursive representation. This was, in fact, the function of fashioning a discipline for both Hirata and Ōkuni: a space to be occupied by those who had not formed their own discourse.

"Men of high rank," Hirata wrote in the *Ibuki oroshi*, "have the leisure time to read a great many books and thus the means to guide people; men of medium rank (*chūtō*) do not have the time to look at books and do not possess the means to guide people."[28] But this is precisely the point of *kokugaku*, and its central function as Hirata came to envisage it. The ruled must be offered assistance and the opportunity to hear about the Way, as he was to conceive it, since it was as relevant to those who might not be able to read as to those who possessed leisure time. "I would exchange a man who reads books for one who listens. For those who hear [the Way] have realized a greater achievement than those who have gained it through study."[29] Clearly, Hirata was demonstrating the necessity to offer representation to the merely ordinary—those whom Motoori spoke about as an ideal but rarely specified in the manner of later *kokugakusha*. His thought would supply meaning for new rural groups but also provide the warrant for another kind of secession.

Kokugakusha such as Hirata and his followers appealed to a reductive strategy to solve the problem of differentness, and yet retained the promise of metaphorical identification. The solution was to dispose of and thus represent the world through reduction in the modality of contiguity, not the continuity that the perception of differentness had denied. The result was to restore the tangibility and wholeness of metaphor. Thus, Hirata and his school saw their task as discriminating among different entities, accounting for discriminations and demonstrating the inevitable connection among all series. Yet it was the ultimate purpose of *kokugaku*, as it was with Mito, to show how connectedness amounted to a kinship of things (wholeness) and the essential similarity of apparent differences. Connectedness showed family resemblances, and family resemblances revealed the relationship of all things, however different they appeared to be on the surface, because of the common and creative powers of the *musubi no kami*.

Crucial to nativist discourse was a concern for language, life (history), and wealth. Such concerns, by virtue of the commitment to a reductive strategy, would be characterized by the search for the genetic origins of the particular object of study. Thus nativism sought out an original, primal language as a universal and translucent form of representation and also as the means to return language to the world of things. Moreover, the *kokugaku* emphasis on history showed not a process or indeed a development, but rather a crucible of different things created by the *musubi no kami*. History, it was apparently thought, would show the web of relations in kinship that holds life together in a continuum of interchanges between gods and men, life and death, production and

---

[28] Tsunoda Tadayuki et. al., eds., *Hirata Atsutane zenshū* 1 (Tokyo, 1912), 2.
[29] Ibid.

growth, and so on. History was the means to express a conception of spatial contiguity; yet for Hirata and Satō Shinen cosmology was the form that called attention to it.[30] Finally, in their search for the origins of wealth, *kokugakusha* reaffirmed the agricultural project. For rural nativists productivity was the presumed solution to preventing disorder and securing self-sufficiency.

Hirata gave *kokugaku* a systematic mapping and a sense of classification designed to represent the relationships among selected objects. His mode of relating was expressed best in cosmological speculation by which he tried to show that it was impossible for dead souls to migrate to the dreaded and foul underworld of *yomi*. The purpose of these speculations was to provide consolation to those among the masses who feared death, and who thus expressed anxiety and unhappiness in activities such as peasant rebellions. To offer consolation Hirata elaborated upon a fundamental division between "visible things" and "invisible things." This classification was presupposed by his cognitive strategy, which related seemingly unrelated objects to one another by showing their shared identity; that is, he apprehended phenomena as related to each other in part / whole relationships, thus permitting their differentiation, but also the reduction of one to a function of another. It is important to note that Hirata and one of his students, Mutobe Yoshika, concentrated on demonstrating the interrelationship between these two worlds (visible and invisible) because both were products of the creation deities.[31] Yet the invisible world of *Kami* affairs was the source of the phenomenal world of visible things. The obvious importance of this division was that by linking the visible to the invisible, and by making one's conduct in the former the basis of judgment in the latter, Hirata and his school were able to offer representation and meaning to groups that remained outside of official discourse. Judgment was based upon morally informed activity, which usually meant work and productive labor. Whatever one did was important—recalling Ogyū's discourse on the little virtues; each individual was thus obliged to perform according to the endowment deposited in him by the heavenly deities.

Hirata's cosmology did much more than enjoin the ruled—the ordinary folk—to fall into line and work hard. In fact, the really important result of his meditations concerning the relationship between divine intention and human purpose was to transform what hitherto had been regarded, in official discourse, as an object into a doing and knowing

---

[30] I have written on Hirata's conception of cosmology in Tetsuo Najita and Irwin Scheiner, eds., *Japanese Thought in the Tokugawa Period* (Chicago: University of Chicago Press, 1978).

[31] Mutobe Yoshika, "Kenyū junkōron," in Saeki Ariyoshi et al., eds., *Shintō sōsho*, 3 (Tokyo, 1897); 4 (Tokyo, 1897); 5 (Tokyo, 1898); 7 (Tokyo, 1898).

subject. He thus demonstrated that the ordinary folk, called *aoihitokusa* by *kokugakusha*, occupied a position of autonomy through the infusion of ethics into their quotidian life and the productivity of their daily labor. By this turn, Hirata made the nativist vision into a powerful projection that others later would normalize into sanctions for secession. His theorizing about the social life world called attention to the centrality of such activities as work and productivity, which formerly had been consigned to the margins of Confucian purpose.

Hirata and his rural followers shifted the axis of attention from the performance of specific behaviors that satisfied norms to the essence of life itself, which was the means of all performance and the indispensable basis of community. The idea of the hidden world took on specific associations: it became synonymous with the sanctuary of the ancestors. Yet the identification between hidden things and the space occupied by the spirits served increasingly as the object of folkic religious practices. The hidden world represented a structural homology with the world of the family, household, and rural community. Symbolized by the tutelary shrines (which in themselves represented the tradition of Izumo and Ōkuninonushi, ruler of the invisible), and thus by the village itself, this world was hidden, powerless in the realm of public authority, yet vibrant with "real" activity. Here, nativist discourse pitted a horizontal realm, close to nature, against the vertical world of the Tokugawa *daikan*, daimyo, shogun and even emperor—indeed, against the artifice of contemporary history itself. The hidden world of village, ancestors, and deities was more "real" than the visible world of power. Without the sanctioning authority of this hidden world the idea of an autonomous village would not have been possible.

Even as this juxtaposition of realms represented Hirata's attempt to dramatize the "real" and the "appropriate," it also offered explosive political possibilities in the environment of late Tokugawa Japan. I can only suggest in this context the obvious implications of elevating the Izumo version of the creation myth over the Ise, and what that could have meant at a later time. Yet at its most fundamental level, the world envisaged by Hirata and his rural followers (Mutobe Yoshika, Miyahiro Sadao, Miyauchi Yoshinaga, Ōkuni Takamasa, Suzuki Shigetane, Katsura Takashige) was one of linkages and relationships, where the microcosm, the village, was informed by macrocosmic organization; where the emperor as living deity of the polity met the tutelary deities and ancestors administered by Ōkuninonushi, who also represented the private communal world of rural Japan; where verticality collided with the horizontal and hidden claims of village life.

Thus *kokugaku*, in its rural appropriation, sanctioned the elevation of the village as substitute for the whole, just as phenomenal life merely called attention to its noumenal and hidden origins. The argument for an autonomous village standing for the whole, apart or separated from the world of public authority, was authenticated by appeals to the Izumo version of mytho-history. Much of it hinged upon the duty to return blessings to the creation deities from which all things literally flowed, and the subsequent obligation to replicate the archetypal creative acts through agricultural work and reproduction. This duty was invariably described as a form of entrustment (*yosashi, mi-yosashi*) which derived its power from scriptural authority and usually had two distinct meanings: literally, the actual event in which the creation gods gave something to other gods or to the imperial descendents; figuratively, the land (*kunitsuchi*) as the object of divine bestowal. Both implied the sense of a trust that must be satisfied, a trust to work the land offered by the gods.[32]

Late Tokugawa *kokugakusha* (invariably village leaders) such as Miyahiro Sadao and Hirayama Chūeimon saw the idea of entrustment as a means of emphasizing the central importance of agricultural life, not to mention their own position in such a world. It was in this context that Miyahiro could propose that agriculture is the base of the realm and the village is the most appropriate means of organizing people to work together. Others saw the village and the *ie* (household) as simply interchangeable. Yet as indicated by theoreticians such as Ōkuni Takamasa, this notion of an autonomous village merged also with the idea of an administration (*minsei*) pledged to taking care of the people (*buiku*). The upshot was increasingly to see *kokugaku* as a method for solving problems in the countryside. Such a method was dramatized in this conception of caring, assistance, and mutual aid, which also could be justified under the aspect of entrustment; in the end, entrustment so conceived became grounds for village self-sufficiency and secession.[33]

All of this was in actuality possible, according to rural nativists, if there existed an administration willing to carry out its "trust" to the people. Writers such as Miyahiro and Miyauchi Yoshinaga proposed ways to bring relief to the rural poor, since these services had been withdrawn or seriously compromised in their areas.[34] Ōkuni's major argument on the importance of work rested upon the premise of mutual self-help as the basis of community and self-sufficiency. But self-suffi-

[32] On the question of entrustment, see the entry "kotoyosashi" in Matsumoto Sannosuke and Haga Noboru, eds., *Kokugaku undō no shisō*, Nihon shisō taikei 51 (Tokyo: 1971), pp. 598-599.

[33] This is the argument proposed by Katsura Takashige in his *Yotsugigusa tsumiwake* (Niigata, 1884).

[34] Miyahiro Sadao, "Kokueki honron" and Miyauchi Yoshinaga, "Tō yamabiko" in Matsumoto and Haga, eds., *Kokugaku undō no shisō*, pp. 292-359.

ciency envisaged larger schemes for the rehabilitation of villages through autonomous action. Essential to self-sufficiency was the relationship between the village leadership and peasantry. Miyahiro, for example, advised peasants to understand and thus preserve the "commands of the *myōshu*, which are no different from public ordinances."[35] Like most rural *kokugakusha*, he saw the village leadership (much like Mito writers talking about domainal leadership) as a substitute for the entrustment represented by emperor, shogun, and daimyo; not as a challenge to officially constituted authority but as a recognition that within the jurisdiction of the village, officials "must have as their chief duty the administration of the peasantry."[36]

It was recognized by most rural nativists that the village—increasingly, and especially in bad years—would be responsible for the extension of relief and assistance. Responsibility fell, according to contemporary reports, to the village official, and although we can discount much of this as self-serving, it would be wrong to underestimate the concern for relief and assistance in certain rural regions. Just as the village—the part—served to recall the whole, so the official—reminiscent of Sorai's prince—was a social official. Indeed, much of the language of rural *kokugaku* referred to the village (and trust) as if it were cut off from other structures. It was precisely in this context that they sought to explain the necessity of self-sufficiency and independent economic determination. Here is Miyahiro, echoing a sentiment shared by all rural nativists: "During times of bad harvest you cannot rely upon the august assistance of the regional lords and officials (*daikan*). One helps oneself with one's savings [or holdings] as well as providing assistance to others. Moreover, one must understand that they should not bother or depend upon the leadership in such times (*tokaku agaru no yakkai ni narazaru kokoroetarubeshi*)."[37]

In this connection, Suzuki Shigetane argued elaborately that officials, like the emperor, "serve with a pure intention to mutually help and to assist . . . to preserve the household enterprises given by the gods, and make substances for food, clothing, and shelter."[38] Indeed, the leadership Suzuki was talking about was the rural elite, which he believed was adequate to administer areas under its jurisdiction. Suzuki went further than most by accepting a division within society in which each sector would exercise trust to fulfill the divine obligations "to make things for other people in these times." Katsura Takashige, a village leader in Niitsu, constructed an argument in which Suzuki's conception of "making the

---

[35] Miyahiro Sadao, "Minke yojutsu," in *Kinsei chihō keizai shiryō* 5 (Tokyo, 1954), 316.
[36] Ibid.
[37] Ibid., p. 317.
[38] Suzuki Shigetane, *Engishiki norito kōgi* (Tokyo, 1900), 1:13-14.

kunitsuchi habitable for the people" functioned to promote the primacy of village jurisdiction; for Katsura the village was the substitute for the *kunitsuchi*, the whole.[39] The point of these meditations was to call attention to the central importance of the village as a space responsible for its own administration and economic well-being. The implication of the proposed arrangement, illuminated by the new religions, was a space that reunited politics and religion as the new shape of secession (again like Mito) and escaped heavy reliance upon structures and institutions.

○

Like *kokugaku*, many of the new religions shared the disposition to mingle elements of myth and contemporary history in order to create new forms of expressibility and interpretation. In the late Tokugawa period, they adhered to the same problematic and the same means by which the nature of the "real" might be apprehended. Their solution, which led to even more radical forms of secession, suggests homology with Mito and *kokugaku*: the extremes that such secessions disclose (especially in the *yonaoshi* outbursts at the end of the epoch) indicate the difference of the groups they sought to represent from those that *kokugakusha* talked about. Despite the reliance of the new religions on comparable mechanisms by which ideology was produced, their constituencies were often the people against whom both Mito and *kokugaku* sought to find protection and to whom they hoped to provide relief and assistance. Like Mito and *kokugaku*, the new religions were also more often than not explicitly unpolitical in their promotion of new relationships and programs. To the established world of public authority and social order they represented displacements rather than challenging replacements. Ironically, these "new" religious meditations, like *Mitogaku* and *kokugaku*, sought to dissolve politics into larger, but autonomous, arrangements—religious spaces, if you will—because of the divisive and stratifying propensities of politics. Yet in establishing the principles of autonomy and wholeness through secession—an act of human will—these new religions offered their interpretation of the problematic of contemporary history and disclosed the possibility for new kinds of social and economic arrangements. Moreover, such an apprehension of the world brought with it a theory of action—the necessity to act as a condition of one's existence, to bring about and indeed secure those communal arrangements that were now considered consistent with new forms of knowledge, human understanding, and human nature. No-

[39] This, it seems to me, is the point of Katsura's "commentary" on Suzuki Shigetane's *Yotsugigusa*.

where was this expressed more extremely than in those groups yearning for "world renewal."

In the bakumatsu, a spate of "new" religions were formed—Tenri, Konkō, Kurozumi, Maruyama, Fuji-kō (as well as the revitalization of more established popular sects)—that sought to realize the promise of horizontal relations by reconstituting themselves as autonomous communities. Indeed, all sought to construct a series of connections ultimately linked to an elemental and original whole that was prior to the vertical world of "names and statuses" valued by the Mito reformists. The new religions were usually characterized by a sharp discrimination between equality and inequality (resembling the samurai emphasis upon merit over ascriptive incompetence), and gave expression to this sense through a form of organization calculated to diminish the reliance upon hierarchy. All, too, projected an image of reform and the equitable distribution of wealth and productivity. Even as the organizational principles called attention to connectedness, representing the resolution of perceived fragmentation in a sense of wholeness, they also expressed the conception of equality that marked so many of these groupings in their most decisive aspects. In the social scale of Tokugawa Japan the new religions sought to give expression to the poor.

Nakayama Miki, foundress of Tenri, came from a wealthy peasant family and was married to a cotton dealer. After his death she apparently fell upon hard times, or so her official biographies relate. (There is reason to doubt the claims relating to her impoverished state.) She did operate in an area that experienced economic hardships, and it is not surprising that she would appeal to those most hard pressed as potential recruits. In her *Ofudesaki* she frequently returns to the theme of poverty, and invites her followers—the poor—to reach the promised state of exaltation, or heaven on earth, and thus attain a release from suffering.[40] Nakayama called her followers together in order to achieve and continue this state of blessedness; cooperation was the key to the economic problem. Indeed, Tenri was originally organized as a kind of financial cooperative—a community of people coming together to resolve their unhappiness, which was interpreted as a form of "unconnectedness." Yet it is clear that unhappiness was very much related to being poor. The same kind of argumentation can be found in the texts of Konkō, Kurozumi, and Fuji-kō.[41]

---

[40] I have relied upon Murakami Shigeyoshi, *Kindai Minshū shūkyōshi no kenkyū* (Tokyo, 1973) for this section. Also Murakami, "Bakumatsu ishinki no minshū shūkyō ni tsuite," in Murakami and Yasumaru Yoshio, eds. *Minshū shūkyō no shisō*, Nihon shisō taikei 67 (Tokyo, 1971). For the Tenri conception of "relief" and "assistance" see especially pp. 180, 189, 192, 200, 210, 211 in the Murakami and Yasumaru volume.

[41] Murakami, *Kindai Minshū shūkyōshi*, pp. 90, 92, 169, 175.

All of the new religions possessed a special perspective on knowledge and the enterprises of learning. Like Konkōkyō, they all invariably replaced learning with "faith" and "belief" as modes of knowing, and proposed that "*gakumon* (learning) without belief will not assist the people."[42] It was faith, Nakayama Miki advised, that would enable people to "know" the exalted state and thus secure relief from contemporary suffering and hardship. Kurozumi Munetada, founder of the Kurozumi sect, advised his followers to forget "worrying about the Way" in order to "know and transmit the virtue of Amaterasu to people of our times."[43] The transmission of such virtue required working and assisting others in community life.

It is interesting to note that many of these "new" religions appealed to local religious practices and traditions in the effort to recruit a followership. All, indeed, struck deep roots in local religious practices loosely associated with Shintō, and derived their authority and appeal from a broadened base of popularist shrine Shintō and village religious practices. Yet this local appropriation obviously betrayed the limited appeal such new groups could enjoy; it also disclosed the relationship between regional hardship and the construction of new religious ideologies. Localism provided a series of linkages between the primacy of the quotidian life, work, and belief as a basis of "knowing" how to achieve the prescribed state of exaltation. Ultimately it can be argued that the impulse prompting the organization of these new religious groupings was the heightened awareness of the necessity for relief and assistance. To supply relief (the state of exaltation) in communal form represented an act of secession, more radical than either the Mito elevation of the domain or the *kokugaku* definition of the self-sufficient village, but homologous to both.

All of the new religions celebrated doctrines calling for relief according to the blessings of a single and all-powerful *kami*, whether it was the Amaterasu Ōmikami of Myorai and Kurozumi, Tenri Ōmikami of Tenri, Tenchikane no Kami (interestingly homonymous with money) of Konkōkyō, or Moto no Oyagami of Maruyama. These primal deities represented the highest of *kami*, and were thus able to offer assistance and relief. The same function, I should add, was attributed to the *musubi no kami* in rural *kokugaku*. In many cases these all-powerful deities were seen as creators of the cosmos and human species. The reliance upon a reliever *kami*, or one who, possessing *kami* character, could bring relief, invariably functioned to explain to the poor, the beleaguered, and the unlettered what in fact was not or could not be explained: the necessity

---

[42] "Konkō ōkami rikai," in Murakami and Yasumaru, eds., *Minshū shūkyō*, pp. 364, 415-416.

[43] Murakami and Yasumaru, eds., *Minshū shūkyō*, pp. 45, 49, 50.

for help and its absence. To offer such an explanation—knowledge of a certain kind—obviously risked provoking conflict with the authority system and its stated responsibility to supply benevolence. Some of the new religious groupings, such as Tenri and Maruyama, developed doctrines announcing the ideal of world renewal in the present. It should further be stated that the world-renewing rebellions and *ee ja nai ka* disturbances frequently coined slogans for their cause in terms of relief and assistance to the people.

Despite the world-renewing project of Fuji-kō, Tenri, and Maruyama, such heady utopianism often called attention to the this-worldly, temporal orientations of these groups. This was even true of the revitalized *nenbutsu* sects such as the *myōkōnin*: all, with the possible exception of Nyorai, spoke of "extreme happiness in this world," a world without illness, poverty, or struggle. Many of the new religious groups stressed consistently the necessity of finding contemporary answers to prayers requesting such things as the "correction of illness and disease." Tenri, like *kokugaku*, insisted upon making "a fresh start beyond death," and actually enjoined its followers to concentrate upon their daily lives in the present without fear or anxious concern for their fate after death. All, too, pointed doctrinally to the idea that humans (not nature) were the standard of action and behavior. This elevation of human capacity and will, humans as subject, which is strikingly reminiscent of earlier epistemological meditations, appeared as perhaps the most common theme among the various groups. Naturally, the primacy of the purely human was intimately linked to the program of relief and assistance to ordinary folk, whose destitute lives constituted the touchstone for recruitment into new religious organizations; not the people of abundance, the rural rich or indeed the leadership, as so many of these new religions insisted, but the diligent and nameless masses regarding whom discourse had been so silent, and whom Tenri identified as the people who inhabited the "bottom of the valley" (*tanizoko*). The importance of these programs was the radical assertion of equality and the promise to redistribute wealth and land; behind this call was the sustaining power of human love and an optimistic reliance upon the essential goodness of human character. The present was the appointed time to establish a new kind of community pledged to mutual love and help.

In Tenri, for example, there was the primary belief that "all are brethren in a row" (*ichiretsu wa mina kyōdai*). *Konkōkyō* announced that all people constitute *kami no ujiko* (members of a divine lineage), while Kurozumi constantly appealed to familistic metaphors to describe the followership. Indeed, dramatized above all else was human equality, without distinctions of class, status, and sex (since many of these groups were founded by women). Tenri's conception of a nuclear family, centered on the partnership of husband and wife, contrasted vividly with the explicit authoritarianism of the patriarchal Confucian family with its propensity for extension in time and space. Others, notably Kurozumi and Konkō, sought to show how the humanness of all men before the primal deity dissolved artifical distinctions of power and class status.

In time, many of these new sects found success in recruiting followers from the samurai class as well. Moreover, many of the new religious constituencies were, owing to their emphasis upon the purely human, steeped in a moral sense characterized by notions of "guilt" and "sin" in terms rich in native associations such as *tsumi* and *kegare*. Konkōkyō rejected popular beliefs and superstitions as harmful and destructive to the masses, and taught what can only be described as a rational life attitude in which an enlightened (calculating) humanness stands as the measure of conduct and judgment. Believers were united according to independent expressions of faith, and brought together in organizations devoted to "mutual assistance and mutual learning." Such was the communitarian form of so many of the new religions—communities of believers or worshipers whose religious lives were not separated from lives of mutual interaction and work. This form of communal organization was noticeably different from the more established modes of religious interaction such as temple groups or parish systems. It resembled most the *kō*, an association of believers who by worshiping, working, and living together had already announced their secession from received and authoritative modes of organization in the Tokugawa system.

The implications of this kind of organization, and the meaning it surely must have emitted for the control system, illustrates best the real nature of conflict in late Tokugawa Japan: the conflict between a conception of authority that was increasingly failing to exercise control, and new conceptions of community seeking accommodation through displacement. In contrast to religions centered on the household, which were based either upon ancestor worship or the worship of some tutelary deity, or indeed village religions that celebrated the continuity of life and productivity for a specific local group, the new religious communities struck dangerously radical sensibilities in late Tokugawa society. Their activity was not merely a form of secession, which itself announced the possibility of collision, but an active enunciation of the ideal of world renewal in the form of universal relief and assistance (*banmin no tame naruzo*). It was this sense of immediacy and urgency that made the secessions something more than mere displacements in the larger context of late Tokugawa history.

o

All of these new groups formulated views on political power, society, and the status of the folk. In Tenri and Maruyama there was clearly manifested a conception of "world-renewal" politics, noting the "decline of Takayama" and the last days of conventional and formal authority; in Konkō's *yo hakawari mono* we have not only a reminder of the relationship between a specific epistemological endowment and cultural form but a widely shared belief in the ebb and flow, and inevitable demise, of established political authority. Indeed, all sought, like *Mitogaku* and *kokugaku*, to unify political doctrine with religious belief in the apparent hope of realizing a new sense of wholeness and overcoming the perceived fragmentation of life. Yet each group saw its "secession" as adequate to a whole whose contours were scarcely, if ever, imagined. The decision to give definitive shape to this conception of the whole was the purpose, if not promise, of the Meiji Restoration.

Finally, the most obvious example of secession, which needs little elaboration, was the *sonnō jōi* (revere the emperor, expel the barbarian) movement of the late 1850s and early 1860s. Under the sanction of violated imperial prerogatives, these activists denounced the Tokugawa as a sham and deceit. Their attack focused upon shogunal failure to meet its responsibility to preserve the peace and maintain order. They dramatized their discontent by withdrawing from the domains, congregating in Kyoto, and forming new kinds of political organizations that were informed by new combinatory strategies and pledged to destroy the bakufu. Destruction of the bakufu was the condition for the reinstatement of a conception of the whole as symbolized in "restoring the emperor." Yet the energy they poured into this activity and the shape they sought to give it clearly represented another instance of the secessionary dynamic characterizing late Tokugawa society, in which groups declared their right to withdraw from the center by claiming first their right to represent themselves ideologically. This form of centering a subject inevitably inspired organizational autonomy, first in action groups and then in the domain as substitutes (part) for the whole.[44] We might recall that much of this activity was explicitly modeled after the earlier Mito secession and sought to promote, in somewhat different organizational format, the relationship between merit and ability and leadership, knowledge of a certain kind and the entitlement of power.

This relationship was reformulated in the late Tokugawa period by such people as Sakuma Shōzan, Hashimoto Sanai, and Yokoi Shōnan. All stressed the importance of acquiring knowledge of a certain kind as a prerequisite to leadership, equivalent to or indeed more important than the achievement of mere moral rectitude. This new knowledge emphasized practicality, utility, and instrumentality as the necessary preconditions for leadership and the attainment of power. The identifica-

---

[44] I have not dealt extensively with this particular group because it is, in part, the subject of Huber's article in this volume.

tion of ability as a manifestation of such knowledge would function as a universal criterion for political recruitment.

It is one of the ironies of late Tokugawa history that in the end this radical secession of *shishi* (restorationists) would, in its failure to install a conception of the whole to replace the discredited shogunal apparatus, be transformed into another form of secession inspired by the Mito example. Surely this is what occurred in the larger domains and what people like Takasugi Shinsaku meant by their promotion of *kakkyoron*.[45] Sectionalist secession, that is, the creation of an autonomous domain as envisaged by Yokoi Shōnan in the *Kokuze sanron*, which would be self-sufficient in economic and military capabilities, was in fact the necessary prerequisite for envisaging the larger whole—what Takusugi called *dai kakkyo*.[46] This form was reworked in ideology to account for a vastly different kind of historicity. By contrast to the earlier Mito argument, the new version was formulated in the environment of *kaikoku*—the opening of the country to foreign contact and trade. Writers like Yokoi were responding to the fact of a new environment and shogunal incompetence to resolve the foreign issue, whereas Mito writers, perhaps more concerned with internal disorder, had sought to forestall the possibility of foreign intrusion. These differing historical conditions prompted people like Yokoi to concentrate on the problem of leadership and its authenticating qualities. Although this is not to say that Mito writers had been indifferent to issues of leadership, concerns for leadership were invariably expressed in the language of ethical rectitude and were displaced in favor of considerations on morality and moral knowledge. Yokoi and the post-*kaikoku* writers turned more to arguments for the acquisition of a certain kind of knowledge as the object of any discourse on leadership and power, often to the exclusion of morality itself. Just as the early Tokugawa sought to divert considerations on power by concentrating on questions of morality and proper behavior, so in the last years of the shogunal order the attainment of specialized knowledge was the means to conceal questions of power and politics. Thus, the self-sufficient domain, a secession responding to a general secessionary impulse, became the part that, in time, would shape the unformed whole.

CODA: THE RESTORATION IN THE REVOLUTION

What I have been discussing in this broadly arched consideration of ideology and the sources of conflict has been the rumor of revolutionary energy in Tokugawa Japan. One of the many possible meanings of the

[45] See Harootunian, *Toward Restoration*, pp. 394-395.
[46] Ibid., pp. 354-379.

Meiji Restoration was the seizure of the central control system in order to stem the perceived political failure and the process of secession which, in itself, gave dramatic expression to the necessity of resolving the question of the whole.

To be sure, it is one of the ironies of late Tokugawa history that this problem of authority was disclosed first in the writings of Mito retainers and in their anxious concern for what they clearly saw as the loss of control in the countryside. Their solution was to sanction a form of secession in order to manage the very people who prompted secession in the first place. Yet this loss of rural control was dramatically evidenced in the writings of *kokugakusha*, and alarmingly illustrated in the formation of numerous religious groupings pledged to establishing new organizations based upon equality and operating free from external control and vertical power. This is, of course, not to say that these secessions eschewed either power or hierarchy. All, in seeking some form of permanence, were compelled to adopt structures and hierarchical arrangements. But such structuring was invariably diminished by the claims of communitarian and horizontalist ties that had offered justification to the appeals of autonomy. For Mitogaku there was the able samurai, expert in instrumental knowledge over mere loyalty; for *kokugaku*, the agricultural sage who possessed useful knowledge and experience as criteria for leadership; and for the new religions, charismatic means to leadership preferment, suggesting the greater possibility for open recruitment. The most extreme expression of this effort to lower the claims of structure and hierarchy was represented by the *yonaoshi* groups at the end of the epoch, but they had no real solution to the desire to sustain epiphany and the liminal moment.

Thus in late Tokugawa times there existed a revolutionary situation among the Japanese peasantry that, far from being incidental to the collapse of the Tokugawa, provided the occasion and the energy by which others were to carry out a seizure of the central control apparatus. Indeed it might be argued that it was precisely because of the loss of control that the contest shifted to a struggle over how the center, and thus the whole, was to be reconstituted. It was fear of continuing failure to stem disorder in the countryside, and indeed arrest the centrifugal motion which secession propelled, that served as the impetus to restructure authority relations. In this restructuring, the struggle was seen increasingly as one between authority and the claims of community, which so many of the secessions seemed to promote in one form or another. Yet the problem was reduced in the end to the belief that too much authority was preferable to too much community. Even *kokugakusha*, occupying the most ambivalent positions in the transformation, ultimately favored this choice in the effort to retain what they possessed against the threat of continuing peasant disorder.

o

Perhaps, then, the Meiji Restoration represented the least radical of the secessions that contemporary history could offer: the Mito solution, with its emphasis upon the primacy of vertical power and its determination to settle rural unrest, promised the most acceptable resolution to the question of authority over the claims of community among the alienated constituencies of late Tokugawa society. Yet the price paid for this conception of authority (which in its original formulation was mediated by strong horizontalist links) was the installation of a new program of knowledge and power that valorized merit, ability, and practicality over mere status ascription; equality and utility over inequality and propriety as enduring evaluative criteria in the management of state and society. The communitarian and human impulses would have to find new modes of expression. Once more they would seek roots and power in the hidden world of rural Japan, which offered, too late, this frayed promise in folklore studies, romanticism and nostalgia, and the rantings of the radical right. One of the last ironies of the later Meiji state was its destruction in the name of a restoration of the proposed balance between authority and community, verticality and horizontality, public and private. The state allowed the former to take precedence over the latter and thus failed to establish the mechanism by which the world of imperial authority might be mediated by the world of communal life, tutelary deities, and ancestors, whose link to the invisible realm, to ritual and to liminality, conferred meaning and dignity upon the mundane details of daily life.

FROM REFORMISM TO TRANSFORMISM: BAKUFU POLICY, 1853-1868

Conrad Totman

The political crisis that preceded the Meiji Restoration was pervasive in its scope and profound in its impact. It discredited almost all the ideological and structural premises of the *bakuhan* system and drove people in all segments of the politically conscious strata of society to reformulate their perception of Japan's future. For some this reformulation constituted a revolutionary intellectual experience involving the abandonment of one perception of the good polity in favor of another, a new choice that might be grasped quite clearly or only in dim outline. For many others the reformulation was essentially a negative experience in which old truths were questioned or abandoned but satisfactory new truths still remained to be found at the time of the Restoration.

This applies to members of the bakufu as well as those of the *han*. What drove bakufu officials to abandon the old order was the intractable set of political problems they faced during the late fifties and sixties. Their regime, the bakufu, was at once a regional and a national polity— both a barony in its own right and the hegemonial element in the larger *bakuhan* system—and it had been able to fulfill both roles reasonably well for the better part of two centuries. However, socio-economic and intellectual developments during the late eighteenth and early nineteenth centuries, such as those Harootunian discusses earlier in this volume, heightened and brought into sharper focus the inherent tensions in the regime's two roles. Then the foreign intrusion at mid-century revolutionized the context of Japanese national politics. It abruptly introduced a set of political demands that the bakufu was utterly incapable of satisfying, and that situation set in motion and helped sustain an internal political disintegration that ruined not only the bakufu but the entire *bakuhan* order.

By early 1867 few influential bakufu officials believed the Tokugawa family could or even should continue to govern Japan through the instruments of the *bakuhan* system. Many officials had no notion of a preferred alternative. Confusion was common, some of its terminal expressions vividly revealed in Steele's study of the Shōgitai. For some officials the best alternative seemed to be to let others—meaning men of the great *han*, court nobles, or both—handle national problems while the Tokugawa attended to their own baronial affairs. It was a view that presupposed the continuation of a larger *bakuhan*-type polity, but one dominated by someone other than the Tokugawa. For others, those who came to dominate the bakufu after mid-1866, the preferred alternative was far more radical in its implication: they worked for a Japan governed by a unitary regime that they themselves would create.

Whatever alternative people envisaged, however, the absence of faith in the existing Tokugawa order was in striking contrast to the faith that had prevailed even a very few years previously, when officialdom had proceeded on the assumption that the system would and should continue to function essentially as it had in the past. The transformation of official attitudes can be seen by a comparison of the bakufu reform effort of 1866-1867 with two earlier efforts, those of 1854-1855 and 1862.

Reformism: The Ansei and Bunkyū Reforms, 1854-1855, 1862

The Ansei and Bunkyū reforms are instructive for both their differences and their similarities. The differences between the two are instructive because they suggest how the larger context of escalating political crisis was radicalizing behavior, the extremity of official actions being roughly proportional to the extremity of the problems perceived. At the same time there was in both a basic similarity of intent on the part of officials, who pursued reform in hopes of strengthening the regime and thereby sustaining the established Tokugawa order. That essentially conservative purpose contrasted sharply with the purpose of the Keiō reformers of 1866-1867, who sought to transform the national polity. The contrast reveals clearly the magnitude of change in political vision that key officials had undergone by 1868. That change is all the more notable if one keeps in mind that those officials who pursued the conservative Bunkyū reform had not been active in the very similar Ansei reform, but that many who played key roles in 1862 were central to the very different reform of 1866-1867.[1] By then the times had so changed them that they tried to change the times.

Abe Masahiro's Ansei reform was a direct response to the treaty imposed on the bakufu by Commodore Perry. There was essential agreement among those who mattered in 1854 that it would have been preferable not to end the policy of seclusion (*sakoku*), but Perry had demonstrated the impossibility of that preference. As a result, such people were driven to the bitter task of deciding how best to accept the unacceptable, and one of the few common denominators among sharply conflicting policy viewpoints was a conviction that defenses must be strengthened. That elemental agreement furnished the core of the Ansei reform. Defense work was expensive, however, and neither bakufu nor *han* had much surplus wealth with which to pay for it. From that situation stemmed the other main thrust of the reform—retrenchment and the elimination of costly ritual.

The character of the Ansei reform was foreshadowed in a list of thirty-seven proposed actions that Abe prepared in mid-1854, just three months after completing treaty negotiations with Perry. Most of the proposals related to economizing and improving coastal defenses, and they demonstrated that Abe was aiming at little beyond reforming and strengthening the existing military system and paying for the effort by trimming unnecessary expenses.[2] In implementation, as in planning, this frame of reference prevailed. A foreign threat having prompted the reform, the most extensive measures were related to maritime defense, notably the promotion of naval training, purchase and construction of warships,

[1] To drop a few names, Abe relied on such officials as Iwase Tadanari, Kawaji Toshiaki, Mizuno Tadanori, Nagai Naomune, and Tsutsui Masanori, of whom only Nagai was active during the sixties. Major figures in the Bunkyū reform, under Itakura Katsukiyo and Ogasawara Nagamichi, included Asano Ujisuke, Jinbō Nagayo, Kawakatsu Kōun, Komai Chōon, Misoguchi Shōnyo, Oguri Tadamasa, Okabe Nagatsune, Ōzeki Masuhiro, and Yamaguchi Naoki. Almost all of those officials were active in the Keiō reform, together with such men as Hirayama Keichū, Inaba Masami, Kurimoto Kon, Mukōyama Eigorō, Ogyū Noritaka, Shibata Masanaka, Takenaka Shigemoto, and Tsukahara Masayoshi.

[2] *Mito han shiryō* (Tokyo, 1970), 1:395-400. To suggest the character of Abe's proposals: one called for a reduction in the size of ceremonial retinues for daimyo and *hatamoto* in Edo; another called for the initiation of military training and naval practice at Hamagoten, a shogunal retreat on the bay adjacent to Chiyoda castle. Most of the other proposals were similar in tone, reformist in the very limited sense of modifying or tidying up specific practices. The most radical proposals included one recommending that the Shinagawa highway station, which was vulnerable to foreign attack, be abolished. Another proposed that rice storage be relocated from coastal Edo back into the hinterland north of the city. Another suggested that unemployed people should be moved to Ezo to settle that frontier area. Yet another proposed that daimyo (mostly *fudai*) in the Kantō area be allowed to take their wives and heirs home from Edo. Other proposals envisioned a sharp expansion of the facilities for study and training in Western civil and military subjects.

erection of coastal fortifications, and emplacement of cannon batteries. Those measures mostly constituted supplemental rather than reorganizational undertakings, however, and so did not entail any complex issues of structural reform.

It was in the area of army reform, where the bakufu already had elaborately organized forces, that strengthening soon acquired serious reformist implications and revealed more clearly official attitudes toward fundamental change. Only one of Abe's thirty-seven points involved the displacement of old practices with new, and that was his instruction to archers to train in the use of firearms. During 1854 army reform consisted of orders requiring men to be frugal, get their equipment in shape, and drill. And in attempts to enforce these orders, the bakufu instituted frequent military reviews within the castle grounds.[3] The following year the vision of reform changed appreciably. Edo leaders began a long-term program to convert their rambling system of pike, sword, and bow-and-arrow forces into a Western-style army using firearms. They established a new training center and limited it to training in the Western style. They decided to set up an armory to cast modern firearms. They ordered all liege vassals (*hatamoto* and *gokenin*) to adopt Western firearms and to master modern cavalry, artillery, or infantry techniques.[4] To my knowledge, however, no real plans for sweeping institutional reorganization were prepared, and the reform meant essentially a change in weapons and field tactics, and limited unit reorganization. That limited program did progress, however, and late in 1856 the senior councilors (*rōjū*) and a crowd of observers were able in one of the frequent inspections to review a force of Western-armed units that numbered some 4,000 men organized in eight ad hoc battalions.[5]

[3] Documents relating to this reform can be found in "Dai Nihon ishin shiryō kōhon" (hereafter DNISK), which is located in the archives of the Shiryō hensanjō of Tokyo University. Many DNISK *kan* dealing with 1854-1857 contain pertinent materials. One observer of a 55/9/26 review, for example, expressed scorn for the effectiveness of the military equipment because so much was ancient and obsolete. DNISK 567 n.p. [ISK, II:113:1:a,c,g,i]. As citations of DNISK *kan* are unpaginated, they require explanation. Each citation is accompanied by reference to the relevant entry in ISK, *Ishin shiryō kōyō* (Tokyo, 1965), which is in effect a published ten-volume seriatum summary of contents of DNISK. Thus the above entry means that the cited entries in DNISK 567 are (in reverse order) the first, third, seventh, and ninth (a,c,g,i) sources listed under the first full topic entry ("Seii taishōgun . . . ," etc.) on page 113 of volume II of ISK. Locating the same topic entry in the indicated DNISK *kan*, one can then usually locate the selection from the source cited without difficulty.

[4] DNISK 494 n.p. [ISK, II:11:1:passim]; 534 n.p. [ISK, II:63:2:a,b]; 542 n.p. [ISK, II:76:3:a]; 544 n.p. [ISK, II:80:4:a]; 556 n.p. [ISK, II:99:4:a,b]; 575 n.p. [ISK, II:122:3:a,b; 123:b,c,e]; 630 n.p. [ISK, II:189:2:a,f]; 654 n.p. [ISK, II:229:2:a,b,d]; 657 n.p. [ISK, II:233:3:a,i,j].

[5] DNISK 675 n.p. [ISK, II:259:6:a,c,d,g]. *Ishin shi* 2 (Tokyo, 1941), 126ff. discusses this bakufu military reform.

Even that modest progress had not been easy, however. Weapons were hard to obtain and unreliable or expensive. Training areas were inadequate, and to acquire better ones, it was necessary to move daimyo about in their Edo mansions, a costly and unwelcome disruption for lords already harassed by other matters. The new, disciplined group training was resented by many samurai. The erasing of inherited status distinctions as men of differing ranks were trained in the new technology created resentment. And quarrels erupted over the relative merits of particular new training styles.[6] The bakufu thus found itself compelled to provide men with funds for the new equipment and training, to repeat its orders from time to time, and in the end to settle for much less improvement than leaders desired.

The experience with army reform was characteristic of the whole Ansei effort. Even the modest reforms proposed were an irritant, an unwelcome expense, a nuisance, and a bother to most of those touched by them. Few felt a sense of crisis sufficient to shake them out of habitual routines. Despite the obstacles, some progress was made on both army and other reform, but in the end the Ansei reform left the *bakuhan* system untouched at its base.[7] The distribution of power and authority was unaltered. Policies of personnel recruitment, promotion, and use were unchanged despite the unusual promotion of a few "able men." The basic military organization was kept intact despite changes in weapons and organization of selected units. Clearly the informing vision of the Tokugawa legacy remained unquestioned.

To stress the unradical character of the bakufu's Ansei reform should not lead to the conclusion that Abe and his supporters were an unusually conservative leadership. They were not. To the contrary, they were

[6] Tokutomi Iichirō, *Kinsei Nihon kokumin shi* (Tokyo, late 1930s), 34:424-426. DNISK 457 n.p. [ISK, I:655:3:a,b]; 544 n.p. [ISK, II:80:4:a]; 575 n.p. [ISK, II:122:3:b]; 648 n.p. [ISK, II:221:1:a]; 657 n.p. [ISK, II:233:3:j]. Katsu Kaishū, *Rikugun rekishi* 1 (Tokyo, 1967), 72-74, 78-79.

[7] Watanabe Shūjirō, *Abe Masahiro jiseki* 1 (Tokyo, 1910), 349. Watanabe sums up the achievements of the Ansei reform in this way. He asserts that Abe was able to
—construct seagoing warships;
—send men to Nagasaki to study naval arts from the Dutch;
—construct coastal batteries at Shinagawa and Nagasaki;
—open military training areas, establish Western rifle units, start military training;
—establish cannon-firing ranges and employ Western methods there;
—allow daimyo to train troops in Edo mansions and keep weapons there;
—estabish the center for Western studies (*bansho shirabedokoro*) and use Western writings there;
—select able men and place them in important posts, despite family backgrounds inappropriate to the office;
—reduce bakufu red tape and the quantity of gifts daimyo had to give the bakufu;
—reduce the number of *han* and bakufu troops and cut associated unnecessary expenses.

more acutely aware of what the foreign threat entailed than was any other organized group in Japan, and as a result they were prepared to make a more radical response than was any other group. Indeed, the bakufu's decision of 1855 to convert its whole army to firearms was probably one of the most extreme reformist decisions of any government in Japan at the time. Abe's regime was in the vanguard of change, but it was the vanguard of a movement that had not really gotten underway. Perry had alarmed many Japanese, but he had moved almost none to a fundamental reexamination of the *bakuhan* system or its component parts.

○

In succeeding years most of Abe's reforms petered out as domestic political disputes overshadowed the foreign military menace. Under the leadership of Hotta Masayoshi, Ii Naosuke, and Andō Nobuyuki during the years 1857 to 1862 the bakufu initiated no significant reforms, being content to accommodate foreign demands out of necessity and to use established political structures and processes for domestic political management. By 1862, however, both the foreign problem and the domestic situation had changed considerably, and the absence of satisfying initiatives from Edo had generated substantial discontent both within and without the regime. In this context of escalating problems and growing alarm, the bakufu was prodded into initiating a new, more extreme reform, the Bunkyū reform.

The Bunkyū reform was at once more ambitious and more ambiguous than the Ansei reform had been.[8] It was more ambitious in the sense that it undertook to make selective major changes in the *bakuhan* system, and it was more ambiguous in the sense that it was implemented for internally inconsistent purposes.

Much of the initiative for the Bunkyū reform came from Matsudaira Shungaku of Fukui and his advisors. During the summer of 1862 Shungaku was able to use pressure emanating from the court, certain great daimyo, and militant samurai to maneuver his way into an unprecedented role at Edo as *seiji sōsai*, a sort of political high commissioner superior to the senior councilors. Using his external political support, and skillfully exploiting bakufu weakness, he was able to impose on a bitterly resistant officialdom a program of political reform that had three crucial aspects. It eviscerated the *sankin kōtai* system by modifying it out of practical existence. It obtained the limited admission of great daimyo into bakufu councils and attempted to secure access to bakufu office for

---

[8] This summary of the Bunkyū reform is based on my extended study, *The Collapse of the Tokugawa Bakufu, 1862-1868* (Honolulu: University Press of Hawaii, 1980).

vassals of those daimyo. It redefined court-bakufu relations in such a way as to give concrete expression to two propositions: namely, that the bakufu was subordinate to the court and that court approval must be secured for all major policy decisions.

Shungaku's reforms served, as intended, to redefine the political relationship of court, bakufu, and great *han*. The old system in which the bakufu supposedly governed in the name of the court and with the obedient support of the *han* was to be replaced by a system in which the court supposedly gave overt approval to policies forged by a governing council composed of major daimyo and nobles who used the bakufu as their instrument of national administration. The term that Shungaku and others used to describe this arrangement was *kōbu gattai*, meaning an alliance of nobles and samurai or union of court and camp.[9] Shungaku's political reform did not, however, go beyond an attempt to redefine the relationship of the three existing categories of court, bakufu, and *han*. It assumed the three would endure. And it assumed that an effectively united national government could be achieved without basic institutional reform, either in terms of abolishing *han* (or bakufu) domanial autonomy or in terms of abolishing the estate system of nobles, samurai, and commoners.

These political reforms of 1862 were the reforms that most interested and gratified Shungaku. But to bakufu officials they were hateful. Senior officials hated them because they stripped them of the hegemonial national role they had enjoyed for so long. Officials in general hated them because they were imposed from without and constituted an assault upon both Tokugawa familial and bakufu institutional authority and interests. And many officials hated them because they constituted a threat to the larger notion of the *bakuhan* system as a valid moral order. Accordingly, whereas Shungaku wished to see the reforms made permanent, the primary concern of officials was to overcome the political weakness that had forced them to accept those unwelcome changes.

Officials recognized, correctly, that it had been bakufu military weakness that compelled them to submit to Shungaku. Military weakness had forced them to accept humiliating foreign demands, and it was capitulation to the foreigners that underlay, directly or indirectly, the political tension and turmoil enabling Shungaku to engage successfully in bakufu politics. Accordingly, the facet of reform that officials worked at most assiduously was military reform. As with the Ansei reform, the Bunkyū military reform required a considerable reallocation of funds, and so the regime undertook a major belt-tightening program whose

---

[9] I have attempted to clarify the term *kōbu gattai* in an essay, "Tokugawa Yoshinobu and *Kōbugattai*," in *Monumenta Nipponica*, 30 (Winter 1975), 393-403.

economizing and administrative rationalizing efforts were far more extensive than those of 1854-1856.[10]

Military reform itself was articulated in terms of the foreign menace, and as in Abe's reform, naval strengthening was given top priority in planning. However, the escalating domestic struggle of 1862, an important facet of which Thomas Huber examines in his essay, steadily shifted official concern from naval to army strengthening. Moreover, as in 1854, it was army rather than naval reform that best revealed the character of official attitudes, because army reform involved reorganizing the established military system, whereas naval strengthening was mostly a matter of adding new forces to what already existed. When one compares the Bunkyū army reform with that of Abe, it quickly becomes apparent that it retraced his steps and then vaulted to a radically new position.[11] Bakufu leaders attempted to legitimize the reform by asserting that they were returning to the "pre-Kan'ei" system of the great founder's day, but by late 1862 they had in fact accepted the necessity of scrapping the hallowed system of Ieyasu in favor of a dual army-navy structure patterned on specific European models. Despite this bold objective, in succeeding months the momentum of military reorganization disappeared even more rapidly than it had developed, and by mid-1863 the reform appeared completely stalled, to the great frustration of those who had been implementing it.[12] It stalled for several reasons, including inadequate knowledge of how to implement it, resistance from personnel in the forces being reformed, and external political complications. Nevertheless, before stalling it did reveal that in the face of more acute political difficulties bakufu officials were prepared for considerably more radical reform than they had been in 1855, and that they wished to forge rapidly a much more completely "Westernized" army than the Ansei reform had proposed to develop gradually.

Even then, however, the bakufu reform vision was hardly revolutionary. Although the military implications of the new international context were far clearer than they had been to officials in 1854, almost no one in Edo was prepared to acknowledge—perhaps they did not recognize—that the very transformation of international context that had rendered the old military order obsolete had also rendered obsolete

[10] I discuss these matters at great length in the extended study cited in note 8. Data on this reform is primarily located in *Zoku Tokugawa jikki* (Tokyo, 1907), 4:1190-1666 passim. Hayakawa Junzaburō, ed., *Kanbu tsuki* (Tokyo, 1915), 1:352-373. Yoshino Naoyasu, comp., *Kaei Meiji nenkanroku* (Tokyo, 1968), 2:839ff. DNISK 1437 n.p. [ISK, IV:85:3:a]; 1501 n.p. [ISK, IV:154:2:passim]. ISK, IV:78ff. passim.

[11] I discuss this military reform at greater length in the extended study cited above. Katsu, 2:129-145, 157-174, 327. Hayakawa, 1:371-373. *Zoku Tokugawa jikki*, 4:1528-1529.

[12] Katsu, 1:88-89; 2:110-112.

the larger *bakuhan* system of which the military order was an integral part. Rather, Edo's military reorganization was intended to facilitate reestablishment of those aspects of the *bakuhan* system disrupted by Shungaku's *kōbu gattai* reform. And within the military effort itself, although reformers did propose to scrap the entire military unit-organization and weaponry of the old forces, their plan was still based on the established system of feudal levies for manpower. The fighting techniques to be developed were the mass-infantry techniques of the West, but the force still was perceived as an elite feudal samurai army, not a mass army based upon the manpower resources of the general populace. As envisaged, then, the Bunkyū military reform, like Shungaku's political reform, was designed to change neither the *bakuhan* system's structurally decentralized political character nor its stratified, hereditary estate system.

○

After the Bunkyū reform stalled and Shungaku fled to Fukui in disgrace, the bakufu entered a long tortured period of bitterly divided and indecisive leadership. Finally in the latter half of 1864 the divisions were overcome and Edo leaders boldly seized the initiative in domestic politics by committing their regime to a vigorously anachronistic policy of reaction. By early 1865 that policy was foundering on internal sabotage and external resistance, and by year's end, in the face of foreign belligerence and defiance by Chōshū, the reactionary leadership had fallen. The discredited leaders were replaced by Itakura Katsukiyo, Ogasawara Nagamichi, and others who had been active in 1862, and who enjoyed the good will of Shungaku and Tokugawa Yoshinobu, the former still ensconced at Fukui, the latter actively participating in bakufu affairs as senior shogunal spokesman in Kyoto.

Despite this change in leadership, bakufu-Chōshū relations continued to slide into war. Accompanying the drift to war was a revived attempt at military strengthening. The goals of that attempt, which began under the reactionary leadership of late 1864, were much more limited than the goals of the Bunkyū military reform. Bakufu leaders were essentially interested in forging an effective striking force for use against fractious domestic elements, in hopes they could thereby reassert bakufu primacy as it once presumably had existed. Accordingly they ignored questions of basic institutional reform, and instead directed their attention to the rapid creation of new units of cavalry, artillery, and infantry. Within the limits of their ambition they were quite successful, forming several infantry battalions that numbered perhaps 5,000 men in all, armed with modern Mini rifles, drilled in unit tactics, and organized in company-battalion fashion.

By the time war with Chōshū erupted in the summer of 1866, these infantry battalions had become the real heart of the bakufu's legions. This new military reality was not, however, matched by a new military vision. The troops continued to be regarded as an army of vassals and rear vassals. And almost all the useless, customary units of liege vassals, notably the swordsmen and pikemen, still existed and still occupied their habitual posts. That they were a worthless expense was recognized by the regime's leaders, but prior to the war with Chōshū officials were unable and unwilling to carry out the painful task of tearing the old system down.

Transformism: The Keiō Reform, 1866-1867

Tokugawa defeat at the hands of Chōshū during the summer months of 1866 was an experience of immense importance to the bakufu.[13] No event since Sekigahara had had a comparable impact on it. That defeat rocked the regime to its foundations, forcing more and more officials to acknowledge what a small but growing coterie had been arguing for three or four years, namely that only through radical changes in the whole political order could they handle menacing foreigners and domestic insurgents, thereby preserving Japanese independence, Tokugawa honor, their own sense of professional competence, and of course their own material interests.

Another view that had begun to appeal to some officals during the previous four years also gained more adherents after the military debacle. That view, a sort of fortress-Kantō mentality, treated the baronial aspect of the Tokugawa role as more important than the national hegemonial aspect. It held that the proper course would be for the shogun to return governing authority to the emperor and channel Tokugawa energy into strengthening the domain sufficiently to preserve the family's feudal autonomy. What made this view attractive was that it seemed to offer solutions to both the regime's domestic and international problems: it seemed a way to appease anti-bakufu proponents of *kōbu gattai* at home while permitting escape from the diplomatic dilemma by the simple expedient of turning it over to others. After a few weeks of

[13] It may be worth noting that the public turmoil of 1866 was only a minor factor in shaping bakufu behavior. In part the turmoil—which actually was widespread and involved vast numbers of people—seems to have had such a slight impact because it was seen as the responsibility of lesser officials: city and district administrators. In part it probably lacked noteworthy direct political impact because most of the incidents did in fact run their course in a few days, as in the past, and so did not present themselves to leaders as a new, unpredictable, and therefore dangerous problem. I discuss this matter at some length in the extended study.

political debate and maneuver in the autumn of 1866, however, bakufu leaders reaffirmed their determination to rule, and the fortress-Kantō alternative did not reappear again until late 1867, when new political crises threatened the whole strategy of radical reform. In those final weeks of crisis after news of the Tosa Restoration proposal reached Edo, the fortress-Kantō alternative emerged with a vengeance, as desperate men frantically proposed one futile strategy after another in hopes of saving something from the disaster that was engulfing them. However, as suggested by William Steele's examination of the Shōgitai affair, which was one of the last such schemes, these eleventh-hour strategies were too insubstantial and too late to save the day.

The last great chance for a revival of Tokugawa fortunes had rested in the Keiō reform, the Tokugawa policy that emerged in the autumn of 1866 and was then pursued for over a year.[14] It was an attempt to build a new order adequate to the new age, and as that statement suggests, it was shaped by a transformational vision. The triumph of that viewpoint during late 1866 and early 1867 led to a fundamental reorganization of bakufu military forces and thrust the tottering regime willy-nilly into a new historical channel. In that channel its leaders repudiated their classic role as defenders of the status quo, a role assumed in both the Ansei and Bunkyū reforms. Instead they adopted a dangerous, partially charted policy of radical reorganization, hoping to regain the initiative in domestic affairs by leading Japan into a new era of national unification.

One of the most noteworthy aspects of the Keiō reform was its remarkable cohesiveness. In sharp contrast to the entire bakufu experience from the time of Ii Naosuke's seizure of power in 1858, it enjoyed the active support of most of the regime's important officials. These officials, who carried out the Keiō reform under the formal leadership of Yoshinobu and Itakura, reflected the several influences operating in 1860s Japan. Some, such as Asano Ujisuke and Komai Chōon, had been involved with Shungaku in the Bunkyū political reform in 1862. Some, such as Misoguchi Shōnyo and Oguri Tadamasa, had been active in the military strengthening efforts of both 1862 and 1864–1865. Some were men who had associated with foreigners in Japan, such as Kurimoto Kon and Yamaguchi Naoki, and others, such as Shibata Masanaka and Mukōyama Eigorō, had traveled on missions to Europe. Most were of *hatamoto* rank because most bakufu administrators were of that rank, but officials of *fudai* daimyo status, such as Ogyū Noritaka and Inaba

---

[14] This discussion of the Keiō reform summarizes an analysis set forth in greater detail in the extended study cited above. It is based primarily on material in *Zoku Tokugawa jikki*, Katsu, vol. 2, and numerous DNISK entries. Specific citations are contained in the larger work.

Masakuni, also played central roles. In a phrase, the Keiō reform was a united bakufu undertaking in a way that was unique to the Bakumatsu period. At a basic level, that unity probably must be attributed to the stress of profound crisis, which had dispelled any lingering hopes for a revival of the old order, and forced the regime's leaders to find in a dynamic new departure a strategy sufficient to the day. The strategy chosen also elicited broad official support because it bridged the gap between the proponents of national governance and fortress-Kantō by entailing policies most of which ultimately could be employed for the latter purpose should the former prove impossible.

The Keiō reform began while the war with Chōshū was still in progress, and it began as a revival of the Bunkyū military reform. As the first news of defeats at the front reached the shogunal headquarters at Osaka, officials exhumed, reviewed, and modified in the direction of greater change the army reform program of 1862. After several days' delay while the problems of Iemochi's death and Yoshinobu's succession were being settled, the military reform got underway. A few days later Yoshinobu abandoned his plan to launch a renewed attack against Chōshū and the war ended, but military reform continued unabated. By the end of 1866 large numbers of liege vassals had been transferred from their old units to new infantry, artillery, and cavalry units. New semirationalized salary arrangements, new uniforms and insignia, and new drill and duty procedures were worked out. New weapons were sought, a new command structure was organized, a new and functional civil-military separation was articulated, and the reform as a whole created most of the system that the Bunkyū reformers had earlier envisioned but failed to realize.

During 1867 the military reform continued. A French advisory mission that had been sought since 1865 finally arrived and began providing more thoroughly Western-style training. Large orders were placed for breech-loading rifles and other modern weaponry. The process of transferring liege vassals to new-style units was completed. Recruitment, salary, and reenlistment arrangements were changed to make military service more attractive. Recruiting campaigns were launched periodically, and by midyear, it appears, the bakufu had a massive army of some 24,000 troops, in forces mostly organized in modern ways and equipped with firearms of recent vintage.

This transformation of the bakufu's legions had not come about easily. Men still resented the changes in fighting style; they chaffed at the threat to their status, and they were outraged by the many subtle and not so subtle ways in which the reformers chipped away at their sources of income and standards of living. The reformers tried to minimize the resistance by recognizing broad status distinctions in their new unit organizations and by allowing salary variations to persist in line with some existing disparities. In contrast to 1862, however, they did not let this general liege vassal displeasure derail their policy, and they succeeded in tearing down completely the old-style military system.

Because liege vassals did resist, and because they were a relatively expensive form of manpower, reformers continued the 1864-1866 policy of anchoring their new army in battalions of infantrymen formed of commoners. Moreover, whereas the fiction had previously been maintained that the infantrymen were rear vassals, beginning in the dark days of the war with Chōshū bakufu recruiters openly and publicly called for commoners to enlist as commoners. During the Keiō reform this public recruitment of commoners from all over the bakufu's domains continued. The largest and best battalions of infantry were formed of commoners, who were recruited, trained, paid, promoted to posts as noncommissioned officers, and otherwise administered in essentially the same manner as the modern mass armies of Europe.

In terms of overall organization, the army had been modernized, and its core was a modern infantry. In other aspects, however, archaic characteristics persisted well into 1867. Liege vassals continued to be paid in a semirationalized manner. A number of large infantry units were feudal in the sense that high-ranking landed *hatamoto* commanded nominally private forces on the basis of their high rank rather than their military competence. Moreover, landed *hatamoto* as a whole continued to be the source of large numbers of commoner troops because of residual feudal military manpower requirements. In the autumn of 1867 in a major and integrated series of reform edicts, the bakufu abolished most of those remaining feudal forms. The private units of high-ranking *hatamoto* were summarily dissolved and the troops reassigned to regular units or sent back to their villages. Landed *hatamoto* as a group were released from all feudal levy and service obligations and ordered to pay heavy money taxes instead, thereby becoming tax-paying landed gentry rather than feudal retainers of the shogun. Further moves were made to rationalize salaries, and the whole bakufu office structure was put on a graduated and fully monetized system. Finally, lesser liege vassals were warned that in due time they too would all be put on fully standardized and monetized salary and tax scales.

These several reforms, which constituted in their entirety a radical internal defeudalization of the bakufu, were paralleled by civil administrative reforms that gave the bakufu many of the characteristics of an embryo national government, and that seemed to be laying the foundations for a claim to the role of national government in a unified polity.

The civil administrative reforms of 1867 involved a basic reorganization of the bakufu's central bureaucratic structure. The old collegial councilor-magistrate (*toshiyori-bugyō*) system that had endured from the days of Ieyasu was replaced by a new ministerial organization. As formulated, individual cabinet members in charge of finances, the interior, foreign affairs, the army, and the navy each headed ministries of subordinate officials charged with elaborately specified functions. In theory men would rise through the ranks, ascending graduated salary ladders to the top ministerial positions. The reform was designed to end the rank-based office system and to make posts at all levels open to talent. Initially the talent would be drawn from *hatamoto* and *fudai* daimyo, the only people who could be trusted to support the reform. However, neither the rhetoric of reform nor the terms of the new system indicated that reformers envisioned that as a permanent situation.

Less visible and less ambitious reforms in Kantō land administration were also carried out. They were designed to strengthen the bakufu's control of its own lands, the lands of *hatamoto*, and the lands of lesser *fudai* daimyo. Those changes, which reflected in part long-standing dissatisfaction with the highly fractionalized land system of the Kantō, also reflected a new desire to destroy the domanial autonomy of greater *hatamoto* and daimyo in general and to bring all the tax resources of the country under the control of a centralized regime. This desire was revealed in the formulation of concrete policies for purchasing private lands—policies that were initially aimed at selected *hatamoto* but that could be applied to daimyo domains whenever that became politically feasible.

The task of financing the new policies precipitated other shorter-range attempts to generate income and trim the costs of governance, and like civil and military reform, these attempts involved ventures very unlike anything tried in the earlier reforms. Bakufu leaders pursued a long-drawn-out but ultimately futile quest for a major French loan. They tried to develop in various forms monopoly trading arrangements with France, and attempted to negotiate a contract with a British entrepreneur for the opening of mines in Ezo. These and many other efforts were insufficient, however, and so Keiō reformers explored ways of terminating the hereditary stipends of incompetent liege vassals and examined with care the possibility of levying regular taxes on lesser daimyo as a means of spreading the costs of government. They also continued to consider, as some had done occasionally since 1864 or even earlier, more direct ways of securing control of the whole nation's land-tax income.

Fiscal need was not the only factor prodding them in that direction: the political climate in general was having the same effect. For example, the bakufu's whole military reform disregarded the daimyo because *han* military forces, which had furnished Edo with its main police and battle forces throughout the Tokugawa period, had proven themselves less and less helpful during the repeated crises of the mid-sixties.[15] Bakufu leaders in 1866–1867, whether themselves *fudai* daimyo or *hatamoto*, recognized that daimyo forces were unreliable or ineffective or, usually, both. They had come to regard such forces not as loyal followers or dependable allies but as obstacles to effective governance. Hence they found it easy to conclude that the best way to turn them to use would be to convert the domains from independent entities into elements in a bureaucratically integrated state. As a corollary they saw *han* productivity as rightfully subject to direct taxation because only thus could it be made accessible to the state.

Cumulatively these acts and analyses involved repudiation of four principles central to the *bakuhan* system: the principles of hereditary status security, obligatory military service to one's lord, feudal domanial administrative autonomy, and domanial fiscal independence. Once these principles had been breached, the very ideological and institutional foundations of the Tokugawa order were undermined. Hence it is not surprising to find that in spelling out the new ministerial system of government in mid-1867 the reformers postulated that the expenditures of the several ministries would be met by taxes gathered from the entire country. Such a proposal would have seemed preposterous and heretical to officialdom in 1854 or even in 1862. But by 1867 it had come to look like a logical part of the most plausible solution to the dilemmas of governance confronting those in charge of the bakufu.

Needless to say, the Keiō reform failed of its larger objective. This was for several reasons: because it generated massive resistance from those bakufu vassals who were bearing the brunt of changes whose outcome offered them no discernible advantages or sense of fulfillment; because it entailed costs that vastly exceeded bakufu fiscal resources; and because such success as it did enjoy provoked resolute counter measures by contenders for primacy, notably Satsuma and Chōshū. The efforts of Keiō leaders to fashion a new order thus served not only to open a new vision of the future to those who worked with them but also to alienate many others, both within and without the regime, and so contributed to the process of systemic disintegration. As a result, once the bakufu's new army had been defeated at Fushimi-Toba, the remaining hulk of the old order in central Japan collapsed abruptly. Moreover, after the civil war had run its course, no viable revanchist sentiment survived among ex-Tokugawa elements. Instead, appreciable numbers

---

[15] I have discussed the 1860s role of *fudai* daimyo in "Fudai Daimyo and the Collapse of the Tokugawa Bakufu," *Journal of Asian Studies*, 34 (May 1975), 581–591.

of people were prepared to move in new directions, a good many of them already having had a foretaste of those directions in the Keiō reform.

One cannot argue from this that Tokugawa leaders destroyed their regime by trying to save it. The old regime would have crumbled regardless of what they did. What they did achieve by resolving to engage in the struggle was to help give the final collapse of the old order a dramatic clarity and definitiveness that it otherwise might well have lacked.

o

When one juxtaposes the Keiō reform against the Ansei and Bunkyū reforms, the magnitude of change in bakufu intentions is readily apparent. The military reform of 1866-1867 was far more sweeping than the most radical visions of earlier years, and it clearly was an instrumental reform functioning as the essential first step in a larger-scale venture designed to transform the bakufu from a feudally organized suzerain regime into a sovereign and unified national regime organized along the bureaucratic lines of Napoleonic France.

This reference to Napoleonic France reminds us that the Keiō reformers, unlike those of Ansei and Bunkyū, had access to a foreign model of a unitary state. That model was France, and it was accessible due to the several bakufu diplomatic and study missions to France and elsewhere and the advisory activities of Léon Roches and other French military, technical, and civil advisors in Japan. Knowledge gained from these several sources was fed directly into the planning and implementation of many key sections of the Keiō reform by officials such as Yamaguchi and Shibata, and it was their knowledge of European models that gave the Keiō reformers, like their Meiji successors, substance for their vision of an altered future.

The European model was not the only reference the Keiō reformers had in mind. A more basic conceptual category was that of a *gunken* or "prefecture-province" system. That term referred to the Chinese imperial bureaucratic system, which Tokugawa Confucianists had long contrasted invidiously with a *hōken* or decentralized "feudal" system. The Tokugawa *bakuhan* system was identified as a *hōken* system, and reformers seeing it as inadequate looked to a *gunken* system as the valid alternative. When, however, they tried to move beyond the vague implications of *gunken* to concrete issues of policy, they found little of substance to work with. The unitary states of Europe seemed to be in a practical sense functioning *gunken* systems, and so reformers looked to them, most notably to the Napoleonic order, for implementive guidance.

Even Napoleonic France was not, however, a sufficient model, and its insufficiency was reflected in lacunae in the reform. Napoleonic France of the Second Empire, after all, was headed by an emperor who was not only chief of state but the forceful director of policy. Subordinate to the emperor was a relatively powerless prime minister and his cabinet associates. That arrangement offered no ready answer to the question of how the Japanese emperor, the shogun, and the senior official in the newly formulated ministerial system would relate to one another. The way Yoshinobu handled political affairs in 1867 suggests, however, that he envisioned himself as an eventual prime minister who would exercise real authority in a state headed by a titular emperor. This self-image is also suggested by the fact that Itakura Katsukiyo, the undisputed leader of the senior councilors and Yoshinobu's most important advisor, was given no new title in the reorganized ministerial system of 1867, even though the title of prime minister was entirely appropriate for him. That omission, which could only have been deliberate, left an uncompromised title available for Yoshinobu, should the occasion arise that he needed one. For our purpose here, however, it will suffice to note that at the heart of the Keiō reform a potentially awkward issue of political relationships remained unresolved, or at least unarticulated, even after the rudimentary structures of a unified national government had begun to take shape.

The awkward problem of integrating court and bakufu notwithstanding, on balance it is the conceptual and institutional changes that were envisioned and undertaken in the Keiō Reform that best indicate the impact of the *bakumatsu* crisis on bakufu officialdom. It had destroyed their commitment to the old order and driven them to attempt the creation of a new one.

Behind this transformation of bakufu policy was a changing perception of structural context that deserves fuller exposition. Back in 1854 bakufu leaders had perceived their task in terms of preserving the *bakuhan* system as a morally and functionally valid order, within which existed Tokugawa patrilineal interests, all as aspects of a legitimate subsystem. The well-being of that subsystem was deemed inseparable from the well-being of the larger *bakuhan* system, which they regarded as the proper structure for "Japan" the nation.

By 1862 foreign intrusion and domestic friction had brought into clearer focus both the notion of Japan as a national entity vis-à-vis other such entities and the notion of the bakufu as a domestic institution vis-à-vis other such institutions, notably the great *han*. Moreover, the rhetoric and content of reform spoke more clearly than before to hard issues of national and bakufu institutional authority and interest. It was still assumed, however, that the preservation of the established bakufu position was essential to the preservation of the national position. If the bakufu should falter, it was asserted, then power would fall into the hands of sectional interests, meaning the great daimyo, or, worse yet, into the hands of *"jōi* fanatics," whose irresponsible behavior would lead the realm to disaster.

On the other hand, in contrast to 1854, by late 1862 preservation of the bakufu position no longer seemed to require reformers to respect the interests of all constituent elements of the bakufu. Rather, it had become a truism among leaders at Edo that, however regrettably, some Tokugawa elements must suffer in order that the well-being of bakufu and nation could be assured. In this new attitude was the beginning of that process wherein bakufu reformers redefined "bakufu" until nothing remained of it except their own political positions and the ideal of an enduring Tokugawa lineage.

This process of eviscerating the concept of "bakufu" accelerated sharply during the crisis years 1865-1866, and by 1867 the regime's leaders had abandoned the old structured ideal. By 1866-1867, too, the reformers' sharper awareness of Japan as a nation among nations had transformed their understanding of its proper structure. They had come to perceive the nation as a structurally unified entity that properly would not tolerate within itself autonomous subsystems, whether that of *han* or bakufu. The internal erosion of their concept of "bakufu" was reinforced by this erosion of its external legitimacy. Although they remained convinced that the bakufu and its larger *bakuhan* system had been legitimate in years past—their anger at the constant accusations of "bakufu selfishness" was deep and enduring—in the new age those arrangements no longer seemed appropriate because they no longer were effective. By the end of 1866 bakufu leaders were no longer attempting to preserve either that cluster of principles and interests that was the bakufu, or that larger cluster that was the *bakuhan* system. To the contrary, buffeted by intractable political problems and forced to formulate new means for handling those problems, the leaders of the Keiō reform found themselves ready to sacrifice both bakufu and *bakuhan* to achieve the purposes they had come to consider valid: securing the well-being of themselves, the Tokugawa lineage, and the nation through formation of a unified polity that would be grounded, somehow or other, in imperial authority.

In short, the crisis of their age had led bakufu leaders through two contemporaneous processes of political reconceptualization. One was a process of role redefinition that led them to divorce their own roles and that of their lord's family from that of the bakufu. Another was a process of structural transvaluation that led them to abandon the *bakuhan* system in favor of a new ideal, that of a structurally unified nation. The old integrated order, in which self-interest and the total public interest were bound together through the values and institutions of bakufu and *bakuhan* system gave way to a situation in which a profound gulf separated the two. Edo reformers bridged that intolerable chasm by envisioning themselves in the Keiō reform as founders and leaders of a new order that would fill with new structures and values the void created by abandonment of the old. That the men whose positions made them the very heart of the old order could be driven by the crisis of their age to abandon that order and desperately try to fashion a new one suggests how deeply the *bakumatsu* crisis had eroded the ideological and structural premises of the *bakuhan* order. It had been a transformational experience.

ACTION AS A TEXT: IDEOLOGY IN THE TENGU INSURRECTION

J. Victor Koschmann

Are there not "marks" on time, the kind of thing which calls for a reading rather than for a hearing?

Paul Ricoeur, "The Model of the Text," *Social Research*, 38 (Autumn 1971), 540.

Each of the three collateral houses (*gosanke*) of the Tokugawa was originally enfeoffed to a son of Tokugawa Ieyasu, the fifth receiving Owari, the tenth Kii, and the eleventh Mito. Mito was by far the smallest of the three domains, having been rated initially at 250,000 *koku* of rice production. Yet what Mito lacked in terms of wealth was soon supplied in prestige. It alone among the Tokugawa-period domains was exempt from the system of alternate attendance (*sankin kōtai*), and the Mito daimyo resided permanently in Edo. Indeed, it was partially as a result of such special treatment, embellished by Mito publicists, that the daimyo of that domain came eventually to be known as "vice-shōgun" (*tenka no fuku-shōgun*).[1]

The second Mito lord, Tokugawa Mitsukuni, further elevated the domain's reputation by gaining personal fame as a "just and capable" lord. His most noteworthy accomplishment, however, was to conceive and initiate the project of compiling an authoritative statement of his-

---

[1] There was no substance to this title, and no evidence that the bakufu ever used the term. For a summary of various sources in which it appears, see Mito-shi Shi Hensan Iinkai, ed., *Mito-shi shi 2 (chū)*, vol. 1 (Mito, 1968), 39-42.

torical orthodoxy concerning the Japanese past, the *Great History of Japan (Dai-Nihon shi)*. The project was continued with varying degrees of commitment by Mitsukuni's successors, but was forcefully revived in the turbulent years of the late Tokugawa period as part of a new effort by Mito to play a leading role in national affairs. More than ever before, in the early to mid-nineteenth century, Mito samurai acted as custodians of the whole, taking upon themselves the task of revitalizing the natural order from which their countrymen had strayed.

Mito house not only claimed a privileged role in defining and maintaining the Tokugawa order. It also reflected, in the poverty, frustration, and divisiveness of its band of retainers, the crisis that confronted the administrative aristocracy as a whole in the late Tokugawa period. Unlike many of the allied (*tozama*) and vassal (*fudai*) houses, whose roots reached deeply into the Sengoku period, the Mito clan was pulled together from disparate elements in the seventeenth century. It always lacked, therefore, a strong sense of continuity and solidarity.[2] In the early nineteenth century this divisiveness was most apparent in factional strife among Mito scholars as they competed for control over the *Great History of Japan* project, and therefore also for the advisory power over domainal administration that such control implied. Reformists soon gained the upper hand in such struggles, and throughout the period from 1829, when their patron Tokugawa Nariaki became the ninth Mito daimyo, until the end of the Tenpō period in 1844, they strove to actualize an archetypal vision of government through widespread institutional reform. Yet factional dissension continued throughout the Tenpō reforms and beyond, gradually intensifying as contending groups allied themselves with supporters in the bakufu and other domains, and took increasingly aggressive positions on national issues.

In the Bakumatsu period the conceit of Mito's rulers that they should play a central role in *bakuhan* affairs and the increasing bitterness of their internal battles combined to create a situation in which Mito effectively incorporated the strife and uncertainty that had infected the nation as a whole. Thus a discussion of the events that literally tore Mito apart in the early 1860s provides an opportunity to explore both the structural features and, more central to the present paper, the symbolic dimensions of conflict as it occurred throughout society in the Restoration era.

CONFLICT AND INSURRECTION

On March 27, 1864, the first year of Genji, a ragged band of Mito samurai, priests, and peasants climbed Mt. Tsukuba in the southwestern

---

[2] For this interpretation, see Inui Hiromi and Inoue Katsuo, "Chōshū-han to Mito-han," *Iwanami kōza Nihon rekishi* 12, Kinsei 4 (Tokyo, 1976), 300.

part of what is now Ibaraki prefecture and announced their dedication to a policy of "revering the emperor and expelling the barbarian" (sonnō jōi). The action initiated an episode known variously as the "Genji disturbance," "Tengu insurrection," or "Tsukuba war," which by year's end was to plunge Mito domain into ruinous civil conflict and consume hundreds of lives.

The occasion for armed action by Mito zealots, culminating in the Tengu insurrection,[3] was provided by bakufu repudiation of domainal reforms that had been carried out in the Tenpō period under Mito lord Tokugawa Nariaki.[4] On April 16, 1844 a Mito elder was interrogated by bakufu senior councilor Abe Masahiro on the pretext of official displeasure regarding such reforms as the conversion of the Tokiwayama Tōshōgū Shrine from Shinbutsu Ryōbu (a Shintō-Buddhist synthesis) to Yuiitsu Shintō (exclusive Shintō), the initiation of construction projects despite the domain's financial distress, and desecration of Buddhist temples. As a result, Nariaki was ordered to Edo and on May 6, sentenced to house arrest. His position as daimyo of Mito devolved to his son Yoshiatsu, but because of the latter's youth, domainal government was placed under the guardianship of three other daimyo: Matsudaira Yoritane of Takamatsu, Matsudaira Yorimasa of Fuchū, and Matsudaira Yorinori of Moriyama. At the same time, a number of Nariaki's high-ranking advisors, including Fujita Tōko, Yamanobe Hyōgo, and Toda Tadaakira, were purged. The conservative leader Yūki Asamichi was left unscathed, however, and his faction subsequently succeeded in reversing many of the Tenpō reforms.

The purge, later known as the "crisis of Kōshin" (Kōshin no kokunan), led to an early instance of direct action on the part of Mito samurai and commoners alike. Groups of gimin (martyrs), often led by village samurai, Shintō priests, or village officials, presented petitions seeking to exonerate and reinstate their former daimyo.

In the ensuing years, the domain was split into increasingly hostile

---

[3] Tengu are mythical long-nosed mountain demons. According to Seya, the name "Tengu faction" was first applied to Mito reformists such as Fujita Tōko and Aizawa Seishisai by conservative opponents during the Tenpō reforms in Mito. Its intended implication was that they were low-ranking retainers who arrogantly held their noses in the air because of their rise to power on the basis of scholarship. Later, Tokugawa Nariaki is said to have actively adopted the name as a designation for the Mito radicals, whom he supported, on the grounds that Tengu were often thought to have superhuman powers and qualities of heroism. See Seya Yoshihiko and Toyosaki Takashi, Ibaraki-ken no rekishi (Tokyo, 1973), p. 181.

[4] The general description of events that follows is based on accounts in Katsuta-shi Shi Hensai Iinkai, ed., Katsuta-shi shi: chūsei-hen, kinsei-hen (Katsuta, 1978); Ibaraki-ken Shi Hensan Iinkai, ed., Ibaraki-ken bakumatsu-shi nenpyō (Mito, 1973); and Seya and Toyosaki, Ibaraki-ken no rekishi.

factions over three major issues: shogunal succession, the signing of a commercial treaty between the United States and Japan, and the Bogo secret imperial decree.[5]

Mito's candidate as successor to the heirless and ailing thirteenth shogun Iesada was Nariaki's seventh son Hitotsubashi Keiki (Yoshinobu). Keiki had studied at the Mito Academy as a child and then succeeded to the house of Hitotsubashi, later becoming the nucleus of a faction that centered on that house. On the other side was the so-called Kishū faction, which supported the daimyo of Kii, Tokugawa Yoshitomi. Since the central figure in the Kishū faction was the Hikone daimyo, Ii Naosuke, the struggle in effect pitted Hikone against Mito.

Mito radicals also confronted both Ii and conservatives in Mito over Japan's signing of a commercial treaty with representatives of the United States following Perry's arrival in 1853. The senior councilor, Hotta Masayoshi, had tried and failed to get a decree from Emperor Kōmei supporting the treaty, but protreaty forces received a boost when Ii attained the post of *tairō*, highest in the bakufu administration. As a result of Ii's influence, the treaty was signed and Yoshitomi (fourteenth shōgun Iemochi) became the heir apparent. It was to protest that chain of events that Nariaki defied confinement orders by taking his son, the incumbent daimyo of Mito, to Edo. In July 1858 Nariaki was again confined, this time to the Mito mansion in the Komagome section of Edo, stimulating another "exoneration movement" on the part of his reformist supporters in Mito.

The third issue of contention involved the so-called Bogo imperial rescript. The Mito representative at court, Ugai Yoshizaemon, had surreptitiously been given the rescript, along with a particularly explicit attachment, on August 8, 1858 by radical partisans in court. Ugai's son then secretly delivered the documents to the Mito mansion in Edo; in the meantime another copy, without the attachment, was delivered from the court through regular channels to the bakufu. The message apparently implied that bakufu actions had been inadequate for a time of national crisis, and also criticized bakufu officials for punishing Nariaki. By way of recommendation, it suggested that the bakufu should attempt to stabilize the situation by moving toward a policy of *kōbu gattai* (unity between court and bakufu) in cooperation with the collateral houses of Owari, Kii, and Mito. Afraid that Mito would leak the document to the other domains, the authorities in Edo ordered that Mito's copy be returned to the bakufu. Heightened bakufu suspicions eventually led to the Ansei purge in which a number of Mito activists, including Ugai and his son, were executed.

[5] This interpretation is from Seya and Toyosaki, *Ibaraki-ken no rekishi*, pp. 172–176.

Ii Naosuke's demand that the rescript be returned to the bakufu fomented a split in Mito not only between conservatives and reformists but among the reformists themselves. The extreme positions were those of the conservatives, who favored return of the document to the bakufu, and the radicals, who advocated its dissemination to the other major domains. Between, or at least circumventing the two extremes, however, was a moderate group led by Aizawa Seishisai, which insisted that the document should neither be disseminated nor relinquished, but rather sent back to the court where it originated. The radicals resolved to resist by force, and when in late December 1859 they feared that the conservatives might attempt secretly to transport the document to Edo, they blocked the Mitsukaidō, which was the main highway between Mito and Edo. In the action, which came to be known as the "Nagaoka tonshū" (Nagaoka occupation), they set up camp and searched all southbound travelers. The incident marked a turning point in the Mito loyalist movement, in that it separated radicals clearly from moderates and neutrals, and brought together a force of hundreds, including peasants as well as samurai. In a negative sense, it fostered unity between reformist moderates and conservatives, who now joined in a pacification campaign against the radicals. Despite repeated calls for dissolution by domainal authorities, the occupation lasted until the middle of the following February.

Following the March 3, 1860, Sakuradamon incident in which a group of Mito zealots, including three Shintō priests, assassinated Ii Naosuke, a large segment of the so-called Nagaoka force dispersed to a number of locations in the southern province of Mito domain. Often making their headquarters at provincial schools, they hid from domainal authorities while collecting funds and training troops for future actions. One of the largest concentrations centered on the Tamazukuri provincial school. The Tamazukuri facility was strategically placed between Mito castle and Edo, and yet sufficiently remote to prevent arrests of rebels who were sought for their part in the Nagaoka and Sakuradamon disturbances. The schools were clearly well-suited to the emphasis on military training that seems to have characterized the rebel bands. Reports on the garrisons by a local official, for example, describe them as so "mad with the Japanese spirit [*Nippon damashii*]" that they trained daily.[6]

It appears that the majority of the Tamazukuri rebels were classified as "peasants," both ordinary farmers without surnames (*hirabyakushō*) and more prominent locals, including village leaders. Contemporary

[6] Seya Yoshihiko, *Mito-han kyōkō no shiteki kenkyū* (Tokyo, 1976), p. 124, quoting *Mito-han shiryō* (Tokyo, 1915), vol. 2 (*ge*).

records estimate, for example, that the Tamazukuri force consisted of about sixteen samurai, one provincial school director, two rustic samurai, two Shintō priests, two Shūgendō practitioners, two local townsmen, and thirty-three peasants, including five with surnames.[7]

Finally, on March 27, 1864, the so-called Tengu band led by Fujita Koshirō, son of Mito reformist leader Fujita Tōko and grandson of the early theoretician Fujita Yūkoku, marched with a force of 150 or so to the top of the famous Mt. Tsukuba. Other leaders included Takeuchi Hyakutarō, a rural samurai, the Shūgendō priest Iwaya Keiichirō, and Mito municipal magistrate (*machi bugyō*) Tamaru Inanoemon.[8] After collecting funds from local farmers and merchants—and apparently also from the Chōshū samurai Kido Kōin (Katsura Kogorō)[9]—they soon moved by way of Nikkō to Mt. Ōhira, where a "Call to Action" (*Gekibun*) was issued and the force expanded to several hundred. After some initial dissension, it returned to Tsukuba and mushroomed into a virtual rebel army of a thousand or so troops. Morale soared when the rebels defeated a force of soldiers from a number of domains, including Shimoosa, Shimodate, Tsuchiura, and Yūki. Meanwhile, conservative forces from Mito under Ichikawa Sanzaemon occupied Mito castle, and a bakufu army was organized against the rebels under the leadership of Tanuma Okinori. In July the Tengu came down from the mountain, camped in the vicinity of Ogawa and Itako, and engaged the conservatives near Mito.

The major struggle, however, occurred between August and October

---

[7] Seya, *Mito-han kyōkō*, p. 127.

[8] Fujita Koshirō (or Makoto) was Tōko's fourth son, born of a mistress. He went to Edo with his father at the age of twelve, was educated there, and subsequently continued his studies with a number of tutors in Mito. He eventually attended the Mito Academy, or Kōdōkan. In 1863, when the Mito daimyo accompanied the shōgun to Kyoto, Koshirō was able to go along. There he met Kido Kōin (Katsura Kogorō) and other *sonnō jōi* activists, and began laying the groundwork for the insurrection. Takeuchi Hyakutarō (or Nobushide), also known as Takenaka Manjirō, was the son of the rich peasant Sen'emon, who eventually purchased rural samurai (*gōshi*) status for 2,500 *ryō*. Hyakutarō studied under Fujita Tōko, participated in such actions as the Nagaoka occupation, and later was a principal director of activities at the Ogawa provincial school where many participants in the insurrection received their training. Iwaya Keiichirō (or Nobushige) was the son of a priest from Shishikura village, which was next to the village where Takeuchi grew up. Also apparently a student of Tōko, he was a principal organizer and trainer at the Itako provincial school. He later deserted Tengu forces during the fighting at Nakaminato. Tamaru Inanoemon (or Shokuin), a Mito samurai, played a central role in the cadastral survey carried out as part of the Tenpō reforms in Mito and held a number of other posts in the Mito administration. He also traveled to Kyoto with the Mito daimyo in 1863. For more information concerning leading participants in the insurrection, see Jōyō Meiji Kinenkai, ed., *Mito bakumatsu fūunroku* (Mito, reprinted 1976), pp. 313-326.

[9] See ibid., p. 325, and Yamakawa Kikue, *Oboegaki: bakumatsu no Mito-han* (Tokyo, 1974), p. 304.

in and around the major port of Nakaminato. When the fighting went against the rebels a contingent of a thousand or so surrendered, relying on a promise of leniency from the conservative side. That promise was subsequently broken: the leaders of the defection were executed, and hundreds of others eventually died in prison. A second group, however, now led by Mito elder Takeda Kōunsai, set out a thousand strong for Kyoto in order to appeal through Hitotsubashi Keiki to the imperial court. After a long trek punctuated by several pitched battles with pro-bakufu domainal armies, the 823 remaining rebels finally surrendered in mid-December in Kaga near the Japan Sea. On February 4, 1865, Takeda and twenty-three others were executed, and in the next few days 328 more met the same fate. About 280 others were banished, some to remote islands. The salted heads of Takeda, Tamaru, Fujita, and Yamakuni Hyōbu were placed on display near Mito castle for three days before being cast into the harbor.[10] Estimates regarding the class membership of Tengu insurgents vary, but commoners appear to have greatly outnumbered samurai.[11]

SIGNIFICANCE AND MEANING

The Tengu insurrection is noteworthy as the major counterpart in eastern Japan to the earlier revolts in Yamato and Ikuno. It dealt an effective blow to the bakufu, tying up manpower, frequently demonstrating the inadequacy of bakufu troops, and costing perhaps more than 330,000 ryō to put down.[12] A recent study by Conrad Totman led him to characterize it as the "most far-reaching, potentially disastrous, sanguinary, and costly insurgency faced by Edo since 1638."[13] It was, therefore, a significant factor in the decline of the bakuhan system.

Yet the insurrection may also be said to have been meaningful in a way not at all dependent upon its causal efficacy in such a sequence of events. The literary historian E. D. Hirsch distinguishes significance from meaning:

The important feature of meaning as distinct from significance is that meaning is the determinate representation of a text for an interpreter.

---

[10] Katsuta-shi Shi Hensan Iinkai, ed., *Katsuta-shi shi*, p. 1048. Yamakuni Hyōbu (or Tomomasa) was Tamaru's elder brother. He had been active in military reform in Mito and was a noted expert in military affairs.

[11] Seya and Toyosaki, *Ibaraki-ken no rekishi*, p. 184; also see Takagi Shunsuke, "Mitohan sonnō jōi undō no sonraku shusshin giseisha," *Ibaraki-ken shi kenkyū*, 13 (1969), 53-78.

[12] Conrad Totman, *The Collapse of the Tokugawa Bakufu, 1862-1868* (Honolulu: University Press of Hawaii, 1980), p. 122.

[13] Ibid., p. 120.

An interpreted text is always taken to represent something, but that something can always be related to something else. Significance is meaning-as-related-to-something-else.[14]

Meaning, in other words, is largely within the boundaries of the text, while significance is located in its relevance to something presumed to be external. By extension, we may postulate a difference between what the Mito rebellion meant in and of itself, on the one hand, and how it related to aspects of the context in which it occurred, on the other. But such a formulation implies an analogy between intentional action and text: the actions that comprised the rebellion must be "read" for the meaning they contain. Probably the most thorough and convincing defense of such an analogy appears in an essay by the phenomenologist Paul Ricoeur. Acts are texts of a sort, according to Ricoeur, because "social reality is fundamentally symbolic."[15] The semiotic or symbolic function—"substituting signs for things and of representing things by means of signs"—is inherent in a social world where we must constantly "read" the meaning of gestures, performances, and responses.

However, Ricoeur also finds in both acts and texts a form of "omni-temporal relevance" that transcends the historical framework of their production.[16] For the historian's purposes, therefore, it becomes necessary to modify Ricoeur's hermeneutic of action by focusing it more closely on historical representations of meaning, in other words, ideology. Harootunian argues elsewhere in this volume that ideology consists in "the practice of representation and the construction of a subject for such representation." If that definition is accepted, and if action may be seen as a text, or form of representation, then it follows that ideology must be accessible in intentional acts as well as texts. The remainder of this paper will be devoted to an exploration of Mito ideology as it was revealed largely in the actions of Mito partisans.

First, events in the 1850s and 1860s clearly indicate that the construction and eventual transformation of a historical subject was a central function of ideology in Mito. There can be little doubt that, as Masao Maruyama points out, the late-Tokugawa Mito school as a whole "produced its theoretical formulation of the Sonnō jōi position from the feudal lord's standpoint."[17] Such contemporary issues as the accumulation of wealth by the merchant class, maldistribution of food, social

[14] E. D. Hirsch, Jr., *The Aims of Interpretation* (Chicago: University of Chicago Press, 1976), pp. 79-80.

[15] Paul Ricoeur, "The Model of the Text: Meaningful Action Considered as a Text," *Social Research*, 38 (Autumn 1971), 559.

[16] Ibid., pp. 543-544.

[17] Masao Maruyama, *Studies in the Intellectual History of Tokugawa Japan* (Tokyo, 1974), p. 357.

dislocation, and peasant rebellion were perceived as symptoms of inadequate performance on the part of the managerial aristocracy. Moreover, solutions were sought initially in what was thought to be the prerogative of that class to redefine and actualize paradigmatic relationships among heaven, land, and society on behalf of the whole realm. The "ignorant [common] people" (*gumin*) were expected merely to respond loyally and submissively, not to act. As Aizawa warns, following the *Analects*, "the people should only be made to depend [*yorashimubeku shite*], never allowed to know [*shirashimubekarazu*]."[18] Nevertheless, the importance of the provincial schools, established by reformists in the Tenpō and Ansei (1854–1860) eras, in fostering the participation of nonsamurai not only in the Tengu insurrection but in earlier actions as well argues that Mito ideology did indeed allow, and eventually encourage, some nonsamurai to "know" and to act.

Second, aspects of the Mito ideology may be read directly in rebel actions, particularly their attempts to associate themselves with central places that had a strongly ritualistic, originary aura, such as the tomb of Tokugawa Ieyasu in Nikkō and the imperial court itself. Major Mito texts such as Aizawa's Seishisai's "A New Thesis" (*Shinron*) had placed heavy emphasis upon the accessibility of natural archetypes of community rooted in a hypothetical conception of origins, and this emphasis was continued by the rebels in their later strategies of action.

Finally, whereas reformist action in the Tenpō period had focused on the establishment of domainal institutions, signifying the viability of the domain as a microcosm of the *bakuhan* system as a whole, action in the Ansei period and after dramatized the emergence of a nationwide political space in which both individuals and the domain itself could act directly upon and for the whole nation.

RECONSTITUTION OF THE SUBJECT

Despite their haughty attitude toward the nonsamurai classes, Mito reformers in the Tenpō period had recognized the political and economic importance of the lower strata of society and spent a good deal of time and effort cultivating their support. Peasant rebellion was recognized as an ever-present threat. Hence in the course of the cadastral survey carried out in 1839 and 1840, for example, they had realized the need to take local differences into account and to include respected members of local communities in survey teams. When samurai were moved out of the castle town onto fiefs of their own, care was taken to clarify rela-

---

[18] Aizawa Seishisai, "Shinron" in Tsukamoto Katsuyoshi, ed., *Shinron, Tekii-hen* (Tokyo, 1931), p. 221.

tions between fief stewards and peasants, and also to lessen the abuse of corvée and other prerogatives.[19]

Moreover, samurai activists often sought out and rewarded locals who had cooperated actively in reform projects such as the cadastral survey. One means of reward was the conferral of semisamurai (*gōshi*) status, including the right to wear swords. Shibahara notes that such treatment must have created a deep sense of gratitude and obligation among recipients and constituted a major factor in the willingness of such individuals to engage in political protest and petitioning on behalf of reformists in the 1850s and 1860s. It was a major element, in other words, in the transformation of a "semifeudal stratum of village officials, landlords and rich peasants" into "political subjects."[20]

Without discounting the psychological factor of gratitude as an incentive for loyalty in this transformation, it is also necessary to recognize the critical importance of the provincial schools established by reformist forces. The three schools created under reformist administration in the Tenpō era—Keigyōkan in the south province, Ekishūkan in the north, and Kōgeikan (later Kashūkan) in the east—and nine more set up in the Ansei period, extended the Mito ideology to an entirely new group of subjects, and thus enabled them to speak and act publicly in a sanctioned, intelligible manner. In other words, the moral, political, and military knowledge imparted through the schools implied the power to act.

As detailed research by Seya Yoshihiko has demonstrated, loyalist radicals were closely involved in the construction of provincial schools in the Ansei period. The school in Machida, for example, seems to have been planned by Takahashi Taiichirō, a low-ranking samurai who studied under a protégé of Fujita Yūkoku and also had a hand in the publication of Aizawa Seishisai's "A New Thesis." Later, Takahashi was an organizer of the Sakuradamon assassination incident and subsequently ended his life by suicide when confronted by bakufu police. He probably also took part in the establishment of two other schools in the northern province.[21]

An analogous role was most likely played in the southern province by the samurai activist Kaneko Magojirō, who had participated in the cadastral survey as a provincial commissioner. Kaneko also led in the revamping of older schools to reflect the Ansei emphasis on military

[19] See Mito-shi Shi Hensan Iinkai, ed., *Mito-shi shi*, 2, vol. 3:788-91; Fujita Tōko, "Hitachi obi" in Takasu Yoshijirō, ed., *Fujita Tōko zenshū*, 1 (Tokyo, 1935), 464-466; and J. Victor Koschmann, "Discourse in Action: Representational Politics in Mito in the Late Tokugawa Period," Ph.D. dissertation, Chicago, 1980, pp. 119-22, 147-48.

[20] Shibahara Takuji, *Meiji ishin no kenryoku kiban* (Tokyo, 1965), pp. 144, 145.

[21] Seya, *Mito-han kyōkō*, pp. 56-57.

arts. The radicals Murata Risuke and Ōta Yasutarō played leading roles in school construction in the east and west provinces, respectively. As Seya observes, once established, the schools consolidated strong vertical links between loyalist samurai, local elites, and even ordinary peasants, thus laying the groundwork for future mobilization.[22]

An early example of the involvement of provincial schools in nonsamurai political activism is provided by the movement to exonerate Tokugawa Nariaki, as noted above. Kashūkan director Kan Masatomo, for example, a strong believer in Shintō and proponent of Aizawa's doctrine of national essence (*kokutai*), led local petitioning together with another school official, Kasukabe Isaji of the Ekishūkan. In a petition drafted in 1846, Kan asserts that the schools had been established for the purpose of exalting the "great Way of the divine sages," and warns facetiously that efforts to "calm the peasants" had been to no avail.[23] The villages in the vicinity of the Kashūkan produced an unusually large number of protesters, who left to join activists from other parts of the domain.

Shintō priests formed an important segment of the movement. Thirty-four clergy associated with the Kashūkan, for example, formed an association called the Green Dragon League (*Seiryūgumi Kairen*). Led by Miyata Tokuchika, a student of the nativist scholar Hirata Atsutane, the organization submitted at least two petitions to the domain calling for Nariaki's release from house arrest, his reinstatement as daimyo, and a continuation of reform.[24]

Undoubtedly, a crucial role in making such activism possible was played by the religious policies pursued by reformists in Mito in the Tenpō and Ansei periods. An earlier system of control, which had forced every citizen to register at a Buddhist temple, was replaced by the Shintō-oriented system of village shrine registration. Shintō funerals were authorized even for nonpractitioners. Moreover, the social status of Shintō and other non-Buddhist holy men was elevated considerably, and they were patronized through offical channels. On February 15 and 16, 1856, for example, a lecture contest was held for Shintō priests at the Mito Academy. Along with prizes for lectures, which because of the Academy's orientation to Shintō-Confucian unity centered on the Confucian classics and the early Japanese mytho-history, *Nihon shoki*, the priests were provided with food, drink, and accommodations.[25]

As Seya points out, such treatment must have been important in fostering solidarity among Shintō practitioners and instilling a sense of

[22] Ibid., pp. 58-59, 72.
[23] Ibid., pp. 104-105.
[24] Ibid., p. 105.
[25] Ibid., pp. 110-111.

gratitude toward reformist authorities. In addition, however, it opened up the major institutional manifestation of Mito discourse to a group customarily excluded from participation, and introduced them to the principles of moral and political action. It is important to note that the education of priests did not stop at theory. Shintō representatives had been allowed since 1840 to take part in military exercises such as the ceremonial bird hunt (Ōitorigari), and they were now organized into seven groups and trained in military arts at provincial schools.[26] The eventual result was a virtually paramilitary force in the service of radical samurai. Priests participated in such later actions as the occupation of the Kogane and Nagaoka stations of the Mitsukaidō, and three were among the assassins at Sakuradamon. Later, in 1863, Shintō and Shūgendō practitioners were mobilized to form a coastal defense corps.[27]

Another institution that linked up with the provincial schools to play an essential role in fostering political subjectivity among the lower orders was the "peasant militia" (nōhei). Suggested in such early texts as "A New Thesis," and initially planned in the Tenpō period, the militia system finally came into existence in September of 1856. According to the formal order, it was to consist of fifteen hundred peasant soldiers, with five hundred in each of three groups: rural enthusiasts (yūshi) who had participated actively in reformist projects, members of the upper stratum of peasants and townsmen who were willing to contribute funds, and ordinary peasants and fishermen who would be assigned to coastal defense units. All were attached to samurai commanders. In 1857 they were granted the hereditary right to wear swords and receive firearms training, thereby achieving the de facto status of country samurai. Their training took place through the provincial schools.[28]

Clearly the schools played a central role in catalyzing radical thought and action in the Mito countryside, thereby broadening and virtually reconstituting the subject of active discourse. Yet it would be wrong, of course, to assume that Mito discourse was transformed into an ideology of peasant rebellion. Although the new subject of action included a broad assortment of rural types, that subject also exploited and oppressed the peasantry in the course of its political activism.

A precedent for such exploitation had been set in the earliest stages of provincial school construction, when both financial and material resources, including books, had been collected from the area served by each school rather than provided by the domain. In the case of the Machida school, such donors numbered 1,284, of whom 45 were of-

---

[26] Ibid., p. 113.

[27] Ibid., pp. 130-131.

[28] See Mito-han shiryō, 1 (jō), kan, 864; Shibahara, Meiji ishin, p. 160; and Seya, Mito-han kyōkō, p. 61.

fered special thanks at the opening ceremonies. Of the 45, 20 were village leaders. Of the remainder, 4 were non-Buddhist religious practitioners, 3 were provincial doctors, and 3 were rustic samurai. As Seya observes, it is difficult to explain such contributions in terms of spontaneous generosity alone, and a certain degree of coercion must have been involved.[29] Outright extortion also seems to have taken place in 1855—the year of the Ansei earthquake in which Fujita Tōko lost his life—when damages to the Mito mansion at Koishikawa, Edo, were repaired in part with monies raised from villagers through the provincial schools.[30]

Perhaps as a direct extension of such methods, it appears that Tengu forces garrisoned at the Tamazukuri and Ogawa schools also supported themselves and their endeavors largely by extortion from the countryside. It was reported that bands of rebels would confront village leaders with demands for a "loan" based on the need to "rid the nation of foreigners." If they failed to come up with an appropriate amount, the intruders would destroy property and wreak havoc in the village. Such raids were by no means limited to Mito, but extended as far as Kasama and the northerly domain of Moriyama. One source, unfavorably disposed to the rebel forces, suggests that monies collected in such a manner by the Tamazukuri force may have totaled as much as thirty thousand ryō. Although that figure is probably high, other sources located by Seya Yoshihiko indicate clearly that an amount close to one thousand ryō was collected in November of 1860 in the vicinity of Minato-mura alone, lending credence to the contention that amounts were indeed substantial.[31]

By the early 1860s, prior to the major Tengu rebellion of 1864, a general state of lawlessness and often indiscriminate plunder seems to have spread across much of northern Kantō. One account reports that

> beginning in early October of Bunkyū three [1863] a large force of Shinto priests, rustic samurai, and peasants gathered at the provincial schools in Naka-minato, Ogawa, and Itako, calling for the expulsion of foreigners [jōi]. They were joined off and on by a diverse collection of hangers-on from other domains. Now and then they would force their way into the homes of the rich peasants and demand contributions toward the establishment of an expulsionist army. More often than not they spent the money in brothels.[32]

[29] Seya, Mito-han kyōkō, p. 72.
[30] Ibid., p. 67.
[31] Ibid., pp. 125-127.
[32] Sakai Shirōbei, Mito kenbun jikki (published together with Takenuma Takeshi, Mito-han matsu shiryō), Tokyo, 1977, p. 132; also quoted in Shibahara, Meiji ishin, p. 175.

Another, more hostile to the radicals, says,

> In broad daylight with lances and swords drawn, muskets primed, they would advance upon the wealthy. They either seized or forcibly borrowed money and grain, and warned that Heaven's punishment [*tenchū*] would be meted out to those who refused . . . [for them,] cutting down a peasant or townsman was no more serious than slicing off a radish shoot.[33]

Such practices were hardly well calculated to attract broad-based support among the rural population, and in some cases peasants reportedly helped the authorities track down and arrest offenders.[34]

Other documents, such as the diary of a roof-thatch contractor in Tsukuba, tend to indicate a certain degree of initial rapport between rebels and local residents,[35] and indeed Shibahara Takuji cites the successful rebel engagement against conservative forces at Mt. Tsukuba on 8 July 1864 as their "first and last" unity with the "masses."[36] Clearly, however, the Tsukuba campaign as a whole was characterized by widespread extortion of money, weapons, food, and labor. Materials from Tsukuba show that a merchant suspected of trading with foreigners through the port of Yokohama was forced to contribute thirty *ryō* to avoid a raid on his life and property, and that Tengu forcibly purchased two guns, six lances, and four swords for the unfair sum of only twenty-one *ryō*. A general report on Tengu movements in the Tsukuba region also includes details regarding their seizure of military equipment, clothing, and funds.[37]

It appears that although the new subject of action was originally from the rural, predominantly peasant, population, it was no longer of or for it. Nevertheless, the participation of rural commoners in political actions such as those recounted above marked a significant departure from the exclusively samurai involvement in the Tenpō reforms.

In short, the disproportionately high level of participation by rural, nonsamurai elites in the radical actions of the fifties and sixties revealed the effects of a form of ideological hegemony through which segments of the population formerly inert politically were provided with a moral and conceptual framework for action and thus constituted as subjects.[38]

---

[33] *Mito-han tōsō shimatsu*; quoted in Shibahara, *Meiji ishin*, p. 183.

[34] *Mito-han shiryō*, 2 (*ge*), 53–65.

[35] Tsukuba-chō Shi Hensan Iinkai, ed., *Tsukuba-chō shi: shiryō shū* (Tsukuba, 1979), pp. 1–70.

[36] Shibahara, *Meiji ishin*, p. 179.

[37] Ibid., pp. 152–162.

[38] On the concept of hegemony, see Antonio Gramsci, *The Prison Notebooks: Selections*, translated and edited by Quintin Hoare and Geoffrey Nowell Smith (New York: International Publishers, 1971), pp. 12–13.

Rather than championing the interests of the rural peasantry, however, this newly "hegemonized" political force collaborated with Mito samurai in the exploitation of the villagers with whom it came into contact.

As I will indicate below, in the course of their transformation into acting subjects, nonsamurai were initiated into an ideological paradigm that had been established by Mito ideologues in the Tenpō era and before. According to that paradigm, political action was to be defined as the representation—through texts, institutions, and performances—of a supposedly natural, self-regulating order. That order would constitute the actualization of the national essence (*kokutai*), and be authenticated by its association with certain cosmogonic archetypes established by the Sun Goddess, Amaterasu Ōmikami. As such, political action would be antihistorical in intent, designed to restore to the present a sense of unity with the Origin, and thus allow an "escape" from history. Whereas in the Tenpō period these ideological precepts had animated the establishment and reform of institutions that were presumed to embody archetypes of order, in the Ansei period and after, the Mito ideology was encoded in a kinetic language of performative gesture.[39]

PILGRIMAGE TO THE ORIGIN

Having gathered at Mt. Tsukuba on March 27, the rebels left almost immediately for Utsunomiya, near Mt. Nikkō, where they arrived on May 5. Mt. Nikkō was the site of mausoleums enshrining the remains of Tokugawa Ieyasu and other shoguns, and was thus among the most sacred spots in the nation throughout the Tokugawa period. On the sixth, Tengu leaders met with sympathetic Utsunomiya samurai and expressed their desire to camp at Nikkō. On the eighth, however, they were told that Utsunomiya commissioner Okura Masayoshi would allow no more than ten people to enter the sacred area, and then only for a single visit. After initial resistance, the Tengu complied, sending a small group of leaders to pay their respects at the tomb of Ieyasu. On the eleventh they repaired to Kanuma in Shimotsuke, and from there to Mt. Ōhira.[40]

In her recent interpretation of those years, Yamakawa Kikue suggests that the Tengu leaders saw Nikkō primarily in military terms as a haven that because of its sacredness would be immune to attack by bakufu troops.[41] That may indeed have been an important factor. At the same time, however, it almost certainly had symbolic meaning as a point of

[39] For an account of the Tenpō Reforms in Mito see Koschmann, "Discourse in Action," chapter 2.

[40] Ibaraki-ken Shi Hensan Iinkai, ed., *Ibaraki-ken bakumatsu-shi nenpyō*, pp. 153-156.

[41] Yamakawa, *Oboegaki*, p. 304.

origin, where the aura of an age prior to historical decay and foreign desecration was still tangible. A suggestion of that aura is captured in a poem reportedly written by Tengu leader Satō Sajiemon as the band negotiated with officials at Utsunomiya:

> The barbarians have invaded eastern seas.
> Yet the soul of the founder is with us
> Even as we shed tears of gratitude
> In melancholy worship from afar—Mt. Nikkō.[42]

Important clues to the symbolic meaning of gestures such as the trek to Nikkō as intentional references to the power of the origin are available in major Mito writings. Texts spell out an antihistorical ideology according to which original archetypes must be reinstituted in order to achieve a state of natural order. "A New Thesis," for example, portrays an ideal condition in which time is collapsed and the primal moment recaptured through ritual practice. For Aizawa, the prototypical rite of restoration is the *daijōsai*, or Great Thanksgiving Ceremony.[43]

The rites of the *daijōsai* are performed at the first harvest following the enthronement of a new emperor, and basically consist in the offering of new grain to Amaterasu. The procedures all reenact mythical themes, particularly the founding of the nation and Amaterasu's benevolent acts on behalf of the people. Most important, however, as the ceremony proceeds, "it is as if the emperor receives anew the mandate of Amaterasu." Indeed, the climax of the rite is a mystical epiphany as Amaterasu appears as the symbol of communal unity and order:

> When the direct descendant of Amaterasu reverently carries out these rites in her honor, an indistinct image of Amaterasu's august countenance rises before the eyes of those present. Neither sovereign nor subjects fail to sense her presence and become profoundly aware of her nearness to them. Therefore, as the officials respect and adore the emperor, they experience the spontaneous and irrepressible feeling that they are adoring Amaterasu herself. As a result, they all feel like descendants of the gods.[44]

In that elusive instant past meets present, the particular becomes universal, and mortals participate in the divine. The conviction of consanguinity injects a strong element of egalitarianism: despite differences in social station, all are minimally authenticated by the divine lineage.

Moreover, the ceremony reaffirms the secure compatibility of man and nature through the medium of a sacred, productive community.

---

[42] Jōyō Meiji Kinenkai, ed., *Mito bakumatsu fūunroku*, p. 335.

[43] Aizawa, "Shinron," pp. 15-16.

[44] Ibid., pp. 19-20.

Long ago, Aizawa says, everyone knew that the grain that sustained their communities originated in seeds distributed by the gods. Hence together they worked hard to develop the productivity of the earth. Their minds were united with "the mind of Heaven and Earth," and "all shared wealth equally."[45] Clearly evident is an emphasis on the Sun Goddess's primal concern for the common welfare. The thanksgiving ceremony is thus associated with a conception of community in which hierarchy, although necessary, need not govern the distribution of resources.

For most people, of course, participation in the *daijōsai* can only be vicarious, but the experiential basis of the national essence as it is manifested in the ceremony is meant to extend beyond that prototypical rite to family ancestral observances, and perhaps even to the variety of mundane rituals such as gift-giving that enable people to interrelate continuously in spontaneous, coordinated movement.[46] The political implications of the religious symbolism that constitutes the *daijōsai* are, of course, central to the ideological statement contained in Aizawa's text. Rites should be symbolically duplicated at all levels of society.[47] The result will be a form of "magical" government in which obedient service comes naturally:

> Filial piety gives rise to a spirit of loyalty to the sovereign and loyalty is the result of following the will of one's ancestors. Hence loyalty and filial piety become one; the education of the people and the refinement of customs is accomplished without a word being spoken. Worship becomes government, and government has the effect of education, hence there is no essential difference between government and the indoctrination of the people. If the people just concentrate on revering Amaterasu and look up to her descendants, they will all face in the same direction and never go astray. Their intentions will converge, and man will become one with heaven. This is precisely what the sovereign relies upon in ruling the four seas, and is the final essence and ground upon which the founder established the nation.[48]

Return to the origin as a model of government, of course, implies a devaluation of history. Hence a large part of "A New Thesis" is devoted to historical surveys that demonstrate the degenerative qualities of time and the periodic need for a restoration. This juxtaposition of a form of historical entropy against a ritualistic conception of the national

---

[45] Ibid., p. 79.

[46] See Herbert Fingarette, *Confucius: The Secular as Sacred* (New York: Harper Torchbooks, 1972).

[47] Aizawa, "Shinron," pp. 19-20.

[48] Ibid., pp. 21-22.

essence recalls Mircea Eliade's description of an archaic mentality. For such a mentality, as for the Mito writers, time contaminates; "history . . . in proportion to and, by the mere fact of its duration, provokes an erosion of all forms by exhausting their ontological substance." Therefore, "the man of archaic cultures tolerates 'history' with difficulty and attempts periodically to abolish it."[49]

The abolition of history for archaic man is accomplished through the repetition of rites that reenact cosmogony: "myths serve as models for ceremonies that periodically reactualize the tremendous events that occurred at the beginning of time." In such ceremonies, "there is an abolition of time through the imitation of archetypes and the repetition of paradigmatic gestures." Thus archaic man is "free to be no longer what he was, free to annul his own history through periodic abolition of time and collective regeneration." He may recover, in other words, a "very distant epoch when men knew neither death nor toil nor suffering and had a bountiful supply of food merely for the taking."[50]

Most significantly for purposes of interpreting the meaning of Tengu orientations to Nikkō, Eliade also observes that a "symbolism of the center" is closely related to the archaic mystique of origins, and the most common representation of centrality is a sacred mountain. A pilgrimage to the center symbolizes the transition "from chaos to cosmos" and thus is difficult but supremely meaningful: "attaining the center is equivalent to a consecration, an initiation; yesterday's profane and illusory experience gives place to a new, to a life that is real, enduring, and effective."[51]

Such insights are extremely suggestive regarding the representational functions of the trek to Nikkō. In the Tenpō period and before, language and institutions had been manipulated as efficient means toward the eventual representation of a natural, unmediated polity. Now, on the other hand, such separation of means from ends is rejected, and action is required to represent directly the possibility of a natural order. In terms used originally by Ferdinand Toennies, there was a transition from arbitrary will, in which means are merely expedient and perhaps even antithetical to ends, to essential will, in which means and ends are an "organic whole."[52]

It is surely possible, therefore, to detect in the Tengu gesture toward Nikkō—as well as in the initial choice of the prominent Mt. Tsukuba,

[49] Mircea Eliade, *The Myth of the Eternal Return or, Cosmos and History* (Princeton: Princeton University Press, 1971), p. 115, 36.

[50] Ibid., pp. xiv, 35, 157, 91.

[51] Ibid., pp. 12-17, 18.

[52] Werner J. Cahnman and Rudolph Heberle, eds., *Ferdinand Toennies on Sociology: Pure, Applied, and Empirical* (Chicago: University of Chicago Press, 1971), p. 66.

and the later trek toward the imperial seat—a strong, symbolic orientation to the "center" similar to that described by Eliade. In the political and religious context of late Tokugawa Japan, the visit to Nikkō could well be interpreted as an attempt to signify—to represent not in texts or institutions but rather in a dramatic gesture—the relevance of original principles in a time of crisis.

It is unnecessary, of course, to deny the importance of what Quentin Skinner would call other "motives" behind the act.[53] For example, Hitotsubashi Keiki recorded retrospectively his view that despite their rhetoric about revering the emperor and expelling the barbarian, Tengu leaders were actually concerned only about the power struggle going on in Mito between radical and conservative factions.[54] Undoubtedly, the Tengu mobilization responded to a number of political, economic, and social considerations, among which were factional conflicts. Such motives, do not, however, affect the proposition that the Tengu leaders intended *in* making the gesture toward Nikkō (if not *by* it) to associate their movement with the aura of original purity and wisdom surrounding Tokugawa Ieyasu, and to suggest a regeneration of the spirit of his administration in order to nullify the degenerative forces of change.

Moreover, intentionality itself is seldom simple or unambiguous. Certainly the strategic significance of Nikkō and all other mountains is undeniable, and virtually all the maneuvers of the Tengu force reveal a strong element of military instrumentality. Yet that is not necessarily the only factor involved. As von Wright has observed, the explanation of collective behavior requires a "second order act of understanding," according to which data about individuals is "colligated" under a general concept. For example,

> I see crowds of people in the street moving in the same direction, shouting things in unison, some waving flags, etc. What *is* it that is going on? I have already understood the "elements" of what I see intentionalistically. The people are "themselves" moving and not being swept by a wind or torrent. They are shouting—and this is to say more than that sounds emanate from their throats. But the "whole" which I observe is not yet clear to me. Is this a demonstration? Or is it perhaps a Folk festival or a religious procession that I am witnessing?[55]

[53] Quentin Skinner, "Motives, Intentions and the Interpretation of Texts," *The New Literary History*, 3 (1972), 400.

[54] Osatake Takeshi, *Meiji ishin*, 2 (Tokyo, 1943), 551.

[55] Georg Henrik von Wright, *Explanation and Understanding* (Ithaca: Cornell University Press, 1971), p. 132.

By the same token, one might ask for purposes of the present interpretive exercise whether the march to Nikkō was primarily a military maneuver or a symbolic gesture in the form of a pilgrimage. For Yamakawa Kikue, as indicated above, it was unequivocally the former, with the sacred aura of Nikkō serving only to insure the Tengu forces against bakufu attack. In the context of the Mito ideology as a whole, however, it is also likely that the action had certain characteristics of a pilgrimage. A movement through space to the "center," in other words, symbolized also a leap back through time to the beginning, and thus dramatized the critical and regenerative possibilities of a restoration.

The work of Victor Turner on ritual and pilgrimage also contains useful clues to the message contained in Tengu attacks. For Turner, "pilgrimages are liminal phenomena"[56] suffused with elements of communitas, which is one of two basic "models for human interrelatedness." The first model "is of society as a structured, differentiated, and often hierarchical system of politico-legal-economic positions with many types of evaluation, separating men in terms of 'more' or 'less.' " The second, which he calls communitas, "emerges recognizably in the liminal period" and connotes "society as an unstructured or rudimentarily undifferentiated *comitatus*, community, or even communion of equal individuals who submit together to the general authority of the ritual elders."[57] Of course, liminality as Turner uses the term is rooted in the *rites de passage* of primitive societies, and the ritual process remains the prototype for communitas. As rituals, therefore, pilgrimages "seem to be regarded by self-conscious pilgrims both as occasions on which communitas is experienced and as journeys toward a sacred source of communitas, which is also seen as a source of healing and renewal."[58]

In the case of the Tengu pilgrimages, however, more is involved than an experience for the pilgrims themselves. Rather than merely self-renewing celebrations, the Tengu actions must be understood as gestures that designated certain referents and communicated a certain content concerning them. The pilgrimage model serves to highlight important aspects of the active "statement" contained in Tengu gestures. A willingness to defy existing laws and conventions, for example, is obviously

[56] Victor Turner, *Dramas, Fields, and Metaphors: Symbolic Action in Human Society* (Ithaca: Cornell University Press, 1974), p. 166.

[57] Victor Turner, *The Ritual Process* (Penguin Books, 1969), p. 82. I employ Turner's conceptualization of communitas despite my dissatisfaction with what appears to be its inherently static bias. In his view, communitas functions primarily to regenerate the "normalcy" of structure (ibid., pp. 169-170). I would argue that in the case of Mito this was not true, and perhaps that indicates that the model should not be used here. On the other hand, Turner's static analysis seems to fit very well with the anti-historical aims of the Mito rebels.

[58] Turner, *Dramas, Fields, and Metaphors*, p. 203.

consistent with the view of pilgrimage as antistructural communitas. The rebel memorial to Itakura Katsushizu, daimyo of Bitchū Matsuyama, for example, stated,

> We sincerely apologize if we should happen to break the law. Nevertheless, even though under present circumstances we may violate a few petty ordinances, justice demands that we obey the great principle of the founder [*sonnō jōi*]. If we do not soothe the imperial heart, how else are we to repay our indebtedness for three thousand years of benevolence?[59]

Whereas in the Tenpō period institutions were seen as necessary vehicles for administration in accord with the Way, the urgency of the new situation demanded that stable structures be set aside in service to the higher duty of actualizing the principle of *sonnō jōi*. As the "Call to Action" asserts, "A deadly disease is not to be treated with common everyday remedies. If extraordinary measures are not adopted, there will be no extraordinary effects."[60]

The general applicability to the Tengu trek of the pilgrimage model is further substantiated by the correlation pointed out by Turner between liminality and status elevation and reversal.[61] As noted above, the Tengu band consisted largely of nonsamurai from rural areas who had been initiated into the Mito ideology through the provincial schools. The leaders, particularly, were of relatively low status, and their own frequent mention of that fact indicates that it was considered meaningful by the Tengu themselves. The memorial to Ikeda Shigemasa, for example, begins, "We are aware that for small men such as we commoners and hermits to exceed the limits of their station and presume to discourse on policy for the realm is no small infraction."[62] The attempt to cultivate an aura of purity and ingenuousness is unmistakable.

Elements of liminality and communitas only suggested by the Nikkō pilgrimage, however, emerge with greater clarity in the later Tengu decision to march westward in an appeal to the court through the good offices of Hitotsubashi Keiki.[63] The immediate political objective was to gain official sanction to serve as part of an imperial force to repel the barbarians. In their earlier memorial to Nariaki's ninth son, Ikeda Shigemasa, for example, they had entreated, "If through your good offices you could intercede on our behalf in order to secure imperial sanction

---

[59] *Mito-han shiryō*, 2:579.

[60] Ibid., p. 576.

[61] Turner, *The Ritual Process*, p. 85.

[62] *Mito-han shiryō*, 2:579–580.

[63] See Osatake, *Meiji ishin*, 2:558 and Jōyō Meiji Kinenkai, ed., *Mito bakumatsu fūunroku*, p. 548.

for our force as the vanguard of expulsionism we should express appreciation with our very lives."[64] Ikeda complied, dispatching memorials of his own to both court and bakufu. In the latter, he referred to the Tengu as the *Yashū ikki* (uprising in Shimotsuke), and while agreeing that the rebellion should be put down, he suggested that in the event the bakufu were to initiate a policy of expelling the foreigner, the Mito rebels should be put in the forefront of an expulsionist force.[65] However, in the case of Keiki, who was now Supreme Commander of Imperial Defense, the rebels misjudged. Not only was he undisposed to provide aid, but he played a major role in their defeat.[66]

The historian Osatake Takeshi is essentially correct in his reading of the intentionality operative in the decision to march toward Kyoto. In his hypothetical reconstruction of rebel thinking, he says,

> If this rebellion had been from the outset designed to fight the bakufu things would be relatively simple. We should struggle to the bitter end, die in battle, or when defeated commit suicide. But we have fought bakufu troops with no intention of destroying the bakufu, so we are faced with a troublesome contradiction. Even so, if we were winning and could expect to keep on winning the issue would probably never arise, but in fact we are now on the edge of winter. We do not want to fight and die needlessly. Nor should we commit suicide, especially not to atone for our sins. All we desire is to *appeal to the realm on the basis of our sincere hearts.*[67]

It should be not be forgotten, of course, that the object of the Tengu appeal was not just the "realm" but the imperial court itself. Ultimately, it was the imperial symbol that provided the major focal point for the relatively unmediated, demonstrative strategy adopted by Mito rebels in the post-Ansei era.

The Tengu appeal to the court brings us full circle, back to the function of the Great Thanksgiving Ceremony as a representation of the origin. As a movement through space to the center which, as with most pilgrimage sites, was the place where "some manifestation of divine or supernatural power had occurred,"[68] the trek toward Kyoto exemplified the spatial counterpart of the backward leap through time in the thanksgiving ceremony. Indeed, Turner's model highlights the profoundly "antistructural" as well as antihistorical mood of the thanksgiving ritual itself. As noted above, that ceremony dramatizes the symbolic consan-

---

[64] *Mito-han shiryō*, 2:581-582.

[65] Jōyō Meiji Kinenkai, *Mito bakumatsu fūunroku*, p. 345.

[66] See Osatake, *Meiji ishin*, 2:561-580.

[67] Ibid., pp. 556-557. Emphasis added.

[68] Turner, *Dramas, Fields, and Metaphors*, p. 189.

guinity of all Japanese as descendants of the gods, and is closely correlated with a notion of ritualistic government transcending all historically
determined, institutional structures. The common focal point of both
rituals—thanksgiving ceremony and pilgrimage—is the imperial presence, itself the major tangible manifestation of the timeless, unchanging
national essence.

Frustrated in their attempts during the Tenpō era to represent natural
forms by shaping institutions, Mito radicals turned to dramatic, often
violent gesture as a means of calling attention to the accessibility of
origins and the possibility of renewal. Nikkō, as the sacred resting place
of the founder of the Tokugawa, provided them with a vivid representation of the need to reform institutions, not only on the domainal level
but for the nation as a whole. In the final analysis, however, institutions, like history, were only relative and conditional, inadequate to a
strategy of unmediated actualization. Hence, even when both domain
and bakufu resisted the restorationist reform of administrative structures, the imperial symbol continued to offer the possibility of a reju-
venating "escape" from history that might provide the basis for a new
start.

New Political Space

Related to the turn to a strategy focused directly on Ieyasu as the founder
of the *bakuhan* system and on the emperor as the symbol of timelessness
and antistructural communitas was an abandonment of the domain (*han*)
as a political field. Implicit, at least, in rebel actions was the production
of a new political space cutting across the barriers to horizontal movement that were characteristic of Tokugawa rule. As Maruyama has pointed
out, the Tokugawa system as a whole relied upon a hierarchical structure in which "the values of the total social system are diffused and
embedded in each closed social sphere." Control is indirect in such a
system, and therefore "any problem . . . must be solved at the place
[*ba*] in which it occurs." Every effort must be made to "prevent the
horizontal extension of incidents."[69]

Obviously, the maneuvering by Tengu from domain to domain, and
particularly the march all the way to Kaga on the Japan Sea, were in
open violation of laws and conventions regulating horizontal movement. In conjunction with the slogan of "revere the emperor and expel
the barbarian," which dramatizes the danger facing not just a particular
domain but the nation as a whole, such movements demonstrated the

---

[69] Maruyama, *Studies in the Intellectual History of Tokugawa Japan*, p. 244.

possibility of a nationwide political arena unfettered by "feudal" barriers.[70] Moreover, by acting implicitly on behalf of the domain, they transformed it symbolically from the representational medium it had constituted in the Tenpō period into an active subject in and of itself. At least through its self-designated representatives, the domain could now act *in* and even *for* the whole. In other words, in place of the Tenpō strategy by which normative principles were to be represented only through the mediation of the domain as microcosm, the Tengu radicals were able to act directly in and on the nation as a whole, implying in the process how that nation might be transformed into something new.

It is certainly true, as Osatake and others have pointed out, that texts related to the Tengu rebellion do not openly employ antibakufu rhetoric.[71] Ieyasu, as the founder of the Tokugawa house and symbolic originator of the principle of "revere the emperor and expel the barbarian," was lionized, as noted above, but even the existing bakufu administration was generally the object of only muted criticism. As in the "Call to Action," Tengu actions were commonly presented as "supplementing the bakufu's judgment" or "assisting the shogun." Nowhere was there even a suggestion that the ultimate objective might be to replace the bakuhan system with anything else.

Yet Tengu actions were clearly a challenge not only to conservative forces in the domain but to the bakufu itself. Despite the absence of anti-bakufu pronouncements, the authorities in Edo did not misunderstand for a moment the threat to the established order posed by the rebellion. They began almost immediately to mobilize forces to put it down. The Tengu hoisted the flag of rebellion on Mt. Tsukuba on March 27, and by April 7 the bakufu had issued the first of many exhortations to domains in the area to prepare for the rebels and, if necessary, to "pacify" them militarily.[72] On July 8 Tanuma Okinori was relieved of his duties as bakufu official in charge of foreign affairs and given command of an expeditionary force. He fought rebels in and around Nakaminato in the summer of 1864, and eventually inflicted the Tengu defeat which led to the decision to set out for Kyoto. Hence, despite the moderate Tengu rhetoric, there could have been no doubt in the mind of any rebel that for all practical purposes the bakufu was the enemy.

---

[70] On the development of a broader political space in the era leading to the Meiji Restoration, see Harry Harootunian, *Toward Restoration* (Berkeley and Los Angeles: University of California Press, 1970), p. 37 and passim.

[71] Osatake, *Meiji ishin*, 2:544.

[72] Ibaraki-ken Shi Hensan Iinkai, ed., *Ibaraki-ken bakumatsu-shi nenpyō*, pp. 153-154.

FROM MEANING TO SIGNIFICANCE

The actions of Mito loyalists in the Bakumatsu era are not to be understood solely in terms of the pursuit of particular interests. They also constituted the practice of representation. They sought to actualize a conception of the whole: to represent as real a natural order, and to provide active subjects who would complete the manifestation and establishment of that order.

Having explored the possible ideological meanings of the Tengu episode, it would seem appropriate in conclusion to return to the question of significance. How did the insurrection as a meaningful event relate to its external context? As already noted, one way to answer such a question is to reinsert the incident into a temporal flow of events. The battles weakened the bakufu and thus no doubt hastened its demise. They also effectively removed Mito *han* from national politics, leaving to western *han* such as Satsuma and Chōshū the glory of actually bringing about a new imperial regime. In that regard, it is ironic that for all their zeal to restore a stable order, the primary short-term effect of actions by Mito partisans was merely to expand disorder and intensify conflict.

Another way to relate the Tengu episode to a broader context, however, is to consider how "expandable" might be the meaning of the active text we have considered. To what extent, that is, might the meaning of the insurrection in the broad sense be taken to represent the meaning of the Restoration itself as a symbolic and highly conflictual event?

As Harry Harootunian has pointed out elsewhere in this volume, secessionist ideologies of the late Tokugawa period grew out of a "discourse on origins" in which diverse groups found legitimacy and autonomy in the belief that they somehow represented the way things had been in the beginning. The Mito formulation of the national origins in terms of the idea of *kokutai* was not only one of the most syncretic and totalizing of such representations, but was also the one that many restorationist partisans found most compelling.

Surely the credibility of restoration as a political movement was to some extent contingent upon an ideological relationship between the "natural" order associated with the Sun Goddess and the persona of her lineal descendant, the reigning emperor. The imperial charisma denoted the purity of origins in the midst of decline and corruption. Hence a restoration of the emperor to the center of power implied the banishment of history and the actualization of the natural order associated with those origins. Under such an order, community would be restored, and the commoner classes would regain a capacity to act not only for themselves but on behalf of a national political entity that had only begun to be constituted.

Such ideological precepts, which link the Tengu insurrection with the Restoration era as a whole, are well exemplified by a sequence in Shimazaki Tōson's novel *Before the Dawn* (*Yoakemae*). The tragic hero, Hanzō, who represents Shimazaki's own father, believed that a Restoration would allow Japan to embark on the "great project of returning to the past, to the age of the gods." It is no accident, therefore, that Hanzō took great interest in the battle that occurred near his home in 1864 between the Tengu force and armies of Suwa and Matsumoto. Perhaps, in Shimazaki's mind, Hanzō's perception that the Mito army consisted largely of peasants was not unrelated to his admittedly paternalistic hope that after the Restoration Japan's new leaders would use their power to meet the needs of ordinary people in provincial areas.[73]

The tragedy of the tale emerges, however, as Shimazaki exposes the hard realities of post-Restoration politics through Hanzō's gradual disillusionment. Dismayed when he is criticized by local peasants, and then dismissed from his position of local responsibility by the new government, Hanzō now begins to feel as if "a chill wind had begun to blow."

> He asked himself, "Is this what the Restoration amounts to?" What he saw unfolding before him was not the restoration of the ancient past, but the beginning of a strange new age.[74]

Meiji Japan was anything but a "return to the age of the gods." Yet visions of a coherent, stable order founded on original principles of religion, education, and administration were prevalent at various levels of society in the Restoration era and entered into ideological practice in widely different roles. For all their diversity, they are noteworthy as evidence of a common regularity throughout sharply conflicting strategies of action. The Mito ideologues and activists did not invent those visions, but rather exemplified their potential power by acting out a particularly vivid and articulate variation. In that sense, their ideology not only had meaning but far-reaching significance for the Restoration and our understanding of it.

[73] Edwin McClellan, *Two Japanese Novelists, Sōseki and Tōson* (Chicago: University of Chicago Press, 1969), pp. 149, 153.

[74] Ibid., p. 156.

"MEN OF HIGH PURPOSE" AND THE POLITICS OF DIRECT ACTION, 1862-1864

Thomas M. Huber

There are many currents of conflict that may run through the history of a nation, conflicts between a regime and its people, conflicts between social classes, or simply conflicts over competing social and religious values. Sometimes these conflicts are minor, flickering occasionally, but not much affecting the momentum of a nation's history. In other cases, these conflicts flare into violence, and can even dominate the future of a nation or a region.

Japan has had her share of this, and many dimensions of conflict have guided her history. One of the periods in which many of these conflicts converged was the Bakumatsu era (1853-1868) marking the final years of Tokugawa rule. The troubles of these years brought many competing interests into the open. Perhaps the best known agents of these conflicts were the "men of high purpose" (*shishi*) who often clashed with the regime and with each other in the 1860s, while the nation groped after an uncertain future. These clashes reached fever pitch in 1862 and 1863, and it is with *shishi* activity in these years that this essay will be concerned. I will argue not only that the violent political actions of the *shishi* played a direct and purposive role in bringing about the new Meiji regime, but also that the value conflict present within the movement revealed cultural attitudes that in themselves would become a major legacy for modern Japanese life.

American scholars have paid little attention in recent years to the activities of the Bakumatsu *shishi*. Their conduct is viewed as colorful but inconsequential. It lacked significant political goals and therefore had few lasting results. The movement is seen as an anomalous sentimental or moral phenomenon that flared for a year or so in time of trouble, but then vanished from view. The Meiji Restoration of 1868 sprang not from the efforts of loyalists, it is argued, but from another source. The new regime was implemented rather by thoughtful bureaucrats of Chōshū and Satsuma, who relied on official armies and Western military techniques. Scholars insist that this movement developed late, and independently of the loyalists' politics of direct action.

In this essay I will argue that the pivotal importance assigned to the *shishi*'s role by many Japanese scholars may be better warranted than some Western commentators have supposed. This is not to say that the sentimental and moral preoccupations noted in the movement by Western observers were trivial. On the contrary, I will suggest not only that this "romantic" element was extremely important as an influence on Japan's future, but also that there coexisted with it in the movement an element that was practical, astute, and highly effective politically. Pragmatism and sentimental loyalism flourished side by side, usually reinforcing each other, but sometimes clashing. Such instances of conflict, although significant in themselves, also mirror a larger meaning for historians. They seem to reflect the same duality of attitudes that would tragically divide the rational Meiji leadership and the Satsuma rebels in 1877. Even the struggle between Control and Imperial Way factions that would rock Japan's military in the 1930s is curiously foreshadowed in some of these encounters.

There are many features of the loyalist movement that indicate that the pragmatic element within it may have had a decisive political impact during the 1860s. Many participants seem to have been keenly aware of the political climate. Many were able to respond immediately to changes in the political environment, and a major power shift on the national stage could bring a *shishi* reaction within hours, sometimes on a very large scale. Concerted action was possible not only because of the high level of political awareness among the *shishi*, but also because of well-developed networks of communication that linked hundreds of their sympathizers. Mass actions by the *shishi* show that although they were not joined by a rigid institutional framework, they were nevertheless "organized" politically: information moved rapidly among them in such a way as to make joint action possible.

Whether or not the loyalists "caused" the Restoration, it is clear that their unique political responsiveness dominated events on the national stage for two crucial years between 1862 and 1864. They decisively undermined the bakufu police power, and for a time in 1863 actually forced the shogunate to renounce its policy of acquiescing in Western treaty obligations. Many later found themselves in positions of responsibility in the Meiji government. Is it possible that the "men of high purpose," even given the divisions among them, may have had a far more profound relationship than we have thought to the emergence of the modern Japanese state?

LOYALTY TO HEAVEN

The Japanese public was badly jolted when Matthew Perry's squadron opened the country in 1853. Many students and "masterless" samurai living in Kyoto were then further dismayed in 1858 at the bakufu's acceding to Western demands for "unequal treaties." Some, who had openly criticized the regime's policies, then fell victim to the grim machinery of the Ansei purge. When the purge was finally relaxed in the early sixties, many more chose to risk their lives and careers rather than acquiesce further in policies that they felt would undermine the social integrity of the country. They turned to a politics of action, and are known in history as the "men of high purpose" (shishi).

In 1862 and 1863 there arose in the streets of Kyoto a pattern of political conduct known as Loyalty to Heaven (tenchū). Popular Japanese works on the subject often choose to highlight the self-sacrificial daring of the movement. Western scholars of late have chosen rather to emphasize the spontaneous and violent quality of the Loyalty to Heaven phenomenon. Despite their youth, the "men of high purpose" were survivors of a hard school. In the late 1850s they had seen Hashimoto Sanai, Rai Mikisaburō, and other popular leaders vanish into Demmachō Prison, not to come out again alive. The loyalists who lived through the discouraging years of 1858 and 1859 had not forgotten what took place, and the main content of Loyalty to Heaven in 1862 was the assassination of those police officials and informers who had played a prominent part in the Ansei imprisonments. They felt that in this way they could undermine the bakufu police power whose workings they had found so distressing, and in this premise they were correct.

Although heroism and violence are both easy to find among the tenchū operatives, we will focus here on another attribute of the movement that, despite its obvious importance, is rarely emphasized: tenchū was unmistakably political in its timing, its objectives, its publicity activities, and its effects. One of the peculiarities of the movement lay in its uncanny timing. There had been an occasional act of political violence before 1862, but the upsurge of direct political action known as Loyalty to Heaven emerged only in the eighth month of 1862. Assassinations, which previously had occurred only once or twice a year, now occurred almost weekly. The rate of political assaults then remained consistently high. From 8/62 to 7/64, a period of twenty-four months, over seventy assassinations took place, almost three a month. After 7/64, however, these activities ceased, subsiding almost as abruptly as they had begun two years before (see Table).[1]

These abrupt oscillations in the assassination rate can easily be explained by reference to concurrent political events. In the eighth month, the vital political role of mediation between the imperial court and the bakufu was taken from the moderate daimyo Shimazu Hisamitsu of Satsuma and given instead to the more radically reformist and procourt leadership of Chōshū. Earlier in the year, Hisamitsu, having won the favor of the emperor, set out for Edo to negotiate with the bakufu on the court's behalf.

During Hisamitsu's absence, however, Chōshū's more innovative leadership sought to displace Satsuma by establishing its own ties with the court. This effort came to fruition on 27/i8, when the court issued a decree ordering Chōshū to negotiate with the bakufu for the "expulsion of foreigners," thereby leaving the Satsuma mediation in the cold.[2] This meant that the more radical Chōshū now had greatest temporal authority in the metropolis, and that the court itself was now for the first time committed to an expulsionist position. It was precisely during these weeks that the tactic of assassination appeared on the streets of Kyoto. The operatives engaged in it were almost certainly responding to the significantly improved political environment that the Chōshū mediation represented.

Later on, Loyalty to Heaven would suddenly subside in the eighth month of 1864. In that month, Chōshū's armies clashed with conservative forces in the Incident of the Forbidden Gate. Chōshū's prestige and power as a sponsor of loyalist activities suffered a decisive blow, thoroughly discrediting Chōshū for a number of years, and leaving the imperial city once more in the uncontested hands of the more conservative domains of Satsuma and Aizu. This development, too, strongly indicates that the activists were responding in a direct and pragmatic way to political circumstance.

If the timing of loyalist violence was politically determined, so were the movement's specific objectives. Although a wide variety of persons were ultimately touched by the movement, high and low, samurai and merchant, all of its victims were said to have offended "Heaven." In more concrete terms, this usually meant that they were implicated in the Ansei purge, or else had been active in implementing bakufu-inspired "Court and Bakufu Unity" (kōbu gattai) policies, such as the mar-

---

[1] See Hirao Michio, Ishin ansatsushi-roku (Tokyo, 1930), backmatter, pp. 1-6. For useful materials on the incidence of violence in the 1860s, see also Nakazawa Michio, ed., Bakumatsu ansatsushi-roku (Tokyo, 1966).

[2] Ishin Shiryō Hensan Jimukyoku, ed., Ishinshi, 6 vols. (Tokyo, 1941), 3:274-275 (hereafter cited as IS). All dates in the text are according to the traditional lunar calendar. Intercalary months are indicated with an "i."

INCIDENCE OF MAJOR POLITICAL ASSASSINATIONS PER YEAR DURING
SELECTED YEARS OF THE BAKUMATSU AND MEIJI PERIODS

Year	Number of Incidents
1857	1
1858	0
1859	1
1860	3
1861	1
1862	19
(1-7 months)	3
(8-12 months)	16★
1863	30★
1864	21
(1-7 months)	17★
(8-12 months)	4
1865	6
1866	0
1867	10
1868	7
1869	5
1870	1
1871	5

★ Intervals of greatest activity.
SOURCE: Hirao, *Ansatsushi*, backmatter, pp. 1-6.

riage of the imperial princess Kazunomiya into the shogunal house. (The
principal exception to this pattern was that of merchants, whose offense
seems to have been profiteering, especially from foreign trade.)[3]

[3] *IS*, 3:250.

Most scholars agree that the earliest manifestation of Loyalty to Heaven was the assassination of Shimada Sakon on 7/20/62. Shimada was a steward of the Kujō house of court nobles, who served as imperial regents (*kampaku*) for the bakufu. During the Ansei purge, Shimada had spied on loyalist critics of the regime and revealed their identities to bakufu agents. This was lucrative work, and Shimada received the fabulous sum of 10,000 *ryō* for his part in it, although it also had the unpleasant consequence of imprisonment and execution for the spokesmen of conscience that he had identified. Shimada was relaxing in his bath one evening in late summer when he heard footfalls in the corridor. His unannounced visitors were samurai from Tosa, Satsuma, and Higo, "men of high purpose," who had come to take his life.[4]

The largest single stroke of Loyalty to Heaven fell a few months later. The four victims were sergeants of police (*yoriki*) under the Bakufu's city commissioner in Kyoto. The commissioner had been in charge of prosecuting the Ansei purge, and nine of his followers had been especially active in this cause. Among them were Watanabe Kinsaburō, Masamori Sonroku, Ōgawa Genjūzō, and Ueda Masunosuke. These men had, in fact, been recalled to Edo for their own safety and had set out from Kyoto on 9/22/62. Characteristically, the *shishi* had informed themselves of this attempted departure, and the next night the four sergeants were attacked in their travel lodgings by twenty-four loyalists, mostly samurai from Tosa, Chōshū, and Satsuma. Three of the four were killed on the spot, while the other escaped only to die of his wounds soon after.[5]

The *tenchū* act that shook bakufu authorities the most, however, was carried out at the expense of wooden images of the Ashikaga shoguns. On the night of 2/22/63, a band of activists entered the Tōji-in temple on the west end of Kyoto and beheaded the statues of the Ashikaga shoguns Takauji, Yoshiakira, and Yoshimitsu. They took the wooden heads with them and absconded. This act was perpetrated at just the moment when the living Tokugawa shogun Iemochi was about to enter Kyoto. This gesture greatly disturbed the authorities because it showed that there were elements in the population that had completely lost respect for the public myths needed to sustain bakufu rule.[6]

If the choice of victims always had clear political import, so did the activities that served to publicize *tenchū* demonstrations. The perpetrators of assassination followed the compelling if grisly practice of posting the head of the victim in some public place, such as at the entrance of a much-frequented bridge, so that as many persons as possible would

---

[4] Naramoto Tatsuya, *Meiji ishin jimbutsu jiten* (Tokyo, 1968), p. 140; *IS*, 3:244.

[5] *IS*, 3:247-248.

[6] Konishi Shirō, *Kaikaku to jōi, Nihon no rekishi 19* (Tokyo, 1971), pp. 266-267.

know what had been done. Always accompanying these displays was a lettered poster (*harigami*) that explained the offenses of the victim, the reasons for his punishment, and sometimes also a warning to his counterparts.

In the case of Shimada Sakon, the victim's head was posted by the river bank in the Fourth Ward over a poster that described him as "a great traitor (*taigyakuzoku*), who has given information to Nagano Shuzen," the bakufu agent. "He is a great traitor, unfit for heaven or earth. Therefore we have punished him." All of this was in the official Chinese script (*kambun*), and a date was thoughtfully added.[7]

A similar fate awaited the statues of the Ashikaga shoguns, whose wooden visages were taken from the Tōji-in in February of 1863. These were placed on a stand by the Kamo River with a message that said, "we are imposing Heaven's Revenge on the disgraceful images of these traitors." At about the same time a paper appeared on the public notice board of Sanjō Bridge, which said that in this world there are many persons whose misconduct is even worse than that of Ashikaga Takauji. If such persons do not "quickly repent their crimes" and "return to the ancient practice of assisting the court," then "the realm's men of high purpose will rise up and rectify these offenses." Statements like these had an ideological quality in that they clearly linked the loyalist movement with the stirring lore of the Kemmu Restoration five centuries before.[8]

Such themes were often sounded without even a symbolic victim. Posters and handbills sympathetic to the loyalist movement proliferated throughout Kyoto and Osaka. They enjoined public officials and even ordinary merchants to be loyal to the court, that is, to support reform within and resistance without.[9] Practitioners of Loyalty to Heaven seem to have been concerned at every step to maximize the public impact of their actions, by public explanation and sometimes by sanguine display. It is very difficult to explain this other than by assuming that they wished to influence public opinion and shape the conduct of their adversaries. In other words, their conduct, though uncouth by later standards, was systematic and purposive.

Finally, there is little doubt that the political effects of loyalist activity were great. When four of the Kyoto commissioner's police agents were assaulted on the night of 9/23/62, consternation among those who remained was profound. They were afraid to carry out their duties, and

[7] *IS*, 3:244.
[8] Konishi, *Kaikaku to jōi*, p. 266.
[9] *IS*, 3:250.

a number of them fled to the countryside to save themselves. The "men of high purpose" in Kyoto had actually dissolved the police power.[10]

The relentless scythe of the bakufu that had cut such a broad swath during Ansei now wavered. So great was apprehension of violent *tenchū* retaliation that no efforts were made by the police to apprehend participants. The Ashikaga statue incident of 2/63 was a partial exception, and nine persons were eventually arrested. The reason seems to have been that this act had even more threatening political implications for the shogunate than attacks on live victims. Even in this case, however, a rumored movement among *tenchū* activists to free the nine forced bakufu authorities to return them to the custody of their own domains.[11]

There were also political results on a larger scale. The loyalist movement, along with radical court nobles and leaders in Chōshū, is usually credited with winning the bakufu's consent to the expulsion of foreigners from Japanese soil beginning on 5/10/63. This was something the bakufu had adamantly refused to do for ten years, yet did here because of the relentless pressure the movement had brought to bear. Moreover, the political momentum of the metropolis caused the balance of influence to swing toward the loyalist faction in many of the individual domains at this time.[12]

Although the proponents of Loyalty to Heaven shared deep feelings concerning the future of their cause, this did not prevent them from acting at every step in a manner that was politically effective. When the time was right, they directed their energies at persons identified by political criteria. They made their actions publicly known in ways that were politically telling. In the end this had a pervasive effect on the political climate, and they accomplished several of their principal objectives.

THE COUP OF 8/18/63

An unexpected feature of the Loyalty to Heaven movement was the similarity in the patterns of action of various incidents even though many different people were independently involved in them. This fact suggests that underlying the political context of these acts was a high degree of communication. Events in the eighth month of 1863 would show even more clearly the remarkable extent to which the activists' communications network had been developed.

In the eighth month of 1863, the emperor Kōmei was becoming ap-

[10] Ibid., pp. 243, 248.
[11] Konishi, *Kaikaku to jōi*, p. 267.
[12] *IS*, 3:252-253.

prehensive of his own somewhat involuntary ties with loyalist activity. Through the offices of Sanjō Sanetomi, Shijō Takauta, and other *shishi* sympathizers among the *kuge*, Kōmei had been issuing decrees promoting the loyalist cause, while also enhancing the temporal influence of his own court. By the eighth month of 1863, the Bakufu had actually agreed to a policy of expelling Westerners in the emperor's name, so that Sanjō Sanetomi and the other loyalist leaders were now talking of a personal campaign led by Kōmei himself against the well-armed outsiders.

At this point, Kōmei began to feel that his involvement with politicized nobles like Sanjō may have gone too far. He therefore invited more conservative authorities—Aizu, Satsuma, and others—to garrison his palace grounds with troops. This was done in great secrecy in the predawn hours of 8/18/63. When morning came, loyalist nobles, sympathetic officials in the bureaucracy of Chōshū han, and *shishi* activists alike, all found that the palace gates were closed to them. The coup was a complete success. Control of the emperor was suddenly lost to the loyalists, and their all-important claim to represent the imperial will was seriously damaged.

The radicals then did a surprising thing. Within hours, several hundred loyalist *shishi*, as well as Sanjō's nobles and the Chōshū leaders, had all gathered at the Myōhō-in east of Kyōto. Their number included Maki Izumi, Miyabe Teizō, Midama Sampei, Hijikata Nansaemon, and many other prominent *shishi* leaders, each accompanied by his own band of followers. A council was held, and after lengthy debate it was decided that all parties, regardless of origin, would withdraw to the one domain of Chōshū. Within a few weeks, over three hundred "men of high purpose" reconvened far away in the town of Mitajiri near the Chōshū coast. They did so even though they came from many different domains all over Japan. The seven radical nobles under Sanjō also made the trip, and along with Maki and other *shishi* personalities served as the leadership of loyalism-in-exile. A teahouse in Mitajiri called the Shōkenkaku served as their headquarters, and gave this group its name.[13]

The new Shōkenkaku establishment consisted mostly of young samurai who had gone up to Kyoto to study martial arts or the Chinese classics, and who had then joined the loyalist movement. The group elected its own governing council, and organized a regimen for itself of lectures, hiking, poetry reading, and so on. News of its existence spread, and *shishi* activists from all over Japan now avoided the hazards of the metropolis and assembled instead at Mitajiri.[14]

The informal organization of "floating" loyalism was in these weeks

[13] Ibid., p. 576.
[14] Hirao Michio, *Nakaoka Shintarō* (Tokyo, 1971), pp. 63-64.

transformed into the semiformal organization of the Shōkenkaku. What had only been a network of common information joining men of common purpose now became a community in a fuller sense. The "men of high purpose" now lived together, studied together, exercised together, and set their political course together.

This phenomenon shows almost beyond doubt that close political ties had been maintained among several hundred activists and groups of activists from all over the country in the early sixties. It was these ties, nourished in the streets and teahouses of Kyoto, that had made the telling actions of the movement possible. The objectives of loyalism were clearly political in quality, and so was the intensive pattern of organizational communication behind it.

The Yamato and Ikuno Incidents

At the same time that large numbers of rank-and-file *shishi* under Maki and Miyabe were deciding to withdraw to Chōshū, smaller and more independent bands of loyalist radicals sought to overthrow bakufu authority in the Tokugawa territories of Yamato and Ikuno. These efforts brought into the open the presence of dual and potentially conflicting value orientations within the loyalist movement. The guiding leadership advocated political expedience and a calculus of results. Leaders of the independent bands argued instead that purity of conduct, a kind of romantic integrity, was the most valid measure of action.

Ironically, the Yamato and Ikuno affairs are also of interest because they represent a stage in the evolution of loyalism toward what would prove the successful military solution of the late 1860s. Many of the "men of high purpose" who began their careers as fugitive assailants in Kyoto would go on to serve in 1866 as officers leading peasant riflemen in Chōshū's new army. The Yamato rising was one of the early experiments in which loyalist partisans actually formed and led a peasant force. This attempt failed, and the reasons that it failed may have encouraged many of the notoriously independent *shishi* who remained to look to Chōshū for a military solution of a similar but more highly structured kind.

The major premise of the Yamato insurgents was that a peasant militia could be raised in a rural area that would be a match for the regular samurai forces likely to be brought against it. In 1865 and 1866, under somewhat altered circumstances, this premise would prove true. Still, these rural insurgencies were strongly disapproved of from the beginning by the more influential national leaders, especially Maki Izumi and Sanjō Sanetomi. The same leaders who condoned even the assassination of Ansei offenders on grounds that it was politically justifiable, opposed the Yamato stroke in the belief that it was reckless and unwise.

When the imperial procession to Yamato was announced on 8/13/63, a band of activists under Yoshimura Toratarō set out the next day for Yamato in the hope of raising an imperial army there. (Sanjō had arranged that Emperor Kōmei would pray before the ancestral shrine in Yamato as a prelude to his personally led campaign against the Westerners.) Yoshimura assumed that his force would dissolve bakufu authority in the Yamato area, welcome the emperor when he arrived, and then participate in the coming campaign against the foreigners.[15]

The young court noble Nakayama Tadamitsu was the nominal leader of this movement, even though the main inspiration behind it was probably Yoshimura's. Yoshimura himself was one of the most outstanding members of Tosa's celebrated loyalist faction, and his ten followers were the core of the Yamato undertaking. Also prominent were Fujimoto Tesseki of Bichū and Matsumoto Kensaburō of Mikawa. A number of local farmers, especially from the Kawachi district, also actively participated. The other Yamato men came from Kurume, Higo, Shimabara, and elsewhere. There were about thirty-eight of them all together.[16]

This youthful band arrived in Yamato on 8/16, confident of success. They prayed at the tomb of Emperor Gomurakami (ruled 1339-1368), and in high spirits fashioned a chrysanthemum banner. They also sent letters to the emperor and four loyalist nobles telling them of their plans. On 8/17, the group invaded the office of the bakufu's deputy at Gojō and easily overpowered him. They then gathered the headmen and village officials of the area, urging them to become the "direct people of the emperor," to serve the "national essence," and to gather peasant troops. In return, they were promised remission of 50 percent of their taxes, a major financial incentive.[17] At the same time, interestingly, the band meticulously reconstituted themselves as an officer corps, designating each man as commander, assistant commander, finance officer, signal officer, quartermaster, lance captain, squad leader, and so on.[18]

Meanwhile, however, cooler heads in Kyoto had heard about all this. Maki, Sanjō, and other prominent leaders were extremely apprehensive that the Yamato affair might turn public opinion against the *sonjō* move-

---

[15] *IS*, 3:584.

[16] Ibid., p. 583. On Nakayama Tadamitsu, see Ōgimachi Suetada, *Meiji ishin no senkusha tenchūgumi Nakayama Tadamitsu* (Tokyo, 1941), esp. pp. 189-281 on the Yamato rising. On Matsumoto, see Mori Senzō, *Matsumoto Keidō* (Tokyo, 1943). For the role of local "men of purpose" in Yamato, see Nigori Tsuneaki, *Tenchūgumi Kawachi-zei no kenkyū* (Ōsaka, 1966). For names, domains, and ages of the Yamato partisans, see Higuchi Saburō, *Tenchūgumi shimatsu* (Tokyo, 1973), pp. 9-13.

[17] *IS*, 3:586-587, 591-592.

[18] Ibid., p. 592; and Nigori, *Tenchūgumi Kawachi-zei*, pp. 337-340.

ment at a critical moment. Maki therefore sent Hirano Kuniomi, a capable young samurai from Fukuoka, to stop it. Hirano reached Yamato on 8/18, only to find Yoshimura's band already celebrating their easy victory over the deputy. Hirano could not get any of the participants to listen to his admonitions, and was forced to return to Kyoto empty handed on 8/19. Even his own companion Azumi Gorō had elected to stay behind with the rebels.[19]

Yoshimura's insurgents now headed for the nearby Totsukawa district, whose farmers were known for their military propensities, being called "Totsukawa of the thousand lances." Sure enough, Yoshimura's men were able to gather a thousand peasant militiamen at Totsukawa by 8/20. The leaders then dispatched a request to the court to take Yamato under its direct jurisdiction, and also petitioned the small nearby domain of Takatori for weapons and provisions. When Takatori declined, the Yamato leaders hurled their newly formed peasant forces into a costly but unsuccessful effort to reduce the castle.[20]

Meanwhile, the bakufu had ordered the domains of Hikone, Tsu, and Kii, as well as smaller domains in the immediate vicinity, to send troops to suppress the rebels. Under these circumstances the peasant soldiers fled, and Yoshimura's followers retreated in the direction of Kawachi. At Washiga-guchi, however, they clashed with large numbers of troops from Hikone and Kii. Nakayama Tadamitsu with seven partisans escaped safely to the Chōshū compound in Osaka, which he entered on 8/27. All of the other leaders, nine of whom would later be given posthumous court ranks by the Meiji government, were killed or captured.[21]

A month after the Yamato rising, there was another that, although conducted by different leaders in a different province, was in some respects curiously similar. In Kyoto, Hirano Kuniomi, who had just returned without mishap from Yamato, was forced by a Bakufu raid on his house on 8/22 to leave the city.[22] With loyalist political hopes dashed by the coup of 8/18 and his personal life thrown into disarray by Bakufu pursuit, Hirano resolved as a last resort to travel to the Ikuno district in Tajima, and there help to raise peasant troops in support of the same Yamato rising that he had recently been dispatched to restrain.

There had already been in Ikuno a strong local interest in forming peasant troops for the purpose of coastal defense. The well-to-do farmer Kitagaki Shintarō and the village headman Nakashima Tarōbei had pe-

---

[19] *IS*, 3:592.

[20] Ibid., pp. 593–596.

[21] Ibid., pp. 597–601. For Yamato casualties, see Higuchi, *Tenchūgumi shimatsu*, pp. 276–79. For recipients of posthumous court ranks, see Nigori, *Tenchūgumi kawachi-zei*, p. 291.

[22] On Hirano, see Haruyama Ikujirō, *Hirano Kuniomi-den* (Tokyo, 1929), esp. pp. 559–591 on the Ikuno rising.

titioned the bakufu for this right, and then had petitioned the court through Maki Izumi. This permission had been granted by the court on 8/16, and Kitagaki returned home to raise the troops. Hirano, leading half a dozen *shishi* from the metropolis, including Midama Sampei of Satsuma, met on 9/19 with Kitagaki and other rural loyalists of Ikuno to plan the formation of a peasant militia.

On 9/28 Hirano visited Mitajiri in Chōshū, where the seven radical court nobles had fled after the coup of 8/18, with the intention of taking one of them back with him to Tajima as commander. Once again, the higher loyalist leadership, Sanjō Sanetomi, Maki Izumi, and others, vigorously opposed this. When Hirano finally persuaded the noble Sawa Nobuyoshi to accompany him, Maki Izumi, two of the court nobles, and several dozen *shishi* followed their boat out into the open sea, calling out and urging them to turn back. Undaunted by this, Kawakami Yaichi, who was a leader in the Kiheitai, and thirty-six other loyalists of various *han*, also returned with Hirano to Tajima.

After arriving back in Ikuno on 10/11, Hirano learned of the failure of the Yamato uprising, and began making the case that a peasant rising would now be of no help to the Yamato men, and have no purpose. Kawakami Yaichi and the *shishi* fresh from Chōshū argued that giving up would be dishonorable, however, so the rebellion went ahead as planned. The Ikuno deputy's office was taken on 10/12, without bloodshed, as the deputy himself had long favored the creation of peasant militia for local defense. Nevertheless, neighboring *han* began mobilizing several thousand troops to suppress the Ikuno rebellion. The loyalists were able to gather two thousand peasant soldiers (brought by their respective village headmen), and promised them a 50 percent reduction in taxes for three years in exchange for their service. A detachment was sent to the north under Kawakami Yaichi and one to the south under Fuji Shirō to counter the invading *han* forces.

Meanwhile, however, there was a failure of will at the headquarters in Ikuno. Many felt that the cause was hopeless, and the noble Sawa Nobuyoshi himself fled on 10/13. Many other leaders, including Hirano Kuniomi, also felt that dispersal of the militia would be desirable. Kawakami, however, on hearing of Sawa's flight, resolved to take his party back to Ikuno and fight to the death, even though his own peasant troops did not relish this prospect. At Miyōken mountain they dubbed him a "false" *rōnin*, surrounded his band, and attacked. Kawakami and twelve others committed suicide rather than do battle with their erstwhile followers. Meanwhile, Hirano had dispersed his band, but was arrested by forces friendly to the bakufu while in flight, and was imprisoned in Kyoto on 10/17. Sawa escaped to Chōshū without harm, although most of the other nonlocal loyalists were either captured by the bakufu or committed suicide.[23]

One of the more interesting aspects of both the Yamato and Ikuno incidents lies in the continuous dialogue that took place between the bands that led them and the larger community of the loyalist movement. This dialogue consisted of splinter leaders such as Yoshimura and Hirano asking for aid, and of metropolitan leaders such as Maki Izumi imploring them oppositely to give up their local uprisings altogether. The Yamato and Ikuno leaders were "more extreme than the extremists." Their activities reveal a large movement with well-developed internal communications, but one that harbored divergent perceptions and values.

After Ikuno, there were no further uprisings of the Yamato type. This line of experimentation was abandoned by pragmatists and romantics alike. These undertakings nevertheless represented one of the earliest efforts of loyalists to organize a military force, and showed that many of the leaders believed in the potential of peasant troops. The uprisings showed the customary courage and self-reliance of the peasants.

The Yamato experience revealed, however, that for military activities to be more successful, it would be necessary to achieve a much higher degree of loyalty and discipline among the peasant recruits and their leaders. From this point of view the attempted risings of 1863 take on added meaning. Despite their anti-authoritarian (and sometimes anti-Chōshū) tendencies, many of the *shishi* who observed the Yamato debacle later chose to serve, nevertheless, in the well-regimented Chōshū militia, where peasant recruits were placed under the direct authority of *shishi* officers, and subjected before combat to a thorough indoctrination in loyalist principles. This result would be hastened by another military experiment, one which in its way also represented a step toward a viable military solution: the battle of the Forbidden Gate.

THE FORBIDDEN GATE

One of the better-known clashes between conservative forces and loyalists took place at the Hamaguri Gate of the imperial palace in 1864. This occasion was the first time that the *shishi* acted together in large numbers within an overarching military framework, although they still did so tentatively. The Forbidden Gate incident (*kimon no hen*) shows perhaps more clearly than any other the duality of values that existed within the loyalist movement. Participants recognized two distinct ideals, one premised on a loyalism of political pragmatism, and the other

---

[23] *IS*, 3:602-621; Konishi, *Kaikaku to jōi*, pp. 313-315.

premised on a loyalism of romantic courage. Most of the *shishi* probably approved of both values, and often the two were not in conflict. Nevertheless there were some circumstances in which the implications of these distinct values were at odds, and in these instances the leadership could become sharply divided. The Forbidden Gate was such a case.

The great majority of Shōkenkaku participants avoided the Ikuno rising in the latter months of 1863 and had remained encamped in Chōshū. The energies of this group were at a high pitch, and most of them were eager to return as soon as possible to the metropolitan arena of Kyoto. It was all that cautious Chōshū leaders such as Kusaka Genzui and Kido Kōin could do to keep the more impulsive of the Shōkenkaku men from marching back to Kyoto immediately. The Chōshū leaders were determined, however, not to return to Kyoto while their enemies were united against them.[24]

Kusaka and Kido were closely monitoring the political situation in the capital, waiting for events to turn in a favorable direction. In the early months of 1864, the so-called *sanyo* council of great domains sympathetic to bakufu-court cooperation (*kōbu gattai*) began to dissolve. By the fourth month most of the participating lords had gone home. Kusaka reported that the phalanx of moderate *han* allied against Chōshū and the loyalist cause was breaking up, and that the time to bring some force to bear in the capital had come. On the strength of this, the Chōshū government made preparations to march. Much of the *han*'s regular army was to be dispatched to Kyoto, along with the new commoner rifle corps of the Kiheitai type that had been organized to cope with Western incursions in 1863.

It occurred to someone that the Shōkenkaku's anomalous presence in Chōshū would be more understandable to everyone if it were reconstituted as one of these new infantry companies, and so it was. The several hundred of *shishi*-in-exile camped at Mitajiri were commissioned by the Chōshū government as a military corps called the Yūgekitai. This company was provisioned by Chōshū and so, in theory at least, was brought under the Chōshū chain of command. Kijima Matabei, a Chōshū official, was named commander of this unit (an appointment that later proved a mistake from the Chōshū point of view). Although many loyalists had been informally affiliated with Chōshū since the Loyalty to Heaven movement of 1862, this was the first time that *shishi* from many domains marched officially under the Chōshū banner.

Chōshū sent four contingents to Kyoto, three advance contingents under *han* elders, including the Yūgekitai, and a large rear contingent under the heir. By mid-July the three forward forces were encamped

[24] *IS*, 4:9-14, 27-29.

on the outskirts of Kyoto, and the bakufu's representatives had asked Chōshū troops to withdraw to the Osaka area while negotiations on the terms of Chōshū's reentry into the city were carried on. A council was called in the Chōshū camp on 7/17/64 to determine whether it were better to withdraw, as the bakufu asked, or to advance on the city. The stage was thus set for an acrimonious discussion that would divide the loyalist leaders. The argument revolved around the issue of whether realistic or romantic considerations should guide their actions.[25]

Kijima Matabei, although a Chōshū official, spoke on behalf of the Yūgekitai and also on behalf of the notion that the *shishi*'s first duty was to conduct himself in a heroic way. He advocated the army's immediate advance, so that it could "remove the evil from the side of the emperor," whatever the cost. Kusaka Genzui spoke for the Chōshū government, but also for the pragmatic notion that the shrewd pursuit of results constituted the highest loyalism. Kusaka argued against a hasty advance. All of them had come seeking to be "pure" in their conduct toward the emperor, he said, but the opportune time had not yet come. It was better first to "pile entreaty on entreaty."

Kijima answered that it was improper to waver and wait, and that duty bade them to launch a firm, courageous, and immediate attack. Kusaka replied with words to the effect that this was impetuous and foolish, whereupon Kijima made an unflattering remark about Kusaka and stormed out of the council. Throughout all this there was an uneasy silence as the assembled commanders listened, not sure which argument was right, or perhaps vexed by the realization that they were both right. Finally Maki Izumi got up and endorsed the view of Kijima. This swayed the others, and the council decided by consensus to march into the city. This would prove to be the wrong decision from a practical point of view. As in the Yamato and Ikuno incidents, the romantic elements in the movement would not be deterred and in their zeal carried others along.[26]

Chōshū forces entered the capital at dawn but were badly defeated at every point. Two of the advancing combat groups, which contained no Yūgekitai men and were perhaps unenthusiastic about the council's decision of the previous day, had not reached the city at all. Other contingents entered, but could not prevail. Kijima Matabei, mounted on horseback, led his troops in a gallant assault on the Hamaguri Gate of the imperial palace, but was shot down before the goal could be reached. This hard-fought but unsuccessful struggle for the Hamaguri portal gave the day its name: the incident of the Forbidden Gate. Kusaka Genzui,

[25] *IS*, 4:35–48; Suematsu Kenchō, *Bōchō kaitenshi*, 2 vols. (Tokyo, 1967), 1:609, 618–619.

[26] Fukumoto Yoshisuke, ed., *Shōka sonjuku no ijin Kusaka Genzui* (Tokyo, 1934), pp. 666–668.

who although he opposed the attack had chosen to accompany the troops, was wounded during the fighting and committed suicide. Maki Izumi escaped with sixteen men to Tenō Mountain, where, when pressed by Aizu troops, he and his comrades also took their own lives. The fighting had ceased by 7/19, though secondary fires detroying 28,000 dwellings raged until 7/21. Once again Chōshū's disconsolate troops and the *shishi* of many domains made their way westward to the relative safety of Chōshū territory.[27]

The tragedy of the Forbidden Gate might have been avoided if it had not been for the remarkable duality of values that characterized the loyalist movement throughout. These values were normally complementary, but could at times point in opposite directions, as they did here, resulting in disunity among the leadership and unwise decisions. The commitment of many *shishi* to romantic heroism in the loyalist cause lent the loyalist movement an unusual vitality, but could also draw it at times into serious errors.

Nevertheless, this experience was a milestone for the loyalist movement. It was the first time that large numbers of *shishi* acted together militarily under the banner of an actually existing political authority, namely, Chōshū. Chōshū's crucial victories over bakufu forces in 1866 and later would be achieved by reliance on a new military into which the "men of high purpose" would be effectively integrated. The Forbidden Gate incident was another step in the evolutionary progress toward this result. At the Hamaguri Gate the loyalists acted in larger numbers and more systematically than they had in Yamato, but still with far less effective order and coordination than they would in the months to come.

The Forbidden Gate marked the end of the colorful interval of "direct action" that began in 1862. Quixotic assaults on offending bakufu officials abruptly ceased when it became clear that the political outcome would now depend only on military success. Valorous but futile episodes such as the Yamato incident and the hasty advance on the Forbidden Gate also were abandoned. Official action would almost entirely replace direct action as the main impetus behind the loyalist movement. Major military encounter would now serve as the political instrumentality of choice, among the loyalist reformers as well as their conservative adversaries.

REALISM VS. HEROISM

How was it that the loyalist movement of the early 1860s was in some respects thoroughly realistic in political terms, while in other respects it

[27] *IS*, 4:85-91.

was startlingly reckless? Why was the movement so divided? The loyalist movement was remarkable for two very different sets of reasons.
It embraced two distinct groups, united by their commitment to loyal
action, and yet seriously divided by their differing perceptions of what
loyal action was. While it is difficult to delineate precisely the mental
attitudes of such large informal groupings as the *shishi* factions, there is
nonetheless considerable evidence to suggest that two basic orientations
guided them, one romantic, and one pragmatic.

The romantic contingent were romantic in the sense that their aim
was not in the external world of concrete results, but lay rather in the
realm of emotional gratification that lay within themselves (but also in
such observers, present or vicarious, as there might happen to be). For
them, such gratification was derived from moral conduct, that is from
exceptional and charismatic acts of loyalty. This usually meant action
that was unconventional and personally hazardous. Such acts were to
be carried out with maximum public visibility, in the name of loyalty
to the emperor, that is, devotion to the communal good. The object
was to achieve a profoundly satisfying spiritual fulfillment, both in the
agent and in the observer. The important thing was how the individual
conducted himself in a given set of circumstances. The direct political
results, if any, had nothing to do with it (although these loyalists may
have hoped to influence public opinion by their dramatic actions, and
thereby achieve indirect political results). The ideological underpinnings
for this attitude almost certainly lay in Ōyōmei Confucianism, Bushidō,
and National Studies thought. This romantic pattern of action, although
sometimes stirring, was always open to the charge by the pragmatists
that the whole procedure amounted to little more than foolish heroics.

The "pragmatic" loyalists constituted the other distinct contingent in
the *shishi* movement. These men wished to enhance the well-being of
the Japanese people in general, not only by seeing to it that they were
spiritually uplifted, but also by protecting them from the threat of colonization (*jōi*) and rescuing them from economic want (*keisei saimin*).
To do this they sought to change the regime. Theirs was a loyalty of
politics, tactics, leverage, and results. Accurate political analysis was
crucial for them, as were organization and finely orchestrated responses
to changing political circumstances. They resorted to drastic action only
where good judgment required it, and were not enticed by great personal hazard for its own sake. Their sophisticated world view relied on
Neo-Confucianism, the Ancient Studies school of Ōgyū Sorai, and such
contemporary reformers as Sakuma Shōzan.[28] Although their approach

---

[28] See Thomas M. Huber, "Chōshū Activists in the Meiji Restoration," Ph.D. dissertation, Chicago, 1975, pp. 72-76, 79-83, 86-89.

to bakumatsu politics was inspired by an incomparable boldness of vision, they were looked down upon by the romantic-heroic element for their apparent lack of daring, and for being petty opportunists.

It is possible that the romantics and pragmatists came out of different social backgrounds, the former being enthusiastic "lower samurai" fencers of *gōshi* or ashigaru rank (*sotsu*), and the latter being well-educated students of Confucian statecraft, from the slightly higher and mostly professionalized ranks of "full samurai" (*shi*). Although most *shishi* were transient students in the metropolis, some devoted themselves primarily to the martial arts (*bu*), and others primarily to the liberal arts (*bun*), and this alone may have generated quite different "ideal interests" among them. Scholars have not yet attempted precise identification of the social backgrounds or educational experiences of the fluid mass of several hundred *shishi*, and it is therefore difficult to offer quantitative evidence that the split in the loyalist movement corresponded to different social types. Nevertheless, it is not unlikely that it did.

Most of the *shishi* were affiliated with particular schools in Kyoto, some of which, like Takechi Zuizan's, were famous for fencing, while others, like Sakuma Shōzan's, were known for Chinese classical and Western studies. The Tokugawa curriculum was in principle divided equally between the martial and literary arts, and all retainers high and low were supposed to study some of both, and usually did. But since the lower ranking ashigaru's lot in life was likely to be manual service or a martial craft, directly martial skills and values were emphasized in his education. The lord's falconers and the keepers of the castle gate were ashigaru, for example.[29] The higher-ranking *shi*, by contrast, was usually destined for an administrative or professional role, and so emphasized social philosophy and literary skills in his education. There were two tiers of elite service in late Tokugawa society, and it is likely that men in each understood and even admired the values of the other. This was probably the case in the loyalist movement in the 1860s. Cadet guardsmen and cadet administrators stood shoulder to shoulder in service to the nation. Perhaps many felt with pride that the loyalty of each group represented only different areas of some larger configuration of loyalty. In practical terms, however, this meant that the participants were committed to different sets of values.

The main problem dividing the two factions was the question of risk. The romantic-heroic element liked to maximize risk, or at least not avoid it, for the simple reason that the more desperate the situation was, the greater the romantic loyalist's opportunity for self-expression. The

[29] See Haraguchi Torao et al., eds., *The Status System and Social Organization of Satsuma* (Honolulu: University Press of Hawaii, 1975), pp. 17-18, 72-73, 153.

pragmatists, on the other hand, abhorred great risk, because it invited political ruin, which was what they most wanted to avoid. This is the issue that brought strife and hard feeling into the movement again and again, at Yamato, at Ikuno, and at the Forbidden Gate. It was in a sense this issue that destroyed the cooperative association of the two groups in the loyalist movement.

After the catastrophe of the Forbidden Gate, the romantic element almost disappeared as an autonomous voice in the ongoing political movement in Chōshū that would eventually lead to Restoration. Some romantic loyalists had died, and the remainder were discredited as a valid source of political counsel. Those who survived either became subordinate to the spokesmen of Chōshū officialdom, or else abandoned Chōshū-sponsored loyalism altogether. The relationship between the Chōshū pragmatists and the diminished number of romantic loyalists who remained in their movement would now be the obviously advantageous one whereby the pragmatists would arrange the strategy, and the romantics would enthusiastically implement it despite the hazards.[30]

The autonomous role of the romantic *shishi* thus came to an end, along with the politics of civil violence in 1864. They left no direct political legacy. This is not to say, however, that they are of no importance to the historian. Their cultural legacy has been great. Mishima Yukio's colorfully staged suicide in 1970 made perfect sense in terms of the value system of the romantic-heroic *shishi*. It is also worth noting that Japan's frantically productive manual worker of today goes about in a crisp military-looking uniform, is proud of his difficult technical skills, and is, according to some, motivated not so much by pay as by an irrational factor: a kind of elite consciousness rooted in self-sacrificial loyalty to company and nation.[31]

The pragmatic element, on the other hand, although it never stirred the popular imagination in quite the way the romantic-heroic element did, was of crucial importance for the immediate political outcome of bakumatsu. The timing and content of the efforts of the pragmatists reflected a prompt and intimate knowledge of public events. They sometimes publicly announced what they were doing and why. They

[30] For a description of later Chōshū campaigns in which *shishi* of other domains participated, see Huber, "Chōshū Activists," pp. 222-229, 231-233, 257-262.

[31] This pattern is understood and cultivated by management. See James C. Abegglen, *Management and Worker* (New York: Kōdansha International, 1973), pp. 157-161; Hazama Hiroshi, "Japanese Labor Management Relations and Uno Riemon," pp. 71-106 in *Journal of Japanese Studies*, 5 (Winter 1979), 88-90; Thomas Rohlen, *For Harmony and Strength* (Berkeley and Los Angeles: University of California Press, 1974), pp. 34-40, 192-207; and George O. Totten, "Japanese Industrial Relations at the Crossroads: The Great Noda Strike of 1927-1928," pp. 398-436 in Bernard Silberman and H. D. Harootunian, eds., *Japan in Crisis* (Princeton: Princeton University Press, 1974), pp. 421, 432-433, 436.

endlessly cultivated socio-political contacts among their fellows, to make politically compelling action on a large scale possible. These ties were strong enough to become the basis for the coalescence of hundreds of *shishi* into the semi-institutional framework of the Shōkenkaku, and later into the fully institutionalized military structures of the Yūgekitai and its successors.

The extreme tactical ingenuity of the pragmatic element did not go unrewarded in the short run. Its strategies dissolved the bakufu police power for a time in 1862, and even steered the reluctant bakufu into a policy commitment to resist foreign influence in 1863. "Direct action" in its many forms dominated the national political stage for most of the twenty-four months that it was practiced. These activities left an important legacy for the mid- and late-1860s, as well. The tendency of the movement in the early sixties was toward ever greater cohesion, with increasing institutional discipline and scale. Step by step, the pragmatists' strategies were moving closer to the use of loyalist peasant armies of the kind that would carry the day in the decisive struggles between Chōshū and the bakufu in the late sixties.

Many of the pragmatist *shishi* would serve as officers in Chōshū's triumphant rifle companies in 1866. Many had close ties with the leading lights of the loyalist reform movement in Chōshū and the court, people like Sanjō Sanetomi and Kido Kōin, who would assume the highest positions in the new Meiji regime of the 1870s. Moreover, a number of *shishi* themselves would later serve as officials in the Meiji bureaucracy.[32] In view of these strong tendencies toward continuity in strategy and personnel between the pragmatic *shishi* and the Meiji government, it is perhaps not going too far to ask whether there may not have been a much closer link between the Meiji regime and these *shishi* than historians have been willing to admit.

The brilliant loyalist movement of the 1860s, although in some respects chaotic, constitutes one of the most striking manifestations of political conflict in Japan's long history. This movement embraced several dimensions of historical conflict, including both clashes over social values and clashes over government policy. The loyalist movement was not a case in which conflict flickered briefly and disappeared, but rather one that left enduring legacies for modern Japanese life.

[32] Bernard Silberman, *Ministers of Modernization* (Tucson: University of Arizona Press, 1964), pp. 105, 108. According to Silberman's study, "non-traditional political activity" was a characteristic frequently found among successful Meiji bureaucrats.

THE RISE AND FALL OF THE
SHŌGITAI: A SOCIAL DRAMA

M. WILLIAM STEELE

PROLOGUE

The Meiji Restoration of 1868 was not universally acclaimed. Like other revolutions, it encountered stiff resistance from groups that identified themselves with the old order. This paper will describe one episode of such resistance: the "social drama" of the Shōgitai. I use Victor Turner's phrase with some reservations. It refers to instances of social conflict that perhaps are best described as such. But Turner does provide a structure of analysis—based on drama and its metaphors—that highlights the dynamics of conflict in a society. According to Turner, the notion of social drama is a device for analyzing episodes that manifest social conflict:

> At its simplest, the drama consists of a four-stage model, proceeding from breach of some relationship regarded as crucial in the relevant social group, . . . through a phase of rapidly mounting crisis . . . to the application of legal or ritual means of redress or conciliation between the conflicting parties which compose the action set. The final stage is either the public and symbolic expression of reconciliation or else of irremediable schism.[1]

Although Turner's model of conflict resolution offers little that is new to historians, his approach is nonetheless useful for the insights it offers

I am indebted to Professors Conrad Totman and Tetsuo Najita for the suggestions they provided in the organization and content of this paper.

[1] Victor Turner, *Dramas, Fields, and Metaphors* (Ithaca: Cornell University Press, 1974), pp. 78-79.

into the motives that underlie conflict. Turner argues that, in crisis situations, individuals are guided not so much by self- or rational interest as by deeply entrenched "root paradigms," which shape the form, timing, and style of their behavior.[2] Action becomes a "social drama."

> Actors who are thus guided produce in their interaction behavior and generate social events which are non-random, but, on the contrary, structured to a degree that may in some cultures provoke the notion of fate or destiny to account for the experienced regulation of human social affairs. Greek tragedy and Icelandic saga are genres that recognize this implicit paradigmatic control of human affairs in public areas, where behavior which appears to be freely chosen resolves at length into a total pattern.[3]

In this paper I will borrow from Turner's methodology to examine the rise and fall of the Shōgitai. In particular, I will attempt to clarify the principles of action that impelled the supporters of the Tokugawa regime in its last hour.

The drama begins with the imperial restoration of 9/12/67.[4] Troops from Satsuma, Chōshū, Tosa, and Hizen seized the Kyoto palace and declared an end to the old regime. On 2/1/68, the former shogun, Yoshinobu, advised that a contest of arms would return the imperial court to Tokugawa control, and ordered some 10,000 troops to advance along the road to Kyoto. Although superior in numbers, the Tokugawa forces lost major battles at Toba and Fushimi. Their defeat destroyed any hope for a restoration of the Tokugawa bakufu.

Yoshinobu fled to Edo, and by the end of 1/68 had decided on a policy of submission. Many of his retainers, however, chose to resist. The Shōgitai and other squads of spirited young men roamed the streets of Edo and harassed the occupying troops. Ōtori Keisuke led divisions of decamped Tokugawa troops in guerrilla activities throughout the Kantō region. Enomoto Takeaki threatened the imperial forces with Tokugawa sea power. Fukuchi Gen'ichirō and other pro-Tokugawa journalists issued pamphlets and other propaganda sheets lambasting the imperial position. Katsu Kaishū attempted to wrest concessions from the imperial command through a series of negotiations.[5] In these ways, To-

---

[2] Ibid., p. 67.

[3] Ibid., p. 67.

[4] Dates appearing in this chapter correspond to the Japanese calendar, and are given in order of day/month/year. The Western calendar year is used in place of the Japanese *nengō*. Intercalary months are preceded by the letter "i."

[5] For details on Katsu Kaishū's negotiations with the imperial command, see M. W. Steele, "Katsu Kaishū and the Collapse of the Tokugawa Bakufu," Ph.D. dissertation, Harvard, 1976.

kugawa loyalists contended with Satsuma and Chōshū forces for the possession of political power.

Within Edo the most militant group of anti-imperial Tokugawa loyalists was the Shōgitai. Three to four thousand young men, responding to an inherited tradition of loyalty and revenge, felt compelled to resist the imperial forces and erase the stigma that had been attached to the Tokugawa family at the time of Toba-Fushimi: the label "enemy of the court" (*chōteki*). They lacked money, manpower, firearms, and national symbols, and stood little chance in a protracted struggle with the superior Satsuma and Chōshū forces. Nonetheless, they were strong enough to cause the imperial side grave concern, and to help shape the eventual outcome of the Meiji Restoration.[6]

ACT ONE: DEFIANCE

On 12/2/68, the former shogun, Tokugawa Yoshinobu, in an attempt to demonstrate an attitude of sincere submission to the new imperial government, voluntarily entered domiciliary confinement at Daiji-in within the Kan'eiji complex atop Ueno Hill. That same day, seventeen of Yoshinobu's personal retainers, led by Honda Toshisaburō, met at the Myōgaya teahouse in Zōshigaya. These seventeen men formed the core of the most vocal group of Tokugawa loyalists, the Shōgitai. Honda had brought them together to protest the collapse of Tokugawa authority. "The present dangerous situation," he declared, "has been brought about by the machinations of a gang of wicked traitors [Satsuma and Chōshū]. This is something I gnash my teeth at and cannot endure. When a lord is disgraced it is time for his retainers to die."[7] It is at this point the drama begins. Honda's declaration initiated a stage of confrontation, or in Turner's words, marked a "breach of regular, norm-governed social relations."

The league quickly attracted interest. A second meeting on 17/2 produced thirty Tokugawa loyalists. Sixty-seven met four days later. At this meeting a pact was drawn up to which all affixed their names in blood:

> Now, at this time when the very existence of the Tokugawa family is at stake, it is the way of the retainer to exert himself in loyalty and patriotism. During the past three hundred years, fighting spirit has

[6] Basic information and documents concerning the Shōgitai may be found in: Yamazaki Arinobu, *Shōgitai senshi* (Tokyo, 1911); Ōmura Masujirō Sensei Denki Kankōkai, ed., *Ōmura Masujirō* (Tokyo, 1944); Ōyama Kashiwa, *Boshin eki senshi*, 1 (Tokyo, 1968); Mori Rintarō (Ōgai), *Yoshihisa Shinnō jikō* (Tokyo, 1908).

[7] Yamazaki, *Shōgitai senshi*, p. 47.

declined to the point where loyalty and patriotism are mere words.
. . . To serve the spirits of our ancestors we must not let our words
contradict our actions. We must devote our lives to erasing the insult
to our lord, exterminate the Satsuma rebels, and, by so doing, serve
loyally the court above and succor the masses below.[8]

A fourth meeting, at Asakusa Honganji on 23/2, gave formal organization to the league. Shibuzawa Sei'ichirō was elected its commander-
in-chief, Amano Hachirō, subcommander, and Honda Toshisaburō
Sunaga Denzō, and Tomokado Gorō, captains. At the same meeting a
new pledge was drawn up, again signed in blood, declaring it the duty
of Tokugawa retainers to protest the innocence of their lord in his attempts to free the court of wicked advisers.[9] It was also at this point
that the name Shōgitai (League to Demonstrate Righteousness) was
adopted. The former title, Sonnō Kyōjun Yūshi-kai (Spirited Men's
League for Respecting the Emperor), was deemed inappropriate, as the
league dropped all pretense of imperial loyalism and justified its actions
purely in terms of loyalty to the Tokugawa family.

Shōgitai members were not representative of the samurai elite, but
rather of what Tetsuo Najita has termed "the voices on the margins and
fringes." They were largely low-ranking Tokugawa retainers and pro-
Tokugawa deserters from domains that had fallen into imperial hands.
Although it was largely a samurai undertaking, some commoners, Buddhist priests, and disaffected nobility also joined. In fact, several Shōgitai leaders were of plebeian origins and had tenuous connections with
the Tokugawa family. Shibuzawa Sei'ichirō and Sunaga Denzō came
from wealthy farming households. Amano Hachirō was the second son
of a village headman. He had studied martial arts in Edo and traveled
throughout Japan before taking up the Tokugawa cause. Other leaders,
such as Honda Toshisaburō and the seven thousand *koku hatamoto* Ikeda
Nagashige, were established Tokugawa retainers. High rank, however,
was the exception; Ikeda was a figurehead.

Young men joined the Shōgitai out of a sense of loyalty to the Tokugawa family. To many there was little consideration of utility or even
of conscious choice. Perhaps in some cases loyalty was a convenient
mask to cover more materialistic interests. The end of Tokugawa rule
threatened the loss of feudal stipends for Tokugawa retainers. In seeking
to restore Tokugawa family fortunes, low-ranking retainers undoubtedly had the preservation of their own status in mind. But on the whole
members in the Shōgitai were motivated by duty rather than choice.
They felt compelled to act out the requirements of a long-standing tra-

[8] Ibid., pp. 48-49.
[9] Ibid., pp. 51-52.

dition of loyal and righteous action. The samurai morality, which had been expounded by writers such as Yamaga Sokō and Yamamoto Tsunetomo (author of *Hagakure*) and dramatized by the revenge of the forty-seven loyal retainers of Akō, had become for many samurai, trapped in the humdrum of a bureaucratic society, a paradigm defining their existence. The *bushidō* myth ("even when I die I will return to life seven times to guard my lord's house") had even more poignancy in the crisis-ridden Bakumatsu period when the existing order was threatened. Thus many Tokugawa retainers responded to news of the imperial restoration with a heightened sense of loyalty to their own lord, the former shogun.

Members of the Shōgitai and similar squads were a rough and ready lot, similar to the pro-Kyoto *shishi* described in Thomas Huber's paper in this volume. They were young men (average age twenty-four)[10] who reacted to the anomie of their times with a reckless yet stubborn dedication. Unlike the members of the Tenchūgumi, however, their cause was the restitution, not the destruction, of Tokugawa family rule: "We seek to destroy Satsuma, the wicked advisor to the throne, and clear Yoshinobu of the false charge [enemy of the court]." They, too, had no vision of reform, justifying their actions simply by protesting uncompromising loyalty to the Tokugawa family. As one nineteen-year-old Tokugawa retainer who joined the Shōgitai put it,

> I was born into a family that has served the Tokugawa family since the days of Mikawa and, although my stipend is not much, my vocation is to serve my lord. The debt (*on*) I owe my lord is great. . . . When a lord is disgraced, his vassals must die. It is my duty to offer my life in an attempt to clear my lord's name and restore the Tokugawa family fortunes.[11]

Ancient regimes do not tumble without protest, and in Japan, as elsewhere, such protest was rationalized in a hyperbolic rendition of traditional values.

The restoration of imperial rule and defeat of Tokugawa forces at Toba-Fushimi by "a gang of wicked traitors" triggered the onset of what Turner calls a "primary process." Resistance to the superior Satsuma and Chōshū troops was both impossible and inevitable. To be sure, some Tokugawa retainers were apathetic, but many were forced, even against their personal preferences, to offer their lives in loyal service to their lord. Resistance acquired, to use Turner's words, "a strange

---

[10] Derived from thirty-three known ages as listed in various sections of Yamazaki; see especially pp. 155-159.

[11] Marumo Toshitsune, "Shōgitai sensō jitsurekishō," *Kyubakufu*, 1:7 (1897), 22-23 (original manuscript, 1868).

processual inevitability overriding questions of interest, expediency, or even morality."[12]

Immediately after the Shōgitai was formed, Tokugawa officials ordered the leaders of the Shōgitai to appear at Edo Castle and explain the nature of the new league. They were afraid that careless acts of violence would injure Yoshinobu's position. Katsu Kaishū, in particular, was engineering a plan of peaceful submission that he hoped would result in imperial pardon and a generous settlement. Shibuzawa Sei'ichirō assured the officials that the Shōgitai was not a gang of ruffians, but a group of men sincerely dedicated to assisting the Tokugawa family. The officials agreed to recognize the Shōgitai, and confirmed Shibuzawa as its head. Beginning on 26/2, members of the Shōgitai, carrying lanterns imprinted with a large red *shō* (demonstrate) or *gi* (righteousness), began to patrol the streets of Edo as an official peacekeeping force.[13] The aim of Tokugawa officials was both to help the Edo city commissioners maintain law and order in an increasingly volatile situation and to contain the activities of the largest force of free-floating anti-imperial activists.[14] The Shōgitai was also given the responsibility of guarding Tokugawa Yoshinobu.[15] For this purpose its headquarters were moved from Asakusa Honganji to Kan'eiji in Ueno.

At the same time that the Shōgitai was preparing to defend the Tokugawa family, leaders of the new government in Kyoto were planning to destroy it. On 11/2, the imperial army left Kyoto with a commission to chastise "the enemies of the court." Encountering no resistance, the main division advanced speedily along the Tōkaidō. By 5/3, it had reached Sunpu. There it paused to plan the siege of Edo Castle. As news of the impending attack reached Edo, membership of the Shōgitai grew. By the middle of 3/68, more than three hundred Tokugawa loyalists had gathered under the Shōgitai banner.

From the outset, however, internal dissensions troubled the Shōgitai. Perhaps acting on suggestions from Edo Castle, Shibuzawa planned to remove the league to Nikkō. Arguing that Edo was too crowded to serve as an advantageous battleground, he solicited contributions from rich merchants to finance the move. Amano Hachirō opposed this plan and maintained that the Shōgitai should remain in Edo to protect the city from imperial attack. He felt that Shōgitai leaders should be given

---

[12] Turner, *Dramas, Fields, and Metaphors*, p. 122.

[13] Yamazaki, *Shōgitai senshi*, pp. 53–54.

[14] This strategy was used again on 3/1 when Katsu Kaishū dispatched Kondō Isami and the Shinsengumi, renamed the Chinbutai (Pacifying Squad), into the Musashi and Kōshū districts to quell peasant unrest, thus removing potential prowar elements from Edo.

[15] For evidence of the Shōgitai's official status, see *Zoku Tokugawa jikki 5 Kokushi taikei*, 52 (Tokyo, 1976 reprint), pp. 402–403.

high office and placed in charge of dealing with the Satsuma and Chōshū traitors.[16] He was suspicious of Shibuzawa's dealings with Tokugawa officials who planned to surrender the castle peacefully. Shibuzawa was able temporarily to control Amano's faction and limit the
Shōgitai to peaceful activities. If hostilities were to occur, Shibuzawa
did not want to endanger the safety of the one million residents of Edo.
Ironically, Shōgitai patrols contributed to the orderly atmosphere that
greeted the imperial occupation of Edo following 15/3/68.

Act Two: Crisis

After the surrender of Edo Castle on 11/4, several related factors contributed to escalate the breach between Tokugawa resistance groups and
the imperial occupying forces, producing a situation of "mounting crisis." First, on the day the official surrender ceremony was held, some
two thousand troops deserted the Tokugawa side. Unable to bear the
humiliation of surrender, they decamped and "formed themselves into
bodies of guerrillas and harassed the troops of the Mikado throughout
the country around Yedo."[17] Shibuzawa Sei'ichirō wanted the Shōgitai
to join the deserters. On 11/4 he led those who would follow him out
of Edo, organized the Shinbugun, and engaged in guerrilla activities in
the Musashino district before joining Tokugawa holdouts in Hakodate.
The core of the Shōgitai, however, refused to decamp from Edo. Under
the militant leadership of Amano Hachirō, the Shōgitai became the largest armed group of Tokugawa supporters in Edo and the most visible
symbol of resistance to imperial rule. At the same time, the size of the
Shōgitai grew rapidly, reaching one thousand members by the middle
of 4/68.

Second, the Shōgitai won the full support of the twenty-two-year-
old imperial prince Rinnōji, the chief abbot of Kan'eiji, following the
surrender of Edo Castle. Rinnōji had earlier attempted to negotiate with
the imperial forces on behalf of the Tokugawa family, but when the
imperial command chose to negotiate with Katsu Kaishū instead, Rinnōji exploded with anger and urged the Shōgitai to initiate hostilities.
He compared the contemporary situation to the An Lu-shan rebellion,
which caused the fall of the T'ang dynasty, and demanded that the flag
of righteousness be raised against the Satsuma traitors.[18]

A third factor encouraged radical sentiment within the Shōgitai. Following the surrender of Edo Castle, the imperial command experienced
administrative, financial, and military setbacks. Even with possession of

---

[16] See Yamazaki, *Shōgitai senshi*, pp. 63-65, for details of their dispute.
[17] Dispatch from Harry S. Parkes to the Foreign Office, June 13, 1868, No. 139.
[18] Yamazaki, *Shōgitai senshi*, pp. 56-57.

the castle, the new government forces were unable to control the city of Edo. On 24/4, the same day that the imperial command established its headquarters within Edo Castle, orders were issued to the former Edo city commissioners to continue their duties as before. Later on 3/i4, admitting its own inability to maintain law and order in Edo, the imperial command tried unsuccessfully to appoint Katsu Kaishū and Ōkubo Ichiō as the joint governors of Edo. Moreover, expeditions against the decamped Tokugawa troops and maintenance of an occupying army in Edo drained the imperial command's financial reserves. Early in 5/68, Matsudaira Yoshinaga recorded the following report on conditions in Edo:

> Things have become truly difficult [for the imperial command]. It does not have even 10,000 *ryō* and the Shōgitai is increasingly violent. It is said that the imperial army cannot go beyond Nihonbashi along the Tōkaidō, that keeping order in the city has been entrusted to former bakufu officials, and that government is carried out under the old laws. The Prince [Supreme Commander Arisugawa] is said to have entered Edo Castle, but there he is a solitary figure with no authority whatsoever.[19]

The military condition of the imperial command also worsened. Peasant uprisings and anti-court guerrilla bands threw the imperial command on the defensive. In Kyoto, rumors circulated that it would require 60,000 to 70,000 troops to bring the guerrillas under control. A report from Utsunomiya on 19/4 warned that it was "difficult to guarantee that what we hold tonight will not be lost tomorrow."[20] Iwakura Tomosada and his brother Tomotsune, the commanders of the Tōkaidō division of the imperial army, wrote back to their father, Iwakura Tomomi,

> The Tokugawa retainers publicly advocate submission; secretly, however, they are plotting treason. Rebels have surrounded Edo, and it is quite clear that they are waiting for an opportunity to launch a large-scale assault. The imperial army is powerless to prevent this. I fear that if we relax but for a moment, we will be overcome by the fervor (*kokoro*) of the rebels.[21]

Finally, suspicions regarding the new government's intentions toward the Tokugawa family, particularly toward Yoshinobu, fanned Shōgitai radicalism. The articles of surrender issued on 4/4 made only vague

---

[19] Nihon Shiseki Kyōkai, ed., *Boshin nikki* (Tokyo, 1925), p. 388.

[20] Ōmachi Masami and Hasegawa Shinzō, *Bakumatsu nōmin ikki*, 3 (Tokyo, 1974), p. 167.

[21] Nihon Shiseki Kyōkai, ed., *Iwakura Tomomi Kankei monjo*, 3 (Tokyo, 1935), 481.

promises of lenient terms of settlement once the articles had been ful-filled. Following the surrender of Edo Castle, therefore, Tokugawa re-tainers anxiously awaited details. When they were not immediately forthcoming, suspicion mounted. Among Tokugawa supporters, one daimyo noted in a memorial to the new government,

> Should the retainers of the Tokugawa family erroneously think that, in spite of Yoshinobu's submissiveness and his endeavors to keep his retainers quiet, your Majesty will not decree any liberal terms but intends to destroy utterly the family and name of Tokugawa, it may follow that they will become desperate and resolve to fight, like the mouse that bites the cat when hard pressed by her, and oppose the imperial forces in arms.[22]

The Shōgitai responded to imperial difficulties and imperial procras-tination with an attitude of increasing contempt. They slipped from Tokugawa control and began freely to harass the occupying troops. As Katsu Kaishū wrote in his diary on 30/4,

> Recently the members of the Shōgitai have repeatedly made inflam-matory remarks [against the imperial command], and their bands have grown larger. There are nearly four thousand men encamped at [Kan'eiji atop] the eastern ridge. They have murdered some imperial troops, and they take delight in sporadic careless and rash acts.[23]

Indeed, Shōgitai membership had swollen following the surrender of the castle. By the middle of i4/68, more than two thousand dissidents were encamped at their bastion atop Ueno Hill. By 5/68, their numbers exceeded three thousand. Organized into a tight military organization composed of some eighteen regular units and sixteen supporting squads, the Shōgitai posed a threat to imperial possession of Edo.[24]

ACT THREE: DEFEAT

By 5/68, the Shōgitai was no longer a peace-keeping force. As a hostile army of spirited warriors, controlled by neither imperial nor Tokugawa forces, it had thrown Edo into a state of crisis. As Harry Parkes noted,

> As the party in Uyeno [the Shōgitai] gained strength their attitude toward the Mikado's supporters became more hostile, and assassina-

---

[22] *Kōko Shinbun*, No. 8, dated 17/i4/68, in Meiji Bunka Kenkyūkai, ed., *Bakumatsu Meiji shinbun zenshū* 4 (Tokyo, 1965 reprint), 35.

[23] Katsube Mitake, ed., *Katsu Kaishū zenshū*, 19 (Tokyo, 1973), 67.

[24] For details concerning the military organization and troop strength of the Shōgitai and its supporting squads, see Yamazaki, *Shōgitai senshi*, pp. 73-101 and Ōyama, *Boshin eki senshi*, pp. 341-351.

tions of the latter were of frequent occurrence. It was evident therefore that they must be speedily dislodged if the mastery of the city
was to remain in the hands of the Mikado's government.[25]

Harry Parkes was not the only one to realize the necessity of "redressive action." Already in 4/68, Etō Shinpei, a Hizen retainer employed by the new government to gather information in Edo, reported
to Iwakura Tomomi in Kyoto that the imperial command was experiencing difficulties in maintaining order in Edo. He criticized the concil-
iatory attitude it had adopted toward the "defeated" Tokugawa family
and warned of the potential danger of the Shōgitai: "Now, if we do not
renew our military spirit and proceed to sweep away the Shōgitai, imperial authority will fall to the ground."[26] Iwakura decided to send a
military advisor to Edo in order to stiffen the posture of the imperial
command. Ōmura Masujirō, a Chōshū retainer and expert military tac-
tician, was the logical candidate for this position. He had consistently
argued for a stronger military stance against the Tokugawa family. On
27/4, Ōmura was appointed military advisor and ordered to depart for
Edo.

Ōmura arrived in Edo six days later, on 4/i4. He attempted to redi-
rect the policies of the imperial command, but encountered difficulties.
The staff officers of the imperial command, Saigō Takamori and Kaieda
Takeji, were conducting a series of negotiations with Katsu Kaishū and
other Tokugawa officials concerning the transfer of power to the new
regime. They realized the limitations of imperial military capability and
the extent of resistance both in Edo and in the Kantō district. Moreover,
they were sympathetic to Katsu's argument that war in Edo should be
avoided at all costs, as it would "cost the lives of countless innocent
people." Unable to agree with the weak-kneed attitude of the imperial
command, Ōmura prepared to return to Kyoto. Before his departure,
an imperial envoy, Sanjō Sanetomi, arrived on 24/i4 with news that
money and reinforcements would be sent from Kyoto.[27] Etō Shinpei,
moreover, supplied Ōmura with fresh tactical arguments. On 1/5, he
submitted an ambitious nineteen-point memorial outlining the means
by which Edo might be established as the capital of a centralized polity.
The first and most important point, he argued, was the subjugation of
the Shōgitai.[28]

Sanjō's arrival helped Ōmura to revive a more aggressive attitude in

[25] Harry S. Parkes to Foreign Office, June 27, 1868, No. 151.

[26] Matono Hansuke, Etō Nanpaku, 1 (Tokyo, 1914), 318.

[27] For details on the dispute between Kaieda and Ōmura, see Kaieda's autobiography,
Kaieda Nobuyoshi, Jitsureki shiden (Tokyo, 1913), Section 8, pp. 30-35. See also Ishii
Takashi, Ishin no nairan (Tokyo, 1974), p. 98.

[28] Matono, Etō Nanpaku, 1:325-328.

the imperial command. The change was reflected in a series of reforms designed to transform Edo from "enemy territory" into the seat of a national imperial government. On 1/5, the Tokugawa family was relieved of the responsibility of policing Edo, and for the first time the imperial command assumed these duties itself.[29] On 6/5, the imperial command ordered all public notice boards set up by the Tokugawa government to be removed and replaced by those of the new government.[30] Finally, on 11/5, the government of Edo was reorganized as a metropolitan district (fu), administered separately from the military command. Ōmura Masujirō was appointed its governor.

On 1/5, formal debate concerning the subjugation of the Shōgitai opened within the imperial command. Saigō and Kaieda argued that the imperial army was ill-prepared to launch an attack. It was outnumbered: the Shōgitai had over three thousand members, whereas commitments to the Kantō and Tōhoku fronts plus the recall of many han troops had reduced the imperial forces in Edo to a mere two thousand men. The Shōgitai, furthermore, had the advantage of position. Imperial troops would have to advance up Ueno Hill to attack Kan'eiji. Nevertheless, Ōmura and Etō maintained that victory was possible and that the current troop strength was sufficient.[31] Moreover, they argued that control of Edo was the key to control of the entire nation: "Since Edo is the center of the nation, it should become established as the permanent national capital in the future. Therefore it is necessary to attack the Shōgitai as soon as possible."[32]

Three factors enabled Ōmura to prevail. First, attempts at conciliation failed. On 3/5, Sanjō reported to Iwakura that efforts at mediation with Rinnōji, the ranking Shōgitai leader, had proven fruitless. He requested that troop reinforcements be sent immediately, as promised. Tokugawa efforts to pacify the Shōgitai also failed. Katsu Kaishū sent a messenger to Rinnōji to plead for forbearance, only to be rebuffed as a "traitor to the Tokugawa family": "Although today's affairs are carried out in the name of the court, in actuality they are the designs of Satsuma and Chōshū. How can you simply wash away and forget in one day the blessings we have received from the Tokugawa family generation after generation?"[33]

Second, Ōmura received unexpected support for his plan to attack the Shōgitai. On 5/5, Ōkuma Shigenobu, a Hizen retainer and ranking

---

[29] Tōkyō Daigaku Shiryōhensanjo, ed., *Fukko-ki*, 5 (Tokyo, 1929), 27. See also *machifure* in Tōkyō-to, ed., *Bannin seidō* (Tokyo, 1973), p. 8.

[30] Tōkyō-to, ed., *Tōkyō-shi shikō: shigai-hen*, 49 (Tokyo, 1959), p. 49.

[31] For their argument, see *Ōmura Masujirō*, pp. 694-697.

[32] Matono, *Etō Nanpaku*, 1:329.

[33] Quoted in *Ōmura Masujirō*, pp. 694-697.

official of the new government's bureau of foreign affairs, arrived in Edo with 250,000 ryō in gold. He was empowered to negotiate the purchase of an ironclad warship, the *Stonewall*, which the bakufu had ordered from America. The warship arrived in Yokosuka after civil war had broken out, and, in accordance with American neutrality, was not turned over to Tokugawa forces. Ōkuma criticized the "state of anarchy" (*museifu no jōtai*) that he found in Edo: "On sea, the former bakufu's warships can obstruct all traffic, and, on land, outside of Nishinomaru, gangs of ruffians are free to come and go. The city is ungoverned. The police are powerless; law and order is absent. . . . This state of anarchy in Edo will eventually cause relations with foreign countries to sour."[34] He concluded that the imperial command should "immediately attack those gangs of ruffians who roam the streets of Edo." On 7/5, he met with American authorities in Yokohama, and, having failed to purchase the *Stonewall*, he returned to Edo and offered the money to Ōmura for use against the Shōgitai. Ōkuma also managed to send nearly one thousand Hizen troops from Yokosuka to Edo to strengthen the position of the imperial command.

Finally, heightened Shōgitai terrorism forced the imperial command to admit the need for strong counter measures. Angered at the removal of Tokugawa public notice boards, the Shōgitai carried out forays against Hizen and Satsuma troops on 7/5. This made even Saigō agree to hostilities in Edo. On 9/5, Sanjō reported to Iwakura that war was unavoidable. On 11/5, the same day that Ōmura was appointed governor of Tokyo-fu, the imperial command decided to attack the Shōgitai at their stronghold in Kan'eiji.

The attack was scheduled for 15/5. On the day before, the imperial command informed the Tokugawa family that it had become necessary to use force against "those contumacious retainers" who had disregarded Yoshinobu's desire that they "submit to the gracious and merciful will of the imperial court."[35] The Tokugawa family was advised to remove all ancestral tablets and other treasures from Kan'eiji. Leaflets were circulated throughout Edo to warn the townspeople of the impending attack:

> For some time past the bands who have broken loose have assembled at the temple of Ueno, frequently assassinating the soldiers of the government, plundering the people of their property in the name of the government forces, and committing acts of increasing violence. They are rebels against the state. . . . They have plundered the property of the innocent populace, and there is no act of violence which

[34] Ibid., pp. 690-691.
[35] *Fukko-ki*, 5:417-419.

they have not committed. As these acts tend to plunge the population into the depths of misery, it has been found unavoidable to use force against them.[36]

At dawn of 15/5, cannon fire echoed throughout Edo. Ten hours of harsh combat ensued. Early reports of Shōgitai victories did not disconcert Ōmura. Confident of the success of his war plans, he gazed intently in the direction of Ueno from a tower within Edo Castle. By nightfall, he was proven correct. Superior strategy and weapons had won the battle. Kan'eiji lay in ashes, the northeastern section of Edo was in flames, and the Shōgitai had fled, leaving over two hundred of their comrades dead, some by suicide.[37]

Although victory "left the Mikado's troops in undisturbed possession of Yedo," as Harry Parkes reported to the British Foreign Office,[38] it was not unanimously acclaimed. A pro-Tokugawa newspaper, Soyofuku kaze, ended its report of the defeat with the following lament:

> Ah! How sad and deplorable is this day! The most sacred spot in all of the Kantō has been, in but an instant, reduced to flames. Fleeing from the disaster, the aged, the young, and the womenfolk of the city wander aimlessly on the roads, filling them with cries of pity. It would seem that the workings of heaven know no right or wrong.[39]

On the other hand, a sense of joy and relief spread through the imperial camp. Iwakura's sons, who had earlier grieved over the helplessness of the imperial army in subduing the rebel bands, wrote to their father on 1/6, after the victory over the Shōgitai, in a different vein:

> Everyone has had a number of worries over reports of a kind of insecurity [we have been experiencing] here, but now things have truly quieted down. It is quite a relief. On the fifteenth of last month, [the imperial army] subjugated a horde of 10,000 rebels who had been creating disturbances throughout Edo and who were encamped at a big temple in Ueno. Since then, things have become truly quiet.[40]

Sanjō Sanetomi also wrote back to Iwakura describing the victory in glowing terms. It was an occasion of "great joy for the nation." Although it had been hard fought and there were many casualties, it had

---

[36] Tōkyō-shi shikō: shigai-hen, 49:55–56.

[37] For details concerning the actual battle, see Yamazaki, Shōgitai senshi, pp. 137–141; Ōyama, Boshin eki senshi, pp. 340–379; Ishin Shiryōhensanjimukyoku, ed., Ishin-shi, 6 (Tokyo, 1941), 218–227; Tokyo-shi shikō: shigai-hen, 49:55–71; Tōkyō-to, ed., Tōkyō-shi shikō: hensai-hen, 5 (Tokyo, 1958), 955–972.

[38] Harry S. Parkes to Foreign Office, July 10, 1868, No. 169.

[39] Soyofuke kaze, No. 7, n.d., in Bakumatsu Meiji shinbun zenshū, 3:408.

[40] Iwakura Tomomi kankei monjo, 4:9.

contributed greatly to "the imperial fortune."[41] Iwakura, relieved at the news of the victory, thanked Sanjō for his efforts:

After reading your letter of 15/5 and the [Kōjō] *nisshin* [both informing me of the plans to attack the Shōgitai], I worried day and night over the results of the campaign. By the 29th, when still there was no news from either the army or the navy, I truly could not eat or sleep in peace. All I did was worry. Finally, when I received your report on the 29th, it was like feeling reborn.[42]

Iwakura's feeling of rebirth was justified. The victory over the Shōgitai represented a major advance in the security of the new government. First, Edo became the possession of the new government. On 19/5, it was absorbed into the new government's administrative network as a military garrison (*chindai*) and placed under the control of the Bureau of Domestic Affairs in Kyoto. The last Tokugawa offices still in nominal operation, the Edo City Office (*machi bugyōsho*), the Temple and Shrine Office (*jisha bugyōsho*), and the Finance Office (*kanjōsho*), were abolished. In their place, Boards of Municipal Government, of Shrines and Temples, and of Civil Affairs were established, placing appointees of the new government in charge of Edo.[43]

Second, on 24/5, the imperial command finally issued the entire terms of settlement. Until that time, the Tokugawa family had only been informed of the item of succession: headship had been transferred to Tayasu Kamenosuke, a five-year-old boy. The other more crucial terms, fief and revenue, had not been announced for fear of resistance. Katsu Kaishū had been working to negotiate a settlement that would have left the Tokugawa family in Edo with a substantial income of 2,000,000 *koku*. Victory over the Shōgitai, however, enabled the new government to order the Tokugawa family to move to a 700,000 *koku* domain in the province of Suruga.[44]

Finally, the battle of Ueno Hill was a turning point in the military fortunes of the new imperial army. With Edo firmly under control, Ōmura Masujirō was ready to "press forward into the northeast" to quell resisters who remained in the Tōhoku region.[45] By the end of 5/68, Ōtori Keisuke's guerrillas had been routed, and relative peace had been restored to the Kantō district. The "northern confederacy" of Tōhoku *han* surrendered to the imperial banner in the middle of 10/68. Enomoto Takeaki held out the longest. On 19/8, he led some two thou-

[41] *Ōmura Masujirō*, pp. 711-712.
[42] *Iwakura Tomomi kankei monjo*, 4:9.
[43] *Fukko-ki*, 5:475-482.
[44] *Fukko-ki*, 5:643-647.
[45] *Ōmura Masujirō*, p. 720.

sand men and eight warships to Hakodate. Enomoto's "republic," however, stood little chance of success. On 18/6/69, he was forced to admit defeat, giving the new government undisputed possession of the nation.

Epilogue

The rise and fall of the Shōgitai has been presented as a social drama, following Victor Turner's scenario of breach, crisis, redressive action, and reintegration. This "dramatistic" approach can be used with profit to place the role of conflict in society on the center stage of historical analysis. In particular, the social drama of the Shōgitai highlights the role of conflict during the Meiji Restoration. Most Japanese accepted the imperial restoration and the collapse of Tokugawa political authority with resignation. But a significant minority of Tokugawa supporters saw no alternative to resistance activities in Edo and its hinterland. Uncompromising loyalty to the Tokugawa family and refusal to decamp from Edo made the Shōgitai the most visible form of resistance to imperial rule. Their actions by no means matched the scale of the Vendée during the French Revolution, but the Shōgitai drama is a reminder that the restoration of imperial rule was not bloodless.

Moreover, Turner's approach helps to generalize the predicament of the Shōgitai. The crises of the 1860s drew responses from all who were politically conscious. Some were forced to redefine the normative basis of loyalty and leadership. Conrad Totman's paper in this volume has detailed the efforts of Tokugawa leaders to transform the bakufu from a feudal to a centralized regime capable of coping with the problems of governance imposed on Japan after 1853. His bureaucrats responded to the crisis of their age by abandoning the old order and seeking a new one. Others, such as the members of the Shōgitai, sought to rejuvenate the ideological underpinnings of the Tokugawa system. The collapse of the bakufu only strengthened their sense of personal loyalty to Tokugawa Yoshinobu, the last shogun. Members of the Shōgitai were angry young men who were willing to stake their lives on proving the innocence of their lord and the validity of the Tokugawa order. Resistance became a desperate attempt to restore meaning in a world that had lost coherence. In this sense, the sonnō-jōi activists described in Thomas Huber's paper had much in common with the Shōgitai. They too were young men confounded by the crisis of their age. They too found solace in total surrender to a grand cause. They had their own "social drama" to perform. Members of the Tenchūgumi and the Shōgitai alike were faithful to the requirements of a tradition of uncompromising loyalty and unequivocal action.

Turner's mode of analysis is particularly useful in isolating the motives of conflict. He argues that conflict does not arise only over questions of interest—"choices of means and ends and social affiliation." Instead, Turner stresses loyalty and obligation:

> Conflict seems to bring fundamental aspects of society, normally overlaid by the customs and habits of daily intercourse, into frightening prominence. People have to take sides in terms of deeply entrenched moral imperatives and constraints, often against their own personal preferences. Choice is overborne by duty.[46]

Young Tokugawa retainers who joined the Shōgitai and similar resistance squads felt they had no other alternative. They rationalized their actions in terms of loyalty and duty and not in terms of victory or defeat. Consciously or unconsciously, they adopted the role of "loyal retainer" and acted out the requirements of this "root paradigm." The Battle of Ueno Hill was in this sense inevitable. Katsu Kaishū and other Tokugawa officials attempted to negotiate a peaceful settlement. They failed not so much because of the intransigence of the imperial forces as because of the strength of the Tokugawa tradition of righteous resistance.

One final consideration is the legacy of Tokugawa resistance. The members of the Shōgitai failed to resuscitate the Tokugawa order. Yet, like the drama of the Forbidden Gate earlier in 1864, the Battle of Ueno Hill had consequences far beyond the defeat of a few thousand dissidents. Victor Turner's study of the abortive Hidalgo Insurrection of 1810 has shown that even movements and revolutions that fail can restructure the political field and leave deposits having potent effects in the future. "It was a failure for Hidalgo the man, but a success in establishing a new myth containing a new set of paradigms, goals, and incentives for Mexican struggle."[47] Similarly, the actions of the Shōgitai in opposing the new imperial regime have left a legacy of loyal resistance that has continued both to inspire and horrify modern Japan. Popular novelists and kabuki playwrights have repeatedly championed their cause. On the one hand, Ueno Hill can be seen as the symbolic birthplace of modern political opposition movements. Using different strategies, the People's Rights Movement of the 1870s and 1880s and the popular parties of the 1890s also attacked the machinations of Satsuma and Chōshū and their arbitrary control over the imperial state. On the other hand, Shōgitai members have been immortalized as exemplars of righteous resistance against overwhelming forces, and have helped to perpetuate the Chūshingura tradition into modern Japan. In this sense,

[46] Turner, *Dramas, Fields, and Metaphors*, p. 35.
[47] Ibid., p. 102.

Shōgitai resistance can be seen as the archetype of Saigō Takamori's revolt in 1877 and the young officers' insurrection on February 26, 1936.

Apart from this psychohistorical legacy, Tokugawa resistance produced extensive social and political change that threatened the success of the new regime. The difficulties experienced by the imperial forces in pacifying Edo and the Kantō region made many domains that had initially sided with the new regime question their decision.[48] Likewise, the strength of Tokugawa resistance disturbed the faith of foreign powers in the new government.[49] This is not to say that a Shōgitai victory could have restored the Tokugawa family fortunes. Tokugawa authority had crumbled; it was economically and politically bankrupt. But sustained political disorder was an alternative to the success of the imperial regime. So was colonization. The prospect of a lengthy civil war, which would "paralyze our commerce," as one British representative put it, was not attractive.[50] These considerations underscore the importance of the Battle of Ueno Hill as a moment of historic crisis. Victory gave the imperial command the ability to regain the momentum that it had lost. Only after this short but hard-fought battle can one conclude that Tokugawa forces were no longer contenders for power and that the imperial will was to prevail.

[48] See Kojima Shigeo, *Kantō fudai han no kenkyū* (Tokyo), for details.

[49] Haraguchi Kiyoshi, *Boshin sensō* (Tokyo, 1963), pp. 191-196.

[50] A. B. Mitford to Harry S. Parkes, Osaka, July 19, 1868. Dispatch from Harry S. Parkes to Foreign Office, No. 188, encl.

THE SOCIAL BACKGROUND OF PEASANT UPRISINGS IN TOKUGAWA JAPAN

Hashimoto Mitsuru

On the eve of the Meiji Restoration, as the Tokugawa system visibly collapsed, peasants tried to reestablish a social certitude from which to interpret their world of fragmenting community. Throughout the Tokugawa period, the relationship between the main and branch lines of the peasant family was the basic normative concept for structuring family and village life and even the political relationship of lord and peasant. Already in the late eighteenth century, when the formal relationship between high- and low-status peasants no longer provided adequate protection to small farmers, the concept of a main-branch family (*honke-bunke*) relationship recurred as the deep structure to reorganize peasant existence in the chaotic world of late Tokugawa Japan. With the disintegration of Tokugawa society, such a relationship became the means for peasants to identify those who were responsible for the crisis and who should be punished. In uprisings, the main-branch family concept helped define the scope, character, and direction of the rebellion; peasants knew who should lead them, how they would be mobilized, and what they would attack and destroy. They obtained this knowledge from the history of their village and they used this historical experience at this critical moment.

The normative structure of the community enabled peasants to recognize the "broken world" (*yo no midare*) of Japan in the late Tokugawa period. What they saw was a world of merciless rulers and avaricious village elites who would not give them the aid they needed. In response, the peasants envisioned the "world of Maitreya" (*miroku no yo*) where they could live in peace and abundance. They organized rebellions for "world renewal" (*yonaoshi*) and joined new religious sects. Chaotic and orgiastic movements represented an opportunity for newly constituting the broken community, an opportunity almost realized in the brief period between the total collapse of Tokugawa rule and the establishment of a new order by the Meiji state.

The purpose of this essay is conceptual rather than empirical or descriptive. It takes its raison d'être from the tendency in much of the traditional monographic literature on the Japanese family to emphasize its integrative, fundamentally harmonious social and political role. Although the validity of such interpretations cannot be questioned, it is also true that family structure is deeply implicated in conflict as it occurred in the rural society of the late Tokugawa period. A good deal of empirical research will be necessary to provide the concrete data and case studies that must undergird fully persuasive judgments, but it is hoped that the following outline will suggest a range of interpretive possibilities and a framework to give impetus to such research.

THE MAIN-BRANCH FAMILY RELATIONSHIP

The paternal structure of the Japanese family extended beyond a single family of consanguine members.[1] Although, strictly speaking, an extended family consists only of members related by consanguinity, this does not necessarily apply to the large "family" in Japan, which also included members who were not related by blood.

The lineage relationship in Japan functioned to transmit property and status from generation to generation within a family and gave hierarchical order to relationships among the various families in the community. In the Japanese lineage system, the family that was considered to be the oldest had the highest status. It generally held a sizable proportion of productive fields and resided in the central part of the village. The family's physical location in the village thus was intertwined with the historical consciousness of the family's origin and the structure of the lineage relationship. Villagers recognized the historical role of the pioneer families of that village and accorded them the highest status in the community.[2] Families regarded as first offshoots of the pioneers could claim the highest status within the village, the second offshoots, the second highest, and so on.

---

[1] Anthropologically, the Japanese family is bilenial, but what is significant here is that Japanese have conceived the family relationship as paternal. See Oikawa Hiroshi, *Dōzoku soshiki to sonraku seikatsu* (Tokyo, 1967), p. 77.

[2] Ariga Kizaemon, "Dōzokudan to sono henka," *Shakaigaku hyōron*, 46 (1962), 3.

Power and authority in the village reflected the subordination of the branch families (*bunke*) to the main families (*honke*) in actual or putative lineage descent. Branches were generally smaller families, derivative from the powerful main families. However, a large branch with a number of smaller families dependent on it could also claim main-family status in relation to them. As such a large branch grew increasingly independent, it would eventually be able to claim main-family status throughout the village. Moreover, the older and more independent among the branch families could claim a higher status than newer and less independent families. In this way, the main-branch relationship structured families into many layers, from the most powerful to the least.

The economic, political, and social benefits associated with family status were many. Economically, the branch family relied heavily on the main family. Most importantly, the latter provided its branch with parcels of land from its holdings. Such parcels were, of course, invariably smaller and less productive than those retained by the main family, and the insufficiency of its holdings was a major factor perpetuating the branch's dependency. Inasmuch as it was forced to depend on the main family for its basic needs, the branch in turn provided the main family with labor service, particularly at sowing and harvesting times. The branch family also assisted the main family in carrying out birth, marriage, and death ceremonies. Besides direct income supplements to branches, the main family also provided manure, water for irrigation, and firewood. This exchange of attentive service for benevolent assistance promoted a world of mutual obligation that permeated community life.

Mutual obligation also functioned in the political sphere.[3] Because of the basic norm of consensus in main-branch family relationships, main families represented branches in the advancement of political demands. Main families felt morally bound to listen to the demands of their branches, just as branch families were expected to follow the lead of the main families. In making decisions about village affairs, therefore, main families could assume that their agreements possessed legitimacy for all members of the community. It was on the basis of mutual obligation between the main and branch families that any agreement by main families of the village was assumed to express the collective will. Indeed, a general consensus attained through the main-branch family relationship was the necessary condition for village administration.

Socially, the main and branch families were hierarchically stratified, but not all relationships within the main-branch nexus were necessarily

[3] Nakamura Kichiji, "Kinsei no kyōdōtai," *Nihon no sonraku kyōdōtai* (Tokyo, 1971); Ariga Kizaemon, "Sonraku shakai no riron," *Dōzoku to sonraku* (Tokyo, 1971).

hierarchical. There were, in fact, peer groups among branch families. In contrast to the hierarchical system, peer groups were organized according to residential location within the village. Five-house groups (*goningumi*) are one example. The *goningumi* network functioned well in carrying out cooperative works such as village road repair and collection of firewood in the mountains. Through such cooperation, families interacted closely and acquired a sense of communal cohesion.

The numerous rituals of village life further integrated groups of families. Hierarchically arranged seats in ritual ceremonies gave the main-branch family relationship tangible form. That relationship was further symbolized in the distance of the seats from the main family's house god (*yashikigami*).[4] Each main family had its own house god, and the branch families constituted the circle of worshipers. The hierarchical structure of the ritual group thus corresponded to the structure of other aspects of village life. In effect, the branch family was not subordinated to the head of the main family as an individual but rather to the main family's house god, which was the symbolic source of family authority. In this way the authority of the house god provided a normative basis for participation in the main-branch family relationship that regulated the status hierarchy in the village.

When one family in the village achieved a dominant position, its house god acquired the status of guardian deity (*chinju*) for the entire village. At the same time, other large families would retain their house gods, which remained ritualistically dominant within the family, even though subordinate to the guardian deity of the village. The village hierarchical system thus involved several house gods, including those that represented authority within families, and also the single guardian deity that symbolized the center of community life and acted as mediator among the major families.

The house god of the branch family was thought to have descended from the main family's house god. Villagers used the term *kamadowake*, the division of the kitchen fireplace, to describe the division of the house god and the establishment of a branch family.[5] The term also emphasized the social subordination of the branch family to the main family. Through the differentiated statuses of all house gods and hierarchically arranged seats at ceremonies centering on the guardian deity, villagers were made very much aware of the relative positions of families and members of their community.[6]

---

[4] Sakurai Tokutarō, *Kōshūdan seiritsukatei no kenkyū* (Tokyo, 1962), pp. 85, 198-199.

[5] Ariga Kizaemon, "Nago no bunrui," *Nihon kazokuseido to kosakuseido* (Tokyo, 1966); Yanagida Kunio, "Ujigami to ujiko," *Teihon Yanagida Kunio shū*, 11 (Tokyo, 1969).

[6] Andō Keiichirō, "Dōzoku ketsugō no bunkai to yashikigami saiki," *Shakaigaku hyōron*, 37 (1959), 65.

The structure of lineage relationships not only regulated the formal aspects of village life, but through the ritual process permeated every aspect of it. With this understanding of their own community in mind, villagers could interpret their everyday life—the roles they should play in the community, and when and where they should participate in village activities. They were ever mindful of their village and the importance of everyday tasks. The history of the peasant community was thus made through the daily activities of mutual help in planting and harvesting, collecting firewood, roofing houses, and conducting initiations and religious rituals. The concept of lineage structured these various activities into a communal unity and created larger groups of peasants for the enhancement of village life and increased production.

DŌZOKUDAN

Once the lineage organization as a visible economic unit (dōzokudan) was established, the main family no longer exercised management power over it. Rather, the main family portrayed itself as the symbol of the whole, and people in the group pledged it loyalty. Responsibility for the enterprise was assumed by managers who began as apprentices and remained as "children" of the main family. Later, these managers also produced branch families that strengthened and developed the group's overall commercial activities, and the ablest of them also formed the top executive group of the whole body. The master of the family entrusted management of the body to this executive group. Though no longer active in administering the enterprise, the main family continued to represent the unit and perpetuity of the whole entity. In that it incorporated the ancestors of the corporate group, the main family occupied the highest status in relationship to its branch families; standing at the apex of the lineage relationship, the main family bound the branches together and made it possible for the enterprise to grow by producing more branches.[7]

The extension of the family organization made hierarchical relationships looser and more flexible than they would have been in a strict lineage pattern. But looseness and flexibility did not eliminate the structure of the main-branch family relationship that formed the conceptual core of the enlarged lineage organization and maintained the unity of the whole. For example, main families produced branch families in order to achieve more effective management. The emergence of branch families resulted from the desire of the main family to increase the effectiveness and productivity of the lineage organization. Main families

---

[7] Nakano Takashi, Shōka dōzokudan no kenkyū (Tokyo, 1964), pp. 50, 74-79, 126-129.

became aware that too close a relationship with the branch family imposed a heavy financial burden on both parties. Moreover, in the course of time, main families gave up more and more parcels of land to branch families.[8] Owing to this shift from direct cultivation of large parcels to cultivation of smaller parcels by branch families, main families were no longer obliged to provide various necessities for the branch families and their dependent laborers, and at the same time the main families could continue to earn profits through rent. Thus, branch families became more economically self-reliant, and dependent laborers often became newly independent peasants. Nevertheless, benevolent supervision and attentive service on the part of the former landholder and tenant remained obligatory in everyday life.

With the attenuation of the inclusive family relationship, the cohesion of the village weakened and the tax system (muraukesei) became increasingly prominent as the major factor circumscribing the village community. That system had been based on the natural village community from its first institutionalization as part of the bakuhan system. Tax payment not only depended on the communal character of the village but later formed an indispensable part of village life.[9]

An annual tax was levied from above on the entire village, but within each village tax payments were assessed from independent peasants according to the size and productivity of their holdings. When a peasant could not pay his share of the tax, he had to rely on a rich and powerful peasant in his village to pay it for him. The village as a whole was obliged to render its tax quota, and the norm of benevolence required a rich and powerful headman (nanushi) to supply the unpaid portion. A common arrangement was that the peasant who could not pay his taxes would go into debt to a wealthy villager. By pawning his land, he would become a tenant (shichiji-kosaku) and enter into a new relationship with the village rich man who had lent the money. Initially, when holdings were pawned for a short time, the rich peasants did not take possession of the pawned holdings. But as the holdings came to be mortgaged for longer and longer periods of time, the village rich and even pawnbrokers outside the village took the mortgaged fields away from the original holders and let them out to day laborers for cultivation. This practice marked the beginning of the landlord–tenant system.[10]

As the circle of peasant activities widened beyond the scope of the village, due to the development of agriculture and the export of special products to towns, the tax system became a strictly economic activity. In this way the system of taxation was distinguished from other com-

[8] Nakamura, "Kinsei no kyōdōtai," pp. 156-157.
[9] Ibid., p. 128.
[10] Ariga Kizaemon, Nihon kazokuseido to kosakuseido, pp. 236-238.

munal activities. It lost its power to integrate the community, and now served only legally and economically to define the borders of the village. On the other hand, peasants freely established communal relations, and peasant communities developed beyond the village's legal borders to organize wider circles of relationships. Communal integration did not depend on legal circumscription but on the necessities of peasant life.

Through the differentiation of daily tasks in the village, new and specified relationships such as that between landlord and tenant emerged from diffuse family ties. Peasants developed functional groups for irrigation and for trading in crops, manure, and special products. Some of these groups were effectively administered by a number of villages together. These new groups provided means for peasants to relate with one another beyond the natural borders of the village. Thus, communal relationships now transcended life in the hamlet, and the peasant sense of community developed a wider frame. This may indicate the disintegration of community, but it also precipitated a new search for the unity that was essential to everyday life.[11]

The new solidarities that extended beyond the village border show the peasants' attachment to the concept of the main-branch family relationship. They could not dispense with that relationship, which provided a natural and reasonable framework for understanding communal activities. Within the context of the newly extended community, families and villages were reordered along the lines of main-branch family links, thus enabling peasants to identify positions of higher status and responsibility. Villages and towns in this wider area were reorganized and reinterpreted as peasants tried to give new meaning to these new relationships, while hamlets lost their autarkic strength. The expanded community involved ties that were more abstract and also weaker than those in the original village. Peasants were unable now to locate the consanguine lineage relationship.

The village no longer adequately represented the arena for peasants' daily tasks. Commerce brought unfamiliar people and new objects from far away. Peasants also acquired knowledge of more productive seeds and farming methods that enabled the poor peasant with small holdings to become more economically independent.[12] Some of the poor peasants engaged in manufacturing and commerce, whereas others developed new agricultural holdings. Their improved economic status did not lead them to deny the main-branch family relationship as the ordering principle of village social and political relationships. They did, however, demand status consistent with their gradually rising power. Through new ex-

[11] Nakamura, "Kinsei no kyōdōtai," pp. 118-120.
[12] Furushima Toshio, *Nihon nōgyōshi* (Tokyo, 1957), pp. 311-312.

periences both within and beyond the village, the established relationships among peasants encountered a crisis that endangered the pattern of mutual obligation.

How did the peasants interpret these new experiences? They had to maintain their village and establish ties with new groups of peasants and traders. Whereas previously the village had been integrated by the system of lineage organization, at the core of which lay the concept of the main-branch family relationship, villagers now felt it necessary to have a new standard for assessing families and individuals. Apparently, leaders could no longer rely on the age of families as a foundation for status and power.

Since wealth was the surest standard for identifying power,[13] main families now found that wealth was their most important characteristic. They had large holdings, owned big houses, and wielded predominant influence over village politics. They elected the village headman from their midst, rationed water for fields, and administered the mountain forests. Nonetheless they could not maintain their status and power generation after generation, and some were replaced by the newly rich in the village. The village community began to raise new families to main-family status. Indeed, wealth eventually became the only qualification for the main families who administered the village with the many dependent branch families under their power. Only the rich could manage their lineage systems as farming enterprises.

Even those who had been unimportant in the village thus organized their power, and they who earlier had been unable to form their own lineage systems came to insist upon having main-family status. The powerful branch family demanded main-family status, and the rising small landholders insisted on their independence. Some moved to newly developed neighboring fields, and by engaging in trade and agriculture on their tiny holdings they had the opportunity to accumulate property. Subordinates (hikan and kakae) who had already accumulated property and established independent lives succeeded the declining main families and achieved the highest status positions in the village. When the village accepted the newly rich as members of the main family group, there occurred a shift of status in the family lineage system.[14]

As the power structure and the relations among families changed, peasants contrived ways of reinterpreting the injured relationships in the community. Once peasants had encountered a more productive and effective way of life, they tended to leave the old relationships, and sometimes even destroyed the traditional ones. They were no longer drawn

[13] Ibid., pp. 306-308.
[14] This shift occurred around the Kansei period. See Ōishi Shinzaburō, *Kinsei sonraku no kōzō to ie seido*, enlarged ed. (Tokyo, 1976), p. 230.

to the old, declining main family that insisted on reciprocity in the relationship between benevolence and attentive service. The reciprocal relationship was burdensome, and both the newly rich and the rising small peasants sought greater independence. Yet because of the peasants' affinity to the concept of a main-branch family relationship, that concept and the system of lineage organization were expanded to accommodate the new groups for which wealth was now the most important qualification for main family status.

THE GROWTH AND DESTRUCTION OF LINEAGE ORGANIZATION

The lineage organization as a farming enterprise developed from the autarkic community and eventually destroyed it. Peasants accumulated capital by combining fields. They also began marketing special products, which liberated them from traditional communal bonds. Even a small family could accumulate sufficient capital to provide for a more independent life. Shifts in the pattern of social relationships occurred as peasants focused on the criterion of wealth as a basis for choosing the main family. As peasants reinterpreted social relationships in terms of economic rationality, critical changes occurred in the social relationships themselves.

The lineage organization became larger and more economically significant, accumulating huge holdings beyond the boundaries of the village. Main families retained their holdings and expected the branch families to be independent in order to create more cultivators for the holdings of the extended lineage system. As branch families scattered beyond the village borders, fewer peasants accepted the legitimacy of the main-branch family relationship.[15] Once separated from the main family, some branch families mortgaged their small holdings to rich, unrelated families and merchants. Often small holders could no longer cultivate their holdings and were replaced by agricultural laborers. They left their fields to work as tenants and lost all hope of buying back their mortgaged holdings. Attachment to their fields and to the personal relationship between main and branch families thus lost its former strength. Contract, not personal ties, became the most crucial aspect of the relationship between landlord and agricultural laborer.

Villagers did not always view the relationship between main and branch families in terms of lineage. They also used another set of terms, *oya* and *ko*, parent and child, to express a tie of mutual obligation and affection between superior and inferior.[16] This set of terms expressed the

---

[15] Nakamura, "Kinsei no kyōdōtai," pp. 153, 156-157.

[16] Kitano Seiichi, "Dōzoku soshiki to hōken-isei," in Nihon Jinbun Kagakukai ed., *Hōken-isei* (Tokyo, 1951), pp. 185-186, 188-189.

sentimental rather than the structural aspect of the relationship. A person of parent status did not necessarily occupy the highest position in the hierarchical system of the village. By this time his superior status was more likely to depend upon skills, experience, and personality. In trade and commerce, merchants and craftsmen would care for their apprentices until they themselves became independent businessmen and craftsmen. The apprentices, in return, would work to pay back the debt incurred during their apprenticeship. Similarly, merchants and craftsmen considered rich customers to be their guardians and would visit them frequently to supply labor services and goods. The large, rich houses would help these small merchants and manual workers in times of crisis, and also provide gifts and aid even at weddings, initiations, and funerals. The small merchants and craftsmen, in turn, compared the rich to their parents and often called them their "main family" (honke).

In the villages, peasants asked powerful and prestigious persons to sponsor their sons at times such as initiation into village society, and to participate as a "parent" in ceremonies related to childbirth, adult initiation, and marriage. Traditionally, men who played the role of ceremonial parent were members of the lineage organization and were usually the most prestigious among them, but this convention changed over time, and eventually sponsors would not necessarily be limited to members of the lineage organization. Villagers could choose their "parent" according to the individual's prestige and their own anticipated benefits. They could even choose from among their colleagues and peers. Thus, peasants were enabled to select "parents" freely from outside the lineage organization.

With the weakening of lineage ties and the emergence of wealth as the principal criterion for main family status, an economic rationale came to dominate social relationships. Rich men were asked to christen children, to be supervisors at initiation ceremonies, and to act as go-between at marriages. Guardians chosen because of their wealth were, moreover, often asked by peasants for guidance in everyday life. Peasants felt it correct, even natural, to ask for such care, and the rich considered themselves morally bound by the symbolic parent-child relationship to do so.

In village politics, headmen (nanushi) held the status of guardian of the village. As representatives of the peasant community, headmen received peasants' demands and represented them in petitions to higher levels of government. When peasants encountered difficulties caused by drought and famine, they petitioned for tax reduction and exemption. Since the peasant was the fundamental producer in the bakuhan system, tax reduction and tax exemption were necessary benevolences when peasants petitioned for the maintenance of their way of life. Peasants petitioned their headman, who petitioned the senior headmen, who in turn petitioned the *han* officials. Petitions followed a hierarchical structure and most petitions that observed the proper procedure were accepted by higher authority. Between peasants and rulers there existed an agreement that those above should act for the peasants' good and that petitions should be presented for the purpose of good government. It was accepted that neither ruler nor ruled should seek private interests, but rather should consider the welfare of the whole *han* and country. Hence, only petitions that followed legal procedure and satisfied these conditions would be judged as reasonable by superiors. With this in mind, the peasants petitioned their superiors with the expectation that rulers would accept their requests.

This sense of mutual obligation between ruler and ruled did not always result in a harmonious relationship, however. Senior headmen and lower officials did not always agree to present peasant petitions or properly represent them to higher officials. Sometimes headmen abused their office in order to exploit peasants through overtaxation. In such cases peasants petitioned directly to upper officials in a form of protest called *osso*.[17] Such actions were illegal, and the leaders of the protest would be executed, even though in most cases petitions were accepted, and both senior headmen and lower officials would be punished for failing to administer their villages properly. Insofar as leaders were prepared to be punished, the tactic of bypassing the headman and going directly to higher authority became an effective, institutionalized form of petitioning.

More radical yet were petitions accompanied by mass demonstrations (*gōso*). A great number of peasants participated in petitioning, and sometimes marched as far as the castle town to demonstrate before the high officials. By the late Tokugawa period, however, protest took even more radical forms, with peasants frequently destroying the houses of officials as well as those of rich villagers whom they deemed morally corrupt. Peasants argued that the rich abused their status and exploited them to such an extent that they could not survive. Absorbed only with increasing their own profits, these "evil" people had opposed the peasants' will and stood against the peasant community. They monopolized special products such as silk thread and indigo, which could easily increase cash income, and raised the tax rates levied on miscellaneous products and labor services.

Peasants, moreover, often considered the village rich and the *han* officials to be in collusion. Higher taxes drove them further into debt

---

[17] Concerning *osso*, *gōso*, and other types of uprisings, see Aoki Kōji, *Hyakushō ikki no nenjiteki kenkyū* (Tokyo, 1966).

while enabling the rich to add to their holdings. Indeed, the rich often used profits extorted from peasants to bribe the *han* officials, who in turn enacted new tax laws on every possible kind of product capable of providing extra income for peasants. Even in cases in which new laws might have been enacted to increase the income of the *han* or to maintain an impoverished *han* treasury, peasants did not think the new laws proper and believed that the rich and *han* officials habitually deceived and exploited the peasants for private gain.

PEASANT UPRISINGS IN THE LATE TOKUGAWA PERIOD

When the headman was both a good guardian and a good representative of the peasants' will, they regarded him as humane, reliable, and benevolent. If bad crops and famine brought the village to crisis, a good headman would offer rice and grain from his own warehouse and plead his village's case before higher officials. Thus, at the lowest administrative level, it was the headman who was in charge of strengthening the moral bond between peasant and ruler, and he was expected by peasants to exhibit the particular morality appropriate to his position as their nearest source of benevolent aid. Actually, of course, no headman could alone sustain his villagers' needs. Demands for tax reduction and exemption could only be granted by higher authority, specifically the daimyo or the overlord. In addition to the satisfaction of their material needs, peasants also demanded that their lord should act morally and benevolently in return for such services as regular payment of taxes. Aid was expected of the benevolent ruler, and if he failed to maintain the peasant community not only at the level of bare subsistence but at the level appropriate to the status of "peasant" (*hyakushō*), villagers would argue that their ruler lacked benevolence and morality.[18] At such times, peasants would seek aid from even higher authorities who they hoped would rectify the situation by bestowing benevolence.

The peasants, moreover, felt that the rich had immorally accumulated wealth and betrayed the expectations of mutual obligation. When the rich betrayed such expectations, the peasants became indignant at disparities in wealth and status that were not conducive to moral benevolence. The village rich and officials, even traders in towns far away, reaped profits and accumulated more wealth than was considered reasonable. Wealth without benevolence, particularly when it was far away and out of the control of the community, became the target of peasant indignation. Peasants responded by attacking the avaricious rich who had broken the moral bond by engaging in single-minded economic

---

[18] Fukaya Katsumi, "Hyakushō ikki no shisō," *Shisō*, 584 (1974), 61ff.

exploitation. The peasants thus imputed avariciousness to the rich who marketed the peasants' products in distant towns, since the economic actions of the rich in their own community no longer met their expectations. Especially in the late Tokugawa period, the avaricious were above all the merchants who engaged in foreign trade at the open port of Yokohama and who exported silk to unknown countries. By this time, therefore, the wealth and benevolence that had once been combined in the main-branch family relationship were clearly divorced, and wealth went to only the immoral rich.

The economic activities of the wealthy drove some peasants into tenancy and others into wage labor. Peasants appealed for redress in petitions: "If we should be left as we are, we will not be able to live on as peasants."[19] Villagers thus demanded the return of their holdings and the reinstatement of old leases that would secure their lives as proper peasants. When *han* officials rejected such appeals along with demands for tax reductions and tax exemptions, peasants came to see their rulers as cooperating with the rich for their own selfish interests, in spite of peasant difficulties, and at the expense of the peasants' welfare. Peasants thus realized that the failure of benevolence was attributable to the conjunction of an immoral economy and immoral politics, and thus felt trapped and helpless.

Peasants inevitably came to realize that they would have to take matters into their own hands in order to change the world. With a desire to level the accumulated wealth and landholdings that no longer coincided with the former status hierarchy, peasants felt it necessary to destroy the prevailing power structure that had brought village life to an impasse and to reinstitute the moral community in which their fathers used to live the life of "peasants." They petitioned for "the continuity of the peasantry."[20] In world renewal movements (*yonaoshi*) they demanded lives suitable to their social status. Acting upon their expectations for world renewal, they destroyed houses, furniture, and goods, the concrete manifestations of insufficient benevolence and the private interest of the rich and powerful. Destruction was an expression of peasants' indignation toward the actual world. In these acts of destruction, however, they warned each other not to steal fine clothes, rice, and money from the rich. They reasoned that the act of destruction was an act for "all the people (*banmin no tame*)";[21] the goods of the rich must be attacked and destroyed but not stolen for private use.

[19] Similar expressions are found in all peasant petitions.

[20] Shōji Kichinosuke et al., eds., *Minshū undō no Shisō*, Nihon shisō taikei 58 (Tokyo, 1970).

[21] "Ōshū Shinobugun Dategun no onbyakushōshū ikki no shidai," in Shōji et al., eds., *Minshū undō no Shisō*, p. 275.

Peasants attacked not only the rich but the officials who colluded with them. In an uprising of 1786 in Fukuyama *han*, peasants destroyed the house of a rich man who had conspired with the relatives of the lord, saying, "he did what he wanted under their protection."[22] In another episode, in the uprising of 1866 in the Shindatsu area, a rich man asked the rioters not to destroy his house, offering them 500 *ryō*, but they refused because he had shown no pity to peasants.[23] Nonetheless, rioters did not attack all headmen. One headman in the uprising of 1786 who had often shown benevolence to the peasants of his village was not attacked.[24] He was famous in his village and throughout the domain, not only for his personal warmth but also for honesty. He had given money and grain to peasants who had difficulty in paying their taxes, and every year he gave food to the poor. Other headmen took advantage of peasants' financial difficulties to enrich themselves through high interest loans.

Destruction and uprising occurred not only on a physical level but on a spiritual one, as well. With the anticipation of a new world, new religious movements also appeared in the Bakumatsu period. These new sects were rooted in the moral life of the community, which formed the basis for peasants' criticism of the morally decaying world. The religions were radical in the sense that they disengaged themselves from the political and economic affairs of everyday life. They mobilized peasants, guiding them in the transition from the particularistic parent-child relationships of the villages to a universalistic concept of guardian and parent—the religious protector whom all peasants should respect and worship as the progenitor of their beliefs. These new religions proclaimed harmony and a restructuring of the family that would lead peasants to salvation. The savior, however, was not to be the house god of a particular family or the guardian deity to a particular village but a deity who would encompass the whole nation, or in its most radical form, the whole world.

Kurozumikyō, the oldest and most conservative of the new religions, was established at the beginning of the eighteenth century. Followers included the ruling class of Okayama *han* as well as peasants, merchants, and artisans.[25] The believers worshiped the sun goddess (*Amaterasu Ōmikami*) as the origin of existence; every human being was derived

[22] "Abe no dōshimon," Mori Kahei et al., eds., *Nihon Shomin seikatsu shiryō shūsei*, 6 (Tokyo, 1968), 359.

[23] "Ōshū Shinobugun Dategun no onbyakushōshū ikki no shidai," p. 281.

[24] "Abe no dōshimon," p. 361.

[25] Murakami Shigeyoshi, "Kurozumi Munetada to kurozumikyō," in Murakami and Yasumaru Yoshio, eds., *Minshūshūkyō no Shisō*, Nihon shisō taikei 67 (Tokyo, 1971), 587-598.

from and modeled after her. As children of the sun goddess, all human beings were thus equal. Devotion to the sun goddess would bring peace and prosperity to the family, clan, and *han*. Most important for believers was to live joyously and energetically, thereby overcoming all worldly difficulties. With an indifference to worldly desires, believers in the sun goddess would never be in need. Death and life, wealth and poverty were all problems of the mind. Truth, selflessness, and honesty dissolved all difficulties. By being honest before the goddess they could realize heaven in the actual world.

These teachings were consonant with the lessons of daily life in the peasant community. Peasants were easily moved by such teachings to criticize the society around them and to believe in the new world that these new religions promised. The preachings of the new religions sounded irrefutable and even natural to the peasants, and provided the allure of an existence that would provide an alternative to their actual life of distress.

The religion of *Tenrikyō* created a more radical state of mind.[26] The founder, Nakayama Miki, reached her religious exaltation after she experienced various personal crises. Born at the end of the eighteenth century, she married a rather wealthy peasant and seemed destined to lead an uneventful and peaceful life. In 1830, a huge religious pilgrimage (*okagemairi*) passed her village on the road to Ise. Two of her daughters died at the beginning of the Tenpō period, and her family suffered during the great Tenpō famine. In the year of Ōshio's uprising in Osaka, she lost her only son. Although she was experiencing considerable suffering in her personal life and watching suffering in the world around her, she worked hard for her family. In 1838, the year after the death of her son, she went into a fanatical state, which has been taken as the beginning of her religious commitment.

To many desperate peasants, *Tenrikyō* offered the way to escape their difficulties. Miki taught them to live happily in order to attain an ideal world. It was in the heaven of this ideal world that they would live a bountiful and peaceful life. Perceiving the cause of the immoral world to be ingrained in the traditional and feudalistic way of life, she defined all people as equal, "on one line." People should all be brothers and sisters and they should not regard any people as unrelated. Believers should consider actual difficulties such as bankruptcy and sickness as opportunities to begin a new life. Even death she interpreted as an opportunity to establish an ideal world. Such beliefs encouraged people who faced disasters, since they had entered the "deep valley," the place to start a blessed life. Believers criticized the ruling class, which did not

[26] Murakami, "Nakayama Miki to tenrikyō," ibid., pp. 599-615.

redistribute its wealth and abused its power; they aimed to destroy the "high mountain" on which the holders of power lived.

Tenrikyō, like *Kurozumikyō*, based its teachings on the morality of everyday life. It taught that the moral way of life, which had disappeared from this world, would relieve people from sickness and poverty. Whereas for *Kurozumikyō* salvation was a problem of the mind, *Tenrikyō* sought renewal of this immoral world and the advent of an egalitarian community. *Tenrikyō* was so radical that it suffered various pressures from other religions and later from the Meiji government. Although *Tenrikyō* and *Kurozumikyō* differed in their attitudes toward the demoralized world, they both relieved their believers from the burdens that were pressed upon them in real life. Other new religions such as *Konkōkyō*, *Miroku* faith, and *Maruyamakyō* in the Meiji period also provided a framework for criticizing the ruling elite and taught the way for world renewal.

The proliferation of new religious movements was but one indicator that peasants sensed something drastically wrong with their world and were trying to radically restructure their lives. Although peasants demanded benevolence from those whom they considered to be in the position of main family or guardian, no main family at this point had sufficient resources to bestow the proper benevolence upon the peasants. The ruling elite was barely able to maintain itself in the face of inflation, and the *han* was powerless even to support the bakufu financially. The ruling class could not be as generous to their subordinates as they once were, and peasants felt that they could no longer rely on their superiors. Peasants thus anticipated the advent of a new benefactor and a new world.

Anticipation of a new world erupted in the form of millenial mass movements. Religious pilgrimages, which were believed to occur every sixty years, provided an opportunity for this eruption.[27] In 1830, there were rumors of a pilgrimage in the coming year, on the sixtieth anniversary of the previous one in the Meiwa period. As the rumor spread, people in towns and villages started on pilgrimages to Ise. Most of them wore straw hats and white clothes and carried ladles in their hands. Sometimes men dressed in female attire, and women wore men's clothes; sometimes, girls danced in the nude; a rich man in Osaka organized a group of geisha and went out with bright clothes and music;[28] rich people in towns and villages on the route of the pilgrimages offered food and clothes, welcoming the crowd as if the pilgrims were gods.[29]

People joined the pilgrimages from almost every corner of the coun-

[27] Fujiya Toshio, *'Okagemairi' to 'ee ja naika'* (Tokyo, 1968).
[28] "Ukiyo no arisama," in Shōji et al., eds., *Minshū undō no Shisō*, p. 359.
[29] Ibid., p. 317.

try. Some organized groups of pilgrims, whereas others started on pilgrimages alone, without telling their parents or employers. The poor and powerless especially escaped for Ise, crying, "we've escaped (nuketa tosa)." In the ee ja naika movements of 1867, most of the pilgrims were unorganized individuals. Not all of them went as far as Ise. Where their charms fell on houses, people danced, drank, and scattered money, crying, "anything's fine (nandemo ee ja naika)!"[30]

When the peasants rose up and attacked the rich, they were entertained by the rich with food and sake as if they were the gods of heaven. Because liberation from the actual world and an abundance of food and drink were a heaven for the peasants, when the peasants were actually surrounded by the abundant goods of the rich, they cried, "it is truly the world of heaven (miroku)."[31] Riots destroyed the houses and warehouses of the rich who had exploited the poor, as peasants cried, "now the gods of the renewed world (yonaoshi) are here to punish them."[32]

With complete confidence, rioters punished ill-doers; a huge crowd of people including gamblers and vagabonds joined this movement of "smashing and breaking (uchikowashi)." Together, they destroyed houses and tore the luxurious goods of the rich to pieces. Destruction was total, and the rioters often went beyond the control of their leaders. They cried, "world renewal (yonaoshi)!" and "for all the people (banmin no tame)!" but what was really going on was chaotic destruction. In the zenith of the destruction of 1866, in the Shindatsu area, the uchikowashi movement was described as the deeds of demons (tengu and tenma).[33] Destruction was orgiastic, as in the ee ja naika movements.

Although there was much destruction associated with these uprisings, peasant action was far from random; the rioters were in some sense controlled and directed by the collective orientation that had integrated the village. Villages mobilized peasants by passing around in other villages a paper called warada kaijō or tengu-jō on which peasants wrote the names of their villages in a circle in order to conceal the movement's point of origin. The paper ordered that all peasants "from fifteen to sixty years old" should participate, and warned that if any peasant failed to join, "the whole village will be burned down."[34] The mobilized peasants carried straw flags and lanterns that identified their villages. In the

[30] "Keiō Ise okage kenbun shokoku fushigi no hikae," in Shōji et al., eds., Minshū undō no Shisō, pp. 374-375.

[31] "Ōshū Shinobugun Dategun no onbyakushōshū ikki no shidai," p. 276.

[32] "Kamo no sawagitachi," in Mori et al., eds., Nihon Shomin seikatsu shiryō shūsei, 6:518.

[33] "Ōshū Shinobugun Dategun no onbyakushōshū ikki no shidai," p. 276.

[34] "Keiō 2 hinoe-toradoshi Chichiburyō kikatsu ikki," in Mori et al., eds., Nihon Shomin seikatsu shiryō shūsei, 6:681; "Nozawa botaru," ibid., 13:52.

uprising of 1866, in the Shindatsu area, rioters wore straw hats, white headbands and white sashes (*tasuki*), red headbands and red sashes, and yellow headbands and yellow sashes, each color identifying their village like a uniform. All of them wore straw coats and carried sickles in their hands.[35] Faced with a demand for mobilization, peasants felt that they had to participate. An episode in the uprising of 1764 along a highway called Nakasendō tells of a young man just married who was mobilized for the sake of the whole village and eventually arrested. Also in the same uprising the parents of a man killed in the tumult were prevented from complaining, since the uprising was for the sake of the village and if they should protest, the leaders of the movement would be identified and punished.[36] The morality of maintaining the village was so strong that they had to follow orders for mobilization.

Personal reasons were inadequate to excuse a peasant from participating in the uprisings. If an individual did not want to join, the decision was made for him by the whole village. In some cases a village that decided not to participate had to fight with the other villages participating in the uprising. Usually, however, peasants were mobilized as if an uprising was just one of the many cooperative works performed by villagers. When faced with a community decision to mobilize, there was no other way but for the peasant to rise up with his fellow villagers to avoid a crisis in the community. Legitimacy was always on the side of the collectivity.

When peasants were mobilized by good leaders, the old communal morality, even in the fragmenting world of bakumatsu Japan, was revived. In an episode in the 1866 Shindatsu uprising, the leader, Hachirō, was fully able to control the rioters, who attacked only the immoral rich and did not destroy pawned goods or steal money. In reviving the old communal morality from such chaos, Hachirō announced, "The officials monopolize power, live a luxurious life, neglect the superiors, and slight all the people. The lower envy and speak ill of the upper. This is what the world is now."[37]

Hachirō criticized the *boshin* war in 1868 and argued that the ruling class would be vanquished by some new power, since the old rulers gave no benevolence to peasants and sought only to benefit themselves. He said that even if they raised huge armies they would have no chance

---

[35] "Ōshū Shinobugun Dategun no onbyakushōshū ikki no shidai," p. 275.

[36] "Tengusōdō jitsuroku," in Mori et al., eds., *Nihon Shomin seikatsu shiryō shūsei*, 6:314–315.

[37] "Hachirō hitori nendaiki," in Shōji et al., eds., *Minshu undō no Shisō*, p. 162. Hachirō denied that he took the leading role in the uprising. Whether he actually led the uprising, however, is less important than his ideas about what a leader should be, and what constituted good peasants and good rulers. He was a legendary leader of the uprising.

of winning.[38] The war was caused by the officials who abused power, craved luxury, and exploited the people, especially those in Aizu and Higo, who conspired to seize power from the shogun. He also criticized the new powers, Satsuma, Chōshū and Tosa, saying that they traded with foreigners, became unmindful of the Buddha, and betrayed the people. He praised the benevolent decision of the shogun to resign and save the whole country from ruin.[39]

Confronted by economic and political crisis in the Bakumatsu period, peasants wanted to live as peasants—cultivating their fields, paying taxes, and living in a peaceful community. The ideal world in their frame of reference was in the "good old days," when they helped each other and when rulers bestowed benevolence. In the contemporary world, however, people with main-family status lacked the means and sometimes the will to bestow benevolence; headmen did not represent the peasants; *han* officials, the rich, and even the lords exploited the peasants and abused their power. Under intolerable burdens of taxes and debt, peasants no longer worked with hope for a secure life. From top to bottom, everything was uneasy and turning upside down. Peasants drank *sake*, gambled all day long, destroyed property, and danced in orgies, crying, "*ee ja naika!*"

To the peasants, "world renewal" was not only a critique of the irresponsible ruling elite but was also a movement back to the time of true "peasant" life. In the fragmenting world, peasants dreamed of bringing the ideal life of the "good old days" into this renewed world. Recovery of "peasant" status meant the reestablishment of the old community where they had worked hard under a benevolent ruler. In order to redistribute wealth and power and restore the morality of the village and the proper relationship between ruler and ruled, they destroyed houses of the rich and the officials.

Restoration of morality in the fallen world thus took the form of rebellion against whoever exploited "good" peasants. In uprisings and in the new religious movements, peasants rejected what had been authoritative and sought a more benevolent and merciful rule. They provided the occasion for formation of a revolutionary ideology, but had no means fully to establish it. Although peasants never obtained any real political power following the Restoration, they nevertheless, through these movements and uprisings and through their criticism of the existing structure of wealth and power, posed a real threat to political authority.

[38] Ibid., pp. 146-147.
[39] Ibid., p. 164.

YONAOSHI IN AIZU

Stephen Vlastos

For nine generations the ancestors of Matsudaira Katamori had ruled
Aizu and rendered loyal service to the Tokugawa shogun. But on November 8, 1868 Lord Katamori's rule came to an end. Abandoned by
his principal allies and on the verge of defeat, Katamori signed a document of unconditional surrender, acknowledging personal responsibility
for the recent war against Japan's new imperial government. The imperial army's month-long offensive against Aizu and the devastating
artillery barrages fired at the castle during the siege of Aizuwakamatsu
had so exhausted the Aizu forces that all the cotton piece goods in the
castle had been cut into bandages; before the ceremonial surrender of
the castle could take place, women had to work late into the night to
weave the white flags. The next day, under the protective guard of the
Yonesawa *han* army, Katamori led the remnants of his once formidable
regiments out of the White Crane Castle, whose towering keep had
long symbolized seignorial rule over the domain.[1]

The subjugation of Aizu was the crowning victory in the five-month
campaign by the newly formed Meiji government to defeat rebel forces
in northeastern Japan and thereby eliminate from the main islands armed
resistance to the imperial coup d'état of January 3, 1868. A few weeks
before the fall of Aizuwakamatsu, the young Emperor Mutsuhito had
chosen the slogan "bright rule" to inaugurate Japan's modern era of
imperial government. In keeping with the spirit of enlightened rule, the
Meiji leaders honored their pledge to spare the lives of Lord Katamori
and his son. Nevertheless, because Aizu troops had led the Tokugawa
counterattack against the palace revolution that brought the new leaders

[1] *Aizuwakamatsu shi* (Aizuwakamatsu City, 1966), pp. 189-192.

to power, the government had early singled out Katamori as the foremost "enemy" of the imperial Restoration, second only to the shogun
himself.[2] It therefore carried out its earlier threat to chastize Katamori:
in the name of the emperor, it confiscated his domain and exiled Katamori and his retainers to a remote northern fief. The consequences of
this decision were far-reaching. Rather than appoint a new daimyo to
rule Aizu, the government seized the opportunity to abolish seignorial
rule and put in its place the personnel and organs of a centralized prefectural system of local government. Prefectural rule under a centralized
government did not come to most rural areas of Japan until the early
1870s, so that in many areas daimyo authority and *han* administration
were not immediately affected by the revolutionary seizure of power of
1868. In Aizu, however, the traditional ruling order was eliminated all
at once, bringing about a dramatic response from the peasant population.

The war and the mobilization that preceded it touched the lives of
many commoners in Aizu; at best it subjected them to new experiences,
but for the most part it caused much destruction of property, disrupted
trade and agriculture, and in other ways imposed great hardship. In the
summer of 1868, as part of a thoroughgoing military reform, Aizu officials for the first time authorized village headmen to raise militia units.
The plan called for mobilizing 3,400 peasant combatants. However, the
domain offered few incentives; peasants were busy with agricultural duties and showed little enthusiasm for the musters and still less for actual
combat. Of greater consequence and concern to peasants was the *han*'s
requisitioning of horses, materiel, and labor just before the harvest to
build defensive fortifications; worse was the devastation of standing crops
and of entire villages that lay in the line of battle.[3] As the siege wore
on, the seizing of food from an already poor harvest by both armies
brought on acute food shortages that were aggravated further by the
blockade thrown up by the imperial army.

In preparing for the assault on Aizu, the Meiji government made a
modest attempt to win over the common people. Handbills distributed
by the army's propaganda agents exhorted them to "work exhaus-
tively" for the imperial cause because the emperor "considers all the
people to be his children."[4] The bills also promised that villages that
supported the war effort would receive substantial reductions in the land
tax. Once the army entered Aizu, however, government soldiers ruth-
lessly seized food, animals, and goods. Though the army issued orders
forbidding improper treatment of the local population, the rape and

[2] Ibid., p. 129.
[3] Ibid., pp. 199-202.
[4] Ibid., p. 199.

rapine of the imperial soldiers became legendary: village women were sexually assaulted, even abducted and taken captive, and merchants came from as far away as Shirakawa, three days' journey to the south, to buy and barter war booty.

It is not surprising, therefore, that with the exception of a small number of peasants, most of whom were from the village headman class, few villagers volunteered their services to either army; neither did they lament the defeat of the *han* army nor cheer the victory of the imperial soldiers. However, peasants were not blind to the significance of the collapse of the established political order and the opportunities that this presented. Indeed, a short ten days after the fall of Aizuwakamatsu, an uprising by the peasants of Takiya department (*kumi*) set in motion a series of local rebellions that continued for the next three months in various localities of the domain. These rebellions were local uprisings that attempted radical changes in the political and economic arrangements in the village. The peasants named this movement *yonaoshi*, literally, "world rectification" or "world renewal." The movement in Aizu in the autumn and winter of 1868 was one of a large number of *yonaoshi* movements in the waning years of the Tokugawa period, and in this essay we will examine how Aizu peasants struggled to change the world around them.

On November 16 two thousand peasants assembled at Gojōshiki village in the mountainous Takiya department of Ōnuma district, south and west of Aizuwakamatsu. During the next several days they marched as a crowd to at least twenty villages, and in each they demolished the homes and offices of the village headman and local moneylenders and merchants. After the attacks, representatives from the villages that had joined in the uprising met to give assent to a list of proposals for changes in land tenure, debt relationships, and village leadership.[5]

The uprising in Takiya department did not spread immediately to other areas of Aizu. Although it set the pattern for subsequent uprisings, the rebellion appears to have been planned and organized as a local movement, rather than as the first stroke of a domainwide uprising. The crowd restricted the attacks to villages in the department, and elsewhere peasants responded thoughtfully rather than spontaneously or impulsively to the initial outbreak of violence. Twelve days elapsed before the next round of attacks, which occurred not in villages immediately adjacent to Takiya but to the north and east in the more populous districts located around the castletown. Here the attacks began on November 28, east of Aizuwakamatsu, in Arai village and in the Takahisa department of neighboring Kawanuma district. Next, we see local re-

---

[5] Tashiro Shigeo, *Shiryō shūsei Aizu nōmin ikki* (Tokyo, 1978), 2:314. Hereafter *SSANI.*

bellions moving in an arc north to Kitakata and east to the Inawashiro region at the foot of Mt. Bandai in the northeast end of the domain. One week after the last attacks were recorded in Inawashiro, violence erupted in distant Minamiaizu in the extreme southwestern portion of Aizu. Beginning on December 12, there were uprisings in four neighboring departments of Minamiaizu—Matsukawa, Narahara, Koide, and Yagoshima—and subsequent uprisings in the Ina region from December 15 to 24. Peace was not fully restored until January 1869.[6]

Looking at the progress of the local rebellions, we see that the attacks were dispersed over a broad geographical area and continued for almost three months. The timing and the locations of the attacks show that peasant violence did not simply spread by "contagion," nor did it unfold in accordance with a consciously formulated plan for a domainwide rebellion. Nevertheless, one may speak of the many local uprisings as a coherent phenomenon because each followed the pattern established in the Takiya uprising: attacks against high-status villagers, and, simultaneously, adoption of a program of radical reform. It is this feature—the combining of attacks, which were common occurrences in late Tokugawa peasant uprisings, with the more unusual activity of formulating programs for political and economic change—that best represents the distinctive character of the *yonaoshi* movement in Aizu. We must look at both the attacks and the effort to bring about more enduring change to understand the import of "world rectification" in Aizu.[7]

[6] Shōji Kichinosuke, *Yonaoshi ikki no kenkyū* (Tokyo, 1971), p. 119.

[7] The Aizu peasant movement was only one of many *yonaoshi*-type movements in the closing years of the Tokugawa period. Most of the large uprisings occurred in eastern and northeastern Japan between 1866 and 1869. It is easier to draw valid generalizations concerning the social and economic character of the uprisings than about their political character. The common characteristic of all of the uprisings was attacks by poor peasants against the wealthy peasant elite, but the political character of the uprisings varied considerably from locality to locality. On the whole the uprisings that occurred in 1868-1869 within the context of the civil war and the visible collapse of daimyo rule, as in Aizu, Echigo, and Kōzuke, were primarily rebellions against the political authority of the village elite, whereas the uprisings in Shindatsu and Bushū in 1866 resembled Tokugawa-period *gōso*, though with millenarian overtones.

The literature on *yonaoshi* uprisings in Japanese is vast; the following provide a good introduction: Sasaki Junnosuke, "Bakumatsu no shakai jōsei to yonaoshi," *Iwanami Kōza Nihon no rekishi* (Tokyo, 1976), 5:247-299; Yasumaru Yoshio, *Nihon Kindaika to minshū shisō* (Tokyo, 1974); and Haga Noboru, *Yonaoshi no shisō* (Tokyo, 1973).

In English-language publications, for discussion of the Bushū uprising see Patrica Sippel, "Popular Protest in Early Modern Japan: The Bushū Outburst," *Harvard Journal of Asian Studies*, 37 (December 1977), 273-322; for discussion of the Shindatsu uprising, see Stephen Vlastos, "Tokugawa Peasant Movements in Fukushima: Conflict and Changing Patterns of Mobilization," Ph.D. Dissertation, California, Berkeley, 1977; and for a general discussion of Tokugawa peasant movements and *yonaoshi* uprisings, see Irwin Scheiner, "Benevolent Lords and Honorable Peasants: Rebellion and Peasant Consciousness in To-

The uprising began with the unleashing of tremendous violent energy against headmen and other well-to-do villagers. A report filed by a group of headmen from the Inawashiro region describes the attacks with which poor peasants began the work of "world rectification."

> Suddenly, without any warning at all, from December 3 to 6, peasants gathered from all over Inawashiro. Raising war cries, blowing on conches, and clanging cymbals, they charged into our houses. They attacked homes, storehouses, and granaries; they cut down the roof supports, ripped up the tatami and floorboards, scattered our stores of rice, split open barrels of miso and soysauce, and snatched up and burned land and tax records and other documents. They filled their sleeves with valuables; they even threatened our lives.[8]

The attacks followed the pattern of Tokugawa-period "smashings" (*uchikowashi*). The leaders and most of the crowd were members of the village community, although they might be joined by drifters, gamblers, *rōnin*, and itinerant laborers; the choice of whom to attack was made in advance and the reasons for the attack were well understood; a large crowd was mobilized, if need be by threat, to demonstrate the collective nature of the violence; and the immediate purpose was to destroy tangible wealth and to confiscate or destroy pawned goods, mortgage deeds, debt vouchers, tax records, and other documents. Planned days beforehand, if not weeks, the uprisings usually took the victims by surprise. The fury of the crowd profoundly shocked the people attacked, who, particularly if they happened to be village headmen, were accustomed to thinking of themselves as the benevolent guardians of the men who staged the smashings.[9]

In Tokugawa Japan, rural "smashings" were likely to occur at times of privation and amidst fear of impending famine; the common conditions were harvest shortfalls, hoarding and speculation, and violent price fluctuations that prevented poor peasants from buying grain at the going market price. To a certain extent, the attacks resembled eighteenth-century European food riots in which the poor forced the rich to "donate" rice or sell at a "fair" price.[10] If they refused, the crowd seized what they could and, as punishment, destroyed what they couldn't carry off.

The attacks in the Aizu peasant movement share some of the characteristics of food riots, but they had greater significance within the

kugawa Japan," in *Japanese Thought in the Tokugawa Period 1600-1868*, edited by Tetsuo Najita and Irwin Scheiner (Chicago: University of Chicago Press, 1978), pp. 39-62.

[8] *SSANI*, p. 332.

[9] Yasumaru, *Nihon kindaika to minshū shisō*, pp. 158-172.

[10] E. P. Thompson, "The Moral Economy of the English Crowd in the Eighteenth Century," *Past and Present*, No. 50 (February 1971), pp. 71-133.

context of Tokugawa rural society. It was a political act to attack the headman whose family, in all likelihood, had governed the village for generations and who, at least in his normative role, was the spokesman, agent, and benefactor of both individuals and the corporate community. The moneylenders, pawnbrokers, merchants, and landlords were also leading members of the village community. Unlike many peasant societies in which ethnic or religious minorities controlled commercial capital, they were the "old" families of the village and the heads of lineage and patron-client networks.

In many of the peasant uprisings of the late Tokugawa period it is difficult to document the degree to which "smashings" were consciously political acts. It can be demonstrated, however, that in the Aizu uprisings, the peasants knowingly and profoundly rejected the traditional village leadership and the economic arrangements through which the elite dominated the local economy. The nature of the rebellion and the underlying causes of conflict will become clearer when we examine the popular movement that followed the attacks. The data on this movement are to be found mainly in extant records of the resolutions that were adopted by peasants' assemblies in localities where the uprisings occurred. They are singularly important documents because they do not emanate from the elite stratum of headmen, merchants, intellectuals, and prosperous farmers whose household records, official reports, and private letters and diaries make up all but a fraction of the extant documentation on Tokugawa village life. In the resolutions of the assemblies, the many small proprietors who struggled daily merely to keep their land, pay taxes, and thus maintain their status in the village community, proposed specific and practical changes in the political and economic relationships that were of greatest consequence to their well-being. Drawing on the extensive research of Shōji Kichinosuke,[11] we will use these and related documents to analyze the conflicts that led to the attacks and the aims and aspirations of the peasants once they gained control of the village.

Early in December peasants from a number of villages in the Narahara department of Minamiaizu met to draw up a list of resolutions that defined the aims of their local movement. They resolved that: 1. *yonaoshi* is a matter to be decided by each department (*kumi*); 2. all village officials shall be replaced; 3. all the old land records and other village documents shall be confiscated; 4. small cultivators shall also be able to serve as chief headmen; 5. with the exception of land, which is to be

---

[11] The importance of Shōji Kichinosuke's pioneering research on regional peasant movements in the Tokugawa period cannot be overstated; I acknowledge my indebtedness to Professor Shōji's scholarship and particularly to *Yonaoshi ikki no kenkyū* (Tokyo, 1971).

dealt with separately, all pawned goods shall be redeemed without interest in five-year installments starting from this year, and the goods themselves shall be returned now; land is a matter to be deliberated upon by each department; 6. cash loans shall be repaid without interest in ten-year installments starting from this year; and 7. a meeting shall be held on December 20 at Yubara, and each village is expected to send two representatives.[12]

In other localities peasants convened assemblies and passed resolutions to give concrete expression to their aims. Documentation of the meetings is spotty and comes from five or six assemblies. A comparison of these materials reveals differences in the specific solutions proposed, but more importantly they reveal a concurrence of interest in several principal issues: they were concerned with the proper constituency of the movements, with reform of village government, with settlement of pawned goods and outstanding debts, and with a just treatment of mortgaged land and debt-tenancy (shitchi-kosaku).

As in the attacks against high-status peasants, the convening of popular assemblies occurred at the department level. Departments were administrative precincts whose boundaries were drawn early in the Tokugawa period. Each department contained lands with an official assessed output of 10,000 koku,[13] which in most areas represented twenty to thirty villages. In all, there were twenty-nine departments in Aizu proper, and twenty-seven that Aizu administered on behalf of Tokugawa government.[14]

The significance of the assemblies appears to be twofold: on the one hand, peasants gave popular sanction through formal (if temporary) organizational structures to the changes they wished to carry out; on the other hand, as Shōji Kichinosuke observes, the fact that mobilization occurred at a higher level than the village shows that they possessed more sophisticated political awareness and broader vision than is commonly ascribed to Tokugawa peasants.[15] It should be pointed out, however, that there is no evidence that they attempted to mobilize beyond the department. The small cultivators who carried out the movement in Aizu were not the parochial rustics who according to lore "knew nothing beyond the village hedges," but they were apparently not ca-

---

[12] SSANI, p. 360.

[13] A koku was a traditional unit of measure equal to 44.8 gallons. Under Tokugawa administration, landholdings were expressed in estimates of the yearly productivity, converted into koku of rice.

[14] Shōji Kichinosuke, Shiryō Tōhoku shohan hyakushō ikki no kenkyū (Tokyo, 1969), p. 8.

[15] Shōji, Yonaoshi ikki no kenkyū, pp. 120-121.

pable of organizing a domainwide movement. Perhaps they did not see the need.

The most radical action of the Aizu peasant movement was the wresting of village office from hereditary headmen. Unlike more economically advanced rural areas of Japan, where by the latter half of the Tokugawa period the election or rotation of the head village office had supplanted family succession, in Aizu the office passed from father to son within the oldest and wealthiest household in the village.[16] The rule by hereditary succession was strictly enforced by the *han*, which also granted headmen the right to have surnames and to bear arms—privileges normally reserved for members of the warrior class. Headmen possessed great power over the political and economic affairs of the village because they were the sole individuals qualified to represent the community in political appeals and financial transactions: the headman kept all village financial records, assessed and collected taxes and dues, sponsored all petitions and civil suits, mediated controversies within the community, and exercised magisterial powers in a wide variety of village affairs.

The wholesale ousting of headmen shows that small cultivators were dissatisfied with the system of village government in which authority was in effect part of the patrimony of the family that boasted the longest lineage and possessed the largest fields. They chose, moreover, to replace the old headmen with their social peers. Data on the holdings of the former headmen and those who came to power after the uprising reveal that the mean holding of the old headmen was twenty-five *koku*, compared to twelve *koku* for the new village leaders.[17] The difference was more than a difference in relative wealth. In Aizu, twelve *koku* represented the average household's holding and the amount of land that a family could cultivate with its own labor. To cultivate a twenty-five *koku* holding, on the other hand, required tenants, hired seasonal labor, or the services of household servants and poor relatives who were still economically dependent on the main branch of the family. Thus, the taking of office by the new headman marked the transfer of local political power to a class representative of the majority of the village community, and the process through which they came to power revealed a new concept of representation sanctioned by popular assemblies rather than by the decrees of the ruling class.

In addition to attacking the authority of the traditional village leaders,

---

[16] Professor Andō Seiichi pointed out to me that the persistence of the domination of village government by hereditary headmen in northeastern Japan may help to explain why *yonaoshi*-type uprisings occurred in this region but not in western Japan, where headmen were usually elected by the members of the village community.

[17] Shōji, *Yonaoshi ikki no kenkyū*, pp. 130-131, 135.

the assemblies also attempted to legislate more just economic relations within the local market economy. Their main concern was usurious short-term credit and the frequent loss of land and movable property as a consequence of peasants' inability to repay high-interest loans. Not all the proposals were the same, but without exception the assemblies demanded the immediate return of pawned goods. The assemblies that were convened in Takiya department of Onuma district and in the Ina region of Minamiaizu ordered the return of movable property without any compensation to the pawnshop owner; in Narahara, also in Minamiaizu, peasants acknowledged the obligation to repay the principal of the loan but not the interest. Some variation can also be seen in the resolutions dealing with outstanding debts. The Ina assembly canceled all past debts; the Takiya assembly canceled debts of more than two years' standing and ordered that other debts be repaid in ten-year installments; and the Narahara assembly ordered that all debts should be repaid without interest over the next ten years.[18]

As we saw earlier, the resolutions distinguished between mortgaged land and movable property. There was a broad consensus with respect to the treatment of pawned goods, but greater difference when it came to the land problem. Consistently the most radical, peasants in the Ina region of Minamiaizu ordered that the land be returned to the former owners. In Takiya department, however, the land was to remain in the possession of the mortgage holder and the rent canceled for one year. In Narahara, as we have seen, the resolution simply stated that the question of land was to be treated as a separate issue to be decided by each department. The intended meaning and the practical consequences of this are not entirely clear. Shōji Kichinosuke argues that the peasants intended to return all land lost through unredeemed loans to the original owners. As a legacy of Aizu's Kansei reform movement, each village kept two sets of land records. One showed the holdings recorded in 1813 when the domain attempted to equalize village holdings, and the other recorded the transfer of land through purchase and foreclosure. Shōji suggests that the peasants confiscated village land records with the intention of restoring to the holder of record in the 1813 surveys parcels of land lost through foreclosure.[19] However, except for the resolution passed by the assembly in the Ina region, there are few data to argue the point, and it does not appear that land redistribution was actually carried out.

The imperial army and the officials appointed by the Meiji government to administer the domain at first adopted a neutral attitude toward

---

[18] Ibid., pp. 120-121.
[19] Ibid., pp. 122-123.

the peasant movement. Some of the uprisings took place far from government troops. But even where soldiers were billeted nearby, as in Inawashiro, they did not attempt to protect the headmen or punish the attackers.[20] Probably recognizing that the movement was a series of local rebellions against village leaders rather than a domainwide uprising against their government, officials were more interested in restoring orderly administration than in intervening in intravillage disputes. When thirty-seven ousted headmen from Takahisa department petitioned the local government office (*minseikyoku*) asking to be reinstated, the officers replied that it was not an opportune time to make changes, since the villages were busy collecting taxes. Moreover, the new headmen had not proven themselves to be delinquent in the performance of official duties or to be guilty of improprieties.[21]

However, the hereditary headmen did not abandon their efforts to regain office. Acting individually and in concert, they used their very considerable wealth and political skills to recover their former positions. At the village level they employed a variety of stratagems, ranging from acts of public repentance and genuine conciliation to bribery and a barrage of civil suits.[22] They also campaigned at the department level to persuade the new regime, as they boasted in one petition, that "because for generation after generation we have continuously served the lord of the domain, we are knowledgeable in the ways of controlling peasants."[23] They received strong support from the former *gōgashira* (department intendants), hereditary officials of *gōshi* (country samurai) status who under the *han* had supervised the day-to-day administration of rural affairs. Unlike the headmen, the *gōgashira* had early been reappointed by the Meiji authorities, since without their assistance it would have been extremely difficult to carry out normal government functions.[24]

As noted earlier, the political struggle for village office paralleled the sharp division within the village between the wealthy elite of large landholders and moneylenders on the one hand, and the majority of small proprietors on the other hand. The eagerness of the old headmen to return to office was without question due in large part to the desire to protect their financial interests in the village, and the resistance to their campaign showed an equally strong desire on the part of poor peasants to protect their earlier gains.

At the same time, there was an ideological clash between two com-

[20] *SSANI*, pp. 332-333.
[21] Shōji, *Yonaoshi ikki no kenkyū*, p. 145.
[22] Cf. ibid., pp. 157-158; *SSANI*, pp. 332-333.
[23] Shōji, *Yonaoshi ikki no kenkyū*, p. 145.
[24] Ibid., p. 142.

peting notions of what constituted the legitimate basis for the exercise of local authority. The authority of the new headmen rested on the revolutionary act of ousting the old headmen and convening assemblies to give popular sanction to the election of new officials. The old headmen relied upon an entirely different set of normative principles to justify their claim to be the rightful representatives of the village. They admitted without apparent embarrassment that "the new headmen serve in accordance with the wishes of the villagers."[25] They argued, however, that their families' history of service to past rulers of the domain and their paternalistic concern for the welfare of the peasants made them uniquely qualified to serve as headmen:

> There are among us both ancient and more recently established lineages, but the great majority of us have ancestors who settled the villages and in this way came to serve as headmen. They were appointed to this office by the former lords of the domain, and for generation after generation the sons have been appointed to carry out the office. . . . Following the customs of old, we devoted ourselves to reclaiming fallow land and to increasing the number of people and horses within the realm. Though insufficient, we devoted ourselves wholeheartedly to the duty of nurturing the peasants under our rule.[26]

The *yonaoshi* movement in Aizu that followed the collapse of daimyo rule was a revolutionary movement by small proprietors and poor peasants who violently rejected the notion that the traditional political and economic hierarchy in the village adequately protected their vital interests. As we shall see, the peasants did not go one step further and attempt to "rectify" the larger relationships between themselves and the national polity. Nevertheless, it was a genuinely revolutionary movement because at the level of the village, as well as the domain, the ideology of Tokugawa rule rested on the norm of benevolence and the assumption that the obligation of superiors to render benevolent attention to the needs of their charges transcended class interests.[27] When the institutions of daimyo rule disintegrated before their eyes, in many localities the peasants of Aizu established popular representation in village government and attempted to legislate changes in economic relationships that were designed to protect their interests as small proprietors.

The "world" of the revolutionary peasant movement in Aizu, however, was the village and not the state. When the peasants petitioned the Meiji authorities to ask for changes in the government's regulations and policies, their appeals were in form and content similar to the demands

---

[25] *SSANI*, pp. 332-333.
[26] Ibid.
[27] Scheiner, "Benevolent Lords," pp. 50-52.

frequently voiced in Tokugawa peasant appeals. They did not confront the new government with radical demands such as equal legal status with samurai, representation in the national government, or an end to feudal taxes and dues. Rather, their petitions stayed well within the bounds of traditional peasant demands. They asked for tax reductions because of the poor harvest, the devastation of crops, and the requisitioning of food; they requested changes in the procedures for tax collection to prevent speculation by middle-level officials; they appealed to the government to abolish monopolies on wax, lacquer, and other special products; and they demanded compensation for the services they rendered to the imperial army.[28] In essence, they made the same kind of appeals to the Meiji government that they were accustomed to making to seignorial authority.

It has been shown that in the *yonaoshi* movement peasants put forth new norms for the exercise of local political power. As would be expected of a bold assertion of rights, the resolutions adopted by the popular assemblies were declarative sentences; for example, "*Nanushi yaku . . . subete tatekae*" (all headmen shall be replaced).[29] In accepting the authority of the Meiji government, however, peasants appear to have assumed the same political and psychological posture toward the new state as they had toward seignorial authority. The petitions were rendered in the subjunctive: "*Onengu no gi, tō ikka nen wa nengunashi ni osetsukekudasaretaku*" (it is [our] hope that [those above] will order the suspension of taxes for one year).[30] They still looked to the state for benevolence.

By emphasizing the political and ideological dimensions of the Aizu peasant movement, I have argued that it was a revolutionary movement and noted that it occurred at the very moment that on the national level Japan was shedding its feudal past. However, there were precise limits to the "revolution." It was a revolt by small cultivators and the poorer members of the village community against the political and economic elite. In the disturbed economic conditions of the closing years of the Tokugawa period, the primary concern of the participants in the movements was to protect their status as small peasant proprietors against the forces that posed the greatest threat to their daily survival.[31] As a

[28] Shōji, *Yonaoshi ikki no kenkyū*, pp. 120-121.

[29] *SSANI*, p. 360.

[30] Ibid., p. 361.

[31] Sasaki Junnosuke's skillful and imaginative class analysis of *yonaoshi* uprisings contributed greatly to my understanding of the Aizu peasant movement. In addition to his earlier cited work, see "Yonaoshi no jōkyō," *Kōza Nihon shi*, 5 (Tokyo, 1970), 87-112. Professor Sasaki characterizes *yonaoshi* as movements that mobilized peasants who lived in constant and acute fear that they would lose their land and movable property and thereby be reduced to landless laborers. The overriding concern of most peasants in the

consequence, peasant violence turned against high-status peasants rather than against seignorial and state authority. The goals of the movement in Aizu were political as well as economic, but the boundaries of the movement reflected the particular class interests of peasants with small or marginal holdings. We end, therefore, with the phenomenon of the peasants who sacked village officials and convened popular assemblies appealing to the Meiji government for benevolence.

---

late Tokugawa period was therefore to maintain and protect their status as independent cultivators working their own holdings. This concern limited the political character and potential of *yonaoshi* movements to the "restoring" of the village community; the "small producer" class character of the *yonaoshi* movements determined the limits of the rebellions.

PURSUING THE MILLENNIUM
IN THE MEIJI
RESTORATION

George Wilson

Great events in world history do not merely leave traces. They erupt onto the scene as stunning transformations generated out of the existing structures and resources of society. So it is with the Meiji Restoration of 1868 in Japan. The date is too limiting, the concept of "restoration" too narrow, to comprehend so vast a transformation.

But analysts of the Restoration have seemed to be preoccupied with the nature of the transition from bakufu to imperial rule, from a late feudal military system headed by the Tokugawa house at Edo to an early national state led by a "sovereign emperor." Whether praising or condemning the outcome, Restoration scholars rarely fail to dwell on the smoothness of transition, the relatively bloodless ease with which the new regime came to power and began to act. In explanation of this ease of transition, they point to the docility of the Japanese people, to their traditional habits of discipline, or to the frustration of the forces of bourgeois revolution.[1] Yet in the wake of the Meiji Restoration, Ja-

[1] The most representative composite analysis of the state of the art in recent Meiji Restoration studies by leading Japanese scholars is Ōishi Ka'ichirō et al., *Meiji ishin*, vol. 5 of *Kōza Nihon shi* (Tokyo, 1970). A joint product of two influential organizations of Japanese historians, the Rekishigaku Kenkyūkai and the Nihon Shi Kenkyūkai, this volume is part of a set of ten volumes that tell much about prevailing Japanese standards and perceptions of historical study. The conflict model of social change, which is evident throughout the volume on the Meiji Restoration, derives from a basically Marxist dialectical approach to history. It has characterized Japanese historiography since the 1930s and especially since the end of World War II. Western writers on the Restoration have tended to use a consensus model of social and historical change, thereby emphasizing the strong

pan changed from an insular society into a world power within four decades. The magnitude of the Meiji Restoration's consequences compels us to seek a more dramatic answer than docility or discipline to the conundrum of Japan's smooth passage from a feudal polity to a new nation. The two decades prior to the Restoration are known by the generic periodizing code word bakumatsu—"the end of the bakufu." And these bakumatsu years had witnessed the release of great intensity and energy that did not simply dissipate as a result of invoking the symbolic authority of the Japanese imperial house in order to unify Japan. Sir George Sansom was right to note the mystery: "From this welter of contradictions a solution presently emerges, nobody can say exactly how or why. Things and ideas cease their demented gyrations and fall into their appointed place." But Sansom was wrong to adduce the analogy of a dream, as if waking up could dispel the confusion: "The dream is over, and the country is united under one leadership."[2]

The temptation to rest with easy answers perhaps arises from the rational cause-and-effect procedures of narrative reconstruction by means of which historians of sharply differing ideological persuasions look at the Meiji Restoration. They see the Meiji leaders enmeshed in Machiavellian politics, and they know that there were people who harbored various kinds of discontent roaming the land, stirring up rural as well as urban turmoil. The resolution of struggles within the elite, and the suppression of political countermovements, made the new government's tasks look deceptively simple. What is missing here is attention to the much more dynamic manifestations of the popular anxiety that permeated the entire atmosphere of these tumultuous years. Throughout the country in the mid-1860s, throngs of pilgrims congregated at religious sites, especially the temple complex at Ise in central Japan, where the regalia and mystique of the mythical past of Japan's imperial house resided. Public pilgrimages to sacred places such as the Grand Shrine at Ise were periodic features of Japanese history that had gone on at least since the late sixteenth century.[3] What changed in the 1860s was

collective ethos of Japanese groups and communities. For an overview of the Restoration period, see Marius B. Jansen, "The Meiji State: 1868-1912," in James B. Crowley, ed., *Modern East Asia: Essays in Interpretation* (New York: Harcourt, Brace and World, 1970), pp. 95-121. For another statement of the historiographical division—similar to the one presented here—see John Whitney Hall, "Japanese History in World Perspective," in Charles F. Delzell, ed., *The Future of History* (Nashville: Vanderbilt University Press, 1977), pp. 183-184.

[2] G. B. Sansom, *The Western World and Japan* (New York: Alfred A. Knopf, 1950), p. 281.

[3] Yasumaru Yoshio, " 'Okagemairi' to 'ee ja nai ka,' " in Shōji Kichinosuke, Hayashi Motoi, and Yasumaru Yoshio, eds., *Minshū undō no shisō*, vol. 58 of *Nihon shisō taikei* (Tokyo, 1970), p. 494.

the intensity of the pilgrims, whose behavior often verged on the hysterical.[4] The last mammoth convergence of pilgrims on Ise had occurred in 1830, but in the 1860s new or revitalized religious sects exploded onto the scene in central Japan, along with the usual crowds of pilgrims. Peasant uprisings (hyakushō ikki) rose in number until the peak year of 1866, displaying utopian or yonaoshi features that were uniquely intense during this decade.[5] Meanwhile, urban carnivals competed with riots, burnings, and trashings for public notice, and revelers or rioters made a shambles of many a downtown area as they danced and sang about a better life to come. Victor Turner calls pilgrimages and related communal movements "liminal phenomena," associated with revival, or sometimes with rejection, of the existing order: "A limen is . . . a 'threshold.' A pilgrimage center, from the standpoint of the believing actor, also represents a threshold, a place and moment 'in and out of time,' and such an actor . . . hopes to have there direct experience of the sacred, or supernatural order."[6]

These are the signs of millenarianism. Yet they tend to be neglected in the explanatory strategies of social scientists and historians. Western theorists of millenarian activity are partly to blame for this omission, because some of them have argued that Buddhist theology is passive and cyclical in nature, and therefore precludes the coming of the millennium even if salvation can be accessible in another life.[7] Millenarianism, or millennialism, as used in this essay, follows the sensitive and profound treatment given to the subject by the sociologist Yonina Talmon.[8] At the most fundamental level, she defines millenarian as an attribute applied "typologically, to characterize religious movements that expect imminent, total, ultimate, this-worldly, collective salvation."[9] Another definition applicable to the usage in this essay is Peter Worsley's: "I use the term 'millenarian' to describe those movements in which there is an expectation of, and preparation for, the coming of a

[4] Ibid., pp. 495-496. For a survey of "thanksgiving" (okagemairi or nukemairi) pilgrimage phenomena during the entire Tokugawa period, see Fujitani Toshio, "Okagemairi" to "ee ja nai ka" (Tokyo, 1968), pp. 35-103.

[5] Classic statements on these risings are Hayashi Motoi, Hyakushō ikki no dentō (Tokyo, 1955) and Zoku hyakushō ikki no dentō (Tokyo, 1971); and Shōji Kichinosuke, Yonaoshi ikki no kenkyū, 2nd ed. (Tokyo, 1970).

[6] Victor Turner, "Pilgrimages as Social Processes," in his Dramas, Fields, and Metaphors: Symbolic Action in Human Societies (Ithaca: Cornell University Press, 1974), pp. 166, 197.

[7] For example, Yonina Talmon, "Millenarism," International Encyclopedia of the Social Sciences (New York: Macmillan-Free Press, 1968), 10:357; and E. J. Hobsbawm, Primitive Rebels: Studies in Archaic Forms of Social Movement in the Nineteenth and Twentieth Centuries (New York: Frederick A. Praeger, 1963), pp. 57-58.

[8] Talmon, "Millenarism," pp. 349-362.

[9] Ibid., p. 349.

period of supernatural bliss. . . . The term, in my use, includes both those movements which anticipate that the millennium will occur solely as a result of supernatural intervention, and those which envisage that the action of human beings will be necessary."[10] Worsley adds a pointed reminder: "Millenarian beliefs have recurred again and again throughout history, despite failures, disappointments, and repression, precisely because they make such a strong appeal to the oppressed, the disinherited and the wretched. They therefore form an integral part of that stream of thought which refused to accept the rule of a superordinate class, or of a foreign power, or some combination of both, as in Taiping China."[11]

APOCALYPSE AND ARTIFICE IN LIMINAL PERIODS

The revolutionary potential of the Japanese social fabric may be inferred from a study of the millenarian combination of conservative and innovative impulses that culminated in the Meiji Restoration. Looking not at the origin or development of Japanese millenarian phenomena but at their eruption into the ambience of foreign and domestic strife during the 1850s and 1860s, I will contend in this essay that the reformers associated with the bakufu and the fanatic imperial restorers whose activities helped make way for the new regime must be viewed in context with the many hundred thousands of rural and urban people whose millennial aspirations expressed their anxiety about their own future and that of Japan. Both the samurai elite and the popular movements were groping for a new and stable order.

Millenarian movements partake of both historical and mythical time, accepting history as linear but believing that divine intervention will somehow stop an intolerable present and restore political and social well-being.[12] In the context of the social hierarchy of the Tokugawa period, millenarian pressure from "lower" status groups may have emboldened unhappy elements within the samurai elite and diminished the effectiveness of the gradualist reforms pursued by the Tokugawa bakufu and its allies. The survivors—those "zealots" (shishi) who had to build the new order—may not have been fanatics, but they did inherit the millenarian ardor of their fallen comrades who had glorified mythic Japanese tradition and called for political power to be returned to the emperor. The Meiji leaders thus found it both expedient and legitimate to manipulate the imperial symbol as they worked to construct a new order that was at once revolutionary and traditional because of the transformed nativ-

---

[10] Peter Worsley, *The Trumpet Shall Sound: A Study of "Cargo Cults" in Melanesia*, 2nd ed. rev. (New York: Schocken Books, 1968), p. 12.

[11] Ibid., p. 225.

[12] Talmon, "Millenarism," pp. 351-352.

ism (*kokugaku*) on which it was based.[13] If the revolutionary component in this mixture was muted because traditional values played so large a part, it was nonetheless present, and it was also a constant threat to erupt again among unstable or ambitious groups within the populace.

It is true, of course, that strong and visionary leadership came to the fore from among elements of the samurai status group, and without such leadership Japan might have foundered in the effort to deal with challenges both at home and abroad.[14] It is also evident that decades-long social change in city and countryside had prepared Japanese of many walks of life to assume new roles suitable for rapid industrialization.[15] These conditions of elite readiness and a general distribution of skills, including literacy, throughout the populace do not, however, suffice to account for Japan's sudden conversion into a new nation.

Turning outside Japan, any attempt to identify the Western powers as colonialist precipitants or catalysts of change in Japan only compounds the problem. Such causal attribution to the foreigners has the effect of mistaking the catalyst of many confused reactions for the producer of one vast "national" response. If anything, the external threat heightened internal tensions, reduced the normal capacity of the political system to cope with divisive issues, and led to a stalemate in politics just when social and economic change was quickening. The chaotic situation yielded what Conrad Totman has newly characterized as a "systemic crisis" precipitated by the Western "imperialist intrusion" of the 1850s and 1860s, and by the novel demands placed upon the bakufu by Japanese who were anxious to respond to this intrusion.[16] But the West deserves no credit for causing a powerful centralized system to constitute itself out of a social and political structure in disarray: it was the

[13] Ibid., pp. 353, 360; Talmon argues forcibly that millenarian movements are both revolutionary and traditional: yearning for a lost past, they await an entirely new future.

[14] See, for example, John Whitney Hall, *Japan: From Prehistory to Modern Times* (New York: Delacorte Press, 1970), pp. 265-272.

[15] The leading Western architect of the thesis that the Tokugawa period witnessed the gradual but sure rise of the socioeconomic preconditions for effective and sustained industrial development is probably Thomas C. Smith; see especially his *The Agrarian Origins of Modern Japan* (Stanford: Stanford University Press, 1959) and *Nakahara: Family Farming and Population in a Japanese Village, 1717-1830* (Stanford: Stanford University Press, 1977). See also Susan B. Hanley and Kozo Yamamura, *Economic and Demographic Change in Preindustrial Japan, 1600-1868* (Princeton: Princeton University Press, 1977).

[16] Conrad D. Totman, *The Collapse of the Tokugawa Bakufu, 1862-1868* (Honolulu: University Press of Hawaii, 1980), pp. xiii-xv, 479-481. This argument can be strengthened by applying the concept of systemic crisis elaborated by Jürgen Habermas, *Legitimation Crisis*, translated by Thomas McCarthy (Boston: Beacon Press, 1975), parts 1-2, especially "Theorems of Legitimation Crisis" (pp. 68-75) and "Theorems of Motivation Crisis" (pp. 75-92).

disarray—not the new regime and its actions—that stemmed from the Western intrusion into Japan.

Why should any part of the ruling elite pursue radical political reorganization and put its own status at risk?[17] What was it that so alarmed some Japanese leaders that they experimented with drastic new policies, even though they clothed them fastidiously in the raiment of tradition? One of the answers to these questions is that popular millennialism on a wide scale affected both popular consciousness and the samurai sense of propriety, chipping away at the authority of the Tokugawa system based on the bakufu at Edo and the more than 250 domains—the "feudal" han. The profusion of millenarian manifestations helps us to understand the slide from anti-bakufu hostility among some samurai to revolutionary action by a new government using "traditional" ideas reworked for mid-nineteenth-century purposes. Popular millennialism frightened all samurai. But those samurai whose own ideas made them receptive to substantive change could alter their programs to accommodate a modicum of popular hopes; at the same time, they could still keep the lid on revolutionary violence. Some of the more radically disaffected samurai who were influenced by the thinking of the late Mito school fit this pattern.[18] The acts that the Japanese feared the imperialists might commit, which inspired millenarian dreams of redemption and utopia, would demand rapid responses. This situation prevented the popular movements from gaining either the time or the space necessary to organize altogether novel policies. Japan's reconstruction by means of transforming extant sociopolitical mechanisms was more important than laying master plans for a new society. Yet the result might have seemed to be the same, so sharp were the Meiji state's departures from past practice. Its mixture of revolutionary energy and traditional values met the demands of the situation. And as the new state built up its authority, not only popular ambitions but also those of the samurai themselves were sacrificed in the name of national unity and industrial development. The old elite thus had to transform itself as well as the country, but it did so in accord with the latent potentialities that were generated within the matrix of Tokugawa society.[19]

[17] See Thomas C. Smith, "Japan's Aristocratic Revolution," Yale Review, 50 (1960-1961): 370-383. Smith answers this question along comparative lines, contrasting the landless condition of the Japanese samurai with the landholding privileges of the French aristocracy. The samurai as a status group, in fine, had less to lose than other elites elsewhere, so they revolutionized the country before the new situation could sweep them aside.

[18] This is the gist of a canny argument put forward by Ueyama Shunpei, "Meiji ishin no kakumeisei: ishin to sonnō jōi shisō," in his Meiji ishin no bunseki shiten (Tokyo, 1968), pp. 7-41, especially pp. 20-37 passim.

[19] In English there are now many books and articles that illustrate the range and depth of social change in Tokugawa Japan. The best volume drawing together a persuasive

No one can find it surprising that the years from the melodrama of Commodore Matthew Calbraith Perry's arrival in 1853 to the consummation of political reorganization in 1868 and thereafter witnessed an explosion of millennial hopes and dreams among the Japanese people. The times were already in transition: to underscore the temporal notion of threshold as used by Victor Turner, we may say that a liminal period of uncertain duration had come to Japan.[20] Folkways and politics both suffered from disturbances of routine, and stirrings of nationalism affected people far and wide, high and low. Cities underwent calamitous changes, fortuitous as in the great Edo fire of 1855, and disingenuous as in Edo's depopulation after the bakufu's 1862 edict relaxing alternate attendance (sankin kōtai) obligations on the part of the domanial rulers, the daimyo. Economic competition fired by the coming of foreign trade disrupted local industries and regional commercial networks. The movement of farmers from place to place unsettled a populace that had never dealt with outsiders or an infusion of nontraditional values. A paradigm of a way of life was in danger of decomposing, and although most responses fell within accepted norms there were many others that did not.

The frightened, the frustrated and humiliated, and the economically deprived and distressed segments of Japanese society looked to millennial hopes for respite from their plight, and they anticipated a renewal of peace and tranquility. These phrases with differing emphases resonate through both elite and popular tracts for the times.[21] Not a few authors

sample of articles in this vein is John W. Hall and Marius B. Jansen, eds., *Studies in the Institutional History of Early Modern Japan* (Princeton: Princeton University Press, 1968).

[20] Turner, "Pilgrimages as Social Processes," p. 197. See also Victor W. Turner, "Myth and Symbol," *International Encyclopedia of the Social Sciences* (New York: Macmillan-Free Press, 1968), 10:576-577.

[21] An enormous published body of literature exists in Japanese to illustrate this matter of "tracts for the times." The most cogent and accessible starting point may be Iwanami's massive *Nihon shisō taikei*, 67 vols. (Tokyo, 1970-   ). Many of the later volumes in this huge set gather and present the essays of theorists and politicians and pundits as well as the documents relating to the rise of new religious sects, riots and uprisings, trashings and burnings, political trends, and other manifestations of social change. Important volumes in this regard include: vol. 50, Tahara Tsuguo et al., eds., *Hirata Atsutane / Ban Nobutomo / Ōkuni Takamasa* (1973); vol. 51, Haga Noboru and Matsumoto Sannosuke, eds., *Kokugaku undō no shisō* (1971); vol. 52, Naramoto Tatsuya and Nakai Nobuhiko, eds., *Ninomiya Sontoku / Ōhara Yūgaku* (1973); vol. 56, Yoshida Tsunekichi and Satō Seizaburō, eds., *Bakumatsu seiji ronshū* (1976); vol. 58, Shōji, Hayashi, and Yasumaru, *Minshū undō no shisō*; and vol. 67, Murakami Shigeyoshi and Yasumaru Yoshio, eds., *Minshū shūkyō no shisō* (1971). Excellent commentaries accompany the texts, and three such commentaries that are crucially important to the theme of this essay are: 1. on popular movements in general, including pilgrimages, Yasumaru Yoshio, "Minshū undō no shisō," 58:391-436; 2. on the relation of nativism (kokugaku) to "world renewal" (yonaoshi) phenomena, Haga Noboru, "Bakumatsu henkaku ki ni okeru kokugakusha no

found it convenient to depict utopian solutions to remedy present dislocations. Others, like the anonymous Osaka physician who chronicled
the turbulence of the age in *Ukiyo no arisama* ("The Way the Floating
World Is"), chose to record the events that animated people's anxieties
without much comment on how they might be ameliorated.[22] Among
disenchanted elements of the samurai elite as well as the general public,
various beliefs arose about the ways in which a new dispensation might
be revealed.

MILLENNIAL DREAMS AS MODELS OF SOCIAL ACTION

Tradition suffuses millenarian movements just as surely as utopia colors
all revolutionary programs. Relief from deprivation or frustration stands
as a ubiquitous millennial goal.[23] Its achievement may come about in
many ways, sometimes involving the public at large, sometimes only
the true believers, sometimes just the activist few. The agent of millennial dreams may be a prophet or a messiah. Consider, for example, the
astonishing role of Amakusa Shirō Tokisada, a veritable masculine Japanese version of Joan of Arc in the so-called Shimabara Rebellion of

---

undō to ronri: toku ni yonaoshi jōkyō to kanrensasete," 51:662–714; and 3. on new religions and cults, Murakami Shigeyoshi, "Bakumatsu ishin ki no minshū shūkyō ni tsuite,"
67:563–570; Murakami here stresses the politicization of the new religions, especially Tenrikyō, and their utopian, *yonaoshi* type of orientation (see p. 569).

[22] Some new historians such as Michel Foucault tell us that we need not know the
author of a text, or even the author's background and probable intent in writing a text.
See, for example, Foucault's "What Is an Author?" in his *Language, Counter-Memory,
Practice: Selected Essays and Interviews*, translated by Donald F. Bouchard and Sherry Simon
(Ithaca: Cornell University Press, 1977), pp. 113-138. *Ukiyo no arisama* is a case in point.
With no special fanfare it records the tides of popular thinking and general Japanese reactions to famines, earthquakes, sightings of foreign ships, and *okagemairi* phenomena
from 1806 to about 1845. All we know is that the author was a fairly affluent physician
who practiced in Osaka and originally hailed from Katsuyama *han* in Mimasaka. Yasumaru, " 'Okagemairi' to 'ee ja nai ka,' " pp. 497-498. The text of that part of *Ukiyo no
arisama* which deals with *okagemairi* and *hyakushō ikki* across most of the four decades
covered by the work is contained in Shōji, Hayashi, and Yasumaru, *Minshū undō no shisō*,
pp. 307-372.

[23] Deprivation that is absolute may elicit less fervent manifestations of millenarianism
than "relative deprivation": when expectations are not fulfilled and ordinary conditions
of life deteriorate, the immediate losers react more fiercely than do society's perennial
outcasts. See Talmon, "Millenarism," pp. 354-355, and David F. Aberle, "A Note on
Relative Deprivation Theory as Applied to Millenarian and Other Cult Movements," in
Sylvia L. Thrupp, ed., *Millennial Dreams in Action: Essays in Comparative History* (The
Hague, 1962), pp. 209-214. But see Worsley, *The Trumpet Shall Sound*, pp. xxxix-xlii,
for a theoretical consideration of "deprivation" versus "relative deprivation" and a spirited
defense of his own thesis that "the disinherited" are the typical carriers of millenarianism.

1637-1638.[24] The rising of Shimabara, an economically deprived provincial community of embattled converts to Catholic Christianity in a forsaken corner of western Kyushu, provoked so savage a destruction by the Tokugawa forces that Tokisada's Christian banner, tattered but whole, was one of the few relics (or even "rebels," for that matter) that survived. Though he and the 37,000 people he led could not prevail over the vast forces that the bakufu deployed against them, Tokisada reflected millennial hopes of redemption in an impossible situation and is remembered as a tragic hero in the annals of Japanese history. This is so even though the faith he died for was alien to Japan, a fact that George Elison remarks when he writes, "Tokisada [was] spiritually twice beyond the pale"—in the eyes of Rome, a "new Christian" (that is, former heathen) and also a chiliast.[25] Indeed, Tokisada was doubly antinomian, too, in the eyes of Edo—convert to an alien religion and rebel against the social order.

But more often the agent of millennial dreams is a collectivity. The mid-nineteenth century Japanese conceptions about relief may be seen in phenomena ranging from the rise of new religious sects and cult behavior to mob outbursts and mass pilgrimages and carnivals in the city streets. Long the realm of religious studies specialists, these phenomena fit into types of active and passive millenarian behavior that could at the time serve as models to be followed.[26] Such action models also provoked countermeasures designed to exploit, contain, or combat them. Historians should also take a hand in studying them and working them into the modes of historical explanation and interpretation that are used in treating this period of Japanese history.

In the countryside, the millennial aspirations of farming communities appeared as efforts to reorganize and improve agriculture. Increasingly, too, there were pilgrimages of thanksgiving (okagemairi or nukemairi) to local, regional, and "national" cultural and religious centers, such as the Grand Shrine at Ise.[27] The foremost nativist scholar (kokugakusha), Mo-

---

[24] On Tokisada and his role in the "rebellion" at Shimabara, see George Elison, Deus Destroyed: The Image of Christianity in Early Modern Japan (Cambridge: Harvard University Press, 1973), pp. 217-221. See also chapter 7 of Ivan Morris, The Nobility of Failure: Tragic Heroes in the History of Japan (New York: Holt, Rinehart and Winston, 1975), pp. 143-179.

[25] Elison, Deus Destroyed, p. 221.

[26] On the distinction between "active" and "passive" millenarian movements, see Worsley, The Trumpet Shall Sound, pp. 12, 236. A generally similar line of argument is advanced by Tanaka Akira, Meiji ishin, vol. 24 of Nihon no rekishi (Tokyo, 1976), pp. 33-35, where Tanaka adapts from the scholarship of Nishigaki Seiji.

[27] See W. G. Beasley, The Meiji Restoration (Stanford University Press, 1972), pp. 217-218, for a discussion of a high-level plan to mount an imperial pilgrimage to Ise in the early 1860s, which had to be called off because of the dangers involved.

toori Norinaga, who lived from 1730 to 1801, was so impressed by the numbers he found recorded in documents he was studying that he left his own account of the coming of huge throngs of pilgrims who had arrived at Ise in 1705, when 3,620,000 people are said to have visited the temple complex in one fifty-day period.[28] Pilgrims also clogged the roads in the 1860s, even as new religious sects such as Tenrikyō and Konkōkyō began to attract mass followings.[29] Central Japan, as access and egress for Ise and the site of the rise of most new religious movements, was particularly affected. But riots, ostensibly concerning economic issues, also marked the bakumatsu years. Food prices climbed, tax collection too often became arbitrary, and local market relations sometimes fell into a disheveled state. The number of peasant uprisings rose sharply in the decade before the Restoration, reaching a high point in the year 1866, when at least 106 outbreaks qualify as *hyakushō ikki*.[30] A millennial content infused these 1866 risings when they called for a kind of utopian *yonaoshi*—"world renewal."[31] Only at their peril could bakufu and *han* authorities overlook such uprisings, yet they proved

[28] Motoori offered his observations in an extended exercise in social commentary entitled *Tama katsuma*, written during the final decade of his life. Yoshikawa Kōjirō, Satake Akihiro, and Hino Tatsuo, eds., *Motoori Norinaga*, vol. 40 of *Nihon shisō taikei* (Tokyo, 1978), p. 82. *Okagemairi* and *nukemairi* are virtually synonymous. The distinction between them is a subtle one involving intrafamily relations; it is discussed in the commentary found ibid. See also Fujitani, *"Okagemairi" to "ee ja nai ka,"* pp. 38-48.

[29] The new religions require attention that I cannot pay them here. For a full rehearsal of the rise of all the new religious movements in the nineteenth century, see Murakami Shigeyoshi, *Kindai minshū shūkyō shi no kenkyū*, 2nd ed. rev. (Tokyo, 1963); and, in English, Murakami's *Japanese Religion in the Modern Century*, translated by H. Byron Earhart (Tokyo, 1980), pp. 4-32, 44-51.

[30] Shibahara Takuji, *Kaikoku*, vol. 23 of *Nihon no rekishi* (Tokyo, 1975), p. 332.

[31] See Irwin Scheiner, "Benevolent Lords and Honorable Peasants: Rebellion and Peasant Consciousness in Tokugawa Japan," in Tetsuo Najita and Irwin Scheiner, eds., *Japanese Thought in the Tokugawa Period, 1600-1868: Methods and Metaphors* (Chicago: University of Chicago Press, 1978), pp. 39-62 passim. It was Scheiner who coined "world renewal" as a translation for *yonaoshi*: "The Mindful Peasant: Sketches for a Study of Rebellion," *Journal of Asian Studies*, 32 (1972-1973): 582. A word almost identical to *yonaoshi*—*yonaori*—was often used as a synonym, depending partly on regional variations of word usage within Japan. There is a difference, perhaps, in the sense that *yonaori* connotes the normal changes of rural and agricultural life, not the radical departures that natural disasters such as floods, famines, or earthquakes and social upheavals brought about. *Yonaori* might as well be translated into English as "world renewal"—just as *yonaoshi* is—but with the awareness that *yonaori* implies the cyclical changing of the seasons and the "times of this world," and not the revitalization concept embedded in the notion of *yonaoshi*. This distinction, common in Japanese secondary sources, is clearly rendered by Miyata Noboru, "Nōson no fukkō undō to minshū shūkyō no tenkai," in *Kinsei 5*, vol. 13 of *Iwanami kōza Nihon rekishi* (Tokyo, 1977), pp. 230-233. The distinction between *yonaoshi* and *yonaori* is also considered by Takagi Shunsuke, *Ee ja nai ka* (Tokyo, 1979), pp. 228-231.

impossible to suppress altogether, and they went on happening even after the Restoration. Despite the prevalence of destruction over construction as a goal of such outbursts, and despite the important role of frustration in triggering them, they did afford opportunities to vent the tensions within a community, and they became "causes" with which to identify in opposition to the existing system.

In the cities, violent demonstrations (*uchikowashi* or *yakiharai*) were directed against rice merchants, sake dealers, pawnbrokers, absentee landlords and others who were seen as exploiters of the urban poor.[32] Even the less violent but strictly antinomian behavior of city crowds as the old order ended in 1867 and 1868 struck fear into the authorities, perplexed the foreign observers, and maintained an underlying destabilization that prompted the adoption of firm new political policies after the new government took power. The appearance of carnivalers in the streets on the eve of the Restoration, shouting crude rhymes ending in catch phrases like *ee ja nai ka* ("Isn't this great!" or "Right on!") and engaging in transvestite and hysterical trancelike behavior, led to summary suppression once the Restoration had occurred.[33]

The crucial importance of these *ee ja nai ka* outbursts has not received adequate attention. Occurring in the cities that the bakufu had to control at the time when its political authority was unraveling, the orgiastic hysteria of the *ee ja nai ka* carnivalers created havoc for leaders who were attempting in vain to return Japan to some sort of stability under

[32] Shibahara, *Kaikoku*, pp. 332-333, graphs thirty-five urban disturbances onto his narrative about the peak year of 1866.

[33] Western writers rarely linger to consider the potency of *ee ja nai ka* and related signs of popular energy. (An exception is E. H. Norman, "Feudal Background of Japanese Politics," a paper presented in 1945, in John W. Dower, ed., *Origins of the Modern Japanese State: Selected Writings of E. H. Norman* [New York: Pantheon Books, 1975], pp. 342-352.) *Ee ja nai ka* is mentioned by Beasley, *The Meiji Restoration*, pp. 292-293, and by Totman, *The Collapse of the Tokugawa Bakufu*, pp. 377-379. Totman goes on to call *ee ja nai ka* "qualitatively different" from *yonaoshi* movements (ibid., pp. 531-532 n. 9). But Japanese historians who pause to reflect on *ee ja nai ka* are not so quick to separate the basically joyous, carnival-like atmosphere of the city revels from the utopian disturbances in the countryside. Takagi, *Ee ja nai ka*, p. 233, agrees that the *hyakushō ikki* have a different character from that of *ee ja nai ka*, but he also calls *ee ja nai ka* "one essential element" in the *yonaoshi* situation (ibid.). He adds that the *ee ja nai ka* crowds of mid-1867 through spring 1868 even had political overtones in that the urban revelers welcomed Satsuma and Chōshū troops who went against bakufu forces in 1868. And Tanaka, *Meiji ishin*, pp. 32-33, calls *yonaoshi* and *ee ja nai ka* "indivisible," but he does point out that no matter how the anti-bakufu forces might have manipulated the urban demonstrators, or used them as a "smokescreen," they were far too widespread to be mere fabrications (ibid., pp. 31-32). See also Yasumaru, "Minshū undō no shisō," p. 391: "As the apex [of popular ambition to break away from the old order], there is the series of *yonaoshi* uprisings of 1866, and there is '*ee ja nai ka*' of 1867, which expressed *yonaoshi* aspirations in a form different from [that of] the uprisings."

bakufu auspices. Yasumaru Yoshio goes so far as to say that the *ee ja nai ka* frenzies "had the effect of temporarily paralyzing the bakufu's system of rule" and constituted a "gusher" of popular millennial aspirations coincidentally spouting forth right in the "central region [where the] bakumatsu political wars" were being played out.[34]

The rabble and hoi polloi found unwilling allies among samurai who had become enraged by the bakufu's tolerance of foreign intervention in Japanese affairs. Cut off from the realities of high-level politics and international negotiations, samurai agitators began calling for a crusade of ethnic redemption that embraced all of Japan.[35] The nativist impulse for such feelings, justified earlier on a rational level by Confucian precepts holding that things must bear their right names and people assume their proper relationships, easily shifted into Japanese nationalism, a supradomainal, suprafeudal political faith requiring new forms of organization and renewed traditional institutions that would raise Japan's reputation in the eyes of a predatory world. To save the country's honor became an unintentionally revolutionary goal—and a decisively millenarian one.

Crisis and the Ironic Fate of the Bakufu Reformers

Most accounts of bakufu and *han* politics during these years stress the vacillations and indecision of policy makers. We need not be so condescending. Faced by unprecedented problems from abroad and a cacophony of demands at home, leaders responded in various ways to meet constantly changing circumstances. These responses were neither good nor bad—just effective or ineffective—and more often than not demonstrated greater knowledge and willingness to make changes than critics recognized or would have favored. Caught in the vortex, obliged to make decisions, the reform-minded bureaucrats who prepared most bakufu policies in Edo adopted programs intended to change Japan, but the inevitable confrontations of the age had rendered this kind of gradualism both unattractive and unattainable. The time constraints were too rigid; they demanded quick action. The fate that befell the establishment was a function of routine processes overtaken by the imperatives of catastrophic events. No matter how affirmative the responses were meant to be, their authors could not get them off the ground

[34] Yasumaru, " 'Okagemairi' to 'ee ja nai ka,' " p. 496. It is ironic that the urban carnivals occurred during a pause in the upsurge of rural unrest. The graph used by Shibahara, *Kaikoku*, p. 333, shows that only 34 *hyakushō ikki* are recorded in 1867, sandwiched between 106 in 1866 and 108 in 1868—the highest points of the entire decade.

[35] The importance of the "ethnic" (not "xenophobic") aspect of this crusade is emphasized by Totman, *The Collapse of the Tokugawa Bakufu*, pp. 485-486 n. 2.

against the storms of crisis that assaulted Japan's leaders at every turn. Catastrophe outpaced the bureaucracy's ability to act. Erosion of authority, in part a consequence of popular discontent, added to the dilemma by diminishing the system's capacity to dispense even-handed justice and efficient services.[36]

Two examples will illustrate this problem. In 1858 and again in 1866, the bakufu had the authority to take the initiative toward reforming the political system and building an effective national response to the imperialist intrusion. A new shogun, preferably Hitotsubashi Yoshinobu, would have revived a sense of unity in 1858 and turned "open country" (kaikoku) into a positive policy for Japan instead of the tactical retreat that Great Councilor Ii Naosuke (1815-1860) eventually made of it when he seized control of the bakufu at midyear.[37] Success, however, was out of the question because of the confusion and sense of crisis that gripped the bakufu. The rest of the country was unprepared to go ahead with a forward strategy, preferring to reinforce traditional practices and to try and limit the de facto extent of the open-country policy that was accorded the United States consul, Townsend Harris, as an inescapable concession.

In 1866, Hitotsubashi Yoshinobu, a collateral who had now reverted to the Tokugawa family surname, actually did become shogun. Although it turned out that he was to be not only the fifteenth but also the last of the Tokugawa shoguns, he began vigorously enough by approving a series of measures designed to industrialize and arm Japan with French assistance. By 1866, however, opposition to bakufu authority had spread across much of Japan, fanned by flames of popular unrest and disturbances. Seeking a symbolically deeper and more powerful remedy, leaders and followers alike looked to the old imperial house in Kyoto. Satsuma and Chōshū, two han that were traditional rivals but banded together in a campaign to save Japan's honor, seized the palace on January 3, 1868, "restored" the youthful Meiji emperor to direct political rule, and eliminated the bakufu-and-han system as a

[36] See my forthcoming article, "Plotting Bakumatsu History: Multiple Dimensions of Motivation in Japan's Meiji Restoration," for a tentative statement about the different "plots" or "story lines" that historical actors were living out during the confused decade of the 1860s. I could not have drawn these distinctions without benefit of studying Hayden White's formal theory of tropal or rhetorical determinism as the key to modern European historical consciousness. White, Metahistory: The Historical Imagination in Nineteenth-Century Europe (Baltimore: Johns Hopkins University Press, 1973), pp. 1-42, 426-434.

[37] This argument underpins my article, "The Bakumatsu Intellectual in Action: Hashimoto Sanai in the Political Crisis of 1858," in Albert M. Craig and Donald H. Shively, eds., Personality in Japanese History (Berkeley and Los Angeles: University of California Press, 1970), pp. 234-263.

relic incapable of coping with current problems. What the establishment might conceivably have accomplished in 1858, in other words, it could not do at all in 1866, and yet the same political elite groups were jockeying for control in both years.[38] The difference lay not merely in the intensification of imperialist pressures on Japan, but also in the rise of popular agitation, whose auguries were too dire to allow for the perpetuation of the status quo. By 1868 an inevitable transformation was well underway.

THE MILLENARIAN CONVERSION OF SAMURAI NATIVISM

The charge that *shishi* zealots among the samurai coopted popular revolutionary energy and turned it against the existing regime, only to suppress it after the Restoration had succeeded, has found articulate exponents in Tōyama Shigeki, Inoue Kiyoshi, and other authors.[39] It is not an inaccurate interpretation, but it is an incomplete one. So too is H. D. Harootunian's argument that nativism, which derived from an extended revival of interest in Japanese literature and myth, became the engine of the Meiji Restoration.[40] The emperor's role did change suddenly from that of a backstage legitimating principle for the bakufu-and-*han* arrangement to one of an onstage actor in whose office all political authority came to coalesce. From mythical times, the imperial line had served Japanese political needs, and, as a presumed descendant of Japan's divine founding heroes, the emperor occupied a unique position in the troubled political firmament of the mid-nineteenth century. The emperor's position was all the more compelling because the times demanded new options, and the recycling of the emperor as a "principal of politics" (rather than a principle) came to represent an attractive alternative to the old arrangement with the shogun and his bureaucrats in command. In this way, nativist ideas did inhere in the throne, and they

[38] Opposing the view that meaningful change might have resulted from the political strife of 1858 is Totman, *The Collapse of the Tokugawa Bakufu*, pp. xx–xxi. He uses 1862 and 1866 as the "watershed years" in the bakufu's downward swing; see ibid., pp. xxii–xxiii.

[39] Tōyama Shigeki, *Meiji ishin* (Tokyo, 1951); Inoue Kiyoshi, *Nihon gendai shi I: Meiji ishin* (Tokyo, 1951). In English, this line of thought appears in the broadly comparative and highly dialectical conceptions of Barrington Moore, Jr., *Social Origins of Dictatorship and Democracy: Lord and Peasant in the Making of the Modern World* (Boston: Beacon Press, 1966), p. 275.

[40] H. D. Harootunian, "From Principle to Principal: Restoration and Emperorship in Japan," in Hayden V. White, ed., *The Uses of History: Essays in Intellectual and Social History* (Detroit: Wayne State University Press, 1968), pp. 221–245. See also Harootunian's attempt to explain the theoretical basis of his concern with nativism: "The Consciousness of Archaic Form in the New Realism of Kokugaku," in Najita and Scheiner, *Japanese Thought in the Tokugawa Period*, pp. 63–104.

encouraged malcontents to promote the far more demanding idea of political restoration. To the extent that popular unrest set the stage for the Meiji Restoration itself, the new leaders did benefit by energies beyond those of their own making.[41]

But Japanese millenarianism combined historic time and mythic time, embracing traditional virtues such as reverence for the imperial house while simultaneously evincing a strong revolutionary potential in its own right. Popular millennialism both frightened and inspired the more daring among the samurai who were willing to act in search of a simple yet effective solution to Japan's mid-century crisis. People as different as the Chōshū samurai Kusaka Genzui and Takasugi Shinsaku and the Shinto priest's son Maki Izumi all determined at one time or another to go into drastic action in order to bring their hopes to realization.[42] Many thousands of confused samurai faced similar dilemmas of conscience. As their fervor became more and more politicized, so was their nativism converted to a revolutionary nationalism.

This is a powerful combination, one that enabled the Meiji Restoration to take the path it did. Yonina Talmon's scrupulous recapitulation of the importance of millenarianism lays stress on "its composite, 'intermediate' nature": "It combines components which are seemingly mutually exclusive: it is historical as well as mythical, religious as well as political, and, most significant, it is future-oriented as well as past-oriented. It is precisely this [amalgam] of a radical revolutionary position with traditionalism that accounts for the widespread appeal of millenarism and turns it into such a potent agent of change."[43]

[41] Carol Gluck examines the rise of a Japanese school of historiography based on the exploits of "the people" (*minshū*) as opposed to the samurai elite in "The People in History: Recent Trends in Japanese Historiography," *Journal of Asian Studies*, 38 (1978-1979): 25-50. A recent effort to supply the educational and sociological background for the rise of popular economic and political consciousness during the Tokugawa period is Fukawa Kiyoshi, *Kinsei minshū no rinriteki enerugii* (Nagoya, 1976).

[42] H. D. Harootunian, *Toward Restoration: The Growth of Political Consciousness in Tokugawa Japan* (Berkeley and Los Angeles: University of California Press, 1970), pp. 42-43, 251-254, 278-320, 390-391.

[43] Talmon, "Millenarism," p. 360. She had earlier pointed to the bizarre and incongruous quality—for the rational Western mind—of millenarian attitudes toward time: both a linear and a cyclical concept can be sustained, but when the millennium dawns, time must presumably stop altogether as myth becomes reality. Yonina Talmon, "Pursuit of the Millennium: The Relation between Religion and Social Change," *Archives Européennes de Sociologie*, 3 (1962): 130-131. The same conclusion emerges from Worsley, *The Trumpet Shall Sound*, pp. 275-276, where he says that the movements he studied were both backward-looking and forward-looking. The Japanese sense of temporal reality is flexible enough to accommodate a linear orientation as well as an emphasis on the timelessness of powerful Japanese myths. See George Wilson, "Time and History in Japan," *American Historical Review*, 85 (1980): 557-571.

Only a profound concern about popular discontent and a determination to act rather than reflect could have energized the forces that won out in the Restoration. Only their revolutionary zeal can provide a rationale for the thoroughgoing quality of subsequent reforms. But they had too lately come from status elitism, and from a nativistic desire to "restore," for them to turn their attention toward satisfying inchoate popular urges. Their plans focused instead on Japan's broader national needs, perceived through the particular prism of their own background and training, and hence very heavily political.

THE MEIJI RESTORATION AS A WORK OF ART

As the generations pass, the great events of world history are periodically reimagined and reenacted. The drama and human suffering of the moment fade away, but they reappear to some who find the magnitude of the transformation too remarkable to forget and too relevant to disregard. In new times of trouble, the model actions of the past are like amulets summoned to salvage a nation or a people from yet another precarious situation. The men who made the Meiji Restoration were the survivors of a whole series of traumatic events that shaped their attitudes as well as the fate of the entire Japanese nation. Their compatriots who had given their lives to ill-defined but powerfully felt causes were gone like the constellation of political institutions they had helped to demolish. These victims of the Restoration's birth struggles "lived as if they were in a work of art": their ambition was "willingly [to] perish into images" that would fire the spirits of a nation at its founding.[44]

In this sense, the Restoration itself was an artistic creation, an artifice fashioned by historical actors who were driven by a romantic quest-myth.[45] The restoration of imperial rule was the symbolic grail. It could end Japan's agony over foreign depredations. In actuality, an end to that agony was to take a much longer time, but millenarian dreams want immediate resolution, and the Japanese myths, which were available and accessible in like measure to the elite and to the general public, afforded a glimpse of apocalyptic visions.

In a larger sense, too, the Meiji Restoration was the apocalypse and

[44] William Irwin Thompson, *The Imagination of an Insurrection: Dublin, Easter 1916: A Study of an Ideological Movement* (New York: Oxford University Press, 1967), pp. ix-x.

[45] Northrop Frye, *Anatomy of Criticism: Four Essays* (Princeton: Princeton University Press, 1957), 186-206. In Frye's schema, the "quest" is identified with the plot line of "romance." In millenarian movements, a quest-myth is most likely to attract adherents when a "disnomic" situation obtains—a situation in which new standards of value and new bases for action may appeal to a community in disarray. Kenelm O. Burridge, *Mambu: A Melanesian Millennium* (London: Methuen, 1960), pp. 274-275.

artifice that may sometimes spring from liminal periods of history. The vision revealed to the world was that of a new nation, resplendent in its unity and independence but proud of its ancient heritage. Under the emperor, that nation would go forward . . . but to what? Here, state-craft required the use of artifice—the devising of new institutions, disguised as old ones, capable of empowering Japan to survive in a Darwinian international climate where friend and foe alike possessed the magic of industry and empire that were not yet Japan's. Statecraft was an art wrested from chance, made heroic by men who rightly assumed that theirs was an opportunity never to come again. They had shared in the millenarian impulse, and their actions reflected its potency. When they suppressed the utopian hopes of others, they did so in order to gratify their own muse. But the Meiji leaders were also erecting an ideological outlet for these energies. By legalizing and registering the new religious sects, for example, they channeled some of the popular discontent into untested dimensions of educational and military endeavors. Such endeavors were essential to the enterprise of constructing the Meiji state, and the government relied on an energetic populace to continue achieving a variety of goals.[46] The intense mix of tradition and innovation in the leadership is emblematic of millenarian movements in general, and it became the hallmark of Meiji Japan. But in 1868 so distant an outcome was as unpredictable as life itself.

No one then acting in the historical arena—neither *shishi* intriguer nor devout pilgrim, neither furious rioter nor frenzied carnivaler—could have apprehended the total configuration of the splendid synchronic episode in world history that was Japan's epoch of the Tokugawa. Nor could anyone have predicted the full potential for change embedded within that polymathic configuration. Each type of historical actor acted differently, like elementary particles occupying a spark chamber in high-energy physics. Samurai who stood by the bakufu and samurai who agitated for radical reform, farmers and city dwellers made anxious about a suddenly uncertain future, prophets of new dispensations from on high, and even the foreigners who trod Japanese ground all behaved in

---

[46] Every society must build and maintain, or tear down and replace, institutions that can condition the unlimited possibilities and the disorder of ultimate reality, so that communities may lead an orderly existence. "Particular institutions and roles are legitimated by locating them in a comprehensively meaningful world. . . . It is important, however, to understand that the institutional order, like the order of individual biography, is continually threatened by the presence of realities that are meaningless in *its* terms. The legitimation of the institutional order is also faced with the ongoing necessity of keeping chaos at bay. *All* social reality is precarious. *All* societies are constructions in the face of chaos." Peter L. Berger and Thomas Luckmann, *The Social Construction of Reality: A Treatise in the Sociology of Knowledge* (Garden City, N.Y.: Doubleday-Anchor, 1967), p. 103.

particular patterns, generated from their own particular perceptions of reality. As in a particle accelerator, each type of behavior interacted with the behavior of the other types. And it was these interactions and interrelations that finally determined the character of the transformation of the entire historical field that all of them simultaneously occupied.[47] The Meiji Restoration was the crucible through which the Japanese and their ideas had to pass in order to reach a newer world. In this discontinuous passage, dreams of the millennium converged with political ambitions to create an array of images representing a massive—revolutionary—transformative experience.

[47] See Wilson, "Plotting *Bakumatsu* History," passim; and Scheiner, "The Mindful Peasant," p. 589. Scheiner states that the distinction between millenarian and revolutionary movements can never be absolute. *Yonaoshi* rebels, after all, "planned for [the] achievement" of their utopian goals; ibid., p. 587. The difficulty of creating an appropriate unitary narrative form to capture the nuances of such a transformation finds eloquent expression in the words of Siegfried Kracauer: "Modern art radically challenges the artistic ideals from which the general historian draws his inspiration. . . . The pioneers of the modern novel . . . resolutely decompose (fictitious) continuity over time. [Modern writers] seek, and find, reality in atom-like happenings, each being thought of as a center of tremendous energies. . . . The disruptive intentions of modern writers and artists are paralleled by the increasing misgivings of historians and thinkers about the synthesizing narrative, with its emphasis on the 'total exterior continuum.' " Kracauer, "General History and the Aesthetic Approach," in Hans Robert Jauss, ed., *Die nicht mehr schönen Künste: Grenzphänomene des ästhetischen* (Munich: Wilhelm Fink Verlag, 1968), p. 122.

PART II

GENERATIONAL CONFLICT AFTER THE RUSSO-JAPANESE WAR

Oka Yoshitake

"Never since the dawn of world history has the growth of the individual been so respected and material happiness so sought after as in present-day Japan."[1] Obviously exaggerated for rhetorical effect, this 1910 statement by Ukita Kazutami is nonetheless highly suggestive regarding the appearance in Japan of an unprecedented degree of individual self-awareness among youth between the end of the Russo-Japanese war and the outbreak of World War I. Hardly peculiar to Ukita, such sentiments were widely shared by the so-called "well-informed" opinion leaders (shikisha) among his contemporaries.

Postwar Trends

New consciousness of the individual was manifested in a variety of forms, some on a more elevated plane than others. For example, the term seikō (success) gained widespread popularity after the war with Russia, revealing a surge of worldly aspiration, particularly among the young.[2] It is true, of course, that risshin shusse (getting ahead in the world) had been in the popular lexicon ever since the Restoration, and both city

Translation and adaptation by J. Victor Koschmann, from "Nichi-Ro sensō-go ni okeru atarashii sedai no seichō," I and II, Shisō, February and March, 1967.

[1] Ukita Kazutami, "Gendai seikatsu no kenkyū," Taiyō 18, No. 8 (June 1910).

[2] The public in the era after the Russo-Japanese war, particularly the youth, worshiped an idealized image of Theodore Roosevelt. It was often said that "combativeness" was necessary for "success," and Roosevelt symbolized that quality.

and country youths were steeped in a passionate drive for advancement. Nevertheless, I think that the meaning of such terms as they were used following the Russo-Japanese war differed somewhat in nuance from the prewar *risshin shusse*. The earlier term implied an urge to elevate the reputation of one's family (*ie*) and earn laurels in one's home town. It also commonly implied the attainment of a high governmental post. This sense of the term gradually changed until *risshin shusse*, now used in conjunction with *seikō*, severed its implicit connection with household and home town to refer only to the individual. Moreover, it now implied the acquisition of wealth. The tendency symbolized by this subtle development came increasingly to characterize the era following the Russo-Japanese war. Ishikawa Tengai says,

> Since time immemorial, the teachings of saints and sages and the doctrines of religious leaders have been directed to one goal: the furtherance of success in life. Here I do not use the term success to refer only to the accumulation of wealth. The term can be used to describe any case in which one attains a predetermined objective, whether in scholarship, spiritual cultivation, or any other enterprise. When the youth of today bestir themselves, it is because they are anxious to find out how they can succeed. What are the secrets of success? Opinion leaders are always pleased to answer that the key to success is thus and so, or that this is the secret to advancement. But unfortunately the brand of success sought by the young and expounded by their mentors is in fact a minor aspect of success in the true sense. That is, they use the term success to mean only the attainment of wealth. We have here a good illustration of the extent to which people today are infatuated with riches.[3]

In a similar vein, Tokutomi Sohō wrote in 1906 that while the first half of the Meiji period had been the "golden age of government authority," the contemporary era had replaced the ethic of *kanson minpi* (respect the officials, despise the people) with *kinson kanpi* (respect money, despise the officials).[4]

The great strength of the desire for success among youth in the years following the Russo-Japanese war is also evident in the tireless repetition by newspapers and magazines of "success stories" built around the lives of men of distinction. There was also a rash of printed material purporting to reveal the specific principles of "success." Tokutomi remarks, "historical and other accounts of so-called successful men are everywhere in newspapers and magazines these days. I would not pre-

---

[3] Ishikawa Tengai, *Tōkyō-gaku* (1909), in *Meiji bunka shiryō sōsho* 11 [*sesō-hen*] (1960), 452-453.

[4] Tokutomi Sohō, "Fukuzatsu naru shakai," in *Daihachinichiyō kōdan* (1907).

sume to pronounce this the age of success, but it certainly is the age of success stories."[5] Similarly, Kuroiwa Ruikō observes,

There are so many publications propounding guides to life nowadays that it is impossible to look at them all. Some seem to have no other purpose than to repeat over and over the principles of success. Even then, however, the readers never tire of it. They pore over such materials repeatedly as if to hope that a novel formula will leap out and propel them directly to the promised land of success. Their eyes are like saucers as they read. While I cannot help but admire their vast endurance in pursuit of self-advancement, at times the spectacle they offer is pathetic in the extreme.[6]

Second, it appears that *après guerre* youth were of a more hedonistic bent than their predecessors, and this aroused criticism from elders concerning their extravagance and lives of "sensual dissipation." Their values were ridiculed as effeminate and dissolute in comparison with the student spirit of old which had demanded an air of rustic vigor, and they were disparagingly alluded to as the "party of stars and violets."

Third, some youths were swallowed up by scepticism and despair in the course of their search for meaning in life. In fact, that tendency had showed signs of emerging even before the Russo-Japanese war, but it became much more apparent following the cessation of hostilities. It was said to be normal for contemporary youths to express anxiety and doubt.[7] This trend was the polar opposite of the burning desire to "get ahead" and "succeed" that coexisted with it, and it was also different from the ethos of earlier young people who had voiced grave concern for the state of the nation. Writing in 1906, Miyake Setsurei observed that feelings of resentment over national affairs had declined; now one heard only the moans of despair. He interpreted this to mean that "what was formerly national [in orientation] had now become social or individual."[8]

Fourth, an individualistic way of thinking pervaded postwar society. The thought of Nietzsche and Ibsen had been introduced in the early years of the third decade of Meiji (1897-1906) and had become influential among a segment of the youth. Following the war, however, individualistic philosophies gathered increasing strength. In the process, members of the younger generation collided frequently with aspects of

<hr/>

[5] Tokutomi Sohō, "Daikō hon'i" in *Daijūnichiyō kōdan* (1911), p. 66.

[6] Kuroiwa Shūroku (Ruikō), *Daini seinen shisō-ron—ichimei Taishō ishin-ron* (1913), pp. 201-202.

[7] For example, Kamata Eikichi, *Dokuritsu jison* (1911), p. 121.

[8] Miyake Setsurei, "Kōgai otoroete hanmon okoru," *Nihonjin* (July 20, 1906); also included in Miyake, *Sōkon* (1916).

the traditional family system ("familism"). Also involved was the problem of romantic love, and the philosophy of free love found advocates
among the young. In a related development, the magazine *Seitō* (*Blue-
stockings*) commenced publication in 1911 and launched the women's
liberation movement. In September 1913, the monthly *Chūō Kōron*
(Central Review) published a special issue on the "problem of women."
As these events suggest, the liberation of women from traditional, feudal values had gradually become a matter of public concern.

Fifth, the naturalist school of literature that had made an appearance
before the Russo-Japanese war now became the dominant genre in the
wake of that conflict. It was the naturalist era from war's end until the
final years of the Meiji period. While this school inherited a biological
view of man and a thoroughly realistic method from the naturalist school
in Europe, it diverged from its European counterpart insofar as it sought
to liberate the individual from traditional norms. This literature was
loved by a broad cross-section of postwar youth, most likely because
of its affinities to other tendencies displayed by the young. Naturalist
literature also reacted upon those tendencies to augment and strengthen
them.

Sixth, socialist thought, which had already made its appearance before the war, found many sympathizers in a certain segment of postwar
youth. This phenomenon, too, was probably not unrelated to the development of individual self-consciousness among youth as a whole.

It is important to note that the above tendencies evident in the youth
were not necessarily independent of each other. They appear, in fact, to
have been linked in a number of ways. For example, in some cases a
youth may yearn for "success" but when things do not work out in his
favor, he attempts to relieve his frustration through a life of pleasure-
seeking. Or perhaps a young man's awakening to individualism pits
him against the family system, but when faced with the seemingly in-
superable difficulty of acting out his convictions, he lapses into doubt
and despair.

In addition to underlying all the above trends, the development of
individual self-awareness on the part of postwar youth also contributed
to the waning of loyalty to the state. A marked tendency toward apathy
regarding national affairs was often noted even before and during the
war. In a newspaper article written during the war, in September 1904,
Tokutomi Sohō observed that youths prior to the Meiji Restoration, at
least the strong and capable ones, had been virtually without individual
awareness. They had thought of themselves as properties of the state
(or *han* [*kokka*]), and they were willing to go through fire and water in
its name. "Their willingness to sacrifice themselves for the state differed
not in the least from the sacrifice of a martyr for his religion." The

state, in fact, had been no less than a national religion. Meiji youth, on the other hand, at least its most outstanding representatives, differed from their predecessors in having developed an individual awareness. By the same token, the young had lost "all, or at least a major portion of the national awareness" that characterized the pre-Meiji young.[9]

In August of the same year, Sawayanagi Masatarō wrote that when war broke out he had been afraid that youths and students would be carried away with enthusiasm and lose their composure. Indeed, the Ministry of Education had issued a directive concerning such an eventuality. It soon became clear, however, that, "as one individual has pointed out, the energy of Japanese students has somehow been repressed. Those in the real world of affairs are hailing Japan's victories and behaving with extreme fervor, while the students are all too cool and reserved." Sawayanagi believed that, generally speaking, it was fine for students to maintain their composure. But he also felt that in a "truly unusual circumstance" such as this, one should normally be unable to contain the energy welling up within, and be unable to stop oneself from venting it in action. In the Franco-Prussian war, he explained, German students had been "extremely active," but in contemporary Japan such a phenomenon was nowhere to be seen. Surely that was a matter for grave regret. He even noted a growing tendency to flee military duty among those who had received or were in the process of receiving a higher education. If it were, by some chance, true that those with education lacked enthusiasm, this would indeed be an alarming occurrence.[10]

The apathetic attitude toward national purposes noticed by Tokutomi and Sawayanagi became much more conspicuous after the war.

THE ROOTS OF CHANGE

What, then, were the sources of the individual self-awareness and the other related trends that swept through the younger generation following the Russo-Japanese war? In the first place, they related to Japan's victory in that conflict. Ever since the Bakumatsu era and Meiji Restoration, the supreme order of state had been the consolidation of national independence. It was to that end that the ruling class had sought to marshal and direct the energy of the people, and it was likewise for that purpose that the people were expected to spare no devotion or sacrifice. With victory over Russia, however, that goal had basically been achieved. Japan's status in international politics had risen precipitously following

---

[9] Tokutomi Sohō, "Seinen no fūki," *Dairokunichiyō kōdan* (1905).

[10] Sawayanagi Masatarō, "Sensō to kokumin no seishin," *Taiyō* 11, No. 11 (August 1905); also included in Sawayanagi, *Jidai to kyōiku* (1905).

its victory over a major world power, and as their country joined the "first-rank nations," a wave of self-congratulation swept over Japanese society.[11] The sense of crisis that had subjugated the national spirit ever since the late Tokugawa period faded, and the release of tension provided the individual with an opportunity to liberate himself from the state. The earlier crisis-consciousness had been deeply rooted and pervasive, however, so the reaction against it also harbored a certain passionate intensity.

Second, the war had set the stage for rapid development of the industrial revolution and, accordingly, for the transition to a capitalist society. In other words, the emergence of individualism was closely related to the expansion and diffusion of capitalist culture and ideology.

Third, it is possible to understand the increasing organization and institutionalization of social life in this period and the remarkable reduction of social fluidity, or "sociability," as having actually heaped fuel on the burning desire for success that already consumed the young. As noted above, "success" tended to be equated with getting rich, and this new atmosphere of respect for wealth and money was at least augmented by postwar governmental policies and the views of "well-informed" opinion leaders. Japan's low rate of capital accumulation had remained a serious problem during the war and under the so-called postwar administration. In response, postwar governments strongly and continuously urged frugality and personal saving. It was even said that "the rescript, the imperial portrait, and the promotion of saving are the three spiritual pillars of today's elementary education."[12]

Moreover, numerous opinion leaders pointed out that Japan since the war might be powerful, but the status of a rich country was still beyond its reach. The people were zealously urged to reject the Tokugawa legacy of disdain for lucre. They should frugally accumulate and strive for a country of wealth. A book edited in 1910 by Inoue Yasutake records the formulas for success expounded by various contemporary men of distinction. Many of the entries included statements along the lines of the above. According to Kanamori Tsūrin, the day's "great sorrow" was that Japan lacked economic strength and could not be called a wealthy

---

[11] Following the Russo-Japanese war, Great Britain elevated its legation in Japan to the status of an embassy and made the British minister an ambassador; Japan reciprocated. Once that precedent was set, similar arrangements were made with France, Germany, Australia, Hungary, Italy, and the United States. Since the established diplomatic practice until the end of World War I dictated that ambassadors should be exchanged only by great powers, and that ministers would suffice between a great power and a smaller one, or between two small ones, Japan's exchange of ambassadors with great powers such as the above indicated her acceptance as a world power. It was against such a background that the Japanese people displayed their new "great-power consciousness."

[12] Wakamiya Shigenosuke, *Ani ben o konoman ya* (1911), p. 8.

nation, even though its military power graced the four seas. Behind such an imbalance was primarily the "many years of samurai education" that disparaged money. But money earned through painstaking toil should not be discredited. Whether money was despicable or admirable depended only upon how it was used. The view that money is inherently evil, he said, "is fundamentally mistaken." It is especially noteworthy that Kanamori, a well-known Christian pastor, would argue in that manner.

A further example of such a viewpoint was that expounded by Naruse Nizō, then president of Japan Women's University (Nihon Joshi Daigakkō). Naruse observed that Japan had made great progress in the course of its successful wars against China and Russia, but now the country's very survival depended upon whether or not it could emerge victorious from the "war of commerce and industry."[13]

He went on to say that throughout the Russo-Japanese war he had displayed a graph of the relative fighting strength of Japan and Russia and had never failed to record fluctuations. Now, however, he had replaced it with a diagram of the national wealth of the various nations of the world. He admonished people to suppress personal feelings and desires, reject self-interest, and join in cooperation for the good of the state.[14]

OBSTACLES TO PROGRESS

Japan had gained a strong foothold on the continent as a result of its victory in the Russo-Japanese war, and from that time onward the ruling elite strove to strengthen the nation as an imperialist power. For that purpose they planned to take the energy of the people, which up to that point had been consolidated and mobilized for the cause of national independence, and rechannel it toward the goal of national expansion. This endeavor was by no means simple. The people had for a very long time been pressed into enormous feats of dedication and self-sacrifice on behalf of national independence, and they were finally conscious of achieving their goal. There are bound to be difficulties when such a population is asked to turn around and endure the same sort of sacrifices in the service of expansionism. Furthermore, as long as Japan's very independence had been at stake, the ruling elite was able to make passionate appeals to native national instincts and loyalties. Now, however, in order to continue receiving strong national support for expansionism, they were forced to resort to outright manipulation. The obstacles to success were enormous.

[13] Naruse Nizō, *Shinpo to kyōiku* (1911), pp. 7-9.
[14] Ibid., p. 272.

A number of other difficulties stood in the way of progress for post-war "imperial Japan." Japanese leaders were distressed by the recurring nightmare of a second Russo-Japanese war, which would be accompanied by Russian reprisals. The establishment, renewal, and later strengthening of entente with that nation failed to dispel such fears. Japan also had to contend with an imperialist confrontation with the United States over developments in Manchuria. This problem coincided with the appearance in western American states of movements to stem Japanese immigration, and the result was a chronic instability in Japanese-U.S. relations. Indeed, international rumors suggested the possibility of a war between Japan and the United States. The deterioration of relations with the United States sent reverberations through the Anglo-Japanese alliance as well, so that after the treaty of alliance was revised in 1911, Japan could no longer expect aid from Great Britain in the event of war with the United States. Against the background of those international developments, Japan repeatedly expanded her military arsenal despite the extra effort that entailed for a country already suffering from a low rate of savings and constant financial shortages, particularly since the war.

In addition, "imperial Japan" experienced a number of domestic circumstances that intensified the uneasiness of the ruling elite. In 1910 the nation was scandalized to learn of a plot to assassinate the emperor (taigyaku jiken), allegedly involving the anarchist Kōtoku Shūsui; and the following year intense public controversy was touched off by a textbook dispute involving the question of imperial legitimacy during the split between the northern and southern courts in the fourteenth century.

The same year saw the revolutionary overthrow of the Ch'ing dynasty and the establishment of republican government in China. Given China's geographic propinquity and the intimate historical and cultural ties between that nation and Japan, Japanese leaders anxiously wondered what sort of impact that political transformation would exert on the popular mind. Under the repeated shock of such events, the Japanese ruling elite became hypersensitive to the point of morbidity concerning Japan's national origins and "national essence" (kokutai).

In July 1912 the Meiji emperor died. He had been the sacred symbol of a rising imperial nation and the object of national adulation throughout his long rule, so his death had a profound impact on the public spirit. It also further aggravated a sense of insecurity within the power elite regarding the stability of the system. Then, immediately following the accession of the new emperor, there occurred the Taishō political crisis. Events surrounding the collapse of the second Saionji (Kinmochi) cabinet and the formation of the third Katsura (Tarō) government caused great public outcry. The so-called Movement to Protect the Constitution was launched, and antigovernment violence led inexorably to the resignation en bloc of Katsura's new government in February 1913. Formation of the first Yamamoto (Gonnohyōe) cabinet was not the end of trouble, however, for under its purview occurred the Siemens incident, involving corruption in naval procurement. The incident irritated the public and was followed by an outbreak of mass disturbances in February 1914. Such furious and repeated popular uprisings not only drew wide public attention but inevitably strengthened the traditional tendency of the ruling elite to distrust and despise the people.[15] A newspaper editorial in the February 25, 1914 edition of *Tōyō keizai shinpō* observed that the authority of the police had suffered in the face of mass movements, citing as examples the turmoil and demonstrations over the Siemens affair, which had caused the downfall of the third Katsura cabinet, and an insult to the national flag in Nanking, which had placed the cabinet in a dilemma. The article went on to say that the ruling class in general had found these incidents extremely deplorable. Members of that class appeared to believe that in the interests of the people and the country severe punishment must be meted out to prevent such behavior from becoming habitual. The writer also cited a friend with relatively liberal views as sharing that opinion.

People were obviously aware that the masses had become a political force to be reckoned with. Beginning around the time of the Taishō political crisis, one begins to see frequent references to a "Taishō Restoration," meaning the establishment of a system of party cabinets.[16] This development, too, should be understood as related to a climate of opinion influenced by mass political movements.

After the fall of the Yamamoto cabinet, Ōkuma Shigenobu organized his second government in April 1914. While it was not widely known at the time, Ōkuma's political rehabilitation was the result of a plot on the part of the elder statesmen to cripple the Seiyūkai. But Ōkuma's political career since the early-Meiji Freedom and Popular Rights Movement had given him the image of a "statesman of the people," and as a result his cabinet enjoyed a certain popular appeal. Furthermore, some commentators mistakenly opined that the appearance of an Ōkuma cabinet symbolized a new era in which the will of the masses would be more faithfully reflected in government. Four months later, Ōkuma was faced with the outbreak of World War I. His administration was accom-

---

[15] See the essays in the section entitled "Minshū no seiryoku ni yotte jikyoku o kaiketsu sen to suru fūchō o ronzu," *Chūō kōron* (April 1914).

[16] For example, an editorial entitled "Taishō seikai no taisei o ronzu, *Chūō kōron* (January 1915).

panied by the feeling, at least, that Japanese government was undergoing an important transformation.

REACTIONS BY "OPINION LEADERS"

From the standpoint of the ruling elite, such political developments both at home and abroad, in combination with the emergence of individual self-awareness and other trends among youth, gave cause for serious concern and apprehension. Such feelings can be gleaned from the views of the so-called opinion leaders who acted as establishment ideologues. These individuals often called for increased attention to character building and moral training in various publications expounding "rules for young men," "principles of moral cultivation," and "guides for life." Their articles were widely read. As noted above, there also appeared a raft of printed matter on the subject of "success" and "getting ahead," which blatantly subordinated all moral considerations to the standards of social and financial advancement. Since both types of materials usually had the same sort of title, one gets the impression that a number of different prescriptions for life were competing for the attentions of youth.

Establishment ideologues often used strong language in admonishing the young to reconsider the powerful tide of ambition that enveloped them. In his 1907 book *Seikō to jinkaku* (Success and Personality), the newspaper man Tamura Gyakusui argued the need to cultivate character. As long as a person was weak in character, his attainment of even the highest honor and glory must be considered fraudulent, an empty dream that would eventually fade away. Granting glory to the dissolute, he said, was as absurd as "crowning a monkey." Such platitudes were quite common in the literature of the period.

The magazine *Chūgaku sekai* (Middle-school World) published a special issue in September 1906 devoted to the moral education of youth. In one section, a number of luminaries from Miyake Setsurei on down expounded their own views on moral education. Hirai Kinzō, for example, recalled in the context of recommending some reading for his young audience that "I read Samuel Smiles' *Self-Help* as a young man, while I was nursing my sick mother. It is a good book. Nevertheless, it is directed to the youth of today who are enamored of success, and hence has little to say on the subject of moral cultivation." It is essential, Hirai observed, that through character building, a youth "construct a firm foundation on the basis of which he may confidently pursue his destiny."

Similarly, Tatsumi Shōjirō, an educator, writes,

Everyone is familiar with the book *Self-Help*. Probably every contemporary man of distinction has been influenced to some extent by
this book. I myself, however, am not that impressed. Why? It deals
with the ways a poor boy uses to get ahead in the world, and therefore its aims are less than exalted. His later book *Character* (1871), on
the other hand, is argued quite differently. There, one gets the feeling
that it is quite all right to be poor as long as one leads a moral life.
Its aims, in other words, are much more elevated.

Tatsumi felt that, in view of the vain lust for success infecting the minds
of youth, he was no longer able to recommend *Self-Help*, a book which
had enjoyed immense popularity since the early years of Meiji.

The ideologues also expounded frequently on the tendencies of youth
toward doubt and disillusionment. Some concluded that it was just a
temporary fad, others that it was the product of too much leisure time.
Still others held that the young tend to be weak-willed and therefore
readily lapse into doubt and anxiety when their search for success is
frustrated, or they are consumed by romantic passion. Many went on
to advise that for youths of shallow experience to search for the meaning of life was a waste of time, bound to be unproductive. Their own
solution to the problems of youth, however, was limited to recommendations of more manual labor, physical training, and the cultivation of
character. Since they made light of the doubt and despair preying on
the young, their advice was inevitably shallow and careless. Moreover,
their unimaginative approach to the problems of youth naturally led to
deepset mistrust of the younger generation as a whole. Any thought
that such young men would be forced to bear responsibility for the
future filled them with profound uneasiness.

The journal *Shin-kōron* (New Review), for example, serialized in the
July through September issues of 1906 a sampling of views on the subject of "how can we stem the tide of deterioration?" In the introduction,
the magazine explained,

> The so-called pessimism, the so-called anxiety, and suicide, all this is
> the product of an age of decline and has no place in the rising empire
> of Japan. Nonetheless, these damaging trends are swiftly becoming
> the sign of the times. Is this not a problem worthy of serious consid-
> eration by our intellectual leaders?

One contributor, Yamane Masatsugu, suggests that the most destructive of contemporary evils is the "anxious pessimism" fashionable among
young men and women. Rather than being a "problem for individuals,"

this trend constitutes an "issue for the state." His views were representative of those of many of his contemporaries.[17]

Ideologues also often discussed the individualistic philosophy that was spreading among youths. Relatively few commentaries rejected individualism altogether, but many expressed the fear that individualistic ways of thinking would gradually erode the family system, leading to its eventual collapse. In terms of the traditional concept of a family state (*kazoku kokka*), the family system was a bulwark of loyalty to the emperor and therefore of the political establishment as well. It is not surprising, therefore, that they were alarmed at the prospect of its disappearance.[18]

Members of the older generation also found it impossible to tolerate the waning of loyalty among the young people and their growing apathy toward the state. In their own youth, their minds had still been dominated by the image of a "great tide of Western power gradually moving East," and the shock of the "black ships" had not yet faded away. When they compared what they saw among contemporary youth to their own experience, therefore, the result was not only concern but outright disgust and indignation. Takebe Tongo (born in 1871) said during a speech in 1909 that as an elementary school student in 1885 he had read in a newspaper that Burma, "almost next door to Japan, had been annexed by Great Britain and its king incarcerated and dethroned." Later, in February 1893, as a student in the First Higher Middle School, he learned of the collapse of "our Eastern neighbor," the kingdom of Hawaii. "O doomed nation," he felt, "how heart-rending are your cries. Spare us the fate of a homeless race." Such sentiments had gripped his heart. His words might arouse unfamiliar feelings in those less than thirty years of age, he said, but he was speaking of a time when the Japanese people had been completely absorbed in securing revision of the unequal treaties, and students were immersed in politics and foreign affairs. It had been under such conditions that he heard of the fall of the Hawaiian kingdom, he explained, so it is natural that he should have been deeply moved. The Sino-Japanese war then had broken out, followed by the Boxer Rebellion, and finally four years later the Russo-Japanese war. Thus, he says, "from the time we were children, whether asleep or awake, in light or dark, the problems of how our country could be preserved and how the existence of our nation could be pro-

---

[17] Yamane Masatsugu, "Ika ni shite suisei no aku kaikō o bōshi subeki ka," *Shin-kōron* 21, No. 7 (July 1906).

[18] See Takakusu Jūjirō, "Nihon no kazoku hon'i to ōshū no kojin hon'i," *Shin-kōron* (May 1906); and Fukasaku Yasubumi, "Kazoku seido hiken," in Tōa Kyōkai, ed., *Kokumin kyōiku to kazoku seido* (1911).

tected, dominated our minds as the most important problems we could imagine."[19]

Many of the older generation found it impossible to swallow their grief over the state of youth or to suppress their serious concern. And they included more than just the outright nationalists. Matsumura Kaiseki (born 1859) said in 1909 that his generation of young people had been well aware of the existence of the state but actually unconscious of their own existence as individuals. As a result of a number of events and circumstances as they grew up, they had found they could no longer ignore the "problem of livelihood" (seikatsu mondai), but, nevertheless, the concept of sacrifice for the nation that they had embraced as youths never completely disappeared. Perhaps, he supposed, anyone who had spent his or her youth sometime between the pre-Restoration era and the first decade of the Meiji period (1868-1877) had been dominated by a sense of nation (kokkakan) rather than a sense of self (kojinkan). The youths of the present, however, were by and large concerned only with pursuing their personal interests, and only a tiny minority aspired to relate themselves in any way to the fortunes of the state. It did not auger well for the country.[20] He went on to lament the decline of moral spirit among young men and women, saying that the young embraced no high aspirations or great hopes; people's minds had turned completely to the problems of livelihood and practical affairs. He urged, "Ah, young men, open your eyes! The great Japanese empire is awaiting extraordinary individuals in the realms of government, religion, and education. Once born into the world, it is a shame for young men to die in vain. For a man's soul to be captivated by women means only that he has not yet discovered great ambition."[21]

The most representative of those who hurled stern warnings at the younger generation for allowing their loyalty to the state to atrophy and their apathy to grow was Tokutomi Sohō. In 1906 he said that the situation in postwar Japan "forces one to admit to signs of intoxication with idleness, profligacy, and indifference toward national affairs. What I am afraid of are indications that the Japanese people will be content with small successes, lose their high aspirations, and adopt a posture of indifference toward government. . . . Nothing would be worse at a time of great trials for the nation than apathy, laziness, and indifference to national affairs."[22]

[19] Speech entitled "Kokon bōkoku no hanashi," in Takebe Tongo, Shin kōkoku no seinen (1915).

[20] Matsumura Kaiseki, Yōjinroku (1909), pp. 114-115.

[21] Ibid., pp. 19-20.

[22] Tokutomi Sohō, "Mukau tokoro ikaga" (25 March 1906), in Tokutomi, Daihachinichiyō kōdan (1907).

The same year he wrote a long newspaper series entitled "Response to a Provincial Youth."[23] There, in five installments, he purported to describe his correspondence with a young man in the countryside. In the first, Tokutomi acknowledged the youth's complaint that most young people of the day were animated by "extremely vulgar goals" such as "business, entering government service, winning fame and honor, and getting rich." The youth said he had attempted to rise above all that, directing his efforts toward "studying the problem of human life." Things had not gone well, however, and he had become distressed.

Tokutomi consoled the youth that such aims were laudable and claimed that he could not agree more. On the other hand, he pointed out that problems of human life, such as "where has man come from and where should he go? Why has man been born into this world? For what purpose? What sort of world will come after this one?" are insoluble. To turn to such quests, renouncing "what should be done, indeed, what had to be done day by day," to throw one's energies into such a "useless enterprise," was exceedingly imprudent. Spiritual distress was no more than the "idle anxiety of a man of leisure."

In the second exchange of letters Tokutomi noted that the youth, in his response to Tokutomi, had admitted that in fact his distress over the problem of human life is the result of a love affair. Tokutomi responds that "it is, of course, improper for a young man even to mention love affairs, let alone to clamor loudly on the subject, allowing his heart to despair and his thoughts to be troubled."

In the third installment Tokutomi remarks, "let love affairs among the young be as they may. It is absurd to get upset over such trivial matters." Tokutomi says that in his last letter, " 'I told you that if you must have a love affair you should set your sights higher and marry the state,' but in response you say, 'how can I marry the state without falling in love?' Well, some say that in principle a couple should marry only after they fall in love, but in reality the marriage usually takes place first and love develops later. It is the love that develops after marriage that is most reliable and secure. To marry the state means to 'tie oneself to the state and relate [the fortunes of] the state to oneself.' "

In the fourth installment Tokutomi writes as follows: "In your last letter you observed that entities like the state are unable to inspire enthusiasm in today's youth, and loyalty to the sovereign and love of the state are 'outmoded arguments.' You added that in contrast to pre-Restoration youths, 'twentieth-century young people are merely bored by such conventional doctrines.' Nevertheless, whatever Japan has to be

---

[23] Tokutomi Sohō, "Chihō no seinen ni kotaeuru sho" from *Kokumin shinbun* (18 February, 25 February, 4 March, 11 March, 18 March, 1906), in Tokutomi, *Daihachinichiyō kōdan* (1907).

proud of today depends completely upon what you and your friends would call 'conventional patriotism.'. . . To my mind, there is no old or new. For me, while it may be old-fashioned, stubborn, or trite, it is enough to strengthen the state and make the Yamato race the greatest on earth." Surely, he said, if there is even one youth of Meiji who has fallen into your mistaken way of thinking despite the grand enterprises that confront him, it is cause for alarm. "When the people lose interest in the state, the state has already begun its decline, and the eventual result of decline is national ruin."

In the fifth letter, Tokutomi asserts that it is time for the Japanese empire to complete a number of tasks vis-à-vis the rest of the world. "In the forty years since the Restoration and the opening of the country, we expanded the imperial policy laid down by the Emperor Jimmu. We not only overturned the evil custom of *sakoku* (insularism) but actively sought knowledge, even to the ends of the earth, and carried out our grand administration for the purpose of disseminating the great right-eousness. . . . How fortunate we are to have been born in such extraor-dinary times. To be wrapped up in stylish pursuits, absorbed in love, transiency, and so on, is impardonable misconduct." The essential mis-sion for Japan included, first, to make of Japan a model nation for the world; second, to enlighten and guide those who might be called Japan's Far Eastern "brethren in the broad sense of the word," giving to each his proper due; third, to break down the barrier between East and West, to end discrimination between the yellow and white races, and to realize "the unification of world culture" and "complete harmony among races." At a time when Japan was faced with such challenges, to assert that patriotism was useless, to view the state as a nuisance, and to propound "the epitome of unhealthy thought" in the form of the belief, for ex-ample, that labor on behalf of the state is "superfluous toil," was to be "unbelievably perverse." Such sentiments often appeared in Sohō's sub-sequent publications.

A QUEST FOR PURPOSE

Also central to the period following the Russo-Japanese war was a de-bate among the so-called opinion leaders concerning national goals. The goal of national independence had been substantially achieved as a result of victory over Russia, so it was believed essential that a new national objective be placed before the people, particularly the young. As the establishment of new goals moved to the forefront of public discussion, it tended naturally to involve reflection concerning the past. In an edi-torial entitled "Important Postwar Issues" published immediately after the war, the magazine *Jidai shichō* (Current Trends in Thought) suggested that the war had concluded the first stage of Japan's national development. The task for the future would now be the achievement of independence in "the true sense of the word." In other words, to think of independence merely in terms of politics and military strength was much too shallow. Real independence was a matter of civilization, thought, and religious belief. Construction of the new Japan must await the accomplishment of this "humanistic sense of independence" (*jinbun-teki dokuritsu ishiki*). "To Eastern civilization, which we have already melted down and recast, must be added the essential aspects of European and American culture as it has developed over the past several hundred years. Our task for the future is to allow Japan's uniqueness to shine forth brilliantly in this manner."[24]

It was often remarked that Japan had gained international recognition in the postwar period because of military might alone, whereas non-military areas of national life were still destitute. The augmentation and perfection of those areas should occupy the Japanese people in the future. Such arguments were delicately tinged with the "pathos of victory." In an article in 1913, for example, Hasegawa Tenkei noted that calls for a new sense of national self-awareness had surfaced often since the war. He was referring to the realizations that Japanese were equal in ability to Westerners, and that Japan was qualified to stand among the great nations of the world. The Japanese people certainly had rejoiced when Japan joined the world's first-ranking nations, and the rise of self-confidence as a result of that "self-awareness" was no doubt to be welcomed. Nevertheless, he observed, an appraisal of the state of Japan now, not even ten years after the war, could not fail to make one question Japan's status. Had not the Russo-Japanese war actually ended in a draw? And had not the Japanese people in fact developed "an insincere, meaningless self-awareness" as a result of having deluded themselves into considering it a victory? A look at the state of philosophy, religion, and the theatre certainly revealed the poverty of the Japanese "inner life," but even Japan's financial affairs, industry, and trade were inferior to those of second-class European nations, and the general standard of living was low. Foreign policy lacked the firm principles appropriate to a first-class nation. Domestic government as well, although parliamentary in name, was actually controlled by the elder statesmen (*genrō*). Such incongruities in the life of the nation made it unworthy of first-class status, and hence the new "national self-awareness" proclaimed since the war was nothing more than a false brand of "self-adulation." "We must become enlightened," he urged, "to the fact that the Japanese in no way qualify as the people of a first-rank nation."

---

[24] Editorial, *Jidai shichō* 2, No. 21 (October 1905).

It was the task of the new revolution of national self-awareness to bring home that knowledge.[25]

In 1906 Sasakawa Kiyoshi wrote, "We have often heard of harmony between Eastern and Western cultures, and been told that Japan's divine calling is the unification of those two worlds."[26] Indeed the view was widespread that the reconciliation of East and West was the national mission of the Japanese. In 1908, Yokoi Tokio proposed that Japan's national destiny and mission vis-à-vis the rest of the world was the integration of Eastern and Western civilizations. Such a role was appropriate to a nation that could claim very little in the way of truly indigenous culture. Japan must preserve traditional thought and at the same time absorb the best in philosophy from the rest of the world. The Japanese people should look forward to the day when they would be recognized by the world as truly cosmopolitan.[27]

Writing again the same year, Yokoi observed that as a result of such inherited propensities as exclusionism and resentment toward the unequal treaties, the Japanese retained a tendency toward exclusiveness. Nevertheless, postwar administration depended heavily upon the participation of foreign capital, and it was incumbent upon the Japanese to cultivate an "international perspective." They should cooperate with the world powers on the basis of reciprocity and set to the development of Far Eastern resources. Of course, in view of the contemporary "imperfections in international relations," it was necessary that arms be maintained for survival, but Japan should take a lesson from the Russo-Japanese war and bear in mind the tragedy of international conflict. In that frame of mind, the Japanese must take the initiative with the powers in advancing a "policy advocating plans for the limitation of weapons and the termination of war." This was the "humanitarian duty that the less developed, military countries owe to the advanced world powers." If, on the other hand, Japan "were to become drunk with the glory of victory and give in to an adventurous spirit by moving increasingly toward militarism; in other words, if Japan were to earn the reputation of a warlike nation, the future could only be anticipated with great foreboding." As a country that had already gained military laurels, Japan should now set out on a "path toward the maintenance of peace." "The adoption of a worldwide perspective requires that the Japanese

---

[25] Hasegawa Tenkai, "Kokumin no daini jikaku," *Taiyō* 19, No. 1 (January 1913). Also see Kuroiwa Ruikō, "Shisō no seiryoku" in Kuroiwa, *Jikkō-ron* (1915); Asada Tadamura, "Sametaru Nihon, nemuretaru Nihon," *Taiyō* 16, No. 6, May 1910); and Uchida Roan, "Taishō jidai no shimei—Taishō jidai-kan," *Chūō kōron* (February 1914).

[26] Sasakawa Kiyoshi, *Taikan shōkan* (1908), p. 45.

[27] Yokoi Tokio, "Shinpo no taisei ni taisuru shōhandō no jidai," *Shin-kōron* (November 1908).

not forget for a single day that for them the only way is to champion brilliantly the cause of humanity and peace."[28]

Yokoi's high-minded ideals were by no means unique, but the most usual approach to the debate on new goals was to advocate that Japan press on toward national expansion. Participants called variously for expansion northward, southward, and omnidirectionally, but as is well known, a prominent role was played by the division between the "march north" and the "march south" positions.

DISSOLUTION OF CONSENSUS

The perspectives represented regarding future goals were diverse. Worthy of particular emphasis, however, is the disappearance after the war of the active and broad national consensus regarding goals that had held fast ever since the Meiji Restoration. As the death of the Emperor Meiji ushered in the Taishō era, many commentators lamented the passing of broad agreement as they nostalgically relived the days of the Meiji period. In his 1915 book entitled *On Ambition*, Sawayanagi Masatarō explained ambition as consisting of passionate hopes and ideals, an unyielding will, and an irrepressible heroic spirit. The people of Meiji, both as individuals and as a nation, had embraced such an ambition and had striven to translate it into action. The Taishō Japanese, however, let it slip. When people had ambition, a country would prosper; when they did not, nothing more than maintenance of the status quo could be expected. From the Meiji Restoration until the Russo-Japanese war, the Japanese people had achieved remarkable advances. Behind that progress was a willingness to spare no effort in carrying out the four great objectives: treaty revision, solution of the Korean problem, establishment of constitutional government, and the induction of Western civilization. By 1907, however, all those goals had been accomplished, and it seemed that both the state and the people had lost their "great hopes, great goals, and great ambitions." The nation had lost its energy. People had surrendered themselves to indolence and acquiesced in the status quo.

No apparent progress had been achieved in the ten years since the war. Not only that, but a series of regrettable circumstances emerged socially, politically, and morally, giving rise to a school of pessimism regarding the future of the empire. In order to make the future bright, the people must have "great aspirations, high ideals, passionate hopes, in other words, ambition." If the youth of the day could be presented with great national issues and high goals, they "would never devote

---

[28] Yokoi Tokio, "Sekaiteki Nihonjin-taru no shisō," *Jidai* 3, No. 26 (April 1906).

themselves to sweet pleasures and immerse themselves in idleness. They would no longer stay aloof from society, flatter themselves, or become addicted to sentimental literature; they would not run to individualism or unwholesome thought, nor would they become intoxicated with lewd songs of renewal (*fukkatsu no uta*)." Accordingly, opinion leaders must provide the people with national objectives. As one such objective, Sawayanagi proposes solution of the China problem and, beyond that, the realization of a "greater Asianism" with Japan in the lead.[29]

Similarly, Kayabara Kazan wrote in 1915 that from the Meiji Restoration to the Russo-Japanese war, the Japanese had shared a certain common enthusiasm. That disappeared after the war against Russia, however, when a "degenerate materialism" spread through intellectual circles and people in all stations of society fell into a spirit of living for the moment. Hence, "there are no ideals, no organized national priorities and, accordingly, no sense of national purpose." If the country were to go on like this, it would lose its right to life as a nation. The country should unify its people under the banner of world empire or national doom and establish a "great determination to advance southward." A new Japan should be built spanning both north and south from the equator.[30]

THE GOVERNMENTAL RESPONSE

Having explored some views put forward by ideologists who took their stand on the traditional values of the establishment, it would be well to have a look at the policy of the government. In April 1906, the year following conclusion of the Russo-Japanese war, Makino Nobuaki, Minister of Education in the first Saionji cabinet, told a gathering of prefectural governors that the government would place increasing emphasis on ethical education. He said that the objective would be to "foster wholesome minds in children and students and thereby cultivate a nation of people whose moral energy is directed toward sincerity and honesty." The future of the state rode on the sincerity of the people. Material progress caused public morality to decline, leading to luxury. In fact,

the young have recently taken to extravagance, receiving inappropriate amounts of money for school expenses and using up other large sums as well; some also take an interest in empty doctrines and philosophies and soon lapse into a pessimistic view of life. This state of

---

[29] Sawayanagi Masatarō, *Yashin-ron* (1915): preface and pp. 2-4, 100-126, 136-141.

[30] Kayabara Kazan, "Kangeki naki jidai—ika ni seinen no jisatsu o mirubeki ya," *Chūō kōron* (autumn supplement, 1915).

affairs is hardly conducive to the cultivation of wholesome energy and orderly progress.

Such trends had to be stamped out. The saying that "wholesome thought and enterprises are fostered on the battlefield, while the nation's many ills are born of peace" was most significant. We should realize, he said, that the German empire emerged from war and for the past thirty years had introduced military spirit and discipline into all corners of society in the context of peaceful competition. The country's contemporary prosperity was the natural result. He then enumerated factors that should be heeded in education. In discussing women's education, he stated that its objective must be "good wives and wise mothers." The praise and favor heaped upon female scholars and businesswomen by the public and newspapers was therefore to be deplored.

In June of the same year, Minister Makino issued a set of official instructions providing that the duty of students is to maintain wholesome thoughts and "solid objectives," devoting present efforts to the attainment of future growth. Expectations were particularly high for students, in whose hands would rest the administration of the postwar state. Nevertheless, a tendency toward "depressed spirits and degeneration of discipline" was regrettably becoming evident among young men and women. There were young people in school "who are satisfied with small successes, who crave luxury, and who worry themselves over idle fancies and therefore neglect the serious business of learning how to get on in the world. They are sometimes extremely licentious and lax in conduct, with no sense of duty or propriety." If something were not done right away about such tendencies, there could be no telling where they might lead.

He also held that when certain segments of society tended toward frivolity, the temptations affecting youth became more numerous and powerful. An investigation of printed materials revealed tracts expounding radical views, materials advocating pessimistic philosophies, literature portraying all manner of vulgar situations. Many such materials were extremely damaging from the viewpoint of education. Hence very careful guidance with regard to reading matter for students was essential.

Moreover, he cautioned, "individuals propounding extreme forms of socialism" had recently appeared in various quarters and had tried by any available means to attract teachers and students to their views. The currency in educational circles of "dangerous thought, which makes light of the founding of the nation and disrupts the social order," did not auger well at all for the future of the state. Those involved with education should maintain discipline, root out radical prejudices, and nip evil in the bud. Students as well as teachers should spare no effort to see that education had its desired effect.[31]

The Boshin Imperial Edict (*Boshin shōsho*) was promulgated in October 1908 under the second Katsura cabinet. Clearly indicating contemporary concerns, it read,

> Only a short while has passed since the war, and governmental administration is increasingly in need of new vigor and discipline.

> We desire that all classes should be united in mind and spirit, devoted to their callings, diligent and frugal in their work, faithful, and dutiful. They should cultivate courtesy and warmheartedness, avoid ostentation and adhere to simple realities, guard against laxity and self-indulgence while undertaking arduous toil.

> The heritage of our divine ancestors and the illustrious history of our nation shine like the sun and stars. If our subjects cleave to that tradition and sincerely strive for its perfection, the foundation for national development will largely have been secured.

Apprehensive about postwar tendencies and the mood of youth, the ruling elite resorted to an imperial show of concern. Obviously, they hoped the emperor's authority would restrain the impulses of their countrymen and stabilize the structure of power.

It was no doubt with similar aims in mind that the ruling class sought to mobilize the power of religion. Their effort is best exemplified in the scheme to "bring together the three religions," which was formulated primarily by Tokonami Takejirō, home minister in the second Saionji cabinet. Tokonami explained the objective of the movement by saying that the cultivation of national morality can only be carried out adequately through education and religion together. Accordingly, it would be extremely desirable for educational and religious parties to cooperate on behalf of national education. "The civilization and enlightenment of a country" requires progress on both the material and spiritual fronts. Nevertheless, relations had worsened recently in the city between workers and capital, and in the countryside between landlords and tenants. The "warmth in relations between the various classes" appeared gradually to be disappearing, and this lack was particularly evident within the families of the rural poor. Surely such circumstances were most deplorable. The problem, however, was that a solution could not be attained through economic means alone. It was also necessary to provide such people with the spiritual solace of religion. By the same token, a school education alone did not suffice to preserve firm moral

---

[31] Ministry of Education Directive No. 1 (*kunrei daiichigō*), (9 June 1906).

fiber throughout the life cycle. A form of continuous social education was essential, and the bulk of that had to be provided by religion.[32]

In order to carry out such a plan, Home Minister Hara Takashi held an audience with representatives from the Shinto, Buddhist, and Christian faiths in February of 1912. Prime Minister Saionji was absent on account of illness, but it was a large gathering, including the ministers of justice, telecommunications, and navy, along with related administrative personnel. The three religious leaders met again the following day, and proceeded, with Tokonami's participation, to draw up a resolution. It provided that in recognition of the government's interest in joining together the three religions, "We will bring our respective doctrines into full play in order to aid the prosperity of the imperial throne and to promote the elevation of the national morality." Furthermore, "we wish to be able to enhance the respect of the authorities for religion; the reconciliation of politics, religion, and education; and the fulfillment of the national cause."[33]

A meeting was subsequently held among representatives of the three religions, scholars, and educators, through the good offices of Anezaki Masaharu. Tokonami wanted to have such meetings on an annual basis,[34] but that ideal was never realized as a result of a cabinet reshuffle the following year. It is noteworthy that the next such meeting was held soon after the imperial assassination incident.

The ruling elite also became seriously involved with provincial youth organizations (seinendan). They encouraged the formation of such groups, made an effort to foster their growth, and, by guiding their activities sought to link provincial youth firmly to the traditional power structure. In April 1910 a national convention of such groups was held in Nagoya and attracted 1,900 participants. The convention passed a list of twelve by-laws (seinendanki jūnisoku) and a set of objectives (jikkō subeki yōmoku). The former included such items as "obey the purport of the Imperial Rescript on Education and the Boshin Imperial Edict," "cultivate a spirit of loyalty to the sovereign and love of country," and "revere the kokutai and respect our ancestors."[35]

SYMPATHETIC UNDERSTANDING

In a May 1880 speech, Kiyama Kumajirō confessed to having agonized over the problem of how man should live. He asked his older school

[32] Tokonami Takejirō, "Sankyō ni kansuru shiken" in Maeda Renzan, *Tokonami Takejirō den* (1939), pp. 252-259.

[33] Ibid., pp. 270-275 for the text of the speech.

[34] Ibid., p. 281.

[35] See Yamamoto Takinosuke, *Chihō seinen dantai* (1909), included in *Yamamoto Takinosuke zenshū* (1931). Also Kumaya Tatsujirō, *Dai-Nihon seinendan-shi* (1942).

mates, scholars, and religious leaders for a solution but was unable to get a satisfactory answer. Finally, he came to believe that such people "ignore the experiences of young people and therefore cannot understand the way we think." He went on to argue as follows: I am not alone in embracing such doubts. Many young people share my feelings. I have been perplexed by a number of problems, one of which has to do with the issue of "what should we be doing? In other words, what should we believe in as the basis for human action?" But my elders, scholars, and religious men have never experienced anxiety concerning fundamental problems of human existence. They are content, therefore, to say that such issues are "an extravagance; it would be better to turn your attentions elsewhere," they say. Aside from whether the apprehensions of youth are right or wrong, they do not even address the issue and make no effort to understand our suffering. They merely criticize and are completely unsympathetic. Another problem which has vexed us is how we should react to socialist thought. Again, there have been no serious essays criticizing socialism on the basis of Japanese social realities and offering alternative ways to reform social ills. Third, in the three-odd years since I graduated from school I have agonized over the problem of people's livelihood. The misery and ugliness of the world have made me unable to suppress an inner sense of anxiety. Also, I have had grave doubts about the "issue of success" which is so popular these days. Success is generally thought of in financial terms, but no one has convincingly addressed the problem of "what is beyond success" and what is "true success from the perspective of human life in general." There is an incessant war in my heart "between success and something beyond success." Finally, there is the problem of romantic love which has been so widely discussed without generating any real answers. Altogether, those who are in positions of leadership "do not understand properly the experiences of young men" like myself who are perplexed by these problems. In other words, he says, the present age is a transitional one characterized by a head-on clash between old and new ways of thinking.[36]

The above speech was included in a collection of Kiyama's works with an introduction by the ethical scholar Ōshima Masanori. Ōshima said, "I have been asked to review these selections because I not only know Mr. Kiyama but am familiar with today's youth. As a contemporary man himself, Kiyama is most sensitive to the dynamics of the contemporary age, and as a youth he is able to sympathize with the standpoint of today's young people." Regarding the above speech, he

[36] Kiyama Kumajirō, *Kiyama Kumajirō ikō*, pp. 64–89.

says, "Kiyama has spoken straight from the heart regarding the viewpoint of youth."

Despite Kiyama's experience, people who adopted a sympathetic attitude and sought to understand the trends that swept through the younger generation in the years after the Russo-Japanese war—who, moreover, tried to find beneath such trends the pulse of a new age—were not entirely absent from the older generation. That fact is illustrated by a 1908 anthology of critical pieces written after 1906 by Togawa Shūkotsu. In it, Togawa reviewed the admonitions of Education Minister Makino which, as noted above, were issued in 1906. He pointed out that Makino's rules forbade the corruption of public morals, pessimism, socialism, and luxury, and their tone throughout was entirely negative and passive. In Togawa's view, however, "to the extent that one believes in a positive approach, luxury should be affirmed, socialism should be welcomed, and pessimism a cause for rejoicing. If we allow ourselves to be disconcerted by diversity among moral codes we will find ourselves totally ignorant of the spirit of the age and the trend of the times."[37]

Togawa went on to say that the youth had become a focal point of criticism. But no matter how dissolute they might have become, they could not hold a candle in that regard to the politicians and educators of the time. We must ask, he said, why the youth have attracted such bitter diatribes. In the first place, the public ridiculed the gentleness of youth by calling them the "party of stars and violets" and other names. But the trend among youth they sought to highlight was the result of the introduction of Western thought. Moreover, members of the "party of stars and violets" knew things that "their Meiji elders find themselves unable to sample." "Leaving aside for a moment the question of their relative merits, these things are quite different from those of the previous generation." "It is only to be expected," he said, "that just as the new generation finds it impossible to understand the old, those raised in earlier times are unable to comprehend the stars and violets of the younger generation."

Because they are unable to comprehend, Togawa says, they inevitably misconstrue. The "elderly" saw the "devotees of stars and violets" as incontrovertibly corrupt and dissolute and therefore could not conceive of the young as the harbingers of something new. Young men and women might indeed be indecisive and on the verge of corruption, but they were also the products of new trends and natural currents. If they were guided properly, they would cause something new to spring up. There was even then something new arising in place of the "party

---

[37] Togawa Shūkotsu, "Kijō shōkan—Saionji naikaku no bunsei," *Chūō kōron* (August 1906); also in Togawa, *Jidai shikan* (1908).

of stars and violets." The relative merits of that new phenomenon depended upon how it was guided. Perplexity and suicide were certainly phenomena of the new age, and at first glance they seemed undesirable, but beneath them there are elements that should be welcomed, and those were the "signs of progress." He, for one, would have liked to see in perplexity and suicide "the overflow of youthful vigor into new dimensions."

Second, he says that compared to ten years ago Western thought was extremely widespread among the young, and accordingly the hold on young minds of Confucianism and *bushidō* had weakened immeasurably. When viewed from the perspective of the old, for whom a brand of morality transcending loyalty and filial piety was unimaginable, this could only be interpreted as a sign of youthful dissipation. But times were changing. When change is precipitous it inevitably would give rise to abhorrence accompanied by a disparaging attitude. Nevertheless, he believed that for the intellectual world such changes marked "the welling up of an exalted spirit" and a "step toward great progress." One should not stand in its way.

Third, the so-called wise men were concerned that a wave of extravagance would overcome society. Virtually all of those in positions of leadership had advanced to their contemporary state of eminence only after a poverty-stricken student life. Nevertheless, there was nothing inherently beneficial in such suffering. Also, the contemporary standard was far above that of the past, and it was natural that this trend should have transformed "the smoldering vigor of youth." Moreover, the new generation of youths used its brain power to get along, whereas the earlier generation had been able to get by on their ragged appearance. In the West, English and American university students "live no differently from real gentlemen," and it was not only natural but desirable that Japanese students should move in the same direction.

Hence, for Togawa, the "elderly" were mistaken in their view that such changes indicated luxury and extravagance, and their agony over the deterioration of youth was misplaced. No doubt it was true, he admitted, that many among the young have lost their spirit and frivolously pursue luxury, but they "will lose out when times change." If the young are now given proper guidance by those in authority, the trends of the time would give rise to a new public morality and a new spirit; a new code of gentlemanly conduct would also emerge. In other words,

> The sick have no appetite. When a patient gains more of an appetite, surely it is an indication that his disease is less serious. Desire is actually life itself. I love desire. I love it as the essential condition of life. Respect for the stars and violets, advocacy of new knowledge,

and taste for beauty—these require no special justification. The misconduct of youth is none other than the discovery of desire. Are they really so decadent? Rather, with only slight exaggeration, their behavior may be said to reveal their capabilities.

If those trends and manners were well guided and their adherents ably led they would provide important elements of the coming society. It was a mistake to think that mere "prohibitionism" would suffice.

> No matter that youth are decadent and the times are corrupt. As far as I am concerned, it is not due to trends among youth that society is withering and dying from corruption. On the contrary, I wonder if they are not actually giving rise to a new life. If those with knowledge and experience would step forward to give guidance it would be all the more fortunate.[38]

In principle Togawa adopted a positive attitude toward the development of individual self-awareness and the various forms of self-gratification which arose from that development. In addition, he found beneath such trends the creative strength to usher in a new era. In the same vein, Ebina Danjō said in 1910 that the age of braggadocio oriented to the secular state had passed. In its place, "a high-toned egoism which gives priority to the individual is swiftly coming to dominate the minds of the young." Of course, excessive egoism was to be avoided, and a spirit of human charity was essential. Nevertheless, to live by one's own labor and care for one's own parents and family was clearly an advance over the life style of the samurai who devoted themselves to an overlord as "hired thugs" in exchange for a stipend.[39]

Again in 1914, Ebina wrote that in contrast to the time of his own youth and before, when young men were arrogant and enraged over domestic and external affairs, the contemporary disappearance of national crisis had allowed the "naturalistic emotions" of youths to subside and had freed them to direct their concern to their households and occupations. Young men had become more sober and down-to-earth in thought, and more realistic. Compared to the "ruffian-like" poses struck by swaggering youths in his own day, they carried themselves with an air of "little gentlemen." Ebina considered this to be a great improvement.[40]

Another who strongly supported the individualistic philosophy of contemporary youth, but from a perspective different from that of Togawa, was Ukita Kazutami. In many books and articles, he passionately propounded a "new morality" based on individualism. He said, for ex-

[38] Togawa Shūkotsu, "Gendai shichō no ichibetsu," *Jidai shikan*, pp. 35–42.
[39] Ebina Danjō, *Shin-kokumin no shūyō* (1910), pp. 7–8.
[40] Ebina Danjō, *Ningen no kachi* (1914), pp. 397–399.

ample, that a religion of ancestor worship had existed in Japan since olden times, and loyalty to the emperor and patriotism were bound tightly to that religious ethos. But when Japan overthrew the feudal system, which ancestor worship had served, and moved toward Western civilization it became necessary to disseminate among the people an ethical framework centering on the absolute value of the individual personality. It was also necessary to develop a parliamentary system of government based on respect for the individual.[41] Although the thought of the older generation was still steeped in the influence of pre-Restoration literature and the Confucian classics, the thought of the members of the younger generation was completely dominated by the philosophy, literature and science of the West. Despite the fact that contemporary young men and women were still educated according to the precepts of filial piety, they followed major currents in society at large by remaining self-oriented in their perception of the world. That inevitably affected their attitudes toward relationships of parent to child, sovereign to subject, teacher to pupil, friend to friend, old to young, and male to female. An increasing proportion of the young had descended into licentiousness, but any use of such all too apparent abuses of freedom as a pretext to reject freedom altogether would only close off the road to national progress and dash all hope of social advancement. It was preferable to rely upon guidance through the medium of wholesome public opinion.[42]

In 1911 Kamata Eikichi observed that the world as a whole was moving from a "militaristic" age to a "commercial" one. As a result, it was almost impossible to find a civilized country ruled by military men. Of course, expansion of the navy was also necessary to protect a country's commerce and colonies. Nevertheless, he said, our education is the same as ever, and many continue to believe that, in principle, as long as order in the form of kokutai is preserved and we remain submissive everything will be all right. But this, he concluded, was fundamentally mistaken. In consideration of the world trends he outlined, Japan had to change to a viewpoint that would "heighten individuality."[43]

In addition, in 1912 the ethical scholar Fujii Kenjirō wrote that the Japanese were living in a transitional era. A new ethics was taking the place of the old one. In content, that new ethic included such precepts as: the people should participate in and manage national government; the rights guaranteed by the constitution should be respected; there should be no distinction between noble and vulgar when it came to occupation, and people should be free to choose their own line of work; women

[41] Ukita Kazutami, "Shōrai no Nihon ni kansuru san dai gimon," Taiyō 14, No. 1 (January 1908).

[42] Other works by Ukita include Jinkaku to hin'i (1908) and Shin-dōtoku ron (1913).

[43] Kamata Eikichi, Dokuritsu jison (1911), pp. 7-12.

were as worthy of respect as men; and so on. All these elements were informed by the spirit of freedom and equality. Freedom meant individual freedom and equality meant individual equality. Hence at the basis of freedom and equality was the concept of the irreducible and inherently valuable human personality. It was only natural that this new ethical spirit should have been challenged continually by the "historical" national philosophy that exalted loyalty, self-sacrifice, and duty.

Fujii tended to approve the new individualistic ethic, but he went on to call for the reconciliation and even unification of freedom and equality with the so-called historical national philosophy. He failed to offer any principle by which this reconciliation could be accomplished, however, so his proposal amounted in the end to little more than a facile brand of eclecticism.[44]

THE SEEDS OF TAISHŌ DEMOCRACY

As I have suggested, the political process from the Taishō political crisis to the advent of the second Ōkuma cabinet definitely conveyed an impression that "the people" were growing into a political force that could no longer be ignored. In a *Tōyō keizai shinpō* newspaper editorial of December 25, 1914, entitled "An Eventful Year," a writer noted that during the period from the resignation of the second Saionji cabinet to the formation of Ōkuma Shigenobu's second government, the masses had often played an important political role. "Mass forces" could now exert strong political influence. Nevertheless, since the mass movement had not yet developed a single organizational expression, this trend harbored considerable danger. It was impossible to predict what would come of it. The same sort of uprisings and mass disturbances that Japan had witnessed recently had preceded the French Revolution. He sincerely hoped, he said, that the public would not simply dismiss the power of the masses in politics as spasmodic or uncreative. For the normally liberal *Tōyō keizai shinpō* to express such a concern bespeaks the degree of shock occasioned by the emergence of mass movements in politics.

The April 1914 issue of *Chūō kōron* collected the views of a number of "opinion leaders" on the subject of mass politics. In one selection, Hayashi Kiroku said that since the Hibiya riots of 1905 it had been customary to seek a solution to political problems in the emergence of mass demonstrations. That trend of thought indicated that average people were beginning to see government as their own business and to have sensitive feelings about political issues. As such, he proposed, it should be welcomed as the "current of a new age."

[44] Fujii Kenjirō, "Shinrai shisō to rekishi shisō to no chōtotsu," *Taiyō* 18, No. 12 (September 1912).

In another, Ukita Kazutami wrote that it is against the spirit of parliamentary politics for government to be controlled by mass movements. But the masses rose up because the government abused power and there was no public opinion by means of which such abuses could be checked. Hence the movements could be understood as transitional phenomena in the change from an autocratic age to a parliamentary one.

Yoshino Sakuzō said in his contribution that mass demonstrations occur when governmental ills are excessive and cannot be controlled through normal means. They arise from the self-awareness of the masses and, in turn, increase that self-awareness. In the case of the riots that took place under the third Katsura cabinet in 1913 and the first Yamamoto cabinet in 1914, a small minority was able to manipulate the masses, and therefore those movements were disparaged. Aside from that aspect, however, they were welcome events to the extent that they contributed to the heightening of self-awareness on the part of the people.[45]

World War I broke out about four months after the formation of the second Ōkuma cabinet, and it was in the latter stages of that conflict that what came to be called the Taishō democratic movement made its appearance. It is obvious that the movement found its direct impetus in a whole complex of international and domestic factors. But when we orient our search for antecedents to the political realities of the time, we are led to the image of the masses projected by the political disturbances that occurred after the Russo-Japanese war. On the other hand, if we direct our search for antecedents to the intellectual realm, we are reminded of the growth of individual self-awareness that was characteristic of youth culture following that conflict. In that regard, it is significant that, as we have seen, Fujii Kenjirō found the basis for a new ethics in a belief in freedom and equality grounded on an ethos of respect for the individual personality. It is also suggestive that Ukita Kazutami, who adopted a very positive attitude toward the individualism espoused by the youth of his day, and called for a "new morality" centering on the absolute value of the individual, went on in later years to participate in the Taishō democratic movement. Even though the growth of individual self-awareness among youth following the Russo-Japanese war was viewed by members of the ruling class and various ideologies as highly prejudicial to the power structure and as a disharmonious force in society, it can be argued convincingly that it was this very trend among youth that contained the seeds of Taishō democracy.

[45] This essay is also included in a collection of Yoshino's works entitled *Sūfu to naikaku hoka* (Tokyo: Asahi Bunko 16, 1950).

THE BUREAUCRATIC STATE IN JAPAN: THE PROBLEM OF AUTHORITY AND LEGITIMACY

BERNARD S. SILBERMAN

INTRODUCTION

The modern Japanese state between 1868 and 1945 shared at least one problem with the industrializing and industrialized states of the West. It too was under siege. Despite the accumulation of enormous resources and extensive police powers, industrializing states found themselves with few exceptions faced with the fear and problem of ungovernability. Indeed, it would not be too much to say that, as such widely different thinkers as Tocqueville, Marx, and Durkheim observed, the central problem of the nineteenth and twentieth centuries was the governability of society. From this recognition of the potential of society for ungovernability as reflected in the seemingly unquenchable propensity toward association, conflict, and violence in the nineteenth century body politic grew the "policy sciences"—political economy, government, sociology, jurisprudence, and anthropology (colonial governability). Whatever the analytical mode, they were all informed by the central notion that the problematic character of social order was directly the consequence of the Western and therefore capitalist experience of industrialization. The increasing social division of labor created disjunction, leading to differentiated life and work cycles that were malintegrated. From this malintegration rose conflict, sometimes defined in terms of class, sometimes in terms of role, sometimes in terms of party, and sometimes in terms of all three. In all of these views the state has been seen as primarily a dependent factor or variable. The state has been viewed as the creation or the executor of dominant class interests or as rising from the functional necessities of integrating ever greater complexity in social roles. The state either represses conflict in the interest of class or mitigates it by acting as the integrator of conflicting, specialized, and differentiated roles or interests.[1] In short, conflict is seen as essentially a social rather than political characteristic. Durkheim perhaps summed this up best: "political questions have lost their interest"; they affect only "a small party of society," never the "vital part." We must look "under this superficial covering" to find "how the great social interests exist and act."[2]

At the heart of the matter is the role of the state in its relation to civil society. Is it, in fact, the case that the state in its various administrative, bureaucratic forms merely reflects passively, integrates, or mediates the hierarchy and conflicts of interest that exist in civil society? The question itself is raised by the experience of a large number of societies in which the state appears to have been and is a primary actor in the formation of interests and of civil society generally. The very intervention of the state in the organization of civil society, as a wide range of writers has noted, has become an identifying characteristic not simply of noncapitalist but of modern capitalist political systems as well. Indeed, since the turn of the century such countries as Germany, Italy, Japan, Spain, Portugal, and large numbers of Latin American countries and other newly developing societies have seen the state emerge at varying times to assume the predominant role in organizing interests, while still retaining a capitalist economic form.[3] One of the major anomalies of this process of intervention has been that the rationale for such intervention, the

---

[1] The former view is still summed up best by Marx's and Engels' formulation: "The executive of the modern state is but a committee for managing the common affairs of the whole bourgeoisie." Karl Marx and Friedrich Engels, "Manifesto of the Communist Party," in Saul K. Padover, ed. and trans., *On Revolution* (The Karl Marx Library, vol. I), (New York: McGraw Hill, 1971), p. 82. See also, Ralph Miliband, *The State in Capitalist Society* (New York: Basic Books, 1969). The neo-Marxist view is also represented by Nicos Poulantzas, *Political Power and Social Classes* (London: NLB and Sheed and Ward, 1978). The latter view is represented by Talcott Parsons, *The Social System* (New York: Free Press, 1951), p. 162. See also R. A. Dahl, *A Preface to Democratic Theory* (Chicago: University of Chicago Press, 1956); also Samuel P. Huntington, *Political Order in Changing Societies* (New Haven, Yale University Press, 1968). These latter stress the integrative conception of the state.

[2] Emile Durkheim, *La socialisme* (Paris, 1928), p. 213.

[3] Generally on this question see, Andrew Shonfield, *Modern Captalism* (London, 1965); P. Schmitter, "Still the Century of Corporatism," *Review of Politics*, 36 (January 1974): 85-131; C. Maier, *Recasting Bourgeois Europe* (Princeton: Princeton University Press, 1975); L. Lindberg et al., *Stress and Contradiction in Modern Capitalism* (Lexington, Mass.: Lexington Books, 1975); D. Schoenbaum, *Hitler's Social Revolution* (Garden City: Doubleday, 1966); Gaetana Salvemini, *Under the Axe of Fascism* (New York: Viking Press, 1936).

problem of governability—the actual or potential consequences of un-mitigated conflicts of interest—has not reduced levels of conflict for very long periods of time. On a number of occasions this conflict has led to situations in which the state has sought to monopolize completely the process of public policy making by organizing public interests in a hi-erarchical, well-defined, functional structure, subordinated to state administrations. This has raised the question of whether the state has an interest of its own.[4] That is to say, when the state through its structural representation, the bureaucratic administration, enters into the process of organizing interests and ends by dominating those interests and trans-forming them into public ones, it appears as if the state were a compet-ing interest group itself. Even in those systems where state intervention has not assumed a predominant role—the United States, Great Britain, Sweden, Norway—it has become clear that private interests have come increasingly to deal directly with the state bureaucracy and have in the process bypassed legislatures and political parties.[5] The state thus ap-pears increasingly to be a direct participant in the negotiation of interest.

This seemingly secular trend of the state's direct participation in the negotiation and organization of interests suggests that it is in fact a ma-jor contributor to the problem of governability. By its active interven-tion in the process of ordering interests, the state appears to claim for itself the privilege of determining the legitimacy of interests, thereby creating the conditions for conflict. Each interest seeks to establish its legitimacy. But the state by establishing itself as a determinant of legit-imacy seems to have created a zero-sum game in which the legitimacy of one interest must be purchased at the expense of another. Is this in fact the case? Does the intervention of the state in civil society result not in the elimination of conflict but rather in its maintenance? Or, in some-what different terms, are there inherent constraints in the structure of the modern state that lead to the institutionalization of conflict?

[4] See, Poulantzas, *Political Power and Social Classes*; Jurgen Habermas, *Crisis of Legitimacy* (Boston: Beacon Press, 1975); Claus Offe, "Introduction to Part II," in L. Lindberg et al., *Stress and Contradiction in Modern Capitalism*; H. A. Winkler, ed., *Organisierter Kapitalismus* (Göttingen: Vandennoeck and Ruprecht, 1974).

[5] Theodore J. Lowi, *The End of Liberalism* (New York: Norton, 1969), pp. 55-100, 287-296; Henry Ehrmann, ed., *Interest Groups in Four Continents* (Pittsburgh: University of Pittsburgh Press, 1958); Nigel Harris, *Competition and the Corporate Society* (London: Methuen, 1972); Joseph La Palombara, *Interest Groups in Italian Politics* (Princeton: Princeton University Press, 1964); R. E. Pahl and J. T. Winkler, "The Coming Corporatism," *Challenge* (March/April 1975), pp. 28-35; Olaf Ruin, "Participatory Democracy and Corporatism: The Case of Sweden," *Scandinavian Political Studies* 9 (1974), 171-186; Samuel H. Beer, *British Politics in the Collectivist Age* (New York: Knopf, 1969); Roland Huntford, *The New Totalitarians* (New York: Stein and Day, 1972); Gerhard Lehmbruch, "Liberal Corporatism and Party Government," *Comparative Political Studies*, 10 (April 1977), 91-126.

An analysis of the emergence and development of the state in Japan after 1868 provides one means of examining this question. From the very beginning of the Restoration, the state played a dominant role in the organization of interests and the determination of public policy. It is clear that the representatives of the state, the Meiji leaders and their bureaucratic successors, were continually concerned with the problem of the governability of society.[6] Each presentation of new or old interests—farmer, business, labor, industry—provided an occasion for new concern over the viability of society. It is even more noticeable that the state's actions and concerns over interests did not result in a noticeably orderly society until the mid-1930s, when the state foreclosed on all concepts of interests. The peasant unrest of the Meiji was joined by other forms as the nineteenth century ended and the twentieth century progressed: urban conflict, the demonstrations accompanying the Sino-Japanese and Russo-Japanese treaties, the rice riots of August–September 1918; labor unrest—the growth of industrial and tenant unions and strikes; business unrest—the attempts from 1900 on to organize business and industry in order to resist some state intervention and policies. To these must be added the unruliness of the ultranationalists and their sympathizers in the military. In short, a close look at prewar Japan suggests that despite a state with vast police resources, a society with a formal ethic of social harmony, and a supposedly firm social commitment to the values of authority, hierarchy, and obedience, Japan was as unruly a modern state as might be found.

In this regard, Japan's experience after 1868 embodies the major paradoxes of the modern capitalist state: centralized power along with unruliness; hierarchical organization of interest combined with market conceptions of interest; public policy formation by narrow elites despite mass participation in politics; formal systems of representation based on notions of individual equality coexisting with informal systems of representation based on the organization and priority of interests. The paradoxes and the conflicts thus generated appear to be centered around the relationship of state to civil society. Insofar as this is a valid inference, the central question can be framed by examining the conditions of the growth and development of the Japanese state. Japan, therefore, provides not merely a case study but a means of posing or suggesting some tentative conclusions about the modern bureaucratic state and its relations to civil society.

[6] See, for example, Kenneth B. Pyle, "The Technology of Japanese Nationalism: The Local Improvement Movement, 1900-1918," *The Journal of Asian Studies*, 33 (November 1973), 51-65; also Ito Hirobumi, "Instructions Addressed to Governors of Cities and Prefectures, September 1887," in W. W. McLaren, "Japanese Government Documents," *Transactions of the Asiatic Society of Japan*, 42 pt. 1 (1914), 324-330.

State Bureaucracy and Legitimacy

Specifically, the problem of the state and its relation to civil society in Japan arises out of several universally recognized paradoxes in Japanese political development. The seizure of power by a new group of leaders in the Meiji Restoration by no means resolved the problem of governability that had arisen in the late Tokugawa period. Indeed, the problem of governability—authority, legitimacy, and obedience—was clearly the primary problem to which the new leaders addressed themselves. Despite serious challenges, the Meiji leadership did appear to have established the authority of the state through the creation of a powerful centralized state bureaucracy by the mid-1880s. The promulgation of the constitution in 1889 seemed to provide the formal capstone to what had already been achieved—a monopoly for the state bureaucracy in organizing society's wants and thus also in establishing the priority of interests. It was with some dismay, then, as the bureaucracy seemed to achieve stability in terms of organization and legitimacy, that the bureaucratic leaders found themselves faced at the end of the century with the emergence of interests with claims to legitimacy that did not have their source in bureaucratic allocation. Political parties, business organizations, and social groups pressed forward their claims in a manner that the bureaucrats found, to their puzzlement, increasingly difficult to reject. At the turn of the century, just as the bureaucracy had become a completely integrated and almost autonomous structure characterized by the possession of Max Weber's legal-rational characteristics, it was forced to retreat from its monopoly over the formation of public policy. Over the next three decades the bureaucracy was forced to admit one claimant after another as having sufficient autonomous priority of interest so as to allow their participation in the process of policy making. It is not too much to say that the period from 1900 to approximately 1936 was one of limited pluralism, to use Linz's phrase.[7] Thus the first paradox: a powerful state bureaucracy created and designed quite consciously to maintain a monopoly over policy making was forced, as it achieved rational organization, to share the process of allocating values and resources with private interests.

The second part of the paradox is equally puzzling. The developments of the 1920s seem to bear out the notion that modern capitalist industrialization was a secular force that would produce ever wider participation of interests in the determination of public wants and their satisfaction. The mid-1930s put an end to this notion as the civil and

---

[7] Juan Linz, "Totalitarian and Authoritarian Regimes," in Fred I. Greenstein and Nelson W. Polsby, eds., *Handbook of Political Science* (Reading, Mass.: Addison Wesley, 1975), vol. 2.

military bureaucracies cooperated to foreclose the whole notion of private interests and sought with considerable success to incorporate those private interests into a public one dominated by the state bureaucracies.

In short, Japan between 1868 and 1945 experienced at least three different means for the authoritative allocation of values and resources. Between approximately 1868 and 1900, authority appears to have rested on the principle of administrative rules—that is, "bureaucratic absolutism." From about 1900 to 1936, authority rested on the principle of organizational consensus: a general agreement among public and private bureaucratic organizations that took the form of what might be called limited pluralism. Finally, between 1936 and 1945, there emerged a structure of authority the basic principle of which was bureaucratic or organizational rationality—something very closely approximating state corporatism. Indeed, it would not seem too extreme to draw the conclusion that authority structures were arbitrary in origin and their principles arbitrary in selection.

The crowning paradox is that despite such pendulum shifts, the bureaucracy continued to enjoy the highest status and the most powerful place in the formation of public policy, a place it continues to enjoy today under a quite different structure of authority. This paradox suggests what others have noted in somewhat different ways, that the state bureaucracy's claim to legitimacy was never seriously challenged. One is forced to conclude that a central characteristic of prewar Japan's political structure was a continued disjunction between legitimacy and authority. To put it another way, the bureaucracy's claim to make public policy was legitimate but somehow not completely authoritative—the basis of legitimacy did not have inherent in it a sufficiently narrow criterion for constraining or allocating legitimacy to only one structure, the state bureaucracy. This helps to explain why Japan could appear to be extraordinarily stable, that is, predictable in terms of the relationship of individuals to the state, but unpredictable with regard to the relationship of groups or interests to the state. Seen in this light, the central problem for Japan after 1868 was, and perhaps still is, the search for an appropriate structure of authority, a problem seemingly focused on the question of integrating the state bureaucracy into society.

The legitimacy of the state bureaucracy's right to organize society's wants in some structure of priorities appears to stand at the center of the problem. On the one hand, whatever its claim to legitimacy, it alone was not sufficient to insure a monopoly, despite the design of its founders. On the other hand, however, its claims have been sufficiently strong to resist attempts to subordinate it, and durable enough to maintain its predominant position of no less than primus inter pares. One can only conclude that the very basis of the bureaucracy's legitimacy contained constraints that did not allow the bureaucracy to subsume society in any permanently institutionalized fashion. But what constraints were present that enabled and seemingly required the bureaucracy to resist a position of either equality or subordination to other organizations in society?

A clue to the answer is provided by the fact that the three structures of authority that emerged between 1868 and 1945 have some consistent similarities and differences, which suggests that although authority structures were arbitrary they were not random developments. First, all three appear to derive their legitimacy from bureaucratic, utilitarian premises, that is, that public policy is best made by "experts." Second, in each the state bureaucracy plays a dominant if not monopolistic role. Third, each is characterized by quite different forms of decision and policy making. From this I think it is possible to conclude that the problem is centered around the development of the bureaucracy as an organization facing quite different decision-making situations. The fact that the bureaucracy emerged and continued to play the dominant role, but did so in varying forms, indicates that the transformation of authority was constrained primarily by organizational and historical contexts in which the bureaucracy sought to maintain its primacy, and thus became itself a primary constraint. The absence of a single principle of institutional authoritativeness suggests further that the basis of bureaucratic legitimacy was itself a product of bureaucratic interest and development that was only an ex post facto constraint. Thus authority in Japan appears to have been purely arbitrary, changing as the bureaucracy itself faced new situations. That fact was of serious concern to a whole generation of constitutional theorists and political activists in Japan.

What, then, was the source of this arbitrariness whose distinctive feature was the powerful role of the bureaucracy? The answer must logically lie in the emergence and development of the bureaucracy as an organization persistently seeking to maintain its influence and authority; the implication is that the state bureaucracy itself is an independent and not simply a dependent variable. In short, if we view the bureaucracy as a complex organization seeking to establish and maintain itself over time as the authoritative institution of Japanese society, then the seemingly arbitrary changes in the structure of authority may be seen as a consequence of the bureaucracy's attempt to resolve, as all organizations seek to do, the uncertainties of its environment.

Specifically, we can suggest that shifts in the structure of authority after 1868 were constrained by the "sunk costs" produced by the wide range of uncertainties emerging out of the Meiji Restoration. The form of resolution provided by the Restoration to the problems of authority and legitimacy was to produce in dialectical fashion a series of developmental problems. Each solution to a problem was to produce a new challenge to bureaucratic and thus state authority. Out of this process emerged not only short-term conflicts, but also the sort of increasing awareness of the arbitrary nature of the bureaucratic state that would be sufficient to produce persistent, long-term conflicts.

The total turnover of leadership accompanying the Restoration created the central problem. The seizure of power by the new leadership left their claims to authority and legitimacy open to question. In their attacks on the Tokugawa regime, the new leaders had appealed to higher moral authority: the emperor. As such appeals are always likely to do, they raised the problem of equality both on the day-to-day level of administration or governance and on the more fundamental level of legitimacy of leadership. By appealing to imperial will, the new leadership denied the possibility of a governmental leadership based on a natural, ascribed hierarchy of governors and governed. At the same time the diversity of social and educational backgrounds from which new leadership was drawn eliminated the possibility of appealing to a natural order of superior men. Indeed, before the emperor there could be no "great names": all men were equal before him. On the general level of legitimacy there was nothing to restrain individuals, either in or out of government, from challenging the authority of those in power by making a similar appeal to higher moral authority. On a day-to-day basis, no problem might have arisen had there been homogeneity of leadership. But when combined with the possibility of resorting to solipsistic appeals to imperial will, the diversity of backgrounds represented in the leadership implied the potential appearance of conflicting views regarding the authority, meaning, and implementation of decisions. This potential for conflict was confirmed when individuals inside and outside the government actually claimed legitimacy for their conflictual behavior by making appeals to imperial will. The most important examples were conflicts among the leaders over Korea in 1873, leading to the Satsuma Rebellion; over the nature of participation in the structure of decision-making that resulted in the emergence of the freedom and popular rights movement (jiyū minken undō); and over the nature of the constitution in 1880-1881 that resulted in the expulsion of Ōkuma and the final settlement of membership in the group of elder statesmen (genrō).

In terms of governmental administration and organization, these conflicting appeals to imperial will created the problem of how to enforce adherence to superior authority. In broad political terms, the questions of authority, legitimacy, and leadership consensus created the problem of social or ideological orthodoxy. These problems could be resolved, as Gouldner has pointed out, only by the techniques of informal solidarity and/or impersonal routinization.[8] If the new leaders were to survive in office they had no choice but to create new structures of informal solidarity by strategically replacing the traditional local leaders and governmental structures. This led to the dissolution of the domains in 1871 and their replacement by prefectures governed by men appointed directly by the new leaders. It is no coincidence that the new governors shared the social, educational, and political characteristics of the central administrative leaders.[9] While this process was going on in the early 1870s, the leadership also sought to eliminate the effects of the absence of homogeneous administrative norms by resorting to rules regarding the boundaries of official authority and the structure of responsibilities. Between 1868 and 1878, the whole structure of local government and its relation to central government, as well as the duties and responsibilities of office holders throughout the hierarchy, were legally defined and enumerated with increasing precision.[10]

Out of this process of role rationalization and strategic replacement emerged the structure of oligarchic decision making. The criteria for appointment in the new government were ambiguous at best. A basic requirement was loyalty to the new regime as indicated by participation in the Restoration movement. Beyond this, there were no explicit criteria or rules regulating appointment, tenure, or advancement. This ambiguity created widespread insecurity and tension reaching to the highest levels of officeholding. The problem was resolved between 1868 and 1875 with the emergence of cliques (as is often the case in such organizational situations).[11] The cliques were organized around a small number of men who held second-level offices in the new central government, and who sought to insure their positions by arranging for the appointment of lower-level officials on the basis of personal loyalty. By 1875 these men had become indispensable. As clique leaders they provided an informal means for securing tenure and advancement for themselves and their subordinates on a more or less predictable basis. At the same time, the clique structure informally solved the problem of the

[8] Alvin W. Gouldner, "The Problem of Succession in Bureaucracy," in Alvin W. Gouldner, ed., *Studies in Leadership and Democratic Action* (New York: Russell and Russell, 1950).

[9] Bernard S. Silberman, "Bureaucratic Development and the Structure of Decision-Making in Japan, 1868-1925," *Journal of Asian Studies*, 29 (May 1970), 347-362.

[10] Jichichō, ed., *Chihō kōmuin seido shiryō* (Tokyo, 1955), 1: 1-88. See also Bernard S. Silberman, "Structural and Functional Differentiation in the Political Modernization of Japan," in Robert E. Ward, ed., *Political Development in Modern Japan* (Princeton: Princeton University Press, 1968), pp. 353-362.

[11] See Anthony Downs, *Inside Bureaucracy* (Boston: Little, Brown, 1967), pp. 67-88, for a description of the emergence of cliques in large-scale bureaucracies.

ambiguity of authority by becoming the mechanism for enforcing the implementation of policy decisions in a uniform manner.[12]

The resolution of these major problems through structures of informal solidarity on the one hand and the use of rules on the other created new developmental problems. Foremost was the problem of continuity in organization and leadership, or the more general problem of legitimacy. The informal structures for determining leadership could not be perpetuated because the original basis for bureaucratic appointment and informal group membership could not be replicated. If bureaucratic leadership was to sustain itself, succession would have to be rationalized and routinized, and a new basis for leadership and organizational legitimacy would have to be found.

The Meiji leaders had few alternative means of resolving this problem. Since they were already committed to a conception of equality and therefore of an equality of wants, essentially they had only two possible choices for the structuring of succession.[13] One alternative was "subjective," rational determination of what was an appropriate leader; that is, all individuals capable of rational choice participate through some form of voting process, selecting the one who most closely represents their rational desires. The other was some selection process that was not inherently discriminatory and based on a notion of "objective rationality," that is, some systematic and scientific method of determining and organizing individual wants or interests for society as a whole that obviates the necessity for each individual to select an appropriate leader. Both are clearly utilitarian notions. The former rests on the assumption that the only way in which the greatest good for the greatest number can be achieved is by counting individual rational choices. The latter rests on the assumption that the greatest good is an emergent property of society taken as a whole, and as an emergent property can only be determined by a science of society and/or a science of wants or economics.[14]

For the Meiji leaders, the first notion was clearly anathema. To opt for subjective notions of rationality would undermine the legitimacy of their own seizure of power, which was, minimally at least, based on some solipsistic notion that they possessed an objective understanding

[12] Hasegawa Ryō, *Meiji ishin ni okeru hanbatsu seiji no kenkyū* (Tokyo, 1966), pp. 63-183.

[13] Robert Dahl suggests three possible alternatives. However, the third, economic rationality, seems to lack the basis of an autonomous choice mechanism. That is, economic rationality may be derived from only subjective assessments of utility or from objective models of utility. See Dahl, *After the Revolution* (New Haven: Yale University Press, 1970), p. 8-55.

[14] John Rawls, *A Theory of Justice* (Cambridge: Harvard University Press, 1971), pp. 25-28.

of the greatest good, whereas all others were mired in false consciousness. Equally important was the fact that to opt for such a solution would undermine the fragile structure of authority built on the twin pillars of informal group structure and a nascent notion of positive administrative rules or law. The first pillar was fragile because it could not be replicated; the second because it relied almost entirely on the notion of imperial will—which, as the Meiji leaders had good reason to know, could be invoked by others. In sum, the Meiji leaders had no choice but to opt for the objective conception of rationality as the basis for selecting leaders and providing continuity in organization.

In the course of institutionalization, this view had to meet specific requirements. It had formally to meet the demand of the equality of wants, while at the same time avoiding an "anarchy" of wants. It had to meet the demand for decision making by a limited group; and, finally, it had to meet the requirement of a routinized and orderly succession of decision makers. Only by a resort to concepts of expertise and impartiality—based on the idea that individual wants could be determined and organized into a social system of wants by scientific observation, knowledge, and application of the rules of economy and society—could the first two of these demands be met. Only by the creation of an autonomous organization based on observable and evaluative criteria, and rules for entrance and orderly rise to leadership, could the last requirement be met. In this sense, indeed, the Meiji leaders were compelled to continue to pursue rationalization not only because they valued it but because they were constrained to do so if they wished to retain the legitimacy of their own actions and status.

It was this situation that led, I would suggest, to the complete rationalization of a structure for recruitment, tenure, advancement, and retirement in the civil bureaucracy in the period 1884 to 1899. By 1900 the majority of upper civil servants were the product of a university education in law, had passed required civil service examinations based on law and jurisprudence, followed a well-defined career and promotion pattern, and were assured tenure.[15] Thus at the end of the century the problem of succession in the leadership within the bureaucracy had been resolved. The routinized career structure with its corresponding educational requirements produced a leadership that was exclusive, astonishingly homogeneous in outlook, and committed to the organization and its role in the political system. Moreover, the career structure itself be-

---

[15] Robert M. Spaulding, Jr., *Imperial Japan's Higher Civil Service Examinations* (Princeton: Princeton University Press, 1967); Bernard S. Silberman, " 'Ringisei'—Traditional Values or Organizational Imperatives in the Japanese Upper Civil Service: 1868-1945," *Journal of Asian Studies*, 32 (February 1973), 251-264.

came highly predictable through dependence on formal rules, thus rein-forcing organizational as opposed to personal authority.[16]

This resolution of the problems of the continuity and legitimacy of state leadership and organization was to have profound consequences for the structure of authority. Forced to make use of objective criteria for determining appropriate leadership and organization, the Meiji lead-ers could no longer base the authority of bureaucracy on informal or-ganization or appeals to imperial will as the basis of positive law. Rather, they would now—by the appeal to expertise and impartiality—be re-quired to find a new basis for authority. However, the basis for legiti-macy—expertise—provided the state with no inherent claim to a mo-nopoly over the organization of society's interests, since other organizaions could recruit experts, as well. As a consequence, some other means would have to be found to maintain the monopoly. Again, very few solutions to the problem were available. Clearly, if the state bureau-cracy, or more specifically its leadership, wished to have a monopoly over policy making, the only way to achieve it was to create a monop-oly over expertise and impartiality. The problem for the state was how to institutionalize such an arrangement in a way that would meet the requirements of formal equality while holding, in fact, such a monopoly and thereby creating inequality. The requirements of equality meant that the acquisition of expertise could not be arbitrarily assigned to any one group. The requirement of expertise and impartiality (and its ob-jective content) meant that it could not be assigned on a subjective basis. In short, expertise had to be acquired through an education capable of being objectively evaluated, and it had to be theoretically open to indi-viduals on an equal basis.

How then to insure a state monopoly? The answer the Meiji leaders produced (with not inconsiderable guidance from European examples) was to create an educational system in the form of a step pyramid. The system was designed not so much to educate as to weed out. Each step upward required a competitive entrance to a narrower and narrower number of schools that the state accepted as capable of producing ex-pertise. The top was so narrow—Tokyo Imperial University—that the state had little trouble adjusting its own structure to absorb the product almost totally. Indeed, it was not until the early 1920s that demand from private organizations grew so great that the state had to increase the number of acceptable schools providing expertise.[17] The state in effect

[16] Ibid., pp. 257-260.

[17] Mombushō, ed., *Gakusei 80-nen shiryōhen* (Tokyo, 1952), pp. 230-255; Herbert Pas-sin, *Society and Education in Japan* (New York: Columbia Teachers College Press, 1965); Ulrich Teichler, *Geschichte und Struktur des Japanischen Hochschulwesens* (Stuttgart, 1975) band I, pp. 100-118.

partially established its authority on its monopoly over expertise through careful control over the reproduction of that quality.

The requirement of impartiality in the application of expertise necessitated enormous emphasis on the extension of rule-making. If the impartial ordering of interest was to be legitimate, it had to be capable of being objectively evaluated. The only means for doing so was to establish precisely the boundaries of all social interests through law. Expertise thus became synonymous with expertise in law and the science of its application, jurisprudence. In this fashion law became the monopoly of the bureaucracy, thereby establishing it as the instrument of social and political orthodoxy. The bureaucracy sought to institutionalize this monopoly through the Meiji Constitution of 1889. The constitution, along with various legal codes promulgated during the following decade, made it clear that positive law was the linchpin of authority in Japanese society. Authority was necessary both in the state and in all the nonpolitical relationships that made up society. Religion, family, and community were all forms of authority binding on the individual who owed them duty and obedience. The codes and the constitution were the instruments that precisely defined these duties, thus making it possible to organize systematically a societywide system of wants and interests, with interests themselves defined by law. On a more general level, this secularized all social organizations. Family, community, and organizations were removed from their bedrock of custom and anchored in a law that made them subject to the arbitrary, utilitarian purposes and aims of society as interpreted by the state bureaucracy.[18]

In dialectical fashion the very conditions of the bureaucracy's success in resolving its major problems raised new ones whose resolution had equally profound consequences. If routinization of the career structure resolved the problem of succession and homogeneity in the leadership, it created some new problems. Foremost among them were differentiation, specialization, and recruitment of personnel. Routinizing careers through administrative rules served organizational authority by making behavior predictable both in the long and short terms. But authority was also constrained by the necessity of maintaining a monopolistic control over a steady flow of uniformly trained candidates. Careers thus had to be made attractive. Predictability of tenure and advancement emerged as solutions. The first was the object of formal rules, whereas the latter was an informal structure that emerged as the consequence of having to deal in the 1890s with pressures from the lower level of the senior civil service now inhabited by the first generation of university-

---

[18] Wada Hideo, "Saiban," in Ukai Nobushige et al., eds., *Nihon kindai hō no hattatsushi* (Tokyo, 1958), 3: 87-88; Ukai Nobushige, *Gyōseihō no rekishiteki tenkai* (Tokyo, 1952), p. 111.

trained officials.[19] Clearly unhappy about both the level and rate of advancement, they sought to dispel their insecurity through the formation of peer-group cliques associated with superior departmental officials. The response to these pressures took two forms: an informal but highly routinized and rapid succession rate culminating in early retirement for senior officials (usually in their late forties or early fifties), and career specialization as the means for acquiring high-level expertise.[20] The former delineated the predictability of the rate for advancement, whereas the latter delineated the career path and level of advancement. Rapid, routinized succession provided a predictable number of positions available for promotion. Career specialization provided a badly needed criterion for categorizing and delimiting the pool for promotions in a predictable manner, namely, experience in a single area of administration. By limiting careers and promotions to a single area of a ministry, seniority could be used as an objective and predictable standard for promotion. Interestingly enough, seniority and career specialization solved the problem of increasing demands for expertise without undermining the solution already arrived at for creating homogeneity—generalist training in law.

The routinization of succession and career specialization transformed the basis for organizational integration. The emergence of these patterns reflected the substitution of legal-rational for personal modes of integration. With this substitution, the basis of oligarchic administrative power dissolved, and it is no coincidence that the oligarchy retired in 1900 from day-to-day supervision of policy making.[21] This dependence on rules and routinized patterns as the source of organizational integration left the bureaucracy bereft of a mechanism capable of authoritatively selecting and ordering priorities. Routinized succession removed the possibility of a long-term, stable leadership while career and departmental specialization produced the now familiar pattern of sectionalism—officials were now entirely committed to their own ministry's priorities.[22] The qualification of career and departmental specialization through administrative rules produced, ironically, precisely those con-

---

[19] Bernard S. Silberman, "The Bureaucrat as Politician in Japan, 1899-1945," in B. Silberman and H. D. Harootunian, eds., *Japan in Crisis: Essays on Taisho Democracy* (Princeton: Princeton University Press, 1975), pp. 183-216.

[20] Ibid.

[21] Roger F. Hackett, "Political Modernization and the Meiji Genro," in Robert E. Ward, ed., *Political Development in Modern Japan* (Princeton: Princeton University Press, 1968), pp. 85-87. Also Bernard Silberman, "Bureaucratic Development and the Structure of Decision-making in the Meiji Period: The Case of the Genro," *Journal of Asian Studies*, 27 (November 1967), 93.

[22] Uzaki Kumakichi, *Chōya no godaibatsu* (Tokyo, 1912), pp. 1-182. This early work still provides an excellent description of the emergence of bureaucratic sectionalism.

ditions by which official and department could and did establish their autonomy. The very rules created to establish the subordination of individual and department to organizational authority now became the basis for establishing the autonomy of individual and departmental goals. The axiom that rules may provide subordination but also produce autonomy was extraordinarily well illustrated here.

Thus, at the turn of the century, the state bureaucratic leaders found themselves faced internally with the crucial problem of how to determine priorities in policy making. The solution to this problem turned out to be typical of such situations: the development of a routine pattern of negotiation and compromise. The pattern was clearly reflected in that most explicit expression of priority ordering, the budget. By 1900 the process of budget formulation was a product of complex, year-long negotiations and compromise.

In this context, a Diet prerogative that had originally seemed unimportant surfaced as a potent weapon. The constitution had given the Diet only the most insignificant of powers. With regard to the most crucial power, control of the budget, the Diet had only the power to refuse, and even this veto power was vitiated by the bureaucracy's constitutional power to bring into force the previous year's budget with certain emergency items added on. So long as the oligarchy acted authoritatively to allocate priorities, the veto power was essentially meaningless. With the removal of the oligarchs, however, the latent centrifugal forces of specialization and sectionalism surfaced. Rejection of a budget by the Diet now meant that bureaucratic leaders had to renegotiate the distribution of funds on the basis of the previous year's budget. The problems thus raised are self-evident.

The only way to avoid this kind of bottleneck was to attempt to preclude the possibility of Diet rejection of budgets. After several attempts at outright repression, the problem was settled by coopting party leaders in the Diet. The compromise reached with those leaders was to last for the next thirty years, and in some aspects continued on after World War II. Parties were given a limited voice in distribution from the pork barrel, but in return they had to accept the bureaucratic version of proper leadership, that is, ex-bureaucrats. The assumption of political party leadership by Itō in 1900 signaled the institutionalization of this compromise. For the next thirty-odd years, nonbureaucratic participation in the structure of formal policy making was limited to the conservative parties, whose senior leadership was composed almost exclusively of former bureaucrats. Even in the heyday of party government, during the 1920s and early 1930s, at least 85 percent of all cabinet ministers were drawn from the ranks of retired or former senior bureaucrats. In sum, the participation of the political parties in decision making after 1900 may be seen as a consequence of changes occurring within the bureaucracy rather than as a consequence of the growth of pluralism in the private sector. The parties achieved institutionalization through cooptation, a process in which the dominant Diet parties were given a monopoly of representation and some participation in decision making, in return for which the bureaucracy retained an informal but effective veto power over leadership and party demands. To put it another way, the emergence of this very limited pluralism appears to have been the product of the bureaucracy's own attempts to retain its monopoly over policy making. Although for just a moment in 1900 Yamagata in a fit of pique was more than willing to crush the parties by sheer force, the bureaucracy was constrained to recognize that by its own criteria of legitimacy, the political parties, so long as they were led by bureaucrats, met the conditions of impartiality and expertise. Itō's act marked a fatal recognition that the bureaucratic monopoly over policy making did not have a basis in legitimacy, but only in power. The price to be paid, however, by political parties or any other private interest was the depoliticization of those interests. Participation in policy making could only be purchased by adhering to the state bureaucracy's notion of impartial expertise.

Significantly, one of the major party demands that was depoliticized in this process was the institutionalization of cabinet responsibility to the Diet. There was never a formal routinization of cabinet succession. Cabinet dissolution and formation were entirely the result of an informal, ad hoc, and generally unpredictable process. Each cabinet was the product of exigency, with its legitimacy resting in a delicate compromise. It is in this respect that the rules of the game were removed from public politics. As cabinets were placed in a "transcendental" domain, any group could demand entrance or exit. It is not surprising, then, that the average life of a cabinet between 1900 and 1945 was fifteen months.

At the turn of the century the bureaucracy found that the attempt to insure its own authoritativeness by monopoly over expertise and law had somehow misfired, just as the edifice designed for that purpose seemed to have been completed. At the heart of this failure were two causes. First, by resorting to positive rules and law as the objective signs of impartiality in the organization of interests, the bureaucracy had created within its environment that most dreaded of all organizational problems, career and departmental autonomy. Protected by rules invoked to subordinate their interests, career officials and departments were able to establish limited autonomy, thereby forcing the bureaucracy as a whole into achieving authority through organizational compromise. Second, the use of the same strategy with regard to its external environment created the same problems. By attempting to define in law all social and economic structures of authority, and thereby subordinating them to the state, the bureaucracy by its own logic was creating precisely the condition that it sought to avoid. The problem would not have been critical had the basis of bureaucratic legitimacy provided an inherent monopoly over authority. Since it did not, as the political parties in 1900 showed, it was possible for other organizations to claim legitimacy by fulfilling two requirements: recognition by law and acquisition of either bureaucratic leadership or bureaucratic organization. That the bureaucracy was in fact aware of this fatal flaw was reflected in its concern over the growth of groups that had legal recognition or the right to associate. The bureaucracy sought to correct this flaw by applying to emerging social and economic interest groups the same strategy which it had worked out internally and with the political parties—a strategy of cooptation that provided limited autonomy and thus limited access to decision making in return for adherence to bureaucratic values of leadership and organization.

Just as bureaucratization and cooption of the political parties had turned out to be the means by which the bureaucracy sought to maintain dominance over policy making and fiscal resources, so bureaucratization of potentially large-scale social movements and voluntary associations proved to be the means by which the bureaucracy resolved the problem in social terms. In the period between 1868 and 1900 the problem of organizing interests had largely centered around subordinating the traditional social organizations of authority. By 1900 the family, local community, religion, and the whole socialization process had become the objects of an unchallenged legal definition, and therefore subjects of the administrative system, primarily the administrative courts.[23] However, the very rationality with which the bureaucracy had addressed itself to the subordination of social organizations began to bear a new kind of fruit in the first decade of the twentieth century. By diminishing through law the local or customary basis of organization and authority, the bureaucracy had created a situation in which local voluntary groups and associations were free to sustain themselves by groping for larger, translocal organizational forms. Military reserve groups, youth leagues, farmers groups, economic associations, and the like began to form national organizations.[24] In the period between 1900 and 1919 all these voluntary

[23] Minobe Tatsukichi, *Gyōsei saiban hō* (Tokyo, 1929), pp. 20-21.

[24] Nagata Masaomi, *Keizai dantai hattenshi* (Tokyo, 1956), chapters 1 and 2; Sato Mamoru, *Kindai Nihon seinen dantaishi kenkyū* (Tokyo, 1970), pp. 1-16, 79-103, 535-540; Richard Smethurst, *A Social Basis for Prewar Japanese Militarism: The Army and the Rural Community* (Berkeley and Los Angeles: University of California Press, 1974); Teikoku Nōkai Shi Kohen, eds., *Teikoku nōkai shikō* (Tokyo, 1972); Nōseikyoku Nōgyōkyōdōbu, eds., *Nihon no nōgyō dantai to nōgyō kyōdō kumiai* (Tokyo, 1952).

associations were taken under the bureaucratic wing and given monopoly status, as well as governmental leadership and regulation. Interest groups were thus coopted into the administrative structure.

In the first decade of the twentieth century, then, it is possible to see the outlines of a new structure of authority. Primarily as a consequence of the bureaucracy's response to the problems created by its own development, the bureaucratic leadership found itself seeking to maintain its control over policy making by cooption. This new pattern of authority had two major characteristics. Organizations of interest were on the one hand provided with legal existence and for the most part a legal monopoly over the interests represented, as in the case of the Agricultural Association, the Reserve Association, and the Chambers of Commerce. They were also provided with governmental supervision and subsidies by appropriate ministries, thereby establishing administrative links to the bureaucracy. Equally important was the fact that the bureaucracy invoked a veto over the leadership of such groups, thereby creating an informal linkage through the creation of a homogeneous elite. Authority came to be increasingly exercised through ministerial administrative links and legitimate elite status. State bureaucratic authority now came to be shared in part by transforming private interests into public ones. Interest groups came to be viewed as channels for implementing state policy. This type of linkage had the added attraction of declassing social and economic interests. By coopting a whole range of private interests, predominantly rural in character, the state bureaucracy not only sought a structural means of control, but also sought to split the rural countryside into a series of autonomous interests that would eliminate the possibility of forming classes. If interests were organized around age groups (*seinen dantai*), military experience (*zaigō gunjinkai*), and occupation (*nōkai* and Chambers of Commerce), then the possibility of class formation and class ties to urban society were obviated.

This emergent structure of authority was not without its problems. First was the general problem of state integrity and its converse, arbitrariness. The bureaucratic attempt to maintain control over the organization of interests by the strategy of cooption created the problem of state boundaries. If private interests were given public status and allowed thus to participate in policy making merely by their existence, then there was a real possibility that the state might be subsumed by society as more and more interest groups achieved a public and legitimate status. The problem did not go unnoticed, and indeed was the focus of conflicting interpretations of the constitution as represented by Uesugi Shinkichi, Hozumi Yatsuka, and Minobe Tatsukichi. The former recognized correctly that the public status of interest groups posed a threat to the integrity of the state ("if the state does not develop it will be destroyed").[25] Uesugi's strategy was in effect to fall back on the notion of imperial will as voiced directly through his bureaucratic ministers.[26] Hozumi was equally concerned with maintaining the state's integrity vis-à-vis private interests. Hence his famous remark, "it is a misinterpretation of theory to think that administrative adjudication was instituted for subjects to carry on disputes with officials over rights and duties and to provide private protection for the subjects."[27] Minobe saw the problem as it was, in fact, unfolding before his eyes: a form of legitimacy that had no institutional principle of authority other than imperial will had to have as its guiding principle the notion that what was rational was real. The only way to make this possible was to argue that the emperor was constrained by his own rationality—that is, the emperor had to use any appropriate means to achieve society's wants.[28] The corporate, or organic, view that Minobe represented was perfectly in accordance with the emergent structure of authority. Furthermore, it allowed the state to avoid inundation by private interests. As he defined the state in terms of functional organs that expressed the will of the state, he also defined the boundaries of what would constitute a state organ. Every organ has its own competence, which is exercised by the display of its will, a legal will. "The will of an organ has the effect of state will only when it is given by state law the competence to determine the will of the state, and only when that will is displayed in the manner prescribed by state law."[29] In other words, the appropriate state organ could incorporate or exclude any aspect of social life from participation by the use of positive law. It was then no coincidence that Minobe's view of state authority became the one taught to and maintained by a generation of bureaucrats between approximately 1915 and 1934.

The second problem created by the structure of authority and the criteria for acceptance of private interests as legitimate was the automatic exclusion of two types of interest: labor, and those organizations too small to employ bureaucratic rationality and/or leadership. Both were to suffer the bitter experience of systematic exclusion from legitimacy through the first three decades of the century. Indeed, it was this systematic exclusion that led both types of interest into constant conflict with the state. That conflict presented an especially worrisome challenge to the bureaucratically dominated, pluralist structure of authority, since

[25] Uesugi Shinkichi, *Kempō jutsugi* (Tokyo, 1924), preface, p. 6.

[26] Ibid.

[27] Hozumi Yatsuka, *Hozumi Yatsuka hakase ronbunshū* (Tokyo, 1943), p. 162.

[28] Minobe Tatsukichi, *Nihon kempō* (Tokyo, 1924), pp. 127-140; Minobe, *Kempō kōwa* (Tokyo, 1914), pp. 2-8.

[29] Minobe, *Nihon kempō*, pp. 294-298.

the claims of labor and small organizations to equity in the structure of interests were based on notions of justice as fairness rather than as social utility. Given the equality, at least formally, of wants in the Japanese polity, such claims had considerable appeal and not a little justification.

The bureaucracy's response to these conflict-laden claims was constrained by a number of factors. First, the level of demand for equity had risen sharply as a consequence of World War I, during which there was a high demand for labor and the work of small and middle-sized enterprises. The end of the war, and the return to more normally competitive domestic and world markets by the mid-1920s, resulted in declines in labor demand, underutilization of marginal enterprises, and fears about a loss of exports.[30] This timing set an agenda. As these elements of the economy were squeezed, their claims for equity increased. A second constraint stemmed from the necessity on the part of the bureaucracy to reject any notion of fairness as a criterion for determining the priority or legitimacy of interests. Such a view clearly would undermine the bureaucratic conception of an objective—scientific determination of utility—and thus would amount to an attack on its position as the allocator of priorities of interest. Nevertheless, the bureaucracy was also constrained by its commitment to the notion of equality, thereby making it impossible to completely dismiss demands for equity. Third, the bureaucracy was constrained to reduce conflict and demands on counts of both legitimacy and authority. In terms of the former, the claims of systematic exclusion from interest priority challenged the bureaucratic claim that it could achieve a net balance of satisfaction of wants over the sum total of society's members. In terms of the latter, continued cases in which authority was rejected could only undermine the authoritativeness of the system.

All of these constraints produced movement in a single direction. In order to meet the requirements that notions of fairness be dismissed and conflicts eliminated, the bureaucracy was led consistently to suppress the labor movement and the demands from marginal operators. Outright force was used with regard to the former, whereas in the case of the latter the depressions of the early postwar period and the late 1920s were allowed to eliminate marginally efficient operators.[31] At the same time, in order to meet the requirements of recognizing equality and of refuting the argument of systematic exclusion, the bureaucracy had to

[30] See William W. Lockwood, *The Economic Development of Japan* (Princeton: Princeton University Press, 1964), pp. 57-61; Kanazawa Yoshio, "The Regulation of Corporate Enterprise: The Law of Unfair Competition and the Control of Monopoly Power," in Arthur T. von Mehren, ed., *Law in Japan: The Legal Order in a Changing Society* (Cambridge: Harvard University Press, 1963), p. 482.

[31] Kanazawa, "Regulation of Corporate Enterprise," p. 482.

find means of legitimately including such interests. The only solution was somehow to *absorb* rather than coopt these interests into a structure of legitimate authority. In the case of labor, this meant that even a state-dominated, national labor movement was obviated, since to create such an organization was in fact to recognize its interest and, even worse, to recognize and institutionalize the class basis of such an interest. The only answer was in effect to declass labor, as had been done in the rural sector, by splitting up the class into a series, indeed almost an infinite series, of autonomous interests on the basis of enterprise—thereby, at the same time, making the interest into an organizational one with no basis in class. In doing so, however, the bureaucracy had to recognize the legitimacy of large-scale economic enterprises as participants in the structure of authority. Briefly put, the labor movement was legitimized and made passive by forcing it to be absorbed into the organizational structure of large-scale enterprise. By becoming an integral part of large-scale enterprise, labor would have to admit the legitimacy of the criteria of expertise and impartiality that dominated such organizations.

The problem for the bureaucracy was to find a means by which labor could be enticed to accept such a situation. The answer emerged relatively early. The founding of the Kyōchōkai (Conciliation Society) in 1919 under bureaucratic patronage marked the opening of a campaign to get large-scale economic enterprises to purchase the passivity of labor with some economic benefits built around the enterprise itself.[32] Benefits such as tenure, housing, medical care and leisure that were directly associated with initiative by the enterprises became substitutes for the benefits such as higher wages associated with unions. In effects, large-scale enterprises became instruments of state authority and policy.

The state bureaucracy had little to lose because since the early 1900s large-scale enterprises had increasingly modeled their organization on the pattern of state bureaucracy. By the early 1920s most of the large-scale economic organizations had patterns of recruitment and advancement as well as organizational structures that mirrored those of the state bureaucracy, even down to the use of examinations to recruit managerial officials.[33] In this sense they met the test of legitimate interests, a status that they did in fact use to seek participation in the setting of

[32] Sumiya Mikio, *Nihon rōdō undōshi* (Tokyo, 1966), pp. 181-183. The Kyōchōkai was founded in 1919 by Shibusawa Eiichi and other business leaders with the active cooperation of the government. It is the predecessor of the present Nikkeiren (Japanese Federation of Employers' Associations). Nihon Keieisha Dantai Remmei Ritsu Jū Shunen Kinen Jigyō Iinkai, eds., *Jūnen no ayumi* (Tokyo, 1958), pp. 1-5.

[33] Hazama Hiroshi, *Nihon rōmu kanrishi kenkyū* (Tokyo, 1964), pp. 488-490; Hyodo Tsutomu, *Nihon ni okeru rōshi kankei no tenkai* (Tokyo, 1971), pp. 420-422.

policy.[34] They argued that their rational organization and leadership indicated that the interests they pursued were public and social, not simply individual and private.

The inclusion of large-scale economic organizations in the structure of authority was reflected in the enactment in 1925 of the first of a series of laws designed to give them authority in the marketplace. These laws allowed associations of exporters and producers to be formed, with the power to set prices, establish quotas, curtail production, and allocate markets. Furthermore, the laws provided that the minister having jurisdiction over the particular trade in question had the power to order firms not party to the association agreement to abide by its terms, thereby forcing marginal operators into dependence upon large-scale enterprises. This pattern was extended to almost the whole range of industry by the Industrial Association Law and the Control of Important Industries Law of 1931. The bureaucracy's power was enhanced in these laws by the power to modify unilaterally any association agreement and to enforce its observation by members and nonmembers alike.[35] By the early thirties, therefore, industrial and commercial organizations at all levels had been effectively brought into the purview of bureaucratic administration. The structure was to be further centralized in the late thirties and early forties under the aegis of war. The National General Mobilization Law of 1939 established compulsory control organizations for all industries, and even some subdivision of industries.[36]

By at least 1931 the high-water mark of limited pluralism as a structure of authority had been reached and this pluralism was already being transformed. The transformation was taking place by the very success of the bureaucracy in delimiting the boundaries of legitimate interests. Already by the mid-twenties the rural sectors of interest, despite discontent over questions of tenancy and the import of colonial agricultural products, had been sufficiently atomized and coopted so as no longer to pose a serious problem in terms of a class-based interest. By the early thirties labor and small-scale, marginal enterprises had been conflated into the structure of large-scale economic organizations, where they were reduced to passivity and subject to control.

Large-scale enterprise might well have offered the only significant challenge to this bureaucratically dominated structure of pluralism. Yet, fearful equally of the challenges to its authority on the part of labor and the exigencies of the world market, large-scale enterprise was willing to

[34] See Nihon Kōgyō Kurabu, eds., *Nihon kōgyō kurabu nijūgonenshi* (Tokyo, 1943). Also see Byron K. Marshall, *Capitalism and Nationalism in Pre-War Japan* (Stanford: Stanford University Press, 1967).

[35] Kanazawa, pp. 482–483.

[36] Ibid.; also Kojima Seiichi, *Nihon seiji sangyō tōsei ron* (Tokyo, 1941).

trade off some autonomy in return for a more stable economic environment, as reflected in support of government-regulated cartels. The emergence by the early 1930s of a direct and stable relationship between the bureaucracy and commercial and industrial organizations deprived the political parties of their only major support outside of the bureaucracy. It is not surprising, then, as Japan became increasingly embroiled upon the Asian continent, that the civil and military bureaucrats became impatient with party demands. The military bureaucracy, concerned about the diversion of resources and the necessity of using military expertise to determine priorities, finally succeeded in 1936, with the consent of the civil bureaucracy, in removing the parties from direct participation in decision making.

The structure of limited pluralism, constrained as it was by the commitment to bureaucratic values, had provided the basis for the emergence of a new structure. Because of the institutionalization of these values and its very basis of legitimacy, the bureaucracy had been forced to recognize some interests as legitimate. By the same token, however, it had been able to repress, atomize, and conflate a wide range of others. By the early 1930s the administrative and elite links between the bureaucracy and a few legitimate interests had become tightly woven. All that was required to legitimize fully the civil and military bureaucracies' claims that a monopoly over policy making was required was the economic and international crisis. From this crisis emerged a structure that closely resembled a state corporatism in which all organizations and interests were systematically aggregated under administrative direction. Administration had come to be substituted for politics at last.

General Implications: Bureaucracy and Conflict

A number of general and specific postulates can be drawn from an analysis of the disjunction between authority and legitimacy arising from the creation of a bureaucratic state in Japan. First, I think we can conclude that this disjunction and the resultant search for an appropriate structure of authority stemmed directly from the seizure of power that the Restoration symbolized. The new leaders were forced, if they wished to retain their status and maintain the legitimacy of their act, to commit themselves to utilitarian notions as the basis for determining public policy. By their seizure of power, the Meiji leaders had destroyed the last vestiges of ascribed status as the basis for determining leadership eligibility and as a primary prerequisite for determining public policy. Furthermore, their successful attack on the bakufu had been based on the argument that it had failed to represent the good of society as a whole— that in crisis the bakufu had put its own interest in retaining power ahead of the interests of society. This immediately raised the problems of what constituted society's interests and how they were to be achieved. In this regard, the new leaders had little choice. In terms of the former problem, the leaders theoretically had a choice between viewing society's interests as based on the wants, or the needs, of those who made up society. Neither of these could be determined with reference directly to an imperial will, since it would have been impossible for a single individual, without a theory and structure of divine knowledge, to arrive at what constituted the public interest. Thus society's interest had to be based on some determination of what constituted individual wants or needs.

It was clearly not possible to define social interests based on a calculus of needs. To adopt that alternative would have required, minimally, both a conception that all resources were legitimately at the disposal of the emperor and his servants, and a belief that the emperor and his servants were capable of determining such needs. The first prerequisite did not exist de facto. The development of an infrastructure of commercial capitalism based upon private ownership of capital had for all intents and purposes reduced whatever notion of imperial rights had ever existed to a political abstraction summed up in a delegation of powers and de facto prerogatives. Furthermore, even if the new leadership had wished to do away with the notion of private capital and its de facto rights, it had not sufficient power to enforce such a transformation. Indeed, it faced enormous difficulties in simply imposing a central claim on the value of such capital, as shown by discontent over the imposition of a land tax in the early years of Meiji.

It is possible to speculate that herein lies the essential importance in Japan of the emergence of a capitalist mode of organizing resources. It was not that it created a class that sought to pursue its interests logically toward the formation of an appropriate political structure. Rather, the development of commercial capitalism produced so powerful a constraint that a new leadership had to view society's interests in terms of individual wants, that is, it had to accept the conception that society's interests were somehow bound to the right of the individual to hold property, and had to transform this conception into various abstract forms.

The Meiji leaders were led willy-nilly to utilitarian assumptions about the formation of a public interest. That is to say, faced with the incontrovertible condition of the commercial-capitalist organization of property, there was no choice but to assume that at its base was the desire of individuals to satisfy rational wants. Thus, it had to be assumed that an appropriate public policy was whatever in a given context would achieve the greatest sum of satisfaction of the rational desires of individuals. The problem for the Meiji leaders, as for others making the same assumption, was that this notion did not and does not imply any specific institutional arrangement for achieving the greatest sum of satisfaction. Rawls states the problem neatly:

> The striking feature of the utilitarian view of justice is that it does not matter, except indirectly, how the sum of satisfactions is distributed among individuals anymore than it matters, except indirectly, how one man distributes his satisfactions over time. The correct distribution in either case is that which yields the maximum fulfillment. Society must allocate its means of satisfaction whatever these are, rights and duties, opportunities and privileges, and various forms of wealth, so as to achieve this maximum if it can. . . . Thus there is no reason in principle why the greater gains of some should not compensate for the lesser losses of others; or more importantly, why the violations of the liberty of a few might not be made right by the greater good shared by the many. . . . For just as it is rational for one man to maximize the fulfillment of his system of desires it is right for a society to maximize the net balance of satisfaction taken over all of its members.[37]

The Meiji leaders, whether they so willed or not, were not only forced to arrive at a utilitarian conception of public interest. They were also constrained to adopt the view that "just as it is rational for one man to maximize the fulfillment of his system of desires it is right for a society to maximize the net balance of satisfaction over all its members." To adopt the view that the net satisfaction of members of society ought to be assessed by counting each individual's system of desires and arranging priorities on some system of majority choice would have, as I had suggested earlier, subjected the Meiji leaders to a test that very well might have denied the legitimacy of their authority and seizure of power. This led them to accept and to promote the notion that society was more than the sum of its parts and was thus obligated and able to maximize the net balance of satisfaction taken over all its members.

From this point of view, the Meiji leaders and their successors were forced to arrive at the only means available within a utilitarian framework by which a society could maximize satisfaction. At the same time, they had to retain their status, legitimacy, and power. This could be done only by accepting the principle of rational choice for one man, which implied a conception of the public policy maker as an "impartial spectator" who at the same time is capable of predicting appropriate

[37] Rawls, *A Theory of Justice,* p. 20.

priorities that will maximize the net balance of satisfaction taken over all its members. It is this spectator, as Rawls points out,

> who is conceived of carrying out the required organization of desires of all persons into one coherent system of desire; it is by this construction that many persons are fused into one. Endowed with ideal powers of sympathy and imagination the impartial spectator is the perfectly rational individual who identifies with and experiences the desires of others as if these desires were his own. In this way he ascertains the intensity of these desires and assigns them their appropriate weight in the one system of desire. . . . In this conception of society separate individuals are thought of as so many different lines along which rights and duties are to be assigned and scarce means of satisfaction allocated in accordance with rules so as to give the greatest fulfillment of wants. . . . The correct decision is essentially a question of efficient administration.[38]

Thus the ideal policy maker is the neutral, impartial expert who is trained to know how to maximize society's desires and use rules in allocating rights, duties, and resources. In this context it is clear that the consequence of such a view is to substitute rational administration for politics as a means of allocating satisfaction. In this sense, politics is reduced to administrative functions. Bureaucratization as a socializing phenomenon has two basic value positions: 1. the notion that expertise is synonymous with impartiality—it is therefore above politics and symbolic of the state's relation to society; 2. a belief that decision making and implementation achieve their highest form in universally applied administrative rules and routines. In short, the bureaucratized state's highest values are expertise and administrative rules.

The bureaucracy or, more precisely, its leaders if they wished to dominate the determination of public policy, had to seek to institutionalize the values of expertise and impartiality and to do it in a manner that excluded all other organizations from gaining access to the same grounds of legitimacy. Two questions are raised by such a conclusion. The first is derived from what appears to be the fact of a state bureaucracy having its own interest: an interest in acquiring and maintaining a monopoly or something approaching it over the process of decision making. Clearly it is an interest and a monopolistic one: it insists that the rational satisfaction of society's wants is achievable only by the ruleful application of expertise through an authoritative structure. The interest or competitive aspect arises because there appears to be no necessary connection between expertise and its ruleful application, on the

---

[38] Ibid., pp. 26-27.

one hand, and the authoritativeness of the structure in which these values are dominant, on the other. That is, there is no inherent reason why expertise and impartiality can arise only in or be a property only of a state structure. Although expertise and rulefulness may produce in their application a narrow range of possible legitimate forms of decision making, they are by no means subsumed totally in state structure. Thus, for a state bureaucracy to achieve a monopoly it must seek to establish its authoritativeness by other means, and the only way to accomplish this is in competition with other possible alternatives.

Why this should be the case stems from the nature of the criteria for expertise and impartiality and their implied tests or means of evaluation. So long as the state bureaucracy in Japan based its legitimacy on expertise and impartiality, it was required to institutionalize patterns of behavior and/or organizations that could serve as "objective" indicators of whether these criteria were being met. In the case of expertise, a high level of education, some test of knowledge, and a well-defined career experience are the normal tests of eligibility. Impartiality or rulefulness in the organization of society's desires and priorities would seem minimally to require some evidence of two things: universality in the application of rules, and an objective measurement of the fulfillment of society's wants. Neither of these require equitability of results so long as they show that a net balance of satisfaction has been achieved over all its members. All that need be shown is that society's rational wants are increasingly fulfilled and this can easily be indicated by reference to increases in such factors as economic growth, standards of living, longevity, and so on. Nothing in these criteria or their tests provides a basis for the state bureaucracy's monopoly over determining the priority of interests. In effect, any organization that meets the criteria of expertise and impartiality may thus claim a right to participate in determining the priority of interests. Even more importantly, by using these criteria in organizing themselves, such private organizations can and must claim a public and therefore authoritative status. Insofar as they claim to allocate values on the basis of expertise and impartiality and exhibit characteristics by which these claims can be validated—for example, a leadership chosen on the basis of education, tests, and experience, and a contribution to the fulfillment of social wants in the form of economic growth or other public good—then such organizations in Japan could and did claim that they were appropriate instruments for fulfilling society's wants. The state bureaucracy, although seeking a monopoly over determination of the public interest, created the very criteria for establishing organizations of interest that could also claim legitimacy and priority for interests. This is clearly evident in three developments after 1900: the emergence of large-scale economic organizations modeled almost exactly after the state bureaucracy, right down to recruitment and career patterns; the emergence of organizations, primarily political parties, whose leadership was dominated by ex-bureaucrats; and the cooption of organizations by the state bureaucracy.

By appealing to criteria and measures of evaluation that had to be based on objectively and publicly measureable standards of performance, the state bureaucracy was forced to institutionalize the means for acquiring the criteria in such a way as to make them available to others. No test of expertise, for example, could be met if all who acquired an appropriate education became officials or if education was limited to those somehow preselected for officialdom. It would appear that the criteria had validity precisely because they were not the specific property of any one group and they were capable of being objectively evaluated.

In institutionalizing the values appropriate to this utilitarian set of assumptions, the Meiji leaders created a basis for the bureaucracy to dominate public policy, but only so long as the bureaucracy could maintain a monopoly over expertise. This monopoly was not, however, inherent in the commitment to objective rationality. No argument could be made for the monopoly of a single structure over the means of acquiring and using expertise. Authority thus had to be constructed out of the means at hand: the bureaucracy's almost complete monopoly over the structure of education and its monopoly over law—in other words, the organizational properties that could secure power.

The flaw, however, existed, and we can generalize from this that it was by its own construct of legitimacy that the bureaucracy was forced to accept other interests as legitimate as they acquired similar characteristics. It was precisely this flaw—the absence of authoritativeness in the basis of legitimacy—that was, I would suggest, the source of the crisis of authority that accompanied the new century in Japan. The crisis was shaped by the bureaucracy's resort to positive law to define the legitimacy of the social system of interest, a necessity if it wished to avoid inundation by private interests. In this process, administrative law and its implementation became the means by which a wide range of social organizations, such as the family, local groups, and private organizations of interests as well as community itself, were secularized and subordinated to bureaucratic jurisdiction. As bureaucratic leadership placed high value on particular strategies for resolving organizational problems, it encouraged or required organizations that it had subordinated or coopted to adopt similar organizational strategies and structures. Bureaucratic values thus became social organizational values.

Secular differentiation and bureaucratization tended to bring private interests into the public sphere through administrative recognition, definition, and regulation. But in so doing the bureaucracy created the conditions for a new state of complexity and transformation. This process of differentiation produced greater formal organizational specificity. Out of it emerged at least a minimal level of autonomy, as in the case of bureaucratic ministries and the political parties, because the more sharply delineated boundaries were not so easily penetrated. That is to say, formal and informal rules, although creating the conditions of subordination and hierarchy, also provided those subordinated with some protection from outside interference.

Seen in this light, the period of democratic experimentation, "Taishō democracy," was a period of limited pluralism at best. It was a period in which parties and other organizations within a very narrow ideological range were allowed to compete for a *share* of power and not for control of power. As with all political parties that compete for only a share of power, the Japanese political parties did not need to establish a majoritarian base, and this perhaps explains why the parties never sought to establish a broad social foundation. The parties, along with other associations of interest, traded off the dubious potentialities of autonomy and the large-scale mass organization of the electorate for the certainties of limited access to decision making. In doing so, the parties were forced to engage in strategies that would insure at best a continued share of power.

The converse of these constraints is equally important. Although the rules of legitimacy provided the possibility for private interests to claim and seek public status, the same rules provided the boundaries for systematic exclusion. All of these interests characterized by appeals to sectoral or individual equity were automatically excluded from direct participation in determining the public interest and, therefore, from establishing any priority of interest. Thus labor, because its claims to legitimacy were based on appeals to justice as fairness rather than appeals to economic rationality, could be and were systematically and legitimately repressed. Only under one condition could labor be viewed as legitimate: when it was coopted by bureaucratic organization. Where unions became company unions or enterprise unions and they did not challenge the legitimacy of the organization, labor was viewed as legitimate. Other groups that could not meet the test of legitimacy, such as tenant farmers and small and medium-sized industries, were similarly excluded. The systematic repression of interests throughout the first three decades of the twentieth century produced not only widespread feelings of injustice and inequity but a series of frustrated and frustrating attempts to seek redress through organization. Such systematic exclusion over long periods of time was bound to raise serious questions of the bureaucracy's and society's intent to provide even a net balance of satisfaction over all of its members.

In other words, the basis for legitimacy of the state bureaucracy contained within it constraints that provided the possibility of conflict from two sources: one that focused on attempts of organizations with bureaucratic values to gain access to the formation of public policy, and one stemming from groups systematically excluded on the basis of their appeal to nonbureaucratic values or their lack of bureaucratic organization. With no inherent claim to sole possession of the right to organize a societywide system of interests, the bureaucracy's basis of legitimacy set in general terms the possibility of competition and conflict over the question of the correct priority of interests. Those groups that accepted bureaucratic values would be able to present almost undeniable claims to priority, whereas the systematic exclusion of others over time would raise the complaint that the bureaucracy was not fulfilling the wants of society, even in terms of a net balance of satisfaction taken over all its members. How long, after all, could some sectors of society be required to give up their satisfactions for the good of society as a whole?

This analysis suggests that bureaucratically dominated political systems are characterized by several structural and processual patterns that are contradictory. With regard to the latter, a pattern of increasing differentiation and autonomy is set off against attempts at reintegration through greater specification of inter- and intra-organizational relationships. Differentiation seems to be a direct product of the resort by bureaucracies to rules and administrative laws to reduce uncertainty. These very rules serve to create not only the conditions of hierarchy but of autonomy as well. Rules not only specify the boundaries beyond which the subordinated may not go, but also beyond which the subordinator may not go. The setting of such boundaries by the state bureaucracy creates the potentiality and actuality of new uncertainties. These uncertainties materialize in the form of "regionalism" within the bureaucracy and "pluralism" outside the bureaucracy. Economically and socially functional interests, such as political parties, youth organizations, labor unions, and business groups, as well as bureaucratic departments, emerge in response to the model and requirements of state bureaucratic rationalization. The state bureaucracy responds, in turn, by using its rule-making powers to subordinate and coopt. Private interests are bureaucratized but not completely eliminated. The state bureaucracy must meet at least the minimal demands of its organized clients. The process seems almost without end. Each new attempt at integration provides the encouragement and model for other sectors of society to seek formal recognition of their interests by rationalization and demands for cooption.

In structural terms there is a constant tendency to produce authoritarian relationships between the state bureaucracy and all private organizations. On the other hand, there is the emergence of ever greater numbers of formally differentiated organizations which, through the rationality of rules, achieve limited autonomy and legitimacy. The end result seems to be the creation of an ever more systematic linkage, through administrative agencies and elites, between bureaucracy and civil society. Such a relationship produces in the bureaucracy the irresistible temptation to reduce all interests to public ones in a formal systematic manner as a means of reducing uncertainty.

o

In a somewhat different direction, I think it is possible to suggest some tentative conclusions regarding the general relationship between revolutionary conditions and the rise of the bureaucratic state. The emergence of Japan indicates that where a revolutionary condition (as indicated by the total succession of leadership) emerges, the outcome must be a form of intense state bureaucratization. The revolutionary condition produces first and foremost for those who come to power the central problem of authority and legitimacy. If those who seize power wish to retain it, these problems can only be resolved, I would suggest, by valorization of the notion of objective rationality and commitment to the maintenance of objective knowledge and rulefulness in its organization. Only through such concepts can the continued power and status of a small group be legitimized while at the same time maintaining that such policy-making structures meet the requirements of equality that the revolutionary seizure of power so clearly implies. The commitment to objective rationality as the means of reconstructing social order arises not only from a need to legitimate a seizure of power but also from the organizational necessity, imposed by revolution, of ordering the administration of power in a uniform fashion. Unless there is a clear, quantitatively-defined set of administrative rules that symbolize a uniformity of purpose and goal, the very legitimacy of the seizure of power is called into question. Power would then seem to be the object of individuals rather than of society. It would seem that state bureaucracy provides the only organizational solution to the myriad problems created by the revolutionary act. By its reliance on rules it creates a necessary uniformity that makes power an organizational rather than an individual property. By its reliance on expertise and impartiality as criteria for selecting decision makers, it resolves the problem of how to legitimize the seizure and retention of power by a small group of people: they seize it in the name of society to achieve society's wants and interests or needs, which can only be known by possessing and using the sciences of society. In elevating these notions to the status of values and institutionalizing them, the problem of equality is also solved. None can be excluded from acquiring such expertise except by the failure of individual intellect. Meritocracy solves the problem of equality as a demand for fairness. For those who seize power, the problem of appropriate organization is thus always resolved by elevating administration to a moral level. Only through administration and the elimination of politics can the greatest good for the greatest number be achieved.

Such a solution, however, provides a constant replication of contradictions. Meritocracy cannot avoid becoming a social value, thereby eliminating the possibility of an institutional monopoly over policy making. Bureaucratic authority then rests on its ability to use its resources to control its environment. Whatever strategy succeeds is thus by definition appropriate. With such a principle, authority must ever seem arbitrary. To escape the accusation of the arbitrary pursuit of power, bureaucratic leaders are forced to appeal to rationality and its concrete expression in rules and positive law. These become the weapons of conflict. For the bureaucracy, the only answer to such conflict is the further rationalization of society. In that sense there appears to be for all revolutionary regimes a dialectical process from which there is no escape. Whatever Max Weber had in mind by his reference to the "iron cage" of bureaucracy, for such regimes there is no more appropriate description.

THE EMPEROR AND THE CROWD: THE HISTORICAL SIGNIFICANCE OF THE HIBIYA RIOT

Shumpei Okamoto

The "Hibiya Riot"

On September 5, 1905, a peace treaty ending the Russo-Japanese war, which had lasted one year and seven months, was signed at Portsmouth, New Hampshire. The treaty signaled Japan's expansion onto the Asian continent and secured for the nation a solid place among the major powers of the world. Japanese policy makers, who knew that Japan's fortunes could only deteriorate had the war been continued, believed the treaty to be the best they could expect. Yet it yielded for Japan neither indemnity nor much territory. The Japanese public, elated by successive reports of victory and uninformed of the actual war situation, had expected that the peace terms would sufficiently compensate the nation for its efforts. The treaty, therefore, disappointed them bitterly. Foreign policy opinion makers, led by minor party politicians, journalists, and university professors, charged that the treaty had nullified the meaning of Japan's victories on land and sea and had failed utterly to allow the attainment of Japan's objectives. Only Tokutomi Sohō's *Kokumin shinbun*, which was generally regarded as official news organ of the Katsura Tarō cabinet, and an extremely small number of socialists and Christians welcomed peace. But the general outcry against the treaty drowned their voices out. The overwhelming weight of Japanese public opinion was against the government for concluding the "humiliating" treaty; many demanded that it be repudiated and that war be continued.

The government at first ignored the public outcry and behind the scenes secretly demanded of Seiyūkai leaders that in return for the reward of power they pledge not to join the popular attack on the government. At the same time, the Kōwamondai Dōshi Rengōkai (Joint Council of Fellow Activists on the Peace Question) took advantage of public indignation to organize a nationwide antipeace movement. The Rengōkai was formed chiefly by several minor party politicians, lawyers, and newspapermen. Its president was the sometime freedom and popular rights (jiyūminken) movement activist Kōno Hironaka. Before the war, the politicians had organized the Tai-Ro Dōshikai (Anti-Russia Comrade's Society) and advocated a strong policy against Russia and an early declaration of war. They had assumed the role of "men of high purpose" (shishi), appealing to the emperor to heed popular aspirations for war. At the outbreak of hostilities, they concluded that their loyal act had successfully moved the emperor to order the "weak-kneed" Katsura cabinet into war. Content with their accomplishment, the shishi had soon disbanded the Dōshikai.

In July 1905, as the Portsmouth conference approached, the activists revived their organization to guide the nation on the peace issue. Thus, the Kōwamondai Dōshi Rengōkai urged the Japanese plenipotentiary Komura Jutarō to exact from Russia uncompromisingly stiff peace terms. It then watched closely the progress of the peace negotiations, and incited a popular clamor for exorbitant gains. Once again, the Rengōkai members posed as shishi, warning the "cowering" government against any compromise with Russia. In mid-August, when they learned of the Japanese peace terms that Komura had presented at the conference, the Rengōkai leaders immediately declared the settlement's inadequacy in light of Japan's war objectives and demanded that the government terminate the peace negotiations immediately. With the news of the conclusion of peace, therefore, the activists quickly resolved that the terms not only "abandoned the fruits of victory" but "gravely damaged the well-being of His Majesty's nation." They rebuked the policy makers for their cowardly act and commenced a vigorous national movement for repudiation of the treaty.

Under the Meiji constitution, diplomacy was the prerogative of the emperor alone, and its execution was entrusted exclusively to an oligarchic decision-making body composed of the elder statesmen (genrō), several cabinet ministers, and top military leaders. By law, the Diet, which to a limited extent reflected public opinion, remained completely outside the foreign policy-making process. As indicated above, the major political parties, which could have demanded a share in the government's peace-making process, early abandoned such intentions in exchange for power. Thus, the oligarchic government's rigid, secret diplomacy provided the Rengōkai with another opportunity to reenact the prewar "precedent." They decided to appeal to the emperor to heed public dissatisfaction with the peace and refuse ratification of the treaty.

On September 2, the Rengōkai issued a proclamation calling for a national campaign against peace. Two days later, President Kōno appeared at the Imperial Household Ministry and submitted a memorial to the emperor. The complete text of the inflammatory document beseeching the emperor to reject the peace was simultaneously made public. The Rengōkai decided also to hold a national rally on September 5 at Hibiya Park in Tokyo, and distributed handbills announcing the event in the city and its vicinity.

The government at last began to worry, as revealed in Katsura's letter to the elder statesman Yamagata Aritomo, that the Rengōkai activities had effectively "agitated lower-class people" and might eventually cause "rickshaw-men and grooms" and "petty merchants" to confuse "affairs of state with affairs of society." Thereupon, it ordered the chief of the Metropolitan Police Board, who was then administratively answerable directly to the prime minister and the home minister, to ban the national rally at Hibiya Park.

The Metropolitan Police Board not only delivered the prohibition to the Rengōkai headquarters but kept several executive members of the group in custody from the early hours of September 5. When the Rengōkai still threatened to defy the order, the police barricaded all the gates of the park and guarded them with some 350 policemen. The Tokyo city council included many Rengōkai sympathizers, such as Mayor Ozaki Yukio, whose anti-Katsura stance was widely known. At the request of the Rengōkai, therefore, several councilmen tried to persuade the Metropolitan Police Board and the Home Ministry to remove the barricades which, councilors claimed, had been unlawfully put up without the consent of the city. Both the police and the ministry rejected the city council's request.

September 5 was an exceedingly hot day. Despite the weather, people continued to gather at the park from early morning. About 11 A.M. the crowd, enraged by the official ban against the rally and the "unlawful" closing of the park, began to clash with policemen. Finally, around noon, the crowd of about 30,000, having overwhelmed the police, rushed into the park shouting, "Port Arthur 203 Meter Hill fell. Banzai!"

Soon the Rengōkai leaders, protected by ruffians and porters, marched into the park behind a huge rally banner and several signs displaying violent phrases. There they distributed small national flags hung with mourning crepe. The assembly began about 1 P.M., with the explosion of a firecracker. It denounced the Katsura cabinet and the plenipotentiary Komura, appealed to the emperor to refuse ratification, and quickly passed resolutions urging the Japanese army in Manchuria to continue fighting and the Privy Council to advise the emperor to reject the treaty. The brass band then played the national anthem, and the crowd shouted "Banzai" three times each for the emperor, the army, and the navy. As another firecracker exploded, the assembly ended without disturbance. The entire procedure took only thirty minutes.

The Rengōkai had originally planned to hold a speech rally at 2 P.M. at the Shintomiza theater in Kyōbashi. President Kōno and several other leaders, however, suddenly altered the schedule and with the rally banner led a crowd of about 2,000 who carried mourning flags toward the imperial palace. Hearing of this, top officials of the Metropolitan Police Board feared that the crowd might resort to a direct appeal to the emperor for the rejection of the treaty. Indeed, they regarded the mass march to the palace grounds with mourning flags to be an act of lese majesty. The board, therefore, dispatched a company of policemen to the palace with orders to disperse the crowd.

Meanwhile, Kōno gathered his followers in front of Nijūbashi. Standing before them, he made a profound bow to the palace and led the crowd in three shouts of "Banzai" for the emperor. Then, as the brass band began to play the national anthem, the police intervened. The Rengōkai leaders resisted, charging that for the police to interfere with the people during a rendition of *Kimigayo* was an act of lese majesty. Soon skirmishes broke out between the crowd and the police, with both sides incurring a number of casualties.

Thereafter, clashes between the crowd and the police quickly spread to other parts of the city. At the Shintomiza Theater a mob of some 2,000 battled the police. A throng of about 4,000, most of whom had attended the national rally, surrounded Tokutomi's *Kokumin shinbun*, and when a melee broke out the police rushed in to defend the press. A throng of about 10,000 surged toward the official residence of the home minister, which was located directly in front of Hibiya Park. The residence was severely damaged by fires set by the mob, and again both police and the crowd suffered numerous casualties.

With nightfall the rioting spread. Mobs concentrated their attack on the police and set fire to police stations and boxes. During the night, the chief of the Metropolitan Police Board was compelled to request the imperial guards and the army's first division to assist in suppressing the riot. The following day, on the authority of an emergency imperial edict, the government declared martial law in the city of Tokyo and vicinity, restricted the movements of citizens, and banned the anti-government press. On the 7th a heavy rain fell, and the riot finally subsided.

In three days more than 350 buildings, including 2 police stations, 9 police branch stations, more than 70 percent of the police boxes in the city, 13 Christian churches, and 53 private homes, were either smashed or burned down. Fire destroyed 15 streetcars. The recorded casualties exceeded 1,000: 450 policemen, 48 firemen and soldiers, and more than 500 among the crowd, including 17 dead. Mobs also stormed the prime minister's official residence, the Foreign Ministry, the American legation, and the Imperial Hotel, but these suffered little damage.[1]

HISTORIOGRAPHY OF THE HIBIYA RIOT

No study was published before the Pacific War on this major metropolitan riot whose suppression required martial law for the first time in modern Japanese history. It was 1938 before a strictly confidential, official investigation was conducted by a public prosecutor as a case study in thought control.[2] This so-called Matsumoto report admits that the riot was directly occasioned by police interference with the national rally, and that the mobs, who regarded the police action as unlawful, focused their attacks on police authorities. Nevertheless, Matsumoto tries to refute the argument that had been presented by defense lawyers in the post-riot trials and later became the standard interpretation of the riot's origins. The lawyers had argued that the riot was an unpremeditated incident provoked by the unlawful interference of the police. Matsumoto, on the other hand, found indirect causes in the prevailing political conditions and the direct cause in the national rally itself. He concludes that popular discontent had inevitably accumulated during the long reign of the Katsura cabinet, and the government's secret diplomacy had provided scheming politicians with an opportunity to incite the public. When the thoughtless masses blindly followed the demagogues' call, and thronged to the national rally, the riot resulted. Matsumoto thus regarded the police authorities, who were charged with the task of preventing the rally, as essentially the victims of prevailing political conditions.

After the Pacific War, in 1952, Matsui Shigeru's memoirs were made public.[3] Matsui was first division chief of the Metropolitan Police Board at the time of the Hibiya riot, and his memoirs contain materials that were apparently written or collected right after the event. Matsui's interpretation of the riot, however, seems to have been added in about 1940-1941. He was motivated much more strongly than Matsumoto by

---

[1] The most recent summary of the incident, based on a number of primary sources, is Amamiya Shōichi, "Hibiya yakiuchi jiken," in Wagatsuma Sakae ed., *Nihon seiji saiban shiroku Meiji go* (Tokyo, 1969), pp. 379-423.

[2] Matsumoto Buyū, *Iwayuru Hibiya yakiuchi jiken no kenkyū* (Tokyo, 1939).

[3] Matsui Shigeru, *Hibiya sōjō jiken no tenmatsu* (Tokyo, 1952).

a desire to refute the notion that the riot was caused by "unlawful police intervention and brutality." Although conceding that the police might not have acted perfectly, Matsui contends that fundamentally the police were made scapegoats for the popular indignation invited by government secrecy about the peace negotiations. He concludes that the immediate causes of the riot were blind mass action and the lack of sufficient police power to suppress it.

Another police-related author, Takahashi Yūsai, published a detailed study of the riot in 1961 based on abundant sources, including the above two works.[4] Unlike his predecessors, however, Takahashi places the responsibility for the riot on the Metropolitan Police Board. He believes that the board mishandled its charge, and goes so far as to suggest that if it were not for police intervention there might have been no riot.

These three works, albeit from different perspectives, are primarily concerned with the issue of police responsibility. In their views of the crowd, they agree wholeheartedly with Prime Minister Katsura that the participants in the riot were simply villainous mobs. George Rudé writes that when the crowd in history is considered unworthy of serious study, the analysis of its motives remains superficial and the explanations of why crowds riot tend to be greatly affected by the values espoused by the investigator.[5] Analysis of the motives of the Hibiya crowd in the three police studies indeed remained shallow. Nevertheless in their use of source material they excelled every study of the riot by later historians who, although critical of these earlier studies, relied heavily on them for factual information.

Hasegawa Nyozekan, a leading liberal polemicist of the Taishō period, stated flatly that the Hibiya riot was caused by a petty scheme of anti-government politicians, and that since it was neither a political nor a social movement it had no significance in relation to so-called Taishō democracy.[6] On the other hand, Yoshino Sakuzō wrote in 1914, admittedly in a highly ambiguous fashion, that the Hibiya riot signaled the emergence of the Japanese masses on the political stage.[7] Similarly, studies of the riot by postwar Japanese historians can be divided roughly into two categories, depending upon whether or not they find in the riot a struggle against the ruling power and whether the struggle is believed to constitute the starting point for Taishō democracy.

With some variation in reasoning and emphasis, a minority of Japanese scholars characterizes the Hibiya riot as a manifestation of popular

[4] Takahashi Yūsai, *Meiji keisatsushi kenkyū: Meiji sanjū hachinen no Hibiya sōjō jiken* (Tokyo, 1961).

[5] George Rudé, *The Crowd in History* (New York: John Wiley & Sons, 1964), p. 214.

[6] "Meiji, Taishō, Shōwa sandai no seiji," *Bungei shunjū* (October 1961), p. 326.

[7] Mitani Taichirō, ed., *Yoshino Sakuzō* (Tokyo, 1972), pp. 65, 77.

nationalism and chauvinism, with little or no antiestablishment intent.[8] On the other hand, the predominant—one might say the "consensus"— view of the Hibiya riot among present-day Japanese historians is that it constitutes an instance of the "people's struggle against despotic ruling powers." Regarding the "people" as the motive force in history, these historians generally perceive a growing class consciousness in the Tokyo crowds and interpret the riot in terms of a theory of class struggle. Their most explicit spokesman, Inoue Kiyoshi, writes,

> How symptomatically imperialistic it was that the Portsmouth treaty, which one might term an international license to establish Japanese imperialism, had to be guarded, from its signing to ratification, by martial law over the city of Tokyo! The people who had been instigated by the demagogues, who were more militaristic than even the government of Japan at that time, soon transcended the demagogue's intention and rushed headlong into a great uprising against the clan government. Thus was announced the arrival of a new era in modern Japanese history. At the same time in Russia, with which Japan had negotiated the peace treaty, great revolutionary movements against the imperial regime were developing day by day under the leadership of the working class. The Japanese socialist organ, *Chokugen*, comparing this uprising by the Japanese people with the revolutionary movements in Russia, stated, "the revolutionary movements in Russia display unity and consciousness. The Japanese uprising has neither unity nor consciousness. In its essence, however, the riot in Japan is similar to the revolution in Russia. We might say that the people in Japan are unconsciously nurturing a spirit of revolution." Indeed, there is a qualitative difference between united and conscious revolutionary movements guided by a powerful socialist party and a mass riot, without unity or consciousness, that is initially instigated by militarists. The Hibiya riot, however, was the first instance in Japanese history in which the people transcended the chauvinistic demagogues and bodily clashed with the power of the state. The *Chokugen* was correct in observing that in the Hibiya riot the people in Japan were unconsciously nurturing a revolutionary spirit.[9]

First, these scholars assert that the basic cause of the riot was not popular dissatisfaction with the peace treaty itself. Rather, the riot represented an explosion of indignation against a despotic government that had imposed upon the people the agony and misery of war and left

---

[8] For instance, Sumiya Mikio, *Nihon no rekishi 22: Dai Nihon teikoku no shiren* (Tokyo, 1966), p. 318; Komuro Akeomi, "Hibiya yakiuchi jiken no saikentō," *Kindai Nihonshi kenkyū*, No. 4 (April 1958), pp. 9-16.

[9] Inoue Kiyoshi, ed., *Taishōki no seiji to shakai* (Tokyo, 1969), p. 1.

them to face an insecure livelihood at war's end. Second, because the people lacked their own leadership and organization, their anger was initially mobilized by nationalistic and chauvinistic demagogues who directed the energy of mass outrage against their political rivals in the form of a chauvinistic antitreaty movement. Third, however, on September 5 the people surprised both their "outside" leaders and those in power by transcending the objectives of the rally's organizers and developing it into an antiestablishment riot. Fourth, the people had no leadership or organization of their own and they therefore failed to achieve their objectives. Nevertheless, Inoue and others assert, their actions signaled the emergence on the Japanese political scene of revolutionary urban masses.

The interpretation of the Hibiya riot as an instance of the popular struggle against the ruling elite presents a number of ambiguities. First, it is not clear who "the people" are or what are their class characteristics. The primary source used by the people's revolution theorists to demonstrate the class characteristics of the supposed participants in the antipower struggle is a list of those indicted by the police as a result of pretrial interrogations. This list is included in Matsumoto's confidential report. However, it contains only 308 names.[10] The police had originally picked up more than 2,000 people. In principle, of course, rioters must be arrested in the very act of rioting. In the case of the Hibiya incident, however, police records show that very few were actually arrested in the act. The records also show that the police arrested many victims of the riot, used their wounds as evidence, and forced them to confess their "crimes." Of the 308, as few as 10 were charged with arson; the rest with instigation or attendance. This obviously fails to reflect that the most prevalent act of the rioters was arson, which destroyed more than 350 buildings and 15 street cars at various locations in the city. Moreover, those indicted included several beggars who "confessed their crimes" to get free food and shelter while in police custody.[11]

Some scholars arrive at their characterization of the participants in the riot by tabulating the occupations of the 117 people who were judged guilty, including only 8 for arson. Their occupations, however, range so widely that no category is conspicuous. About 10 were listed as factory workers, and only one was a student. Broadly speaking, craftsmen were most numerous.[12]

Available materials other than trial records provide us with highly fragmented descriptions of the crowd at the riot sites, without exact numerical information: "construction laborers," "rickshaw-men,"

[10] Matsumoto, *Iwayuru Hibiya*, supplement, pp. 8-27.
[11] "Kyōto shūshū hikoku hiken yoshin kiroku," unpublished.
[12] Matsumoto, *Iwayuru Hibiya*, supplement, pp. 8-15.

"craftsmen types," "farmerlike," "a newspaper deliverer," "ruffian type," "a politician type," and "an apparent gentleman with a Panama hat and a stick." In conclusion, the sources are too unreliable and insufficient to allow us to know the "faces" of the participants and the class characteristics of these "revolutionary people."

Virtually the sole piece of concrete evidence presented by the people's revolution theorists in support of their contention is that the rioters' attack was clearly focused on the organs of the state power, namely, the home minister's official residence, police stations, and numerous police boxes. In presenting this fact as evidence, of course, they continue to assume that the masses who participated in the national rally actually intended from the beginning to rebel against the ruling powers, transcending the objectives of their demagogic "leaders." On the other hand, overwhelming evidence suggests that the direct cause of the antipolice riot was police intervention in the mass demonstration.[13] In other words, initially the crowd had no intent to riot, and in the absence of forceful police action it never would have attacked the police.

It may be true, as Katsura himself noted, that for one reason or another, antipolice sentiment was prevalent among the people. Even so, the people's revolution theorists are no more persuasive than those who would straightforwardly attribute the cause of the widespread attacks to mass indignation over the persistent official interference with mass demonstrations and to the widely criticized behavior of some policemen, who with their drawn swords apparently caused most of the seventeen deaths among the people. It must also be noted that in other cities, too, crowds attacked police stations and boxes only when the police interfered with mass rallies.

Another weakness of the people's revolution theory is that at the national rally and thereafter the crowd appealed to His Majesty to reject the treaty with their repeated shouts of "Banzai" to the emperor, to the imperial army, and to the navy, accompanied by the national anthem. It is difficult to interpret this as behavior directed against the ruling elites. The imperial army and navy were at the time predominantly under the command of the Satsuma-Chōshū oligarchs. Moreover, the mobs greeted with a shout of "Banzai" the soldiers who had been dispatched to restore order in the city. Indeed, the people so often provided the soldiers with food and other articles that the military authorities felt

---

[13] Hanai Takuzō, *Shōtei ronsō* (Tokyo, 1930), pp. 6, 14, 40, 113; Minobe Tatsukichi, "Kenryoku no ranyō to kore ni taisuru hankō," *Kokkagakkai zasshi*, 19 (October 1905); *Japan Daily Herald* (September 6, 1905); *Japan Weekly Mail* (September 9, 1905); *Eastern World* (September 6, 1905); George Kennan's eyewitness report, "The Sword of Peace in Japan," *Outlook* (October 14, 1905), pp. 357-365.

obliged to issue an order against such acts.[14] We can only conclude that the masses resented the police who had interfered with their rally, not the organs of state power in general.

The mobs destroyed many Christian churches, which at the time were themselves symbols of opposition to state power. Furthermore, no socialist who openly opposed the ruling class participated in the antipeace movement. In fact, socialists and most Christians had been against the war and welcomed its termination. The Japanese masses therefore judged them traitorous.[15] The people's revolution theorists generally ignore these facts or fail to explain them convincingly.

In short, unless one uncritically upholds a specific class-struggle interpretation of history, one cannot accept the view that the Hibiya riot was a mass struggle against the ruling power. In this connection, it is noteworthy that some popular revolution theorists even hypothesize that the riot could have been deliberately instigated by the government, which feared rising popular opposition and prompted mob action as an excuse to exercise suppression.[16] Official conspiracy may indeed have played a role in instigating crowd action at various points in history, but overwhelming evidence regarding the Hibiya riot renders a conspiracy theory too far-fetched to merit serious consideration.

Although similarly upholding the class-struggle interpretation of history, some younger historians have tried to improve critically upon the works of their elders, such as Inoue. Miyachi Masato, for example, accepts the basic premise that the riot was against the ruling powers.[17] The main thrust of his impressive research is, therefore, to explain more convincingly the causes of the uprising through a broader analysis of the existing "objective conditions"—political, economic, and social. At the same time, he departs from Inoue's contention that in their actions the people transcended the stance of antipeace leaders. On the contrary, Miyachi places the leaders in the role of "a unique political faction." Albeit unconsciously, this faction provided an opportunity for rebellion to the urban masses, whose state of "perpetual insecurity" had already established the objective conditions for an uprising.

By the beginning of the twentieth century, Miyachi maintains, urbanization and developing capitalism had transformed Tokyo from a

---

[14] Takahashi, *Meiji keisatsushi kenkyū*, p. 181.

[15] Matsumoto, *Iwayuru Hibiya*, p. 22. Yoshikawa Morikuni, *Keigyaku seisōshi* (Tokyo, 1957), p. 58.

[16] Uesugi Jūjirō, "Hibiya yakiuchi jiken no kenkyū no tame ni," *Rekishigaku kenkyū* (June 1955); Shinobu Seizaburō and Nakayama Jiichi, eds., *Nichi-Ro sensō no kenkyū* (Tokyo, 1972), p. 439.

[17] Miyachi Masato, *Nichi-Ro sensōgo seijishi no kenkyū* (Tokyo, 1973); Miyachi Masato, "Nichi-Ro zengo no shakai to minshū," in Rekishigaku Kenkyūkai and Nihonshi Kenkyūkai, eds., *Kōza Nihonshi 6: Nihon teikokushugi no keisei* (Tokyo, 1970), pp. 131-170.

premodern into a modern city. The process had affected the life patterns of the working class in such a way as to produce extreme instability in city life. There emerged a work force that was transitional in terms of standard class categories and that was prone to resort to spontaneous rioting against the capitalists: a vast number of day laborers, coolies, and craftsmen bewildered by the flux of the premodern environment, and the massive convergence of rural population upon an already expanding urban slum. In pursuit of their imperialistic ambitions, the rulers imposed upon the urban masses exploitative policies that caused high taxes, inflation, and particularly high prices for rice. The result was to make even the petit and middle bourgeoisie resentful toward the government. The traditionally antigovernment press capitalized on the urban plight in pursuing its attack on the regime. Based on these observations, Miyachi, like Masumi Junnosuke a few years earlier,[18] defines the period between the Russo-Japanese war and the rice riots (1905-1918) as "a period of urban mass riot."

The war, Miyachi asserts, only exacerbated conditions of perpetual urban insecurity by adding conscription, emergency taxes, public bonds, and the assessment of "voluntary" contributions. Out of patriotism, bordering at times on intense chauvinism, the people struggled to adjust to additional wartime burdens. Yet in striving to achieve their imperialistic objectives, the ruling powers ignored the people's plight. Moreover, the established political parties fundamentally supported the government. Thus it was impossible for the socialists, with their antiwar stance, to turn a chauvinistic populace against the exploitative government. Under such circumstances, only the antipeace and antigovernment Rengōkai could appeal to the latent resentment of the people toward the regime and mobilize the indignant masses in a nationwide movement. "The public excitement over the peace issue was ultimately to turn into a riot," Miyachi concludes, "even when it was not intended as such by the rally organizers."[19]

Miyachi discusses a number of interesting facts concerning the economic and social insecurity of the masses in Tokyo at the time of the Russo-Japanese war, and demonstrates the potential for mass rioting. His analysis of the various activist groups that stood ready to lead the insecure masses to collective action is also illuminating. In explaining the Hibiya riot, however, Miyachi's detailed study still lacks the vital link that is needed to connect persuasively the existing "objective conditions" for rioting with its actual occurrence. He relies on a strict materialism in assuming a one-to-one relationship between the environ-

---

[18] Masumi Junnosuke, *Nihon seitō shiron*, 4 (Tokyo, 1968), 92.
[19] Miyachi, *Nichi-Ro sengo seijishi no kenkyū*, pp. 248-249.

ment of the urban dwellers and their political consciousness and action. Similarly, even if one accepts his explanation as to the leaders' objective in mobilizing the insecure urban masses, Miyachi's explanation for the masses' response to the leaders' call is largely dependent upon a form of "circumstantial determinism." Such difficulties also weaken his attempt to link the occupational and class composition of the supposed participants with the regional distribution of types of workers across the city of Tokyo on the basis of the aforementioned limited pretrial police records. He writes, "as we analyze the social strata of the participants in the riot, it is readily apparent which social classes bore the heavy burden of the wartime economy."[20] Thus, in the end, Miyachi fails to refute decisively Nezu Masashi's earlier observations on the riot to the effect that "the people in a miserable plight can be led and instigated in any direction. The rigid view that the people must always be correctly progressive has no factual basis. It is tantamount to subjectivism, an example of wishful thinking."[21]

Matsuo Takayoshi defines Taishō democracy as a democratic tendency that appeared conspicuously in political, social, and cultural spheres from 1905 to 1925. The trend was promoted, Matsuo asserts, by "various broad mass movements to attain and protect political rights and civil liberties." He attempts to justify placing the Hibiya riot at the forefront of this series of mass movements, although he admits that the riot at least partially represented a "reactionary movement" for chauvinistic expansionism.[22] He contends that it contained an element of protest against "despotic clique (*hanbatsu*) rule," and asserts that this characteristic of the antipeace movement becomes clearer when viewed from the broader perspective of the nationwide movement that emerged following the Hibiya riot.

Matsuo further maintains that the Hibiya riot in and of itself was a protest against the regime and its "claw," the police, which deprived the people of the freedoms of speech and assembly. As proof, he points out that the riot began with attacks on the police, the official residence of the home minister who presided over the police, and the government mouthpiece, *Kokumin shinbun*. He also notes that the ensuing riot concentrated on the police stations and boxes all over the city.[23]

Matsuo's argument is no more compelling than the claims of others that it was out of chauvinism that the rioters attacked the police, who interfered with their antipeace movement, and the newspaper, which supported peace. Matsuo is more explicit than Miyachi in attaching sig-

[20] Miyachi, "Nichi-Ro zengo no shakai to minshū," p. 151.
[21] Nezu Masashi, *Hihan Nihon gendaishi* (Tokyo, 1958), pp. 267 and 303.
[22] Matsuo Takayoshi, *Taishō demokurashii* (Tokyo, 1974).
[23] Ibid., p. 15.

nificance to the antiregime sentiments of the Rengōkai leaders. Indeed, he seems to credit the masses only to the extent that they joined Rengōkai leaders in the antiregime movements. Yet his argument ignores abundant evidence, including trial records and the statements of the Rengōkai leaders themselves, which clearly establish that the Rengōkai leaders played no part in the rioting.

As we have seen, Inoue and others valued the so-called popular struggle against the ruling powers precisely because the people "transcended" the intentions of the Rengōkai leaders. Matsuo is caught in a basic contradiction when he tries to attach equal significance to the intentions of the Rengōkai leaders and to the actions of the rioters. This contradiction leads him to convoluted efforts to establish a seeming duality within the Rengōkai, and the masses as well, in order to find an antiregime element in both. Matsuo assigns chauvinistic and antiregime characteristics to both the Rengōkai leaders and their followers. Moreover, he approves of both for being antiregime, but criticizes both for their chauvinism. Matsuo's effort to discuss the antipeace movement on a nationwide scale makes a valuable contribution, but his presupposition that there is a clear element of political reformism in the Hibiya riot results in considerable ambiguity.

Needless to say, evaluations of an historical event are always colored by preconceptions. Such preconceptions are obvious in government and police-related views of the Hibiya crowd as a "bunch of undesirable elements." Yet later historians have rigidly followed a class-struggle interpretation of history in their fervent desire to make of the Hibiya riot a distinct starting point for so-called Taishō democracy. Most have portrayed the series of mass actions from September 1905 to the rice riots of 1918 in the image of a "recurrence of Hibiya," and have attributed to the Hibiya riots the character of conscious democratic struggle against the ruling elite. Despite their broader scope and wealth of factual information, the rigid preconceptions adhered to in these studies make them ultimately unconvincing.

IN SEARCH OF THE HISTORICAL SIGNIFICANCE OF THE HIBIYA RIOT

The motives behind a riot are perhaps as numerous as the participants. What we must search out, therefore, is not a variety of personal motives but rather the prevailing mentality that shapes the collective behavior of divergent individuals and allows participants to justify their actions.[24] Thus, the first step toward an understanding of the mentality of the

[24] Neil J. Smelser, *Theory of Collective Behavior* (New York: Free Press of Glencoe, 1963), pp. 79-130 and 222-269.

crowd in the Hibiya riot must be the most straightforward, unadorned examination of its behavior that is allowed by available factual information.

Certainly many of the riot participants were disgruntled with the additional wartime burden of high taxes, "voluntary" contributions, conscription, and inflation. Privately, they harbored a strong sense of economic and social deprivation. They were therefore anxious that the results of war should sufficiently compensate for their wartime toil and assure a better life in the future. To that extent, private survival instincts conditioned the masses to be dissatisfied with a peace treaty that provided no indemnity and only a small territorial gain.

A sense of deprivation and survival instinct alone, however, do not explain the immediate occasion for the violent explosion and its pattern.[25] It was necessary that private discontents be ideologically channelled into action. The behavior of the participants, who manifested sufficient consciousness of public issues to attend the national rally, suggests that they were loyal and patriotic subjects prone, whenever the opportunity arose, to cry "Banzai" for the emperor, the army, and navy, and to play the national anthem. Whatever private discontents they might have harbored, the participants identified readily with what they believed to be the interests of the state, and engaged in a movement to promote a public cause. In their antipeace activities, the masses were not directly in pursuit of private gain. Why, then, did they so readily identify their private concerns with a public issue?

It is generally agreed that in no other period was the idea of resistance to state power as widely held as during the popular rights movement of the Meiji teens, when a dynamic middle stratum still maintained its independence from the authority of the state. By 1890, however, the movement had been suppressed, and the orthodoxy of the imperial system was steadily established through the Imperial Constitution, the Rescript on Education, and the reorganization of the local administrative structure. Prior to that time, both power holders and people had understood rather clearly that the mobilization of loyalty was a political issue. Now, however, as the state's assimilation of its subjects was more or less completed by the beginning of the twentieth century, the emperor became the sole, symbolic focal point for popular loyalty, and the political nature of the state was concealed in an image of a family-state with the emperor as father figure. Loyalty to the emperor became synonymous with loyalty to the state, and thus the government held a monopoly on the prerogative to determine what was a loyal act.[26]

[25] Ted Robert Gurr, *Why Men Rebel* (Princeton: Princeton University Press, 1970), pp. 13-51 and 155-231.

[26] Maruyama Masao, "Chūsei to hangyaku," *Kindai Nihon shisōshi kōza*, 6 (Tokyo, 1958), 443-447. Banno Junji, *Meiji kempōtaisei no kakuritsu* (Tokyo, 1971).

By the time of the Russo-Japanese war, therefore, a dual character had been created for the emperor: as manipulated by the ruling oligarchy, he was both constitutional monarch and absolute "father" of the nation. Yet only the latter image was presented to the general public.[27] The war crisis intensified the people's devotion to their father, the Meiji emperor, and drove them to exert their utmost for the successful execution of war.[28]

In the view of such loyal subjects of the emperor, the government leaders who had concluded the "humiliating peace" were, as Kōno's September 4 memorial stated, "criminals to His Imperial Majesty" and "to the people."[29] Loyalists quickly became convinced that it was their duty to join the national movement, reject the peace, and chastise the "criminals." Thus public response to the rally came as a pleasant surprise to the Rengōkai leaders, who had feared that their call might go unheeded. People traveled to Tokyo from the countryside, and many sent contributions and letters of indignation, some written in blood, to Rengōkai headquarters.[30] In short, the prevailing mentality of the crowd that gathered at Hibiya on September 5 was, as Yamaji Aizan wrote, one of "sincere loyalty and patriotism." People suppressed their private interests for the sake of the public. Their behavior clearly manifested the uncritical belief in a state orthodoxy of personal imperial rule that they had been taught.[31] Kita Ikki, who was in Tokyo during 1905, was strongly affected by the mass antipeace movement, which he characterized in terms of the late-Tokugawa loyalist slogan of "revere the emperor and expel the barbarian" (sonnō jōi).[32] Dominating the mind of the crowd was not political reform but a simple and direct opposition to those who were "criminals" against the emperor and themselves.

For this reason, the crowd regarded police intervention at Hibiya Park and at Nijūbashi as an act of disloyalty. Policemen had interfered with the people's execution of their duty as loyal subjects of the emperor, and the people therefore concentrated their attacks on the police. In short, the Hibiya riot should be defined as a mass riot for public justice

---

[27] See Kuno Osamu and Tsurumi Shunsuke, *Gendai Nihon no shisō* (Tokyo, 1956), pp. 132-133.

[28] Even the champion of "people's history," Irokawa Daikichi, who is critical of Maruyama's view of the emperor system, agrees with him on the nationalistic chauvinism of the Japanese people at the time of the Russo-Japanese war. Irokawa Daikichi, *Meijijin* (Tokyo, 1965) and *Meiji no bunka* (Tokyo 1970); Ubukata Toshirō, *Meiji Taishō kenbunshi* (Tokyo, 1926), pp. 155-226.

[29] *Tokyo asahi shinbun* (September 5, 1905).

[30] Ogawa Heikichi bunsho kenkyūkai, comp., *Ogawa Heikichi kankei bunsho*, 1 (Tokyo, 1973), 196-200.

[31] Tōyama Shigeki, *Nihon kindaishi*, 1 (Tokyo, 1975), 290-293.

[32] Kita Ikki, *Kokutairon oyobi junsei shakaishugi* (Tokyo, 1969), p. 433.

under the banner of the emperor. As a "church and king riot," its fundamental orientation was naturally traditionalist and conservative.[33]

Participants in the mass protest movement, however, unwittingly exposed a grave conflict that had been hidden within the Meiji political system. They touched on the contradiction between the public façade of an absolute emperor's personal rule and the actual role of the emperor as a constitutional monarch to be exploited by the ruling oligarchs. A few years after the Hibiya riot, Tokutomi Sohō commented that "in the event, both the attackers and the attacked had legitimate reasons."[34] The riot was a "loyalty contest" between the people and government leaders, both upholding their own notion of the emperor.

As the competition progressed, it became evident that members of the "family state" differed hierarchically in the meanings they attributed to imperial loyalty. In other words, the "purity" of one's loyalty to the emperor corresponded to one's distance from the throne. The nearer one stood, the less pure and the more politically tainted was one's loyalty. In relation to the peace issue, no one close to the throne, including the elder statesmen and the cabinet decision makers, doubted that the emperor would ratify the treaty. The major party leaders, who expected to succeed momentarily to the reins of government, also understood the workings of the imperial system. Therefore, none of them seriously contemplated joining the masses. Only the minor party members who were politically ambitious spearheaded the mass movement in appeal to the emperor. Yet even their notion of the imperial system was sufficiently pragmatic that they withdrew smoothly from the scene of protest soon after the Hibiya rally.

At the point furthest from the throne stood the masses, who wholeheartedly participated in the antipeace movement. They were, in Kita's words, "the plebians who would die with utmost sincerity for the cause of sonnō jōi."[35] Identifying with the imperial personage and the cause of his state, the masses, who had little knowledge of foreign affairs, blindly manifested their emperor-centered chauvinism. Popular enthusiasm for the war permeated the ranks not only of the unsophisticated but also of the well-educated. This unbridled, nationalistic, Meiji mentality can be amply and vividly observed in numerous contemporary documents, such as philosopher Nishida Kitarō's diary, poet Ishikawa Takuboku's notes, and the wartime letters of Hirano Tomosuke, who was selected by historian Irokawa Daikichi as the prototypical "Meiji man."

[33] Rudé, Crowd in History, pp. 135-148. E. J. Hobsbawn, Primitive Rebels (New York: Norton, 1959), pp. 108-125.

[34] Tokutomi Iichirō, Taishō seikyoku shiron (Tokyo, 1916), p. 156.

[35] Kita, Kokutairon oyobi junsei shakaishugi; Maruyama Masao, Gendai seiji no shisō to kōdō (Tokyo, 1964), pp. 162-163.

During the war, the government vigorously stimulated popular loyalty to the emperor for the sake of national mobilization. Now, at war's end, it had to face the real consequences of the popular chauvinism that government itself had encouraged and exploited. When the masses' sincere loyalty was organized by political activists into a national antipeace movement, the government was compelled to repress it with force. Yet the government underestimated the vigor of mass nationalism, which had been further invigorated by the wartime experience itself.

Since they had been led to believe in the emperor's own infallibility and his personal concern for his subjects, the people could attribute conclusion of the "humiliating" peace solely to the evil ministers around the throne. As a result, they rose up in anger, revealing the double-edged nature of the imperial system. Thus the Hibiya riot demonstrated both the successes and the dangers of indoctrination under the Meiji state.[36]

The mass movement achieved none of its conscious objectives. In its wake, however, it left a number of far-reaching consequences. Some conclude that the event inevitably created a sense of disillusionment and even suspicion toward the "father-emperor" who failed to respond to a sincere popular appeal. The Meiji emperor himself, who heard the riotous commotion outside his palace, composed a poem: "Directions may differ / But the sincerity of Our subjects toward the state / Must be one."[37] Yet despite his optimism and expectations, the war that had ended in unprecedented riots in the capital city was to render an increasing number of minds more complex and reflective over the issue of the state. Some noted the growth of considerable apathy toward public affairs in the postwar years, as shown in the works of Sōseki, Roka, Doppo, Katai, and Ōgai. A new generation was to appear that asserted individuality more openly and consciously than did its parents.[38]

Such trends drove the ruling authorities to redouble their efforts to indoctrinate the people with the notion of a family-state centering on the emperor. The government initiated a renewed indoctrination program as early as October 1905, beginning with celebrations marking the triumphant return of the imperial navy. On that occasion, the main streets of Tokyo were decked with triumphal arches (including one right next to Hibiya Park), trolley cars were decorated, and the entire city turned out. The celebration rally at Ueno Park was presided over by

[36] Marius B. Jansen, "Monarchy and Modernization in Japan," *Journal of Asian Studies*, 36 (August 1977), 621.

[37] Sasaki Nobutsuna, *Meiji tennō gyoshū kinkai* (Osaka, 1927), p. 306.

[38] Oka Yoshitake, "Nichi-Ro sensōgo ni okeru atarashii sedai no seichō," part 1, *Shisō*, no. 513 (February 1967), pp. 137-149; part 2, *Shisō*, no. 513 (March 1967), pp. 361-377. See Oka, "Generational Conflict After the Russo-Japanese war," in this volume.

the emperor himself, with the attendance of one quarter of a million people, giving an indication both of the enthusiasm of the government for the renewed propaganda campaign and the as yet fundamentally unchanged mentality of the Meiji Japanese.[39]

Government efforts on behalf of the reindoctrination program were further evidenced by a stream of imperial edicts. One in particular, issued on the occasion of ratification of the peace treaty, deliberately stated, "We, the Emperor, examined the peace terms our plenipotentiary had concluded and found them meeting Our wishes in every detail." At the same time it admonished the people against indulging in "an insolent and negligent sentiment." Other edicts profusely commended the military commanders and the plenipotentiary on his return from Portsmouth. The Home and Education Ministries instructed the people in one directive after another to make further efforts in the service of the state. Shintō priests were mobilized to celebrate the victory at shrines all over the country and to rededicate the populace to the cause of the divine nation.[40] Such government efforts were soon extended, on the one hand, to the reorganization and "revitalization" of towns and villages, and on the other to the suppression of dissent among the people, which culminated in the High Treason case of 1910.

The impact of the Hibiya riot was not felt by the ruling oligarchy alone. The crowd action also impressed those who were more clearly conscious politically and suggested to them the potential of the masses as a political force. Its ripple effects were observed in the postwar parliamentary debate on the issue of the "recuperation of popular vitality and livelihood." As a form of political protest the riot set a precedent for later mass mobilizations that would reveal heightened political consciousness in pursuit of immediate private interests. Moreover, the Hibiya protest was to bequeath its legacy not only to those of liberal and leftist orientations. As exemplified in Kita's later career, the riot also was remotely but undeniably echoed in the Shōwa Restoration movements of the young right-wing officers in the 1930s.

In the narrowest sense, the Hibiya riot was little more than a blind outburst, and its basic orientation was toward nationalistic chauvinism. Its participants were only remotely concerned with political reform. Nevertheless, when the masses challenged a political decision of the ruling oligarchs out of their "pure" sense of loyalty, they unwittingly exposed the vital weaknesses hidden within the Meiji imperial system.

[39] Miyake Setsurei, *Dōjidaishi*, 3 (Tokyo, 1950), 455.
[40] *Tokyo asahi shinbun* (September–October 1905).

GROWTH AND CONFLICT IN JAPANESE HIGHER EDUCATION, 1905-1930

BYRON K. MARSHALL

In the two decades following the end of the Meiji period, Japanese higher education experienced severe conflicts as government, faculty, and students fought over a wide range of issues involving political rights and academic freedom. This conflict has most often been seen, on the one hand, as the result of the predisposition of an authoritarian regime to suppress intellectual freedom and, on the other hand, as the consequence of ideological ferment in a shifting international climate of opinion made turbulent by the First World War and the Russian Revolution. Thus academic intellectuals are viewed as the hapless victims of a state machinery of thought control triggered as the winds of Western liberalism and Marxist radicalism swept over a society undergoing the strains of rapid industrialization.[1]

This essay does not deny the validity of explanatory insights gained from such perspectives, but rather seeks to extend our understanding of such conflict by placing it in the light of a somewhat different perspec-

[1] See, for example, Ienaga Saburō, *Daigaku no jiyū no rekishi* (Tokyo, 1962); Itazaki Akio, *Daigaku no jisei no rekishi* (Tokyo, 1965); Tanaka Kōtarō, Suekawa Hiroshi, Wagatsuma Sakae, Ōuchi Hyōe, and Miyazawa Toshiyoshi, *Daigaku no jiji* (Tokyo, 1963); Tsurumi Shunsuke, et al., *Tenkō*, 3 vols. (Tokyo, 1960-1962); and, in English, Michio Nagai, *Higher Education in Japan: Its Takeoff and Crash* (Tokyo, 1971), and Doo Soo Suh, "The Struggle for Academic Freedom in Japanese Universities before 1945," Ph.D. dissertation, Columbia, 1953. Two more recent and analytical treatments of some aspects of the topic are Henry D. Smith II, *Japan's First Student Radicals* (Cambridge: Harvard University Press, 1972), and Richard H. Mitchell, *Thought Control in Prewar Japan* (Ithaca: Cornell University Press, 1976).

tive—a perspective derived from the studies of organizational change and elite conflict. Stated in its simplest terms, it argues that turmoil within the Taishō system of higher education is better understood if our attention is directed to processes of growth and change that eroded an earlier cohesion between a bureaucratic elite within the government and an intellectual elite within academia—processes that led in this period to a partial breakdown of the mechanisms of coordination and control of universities by the state and thus caused a crisis of governance.[2]

Japan's modern system of higher education began with the founding of Tokyo Imperial University as the primary agency for the importation of new knowledge deemed necessary for transforming Japanese society into a modern state, and as the apex of a system of government-sponsored schooling intended to instill loyalty to that state. During the Meiji period, Tōdai and, to a lesser extent, its sister institution in Kyoto served as integral parts of a bureaucratic system of cultural management—the product, in Harry Harootunian's terms, of a "cultural policy" aimed at the "political management" and "bureaucratization" of Japanese intellectual life.[3] In this early period, the Tōdai faculty was granted high status and critical roles not only in the recruitment, training, and evaluating of future elites but also as a reservoir of expertise for decision making on a wide range of public policy issues as well as of defenders against ideologies that might challenge the Meiji authority structure.[4] By the 1920s, however, this system had undergone far-reaching changes, and the challenge to governmental authority as often as not came from these universities themselves.

GROWTH AND SEGMENTATION IN HIGHER EDUCATION

As Tables 1 and 2 indicate, the 1910s and especially the 1920s were decades of extraordinarily rapid expansion in the Japanese system of

[2] For this perspective, see Neil J. Smelser, "Epilogue: Social-Structural Dimensions of Higher Education," in Talcott Parsons and Gerald M. Platt, *The American University* (Cambridge: Harvard University Press, 1973), pp. 389-422, and "Growth, Structural Change and Conflict in California Public Higher Education, 1950-1970," in Smelser and Gabriel Almond, eds., *Public Higher Education in California* (Berkeley and Los Angeles: University of California Press, 1974), pp. 9-141; J. Victor Baldridge, *Power and Conflict in the University: Research in the Sociology of Complex Organizations* (New York: John Wiley & Sons, 1971); Suzanne Keller, *Beyond the Ruling Class: Strategic Elites in Modern Society* (New York: Random House, 1963); and Bernard Silberman's contribution to the present volume.

[3] "A Sense of Ending and the Problem of Taishō," in *Japan in Crisis: Essays on Taishō Democracy*, edited by Bernard S. Silberman and H. D. Harootunian (Princeton: Princeton University Press, 1974), pp. 3-28.

[4] For evidence to support this generalization, see my "Professors and Politics: The Meiji Academic Elite," *Journal of Japanese Studies*, 3 (Winter 1977), 71-97.

higher education. The total number of students enrolled in universities (*daigaku*), colleges (*semmon gakkō*), and higher schools (*kōtō gakkō*) increased at rates as high as 64 percent over five-year periods for a total jump of over 240 percent between 1913 and 1933. The expansion of officially recognized universities was even more dramatic, although in part this was due to the upgrading of existing *semmon gakkō*. Although such segmentation was the primary means of accommodating to growth in scale, the imperial universities at Tokyo and Kyoto both also experienced large increases in their student bodies (see Table 3).

BUREAUCRATIZATION AND DECENTRALIZATION OF AUTHORITY

Such rapid growth in scale and segmentation of any social system poses serious challenges for coordination and control, and given the inadequate response to these challenges, it is not surprising that the Japanese system of higher education became more vulnerable to conflict in this period. On the one hand, there was an increasing trend toward bureaucratization (in the sense of administrative rule-making and career routinization) within the Ministry of Education, and, on the other hand, a steady drift away from effective centralized authority within the universities.

One measure of the bureaucratization of authority vis-à-vis the universities is the proliferation of formal rules intended to standardize procedures of governance within the system (see Figure 1). This proliferation of standardized rules was, in part at least, a response to a system becoming increasingly complex merely because of its growth in scale and segmentation. It is also an indication of a fundamental shift toward more formal mechanisms of coordination between the Mombushō and the universities necessitated by the inadequacies of the informal channels of communication that had functioned in the Meiji period.

At the end of the Meiji period, as the staff of the Mombushō grew and became more professionalized, there took place a clear differentiation between its personnel and the faculty at Tōdai. Although the Mombushō and the imperial universities had been formally distinct from at least the time of the reorganization of Japanese government in 1885, until 1905 administrative personnel were actually often treated as if they were interchangeable. The Bureau of Higher Education (the *Semmon gakumu kyoku*) between 1880 and 1905 was headed almost exclusively by men with prior experience as administrators and/or faculty from the imperial university: long-time Tōdai administrator Hamao Arata from 1880 to 1885, and again in 1886-1893; law professor Kinoshita Hiroji between 1893 and 1897; literature professor Ueda Mannen from 1897 to 1903; and agriculture professor Matsui Naokichi from 1903 to 1905.

TABLE 1. Expansion of Higher Education 1908-1933

No. of	Daigaku	Semmongakkō	Kōtōgakkō	Total Students	% Increase (5 years)
1908	3	65	8	46,504	
1913	4	86	8	53,188	+14.4
1918	5	96	8	65,180	+22.5
1923	31	121	25	106,698	+63.7
1928	40	153	31	165,885	+55.5
1933	45	171	32	181,455	+ 9.4

Source: Mombushō, *Wagakuni no kōtō kyōiku* (1964), Table 1, p. 254; Table 2, pp. 262-267.

TABLE 2. Expansion of Universities 1908-1933

	Schools	Students	Faculty	Faculty/ Students	Expenditures (1000s of 1961 yen) Total	Expenditures (1000s of 1961 yen) Per Student
1908	3	7,517	533	1:13.6	1,744,031	232
1913	4	9,472	815	1:11.7	2,553,824	267
1918	5	9,040	970	1: 9.3	2,170,884	240
1923	31	38,731	3,224	1:12.0	9,668,734	250
1928	40	61,502	4,905	1:12.4	14,233,584	231
1933	45	70,893	6,285	1:11.3	19,645,558	272

Source: Calculated from Mombushō, *Wagakuni no kōtō kyōiku*, Table 1, p. 254; Table 2, pp. 262-267; Table 8, pp. 290-291; Table 12, pp. 184-185.

TABLE 3. Growth of Tokyo and Kyoto Imperial Universities 1913-1933

	Tokyo Students	Tokyo % Change	Kyoto Students	Kyoto % Change
1913	5,223		1,791	
1918	4,904	− 6%	2,033	+ 14%
1923	5,981	+22%	2,548	+ 25%
1928	7,820	+31%	5,170	+103%
1933	8,269	+ 6%	5,710	+ 10%

Source: *Nihon Teikoku tōkei nenkan*, vols. 45, 49, 50, and 54.

Nor was it rare to find Tōdai personnel even in the top post of education minister. Hamao served briefly in the Ito Cabinet of 1898, as did sociologist Tōyama Masakazu. When Prime Minister Katsura Tarō made his first appointment to that post in 1903, his choice was science professor Kikuchi Dairoku. After 1905, however, the minister's post became increasingly politicized as prime ministers in the Taishō period used the education portfolio to draw influential civil servants (such as Makino Nobuaki, 1911-1912; Okuda Yoshihito, 1913-1914; Ichiki Kitokurō, 1914-1915; Okada Ryōhei, 1916-1918) or political party supporters (such as Nakahashi Tokugorō, 1918-1922) into the cabinet. These

FIGURE 1. Index of New Edicts, Regulations and Ordinances for Higher Education, 1895-1930 (Ten-year Averages)

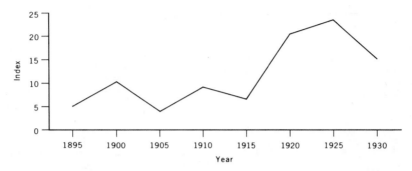

SOURCE: calculated from Mombusho, *Daigaku kankei hōrei no enkaku* (Development of Laws and Ordinances concerning Colleges and Universities), Tokyo, 1945-1950, four volumes.

were men whose views on educational policy were often at odds with that of the Tōdai leaders, as were sometimes those of the occasional academic drawn from private schools to serve as head of the Mombushō in these years (such as Takada Sanae, 1916, president of Waseda; Kamata Ekichi, 1923-1924, president of Keio). Simultaneously, recruitment to the bureau chief of higher education became routinized as part of the bureaucratic process of promotion within the permanent staff of the ministry. Thus Fukuhara Ryōjirō, a career Mombushō bureaucrat, headed that bureau from 1905 to 1911, when he moved up to be vice minister. His successor, Matsuura Shinjirō, was also eventually promoted to vice minister in 1924, turning the post over to the then chief of the bureau of technical education.[5]

[5] Another measure of the professionalization of Mombushō staff in these years can be seen in the relative stability of tenure in the posts of Vice Minister and *Futsū gakumu kyokuchō* (Chief of the Bureau of Education):

	Average Years in Post	
	1886-1906	*1906-1926*
Vice minister	1.7	2.9
Futsū gakumu kyokuchō	1.7	2.9
Semmon gakumu kyokuchō	2.2	6.7

SOURCE: Ijiri Tsunekichi, ed., *Rekidai kenkan roku* (Tokyo, 1967).

For yet another indication of the decline of Tōdai's influence on educational policy, compare the proportion of Tōdai faculty on the *Kōtō Kyōiku Kaigi* of 1897-1901 with the list of participants in the government conferences of 1910 and 1918: Kaigo Tokiomi, ed., *Rinji Kyōiku Kaigi no kenkyū* (Tokyo, 1960), pp. 1018-1036; Mombushō, *Meiji ikō kyōiku seido hattatsushi*, rev. ed. (1964-1965), 5:1139ff., 6:1177; Mombushō, *Gakusei hachijūnenshi*

If the Bureau of Higher Education became more professionalized and differentiated from the Tōdai faculty in these years, there are also indications that its relative position within the Mombushō was reduced as other units grew in size and budget. Although it is true that expenditures for higher education rose rapidly in the Taishō era, expenditures for other parts of the school system grew even faster. The Bureau of Higher Education, one of only four ministry bureaus in 1908, was only one of seven by 1928; and the size of its staff, which constituted approximately 13 percent of the ministry higher civil servants in 1906, grew so slowly that it represented less than 6 percent in 1926 (see Table 4).

These changes within the Mombushō were accompanied by an even more significant trend in the governance of the imperial universities—a trend toward decentralization and delegation of authority, marked by greater participation by faculty in the selection of presidents and deans and in a variety of other critical matters. Prior to 1897, Tōdai presidents had been men not only selected by but also with close ties to the Meiji political elite. Katō Hiroyuki, who served a total of twelve years in two separate terms, was a model of what has been labeled the "service intelligentsia" of early Meiji.[6] Watanabe Kōki (1886-1890) had been the chief administrative official for the city of Tokyo before being appointed by Minister Mori Arinori. Hamao Arata (1890-1897) had long

TABLE 4. BUREAU OF HIGHER EDUCATION WITHIN THE MOMBUSHŌ

	1906	1908	1913	1918	1923	1926	1928	1931
A. Expenditures on universities (in 1000s yen)		4,706	5,841	6,274	29,074		33,083	
B. As % of total ministry budget		61.5%	55.5%	25.5%	28.9%		24.5%	
C. Bureau salaries (in 1000s yen)	9.7			18.9	33.5	28.6		31.3
D. C as % of total ministry salaries	12.9%			14.1%	6.0%	5.5%		3.9%
E. Bureau staff	18			20	29	24		23
F. E as % of total ministry staff	13.3%			10.0%	5.0%	5.3%		3.5%

SOURCES: A & B calculated from Mombushō, *Meiji ikō kyōiku seido hattatsushi* (rev. ed., 1964-1965), IV, 730-740; C, D, E, & F calculated from *Nihon Teikoku Mombushō nempō*, various years.

(1954), pp. 164-165; and Abe Isoo, ed., *Teikoku Gikai giji kyōiku sōran*, 4 vols. (Tokyo, 1932-1935), 1:112-113, 2:266-273.

6 David Abosch, "Katō Hiroyuki and the Introduction of German Political Thought in Modern Japan," Ph.D. dissertation, California, Berkeley, 1964.

held posts in the Ministry of Education as well as within the Tōdai administration. From 1897 on, however, the government turned to academics from among the faculty itself: first Professor Tōyama Masakazu, then Kikuchi Dairoku and Yamakawa Kenjirō. In 1905 Hamao Arata was brought back to office in the wake of the confrontation between the Katsura Cabinet and the Tōdai faculty over the government's attempt to fire law professor Tomizu Hiroto in the so-called *Shichi hakase jiken* (the Affair of the Seven Professors). But Hamao's reappointment was less a reversion to previous patterns of nonfaculty presidents than a temporary compromise with the Tōdai faculty, who accepted Yamakawa's firing in return for the removal of Education Minister Kubota Yuzuru and the reinstatement of Professor Tomizu.[7]

The Tomizu Affair of 1905 ignited long-smouldering issues concerning the governance of imperial universities. In particular, the Tōdai faculty leaders desired more formal and direct influence on the selection of school presidents. In 1907 they supported the successful efforts of their colleagues at Kyoto (many of whom were originally from Tōdai) to oust the Mombushō-appointed bureaucrat, Okada Ryōhei, from the Kyōdai presidency. In 1913 Tōdai faculty succeeded in having Yamakawa Kenjirō reappointed to the Tōdai presidency, but the Mombushō also chose to appoint another career bureaucrat, Sawayanagi Masatarō, as head of Kyōdai. In the face of threatened resignations by a number of prestigious Kyōdai professors who objected to Sawayanagi's heavy-handed personnel policies, the Mombushō backed down and compromised by allowing Yamakawa to serve concurrently as president of both schools over the next two years. In 1915, the Mombushō admitted defeat and permitted Kyōdai to nominate its own candidate from among the faculty. Finally, as part of the 1918 reforms, faculty balloting for the presidency became the accepted norm, and neither Tōdai or Kyōdai was ever again headed by anyone other than the majority candidate of its respective faculty.[8]

The delegation of this important authority to the faculty was only one of a number of steps toward greater self-government taken over the years between 1905 and the 1920s. Indeed, there took place a marked shift from the "authoritarian-bureaucrat" pattern of Meiji to one much closer to "collegial" or "participatory" governance within the imperial universities.[9] This can be seen quite clearly in two related developments: the expansion of the membership and powers of the University Senate

---

[7] For an account of the Tomizu Affair, see below and "Professors and Politics."

[8] For further details on this, see my "The Tradition of Conflict in the Governance of Japan's Imperial Universities," *History of Education Quarterly*, 17 (Winter 1977), 385-406.

[9] These terms are used in the sense used in Baldridge.

(*Hyōgikai*) and more formal faculty participation in the selection of deans or (more accurately after 1918) departmental chairmen.

The University Senate at Tōdai could trace its formal origins back to 1881, when it had functioned briefly as an assembly of all senior faculty. As reorganized in 1886 by Education Minister Mori Arinori, however, it had been reduced in size and included only appointees of the Mombushō. Between 1902 and 1919, advocates of academic self-government won a series of victories that turned the Hyōgikai into a representative body with a wide mandate for consultation on university affairs, including after 1907 that large portion of the budget over which the Mombushō had granted jurisdiction to the school. Under the terms of the 1919 university regulations, two-thirds of its members were elected by the faculty, with the remaining third consisting of departmental chairmen sitting ex officio. These departmental chairmen (*gakubuchō*) were themselves elected by formal vote by the faculty of their units. Although this change is often considered an innovation in 1919, there is evidence to support the contention that what actually took place in these reforms was the legitimization and formalization of practices that had developed over the preceding decades. For instance, between 1893 and 1919 three-quarters of all the heads of the faculties of law, letters, sciences, engineering, and agriculture (that is, all units except the medical school) won election to the Hyōgikai either prior or subsequent to election as unit head. It can therefore be argued that these were usually men with solid support from among their peers.[10] Moreover, even the Hyōgikai and the departmental chairmen were accountable to their faculty constituencies, particularly on basic issues such as curriculum and personnel matters, for these were subject to formal votes within each unit of the university. In effect, real decision-making power (if not formal authority) over a wide range of crucial issues had come to rest with the faculty meetings of the separate departments. Here, although only full professors usually voted on personnel matters, the entire faculty participated in departmental discussion; and, once a department had taken a firm stand on an issue within its expertise, neither the president nor the Hyōgikai usually saw fit to challenge it. The Mombushō, in turn, deferred to the university on matters of internal governance. The result of these cumulative changes was a system in which real power was radically more diffused than its Meiji designers had ever envisaged.[11]

---

[10] See my "Tradition of Conflict."

[11] For a more detailed look at how a Tōdai department conducted its affairs, see my "Academic Factionalism in Japan: The Case of the Tōdai Economics Department, 1919-1939," *Modern Asian Studies*, 12 (October 1978), 529-551.

CHANGES IN FACULTY ROLES

If the growth and structural changes in the system of higher education rendered it more vulnerable to conflict because of the difficulties in coordination and control, there were also shifts adversely affecting the circumstances of the faculty and students that increased the potential for conflict. Although more research needs to be done on such aspects as the perceptions of individuals within the system, there is sufficient evidence to suggest how this growth and change were accompanied by at least partial losses in some key roles that the academic elite had come to expect to play.

The easiest to quantify of these changes was the erosion of Tōdai jurisdiction over the recruitment and supply of future elites. In the Meiji period, Tōdai professors had served as mentors to youths whose Tōdai credentials gave them tremendous advantages in vying for positions in the higher civil service and other elite structures within Japanese society. This was far less the case in the 1920s. The expansion of the total supply of university graduates that resulted from the expansion of the system of higher education could hardly have come at a worse time in terms of market demand. Although the government bureaucracy as a whole continued to grow in this decade, the pace of its growth was much slower than in the Meiji period, and Tōdai graduates increasingly tended to seek jobs in the private sector. But opportunities became more limited here also as the Japanese economy suffered through a series of sharp business cycles in the 1920s. The result was an excess of supply and thus unemployment (as well as underemployment) for university products, as is reflected in the statistical data (see Figure 2 and Tables 5 and 6). The situation was particularly acute for degree holders in hōgaku (law) and keizaigaku (economics); yet over 40 percent of the student body at both Tōdai and Kyōdai continued in the 1920s to major in these "policy science" fields, despite the relative decline in employment opportunities (see Table 7).

By the end of the 1920s, the unemployment problem had come to be seen by academics as well as others as a major cause for student discontent and for the growth of Marxist influence on campus. For Marxist academics such as Ōmori Yoshitarō, the crisis at least had the salutary effect of freeing students from the "delusion" that Japanese higher education was truly dedicated to higher learning:

> The prestige of the schools as well as that of the faculty has been totally destroyed. . . . [Students now realize that] the higher schools and universities are nothing more than organs like the military and police for maintaining control by the ruling class, and the faculty

FIGURE 2. Employment Rates of New University Graduates, 1918-1933

SOURCE: Ministry of Education, *Demand and Supply for University Graduates*, Tokyo, 1959 revised edition, Figure 19, p. 17.

TABLE 5. EMPLOYMENT OF COLLEGE GRADUATES IN 1920s (AS PERCENTS)

	1923	1924	1925	1926	1927	1928	1929
All Departments	84	75	66	59	64	54	54
Law and Economics	72	62	55	52	65	48	38

SOURCE: Abe Isoo, *Shitsugyō mondai* [The Unemployment Problem] (1929), p. 195 (from Appendix XII, p. 392, in Nobuya Bamba, *Japanese Diplomacy in Crisis* [Vancouver, 1972]). For comparable figures, see Henry Smith, *Japan's First Student Radicals*, p. 214.

(with the exception of a few red professors) are merely watchdogs for the learning of the ruling class.[12]

[12] Ōmori Yoshitarō, "Gakkō sōdō uraomote," *Chūō kōron*, 45 (August 1930), 213-220. The author, previously an associate professor of economics, had resigned from the Tōdai faculty in 1928 as a result of pressures brought to bear in reaction to his leftist political activities.

Some non-Marxists, such as Kawai Eijirō, used language almost as strong in arguing that the unemployment crisis signaled the time for basic reform, albeit not as radical as that envisaged by Ōmori. For Kawai what was needed was a different type of product. Whereas in Meiji times "the universities, especially the imperial universities, were necessary organs for training assistants" to serve in subordinate roles under the great "pioneers" within the government and business, this was no longer the case:

TABLE 6. SHIFTS IN OCCUPATIONS OF TŌDAI GRADUATES

	September 1908		September 1917		March 1933	
	Law and Economics	All Depts.	Law and Economics	All Depts.	Law and Economics	All Depts.
Total number	3,042	9,237	7,108	18,479	18,479	41,674
% government officials	36.6	12.7	29.6	12.1	18.5	8.9
% government technicians	—	19.9	—	16.6	—	12.9
% school teachers	2.2	18.6	0.2	15.2	4.3	15.4
% lawyers, doctors and other professionals	6.6	5.9	11.2	9.9	7.4	3.7
% banking and business	12.5	13.8	21.5	9.2	28.7	23.4
% other occupations	7.6	4.0	12.3	8.7	16.7	9.0
% not determined	12.6	6.1	12.1	8.9	21.2	12.3
% deaths and miscellaneous	21.9	19.0	15.1	10.4	3.2	14.4

SOURCE: Ōuchi Hyōe, "Tōdai gakusei seikatsu no ichidammen" [One Aspect of the Life of Contemporary Students], Kaizō 17 (August 1935), 8.
NOTE: Law and economics were in the same department prior to 1918.

TABLE 7. ENROLLMENTS BY DEPARTMENT, TŌDAI AND KYŌDAI 1918-1933 (AS % OF TOTAL STUDENTS)

	1919	1923	1928	1933
Total Tōdai	4,904	5,981	7,820	8,269
Law	34	31	29	28
Economics	10	13	15	16
Total Kyōdai	2,033	2,548	5,170	5,710
Law	32	20	28	32
Economics	21	27	18	16

SOURCE: Nihon Teikoku tōkei nenkan, various years.

the universities consciously or unconsciously came to consider their function that of producing technicians for society . . . graduates who were nothing more than assistants. . . . Now the supply of such narrowly trained products has increased beyond the demand [because], in addition to the oversupply of university graduates, the supply from outside the universities has also increased. The university student cannot retain a monopoly [because] numerous competitors have appeared from outside the university.[13]

Thus by the end of the 1920s, the unemployment problem proved quite disturbing to faculty members at elite schools such as Tōdai who had once had reason to believe that their students would move all but automatically into roles with considerable potential for influencing the affairs of state and their society. In short, the Tōdai faculty were faced with a very real erosion in their roles as mentors to future elites.

Nor could this loss be considered the unintended consequence of incremental policy making in relation to the higher civil service examination system. As Robert Spaulding has shown, the privileged position of Tōdai as the personnel agency for the bureaucracy had been under steady attack from the 1890s, although opponents of such *teidai tokken* (imperial university privileges) as exemptions from certain examinations were unsuccessful until 1910 in forcing any actual reforms. In 1910, however, the Lower House of the Diet passed a bill extending exemptions to graduates of the private law colleges. Although the bill was resisted by the government and did not survive the House of Peers, Spaulding points out the underlying significance of the Lower House vote: "After 1903 [the anti-imperial university] cause was taken up by . . . private university alumni already established in a profession or business, moving into political parties and the lower house of the Diet. . . . The new critics gave the protest movement the respectability, continuity, and political influence it had [previously] lacked."[14]

In 1914 such pressure began to produce results, as men such as Hara Kei, then home minister, gave support to the attempt to reduce the rule of Tōdai, apparently as part of a larger effort to open the top echelon of the civil bureaucracy to more party supporters. When the govern-

[13] Kawai Eijirō, "Shūshokunan to daigaku kyōiku," *Teikoku daigaku shimbun*, January 19, 1931; reprinted in Kawai's book published in 1931, *Daigaku seikatsu no hanrei*, and included in *Kawai Eijirō zenshū* (Tokyo, 1968), 19:176-181. In addition to articles cited here and in notes above, see the discussion and references in Doo, "The Struggle for Academic Freedom," pp. 283-300.

[14] Spaulding, *Imperial Japan's Higher Civil Service Examinations* (Princeton: Princeton University Press, 1967), p. 139.

ment stalled in implementing the 1914 reform, which would have ended special privileges in the examinations for imperial university graduates, it triggered mass demonstrations by private college students outside the Diet and more vehement attacks on policy favoring the imperial universities from members within the Diet. The government gave ground, though slowly, in 1918 and again in 1923. By this time, of course, official university status had been granted to most of the private schools involved in the original campaigns. Spaulding's exhaustive research on the subject did not yield hard data on relevant numbers of Tōdai graduates affected, but competition from graduates from other schools was significant. Moreover, the role of Tōdai professors as civil service examiners was reduced somewhat as the overall proportion of civil bureaucrats and others increased during the 1920s (see Table 8).

TABLE 8. Higher Civil Service Administrative Examiners (as percents)

	1906-1917	1918-1928
Tōdai faculty members	66.0	44.6
Faculty from other schools	23.2	25.0
Government officials	10.8	30.4

Source: Spaulding, *Imperial Japan's Higher Civil Service Examinations*, Table 34, p. 249.

The role played by the Lower House of the Diet in bringing about the Taishō reforms in civil service recruitment in particular and the expansion of higher education in general was part of a larger shift in the political environment that adversely affected the political position of the Tōdai academic. As political parties gained strength in the late Meiji and Taishō periods, the Diet became more and more the central forum for public debate over social legislation. Simultaneously, the civil bureaucracy, which still drafted as well as implemented much of such legislation, grew increasingly independent of the older Meiji style of oligarchic coordination as it moved toward greater specialization and autonomy. This emergence of political parties and the maturation of the civil bureaucracy in the Taishō period altered the processes of policy making in a way that reduced opportunities for academics to exert the type of direct influence on the broad range of social policy (as well as specific educational issues) that they had enjoyed in the Meiji period.

One indication of this reduction in the influence of academics upon the civil bureaucracy—the differentiation between Tōdai professors and the Mombushō staff—has already been described. A similar trend took place within the Justice Ministry, whose personnel had once frequently appeared as instructors in the Tōdai Hōgaku classrooms and had turned regularly to Tōdai academics for expertise in revising the law codes of mid-Meiji. In the Taishō period such interchange of personnel was rare. Moreover, as the Hiranuma clique gained power within the Justice Ministry in this same period, relations between that ministry and the Tōdai faculty were to become increasingly strained.[15]

Yet another important sphere in which academic expertise carried less weight in the Taishō period was that of industrial relations and labor legislation. In the Meiji period, Tōdai professors had been ex officio participants in major government-sponsored conferences on labor policy, and, as members of the influential Shakai Seisaku Gakkai (Social Policy Association), had taken a leading part in pressuring the bureaucracy for action on factory legislation. By the early 1920s, however, the Shakai Seisaku Gakkai had been disbanded, and bureaucratic agencies within the Home Ministry and the Ministry of Agriculture and Commerce, as well as the quasi-official Kyōchōkai (Conciliation Society), had taken over much of the function of preparing policy positions for Diet action.[16]

The historian Tsurumi Shunsuke has summarized succinctly these trends in his comments on the frustrations of academic intellectuals in the 1930s, although I would date the change somewhat later and the frustration somewhat earlier: "Between the Meiji Restoration and the mid-Meiji period was an era in which specialized scholars [*semmonteki gakusha*] had participated fully in national policies as they took shape in the government. But this contact turned into one of an exchange of mere formalities."[17] What Tsurumi does not mention here was that, ironically, this change was made possible by the increased supply of university-trained expertise within the Taishō bureaucracy.

These changes in the political environment did not go unrecognized by academic activists such as Takano Iwasaburō. He first took part in an effort during the 1910s to establish a separate economics department that would be distinguished from its parent Hōgakubu by greater attention to the application of scholarship to social problems. Although this effort eventually bore fruit in 1918, Takano remained frustrated, and in 1919 he gave up his Tōdai professorship to pursue his goals more directly through the privately funded Ōhara Institute for the Study of Social Problems. His ambivalence toward the potential of the university as a base from which to influence social reform, however, is revealed in

[15] For the Meiji period, see "Professors and Politics" cited above; for the Justice Ministry in the Taishō period, see Mitchell, *Thought Control*, pp. 34ff.

[16] In addition to "Professors and Politics," see my *Capitalism and Nationalism in Prewar Japan* (Stanford: Stanford University Press, 1967), chapters 4 and 5; and Kenneth B. Pyle, "Advantages of Followership: German Economics and Japanese Bureaucrats, 1890-1925," *Journal of Japanese Studies*, 1 (Autumn 1974), 127-164.

[17] Tsurumi et al., *Tenkō* 2:179.

his advice to his younger colleagues when they were considering resignation as a group in protest to the Morito Incident of 1920: "The goal is the construction of a more rational society; the method, gradualism; the place, the university as the agency for research into truth; the time, too early when the research is not yet accomplished and our colleagues are [too] few."[18] In 1924 Yoshino Sakuzō, another prominent Tōdai professor committed to political reform, also chose to relinquish his academic post in order to work for change through the Social Democratic movement. Most academic activists, including the celebrated Kawakami Hajime at Kyōdai, however, attempted to remain within academia. But they came to devote a larger and larger share of their time and energies to political causes outside the campus, as did the left-wing student groups that they did so much to encourage.[19]

ATTEMPTS TO REASSERT GOVERNMENT CONTROL

The gradual breakdown of the Meiji system of bureaucratic management of intellectual life did not go unnoticed within the government. The primary response, however, was one that progressively reduced the role of the Mombushō and further fragmented bureaucratic control. Beginning in 1911 with the expansion within the Home Ministry of the Special Higher police (*Tokubetsu Kōtō Keisatsu*), a unit charged with censorship of the press and investigation of ideological crimes, and continuing through the 1920s with the creation in 1926, for example, of the Shisō (Thought) Section of the Justice Ministry, the problem of controlling heterodoxy on campus shifted away from the Mombushō. During this process, strong interagency rivalries over jurisdiction and vigorous disagreements over tactics posed serious obstacles to coordinating government efforts.[20]

When the sudden outburst of student and faculty activism following World War I stirred conservatives in high places to take action, these opponents of academic freedom recognized the difficulties of relying on Mombushō administrative procedures to curtail such dissent. The delegation of power within the system to school presidents, faculty senates, and individual departments had progressed too far to be reversed easily. Instead, they moved to bypass the Mombushō where necessary and to resort to control measures that were more direct. Thus the pattern of control changed abruptly beginning with the "Morito Affair" of

[18] "Takano nikki (shō)," reprinted in *Kappa no he*, edited by Suzuki Kōichirō (Tokyo, 1971), pp. 321-322; see also Ōshima Kiyoshi et al., *Takano Iwasaburō den* (Tokyo, 1968), p. 183; and my "Academic Factionalism."

[19] On Kawakami, see Gail Bernstein's biography, *Japanese Marxist* (Cambridge: Harvard University Press, 1976).

[20] On this point see Mitchell, *Thought Control*, and Smith, *Japan's First Radical Students*.

1919-1920. This change is evident in even the briefest of comparisons between the incidents of the 1919-1930 era and the "Tomizu Affair" of the late Meiji period.

In 1903, when Tomizu and his six colleagues began to earn the hostility of major government figures because of their outspoken criticism of policy toward Russia, the Katsura Cabinet first attempted to discredit the professors by leaking damaging versions of their position to the press. When the group responded with even more vehement protests, Education Minister Kubota Yuzuru prevailed upon Tōdai President Yamakawa Kenjirō to instruct his faculty on proper behavior, which Yamakawa did in several conversations with the individuals involved, despite Yamakawa's own sympathies with the group. When the war with Russia stimulated the group to new attacks on the Katsura Cabinet, Minister Kubota paid a personal call on Tomizu to warn him, and the Foreign Ministry relieved three of the academics from their advisory posts within that ministry. When this type of pressure failed, the government used the ultimate weapon in its administrative arsenal by suspending Tomizu from his professorship under the authority of the Ministry of Education regulations for personnel matters.[21]

In 1919, by contrast, when assistant professors of economics Morito Tatsuo and Ōuchi Hyōe were brought under attack because of a scholarly article published on anarchist thought (a much less overtly "subversive" act than many of Tomizu's), the government adopted very different tactics. According to the diary of Prime Minister Hara Kei, the lead was taken in this instance by Procurator General Hiranuma Kiichirō.[22] The Mombushō, represented in the Hara Cabinet by former businessman and party stalwart Nakahashi Tokugorō, was decidedly cool to Hiranuma's urging that the Tōdai faculty be taught an object lesson. Hiranuma, however, had never intended to rely solely on such administrative channels, and turned instead to the powers of the Home Ministry, which banned the objectionable issue of the Keizaigakubu departmental journal, and of the Justice Ministry, which issued indictments for the two professors under the press laws.

The differences in the part played by Tōdai President Yamakawa in 1903-1905 and the same President Yamakawa in 1919-1920 is also instructive. In the former case, Yamakawa, at the insistence of the Mombushō, had undertaken to resolve the issue by dealing directly with his faculty members. In the latter case, when warned by the Mombushō of Hiranuma's intentions, Yamakawa sought the intervention of the three senior economics professors to persuade Morito to offer an apology.

[21] "Professors and Politics," cited above.

[22] Hara Keiichirō, ed., *Hara Kei nikki*, 9 vols. (Tokyo, 1950-1951), 8:453-457; for further details and sources on the Morito incident, see the articles "Academic Factionalism" and "The Tradition of Conflict" previously cited.

When that failed, Yamakawa requested a special meeting of the economics faculty in deference to the principle of departmental jurisdiction over personnel matters. It was thus the full professors of the Keizai-gakubu, rather than either the Mombushō or the Tōdai president, who voted to suspend Morito and Ōuchi. Both men were subsequently prosecuted by the Justice Ministry and convicted by the courts, but Ōuchi at least was reinstated by the Economics Department after spending his year of probationary sentence studying abroad.

This new pattern of attempts to assert control over imperial university faculty became even clearer at the end of the 1920s in the so-called "March 15th Affair" of 1928. On that day, the police under the Home Ministry carried out a massive roundup of suspected communists. The following month, the Education Ministry, which apparently had not been privy to police plans, agreed with the Tanaka Cabinet that the shocking number of university students arrested in the roundup warranted more vigorous steps to suppress radicalism among the faculty. Among those on the ministry's list were three assistant professors at Tōdai, Professor Kawakami Hajime at Kyōdai, and three members of the faculty at Kyushu Imperial University. At Tōdai, President Onozuka Kiheiji responded to the Mombushō by saying that his university would handle its own internal affairs. Onozuka did admonish two of his young faculty—Ōmori Yoshitarō and Hirano Yoshitarō—for their off-campus political activities, and Ōmori subsequently decided to resign. But Onozuka also told the University Senate that such matters were to be left to the departments, which in this instance took no action. At Kyōdai, President Araki Tomosaburō, while less committed to academic freedom, nonetheless respected the principle of departmental autonomy sufficiently to obtain Kawakami's resignation by the stratagem of claiming that his department faculty had requested it. President Araki then presented the fraudulently obtained resignation to Kawakami's department, which duly voted to accept it as a fait accompli. A similar stratagem was used in Kyushu to oust Assistant Professor Sakisaka Itsurō and two colleagues.

The resistance to Mombushō authority by Onozuka at Tōdai and the convoluted procedures used at the other imperial universities did not satisfy hardliners within the government, and in 1930 the Justice Ministry once again took matters into its own hands. Using the expanded powers granted it under the 1925 Peace Preservation Law, the Justice Ministry indicted assistant professor of economics Yamada Moritarō and assistant professor of law Hirano Yoshitarō, two of the young Tōdai faculty whom Onozuka had protected in 1928. Under the civil service regulations that covered academics at the imperial universities, such indictments carried with them automatic suspension from teaching. Thus the Justice Ministry circumvented the issue of university autonomy.[23] But only by treating academic dissent as criminal behavior and bringing professors to trial through the court system could control be reasserted over the academic elite within Japan's system of higher education.

CONCLUSION

The story of the continued struggles during the 1930s to resolve this crisis of governance in Japan's system of higher education lies outside the scope of this paper, although it should be noted that it was not until the outbreak of war with the United States in 1941 that this conflict subsided. What remains here is to summarize the conflict as it developed from the end of the Meiji period down through the 1920s in the context of the other contributions to this volume.

Prior to the Russo-Japanese war, relations between the Meiji government and the academic elite at Japan's imperial universities were generally harmonious—coordinated through an Education Ministry, which was most often under the influence of men with close ties to Tokyo University, and marked by a consensus on ultimate goals shared by the senior Meiji bureaucrats and the leading members of the faculty. Tensions between government and university in the years prior to 1905 arose primarily over how to formalize this relationship in legal administrative terms, and conflict was minimized through compromise using informal channels. Those tensions erupted into open conflict in the "Tomizu Affair" of 1905, a dramatic break with past patterns of conflict resolution and the first clear indication of the severe strains building within the mechanisms of coordination and control within the system of higher education.

The Tomizu Affair, however, differed from the conflict of the Taishō period in several significant ways. In 1905 the main struggle was over the place of the imperial university *within* a bureaucratic system of cultural management. Despite the strains, the consensus between bureaucratic and academic elites that had characterized the early Meiji was still largely intact. Tōdai spokesmen challenged the Katsura Cabinet but not the concept of an administrative state as described by Bernard Silberman.[24] Tomizu's supporters accepted the ideals of an impartial bureaucratic elite and a neutral state, affirming the identity of the polity and society. If these scholars sought greater autonomy for the university, it was to ensure its independence from the partisan politics of cabinet government and protection from Diet party interference. The chief argu-

[23] Ibid.
[24] "The Bureaucratic State in Japan: The Problem of Authority and Legitimacy," in this volume.

ments set forth in their attempt to legitimize freedom of speech for the dissenting academic was an elitist justification that defined the scholar as impartial expert who stood above the partisanship of political or social conflict.

During the Taishō era, conflict between Japan's elite universities and the government authorities took on a very different character. As Peter Duus has pointed out, deep cleavages developed within the intellectual community of the 1910s and 1920s, as political thinkers were compelled to come to grips with the question of the neutrality of the administrative state and to rethink the role of the intellectual in Japanese politics.[25] Those cleavages were reflected in the dissension that plagued Tōdai and other elite universities in the 1920s. The view of the academic as a nonpartisan expert cooperating in the bureaucratic management of society was challenged by activist professors who sought to create a new social order. The issue of academic freedom thus became inseparably linked with that of the legitimacy of political conflict in the wider society despite the reluctance of the liberal intellectual to abandon the consensual model of society.

Underlying these cleavages over ideological issues were two fundamental changes in the relationship between the state and the university that created tensions even for those academics who might otherwise have been content to work within the old system. First, as the civil bureaucracy matured as an increasingly specialized body of experts, the academic elite found its role within an administrative state reduced proportionately. This added to the pressures on those academic intellectuals who sought to influence public affairs to operate outside the bureaucratic channels that had been open to them in the Meiji era. Second, and closer to the main focus of this paper, the breakdown of coordination within the educational system created a crisis of governance that stimulated conservatives within the bureaucracy to adopt new measures in an attempt to reassert control over the university. The Meiji style of mediating disputes through ties between the Mombushō and the academic elite gave way to Home Ministry censorship and criminal proceedings instigated through the Justice Ministry. Such measures were to prove ineffective in the 1920s in suppressing radical dissent on the campus, and only further polarized the issues surrounding the role of the academic in his society and the place of the university in an administrative state. Thus the inability of the Taishō government leaders to accommodate to the processes of growth and organizational change within the system of higher education insured the ultimate breakdown of earlier Meiji patterns of bureaucratic management of intellectual life, and set the stage for an even more intense struggle in the 1930s.

[25] "Liberal Intellectuals and Social Conflict in Taishō Japan," in this volume.

SCIENCE, BUREAUCRACY, AND FREEDOM IN MEIJI AND TAISHŌ JAPAN

JAMES R. BARTHOLOMEW

Sir Francis Bacon in the seventeenth century once described scientific research as the antithesis of political action.[1] The Marquis de Condorcet in the eighteenth century called science the most important "natural threat" to the seekers of political dominance.[2] In 1931 Lord Bertrand Russell told scientists that as "servants of truth" they must willingly suffer "privations and persecutions" to defend their professional freedom,[3] whereas Robert K. Merton in 1948 claimed that scientists have typically avoided becoming "handmaidens of state" by invoking what he called the "pure science sentiment."[4]

Japanese science seems anomalous in this context because so many writers consider it merely a "tool" of public policy. Impressed by what he called a "preponderance of power" in Tokugawa society, Fukuzawa Yukichi in his *Outline of Civilization* called Japanese scholarship a "mere adjunct of government."[5] The chemist Sakurai Joji wrote in 1927 that Japanese scientists were "constantly humiliated" by an almost total "in-

[1] Refer to Joseph Haberer, *Politics and the Community of Science* (New York: Van Nostrand Reinhold, 1969), p. 46.

[2] Quoted in Keith Michael Baker, *Condorcet: From Natural Philosophy to Social Mathematics* (Chicago: University of Chicago Press, 1975), p. 79.

[3] *The Scientific Outlook* (New York: W. W. Norton, 1962), p. 99.

[4] *Social Theory and Social Structure* (Glencoe, Ill.: Free Press, 1949), p. 299.

[5] Quoted in Maruyama Masao, "Fukuzawa Yukichi no jukyō hihan," in *Tōkyō Teikoku Daigaku gakujutsu taikan: Hōgakubu, Keizai Gakubu* (Tokyo, 1942), p. 415.

ability to influence the government authorities."[6] And in 1961 the physicist and historian of science Yuasa Mitsutomo lamented what he saw
as the "vulnerability of Japanese scientists to excessive government interference."[7] Indeed, if prominent characteristics of Japanese society and
government are correctly diagnosed, one can scarcely avoid affirming
these rather cynical judgments. Anthropologist Nakane Chie has described Japanese society as a constellation of mutually exclusivist small
groups whose competitive interaction helps insinuate state power into
its every nook and cranny.[8] Similarly, Bernard Silberman believes the
Japanese government tried to bureaucratize all private interests in the
modern period as a means of destroying their power.[9]

Nakane regards science as historically weak in Japan and attributes its
weakness to the nature of social structure. In her analysis, all social
organization in Japan consists of a leader and two or more followers,
arranged in a relationship of unqualified loyalty and dependence but
similarly mediated by quasi-contractual elements. That is, followers give
unqualified loyalty to leaders, but anticipate certain benefits and returns.
A senior scientist as group leader will be expected to help younger scientists acquire the expertise required for professional success. He will
help clients find suitable employment. And as the situation demands, he
may even help find spouses for the students that he trained. The relationship is thus one of intimacy and reciprocal support and loyalty. State
power enters in the competitive interaction between one scientific group
and another. Each of many groups will seek to achieve autonomy. Each
of many groups will seek to become exclusive. And each and every
group will cling to its own prerogatives and privileges. Because each
group is closed and suspicious of those outside, there is no possibility
of a coalition in the face of external forces. Thus, by an effective policy
of dividing and conquering, state bureaucratic agencies can manipulate
and subvert and thereby preclude the attainment of institutional autonomy for science.[10]

Silberman's analysis does not reflect the experience of Japanese science, but nevertheless has implications for our historical understanding
of it. Like Nakane, he is concerned with issues of social stasis and conflict, but his discussion focuses directly on the problems of governing
society. Special circumstances existing between 1868 and 1945, as he

[6] *Omoide no kazukazu* (Tokyo, 1939), p. 113.

[7] *Kagaku shi* (Tokyo, 1961), p. 282.

[8] *Japanese Society* (Berkeley and Los Angeles: University of California Press, 1970),
p. 102.

[9] "The Bureaucratic State in Japan: The Problem of Authority and Legitimacy," in this
volume.

[10] Nakane, *Japanese Society*, pp. 87-103, 133-134.

sees it, made this a difficult task at best. First of all, the Restoration government was a revolutionary regime. It had seized power in the emperor's name but its claims could be challenged by other political claimants. Second, it claimed to perceive reality correctly, but its judgments were manifestly subjective throughout. Third, its revolutionary leaders were few and could not reproduce their pattern of selection. Finally, their desire to monopolize policy making led them deeper into conflict with society. To surmount these problems and difficulties they chose a strategy of bureaucratization. Appeals were made to expertise and impartiality as the basis of political authority. There was an enormous emphasis on the extension of rule making. The boundaries of all social interests were determined through law. And efforts were made to coopt any private interest that even remotely appeared to be threatening.[11] If bureaucratization obstructed institutional autonomy in science, it would have been precisely through this policy of cooptation. Financial subsidies may have given the state influence over research and personnel appointments. Conferrals of legal or monopoly status may have diminished invaluable competition. Freedom may have been compromised by recipients' conversion into instruments of state control. Most of all, reliance on rules and law may have rendered institutional procedures inflexible.

This essay focuses on a particular scientist's career in which these issues are sharply drawn. Kitasato Shibasaburō (1852-1931) was a microbiologist with a kind of "antiestablishment" background. He came from the Kumamoto domain, where he was exposed to anti-Restoration and anti-Confucian ideas and values in the 1860s and 1870s. He was noted for challenging authority as a student at Tokyo University (1875-1883) and an official in the Bureau of Public Health (1883-1885), and he continued to challenge authority while studying at Robert Koch's laboratory in Berlin (1886-1892). Kitasato was also a vigorous proponent of innovative ideas and conceptions in science. Under Robert Koch's influence he became committed to the germ theory of disease and drew on it heavily for practically all of his scientific work. In 1889 he isolated a pure culture of the tetanus bacillus. In 1890 he discovered the principle of antitoxic immunity with Emil von Behring. And in 1894 he similarly isolated the bacillus of plague in Hong Kong.

Throughout the remainder of his long and distinguished career, Kitasato championed what has properly been described as a new tradition in medical science.[12] Because of his German mentor's experience and his personal observations, Kitasato sought a fusion of basic and clinical

[11] Silberman, "The Bureaucratic State in Japan."

[12] Peter Buck, *American Science and Modern China, 1876-1936* (Cambridge, England, 1980), p. 41.

medicine. This position, however, ran counter to medical traditions in Germany as well as Japan, and was opposed by the faculty of Tokyo University and most officials in the Japanese Education Ministry. Moreover, Kitasato used techniques for promoting these views that bureaucratic opponents and some medical scientists found particularly reprehensible. He exploited political sensitivities about the Education Ministry and the university to get a laboratory that was institutionally isolated from both. He played the rivalries of the Education Ministry and the Ministry of Home Affairs off against each other to maintain his autonomy as director of the Infectious Diseases Institute. He risked criticism about "mixing public and private interests" to accumulate wealth as a hedge against cooption by the Ministry of Education. And he relied extensively on factional loyalties and political maneuvering to secure his professional autonomy.

KITASATO'S EARLY YEARS

Kitasato came by independence, suspicion of authority, and a pragmatic conception of learning early in his life. His parents, a village headman who belonged to Kumamoto's warrior class and a domain official's daughter raised in Edo, boarded their oldest son with relatives as a way of encouraging independent behavior. Avid devotion to martial arts and a tendency to reject discipline created conflicts with family members, and he was slow to appreciate book learning. He was subsequently exposed to medicine as a youth while living with Chinese-style doctors on two separate occasions, but he only developed a serious interest in the field after studying with the Dutch physician C. G. von Mansveldt at the Kumamoto medical academy.[13] His other associations suggest that the pragmatic view of science and wariness of officials that subsequently typified his outlook may also have been products of the Kumamoto years (1867-1874). For example, one of his associates was an anti-Restoration activist whose students later participated in the Shimpūren uprising of 1876; another was a moral philosopher who defended the legitimacy of private interests and condemned "impractical" learning.[14]

[13] Miyajima Mikinosuke, *Kitasato Shibasaburō den* (Tokyo, 1931), pp. 240-241.

[14] See ibid., p. 10 regarding the influence of anti-Restoration ideology on Kitasato. The other major influence is likely to have been Takezaki Ritsujirō (or Sadō), brother-in-law of Yokoi Shōnan (1809-1869). Takezaki taught ethics at the Kumamoto Medical Academy (Igakkō) and its Western Studies School (Yōgakkō) during the period 1869-1873. Although he functioned within the Confucian tradition, he was scarcely the hidebound traditionalist. Socratic dialogue, rather than lecturing, was his principal mode of instruction. Students were encouraged to interpret Confucian texts for themselves, and knowledge of fact or value was described relativistically in terms of its social consequences. This indi-

Medical studies at Tokyo University (1874-1883) may have reinforced his earlier leanings. Contrary to the theoretical, research-oriented cast it later acquired, the medical program of Kitasato's day was heavily practical in nature and geared to producing clinicians. Most of the professors were German, but the highly professional, German-style curriculum of the late Meiji era was not yet in evidence. Research was not emphasized, and even German faculty members taught clinical and basic medical subjects interchangeably. In 1880 President Katō Hiroyuki took steps to promote greater student interest in research, but these were slow to achieve results and did not affect Kitasato significantly.[15]

The conflicts that so embittered later relations with Tokyo University professors also seem to have begun in his medical student years. Kitasato was assertive, even arrogant in dealing with superiors. In 1881 he led a boycott against Professor Wilhelm Schultze, who had angered students by examining them on material that was not covered in lectures. Schultze abandoned the practice after the students demonstrated against him, but Kitasato would not apologize for his actions even when the dean requested that he do so. Although his academic performance was respectable, the inordinate time he spent on martial arts, public speaking contests, and part-time jobs prevented him from graduating higher than eighth in his class.[16] Since third place was the usual cut-off for those with the highest aspirations, he seemed to have no possibility of marrying a professor's daughter, joining the university faculty, or studying in the West at the Japanese government's expense.[17]

Even so, the value of his diploma by virtue of scarcity offered some attractive opportunities. In 1883 Kitasato joined the Bureau of Public Health in the Home Ministry, where he quickly became involved in medical administration. Despite a small salary and an unimpressive title, he had major responsibility for preparing the state medical examinations, for choosing the examiners, and for investigating foreign systems

vidualistic, and at the same time instrumentalist, conception of knowledge probably did affect Kitasato, but there is no way to be certain because attendance at Takezaki's classes was voluntary for Igakkō students and because Kitasato himself never acknowledged any such influence. The connection, however, was made by Kiyoura Keigo, a Kumamoto native who became prime minister in the 1920s. For details on the Kumamoto Igakkō, see Yamazaki Masataka, *Higo iiku shi* (Kumamoto, 1929), passim. For Kiyoura's remarks, see his essay, "Yon dai-onjin," in Miyajima, *Kitasato Shibasaburō den*, pp. 239-250.

[15] *Tōkyō Teikoku Daigaku gojū nen shi* (Tokyo, 1932), 1:479-483.

[16] Iwasaki Katsumi, *Kōmoto Jūjirō den* (Tokyo, 1943), p. 50; and Miyajima *Kitasato Shibasaburō den*, p. 23.

[17] For information pertinent to informal aspects of the foreign study selection process, see Miura Norihiko, ed., *Ichi igakusha no seikatsu o meguru kaisō* (Tokyo, 1955), p. 38. Criteria affecting the appointment of professors in the faculty of medicine are discussed in "Batsu no Ika Daigaku," part II, *Tōkyō Asahi Shimbun* [hereafter *TAS*], No. 10159 (October 29, 1914), p. 5.

of health and medical care. He also gave lectures on public health matters. The prestige these activities gave him is well illustrated by a trip he made to northeastern Japan. A certain local journalist sympathetic to the Popular Rights movement hoped to embarrass the Tokyo government by asking the head of Kitasato's delegation to deliver a lecture on a public health topic. Unable to refuse because of his job title, the man turned in desperation to Kitasato, who agreed to give the lecture but only if requested, not ordered, to do it. At the banquet that followed the lecture, Kitasato then assumed the place of honor and shunted the nominal delegation head to the rear.[18]

Employment in the Bureau of Public Health also marked the beginning of his interest in bacteriology or microbiology. Research in this field had begun in Japan some six months earlier, when Ogata Masanori returned from Max von Pettenkofer's Hygiene Institute in Munich and accepted a post at the Tokyo Hygiene Laboratory. The Public Health Bureau loaned Kitasato to Ogata as an assistant, and he began doing research while continuing other duties. His studies of cholera in chickens attracted favorable attention and led Bureau Chief Nagayo Sensai to recommend him for a Home Ministry fellowship at Robert Koch's laboratory.[19]

MICROBIOLOGICAL STUDIES IN GERMANY

Kitasato's years in Germany (January 1886–October 1891) were the most decisive of his life. He developed a strong commitment to his field, and he made fundamental contributions to knowledge. He became a researcher of international renown. He formulated controversial opinions about the conduct of science and about the nature of research institutions. All of these developments were affected by his deep loyalty to and intimate friendship with his German teacher, Koch. Koch's analytical precision, Teutonic stubbornness, and intellectual creativity became the model for Kitasato's research strategy. His espousal of the germ theory of disease provided intellectual guidelines and a professional role conception. And his personal tribulations shaped Kitasato's views on the relationship of bacteriology to the Japanese university system. Moreover, the sum of these political and intellectual commitments led some Japanese officials to consider Kitasato a cultural rebel and a dangerous political opponent.

The strength of Kitasato's loyalty to Koch was first tested in 1887, when Bureau Chief Nagayo ordered him to leave Berlin for Munich.

---

[18] Miyajima, *Kitasato Shibasaburō den*, pp. 170-171.
[19] Ibid., pp. 31-32.

As explained to him by a Japanese medical delegation, the purpose was to allow the bureau's other exchange student to work with Koch while Kitasato would work with the founder of modern hygiene, Max von Pettenkofer. This was not acceptable to Kitasato because of Pettenkofer's scientific opinions.[20] Whereas Koch attributed disease to the specific pathogenic effects of discrete microorganisms, Pettenkofer pointed instead to deficiencies in public sanitation. He rejected the germ theory of illness altogether, constantly attacked the findings of Koch, and even consumed a pure culture of cholera bacilli to "prove" his case in 1883![21] Kitasato informed the Japanese study team of these facts, argued that a transfer to Munich would destroy his career, and threatened to abandon his stipend if the order were not rescinded. Fortunately, his views were accepted by an influential delegation member, Dr. Mori Rintarō, who had previously studied microbiology, explained the significance of the Koch-Pettenkofer debate to Nagayo, and Kitasato was permitted to remain in Berlin.[22]

Scientific values and research strategy were another area of agreement between Koch and Kitasato. Both impressed associates as serious-minded, distant, and aloof; but these qualities were a measure of professionalism and mutual respect. Koch had attained his professorship only after a long and arduous struggle, and unquestionably appreciated Kitasato's neglect of recreation and his eighteen-hour days in the laboratory. It was probably this friendship that assured Kitasato's compliance with a suggestion Koch made about professional responsibility in 1886. The occasion was a scientific conflict over beriberi that turned on the matter of aetiological origin and pitted Kitasato against his former associate Ogata, now professor of hygiene at Tokyo University. Ogata had published a paper declaring beriberi a bacterial disease, and said he had isolated its particular causative agent. Robert Koch read the Ogata paper, decided the claims were spurious, and asked Kitasato to publish a rebuttal in Japanese. Kitasato hesitated, saying a direct criticism would be poorly received in Japan because he was considered a pupil of Ogata by virtue of their earlier association. However, Koch told him the commitment of scientists to intellectual progress made the intrusion of such personal feelings inappropriate, so Kitasato prepared critiques in German and Japanese and sent them off to prominent medical journals.[23]

[20] Ibid., pp. 40–41.

[21] Claude Dolman, "Max von Pettenkofer," in Charles S. Gillespie, ed., *Dictionary of Scientific Biography* [hereafter *DSB*], 10 (New York: Charles Scribners' Sons, 1974), 556–563.

[22] Miyajima, *Kitasato Shibasaburō den*, pp. 40–41.

[23] Ibid., pp. 38–39; Kitasato Shibasaburo, "Ueber die Reincultur eines Spirillum aus

The beriberi dispute was a commonplace affair by the standards of Western science. It focused on an intellectually challenging problem, and was conducted in an orthodox fashion. Beriberi was a very difficult subject for biomedical scientists. There was rampant speculation about its cause in the late nineteenth century, and research findings seemed contradictory. In fact, there were five categories of explanation to be found in the international medical literature, and the real cause—Vitamin B_1 deficiency—was not fully established until 1936.[24] Like Ogata, Kitasato favored a bacterial explanation but dissented from Ogata's particular claims. He took Ogata to task for incomplete description of the alleged pathogen, for relying excessively on the inconclusive Gram coloration test, and for failing to reproduce bacillus cultures in blood serum from the bodies of beriberi victims.[25] Despite the cautious, even understated tone of the review, critics were soon up in arms. Tokyo University's president, Katō Hiroyuki, asserted that Kitasato's criticism showed he "did not understand the way of the student."[26] Two medical faculty graduates employed in the War Ministry accused Kitasato of jealousy in a privately circulating pamphlet.[27] Medical Affairs Bureau chief Mori Rintarō in a letter to the *Tokyo Iji Shinshi* absolved Kitasato of "shamelessly expressing his own views" but said he was guilty of "overemphasizing science and neglecting human feelings."[28] And the Ministry of Education avenged the supposed slur on Tokyo University's reputation by snubbing Kitasato on a tour it sent to Koch's laboratory in 1890, and by refusing several requests that it assist his researches.[29]

Intellectual commitment to Koch's ideas is also apparent in Kitasato's scientific research. His first major project, on tetanus, was undertaken because of an implied threat to the germ theory by a professor at the University of Gottingen. Dr. Karl Flugge, a former Koch student, argued in 1888 that Arthur Nicolaier's bacillus, the suspected pathogen of tetanus, could not be grown in a pure culture because he and several other researchers had failed at such a task. Koch was disturbed by the ammunition this report gave to his many academic critics and urged

---

faulendem Blute, Spirillum concentricum n. sp.," *Centralblatt für Bakteriologie und Parasitenkunde*, 3:3 (II. Jahrg 1888), 76-78; and "Zai Doitsu-koku Igakushi Kitasato Shibasaburō shi shokan," *Chūgai Iji Shimpō*, No. 212 (25 January 1889), p. 105.

[24] Robert R. Williams, *Toward the Conquest of Beriberi* (Cambridge: Harvard University Press, 1961), p. xviii.

[25] Kitasato, "Ueber die Reincultur," pp. 76-78.

[26] Ogata Norio, "Kitasato Shibasaburō ryaku den," *Igaku Shi Kenkyū* [hereafter *ISK*], No. 2 (1962), p. 42.

[27] Kitajima Ta'ichi, *Kitajima Ta'ichi jiden* (Tokyo, 1955), pp. 24-25.

[28] Mori Rintarō, "Tōkei ni tsuite no bunsō," *Tōkyō Iji Shinshi* [hereafter *TIS*], No. 562 (June 8, 1889), p. 2.

[29] Takano Rokurō, *Kitasato Shibasaburō* (Tokyo, 1965), p. 209.

Kitasato to enter the debate. Although the solution to the tetanus problem proved to be very difficult, Kitasato did achieve a pure culture in 1889 and gained a wide reputation for his work.[30] The solution also led him to a very significant discovery. By carefully manipulating amounts of toxin injected into laboratory animals over time, he demonstrated the existence of substances in the blood serum of the body that are capable of neutralizing foreign materials. This discovery of antitoxic immunity, achieved jointly with Emil von Behring in 1890, became the foundation stone of immunology and made both men world famous.[31]

Scientific ideas apart, Koch's most decisive influence on Kitasato probably lay in his conception of the scientist's social role. Whereas most German biomedical scientists were socially aloof and dedicated exclusively to research, Koch was socially engaged and concerned with clinical treatment. Many German scientists, of course, objected strongly to his ideas. He was the leading German proponent of the bacteriological conception of disease at a time when many continued to attribute illness to complex cellular imbalances. Then there were differences about appropriate professional credentials. Most German biomedical scientists holding professorships also had the Ph.D. by this time; Koch had only an M.D. from the University of Gottingen. And there were disagreements about clinical medicine's place in the contemporary academic setting. German academic medicine had tended to separate clinical medicine sharply from basic medicine by segregating clinicians and researchers in different professional associations and limiting research opportunities to professors; but Koch, as a former district physician at Wollstein, East Prussia, had created bacteriology in the first place by linking his researches on anthrax to the practical or clinical needs of his patients.[32]

What most disturbed Koch's German academic colleagues was the nature and extent of his nonacademic contacts. Because of the very authoritarian socio-political system in which Prussian universities existed, few professors were committed to a liberal conception of society; most wanted to emphasize impractical lines of research as a way of avoiding outside demands and interference.[33] Their commitments to the cellular imbalance theory of disease were compatible with an ivory tower philosophy because they implied that effective means of treatment were

---

[30] Miyajima, *Kitasato Shibasaburō den*, pp. 44-45.

[31] Thomas Brock, ed., *Milestones in Microbiology* (Englewood Cliffs, N.J.: Prentice Hall, 1961), pp. 138-140; and William Bulloch, *The History of Bacteriology* (London, 1938), pp. 260-261.

[32] Joseph Ben-David, "Roles and Innovations in Medicine," *American Journal of Sociology*, 65:6 (1960), 562-563.

[33] Fritz Ringer, *The Decline of the German Mandarins* (Cambridge: Harvard University Press, 1970), p. 113.

difficult at best, but Koch's conception of illness had very different implications. The demonstration that a wide range of diseases might result from specific microorganisms meant that precise measures of prevention, treatment, and eradication were now possible. Thus, military leaders and government officials became interested in Koch's research and actively began to promote his academic career. Such sponsorship led to his directorship of the Physiological Laboratory at the Imperial Health Office in 1880, and in 1885 to a professorship of hygiene at Berlin University.[34]

Koch's subsequent abandonment of his professorship in 1891 was an unintended and ironical consequence of these same nonacademic connections. The trouble began when he announced his discovery of tuberculin, a substance elaborated by the tubercle bacillus, at the Tenth International Medical Congress in Berlin (1890). Such scientific presentations were generally commonplace and routine, but this one was quickly beset by a number of special problems. The Prussian Education Ministry, which was partly hosting the congress, pressed Koch for a spectacular announcement as a way of making propaganda for Germany. Tuberculosis and the quest for its cure were matters of intense public interest. And Koch's findings seemed to imply the existence of a cure, but were actually inconclusive. Thus things began to go badly when clinical tests falsified his claims. The wealthy tubercular patients and doctors who flocked to Berlin were intensely disappointed and angry. The Prussian Education Ministry was embarrassed. And Koch was publicly attacked and ridiculed.[35]

Koch responded to this setback with a complete professional volteface. Heretofore he had been consultant to and subject to the authority of the Prussian Ministry of Education as a professor of basic medicine. But because the influence of German academic physicians was so strong in the university and the ministry, he decided to remove his work to a new setting and to establish a new relationship with the bureaucracy. In 1891, therefore, he resigned his academic appointment and requested both the establishment of a new, independent laboratory and a transferral of his public health consulting functions from the Education Ministry to the Imperial Health Office. These steps removed a source of major intellectual discontent, namely, the characteristically German separation of basic research from clinical medicine. As a professor of basic medicine at Berlin University, Koch had been obliged to entrust the clinical

---

[34] Fielding H. Garrison, *A History of Medicine* (Philadelphia: W. B. Saunders, 1929), pp. 581-582.

[35] Claude Dolman, "Heinrich Hermann Robert Koch," in *DSB*, 7, p. 426.

tests for tuberculin to two members of the clinical faculty.[36] This was, of course, a routine arrangement in the German academic medical setting, but the circumstances of Koch's career made it an obnoxious procedure for him. He was a leading proponent of a professionally unpopular theory being subjected to pressure from Prussian Education Ministry officials. He had entered academic life from the field of clinical practice, and he had dragged ivory tower academics into the vortex of sociopolitical involvement. Thus, when the clinical tests falsified his claims for tuberculin, he considered the results as virtually an act of professional sabotage. Because of these facts, he quite naturally asked the government to create an independent laboratory built explicitly for him and to his personal specifications.[37] This institution, called the Prussian Institute of Infectious Diseases, came into existence in 1891, but only because his supporters managed to override the objections of other scientists such as Rudolph Virchow, who was both a Reichstag member and a pathology professor opposed to the germ theory of disease.[38]

FOUNDING OF THE JAPANESE INSTITUTE OF INFECTIOUS DISEASES

Japanese developments in the field of contagious diseases superficially resembled the major developments in Germany. There were large-scale epidemics in each country. Officials and scientists moved to confront them. Tuberculosis and its conquest became a focus of special attention. And the leading scientist in the field was a forthright, independent maverick. Yet despite the apparent similarities, the differences stand out even more. An absence of peers gave Kitasato greater influence in Japan than even Koch had in Germany. Koch was generally disliked for his ideas, whereas Kitasato was mostly disliked for his values. Koch was mostly opposed by other scientists, whereas Kitasato was primarily opposed by government officials. Finally, although both men got their way in the formal administration of science, Kitasato's success probably aroused the greater degree of antagonism.

Foundation of a Japanese research laboratory in the field of contagious diseases was a result of several related factors. First of all, Japan was suffering severely from epidemic diseases in the early and middle years of Meiji. There were 108,405 deaths from cholera in 1886. Dysentery

---

[36] The two colleagues were reportedly Carl Gerhardt and Ernst von Bergmann. For details see Kitasato's letter to Dr. Hasegawa Tai read into the proceedings of the Japanese Diet: *Dai Nihon Teikoku Gikai shi* [hereafter *DNTGS*] (Dai Nihon Teikoku Gikai Shi Kankō Kai, 1926-1930), vol. 2: see "Yosan sainyū saishutsu sō yosan an Mombushō jokan," House of Representatives, 4th Diet, 11 January 1893, pp. 760-763.

[37] Dolman, "Koch," p. 426.

[38] Ibid., p. 426.

killed 41,284 Japanese in 1892. And between 1886 and 1891 there were about 7,000,000 reported cases of tuberculosis, of whom over 215,000 are reliably known to have died.[39] Second, the controversy over tuberculin in the context of so many tubercular cases aroused considerable interest in research, even though Koch's claims had been partially rejected as false. And third, Kitasato returned to Japan in the fall of 1892 and immediately began trying to establish a laboratory in the field. Even these factors do not fully explain what happened, however. Basically, Kitasato benefited from competitive pressures in the Japanese political system. Tensions growing out of the Restoration provided a favorable circumstance, as did rivalries in the Meiji bureaucratic arena. On the one hand, he exploited antagonisms between the newly established Diet and a bureaucracy that was not much older; and on the other, he manipulated tensions between the Ministry of Education and the Ministry of Home Affairs.

Kitasato's presence and opinions had a major impact on the outcome. Because he wanted to "repay the Japanese people" for the opportunities they had financed, he returned to Tokyo to seek a suitable position in the spring of 1892.[40] In principle, this should not have been difficult because of the credentials he was able to present: the conquest of tetanus, the discovery of antitoxic immunity, with offers of a professorship at the University of Pennsylvania and of a laboratory directorship at the University of Cambridge. In fact, several professors ignored the beriberi controversy and suggested that he join the faculty of Tokyo University, while Home Ministry officials wanted him to return to the Bureau of Public Health.[41]

None of these offers seemed suitable, however, and he quickly rejected them all. Pennsylvania and Cambridge were outside Japan, where he wanted to work. The research facilities of the Public Health Bureau's Hygiene Laboratory were completely inadequate in scale, whereas the Tokyo University "offer" had several important defects. The invitation was informal, lacking authorization from the Ministry of Education. The dean who extended it was the same man whose request for an apology to Professor Wilhelm Schultze Kitasato had rejected in 1881.[42] And the formal organizational arrangements were definitely not to his taste. Because the German universities were considered the world's most advanced, education reformers in the Ministry of Education had adopted

---

[39] Regarding cholera and dysentery, see Kawakami Takeshi, *Gendai Nihon iryō shi* (Tokyo, 1965), p. 131. On tuberculosis see "Kengi an no kaketsu," *TIS*, No. 778 (February 25, 1893), p. 47.

[40] Miyajima, *Kitasato Shibasaburō den*, p. 56.

[41] *DNTGS*, p. 763.

[42] Ibid., p. 763.

some organizational features of the German academic model. In particular, Tokyo University was in process of instituting a *partial* separation of basic research from the disciplines of clinical medicine. Thus, Kitasato decided to choose an essentially ad hoc arrangement.[43] Through the efforts of Nagayo Sensai, now retired from the Bureau of Public Health, he won sponsorship and support from a private philanthropic organization and two other prominent figures. In September 1892, consequently, there came into being the country's first laboratory for infectious diseases, supported by 3,600 yen from the Great Japan Hygiene Society with land and buildings donated by Fukuzawa Yukichi and 1,000 yen for expenses from the industrialist Morimura Ichizaemon.[44]

The aftermath of the tuberculin controversy had a significant impact in Japan at this point. Koch's original claim for the substance—that it would cure tuberculosis—had been falsified, but other questions remained, and Koch was besieged by requests for test samples of the controversial substance. Two testing programs were in due course established in Japan. Probably through Kitasato's intervention, the Home Ministry obtained a sample in February 1892 and immediately began testing in several affiliated hospitals, and the Ministry of Education got a sample about one month later and began its investigation at Tokyo University. The almost inevitable result was that each ministry submitted a plan to the Cabinet for its own research laboratory in the field of infectious diseases.[45]

Prime Minister Itō Hirobumi's Cabinet chose to support the proposal submitted by the Ministry of Education. This request called for a research laboratory, several barns for the laboratory animals used in making serums, and a hospital for human patients. Tokyo University would supervise the entire operation, with the Education Ministry having final authority. Kitasato was to be named director but would not have either the rank of professor or independent control of finances and staff appointments. And the budget for construction was to be a mere 34,659 yen, as compared to the Ministry of Education's initial request for 100,000 yen.[46]

Negative reactions were quickly aroused when the recommendation reached the Diet. Its most forthright critic was a physician named Hasegawa Tai, who argued that the presence of Ogata Masanori's hygiene laboratory at Tokyo University made the establishment of an infectious

[43] James R. Bartholomew, "Japanese Modernization and the Imperial Universities, 1876-1920," *The Journal of Asian Studies*, 37 (February 1978), 251-271.

[44] Miyajima, *Kitasato Shibasaburō den*, pp. 61-65.

[45] "Densembyō Kenkyū Jo," *TIS*, No. 762 (November 5, 1892), p. 47.

[46] Ibid., p. 47, and "Densembyō kenkyūshitsu setchi no keikaku," *TIS*, No. 747 (July 23, 1892), p. 39.

diseases laboratory 'at that institution superfluous. He noted the history of conflict between Kitasato and the Ministry of Education, and said he thought the ministry would likely interfere in Kitasato's work. And he raised objections against the formal organization of the faculty of medicine itself. In this connection he emphasized the instructional value of Koch's debacle in Berlin, contending that Berlin University's separation of basic research from clinical medicine had sabotaged Koch, and arguing that the same thing would happen to Kitasato if he went to Tokyo University, because it had adopted the same organizational model. Hasegawa further emphasized that Kitasato, for all of these reasons, would refuse to work in such a laboratory in any case. And since a laboratory for infectious diseases without Kitasato "would be like a Kabuki Theater without Danjuro," there was no reason for the Diet to build something which "could not be a feasible venture."[47]

Under Hasegawa's leadership, the Diet then voted to subsidize a laboratory whose specifications Kitasato did favor. The institution to be established would operate under the auspices of the Great Japan Hygiene Society, thereby replacing the existing laboratory, which was already too small. Kitasato would become director with major executive authority. Funding would be private but the government would provide a subsidy. And Kitasato would serve the government as a technical expert (*gishi*) in the Bureau of Public Health. The amount of subsidy requested was supposed to fill the gap between the earlier private contributions and the current operational expenditures. Thus, 20,000 yen was requested for construction and 45,000 yen for operations over a three-year period.[48]

Opposition to the Hygiene Society bill took a number of different forms. Despite the apparent neutrality of Prime Minister Itō's Cabinet, Vice Minister of Education Kubota Yuzuru continued to promote Tokyo University as the most appropriate site.[49] A member of the House of Representatives opposed linking policy to Kitasato's personal wishes.[50] Another said a government affiliation was more appropriate than a private one because Kitasato had attended a state university and had studied in Berlin at the Japanese government's expense.[51] And a third thought his attitude was "harsh" when so many diseases were threatening the

[47] *DNTGS*, pp. 760-763.

[48] *Densembyō Kenkyū Jo annai* (Densembyō Kenkyū Jo, 1911), pp. 1-3.

[49] "Ika Daigaku Densembyō Kenkyū Jo setchi hi," *TIS*, No. 772 (January 14, 1893), p. 36.

[50] *DNTGS*, pp. 764-765.

[51] *DNTGS*, II. Cf. "Dai Nihon Shiritsu Eisei Kai setsuritsu Densembyō Kenkyū Jo hojō ni tsuke kengi an," House of Representatives, 4th Diet, 23 February 1893, p. 1021.

country.[52] But none of these criticisms was as forceful as those enunciated by a former Tokyo University president. Watanabe Koki, who held the office from 1882 to 1886, offered several objections in a speech to the House of Representatives on February 23, 1893. Koch's laboratory in Berlin was government-funded; thus, Kitasato's should be also. Kitasato's career should be assisted by the government in the future because it had been so assisted in the past. The proposed Institute of Infectious Diseases was too important to entrust to private sponsorship. Private sponsorship might make other countries think Japan had little appreciation for science. Moreover, supporting someone whose ties with the Ministry of Education were so tenuous might be a bad idea altogether![53]

Watanabe was so bitterly opposed to the "private" development of science that he led a campaign to block construction of the new institute after the Diet rejected his arguments. He became a leading spokesman for residents of Tokyo's Shiba Park district, who objected to the presence of an infectious diseases laboratory and hospital in their neighborhood for a variety of aesthetic, financial, and hygienic reasons. This movement to obstruct implementation of the enabling legislation began in April and continued through September of 1893. Not all adherents opposed creation of the institute as such, but most demanded relocation of the hospital and some of the laboratory as well. Their immediate objective was thus to force concessions from Kitasato and his sponsors on these points, or failing that, to block the physical construction by any and all means. But the proponents of the laboratory were adamant, and they took several effective steps. Kitasato held endless meetings with delegations of local residents. His medical supporters explained the work of the Koch and Pasteur Institutes in lectures for the general public. And they elicited active support from the major newspapers of Tokyo. It was a measure of their success that Watanabe later said the press had called his movement "irrational" and had subjected him to "indiscriminate riducule."[54]

Why did Kitasato win when the opposition was so determined? For one thing, the Japanese Diet was unusually assertive in the decade of the 1890s. In 1890, the Diet slashed the Yamagata Cabinet's budget by 10 percent. In 1891, it obstructed legislation through filibuster. In 1892, it

[52] *DNTGS*, pp. 764-765.

[53] *DNTGS*, p. 1021.

[54] For Watanabe's remarks, see "Densembyō Kenkyū Jo ni kansuru Shiba-ku kai," *Tokyo Nichi Nichi Shimbun*, No. 6453 (April 29, 1893), p. 4. For details on the antilaboratory movement, see my Ph.D. dissertation, "The Acculturation of Science in Japan: Kitasato Shibasaburō and the Japanese Bacteriological Community, 1885-1920 (Stanford, 1971), pp. 61-71.

came within three votes of impeaching the Cabinet, and in 1893 it sent a resolution to the emperor requesting the dismissal of the prime minister.[55] Some of this behavior was sheer assertiveness for its own sake. The Diet had only been established in 1890. Thus, it was determined to carve out its niche in the Meiji constitutional system by subjecting all government requests to particularly severe scrutiny. Some of it was motivated by a straightforward desire to reduce public expenditure. Hasegawa Tai in particular was a vigorous opponent of excessive spending and actively opposed several education initiatives on these grounds during the decade of the 1890s.[56] And some of it resulted from a desire to curb the spread of bureaucratic influence into different areas of Japanese society.[57] The Hygiene Society subsidy bill on Kitasato's behalf had the great merit, from the Diet's point of view, of combining all three attractions. The Diet could assert its authority by defeating a government budget request. By endorsing Hasagawa's arguments it appeared to be saving money. And in siding with Kitasato the Diet could present itself as the defender of private interests. Such attitudes gave private legislative initiatives greater prospects of success in the 1890s than they enjoyed in later years. Among the seven privately sponsored ad hoc proposals for science considered by the Diet in the decade 1890-1900, three (43 percent) were approved and implemented, but during the two decades between 1900 and 1920, there were only seven such proposals and just two (29 percent) became realities.[58]

Kitasato also benefited from factional divisions in the national bureaucracy itself. Although medical care and treatment were the province of the Home Ministry, and medical education the responsibility of the Ed-

[55] Hugh Borton, *Japan's Modern Century* (New York: Ronald Press, 1955), pp. 198-202.

[56] Terasaki Masao, "Teikoku daigaku keisei ki no daigaku kan," in Terasaki Masao et al., eds., *Gakkō kan no shiteki kenkyū* (Tokyo, 1972), p. 246.

[57] Debate in 1896 on a proposal to award matching funds from the National Treasury to agriculture experiment stations established by the prefectures or by private agencies constitutes one example. Representative Matsuo Kenzo endorsed the proposition in debate, but emphasized that matching funds must never exceed 50 percent of budgeted expenditures, to avoid giving Tokyo undue control over personnel decisions. Representative Komatsu Sansho opposed such grants altogether, saying: "There are so many evils in this kind of assistance. . . . When the government exerts itself to help in such matters, it almost always creates unendurable interference. . . . Gentlemen of the Shimpoto and gentlemen of the Kaishinto, if we want to promote popular rights at all, if we truly wish to defend local rights and achieve our objectives of local autonomy, I am firmly convinced that we cannot ask for state support and at the same time hope to avoid the state interference that will surely accompany this proposal." See *DNTGS*, III. Cf. "Fuken nōji shikenjo kokkō hojo hōan," House of Representatives, 9th Diet, 18 March 1896, pp. 1873-1875.

[58] Calculations are based on information in *DNTGS* and *Teikoku Gikai Shūgiin iinkai giroku* [hereafter *TGSIG*] (Shūgiin Jimukyoku, 1890-1920).

ucation Ministry, curious anomalies existed and jurisdictional squabbles were frequent. The Bureau of Public Health had itself belonged to the Education Ministry prior to 1875.[59] The Central Hygiene Commission, which passed judgment on matters of medical policy, was affiliated with the Ministry of Home Affairs, but it also contained members from the Ministry of Education.[60] Education had once had control over the certification of physicians, but lost it to Home Affairs, and Home Affairs was invariably dependent on Education for staffing the certification panels.[61] Home Affairs did not contest the Cabinet rejection of its laboratory proposal, but was scarcely disappointed when its rival's proposal was defeated in the Diet. Moreover, Kitasato had close ties in the Bureau of Public Health. Hasegawa Tai later became chief of the Bureau of Public Health (1898-1902), and Kitasato's initial sponsor, Dr. Nagayo Sensai, had held the same post for nearly twenty years (1875-1892).[62] As Hasegawa Tai told the House of Representatives Budget Committee during the deliberations, "These ministries are all feudalistic and they are constantly plundering each others' resources."[63]

Broader tensions in Japanese society stemming from the collapse of the old regime may also have aided Kitasato's political success. His own background was at least "nonestablishment" in social and political terms. One of the schools he attended in Kumamoto was suffused with anti-Restoration influences, and his own native region was at best neutral toward the Meiji government. There was also the matter of his disciplinary affiliation. Whereas many fields of science were heavily dependent on the Meiji government and the Tokugawa Shogunate before it, medicine was at least partly independent and was socio-politically "detached."[64] Moreover, his maverick affiliations appealed to certain qualities of mind. Fukuzawa Yukichi's attitude toward the Meiji establishment was certainly "detached," whereas that of Hasegawa bordered on outright hostility. The former habitually refused to serve in the Meiji government and expressed qualified appreciation of certain Tokugawa

[59] Hashimoto Masakiyo, "Meiji jidai ni okeru eisei gyōsei kenkyū sho shi," *ISK*, No. 3 (1963), pp. 20-25.

[60] *Shokuinroku* (Naikaku Insatsukyoku, 1886-1920).

[61] Kawakami, *Gendai Nihon iryō shi*, pp. 105-128.

[62] Ijiri Tsunekichi, ed., *Rekidai kenkan roku* (Tokyo, 1967), p. 117.

[63] *TGSIG* (Shūgiin Jimukyoku, 1893), vol. 4: see "Dai go-ka dai-ichi go Mombushō no bu," House of Respresentatives Budget Committee, 2nd Session, 5th Diet, 8 December 1893, p. 1.

[64] Nakayama Shigeru, "Japanese Scientific Thought," in *DSB*, 15 Supplement 1, pp. 742-743. See also James R. Bartholomew, "The Japanese Scientific Community in Formation, 1870-1920," Lawrence Schneider, ed., *Science in Modern East Asia*, Vol. I (Buffalo: State University of New York, *Journal of Asian Affairs*, Vol. V No. 2, Fall 1980), pp. 62-84.

ideals, whereas the latter actually fought against the Restoration in his native Nagaoka and constantly attacked the policies of the Ministry of Education.[65] On one occasion Hasegawa accused the ministry of violating civil service regulations by personalistic recruitment of officials.[66] On another he attacked it in the Diet as a "mansion full of ghosts."[67] And on yet a third occasion he criticized its aggressiveness, saying it was unusually adept at "holding its [political] ground."[68]

Kitasato also won because the need for his services was great and the practical alternatives were few. There were almost no other bacteriologists in Japan in 1893, or at least none with comparable credentials. Takagi Tomoe and Toyama Chinkichi were old enough and had University medical degrees, but neither had studied abroad nor had any postgraduate training. Asakawa Norihiko, who made a distinguished reputation later, had not studied abroad. Tsuboi Jirō was still in Europe at this time. And Ogata Masanori and Nakahama Toichirō had the formal credentials but not the experience in research. Moreover, both had studied with Pettenkofer and were considerably less competent.[69] Given the dimensions of the medical problems and the economic losses involved, the government might well have met the price of anyone who could guarantee results. And in this case, Japanese authorities had a particularly attractive choice. Kitasato Shibasaburō was not only the top bacteriologist in Japan, he was among the top three or four in the world and had helped to create the discipline of serology on which any effective bacteriological campaign would necessarily have to depend.

THE INSTITUTE'S MISSION AND FUNCTIONS

Considering the magnitude of the challenge and the abilities of the challenger, it is not surprising that the Institute of Infectious Diseases grew steadily in the years which followed its creation. In 1895 the Diet approved a request from the home minister for a continuation of annual subsidies. In 1896 Kitasato was named "consultant" to the government-owned Serological Institute for serum manufacturing. In 1899 the Institute of Infectious Diseases was nationalized, and in 1900 Kitasato assumed the concurrent post of director of the Tokyo Vaccine Station for the production of smallpox vaccine.[70] These activities soon exceeded the

---

[65] Umezawa Hikotarō, ed., *Kindai mei'i ichiyū hanashi* (Tokyo, 1937), p. 373.

[66] *TGSIG*, p. 3.

[67] Yamaguchi Gorō, ed., *Hasegawa Tai Sensei zenshū* (Tokyo, 1939), p. 491.

[68] *TGSIG*, p. 1.

[69] Since Pettenkofer was a dedicated opponent of the germ theory, it is hardly surprising that students of his, such as Ogata and Nakahama, were inadequately trained in bacteriology. See note 21 above.

[70] *Shokuinroku*, 1901, p. 67.

capacity of existing facilities and during the Russo-Japanese war, the government decided to build a larger institute at Shirogane Daimachi, not far from the former institution at the Shiba Park site. The new facility continued the earlier activities of scientific research, medical treatment, teaching, and serum-vaccine manufacturing, and was materially assisted by the adjunction of the Serological Institute and the Tokyo Vaccine Station in 1905.[71] Kitasato at that time became director of all three agencies and thus controlled all Japanese serum and vaccine production for the next decade.

Expansion of activities brought an expansion of staff and greater expenditure of funds. In 1894 there were only four members of the technical staff, including Kitasato himself.[72] By 1899, however, this group had expanded to seven and jumped again to ten in 1900 as a result of nationalization. Thereafter a distinction based on educational qualifications and length of service was fully instituted, with some researchers holding the title of *gishi* (technical expert) and others that of *gishu* (technician). There were four *gishi* and thirteen *gishu* in 1902, and seven *gishi* and twenty-one *gishu* in 1905.[73] The greatly enlarged staff of 1905 did not prove to be permanent, however, because the government found it could mass-produce serums and vaccine of high quality with a smaller staff at less cost. Salary expenditures were partially diverted to research programs. The numerical expansion of the Institute staff therefore slowed, and in the financially troubled years that preceded World War I it declined altogether.

Expanding budgetary outlays nevertheless show continuing government interest. In 1894 the laboratory and its auxiliary facilities took in and spent about 20,000 yen. At the time of nationalization in 1899, its annual budget had reached 56,036 yen; and by 1902 it was 60,540 yen.[74] Adjunction of the Serological Institute and Vaccine Station inflated expenditures after 1905, and in 1912 regularly budgeted spending by the Institute of Infectious Diseases exceeded 210,000 yen.[75] Budget comparisons with Tokyo University provide further indication of the institute's political popularity. In 1894 the disparity in spending between the two (very different) institutions was about 1:25—the university had an authorized spending level at that time of 518,816 yen; by 1902 the margin

[71] Miyajima, *Kitasato Shibasaburō den*, p. 78.

[72] Compiled from information in *Kitasato Kenkyū Jo gojū nen shi* (Tokyo: 1966), pp. 627-692.

[73] *Shokuinroku*, 1906, p. 61.

[74] *TGSIG*, 16:1: see "Dai-ichi rui dai-ni go yosan iin dai-ichi bunkakai kaigiroku dai-ni kai," House of Representatives Budget Committee, 2nd Session, 15th Diet, 17 December 1901, pp. 16-17.

[75] Aoyama Tanemichi, "Tokugakusha no shōrai ikaga," *Ikai Jihō* [hereafter *IJ*], No. 1055 (September 12, 1914), p. 8.

had narrowed to 1:16 and in 1912 it was only 1:6.6. Moreover, between 1912 and 1914 the institute's regular budget increased by 15,599 yen and total expenditures by 71,769 yen, whereas the university in the same period found its appropriations and spending level reduced from 1,380,000 yen to about 1,330,000 yen.[76]

Institutional growth of this magnitude reflected a number of professional achievements. Most conspicuous were those in research and clinical treatment, where Kitasato continued investigations of tuberculosis while staff members worked on subjects like smallpox, dysentery, and diphtheria. The Institute of Infectious Diseases first won world acclaim in the summer of 1894 when Kitasato announced his discovery of the plague bacillus coincidentally with Alexandre Yersin of the Pasteur Institute.[77] In 1897, Shiga Kiyoshi isolated the bacillus of dysentery that has since born his name. And in 1901 the institute's veterinary expert, Umeno Shinkichi, discovered the cause of lymph gland disease in horses. Comparable gains were also attained in the field of clinical treatment. Since Kitasato had created serology and serum therapy with Emil von Behring, Japan became the first country in the world to use serum treatment for cholera, tetanus, and diphtheria.[78] In 1895 Kitasato treated 322 diphtheria patients at the institute hospital with the serum invented by von Behring, and fewer than 9 percent died. The same year he devised a cholera serum that saved two-thirds of the victims in a Tokyo epidemic.[79] And in 1902 Hida Otoichi made a major advance in the treatment of diphtheria. By adding a small amount of sugar and peptone to

[76] Sato Kenzō, *Kokuritsu daigaku zaisei seido shikō* (Tokyo, 1965), p. 293.

[77] Credit for the discovery of the plague bacillus is usually assigned to the Swiss bacteriologist Alexandre Yersin and to Kitasato jointly on the grounds that both men simultaneously isolated the same microorganism in separate investigations. In fact, doubts as to where credit should be assigned have surrounded Kitasato's work rather than that of Yersin. Dr. Norman Howard-Jones, who concluded in 1973 that the bacillus isolated by Kitasato in 1894 was not the true pathogen, is only the most recent commentator on the subject, and his analysis is no more likely to resolve the issue definitively than earlier such efforts. Dr. Fujino Tsunesaburo, whom Howard-Jones does not cite, for example, continues to defend Kitasato's claim on the basis of his own investigation. And the intense factional and institutional rivalries that so often divided the Japanese medical science community in the 1890s at least call into question the objectivity of judgments by some contemporaries of Kitasato on which Howard-Jones places great emphasis. For Howard-Jones' analysis, see his article "Was Shibasaburo Kitasato the Co-Discoverer of the Plague Bacillus?" *Perspectives in Biology and Medicine*, 16 (Winter 1973), 292-307. For Fujino's views, see his retirement address at Osaka University entitled "Nihon saikingaku shi, Meiji-Taishō hen," *Medical Circle*, No. 129 (August 25, 1970), pp. 321-340. Regarding factionalism in the medical community, see my article entitled "Japanese Culture and the Problem of Modern Science," in Arnold Thackray and Everett Mendelsohn, eds., *Science and Values* (New York: Humanities Press, 1974), pp. 109-155.

[78] Miyajima, *Kitasato Shibasaburō den*, p. 70.

[79] Ibid., p. 74.

a burdock culture base, he was able to determine the relationship between the form of the diphtheria bacillus and its reaction to toxicity. This led to the manufacturing of a highly effective serum that Kitasato called "superior to any in Europe or America."[80] Germany and other countries began importing the serum, and the government of Japan hereafter allowed the institute to monopolize all serum production for the country.

An institute function with important political consequences was the teaching of epidemiology. In March 1894 Kitasato began accepting short-term special students called *denshūsei*. Some were medical students, but most were local health officials. At the request of the home minister, the Diet in March 1895 authorized prefectural governors to recommend candidates to the program and appropriated funds to pay for their training. These state-supported *denshūsei* and others who paid their own way studied bacteriology, epidemiology, toxic prevention, microscopy, culture-making and methods of clinical treatment.[81] The number of Kitasato "students" produced by this program numbered 450 by mid-1899, 2,400 by 1914, and was augmented informally by the participation of institute scientists in local campaigns against disease.[82] Several times a year, at the Home Ministry's request, Kitasato or various colleagues would travel to a disease-infested area to supervise the needed epidemiological countermeasures. Besides their medical objectives, these trips had the educational function of persuading local officials to follow the direction of professional medical experts. In 1911 the institute was asked to send an inspector to Korea and Manchuria, where a plague epidemic was raging. Since the delegate in this case had to work with Chinese and Japanese officials, Kitasato agreed to the home minister's request that he make the trip himself.[83] As a result of his participation, the campaign was successful and casualties were minimized. It was typical of all such campaigns in relying very heavily on Kitasato's professional advice.

The institute activities that best guaranteed freedom from the Ministry of Education were serum-vaccine manufacturing and medical consultation. Under the terms of Imperial Ordinance 279 (October 1898), the Bureau of Professional Education was supposed to "supervise and

[80] Kitasato Shibasaburō, "Setsuritsu no shūshi," *TIS*, No. 1900 (December 12, 1914), pp. 2648-2649.

[81] *DNTGS*, III. Cf. "Dai Nihon Shiritsu Eisei Kai setsuritsu Densembyō Kenkyū Jo ni sembatsu kenkyūsei o oku no kengi an," House of Representatives, 8th Diet, 18 March 1895, p. 919.

[82] Miyajima, *Kitasato Shibasaburō den*, p. 80.

[83] Ibid., pp. 109-110, 259.

encourage all the sciences and the arts."[84] The Education Ministry thus had jurisdiction over the imperial universities and all higher schools. It supervised research facilities like the Seismological Study Commission, the Tokyo Academy of Sciences, and the Central Meteorological Observatory. And it could point to the scientific research and teaching functions of the Infectious Diseases Institute as an argument for acquiring control over that facility as well. However, consultations on public health and the manufacturing of serums and vaccine gave Kitasato a rationale for the Home Ministry affiliation. Under the terms of Imperial Ordinances 88 (March 29, 1905) and 104-105 (March 31, 1905), he could justify the existing bureaucratic arrangements by pointing to provisions that the institute serve as a "consultative agency to the Home Ministry with respect to public health" and assume responsibility for manufacturing "vaccine, serums, and other substances for treating bacteriological diseases."[85]

By using these authorizations Kitasato gradually became the single dominant force in the Japanese public health system. In 1895 he persuaded the Diet to revise the regulations on epidemic disease and inspired an 1897 law making epidemiology its base.[86] In 1899 he secured the dismissal of the Bureau of Public Health's section chief for insurance, quarantine, and medical affairs, apparently because the incumbent did not get along with its medical and scientific advisers.[87] In 1903 and 1912 he defeated proposals to reduce the budget of the Institute of Infectious Diseases that emanated from the Ministry of Finance. And in 1914 he instigated the founding of a national network of sanatoria for victims of tuberculosis.[88] In view of these achievements, it is not surprising that the Bureau of Public Health was considered an "extention of the Infectious Diseases Institute," whereas the bureau chief himself "could scarcely do anything without consulting Kitasato."[89]

Limitations on his formal authority made these achievements more remarkable. Kitasato never held a really important office, and the institute's charter was thoroughly hedged by restrictions. He began government service in 1884 at the rank of technician second class (nitō gishu). He rose to technician first class (ittō gishu) in 1886, and to technical expert (gishi) only in 1893. Between 1896 and 1913 his official title was

---

[84] Shokuinroku, 1899, p. 482.

[85] Shokuinroku, 1906, p. 61.

[86] Miyajima, Kitasato Shibasaburō den, p. 117.

[87] "Eiseikyoku to Kitasato shi," IJ, No. 276 (September 16, 1899), p. 759.

[88] Takano Rokurō, Kitasato Shibasaburō (Tokyo, 1965), p. 137. The sanatoria, for the most part, did not materialize until additional legislation was enacted by the Diet in 1918. See Takano for details, pp. 132-138.

[89] "Fuji-Tsukuba: Kitasato to Miyamoto," IJ, No. 1014 (November 29, 1913), p. 2168; and Izawa Takio Denki Kensan Iinkai, ed., Izawa Takio (Tokyo, 1951), p. 109.

councillor (*komon*) and his rank was *kōtōkan nitō*. In 1914 he was raised to the rank of *kōtōkan ittō*, but he only achieved the honorific title of *kun nitō* at the very end of his life.[90] Although none of this mattered on a day-to-day basis, explicit controls were available if anyone dared to use them. Under the terms of a letter to Kitasato from Home Minister Inoue Kaoru dated March 13, 1893, all regulations of the institute, together with any revision or diversion of budgeted items, had to be approved by the minister of home affairs. The laboratory's activities were to be supervised by the chief of the Bureau of Public Health. The home minister had to be informed about laboratory activities each year in writing. And the Board of Audit was empowered to inspect the institute's accounts whenever it wished to do so.[91]

Government officials could not invoke these restrictions, however, because of Kitasato's political power. Four or five of the ten men who served as chief of the Bureau of Public Health between 1891 and 1914 were his personal friends. The Great Japan Hygiene Society gave him money and sponsorship. Hasegawa Tai, with his own scores to settle, helped Kitasato in the Diet. Tanaka Giichi, owner of the medical journal *Ikai Jihō*, and Fukuzawa Yukichi, owner of the *Jiji Shimpō*, gave him a forum in the press.[92] He controlled a majority of Central Hygiene Commission members after 1899, and nearly all Japanese health officials had studied epidemiology at the Institute of Infectious Diseases.[93] Moreover, Kitasato was a politician of more than average ability. He knew how to influence officials. He spent large sums of money on official entertainment. He carefully maintained certain patron-client relations. And he paid close attention to the press.[94] Dr. Kitajima Ta'ichi, the institute's deputy director, said Kitasato had a "very special position in the Ministry of Home Affairs."[95] Dr. Miyajima Mikinosuke, an institute staff researcher, believed that not even the home minister could defy him.[96] Kohashi Kazuta, one-time chief of the Bureau of Public Health, thought Kitasato would have reached the Cabinet had he entered elective politics.[97] And Kubota Seitarō, another Public Health Bureau chief of the

---

[90] Kubota Seitarō, "Kanri Kitasato," in Miyajima, *Kitasato Shibasaburō den*, p. 261. For information on Kitasato's bureaucratic rank, see *Shokuinroku* for the appropriate years.

[91] "Demsembyō Kenkyū Jo hojōhi kafu no meireisho," *TIS*, No. 786 (April 23, 1893), p. 48.

[92] Kitajima, *Kitajima Ta'ichi jiden*, p. 99.

[93] Kawakami, *Gendai Nihon iryō shi*, pp. 251-252.

[94] Kitajima, *Kitajima Ta'ichi jiden*, pp. 99, 107.

[95] Ibid., p. 58.

[96] Miyajima, *Kitasato Shibasaburō den*, p. 82, describes how Kitasato was able to enlist Home Minister Hara Kei's support against bureaucratic opponents in 1911.

[97] Kohashi Kazuta, "Kakuretaru daiseijika," in Miyajima, *Kitasato Shibasaburō den*, pp. 294-295.

period, attributed Kitasato's failure to achieve a higher formal office to "[fundamental] defects in the bureaucratic system."[98]

Kitasato's major political objective was always to prevent the institute's transfer to the Ministry of Education. Shortly after the laboratory was nationalized in March 1899, former Vice Minister of Education Kubota Yuzuru raised the possibility of a transfer in a speech to the House of Peers, but no follow-up action was taken until the spring of 1903.[99] At that time the institute was listed by Okuda Gijin, recently retired chief of the Cabinet Bureau for Legal Affairs, as one of six scientific agencies to be transferred to the Ministry of Education in a major bureaucratic reform. Okuda and the incoming prime minister, Katsura Tarō, were concerned about the rising costs and declining efficiency of government, and apparently decided to relocate these agencies in the Ministry of Education because of its political reputation as an easy mark for budget cutters.[100] Kitasato, however, would have none of it and immediately raised objections. By invoking the support of various friends, planting critical statements in the press, and showing a posture of "unrelenting opposition," he defeated the proposal and preserved the existing bureaucratic arrangements.[101] Nor was the outcome any different when the government raised the issue in 1911 under Saionji Kimmochi or in 1913 under Yamamoto Gonnohyoe. Okuda's ideas were still the guiding inspiration. Kitasato was still adamantly opposed, and he and his supporters were still in a position to prevail.[102]

Nevertheless, forces to produce a different outcome were already in progress. Changes in the formal administration of science and technology were eroding the strength of Kitasato's base in the Ministry of Home Affairs. His monopoly of scarce knowledge was diminishing as Japan acquired more bacteriologists. And a very determined enemy was beginning to challenge his influence in the government. Although clique relations preserved much of his influence in the long run, these changes were palpably detrimental in the short run. They undermined both his right and in some degree his ability to act independently. They provided

[98] Kubota, "Kanri Kitasato," p. 261.

[99] *DNTGS*, V. Cf. "Gakusei chōsa kai ni kansuru kengi an," House of Peers, 14th Diet, 31 January 1900, pp. 111-112.

[100] Okada Tomoharu, *Aa Okuda Hakushi* (Tokyo, 1922), p. 141. For comments on the Ministry of Education, see "Aa Densembyō Kenkyū Jo," *Kyōiku Jiron* [hereafter *KJ*], No. 1063 (October 25, 1914), p. 47.

[101] Uzaki Kumakichi, *Aoyama Tanemichi* (Tokyo, 1930), p. 150.

[102] Yagi Itsuro quotes Kitasato as saying, "When the Yamamoto Cabinet was in office, Education Minister Okuda was planning a transfer, but I asked Home Minister Hara to prevent it. So the Cabinet knew there would be a problem." See Miyajima, *Kitasato Shibasaburō den*, p. 304.

an alternative means of accomplishing socially vital tasks. And they gave opponents leadership and a strategy for political action.

Changes in the administration of scientific agencies created bureaucratic precedents for Okuda's transfer proposals and those of the Education Ministry. As Table 1 shows, there was a steady deterioration in the role of the Home Ministry and a steady rise in the influence of the Ministry of Education in the arena of scientific administration. When the modern cabinet system was established in 1885, the Ministry of Home Affairs controlled 47 percent of the government's 15 laboratories and testing stations that were not affiliated with the university; the Ministry of Agriculture and Commerce controlled 33 percent of these facilities, while three other ministries administered the remainder. When Kitasato established the Institute of Infectious Diseases in 1893, the Agriculture and Commerce Ministry still controlled 33 percent of these facilities, but the Home Ministry's percentage had slipped to 38, whereas that of the Education Ministry had risen to 14. And a year after the nationalization of the Institute in 1899, Agriculture and Commerce had a 35 percent share, the Home Ministry a 23 percent share, and Education had jumped to a 22 percent share. Some of these gains by Education resulted from the founding of new laboratories and stations, but others resulted from transfers away from the Ministry of Home Affairs. In 1890 Agriculture and Commerce ceded to Education control over the Forestry Experiment Station, which had originally belonged to the Home Ministry.[103] In 1896 Education took the Tokyo Astronomical Observ-

TABLE 1. The Bureaucratic Affiliations of Scientific Agencies

Ministry	1885		1893		1900		1909		1915	
	N	%	N	%	N	%	N	%	N	%
Home Affairs	7	47	8	38	7	23	7	17	6	13
Agriculture & Commerce	5	33	7	33	11	35	15	37	15	33
Public Works & Communications	1	7	1	5	2	7	2	5	2	4
Navy	1	7	1	5	3	10	4	10	5	11
War	1	7	1	5	1	3	3	7	3	7
Education	0	0	1	5	7	22	8	20	13	28
Railways	0	0	0	0	0	0	1	2	1	2
Finance	0	0	0	0	0	0	1	2	1	2
Totals*	15	100	21	100	31	100	41	100	46	100

Sources: Yuasa Mitsutomo, *Gendai kagaku gijutsu shi nempyō* (Tōkyō, 1962); *TGSIG*, various numbers.

* Percentage totals may be slightly higher or lower than 100 due to rounding.

[103] *Tōkyō no rikakei daigaku* (Tokyo, 1964), p. 124.

atory away from the Home Ministry. And in 1896 again, the Home Affairs Ministry ceded to Education control over the Central Meteorological Observatory, which had formerly belonged to the defunct Public Works Ministry.[104]

Steady growth in the number of bacteriologists further eroded Kitasato's political position. There were only seven bacteriologists in Japan when the Institute of Infectious Diseases was founded. Within a year after nationalization, the number had increased to twenty-four. There were thirty-one Japanese bacteriologists when Okuda first recommended the Institute's transfer. But by 1910 there were forty-two Japanese bacteriologists, and on the eve of World War I, there were forty-three.[105] Moreover, the percentage of bacteriologists employed in organizations controlled by Kitasato's admirers was steadily declining. As Table 2 shows, 57 percent of Japan's seven bacteriologists worked with Kitasato in 1893, whereas 43 percent worked in the hostile environments of Tokyo University and the Tokyo Hygiene Institute.[106] In 1900, 54 percent of the twenty-four bacteriologists in Japan still worked in

TABLE 2. EMPLOYMENT OF BACTERIOLOGISTS IN ORGANIZATIONS

	Favorable to Kitasato		Hostile or Indifferent to Kitasato	
Year	N	%	N	%
1893	4	57	3	43
1900	13	54	11	46
1910	18	43	24	57
1914	18	41	25	59

SOURCE: Iseki Kurō, ed., *Dai Nihon hakushi roku*, vols. II, III (Tokyo, 1929-1930), and various biographies.

[104] Yuasa Mitsutomo, ed., *Gendai kagaku gijutsu shi nempyō* (Tokyo, 1961), pp. 32-35, 58-59.

[105] "Bacteriologist" is a term defined here by the number of Japanese aged 30 or above who obtained doctorates of science in medicine with a bacteriological specialty during the period 1888-1920. Such estimations invariably rest on a judgmental factor. The primary considerations here were: a. attainment of skills sufficient to conduct research—hence the age factor; b. publication of at least one original piece of research in the field; and c. peer certification of competence by designated colleagues at Tokyo or Kyoto Imperial University. Whatever the plausibility of these criteria, the argument rests less on the exact number of bacteriologists than on the general statistical trend. For additional details, see Iseki Kurō, ed., *Dai Nihon hakushi roku*, 5 vols. (Tokyo, 1930); and Bartholomew, "The Japanese Scientific Community."

[106] For details on the sentiment at Tokyo University, see *Kitajima Ta'ichi jiden*, pp. 40-41. Hostilities at the Tokyo Hygiene Institute stemmed from the presence of Dr. Nakahama Toichiro as director. The degree of his hostility is indicated by an article he is believed to have written: "Kitasato Shibasaburō hyōron," *Taiyō*, 6 (March 1902), 26-28.

institutions or for organizations controlled by his allies; but by 1910 this figure had dropped to 43 percent, and on the eve of World War I it declined further to some 41 percent.

An eroding monopoly of skills and loss of political leverage were what made this trend significant. Although most Japanese bacteriologists before 1900 were both loyal to Kitasato and employed in organizations where they were free of conflicting loyalties, their continuing movement into organizations controlled by politically hostile elements thereafter altered the situation. In 1898 Dr. Yokote Chiyanosuke became an assistant professor of bacteriology at Tokyo University. In 1908 Dr. Ishihara Kikutarō left the Tokyo Higher Normal School to assume the same position. And in 1909 Dr. Futaki Kenzō accepted a junior faculty position at the university.[107] But the most politically damaging institutional move for Kitasato was that of Dr. Saizawa Kōzō in 1913 to the faculty of the Army Medical College, which was subject to the authority of Kitasato's long-time critic, Dr. Mori Rintarō, chief of the Medical Affairs Bureau in the Ministry of War. Saizawa's move was damaging because he had an unusual combination of skills. Yokote, Ishihara, and Futaki were all competent researchers, but none of them had a prior connection with Kitasato or the full range of qualifications required to replace him. By contrast, Saizawa, who had spent two years with Kitasato (1907-1909) and two more at Koch's laboratory (1910-1912) was not only trained in research and clinical treatment but was formally qualified to supervise the production of serums and vaccine.[108] Because Ishihara, Futaki, Yokote, and Saizawa were reasonably well trained—and especially because Saizawa occupied a politically vulnerable position—the Ministry of Education, by allying itself with the War Ministry, was able to assemble a pool of talent that was at least formally capable of replacing the Kitasato staff when they resigned to protest the transfer of the Institute of Infectious Diseases in October 1914.[109]

This transfer was primarily the work of the constitutional law expert Ichiki Kitokuro, a professor in the law faculty of Tokyo University (1894-1905) and a career civil servant. Ichiki's dislike of Kitasato was occasioned by his occupancy of several government posts from which he was able to observe Kitasato's political maneuvering. In 1899, while serving as an ex officio member of the Central Hygiene Commission, Ichiki watched Kitasato use the commission to fire a civil servant he

[107] Tōkyō Daigaku Igaku Bu Hyakunen Shi Henshū Iinkai, ed., *Tōkyō Daigaku Igaku Bu hyakunen shi* (Tokyo, 1967), p. 298; and Futaki Kenzō Sensei Kinen Kai, ed., *Futaki Kenzō Sensei* (Tokyo, 1969), p. 308. Futaki became deputy director of the Komagome Hospital, a Tokyo University-affiliated institution.

[108] Iseki, *Dai Nihon hakushi roku*, 2:218-219.

[109] Yamada Hiromichi, *Gun'i to shite no Ōgai Sensei* (Tokyo, 1934), pp. 383-391.

disliked from the post of section chief for insurance, quarantine, and medical affairs. In 1903 and again in 1911, he tolerated helplessly Kitasato's destruction of the bureaucratic reform plans drafted by Okuda Gijin, his predecessor in the office of cabinet bureau chief for legal affairs. And during the period 1908-1911, while serving as vice minister for home affairs, Ichiki became particularly incensed by the growing national power of the "Kitasato faction" and their apparent ability to disrupt what he considered rational bureaucratic administration. Prior to 1911, Ichiki had always cited the vaccine-serum manufacturing program and medical consultation activities of the Institute of Infectious Diseases as arguments for continuing its Home Ministry association. But after watching Kitasato use Seiyukai connections and the press to thwart the Okuda reforms, Ichiki decided a jurisdictional transfer of the laboratory was the only way to bring him under bureaucratic control.[110]

The Laboratory Transfer Controversy and Its Aftermath

The change in the institute's bureaucratic affiliation that Ichiki engineered was a particularly conspicuous example of bureaucratic interference in, or cooption of, science. It was made possible by Ichiki's appointment to the post of education minister in Okuma Shigenobu's Cabinet. It took place because he planned it in secret and got Okuma's belated endorsement. It was motivated by his narrowly conceived, almost fanatical belief in bureaucratic rationality, and it succeeded because Kitasato had lost some of his earlier political leverage. The political victory had at the same time a number of unfavorable consequences for the Ministry of Education. It further antagonized an already hostile Diet. It exposed the ministry to bitter attacks in the press. It aroused politically consequential suspicions. And it seriously damaged the production of serums and smallpox vaccine.

Transferral of the laboratory was never, of course, justified on political grounds but as a means of strengthening science or government. In a talk to the Dōshikai's Government Affairs Study Committee on November 28, 1914, Ichiki claimed that the transfer would save money, rationalize bureaucratic administration, and further the aim of technological and scientific independence. "Because of the present war in Europe," he said, "it has become impossible for us to send students to study in France or Germany. We are drawing up plans to achieve greater scientific autonomy and hope the transfer of the Institute of Infectious

---

[110] Ichiki Sensei Tsuitō Kai, ed., *Ichiki Sensei kaikō roku* (Tokyo, 1954), pp. 117-127. For further discussion of Ichiki's motivations, see "Denken ikan no hishi," *IJ*, No. 1095 (June 19, 1915), pp. 9-10.

Diseases will help us achieve this goal."[111] Prime Minister Okuma, for his part, had already enunciated these views, going so far as to tell *Ikai Jihō* that Kitasato's group would benefit from the transfer because "Tokyo University sets the standard for Japanese scientific research."[112]

Kitasato's reaction, though tardy, was hostile in every respect. He gave Okuma a noncommittal answer on October 6, when the prime minister first informed him of the transfer and asked that he stay as director.[113] But a few days later he told Ichiki he was "incapable of understanding the way a scientist thinks!" as a prelude to resigning his appointment in the Ministry of Home Affairs.[114] In a speech to colleagues he justified his resignation as follows: first, the transfer decision was wrong because it assumed the Institute to have a nonexistent connection with formal scientific education; second, it was wrong because it ran counter to worldwide trends in public health administration; and third, it was wrong because it threatened to "destroy comprehensive research (*sōgō kenkyū*) at the institute."[115] To his mind the Institute of Infectious Diseases was only concerned with combatting epidemic diseases and advising the government about them. Affiliation of the institute with Tokyo University in particular would contradict the foreign tradition of separate institutes for bacteriology; and the university's organizational scheme would impede the laboratory's ever intimate relations between basic and clinical medicine.[116]

The resignation of Kitasato and those of colleagues that followed posed a serious dilemma for the Okuma administration. No one had anticipated mass resignations, and fully trained successors were not immediately available in all cases. In fact, Okuma betrayed some anxiety about this in his *Ikai Jihō* interview: "Scientists and academics who engage in this kind of work are apt to misunderstand simple facts and cling to ridiculous ideas. We must pay no attention to them. . . . It is perfectly apparent to anyone with the slightest scientific knowledge that this transfer has been carried out in a wholly reasonable manner."[117] Ichiki also admitted that the resignations were "causing certain difficulties," and told a Diet committee he did "not care what ministry or bureau qualified

[111] "Bunshō no ikan mondai benkai," *IJ*, No. 1067 (December 5, 1914), p. 18.

[112] "Okuma Shushō no tenkan iken," *IJ*, No. 1063 (November 7, 1914), p. 10.

[113] Kitajima, *Kitajima Ta'ichi jiden*, p. 42.

[114] Miyajima, *Kitasato Shibasaburō den*, p. 83.

[115] *Kitasato Kenkyū Jo nijū go nen shi* (Tokyo, 1939), p. 6.

[116] On the institutionalization of bacteriology outside Japan, see Ben-David, "Roles and Innovations in Medicine," pp. 561-562; and John B. Blake, "Scientific Institutions since the Renaissance: Their Role in Medical Research," *Proceedings of the American Philosophical Society*, 101 (February 1957), 51-53.

[117] "Okuma Shushō no tenkan iken," p. 10.

successors might belong to."[118] Both officials were troubled by the shortage of serum technicians. Kitasato's staff had trained a number of technicians since 1905, but none wanted to work for the Ministry of Education and few held positions from which they could readily be forced to do so. Saizawa Kōzō, in fact, was reluctant to take the assignment, but his position in the military command chain under Mori left him vulnerable to coercion. Under direct orders from Mori, he thus ignored charges of "betrayal" from other Kitasato pupils and offered his services to the Education Ministry and Tokyo University on October 26.[119]

Home Ministry officials were among those offended by the laboratory transfer decision. For one thing, they resented the lack of prior consultation. Okuma had personally assumed the Home Ministry portfolio when he organized his cabinet and he excluded Home Ministry officials from the transfer planning process out of concern for Kitasato's political influence.[120] Such maneuverings naturally raised anxieties about the ministry's role in the government. Vice Minister Shimo'oka Chūji told Okuma the university might destroy the organizational arrangements of the institute after gaining control of its affairs, and similarly expressed concerns about the administration of public health.[121] Okuma in turn rejected Shimo'oka's first reservation but offered a concession on the second. Somewhat under duress, he added provisions to the transfer documents stating that the Ministry of Education accepted a continuing relationship between the Home Ministry and the university-controlled institute, and that the Ministry of Education would further guarantee the right of consultation with the institute in the epidemiological field.[122]

Members of the Diet also criticized the transfer and the apparent motives of its sponsors. Two members of the House of Representatives said the institute's affiliation with Tokyo University would damage its research program.[123] Another said it would increase the cost of public health.[124] And two others lamented Kitasato's possible subjugation to a

[118] TGSIG (Shūgiin Jimukyoku, 1914), vols. 32-35: see "Yosan iinkai giroku sokki dai nana kai," House of Representatives Budget Committee, 7th Session, 35th Diet, 16 December 1914, p. 75.

[119] Yamada, Gun'i to shite no Ōgai Sensei, p. 386.

[120] Fear of Kitasato's political influence in the Home Ministry as a reason for excluding ministry officials from the transfer planning process is strongly implied, though not explicitly stated, in "Denken ikan no hishi," pp. 9-10. Okuma may also have feared the Seiyukai leanings of some Home Ministry officials and Kitasato doubly, because the latter had connections with both.

[121] "Ōtemachi yori Hitotsubashi e," IJ, No. 1060 (October 17, 1914), p. 11.

[122] "Densembyō Kenkyū Jo kangae," TAS, No. 10145 (October 15, 1914), p. 3.

[123] DNTGS, IX. Cf. "Densembyō Kenkyū Jo ikan ni kansuru shitsumon," House of Representatives, 35th Diet, 15 December 1914, p. 961.

[124] Ibid., p. 957.

hostile section of the government. Dr. Wakasugi Kisaburō, a physician who had also graduated from Tokyo University, blamed the entire affair (erroneously) on the supposed machinations of the medical faculty dean, charging improper manipulation of a friendship with Prime Ministry Okuma.[125] Yagi Itsurō from Nara, who was also a physician, said Okuma and Ichiki were completely ignorant of the "peculiarities of scientific research" and had gravely insulted all Japanese scientists by excluding Kitasato from prior consultations.[126] He and Representative Yoshiue Shōichirō of Hokkaidō further charged the Cabinet with inconsistency and a political double cross. One said the Ministry of Education was capricious in its choice of research facilities to annex, while the other contended that the transfer itself was "nothing but a political act."[127]

A Seiyūkai party manifesto denounced the transfer in the *Tōkyō Asahi Shimbun*. The statement argued that Tokyo University and the Institute of Infectious Diseases were incompatible institutions, since the latter was dedicated to research and the former was interested in teaching. The institute would suffer from association with the university because the latter was shot through with cliques, rigidly organized by chairs, and deficient in research output. Moreover, the Ministry of Education's annexations of research laboratories were illogical, inconsistent, and uninformed by foreign experience, while new institutional procedures imposed on the institute by the transfer would cost more than the old and would probably endanger the production of serums and smallpox vaccine.[128] At the instigation of Seiyūkai leaders, the House of Representatives then voted on the transfer and condemned it by a margin of 187 votes against to 171 in favor.[129]

Reactions from physicians and scientists were as compliant as those from politicians were aggressive. Several prefectural medical societies passed resolutions criticizing the transfer, but most medical and scientific professionals either supported it, stifled misgivings in private, or publically feigned indifference.[130] Koganei Yoshikiyo, professor of anatomy at Tokyo University, came out in favor of the transfer, probably because Mori Rintarō was his brother-in-law, and was belatedly joined

[125] Ibid., p. 961.

[126] Ibid., p. 957.

[127] Ibid., p. 962 and *TGSIG*, p. 66.

[128] "Densembyō Kenkyū Jo heigō wa fukanō," *TAS*, No. 10155 (October 25, 1914), p. 3.

[129] "Shūgiin kaisan: Suisan Kōshū Jo Densembyō Kenkyū Jo," *TAS*, No. 10218 (December 27, 1914), p. 2.

[130] Resolutions condemning the laboratory transfer were issued by medical societies in Tokyo and the Kansai region. For details see "Tōkyō kaigyō igakushi kai no ketsugibun happyō," *TIS*, No. 1895 (November 7, 1914), p. 40 and "Densembyō Kenkyū Jo ikan no nariyuki," *TIS*, No. 1896 (November 14, 1914), pp. 42-43.

by Hirota Tsukasa, professor of pediatrics.[131] Ishiguro Tadanori tried to mediate the conflict from his chairmanship of the Central Hygiene Commission but backed off completely when Okuma rebuked him in person.[132] Nagayo Mataró, professor of pathology, was also opposed to the transfer but decided his university position demanded a public show of compliance.[133] But the most revealing response was that of the president of the Great Japan Hygiene Society, Kitasato's original sponsor. Dr. Kanasugi Eigoró began by calling the transfer—in private—the "result of an insidious plot." He then decided to protest to Okuma and organized a medical delegation for the purpose. But once in Okuma's office his reaction changed completely. As he himself later told a meeting of Hygiene Society members, "It was an extraordinary thing for a mere group of physicians to visit His Excellency the Prime Minister and take up his time discussing this matter. The members should understand that we only did this to save appearances. . . . If you are all dissatisfied and want us to visit him again, we will. But we felt overwhelmed to have said as much as we did to His Excellency on this subject."[134]

The Ministry of Education was not, on the other hand, without some rational or legal basis for its action. Agriculture and Commerce administered many programs with industrial applications. Home Affairs controlled some of the country's biomedical research, whereas Communications had a solid foothold in the field of electrical engineering. But Imperial Ordinance 279 gave the Ministry of Education an unusually broad mandate by directing its Bureau of Professional Education to "supervise and encourage all the sciences and the arts."[135] This meant in practice that Home Affairs, Agriculture and Commerce, and Communications concentrated on fields of research with known practical applications, whereas Education had the upper hand in the areas of "basic research." Thus, the Ministry of Home Affairs controlled such facilities as the Tokyo Hygiene Laboratory, the Osaka Hygiene Laboratory, and the Institute of Infectious Diseases. The Ministry of Agriculture and Commerce supervised the Industrial Research Laboratory, the Tokyo Agriculture Experiment Station, the Institute for Animal Husbandry, and the Sericulture Institute. Communications had jurisdiction over the Electro-Technical Laboratory, the Radio-Telegraph Research Station, and the Railways Research Institute; Education had charge of the Misaki

---

[131] Sakai Tanibei, "Genkan ban nikki," in Kumagai Kenji, ed., *Omoide no Aoyama Tanemichi Sensei* (Tokyo, 1959), p. 414.

[132] Kitajima, *Kitajima Ta'ichi jiden*, pp. 51–52.

[133] Nagayo Hakushi Kinen Kai, ed., *Nagayo Mataró den* (Tokyo, 1944), p. 152.

[134] *Kitasato Kenkyū Jo*, p. 14 and "Dai Nihon Shiritsu Eisei Kai dai sanjūni-ji teiki sōkai kyōkō gaikyō," *Dai Nihon Shiritsu Eisei Kai Zasshi*, No. 379, Part 1 (1914), p. 14.

[135] *Shokuinroku*, 1899, p. 482.

Institute for Marine Life Studies, the Seismological Study Commission, and the Mizusawa Latitudinal Observatory.

Yet many anomalies remained, and critics often found them perplexing. Yagi Itsuro demanded to know why the Brewing Institute was located in the Ministry of Finance rather than the Ministry of Education if the unity of bureaucratic administration were so important.[136] The education journal *Kyōiku jiron* contended that the government ought to transfer the Industrial Research Laboratory to the Ministry of Education "if it is really so concerned about cutting expenditures."[137] Yagi also thought that the Education Ministry's commitment to medical research should have given it control over the Beriberi Research Commission.[138] In fact, the ministry's actions were not unvarying models of bureaucratic rationality. In 1903 the Education Ministry denied Hasegawa Tai permission to call his Zaisei Gakusha medical academy a "higher professional school" as authorized by law because of his association with, and support of, Kitasato.[139] It claimed in 1908 that its loss of control over the Beriberi Research Commission to the War Ministry occurred "because the minister missed the cabinet meeting due to illness on that particular day."[140] Throughout the last years of the Meiji period, Education declined jurisdiction over the Finance Ministry's Brewing Institute, saying its particular research program was "not very academic," yet in 1914 it took control of the Fisheries Institute, which had no greater pretensions to scientific research activity.[141]

This case, in fact, sheds light on the Kitasato affair by documenting the ministry's pattern of political aggrandizement. Apart from the way in which the two conflicts were resolved, the major element of difference between the cases was the far greater commitment to research of the Institute of Infectious Diseases. Both laboratories began as private foundations and later became government facilities. The Fisheries Institute had ties to the Fisheries Association like those of the Infectious Diseases Institute to the Great Japan Hygiene Society; and both carried on vocational education and technical research of practical applicability. As in the case of the Institute of Infectious Diseases, the founder of the Fisheries Institute denounced the Ministry of Education for the takeover; moreover, its director resigned and the students went out on strike.[142] Education backed down to the extent of leaving the testing

---

136 *TGSIG*, p. 81.
137 "Aa Densembyō Kenkyū Jo," p. 47.
138 *TGSIG*, p. 81.
139 Shioda Hiroshige, *Mesu to tate* (Tokyo, 1963), p. 76.
140 *TGSIG*, p. 81.
141 Ibid., p. 81; and "Suisan ikan mondai," *KJ*, No. 1065 (November 15, 1914), p. 36.
142 "Suisan ikan mondai to seitō," p. 38.

and research component with the Ministry of Agriculture and Commerce; but the founder denounced the ministry publically in rather harsh words: "The people who are carrying out this transfer are just bureaucrats playing factional games. They claim they are doing it in the name of unifying educational administration, but actually it is just to increase their own personal power."[143]

Similar motivations operated in the transfer of Kitasato's laboratory. The premium on technical independence created by wartime conditions in Europe was simply used as a rationalization after the fact. It could not have been a cause of the transfer because the action was planned from April, whereas the war began only in August.[144] Moreover, Ichiki despised Kitasato and finally admitted this openly.[145] Then there is the curious matter of Ichiki's December 16, 1914, testimony to the House Budget Committee and the contemporary explanation of the transfer of a Home Ministry official who was hostile to Kitasato.

Ichiki made three notable statements when he appeared before the Budget Committee on December 16. First he observed that "private researchers" were incapable of improving the "unsatisfactory state of bacteriological research and vaccine manufacturing in Japan." Then he remarked that a "government laboratory" had to manufacture serum and vaccine because "no private agencies" were doing so. And finally he said changes had taken place at the institute in 1899 when Kitasato became director of this newly established "national laboratory."[146] Juxtaposition of these remarks yields no meaning because the institute *was* a government institution; Kitasato *was* its director; and *only* the institute produced serums and vaccine at the time. But if political motivations are imputed, Ichiki's statements become coherent. Kitasato was supposedly employed by the government but his attitude suggested he was not. The institute was a government laboratory in name but a private laboratory in fact. Kitasato was thus obnoxious because he wielded an inordinate degree of informal power and not because he had violated any formal regulations. Ichiki himself never admitted that the transfer was designed to destroy Kitasato's power, but Izawa Takio, inspector general of the Metropolitan Police in the Ministry of Home Affairs, made exactly this point in his memoirs:

[143] "Suisan ikan mondai to suisan o," p. 37.

[144] "Denken ikan no hishi," pp. 9-10 reports that Ichiki had decided to transfer the Institute of Infectious Diseases to the University and the Education Ministry even before assuming office in April 1914.

[145] Ichiki Sensei Tsuitō Kai, *Ichiki Sensei*, pp. 65-66. Ichiki in his memoirs calls Kitasato "a kind of a politician" and criticizes him for daring to publicize his opposition in the newspapers.

[146] *TGSIG*, pp. 68-69, 73, 75.

[Prior to its transfer to the Ministry of Education], the Institute of Infectious Diseases was a real barrel of rotten apples. It was supposed to be a state institution, but Dr. Kitasato had made it completely his own property. The chief of the Bureau of Public Health, who was supposed to supervise it, could not do anything without consulting him. Everything at the institute was under Kitasato's control. Since things had been this way for over a decade, one would have to say that the bureaucratic system had been disrupted. The government decided to transfer it to the Ministry of Education because its aims were not being realized where it was, under the Ministry of Home Affairs.[147]

The Ministry of Education thus got control of the Infectious Diseases Institute but only at the cost of sustaining other setbacks. Kitasato managed to establish himself in a situation of even greater autonomy. The ministry lost prestige because of the problems of the institute after the transfer. And it failed to gain control of several new laboratories. Sensitivity to or fear of bureaucratic cooptation was an underlying theme in each of these developments. It manifested itself in the founding of new laboratories as an issue of bureaucratic jurisdiction. In the problems of the institute after the transfer, it appeared in a debate over the quality of serum and vaccine manufactured by the new institute staff. And in Kitasato's activities, one sees these sensitivities in his establishment of a private research laboratory, in his acquisition of a serum manufacturing license, and in his efforts to influence government policy through the Diet.

Kitasato's ability to reestablish himself successfully was the first of the Education Ministry's setbacks. He actually began planning a new research laboratory almost as soon as Okuma informed him of the transfer. The new facility, which soon became known as the Kitasato Institute, though somewhat smaller than the Institute of Infectious Diseases, was essentially modeled on it. It was dedicated to research, clinical treatment, and the production of vaccine and serums. But it also incorporated two notable changes, representing at the same time a broadening of mission and a partial narrowing of focus. That is, the Kitasato Institute directed its research not only to bacterial disease but to human and animal diseases in general, while at the same time emphasizing research on all aspects of tuberculosis.[148] In fact, Kitasato's interest in tuberculosis was a major reason for his opposition to the laboratory transfer and his establishment of the Kitasato Institute. Professors in the Faculty of Medicine at Tokyo University had unequivo-

---

[147] Izawa Takio Denki Kensan Iinkai, *Izawa Takio*, p. 109.
[148] *Kitasato Kenkyū Jo*, pp. 25-27.

cably stated their lack of faith in the efficacy of Koch's tuberculin and their disinterest in the prophalactic approach to the disease long advocated by Kitasato.[149] Establishment of his own laboratory was therefore motivated, in a sense, by a desire for untrammeled intellectual autonomy as well as for institutional freedom.

Money was one of the sources of Kitasato's autonomy. From 1893 onward he operated a private sanatorium for wealthy tubercular patients. Known as the Yojo'en, this facility was built on Fukuzawa Yukichi's land with Morimura Ichizaemon's money, but the enterprise was so successful that Kitasato bought them out after only one year in business. Charges by critics that the Yojo'en's treatment of former institute hospital patients constituted a "mixing of public and private interests" prompted secrecy about its operations, but word filtered out and its reputation grew.[150] No figures are available on the extent of its profits, but Kitasato's ability to bear much of the cost of the Kitasato Institute himself is one indication of their magnitude. The new laboratory cost about 400,000 yen to build, and Kitasato personally paid 75 percent of this sum. By contrast, 400,000 yen then represented about 30 percent of Tokyo University's annual budget.[151]

Two of Kitasato's later achievements indicate the importance of politics in his long-term professional success. One was the acquisition of a government license to produce serums and vaccine. The other was the Diet's enactment of legislation governing the prevention of tuberculosis. Kitasato got the serum and vaccine manufacturing license in clear defiance of the Okuma administration because he had friends in the Home Ministry who continued to resent the Ministry of Education. He got the Diet to enact the legislation on tuberculosis because its physician members distrusted Tokyo University and because the Seiyukai party wanted to embarrass Prime Minister Okuma. Just two days after his meeting with Okuma (October 6, 1914), Kitasato sent Kitajima Ta'ichi, his deputy director, to see the chief of the Third Section in the Metropolitan Police Department, which had legal jurisdiction over public health matters in Tokyo. Kitajima requested and obtained the affixation of the inspector general's seal on documents requesting a license and forwarded them to *himself* as Chief of the Epidemics Prevention Section in the Bureau of Public Health! He then presented them to the chief of the bureau and obtained his approval. The bureau chief then returned the

---

[149] Takano, *Kitasato Shibasaburō*, p. 135.

[150] Ibid., pp. 55-57; and "Dōfudegaoka Yōjōen," *TIS*, No. 819 (December 9, 1893), pp. 40-41.

[151] Miyajima, *Kitasato Shibasaburō den*, pp. 92-93, 313; and Sato, *Kokuritsu daigaku*, p. 293.

documents to the Police Department, which issued the license just a few days later.[152]

Kitasato's ability to push tubercular legislation through the Diet shows strength outside the bureaucracy as well as inside it. Because scientists in the medical faculty at Tokyo University were unenthusiastic about his entire approach to tubercular treatment, the Ministry of Education opposed his initiatives. He began a process of direct political action to thwart such opposition, donating money to certain Diet candidates and making speeches for others.[153] Much of his success depended on Sei-yukai support, but certain physician Diet members also played a role. Some of their support reflected agreement with his medical views; but some of it also reflected their opposition to professors in Tokyo University's medical faculty for blocking the formation of a national medical association in which the latter's minority status among all Japanese physicians would dilute their political impact.[154] Through the coming together of such multifarious interests, the Diet in 1918 finally enacted legislation committing Japan to Kitasato's program of sanatoria construction and to certain sanitary improvements in schools, factories, and various public buildings.[155]

Problems with the production of serums and vaccine were nearly as great a blow to the Ministry of Education as the successful establishment of the Kitasato Institute. Because the new staff had much less experience than Kitasato and his colleagues, questions were immediately raised about the value of their product. Some medical authorities claimed the immunizing capability of their serums had declined, thereby causing higher death rates. Others said the ministry was trying to cover up the problem by lowering the price of the Japanese serums while importing American serum. And still others said the institute's serum production program was losing money because of a loss of public confidence.[156]

[152] Kitajima, *Kitajima Ta'ichi jiden*, pp. 49-50.

[153] For details on Kitasato's electioneering activities, see the following articles in *Ikai Jihō*: "Kitasato ontai no shutsuba," *IJ*, No. 1189 (April 7, 1917), p. 661; "Kanasugi Sensei no go-Seiken," *IJ*, No. 1191 (April 21, 1917), p. 752; "Gojin wa danjite shinzezu," *IJ*, No. 1193 (May 5, 1917), p. 848; "Sōsenkyō go no Dai Nihon Ishi Kai," *IJ*, No. 1195 (May 19, 1917), p. 922; and "Denken kaizen mondai ni tsuite," *IJ*, No. 1195 (May 19, 1917), p. 936. There is no truth to Sakai Tanibei's claim that Kitasato gave the Seiyukai 1,000,000 yen during the 1917 campaign (see n. 131, pp. 413-414), but he did provide several thousand yen to Drs. Yagi Itsurō and Tsuchiya Seizaburō. See Kitajima, *Kitajima Ta'ichi jiden*, p. 93 and Miyajima, *Kitasato Shibasaburō den*, pp. 304-308.

[154] "Ikai dantai undō shi," Parts 4, 12, 15 and 16: *IJ*, No. 1200 (June 23, 1917), p. 1152; No. 1211 (September 8, 1917), p. 1608; No. 1215 (October 6, 1917), p. 1757; and No. 1216 (October 13, 1917), p. 1801.

[155] Takano, *Kitasato Shibasaburō*, p. 137.

[156] *Kitasato Kenkyū Jo*, pp. 21-24; *DNTGS*, IX: see "Densembyō Kenkyū Jo seizō no diphtheria kessei ni kansuru shitsumon," House of Representatives, 36th Diet, 2 June 1915

The Ministry of Education tried to blunt the charges by presenting counterclaims. Although the immunization count of the new serums had indeed dropped, the cure rates had gone up. Prices had been lowered but only for the purpose of promoting distribution. The amount of American serums imported was small and only for "experimental purposes," and the loss of income resulted from price cutting, not the refusal of the pubic to buy.[157]

One should consider the possibility of self-interested motives in weighing each of these arguments. For example, the judgment of Education Ministry critics may have been affected by their friendship with Kitasato. Dr. Hida Otoichi, who raised the issue of immunization capability, was a bacteriologist on the staff of the Kitasato Institute, whereas Dr. Tsuchiya Seizaburō, who leveled the charges of higher death rates from disease, had studied with Kitasato in his epidemiological and public health programs.[158] Moreover, the Kitasato Institute had a competing financial interest in serum and vaccine production. Because the new laboratory was a private venture with no government subsidies, and because income from the Yojo'en was not sufficient to meet all operating expenditures, profits from the manufacturing of serums and vaccine were absolutely essential.[159] But the motives and claims of the other side were equally self-serving, if not more so. A 1915 study asserting the efficacy of the serums is suspect because it was carried out under the auspices of the Education Ministry by a professor of pediatrics at another imperial university.[160] Assertions of improved cure rates were backed up only by a single hospital study at a Tokyo University affiliate (Komagome).[161] And the Ministry of Education tried to defend its share

---

(hereafter "Densembyō' Kenkyū Jo"), pp. 1326-1332; and *DNTGS*, X: "Teikoku daigaku tokubetsu kaikei hō chū kaisei hōritsu an," House of Peers, 37th Diet, 1 February 1916, pp. 67-68.

[157] *DNTGS*, X: see "Teikoku daigaku tokubetsu kaikei hō chū kaisei hōritsu an," House of Peers, 36th Diet, 16 December 1915, pp. 306-310; "Densembyō Kenkyū Jo," pp. 1330-1331; and *TGSIG* (Shūgiin Jimukyoku, 1915-1916), vol. 37:2: cf. "Dai-go rui dai-hachi go yosan iinkai kaigiroku dai-ni kai," House of Representatives Budget Committee, 2nd Session, 36th Diet, 21 December 1915, p. 4.

[158] Iseki, *Dai Nihon hakushi roku*, 3:335-336; and Shūgiin, *Gikai seido nanajūnen shi*, 11 (Tokyo, 1962), 318.

[159] Kitajima, *Kitajima Ta'ichi jiden*, pp. 47-48; and Miyajima, *Kitasato Shibasaburō den*, p. 97.

[160] Dr. Ito Sukehiko, the professor in question, was cited as the author of the report by Fukuhara Ryojiro, vice minister of education and acting director of the Institute of Infectious Diseases following the transfer. For details, see *DNTGS*, IX, pp. 1330-1331; and Iseki, *Dai Nihon hakushi roku*, 2:82-83.

[161] Results of the Komagome Hospital study were announced by Matsuura Shinjiro, chief of the Bureau of Professional Education. See *TGSIG*, vol. 37:2 (n. 157 above), p. 4.

of the vaccine and serum market by overly strict inspection of the Kitasato Institute's production.[162]

The preponderance of evidence, in fact, supports the Ministry of Education's critics. Vice Minister Fukuhara Ryojirō denied all allegations of inept performance in serum manufacturing on the floor of the Diet, but he admitted in the privacy of the Budget Committee chamber that the "limited ability" of the new serum technicians—Saizawa Kōzō and his staff—might very well lead to an inferior product.[163] Others favoring the laboratory transfer were also unimpressed. Dr. Yamakawa Kenjirō, a physicist who was then Tokyo University's president, told Education Minister Okuda Gijin in the winter of 1914 that there was "some question whether serum manufacturing could be carried on at the university."[164] Mori Rintarō wrote in his diary of "anxiety" over the professors' total ignorance of the serum manufacturing process.[165] The chief of the Bureau of Professional Education, Matsuura Shinjirō, told the Budget Committee the pre-transfer diphtheria serum had a higher immunization level than the serum produced by the post-transfer staff.[166] And serum production chief Saizawa himself admitted in 1928 that it had been "very difficult" to obtain the required minimal level of 500 immunization units in the first years after the transfer.[167] In view of such evidence, it is not surprising that Vice Minister Fukuhara had pleaded with the Diet in 1914 for a cessation of criticism on the laboratory transfer issue, arguing that rumors about incompetent performance and higher

[162] On October 12, 1915 the government issued Home Ministry Ordinance No. 12 governing the manufacturing of medical substances and their inspection by the state authorities. The medical community criticized the inspection order as an "attempt to suppress private enterprise." See *Kitasato Kenkyū Jo* (n. 115 above), pp. 23-24. The Ministry of Education, in fact, had already given warning of its intentions when Minister Ichiki testified before the Budget Committee of the House of Representatives on December 16, 1914. He noted that the Kitasato Institute's serums and vaccine sales would very likely produce a loss of income for the Institute of Infectious Diseases, and noted that the Ministry of Education would "have to adopt measures to deal with this probable loss of income." For details see *TGSIG*, vols. 32-35 (n. 118 above), p. 83.

[163] On the floor of the Diet, Fukuhara stated: "We sought the opinions of authorities at ten hospitals regarding the [clinical] results obtained from using both the old and new [diphtheria] serum. They agreed that there was no difference." See *DNTGS*, IX, pp. 1330-1331. Six months earlier, in secret testimony before the Budget Committee, however, Fukuhara had said: "We have appointed a new [laboratory] director and technicians since Dr. Kitasato resigned, of course, but they have limited ability and probably will not produce very good serums." For details see *TGSIG*, vols. 32-35 (n. 118 above), p. 77.

[164] Hanami Itsuyuki, *Danshaku Yamakawa Sensei den* (Tokyo, 1939), pp. 275-276.

[165] Yamada, *Gun'i to shite no Ōgai Sensei*, p. 383.

[166] *TGSIG*, vol. 37:2 (n. 157 above), p. 4.

[167] *Tōkyō Teikoku Daigaku gakujutsu taikan: Igakubu, Densembyō Kenkyū Jo, Nōgakubu* (Tokyo, 1942), p. 446.

death rates from disease were "not good for the [reputation of] the Ministry of Education."[168]

The ministry also fared poorly in administrative decisions about various new laboratories. Its share of government research institutions declined only slightly (from 13 of 46 laboratories or 28 percent on the eve of the war to 18 of 67 or 27 percent at the end of 1920), but this is misleading because three of the five new "mission research" laboratories it acquired came to it only because the government decided in contravention of precedent to locate these facilities at imperial universities. Moreover, the ministry's control was minimal at the most important of this group—the Aeronautics Institute—and even this degree of association was opposed by certain Diet members, military officers, and scientists. Thus, Education had to share control with the War Ministry, and the professors in charge went to considerable lengths to secure their professional autonomy. Finally, two other facilities to which the Education Ministry had a strong legal claim were assigned to the administrative control of other government agencies; and in each case suspicions aroused against the ministry by the Kitasato affair were a major part of the reason.

One of these laboratories was the Institute for Aeronautical Research, founded in 1918. The Education Ministry had a strong basis for claiming control of this facility because the new facility was to carry on basic as well as applied research, and because all of the researchers were faculty members at Tokyo University. But the Ministry of War and the Diet's lower house objected on the grounds of the Institute's prior history and the Ministry of Education's ineptness. The War Ministry argued with some justification that the facility was primarily an outgrowth of the former Ad Hoc Committee on the Military Uses of Balloons, and that much of its research would have military applications.[169] Dr. Tsuchiya Seizaburō, who had earlier challenged Education's administration of serum and vaccine production, saw the principal issues as intellectual freedom and bureaucratic incompetence. In his opinion, the University was not sufficiently oriented toward research, and the research it did do was overly circumscribed by academic divisions. Moreover, the Ministry of Education had proven a lack of respect for science by its treatment of Kitasato and its mishandling of serum and vaccine production.[170] How influential his views were is not entirely clear, but they seem to have affected the resolution of the issue. The Ministry of Education had to share supervision with the War Ministry, while university president Ya-

[168] DNTGS, IX, p. 1329.

[169] Nakamura Seiji, Tanakadate Aikitsu Sensei (Tokyo, 1943), pp. 182-183.

[170] TGSIG (Shūgiin Jimukyoku, 1918), vol. 40:1: see "Tōkyō Teikoku Daigaku oyobi Kyōto Teikoku Daigaku rinji seifu shishutsu kin kuriiri ni kansuru hōritsu an hoka ikken," House of Representatives Budget Committee, 40th Diet, 8 February 1918, p. 32.

makawa Kenjirō took steps to maximize the freedom of the Aeronautics Institute. By attaching it to the university rather than to the ministry directly, as officials there wanted, he was able to avert the possibility of a future administrative transfer; and by divorcing its accounts from the university's general fund, he was able to prevent any sudden diversion of resources. The Ministry of Education did get the right to name the director, but the president and the physicists who ran the institute had to give their assent first.[171]

Factors that obstructed the ministry's control of the Aeronautics Institute similarly influenced disposition of the National Institute for Nutrition. As in the former case, Education had a claim because the mission of the Nutrition Institute was defined as a combination of basic and applied research. But similarities ended there because the government in 1920 was taking over an existing laboratory rather than creating a wholly new one. The factors that appear to have decided the outcome were the background and wishes of the founder, the views of university professors, the attitudes of the Finance Ministry and of certain members of the Diet. The Institute for Nutrition had originally been founded in 1914 by the bacteriologist Saiki Nori, a graduate of Yale University and former staff researcher at the Institute of Infectious Diseases.[172] Saiki, who was interested in the chemical composition of foods, their digestibility, and their role in disease prevention, favored an affiliation with the Home Ministry because of its public health activities and his own ties to Kitasato. Seemingly because Tokyo University professors were disinterested in the field, the Ministry of Education did not actively pursue control of the Nutrition Institute, but the Ministry of Finance favored such a tie-up as a means of saving money.[173] However, an earlier critic of the Education Ministry helped prevent this from occurring. Like Tsuchiya in the Aeronautics Institute case, Dr. Yagi Itsurō argued that Tokyo University was structurally too rigid for cross-disciplinary research, and cited Koch's departure from Berlin—the precedent for Kitasato—as proof of the point. If Education ever hoped for a foothold in nutrition studies, the possibility ended with an exchange between the vice minister of finance and Yagi in the House Budget Committee. The vice minister declared his appreciation for Yagi's analysis and said the government would "consider his views carefully" in its disposition of the issue.[174]

Education's greatest setback related to the Institute for Physics and

[171] Hanami, *Danshaku Yamakawa Sensei den*, pp. 318-319.

[172] Iseki, *Dai Nihon hakushi roku*, 2:161-162.

[173] *TGSIG*, vol. 41:2: see "Kokuritsu Eiyō Kenkyū Jo setsuritsu ni kansuru kengi an iinkai giroku (sokki) dai-go kai," House of Representatives Budget Committee, 5th Session, 40th Diet, 7 March 1919, pp. 17-18.

[174] Ibid., p. 18.

Chemistry. This failure was especially serious because the opposition to its aims was broadly based and because the stakes were very high. The Institute for Physics and Chemistry was the most important and the most prestigious scientific research establishment built in Japan prior to 1945. It carried on applied research for the business community and the armed forces as well as basic research at the behest of academic scientists. Japan's wartime atomic bomb project was partly based at the institute, and its first two Nobel laureates in physics were partly trained there.[175] The institute was built largely because of circumstances relating to the outbreak of World War I. The Allied nations imposed a naval blockade against Germany. Japan lost the major source of its pharmaceuticals, dyestuffs, and industrial chemicals. Leading Japanese industrialists and scientists persuaded the government of the need for technical self-sufficiency and proposed an institute for physical and chemical research as a means to that end. After a series of meetings convened by Prime Minister Okuma and attended by officials, scientists, and industrialists, the decision was made to establish such a laboratory through private gifts and government subsidies.[176]

Bureaucratic jurisdiction came sharply into focus when the subsidy proposal reached the Diet because of the government's clear departure from bureaucratic precedent. Basic research was stipulated as the principal objective of the Institute for Physics and Chemistry, yet control was assigned to the Ministry of Agriculture and Commerce. Several officials tried to explain the contradiction by citing applied research for industry as the facility's principal goal. But this was not convincing because the government's own documents said otherwise, and because Education Ministry officials attended the hearings.[177] Minister of Education Takata Sanae claimed that Agriculture and Commerce had been given control because the institute's industrial backers were accustomed to dealing with that particular agency, whereas Professional Education

[175] For details on Japan's wartime atomic bomb project, see Deborah Shapley, "Nuclear Weapons History: Japan's Wartime Bomb Projects Revealed," *Science*, 199:4325 (13 January 1978), 152-157; and Charles Weiner, "Japan's Nuclear Bomb Project," *Science*, 199:4330 (17 February 1978), 728. The direct importance of the Institute for Physics and Chemistry in the training of Tomonaga Shin'ichirō (Nobel Laureate 1965) and indirect importance in the work of Yukawa Hideki (Nobel Laureate 1949) is indicated by Kaneseki Yoshinori, "The Elementary Particle Theory Group," in Nakayama Shigeru, David L. Swain, and Yagi Eri, eds., *Science and Society in Modern Japan* (Cambridge: MIT Press, 1974), pp. 234-239.

[176] Itakura Kiyonobu and Yagi Eri, "The Japanese Research System and the Establishment of the Institute of Physical and Chemical Research," ibid., pp. 187-189.

[177] *TGSIG* (Shūgiin Jimukyoku, 1916), vol. 37:1: see "Rikagaku o kenkyū suru kōeki hōjin o kokuhō hojō ni kansuru hōritsu an iinkai giroku (sokki) dai-ni kai," House of Representatives Budget Committee, 2nd Session, 37th Diet, 21 February 1916, pp. 3, 7-8.

Bureau Chief Matsuura Shinjirō cited "inadequate facilities for large-scale research in physics and chemistry in the imperial universities" as a factor in the bureaucratic affiliation of the institute.[178]

Admissions like this and a rash of contradictions made the situation more embarrassing for the Ministry of Education. Political Councilor Otsu Jun'ichirō conceded that the ministry "should have done more on behalf of physics and chemistry."[179] Education Minister Takata said the Education Ministry "should have been put in control from the outset."[180] And Minister of Education-to-be Okada Ryōhei, Ichiki Kitokurō's brother, denounced the Agriculture and Commerce tie-up as a "disruption of bureaucratic procedure" and a "violation of the law."[181] Sensitivities aroused by Kitasato's laboratory transfer were an underlying theme in the entire parliamentary discussion. Citing this precedent, one Diet member wanted to know what role Education saw for itself regarding the Institute for Physics and Chemistry.[182] Another cited Kitasato's having been "driven" to establish an independent laboratory as proof of Education's failure to encourage scientific research.[183] A third said the Ministry's "take-over" of the Infectious Diseases Institute showed bureaucratic control, rather than science promotion, to be its fundamental, underlying concern.[184] And Agriculture and Commerce Minister Kōno Hironaka told the press the major reason for the Agriculture-Commerce tie-up was a fear that Education "might take over this laboratory the way it did the Institute of Infectious Diseases."[185]

SUMMARY AND CONCLUSIONS

Kitasato's career implies several conclusions about the problem of science and the Japanese state. It casts doubt on the claim that competitive group interaction was necessarily incompatible with the establishment of institutional freedom. Kitasato used factional ties and politics with extraordinary and impressive success. He formed a potent coalition to defeat the Education Ministry's laboratory proposal to the Diet in 1893. He used factional ties to secure and to enhance the work of the Institute

---

[178] Ibid., p. 8; and *TGSIG* (Shūgiin Jimukyoku, 1916), vol. 37:1: see "Rikagaku o kenkyū suru kōeki hōjin o kokuhō hojō ni kansuru hōritsu an iinkai giroku (sokki) dai-san kai," (hereafter "Rikagaku"), House of Representatives Budget Committee, 3rd Session, 37th Diet, 22 February 1916, p. 18.

[179] "Rikagaku," 22 February 1916, p. 20.

[180] Ibid., 21 February 1916, p. 8.

[181] "Dakyō an kaketsu," *TAS*, No. 10644 (26 February 1916), p. 3.

[182] "Rikagaku," 22 February 1916, p. 20.

[183] Ibid., 21 February 1916, p. 7.

[184] Ibid., 22 February 1916, p. 22.

[185] "Rikagaku kaketsu," *TAS*, No. 10641 (February 23, 1916), p. 3.

of Infectious Diseases for more than twenty years. And he used the same factional ties to reassert his autonomy following the 1914 bureaucratic and political debacle. Needless to say, concerted efforts were made to contain the power of his particular interest group through the processes of bureaucratic cooptation. His laboratory received subsidy payments for several years before its nationalization. It enjoyed a ten-year monopoly over the manufacturing of serums and vaccine. The terms of his appointment as director implied the possibility of a state veto over the direction of the laboratory's research. And both the institute and its directorship were legally authorized mechanisms for the implementation of public health policy. However, the bureaucratization thesis falls short of a fully accurate description in two significant respects. It treats the bureaucracy as a monolith, rather than an aggregation of competitive fiefdoms. And it describes as "private interests" social entities with ambiguous activities and images.

Several facts seem pertinent to these two particular issues. First, Kitasato did *not* after 1899 represent a "private interest" in any sense other than moral. He was a government employee. His laboratory was owned by the state. And his duties were specified by law. Second, the Japan Hygiene Society, which supported his work before the laboratory nationalization of 1899, though a private entity under the law, was deeply involved with the state. It materially assisted the state's epidemic control efforts. It helped certify doctors for practice. And it helped to maintain public health standards throughout the country.[186] Third, cooptation was not directed at Kitasato by the bureaucracy in general but by two of its ministries in particular. What Home Affairs possessed, Education could envy, and what Education could acquire, Home Affairs might covet. Precisely because two ministries were involved, Kitasato could always balance the pretensions of the one against the claims of the other in a way that enhanced both his personal aspirations and his scientific or professional goals.

Other scientists, however, may not have resisted or manipulated bureaucratic power in the same effective manner. Ishiguro Tadanori and Kanasugi Eigorō retreated in the face of rebukes from Okuma. Pathologist Nagayo Matarō elected to stifle his discontents. Hirota Tsukasa actually supported the laboratory transfer, and anatomy professor Koganei Yoshikiyo gave his support out of concern for family loyalty. Moreover, these five men represented what was institutionally the strongest tradition in the Japanese scientific world. Japanese medical science, though not a conceptual outgrowth of its Tokugawa predecessor, was substantially indebted to Sino-Tokugawa medicine at an institu-

---

[186] Nagayo Sensai, *Shōkō shishi*, 1 (Tokyo, 1902), 38-39, 42.

tional or socio-psychological level. Tokugawa and modern medicine were broadly popular and widely diffused in society. Both were viewed as having practical benefits. Both enjoyed private and public patronage. Both allowed practitioners to earn a living through medical practice. And both were relatively autonomous.[187] In short, the Japanese medical tradition embodied the kind of professional or para-professional elements that would seemingly have facilitated attainment of institutional and political autonomy.

Physical and other scientific or protoscientific traditions, by contrast, were somewhat weaker in various institutional respects. Their status had been impaired before the Restoration by lingering suspicions about Christianity. Schools offering instruction in sciences other than medicine were a late Tokugawa development, coming only in the 1850s on any notable scale. These fields were heavily dependent on the state for such support as they happened to receive. Many of their practitioners were considered government officials. Few Japanese made a living *before* the Restoration based on competence in nonmedical sciences. And their traditions embodied few elements of professionalism in an institutionally meaningful sense.[188] To suppose, therefore, that scientists in fields other than medicine might have effectively challenged the government on a significant intellectual or professional issue in the Meiji period requires a leap of faith for which the institutional history of nonbiomedical science provides relatively little justification.

Nevertheless, some Japanese scientists in fields other than medicine *did* achieve autonomy beyond that of most university professors. Yamakawa Kenjirō, Professor of Physics at Tokyo University, was able to secure financial autonomy for the Aeronautics Institute because of his position as university president.[189] Ikeda Kikunae, professor of chemistry at the same institution, achieved an unusual degree of autonomy through his intellectual labors. In 1908 he discovered and patented a technique for producing glutamine acid salt by hydrolyzing protein, from which developed the food seasoning product called "Aji-no-moto" in Japan and "Accent" in the United States.[190] In much the same manner, Honda Kotarō, professor of physics at Tohoku University, built a quasi-independent laboratory, the Institute for Metals Research, at his home institution on the strength of contributions from the Sumitomo industrial family. Thanks to his development of the structurally superior K-S steel, Honda was so secure in his academic bailiwick that he could

---

[187] Nakayama, "Japanese Scientific Thought," pp. 742-743.

[188] Bartholomew, "The Japanese Scientific Community."

[189] Hanami, *Danshaku Yamakawa Sensei den*, pp. 318-319.

[190] *Tōkyō Teikoku Daigaku gakujutsu taikan: Rigakubu, Tōkyō Tenmon Dai, Jishin Kenkyū Jo* (Tokyo, 1942), pp. 129, 131.

willfully ignore Education Ministry officials or even steel company executives as circumstances might prompt him to do so.[191]

At the same time, physics, chemistry, and other fields shared, or were in a position to benefit from two structural conditions favoring institutional autonomy in general. One was the lingering presence of tensions and antigovernment resentments derived from the period of the Restoration. Fukuzawa Yukichi displayed some of these resentments. Hasegawa Tai was clearly influenced by them. And the Diet as a whole was a hotbed of antigovernment sensibilities. There is no reason whatever to suppose that sciences other than medicine were unable to win support from figures like Fukuzawa, Hasegawa, or various members of the Diet. In fact, both Fukuzawa and Hasegawa declared their interest in all major sciences, not simply microbiology or medicine.[192] Second, all—or nearly all—the principal sciences could have benefited, and did benefit, from competitive tensions within the bureaucracy. Depending on the particular subspecialty, physics could be an area of concern not only to the Ministry of Education but to the Ministry of Agriculture and Commerce, the War Ministry, the Navy Ministry, and the Ministry of Communications. Similarly, chemistry became a focus of interest in Agriculture and Commerce, War, Navy, Communications, Education, Finance, and Home Affairs. Thus, a physicist seeking support for aerodynamic research (as Yamakawa and other Tokyo University physicists did) might attract support not only from the parent Education Ministry but from the War Ministry or the Ministry of Agriculture and Commerce. In the same fashion, a chemist seeking support in the pharmaceutical field might consider affiliation with Education, Home Affairs, or the Agriculture and Commerce Ministry.

These observations raise the question of whether Japanese science *is* truly anomalous. The rhetoric of Western science and its Japanese reverberations imply an affirmative answer, but the preponderance of empirical evidence does not. Most Western scientists have historically shunned political involvements. They have often considered science's rational truths so intellectually compelling that ignorance and political

---

[191] Ishikawa Teijirō, *Honda Kōtarō den* (Tokyo, 1964), pp. 113-119.

[192] Among the most revealing indicators of Fukuzawa's view is his declared interest in supporting five to ten "good scientists" out of his own funds "if that would allow them full time for research." For details, see Ishikawa Mikiaki, *Fukuzawa Yūkichi den*, 4 (Tokyo, 1932), 3-4, 10. Hasegawa's views, though less straightforward, were in general very favorable to the needs of scientific research from a broad institutional perspective. Despite his well-deserved reputation as an educational penny pincher, he strenuously defended an expensive 1892 plan to establish a second imperial university (in the Kansai region) on the grounds that researchers at Tokyo Imperial University needed the competition. For details, see *Kyōtō Teikoku Daigaku shi* (Kyoto, 1943), pp. 9-10. See also the penetrating analysis of Terasaki Masao, "Teikoku daigaku keisei," pp. 246-249.

authoritarianism must inevitably disappear. René Descartes argued this point in the seventeenth century. Baron D'Alembert took up the same view in the eighteenth century. Herbert Spencer claimed the same in the nineteenth century. And Bertrand Russell articulated the identical position in the twentieth century. However, the considerable growth of science throughout the world during the past four hundred years has not been accompanied by—let alone caused—a diminution of ignorance, bigotry, or totalitarianism. If anything, these forces may have actually increased their hold on human intellects and institutions. Moreover, as we now know too well from the recent work of scholars such as Joseph Haberer and Alan Beyerchen, scientists themselves have largely been absent from the ranks of freedom's defenders.[193] Although Galileo opposed the Inquisition in the seventeenth century and Sakharov the Soviet regime in the twentieth, Max Planck remained silent against the Nazis in the 1930s and 1940s, and Robert Oppenheimer enjoyed the open support of few scientific defenders in the 1950s. In the opinion of Warren O. Hagstrom, a sociologist of science, science is an enterprise with a strong tradition of rhetorical freedom but very weak institutional freedom; scientists are loyal to scientific truths in the narrow sense, but scarcely at all to the scientific community—let alone the general society—in any broader, active sense.[194] If many Japanese scientists thus remained silent in the face of state bureaucratic power, it seems impossible to determine clearly whether one should ascribe their behavior to their socialization as Japanese or to their enculturation in the Western scientific tradition.

[193] Haberer, *Politics and the Community of Science*; and Alan D. Beyerchen, *Scientists under Hitler.* (New Haven: Yale University Press, 1977).
[194] *The Scientific Community* (New York: Basic Books, 1965), pp. 146, 265, 282.

THE TRANSFORMATION OF THE JAPANESE LABOR MARKET, 1894-1937

RON NAPIER

Economic growth, especially rapid growth of modern sectors of the economy, can drastically alter the balance of supply and demand in various economic markets and lead to a reshuffling of the distribution of income among the various classes that make up a society. The alteration of economic power of a class leads to conflict with the defenders of the status quo as the rising classes attempt to obtain the full benefits of their new position. The transformation of the Japanese labor market around 1917 is a vivid example of economic development changing the fundamental rules of the game and giving the average Japanese worker, for the first time, a significant increase in real income and the ability to choose the form of his economic relationships in the society. The order of classes was not overturned, but the status of the Japanese worker after 1917 was far different from that of his earlier counterpart.

The new status of the worker manifested itself in many ways. Labor's share of the national income increased, leading not only to increased consumption but to changing patterns of consumption; workers asserted their new-found freedom by engaging in job mobility, tenant disputes, strikes, and greater political activity (universal manhood suffrage was instituted in 1925).

The magnitude of the change is not to be underestimated. During the years after 1917, labor's real agricultural wage rose about 40 percent in real terms from pre-1917 levels. The share of national income that went to unskilled labor, which had been declining since the late nineteenth century, sharply rose. At the same time, the structure of the economy also shifted increasingly toward modern forms of organization that combined employed labor and capital, and away from older forms that used self-employed or family labor and little capital. Japan's modern industrial structure was just beginning at this time.

The purpose of this paper is twofold: first, I wish to document the changes that occurred in the labor market from 1917 on and contrast them with the conditions in the earlier years; second, I wish to bring the evidence developed in this paper to bear on the twenty-year-old controversy between classical and neoclassical interpretations over the theoretical nature of the labor market.

This paper will be organized into sections covering the theoretical dispute, testing the hypotheses involved in those theories, examining other forms of evidence concerning changing labor market relations, and finally discussing the implications of the findings of this paper on early twentieth-century Japan in general and on the interpretation of prewar Japanese economic development in particular.

THE THEORETICAL CONTROVERSY

The Japanese unskilled worker and peasant farmer have generally been viewed as powerless pawns in the prewar development of the Japanese economy. Their incomes were set at a subsistence level, and the riots, strikes, and tenant disputes of the period have been viewed as evidence of the frustration and impotence of workers who had been pushed to the limit. The huge numbers of workers in the unskilled urban labor market and in the landless classes in agriculture led to vicious competition among workers, which reduced wages and labor's share to the benefit of landlords and employers. In this view Japan was the embodiment of W. Arthur Lewis's theory of labor surplus development.[1] The beauty of the labor surplus interpretation lies in the resulting portrayal of Japanese economic development. In this interpretation, low-wage labor passively aids development by holding down costs, enhancing profits, and thus speeding capital accumulation and growth. If Japan did not have surplus labor by nature in 1917, then the interpretation of the succeeding years will naturally be more complex, and other factors will have to take over the role of labor surplus in the writing of Japanese economic history. And, further, labor must then be viewed as a constraint on economic growth.

The opposing interpretation, supported by the findings of this paper, suggests that the Japanese labor market, by 1917, had passed into a

---

[1] Arthur W. Lewis, "Economic Development with Unlimited Supplies of Labor" in A. N. Agarwala and S. P. Singh, eds., *Economics of Underdevelopment* (New York: Oxford University Press, 1963).

competitive stage in which wages were not set by subsistence levels. Further, opportunity and choice for workers definitely exceeded the negligible levels suggested by labor surplus theory. The results of analysis based on econometric analysis of the bulge in real wages from 1917 to 1927 and further evidence drawn from such diverse sources as strikes, mobility, land rents, tenant disputes, farm debt, and evolving tenant-landlord relationships are all used to support the competitive labor market interpretation of Japanese economic development. Certain key findings lead to the conclusion that the labor surplus theory interpretation cannot be justified.

The labor surplus theory states that, in a labor surplus economy, economic growth is greatly facilitated by providing large numbers of willing but powerless workers to growing industries at an unchanging and low wage.[2] In a labor surplus economy, it is clear that the balance of power belongs to the owners of the scarce capital and land resources—the entrepreneurs and landlords—and not to the owners of abundant labor resources, the workers. The lack of power results in low income and a lack of alternatives.

However, a close look at the economic relations among the classes reveals a marked change in their tenor around 1917. At that time, formerly powerless unskilled workers, both in urban and rural areas, were able to assert themselves and obtain a significant increase in both income and the ability to choose. I maintain that although strikes, tenancy disputes, and the like are sources of economic power, the fundamental cause of rising real wages and opportunity was the tightening of labor markets due to the special external conditions of that period that converted the unskilled labor of Japan from a poor and powerless group into a relatively well-off and powerful group at the expense of other classes. Thus, the marketplace with its combination of random, cyclical, and long-term events can alter the status quo and give economic power even to the most disadvantaged groups within a society. The strikes, disputes, and other phenomena are evidence of the underlying shift in economic power and not its cause.

W. Arthur Lewis's two-sector model of economic development (modern and traditional or industry and agriculture), hypothesizes the modern sector facing a flat supply curve of unskilled labor from the traditional sector. The supply curve of labor is flat because there are so many workers that labor has no power to raise wages. The wage level (often called the institutional wage) is determined by the cost of subsistence. Labor surplus implies that so much labor is applied to existing land and capital that the marginal productivity of labor in the traditional

[2] Ibid.

sector is quite low—near zero—and definitely below subsistence. Labor can thus be drawn out of the traditional sector into the modern sector with little effect on either the wage or output level of the traditional sector. This low wage level encourages industrialization and capital formation.

The labor surplus economy ends when a sufficient number of workers have been drawn out of the traditional sector that the marginal productivity of labor in the traditional sector exceeds the subsistence wage level. The modern sector must thereafter pay higher wages in order to bid workers out of the traditional sector. The supply curve of labor to the modern sector is now said to be rising and competitive wage determination takes over. The transfer of labor out of the traditional sector is no longer costless; output declines as labor input falls. When marginal productivity in the traditional sector surpasses the subsistence level, the supply curve is no longer flat but rising, and we say that the turning point has been reached.

The turning point is an important event in economic development. Before reaching the turning point, the economy develops with virtually no labor constraint. After reaching the turning point, however, the excess pools of labor have dried up; labor becomes a constraint and rising wage rates directly affect growth.

In the standard book on the application of labor surplus theory to Japan, Minami Ryōshin compares calculations of marginal productivity with wages.[3] He demonstrates that Japanese agricultural wages exceeded productivity measures until 1959, thus placing all of prewar Japanese development and fourteen years of postwar Japanese development under the aegis of labor surplus theory.

o

The labor surplus interpretation has been challenged from its inception. The main point of contention was the bulge in real and nominal wages (including agricultural wages) in the years 1917-1927. During this bulge, real agricultural wages rose 30 to 40 percent above earlier levels, and stayed high until 1927, after which they fell (see Table 1). Agricultural farm laborers are the epitome of all unskilled workers. In a labor surplus economy, unskilled workers are paid more than their marginal productivity, but their wages are not supposed to change rapidly, if at all. The sustained increase in the real wages of these unskilled workers is of enormous interest in understanding the underlying nature of the labor market.

Defenders of the neoclassical (competitive) and classical (labor sur-

---

[3] Ryōshin Minami, *The Turning Point in Economic Development* (Tokyo, 1972).

TABLE 1. INDEX OF REAL AGRICULTURAL WAGES FOR MALE ANNUAL CONTRACT
WORKERS (1914-1916 = 1.000)

Year	Wage	Year	Wage	Year	Wage
1905	0.845	1916	1.036	1927	1.427
1906	0.911	1917	1.009	1928	1.261
1907	0.891	1918	1.021	1929	1.372
1908	0.985	1919	1.191	1930	1.308
1909	0.935	1920	1.129	1931	1.222
1910	1.011	1921	1.270	1932	1.092
1911ᵃ	1.031	1922	1.294	1933	1.077
1912	1.121	1923	1.327	1934	1.102
1913	1.052	1924	1.334	1935	1.117
1914	0.959	1925	1.340	1936	1.144
1915	1.005	1926	1.406	1937	1.245

plus) interpretations of the Japanese labor market have lined up on opposing sides concerning the nature of the bulge. The supporters of the
labor surplus interpretation of Japanese development generally deny the
importance of this eleven-year bulge and, instead, resort to arguments
such as wage rigidity or cyclical aberrations to justify the interpretation
that Japan experienced labor surplus development well into the postwar
period. On the other hand, the neoclassical or competitive position in-
terprets this long-lasting bulge as evidence that the labor surplus stage
of Japanese development ended with World War I.[4] The bulge forms
the central battleground for theorists of numerous labor market and
economic phenomena of the period.

In the labor surplus interpretation, the wage bulge is deemed to be a
"cyclical increase" or an example of "wage rigidity." For example,
Minami has suggested that "these increases were merely a cyclical increase, resulting from the upswing in economic activity during World
War I."[5] Ohkawa Kazushi earlier expressed a similar position:

> During this period [the World War I boom], a shortage of the labor
> supply was felt temporarily; a shift in the labor force from agriculture
> to the rest of the economy was accelerated; and money wages tended
> to rise. The real wage rates thus showed a rise later on due to the
> downward rigidity, as commodity prices turned to fall after the end
> of the war. The turning point, around 1917, suggested by Fei-Ranis,
> in my view, seems to be derived from these swing phenomena. . . .
> The real difficulty, therefore, lies in the task of distinguishing the

[4] See J.C.H. Fei and G. Ranis, *Development of the Labor Surplus Economy* (Homewood,
Ill.: R. D. Irwin, 1964), or Kōji Taira, *Economic Development and the Labor Market in Japan*
(New York: Columbia University Press, 1970).

[5] Minami, *The Turning Point in Economic Development*, p. 263.

trend phenomena from the swing phenomena. We have to refer to the trend phenomena, meaning thereby the lasting structural changes which transcend the swing phenomena.[6]

There are many problems with the explanation of a "cyclical" or temporary rise in wages. First, the cyclical increase is attributed to conditions in World War I. The Japanese economy slumped severely in 1920, as extraordinary war-related export demand collapsed at that time. Wages continued to be high in real terms until 1927, considerably after the war.

The decline in real wages from 1927 on is seen by the supporters of labor surplus as the vindication of their position. Wage rigidity is blamed for the delay of falling wages from 1920 to 1927. Minami elaborates on wage rigidity and the long duration of the bulge by stating simply that "it seems to be difficult to acknowledge the downward rigidity in nominal wages in the labor surplus economy. In my opinion, however, the rigidity is not inconsistent with the hypothesis of unlimited supplies of labor."[7]

It should be noted that the labor and wage rates being considered here are those of unskilled agricultural workers. These workers are the lowest common denominator in a society like that of prewar Japan, and they form the most numerous single occupation. Wage rigidity is not an explanation when applied to unskilled workers in a largely agricultural economy.[8] Wage rigidity would require an explanation itself and, certainly, one could not automatically accept a wage rigidity lasting eight years as a part of the standard labor surplus theory. The subsequent rise of real agricultural wages in the 1930s is another problem facing the labor surplus interpretation.

In support of his labor surplus thesis of Japanese development through the late 1950s, Minami has leaned heavily on estimates of the elasticity of output with respect to labor input.[9] Taking these estimates and mul-

---

[6] Kazushi Ohkawa, *Differential Structure and Agriculture: Essays on Dualistic Growth* (Tokyo, 1972), p. 128.

[7] Ryōshin Minami, "The Supply of Farm Labor and the Turning Point in the Japanese Economy," in Kazushi Ohkawa, Bruce F. Johnston, and Hiromitsu Kaneda, *Agriculture and Economic Growth: Japan's Experience* (Princeton: Princeton University Press, 1970). p. 277.

[8] A small minority of Japanese workers belonged to either industrial or tenant unions.

[9] Minami uses 0.244 as the output elasticity of labor. This figure was obtained from cross-sectional studies of production functions of rice for 1937-1939 and other grain crops for 1940-1941 (together amounting to about 65 percent of the total value of agricultural output) done by Ohkawa Kazushi. A study by Shintani for the 1890s resulted in a 0.215 elasticity estimate. Agricultural wages averaged 70 percent of average labor productivity. In addition, rent levels paid by tenant farmers averaged about 45 percent of total output. It should be remembered that fifteen million agricultural workers were crowded onto an

tiplying them by the average output per worker, one obtains the estimated marginal revenue product of labor, which is consistently below the wage rates actually paid in agriculture.[10] This is Minami's main piece of evidence.

It should be noted that the values of the elasticity of output, with respect to labor, are taken from one study for the 1890s and another for the late 1930s. Other estimates for the output-labor elasticity are somewhat higher than the ones Minami uses, but they still do not raise calculated marginal productivity to the wage levels paid to agricultural workers.[11] Although these results are strong evidence in favor of Minami's interpretation of labor surplus development of the Japanese economy, the evidence that can be amassed on the competitive side is much larger and more persuasive.

The competitive labor market interpretation originates with the work of J.C.H. Fei and Gustav Ranis.[12] They base their conclusion on very few pieces of evidence. Fei and Ranis point to the dramatic and sustained rise of nominal and real unskilled wages during World War I and the 1920s as evidence that Japan had already made the transition from the labor surplus economy. Fei and Ranis proposed a 1916-1919 timing of the turning point from surplus labor to marginal productivity wage determination. They state that "we have convincing evidence that Japan's unlimited supply of labor condition came to an end at just about that time [end of World War I]. . . . The virtual constancy before and rapid rise of the real wage after approximately 1918 is rather startling. We thus have rather conclusive evidence in corroboration of our theoretical framework."[13]

Koji Taira takes a different tack in supporting the competitive interpretation of Japanese labor markets in the prewar period: "I feel that there has never been a Lewisian period in the history of modern Japan. In the first place, the degree of commercialization that characterized pre-Meiji agriculture already suggests a sensitive marginalist calculus on the part of the peasant household, unlike the subsistence sector in the Lewisian economy."[14]

Agriculture had been increasingly commercialized during the Tokugawa and Meiji eras. Farmers increasingly responded to outside profit

---

arable area one-sixth the size of California. Minami, *The Turning Point in Economic Development*, pp. 170-185.

[10] Ibid., p. 200.

[11] Yujiro Hayami et al., *A Century of Agricultural Growth in Japan* (Minneapolis: University of Minnesota Press, 1975).

[12] See Fei and Ranis, *Development of the Labor Surplus Economy*.

[13] Ibid., pp. 263-264.

[14] Taira, *Economic Development*, p. 69.

incentives, as vividly shown by the rapid increases in sericulture from the Meiji period on. T. C. Smith writes about "labor shortages" even in the Tokugawa period.[15] This high level of commercialization of agriculture is inconsistent with the labor surplus view of communal sharing of output implicit in subsistence-level wage determination. To investigate further the effects of commercialization of agriculture (meaning the growing of crops for cash sales rather than for consumption) and of profit orientation on the behavior of both agricultural workers and landlords, one should investigate the implications of a true labor surplus wage determination process.

On the demand side, why should a landlord pay an agricultural worker more than he was worth, that is, his marginal productivity or contribution to output? One can understand the sharing of output among family workers, but the Meiji landlord attained his position only by generating savings that allowed him to acquire land from families forced to sell. Landlords were eager to raise rents, to charge high interest rates on loans, to foreclose on land when loans were defaulted, and to engage in entrepreneurial activities in commerce and industry. Why would the landlord then turn around and consistently pay workers more than their output was worth? If he did so, this would imply that the more workers he hired, the less the landlord's income would be.

Conversely, on the supply side under the labor surplus system, who would not want to become a hired worker? A family with its own land would on average be better off if it hired out its family members rather than have them work on the family farm, since wages, according to Minami, were significantly greater than marginal productivity. The tenant farmer generally crowded his family on a small plot of rented land and tried to make ends meet. Tenant farmers, including tenants who owned some land, made up over half of the agricultural population and about one-quarter of Japan's population. Clearly, the marginal productivity observation for all of agriculture must hold particularly for these small farmholds. Thus, one would expect under the labor surplus framework that wage labor would be more lucrative than tenant farming. However, all the evidence points to tenancy as the preferred occupation to landless agricultural wage workers. We can see from the viewpoints of both the landlords and workers that the labor surplus system, when confronted with competitive market forces, is put under strain. The combination of the profit orientation of landlords and the lack of a queue to become a wage worker weakens the labor surplus theory's validity in Japan.

[15] T. C. Smith, *The Agrarian Origins of Modern Japan* (Stanford: Stanford University Press, 1959).

It is necessary to go one step further and analyze the wage bulge to see if it can be explained. In the process of modeling the wage determination process in Japan, it became apparent that wages were directly related to a number of economic forces and were not set by the subsistence level combined with wage rigidity. The evidence to be revealed by econometric analysis strongly supports the competitive interpretation of labor markets. Further, the analysis reveals striking changes in the dimensions of choice and purchasing power of unskilled workers. The substantial shift in the balance of economic power toward unskilled labor resulted in an across-the-board response in the forms of tenant disputes, industrial strikes, and voluntary mobility from job to job, and from one occupation to another. Those who suffered a loss of power resisted. Employers practiced lockouts, published blacklists of workers who quit in search of higher wages, and promised not to pirate labor from each other. Landlords resisted demands for lower rents, while the government instituted programs to stockpile rice and to increase rice imports from Korea and Taiwan, both Japanese colonies, in order to lower the nominal wage level. The government also delayed implementation of factory labor laws and continued to harass labor-related press and political party activities. It is clear that what is at stake here is not merely the correct theoretical interpretation of the nature and role of the labor market, but also the larger question of the resulting flux in income shares among competing groups within society and the conflicts that arose as a consequence. The tenant income determination model presented below and the analysis of the forces behind it support the competitive labor market interpretation and reveals the shifting distribution of income within the society and the dimensions of conflict involved in arriving at a distribution of income more favorable to labor.

A Tenant Income Determination Model

In this section, a model of tenant income determination will be developed to explain the rise and subsequent fall of real wages of unskilled agricultural workers in the period 1917-1927. Tenants were more numerous than wage workers in agriculture, and their incomes were determined by the same forces, since they were both at the bottom of the Japanese economic ladder. The analysis reveals that the changing distribution of income was exactly the opposite of that predicted by the labor surplus theory. These findings will be linked to patterns of industrial strikes, tenant disputes, mobility, and other trends to substantiate both the increase in economic power and conflict at this time.

First, the close relationship between agricultural wages and tenant incomes is shown. Next, the determinants of the net prices received by tenants are examined, as they are the most important determinants of tenant incomes. This analysis reveals, in succession, the reasons for the sustained rise and the ultimate decline of real wages during the bulge period.

The income of a tenant farmer depends on his physical output of crops, the prices he receives for his crops, the rent and taxes paid, and the costs of necessary farm inputs, such as seeds, fertilizers, tools, and so on. In a labor surplus economy with an agricultural labor force consisting of only landlords and paid workers (no tenants), higher agricultural prices would not necessarily lead to higher real wages. Especially if land ownership is stable and if there is little mobility between landowner status and other labor statuses, agricultural workers' wages should be determined by the subsistence level. Price increases can only affect agricultural real wages if there is mobility between the categories of the agricultural labor force that directly receive revenues from the sale of output (and thus are directly affected by price changes), and landless agricultural workers. If there exists a tenancy system, the combined characteristics of nonpermanent attachment to the land and direct access to the effects of price changes are present. The tenant farmer is like a landlord in that an increase in the price of a crop will benefit him. The tenant farmer's income directly affects the wages paid to agricultural wage labor, since the two groups are good substitutes for each other. Thus, in the tenant farmer we have a way of translating price increases in the product market (that is, crop prices) into wage increases in the labor market.

There are three qualifications in the workings of this mechanism of transforming higher agricultural prices and concomitant increased cash flows into higher real wages for agricultural workers. First, the effects of increased prices on the value added of tenant farmers should not be offset by increased land rents. Labor surplus theory would suggest raising land rents as the method to hold down the real incomes of tenants should prices rise. Second, the increase in tenants' nominal incomes should be in excess of the rise of prices, otherwise real incomes would not rise. Third, tenancy must be an alternative occupational status for unskilled workers; that is, labor mobility must exist in and out of the tenancy occupational category.

If the above conditions are met, the incomes of tenant farmers, real and nominal, become the alternative wage or opportunity cost of unskilled workers throughout the economy. In addition, an increase in crop prices could increase the real incomes of both tenants and landless workers. The relation is somewhat indirect, as agricultural prices affect tenant incomes, which then, in turn, influence agricultural wages.

To sum up, the model presented here focuses on the effects of price changes in the agricultural product market (crop prices) on wages in the agricultural labor market. Prices affect tenants' disposable incomes so long as rents do not absorb the increase, a critical measure of the balance of power between landlords and tenants. Mobility between tenancy and other unskilled occupations creates the link between tenants' incomes and unskilled wages. Thus, if demand forces in the product markets are strong enough, real tenants' incomes and unskilled wages will rise, an outcome inconsistent with labor surplus models.

We now digress to a technical discussion of model specification and estimation. Agricultural incomes and value added per capita are affected by the prices and quantities of both inputs and outputs. In Japan, from 1894 to 1937, the secular trends of output and labor input were basically smooth and with very low annual rates of change, especially when compared to price changes. Thus, price changes provide the source of the bulk of year-to-year variations in agricultural incomes.

The net effects of agricultural input and output prices on farmers' incomes are often represented by a standard index formulation—the output price index divided by the material input price index. This formulation is not a good indicator of nominal or real agricultural incomes. What is needed is an index keyed to income or value added, and not just prices. For example, if prices of both outputs and inputs were to double, *ceteris parabis*, a tenant's income would also double, but the standard formulation would be unchanged.

Instead of the standard index formulation, I used a "value-added" price index. The value-added price index is derived by dividing nominal value added (total sales minus all material costs; equal to the return on capital, land and labor) by real (constant price) value added.[16] Nominal value-added is calculated in current prices, while real value added is obtained as the residual of current output and input quantities at a selected period's prices. The value-added price index represents the net effect of changes of output and input prices on nominal value added and incomes. If output and input prices double, *ceteris parabis*, this index will also double, as will nominal income.

This index can also be converted into a real or purchasing power index by further deflation by consumer price indices. Thus, the effects

---

[16] The value-added price index (VAP) is:

$$\text{VAP(t)} = \frac{\Sigma_i(P_{it}q_{it} - C_{it}M_{it})}{\Sigma_i(P_{i34\text{-}36}q_{it} - C_{i34\text{-}36}M_{it})}$$

Where the subscript t is time, i is the crop, and *34-36* refers to 1934-1936 base year prices. The symbol p is crop output price, q is physical output, c is material input prices, and m is material input quantity.

of input, output, and consumption prices can all be compressed into a single index.

In this paper, nominal wages for male annual contract workers in agriculture are taken as representative of unskilled wages. Their wages should be closely related to tenant farmers' incomes, which, in turn, are determined mainly by net prices received by farmers (the value added price index) and the proportion of output that is paid to landlords as rent. In addition, a lagged value-added price variable was also used to account in both workers' and employers' perceptions and to take into account the fact that these contracts were negotiated annually. The wage determination equation was estimated for the 1903-1937 period due to a lack of rent data for earlier years. The results are as follows:

$$\text{WAGES} = 11.01 + \underset{(7.34)}{11.628 * \text{VAP}} + \underset{(10.98)}{18.596 * \text{VAP}(-t)} - \underset{(-2.77)}{19.288 * \text{RENT/Q}}$$

$$R^2 = 0.967$$

Where "VAP" is the value added price index, "VAP$(-t)$" is the lagged value-added price index (4/7 weight to the previous year's price, 2/7 to that of two years prior, 1/7 for that of three years prior), and "RENT/Q" is the average rent levels for paddy fields divided by agricultural output per unit area. The figures underneath the coefficients in parentheses are t-statistics.

Wages are well explained by movements of the value-added price index and movements in rent proportions. The very fact that agricultural wages can be modeled on such indirectly related items as land rents and agricultural output prices seriously weakens the possibility that these wages were determined by subsistence levels. Wages showed sensitivity to land rent levels; as land rents fell for tenant farmers, the wages of landless workers rose. It is clear that agricultural worker wages were closely related to tenant farmer incomes, which were, in turn, affected by the net prices received and rent levels paid. Figure 1 displays the pattern of wages and the value-added price index (1914-1916 = 1.00). The relationship between the two is dramatic; before World War I, the wage series shows the same cyclical movements as the price series, and the two series climbed sharply together from 1917 on and fell together in the late 1920s only to rise again in the mid-1930s. There is no need to resort to "cyclical" explanations or to "wage rigidity" in order to justify the bulge in wage levels. Wages were determined by tenants' incomes. Thus, if we can explain agricultural prices and land rents, we will have explained the forces behind tenants' incomes, wage levels, and the wage bulge.

Since prices have been isolated as the leading influence on tenants' incomes and are also well correlated with wages, we now turn our attention to explaining the price level. Market price determination equations have supply and demand equations implicit within them. Supply is mainly influenced by past output prices as well as food imports. Demand depends on income levels of consumers and inventory levels of agricultural commodities. The annual movements of the VAP (value-added price) index are well described by a model incorporating lagged prices VAP($-$t), lagged food imports per capita in physical units Qm ($-$t), nominal urban disposable income per capita Yd, and levels of agricultural inventories in physical units I: The results are presented below and in Figure 2, along with the actual VAP index.

$$VAP = 0.2062 - 0.000607 \star I + 0.004013 \star Yd - 0.000901 \star Qm(-t)$$
$$(3.58) \quad\;\; (-2.53) \quad\quad\quad (4.88) \quad\quad\quad\;\; (-3.40)$$

$$+0.4603 \star VAP(-t)$$
$$(4.68)$$

$$R^2 = 0.907$$

The figures in parentheses are t-statistics. The period of estimation is 1894 to 1937.

FIGURE 1. Price and Wages in Agriculture

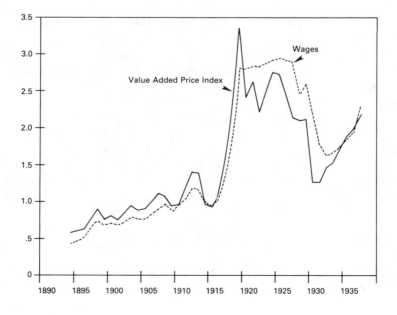

FIGURE 2. Results of Estimation

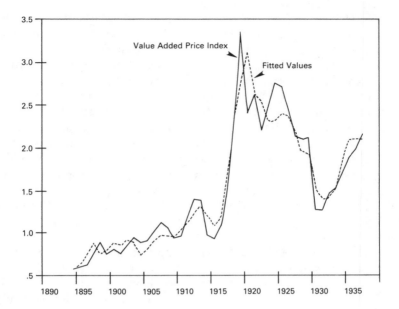

The estimated equation is pretty much as one would expect. The coefficients and t-statistics say that larger inventories tended to depress prices, that higher urban income (including profits, rent and interest income, as well as wages) raised demand and therefore prices for agricultural products, and that farmers responded to higher prices for food by increasing output.

At a deeper level than the value and signs of coefficients of explanatory variables, one must relate the patterns of the underlying forces to the pattern of the variable we wish to explain. The "VAP" index shows the same bulge that wages showed. How do the underlying forces explain the rise, sustained high level, and subsequent decline in this net price measure? The rise in value-added prices around 1917 can be ascribed to two basic forces. The war boom vastly inflated urban purchasing power, which sharply increased demand for agricultural products, causing a rise in prices. In addition, agricultural harvests, which had benefited from exceptional growing weather from 1914 to 1916, returned to normal or less than normal levels for most of the 1917-1926 period.[17] This event depleted inventories and raised prices. Even sharply higher rice imports from the colonies from the early 1920s on had little

[17] Ron Napier, "Prometheus Absorbed: The Industrialization of the Japanese Economy, 1905-1937," Ph.D. dissertation, Harvard, 1979, pp. 37-74.

effect. The sharp deflation and depression that struck the industrial sector from 1920 on lowered agricultural prices from the high 1919 level (see Figure 2), but failed to return prices to pre-World War I levels, precisely because of depleted inventories due to a string of modest harvests. Thus, we have explained the rise and sustained high level of agricultural prices through the mid-1920s. The decline in prices, starting in 1927 and beginning in earnest in 1929, is due to the collapse of the low inventory underpinning of high prices due to a string of consecutive good harvests from 1927 to 1931[18] which, in combination with higher imports caused the sharp fall in prices. Thus external events, namely, the World War I boom and poor harvests, raised prices from 1917 to 1919. The end of the World War I-related boom caused the sharp decrease in prices after 1920, but continued poor harvests maintained prices at significantly higher levels than had prevailed before the war. The string of good harvests from 1927 on forced prices down nearly to prewar levels as, finally, all unusual conditions in the marketplace disappeared.

The story thus far explains the bulge in prices, but tells us little about an increase in economic power and income of tenant farmers and other agricultural workers. Outside factors, such as war booms and weather, seem mostly responsible for the favorable prices. Higher prices certainly increased the total income of agriculture, but this increase does not by itself guarantee that tenant farmers or agricultural wage labor would receive more. Labor surplus theory, in particular, would predict that due to the overwhelming numbers of workers present and the fact that wages already exceeded marginal productivity, increases in prices would be absorbed by landlords in the form of increased rents. This is a reflection of the premise in labor surplus theory that land and capital are the scarce resources that command high returns, whereas labor is abundant and receives little. Thus, the determination of whether labor benefitted from the price bulge modeled above depends critically on the pattern of land rents during this period. If the Japanese labor markets from 1917 on are labor surplus, most of the gains from higher prices would go to the landlords. If labor has a strong economic position, then the incomes of tenant farmers and, in turn, wage workers should have benefited from the higher prices.

Rents for rice paddy fields (in *koku* of rice per *tan* of land where a *koku* is 4.96 bushels and a *tan* is 0.247 acres) are presented in Table 2. Paddy rents increased slowly in absolute terms until 1920 and then declined. Thus, we have direct evidence that rents did not impair the higher

---

[18] G. C. Allen, *A Short Economic History of Modern Japan*, rev. ed. (London, 1962), p. 115.

incomes tenant farmers received due to higher prices. In fact, labor's position after 1920 was strong enough to reduce rents, so that falling rents actually contributed to the incomes of tenant farmers. Landlords were not only unable to siphon off the increased income flowing into agriculture, they actually were forced to cut rents due to labor's stronger position. The labor surplus position fails this vital test of strength, and one must conclude that the Japanese labor market was competitive by this time. It is clear that not only was the labor market competitive but labor realized their new-found bargaining power. This resulted in the high level of tenant disputes of this period, with tenants seeking lower land rents.

A closer look at rents shows that not only did rents fall absolutely from 1920 on, rents fell relatively to output per unit of land area throughout the 1905-1937 period for which we have information on wages.[19] Agricultural output grew 1.64 percent per year from 1892 to 1902, 2.29 percent from 1902 to 1915, 1.33 percent from 1915 to 1931 and 0.79 percent from 1931 to 1938. Area under cultivation increased at an average annual rate of 0.32 percent for paddy fields and 0.67 percent for nonpaddy fields over the period. Paddy rents increased 0.77 percent per year from 1905-1909 to 1915-1919, and then declined 0.48 percent per year from 1915-1919 to 1935-1937 (and fell 0.87 percent per year from 1920-1924 to 1930-1934). Further, nonpaddy rents declined as a proportion of paddy rents, reinforcing the pattern of increasing tenant incomes due to rent reductions.

The combination of war-boom-related demand and poor harvests raised prices of agricultural goods in the 1917-1927 period, causing the celebrated wage bulge of debates on Japanese economic history. On the face

TABLE 2. PADDY RENTS IN *Koku* OF RICE PER *Tan* OF AREA AND NONPADDY RENTS AS A PROPORTION OF THE CASH VALUE OF PADDY RENTS

Period	Paddy Rents	Nonpaddy Rents
1905-1909	0.966	0.406
1910-1914	0.984	0.385
1915-1919	1.043	0.335
1920-1924	1.041	0.292
1925-1929	0.971	0.353
1930-1934	0.954	0.394
1935-1937	0.952	0.282

SOURCE: Umemura Mataji, *Nōringyō*, in Ohkawa Kazushi, Shinohara Miyohei, and Umemura Mataji, eds., *Chōki Keizai Tōkei*, 9:220-221.

NOTE: A *koku* is 4.96 bushels, a *tan* is 0.247 acres.

[19] Umemura Mataji, *Nōringyō*, in Ohkawa Kazushi, Shinohara Miyohei and Umemura Mataji, eds., *Chōki keizai tōkei* 9 (Tokyo, 1966), 220-221.

of it, labor did not cause the wage bulge through direct action. Rather, labor made sure that it benefited from the price hike by forcing a decrease in land rents. The ability to demand reduced rent obligations during a boom period (and thereafter) clearly demonstrates labor's power and forces the conclusion that the Japanese labor market for unskilled workers from 1917 on must have been competitive in nature and not labor surplus. Labor, by this time, had the power to increase its share of income and to translate this power into a wide variety of altered conditions to be discussed below. Labor from 1917 on was a force to be reckoned with, as later patterns of conflict will attest.

OTHER EVIDENCE

An event as important as the increase of the power of labor in its dealings with landlords and business must surface in more ways than in an analysis of the wage bulge and land rent patterns. In this section, we will examine tenant disputes, farmer savings, mobility, and industrial strike activity in the light of our earlier findings.

Tenancy disputes support the findings of increased labor power. The timing and incidence of tenancy disputes suggests that the behavior of tenant farmers from 1917 on was different from earlier behavior. Disputes increased dramatically in the 1917-1931 period over earlier years. According to Ann Waswo, these disputes were not caused by high rent levels or impoverishment.[20] Instead, disputes occurred mainly in areas adjacent to industrial centers with relatively few in exclusively rural areas. The pattern is consistent and unmistakable. Tenants used their new-found power, especially in urban areas where there were more job opportunities. Lower rents resulted from tenants' demands. The trend to lower rents did not end with the war-induced industrial boom, but continued throughout the twenties and early thirties.

Ann Waswo describes the situation of the tenant farmer as follows:

Industrialization and, in particular, the rapid spurt of economic growth caused by World War I affected tenant farmers in several ways. First, the increase in urban job opportunities reduced competition for land among tenants. Where population pressure on the land was high, a landlord could always find land-poor farmers willing to cultivate his fields on almost any terms; if dissatisfied tenants demanded rent reductions, they could be speedily replaced. Where, on the other hand, part of the local population migrated to cities, population on the land

[20] Ann Waswo, "The Origins of Tenant Unrest" in Bernard S. Silberman and H. D. Harootunian, eds., *Japan in Crisis* (Princeton: Princeton University Press, 1974).

declined and tenants could demand lower rents with less fear of reprisal.

Reports from Saitama prefecture (near Tokyo), for example, noted that, "many people abandoned farming recently because of the growth of secondary employment and a great increase in wage. As a result, there is a surplus of arable land, and tenant farmers have become emboldened."[21]

Waswo typifies the tenant disputes of 1917-1931 as numerous, generally close to urban centers, and instigated by tenants seeking lower land rents. The effect of nearby urban employment is thus apparent. The continued strength of tenant disputes beyond the end of the war-boom years suggests that the phenomena of disputes and rent decreases were not merely a temporary change but part of a deeper change in the fundamental position of labor. It is interesting to note that in the 1930s the nature and place of tenancy disputes changed once again. This time, they were in largely rural areas and were instigated by landlords seeking to discharge tenants so that they could farm the land themselves because agricultural prices had fallen so low.

Another indication of change comes from surveys of farm households. The average household farmed only 2½ acres of land. The farmer had expenses year-round, whereas he only sold his crops once or twice a year. Farmers often resorted to borrowing at very high interest rates to tide them over until harvest time. Often farm households were forced to carry debts from year to year. A survey of average indebtedness of tenant and landowner farms from 1921 to 1927 reveals that outstanding debt was steadily reduced from 1921 onward, resulting in net savings for the landowner sample in 1924 and for tenant farmers in 1925.[22] It should be noted that despite the end of the war boom, the financial position of farmers improved from 1921 on. The net asset position of farmers was short-lived, as both groups subsequently became net debtors as agricultural prices fell. The significance of the improved finances of farmers in the first half of the twenties is the obvious correlation it shows with the tenant income determination model and land rent patterns discussed earlier. Tenant farmers benefited to the extent that they were able to eliminate their debt. This event not only substantiates the competitive over the labor surplus interpretation, but also illustrates the changes in relative status of tenant farmers, reflecting their increased status.

Turning to the urban labor market, we will see the same patterns as

[21] Ibid., pp. 382-383.
[22] Kozo Yamamura, "The Japanese Economy, 1911-1930: Concentration, Conflicts and Crises," ibid., p. 306.

TABLE 3. TENANT AND LAND OWNER HOUSEHOLD BUDGETS, 1921-1927 (in yen)

	Owners		
	Income	Expenses	Debt
1921	1,138	1,184	469
1922	912	1,156	242
1923	1,058	1,140	63
1924	1,358	1,392	− 114
1925	1,396	1,530	204
1926	1,174	1,383	605
1927	1,095	1,320	545
	Tenants		
	Income	Expenses	Debt
1921	597	642	190
1922	529	715	170
1923	682	727	60
1924	724	821	38
1925	965	890	− 28
1926	707	928	387
1927	711	885	426

SOURCES: Kozo Yamamura, "The Japanese Economy, 1911-1930: Concentration, Conflicts, and Crises," in Bernard S. Silberman and H. D. Harootunian, *Japan in Crisis* (Princeton University Press, 1974), p. 306.

NOTE: Income is net of production costs, debt is the outstanding balance, negative means net savings.

those exhibited in tenant disputes and savings. A look at strike activity, labor mobility, and consumption reaffirms the changing status of labor within the Japanese economy.

Strike activity was generally at low levels in the Meiji era. Surveys of strikes date back only to 1897.[23] According to this data, in only one year before 1917 did the number of workers involved exceed 10,000 (see Table 4). The World War I boom in Japan brought with it hyperinflation, rapid increases in manufacturing output, and consequent heavy demands for factory labor. Striking workers rose from 8,413 in 1916 to 57,309 in 1917. The end of the war boom in Japanese manufacturing in 1920 resulted in a decline in strike activity and shifted the grievances from demands for wage hikes during the war boom to protests over wage cuts and discharges.

Although the number of striking workers declined after World War I, they remained far more numerous than in the pre-1917 period throughout the 1920s. Worker strike participation rose again in the 1929-

[23] Rōdō Undō Shiryō Iinkai, *Nihon rōdō undō shiryō*, 10 (Tokyo, 1962), 192-207.

TABLE 4. THE NUMBER OF STRIKERS AND MAN-DAYS LOST TO STRIKES, 1897-1937

Year	Strikers	Year	Strikers	Year	Strikers
1897	3,510	1905	5,013	1913	5,242
1898	6,293	1906	2,037	1914	7,904
1899	4,834	1907	11,483	1915	7,852
1900	2,316	1908	823	1916	8,413
1901	1,948	1909	310	1917	57,309
1902	1,849	1910	2,934	1918	6,645
1903	1,359	1911	2,100	1919	63,137
1904	897	1912	5,736	1920	36,371

Year	Strikers	Man-Days Lost	Year	Strikers	Man-days Lost
1921	58,225	1,173,177	1930	64,933	1,085,074
1922	41,503	447,016	1931	54,515	980,054
1923	36,259	421,873	1932	46,025	618,614
1924	48,940	613,144	1933	35,880	384,565
1925	32,472	295,027	1934	42,149	446,176
1926	63,644	698,071	1935	31,853	301,324
1927	43,669	1,177,352	1936	26,772	162,590
1928	36,872	583,595	1937	53,429	353,407
1929	60,084	571,860			

SOURCE: Rōdō Undō Shiryō Iinkai, *Nihon Rōdō Undō Shiryō* (Tokyo, 1962), 10:440-505.

1931 recession. The main causes of strikes in the 1929-1931 period were very similar to those in the 1920-1922 downturn—defensive strikes to protest lower wages and discharges. Despite growing employment in the urban sector in the mid-1930s, strike activity was low, indicating the state of the political climate as well as depressed agricultural conditions.

Data on total worker days lost to strikes are available from 1921 on. Only four years in the 1921-1937 period registered in the neighborhood of a million worker-days lost. These years were 1921, when wages fell and workers were laid off due to the end of the war boom; 1927, when the bitter Noda strike started;[24] and 1930-1931, when labor market conditions were similar to the depressed conditions of 1920-1922. To this list we can probably add 1917-1920, due to the large number of striking workers and the Yawata steel mill strike of 1920.

Strike activity can be demarcated into two periods, before and after

[24] George O. Totten, "Japanese Industrial Relations at the Crossroads: The Great Noda Strike of 1927-28" in Silberman and Harootunian, eds., *Japan in Crisis*.

1917. Before 1917, strike activity was minimal, but after 1917, strike activity remained at relatively high levels through a variety of weak and strong labor markets. The political climate also was changing at this time, and this could also help explain the increased willingness to strike. Strike activity supports the hypothesis of a substantial and permanent alteration of the nature of the labor market around 1917. Workers in both urban and rural areas sensed their changing status at this time and, despite higher real incomes, engaged in tenant disputes and strikes with a much greater frequency than before.

Voluntary job mobility can be seen as a measure of economic opportunity. We can see from Table 5 that the agricultural labor force declined in the 1895-1925 period and was roughly stable thereafter despite substantial growth in population. Clearly, many workers migrated out of agriculture into nonagricultural occupations. Since the level of migration actually reduced the agricultural labor force, some element of the migration must have been voluntary. The extent of migration in Japan is revealed by a 1930 survey, which showed that 49 percent of all male manufacturing workers in Japan were employed outside the prefecture of their birth.[25] In Tokyo, this percentage reached 71 percent, whereas for Osaka it was 69 percent.

Job mobility is also demonstrated by separation rates in manufacturing, which were quite high in the period under study. A high separation rate, especially if separation is voluntary, indicates that workers were aware both of other job opportunities and that by changing jobs one could better one's position. Unfortunately, information on voluntary separation (as opposed to layoffs or firings) is very spotty. The information available is summarized in Table 6. The evidence shows that voluntary quits as a proportion of total unemployment was higher in

TABLE 5. AGRICULTURAL AND NON-AGRICULTURAL LABOR FORCE IN THOUSANDS OF WORKERS, 1895-1935

Year	Agriculture	% Ag.	Non-Agriculture	% Non-Ag.
1895	15482	65	8242	35
1906	15821	63	9161	37
1910	15830	62	9645	38
1915	15075	57	11230	43
1920	13855	51	13405	49
1925	13540	48	14565	52
1930	14084	48	15535	52
1935	13871	44	17340	56

SOURCE: Mataji Umemura, "Sangyō Betsu Koyō no Hendō 1880-1940," in *Keizai Kenkyū*, 24 (April 1973), 107-116.

NOTE: Agriculture is the labor force engaged in agriculture and forestry.

[25] Naikaku Tōkeikyoku, *Rōdō chingin jitchi chōsa* (Tokyo, 1930), pp. 66-73.

the relatively good years of 1924 and 1925 than in the recession year of 1932. It would appear that workers realized their ability to find new and presumably better employment, and exercised this ability rationally in accordance with economic conditions.

Another dimension of the effects of increased worker compensation and economic power is apparent in consumption or lifestyle trends. Japan experienced a "roaring twenties" of its own, albeit mild in comparison to that of the West. Among the observations about this period:

> for the less affluent there were dance halls, whose taxi-dancers provided a cheaper, if untraditional, alternative [to geisha]. Restaurants flourished. And the Japanese became, as they have remained ever since, inveterate travellers. So much so, wrote a British resident, that it came to a pitch where, especially on Sundays and holidays, it was easier to find room in a third-class railway carriage than in the superior classes.[26]

By the end of World War I, further changes had emerged. Standards of living had risen; workers drank beer and soft drinks; and weekly magazines, movie houses, bars, restaurants, and other manifestations of popular culture had appeared. . . . This was the age of the *mobo* and *moga* (*modan boi* and *modan garu*), who strolled on the Ginza or the main thoroughfares of Osaka, boys who wore Harold Lloyd glasses and girls who drank, smoked, and read literature. These were the years of the permanent wave, the bathing suit, the bare-legged chorus line, the dance hall and the cabaret.[27]

TABLE 6. REASONS FOR JOB SEPARATION, 1924-1932 (percentage composition)

	1924	Tokyo 1925	Salary 1925	Labor 1932	Factory 1932	Day 1932
Voluntary quits	38	33	30	17	7	30
Layoffs	19	43	51	65	83	54
Firings	2	0	0	3	0	0
Disaster	0	2	1	0	0	0
Injury, sickness	10	15	12	11	3	9
Military service	2	1	0	1	0	2
Other	31	6	5	3	7	5

SOURCE: Rōdō Undō Shiryō Iinkai, *Nihon Rōdō Undō Shiryō* (Tokyo, 1962), 10:192-207.

NOTE: Salary means salaried workers, labor is production workers, factory is factory workers, day is day laborers, intel is "intelligentsia."

[26] W. G. Beasley, *Modern History of Japan*, 2nd ed. (New York: Praeger Publishers, 1975), p. 219.

[27] John K. Fairbank, Edwin O. Reischauer, and Albert Craig, *East Asia: The Modern Transformation* (Boston: Houghton-Mifflin, 1964), p. 522.

CONCLUSION

In this chapter, a wide variety of evidence, combined with the results of a test of agricultural wage and income levels, leads to the conclusion that labor in the years after 1917 experienced an improvement in its economic position vis-à-vis other classes in Japan. The improved position of labor is demonstrated not only by higher standards of living but also by the patterns of action ranging from job mobility to tenant disputes and strikes. In particular, the landlords of Japan failed the test of their power from 1920 on, when they were forced to cut land rents of tenant farmers (by far the largest occupational group in the country) at a time when total agricultural income was rising. Thus, tenants and other unskilled workers were able to benefit greatly from market conditions that inflated the income of the agricultural sector. The bulge from 1917 to 1927 in agricultural wages and tenant incomes was due to favorable agricultural prices, which, in turn, were due to a complex pattern of wartime boom conditions and the influence of the weather on the size of the harvest and inventory levels.

The results of the study also strongly support the competitive interpretation of the Japanese labor market from 1917 on. The labor surplus model, although appealing, simply rests on too weak a foundation to stand against the wide variety of evidence and test results that support the competitive interpretation. W. Arthur Lewis perhaps foresaw the type of situation that occurred in Japan when he stated that "the most interesting of these possibilities [early end to the labor surplus stage] is that the terms of trade may move against the capitalistic [nonagricultural] sector . . . [capitalistic sector] expansion increases the demand for food in terms of capitalistic products, and so reduces profit. This is one of the senses in which industrialization is dependent upon agricultural improvement."[28]

In a sense, agricultural prices rose because supply capability was inadequate to handle either urban boom conditions or the setbacks of a few poor harvest years. But we have also shown that it was the tenant farmers and wage workers who benefited more than the landlords. The wage and price bulge was much more than a simple change in the terms of trade; it was a thorough alteration of labor market conditions.

The reinterpretation of the Japanese labor market as competitive and of the unskilled worker as a new focus of economic power naturally changes the underlying explanations of Japanese economic history of the period. For example, the relative rigidity of Japanese price levels after World War I, when compared internationally,[29] is clearly due to high

[28] Lewis, "Economic Development with Unlimited Supplies of Labor," p. 432.
[29] Allen, *Short Economic History*, p. 101.

agricultural price levels and concomitant high wages. The success of Japanese exports in the midst of the Great Depression can be partly attributed to lower costs due to lower wages for unskilled labor from 1927 on, before the start of the Depression. A further study of the relation of industrial and agricultural wages shows strong correlations with the more labor-intensive manufacturing industries (which accounted for most of manufacturing employment), thus enlarging the applicability of the tests used in this paper.[30]

The rise of unskilled labor affected the profits of both landlords and capitalists, partly explaining the relatively slow rate of capital accumulation during the bulge period.[31] The changing balance of power within the economy, which led to strikes and tenant disputes, was due to workers attempting to actualize their new position. The overall interpretation of Japanese economic history must take into account that unskilled labor was not passive but was a restraint on growth, as are all scarce resources. Thus, labor did not simply lubricate the growth process but, instead, was an active participant that sought to better itself, as all other groups also did.

This paper has sought to demonstrate that labor underwent a vigorous expansion of both its income and relative position within the economy. The wage bulge of 1917 to 1927 was a fascinating interlude in Japanese economic history that adds greatly to our understanding of the process of growth. Labor played a vital role in the economic development of the country. The results of this paper cast that role in a somewhat different light. Labor used its enhanced position to increase its own share of national income in the 1917-1927 period, resulting in conflict and change in the economy and society. Labor cannot be viewed as passive and powerless but, instead, as an aggressive and scarce factor in Japanese development.

[30] Ron Napier, "Prometheus Absorbed," pp. 113-148.
[31] Ibid., pp. 234-256.

IN SEARCH OF EQUITY:
JAPANESE TENANT UNIONS
IN THE 1920s

ANN WASWO

That the Japanese bureaucracy sought to extend its control to the very
lowest reaches of rural society and to prevent the emergence among the
rural population of organizations based on social class is beyond doubt.
That these goals were easily achieved is another matter entirely.

From its inception in 1900, the government's local improvement
movement, a series of initiatives designed to integrate rural communities and preexisting rural interest groups more fully into the central
administrative structure of the state, met with both active and passive
resistance. The effort to merge the Shintō shrines of individual hamlets
into one central shrine for each administrative village in the country
aroused considerable opposition among hamlet residents, as did the effort to transfer control of hamlet common lands and forests to the villages. In both cases the bureaucracy found it necessary to scale down its
original objectives. Similarly, many administrative villages responded
without enthusiasm—or failed to respond at all—to the bureaucracy's
request for comprehensive local development plans.[1]

Nor did efforts to "declass" social and economic interests in the countryside proceed without setback. By early Taishō the bureaucracy had

I wish to thank Nishida Yoshiaki, Yoshioka Yoshinori, Kawai Satoru, Inoguchi Ku-
niko, Inoguchi Takashi, and Carol Gluck for their very generous assistance in collecting
and/or deciphering many of the materials on which this paper is based.

[1] Kenneth Pyle, "The Technology of Japanese Nationalism," *Journal of Asian Studies*,
33 (November 1973), 58-60, 65; Fukutake Tadashi, *Japanese Rural Society*, translated by
Ronald Dore (Tokyo, 1967), pp. 169-170.

indeed acquired a high degree of control over a number of grass-roots organizations in the countryside—for example, the youth groups that had long existed at the hamlet level and the associations of ex-servicemen that had appeared in increasing numbers after the Russo-Japanese war. Yet at the same time the bureaucracy was confronted with the emergence of the very sort of class-based organizations its social policy had been designed to prevent. These were of two kinds: organizations of landlords, which the bureaucracy did not find especially troubling,[2] and organizations of tenant farmers, which it did. My concern in this paper is with the latter—with the internal organization, activities, and goals of tenant unions.

My focus will be on the 1920s. After a general description of tenant unions, I will present a detailed analysis of tenant unions and the tenant movement in the Izumo region of Shimane prefecture. Finally I will discuss the ways in which the bureaucracy dealt with tenant unions. Before I turn to these topics, however, I should comment briefly on the dimensions of the phenomenon I am considering.

o

Roughly 50 tenant unions had been established in Japan by 1908, the first—in Gifu prefecture—as early as 1875. Thereafter unions began to multiply at a faster rate. By 1917 some 173 unions were known to exist; by 1921, 681, and by 1923, 1,530. In 1923, the first year for which membership figures are available, 163,931 tenant farmers, or 4.3 percent of all tenant farmers in the nation, belonged to unions. Four years later, in 1927, the figure had risen to a peak of 365,332, or 9.6 percent of all tenant farmers.[3]

In common with popular movements in other times and places, the tenant movement in Japan was unevenly dispersed throughout the country. Some prefectures, primarily those in northeastern Japan and Kyushu, had few unions, whereas others, primarily those in central Honshu and the Inland Sea region, had large numbers. In many of the latter a considerably higher than average percentage of the tenant population was unionized. In 1927, for example, over 41 percent of the 4,582 unions in existence were located in only seven of the nation's forty-seven prefectures. The percentages of tenant farmers in those pre-

---

[2] As I will discuss later, bureaucrats believed in early Taishō that landlords acted on behalf of rural society as a whole. Not until the 1920s did they begin to perceive that landlords, too, had class interests that landlord unions (*jinushi kumiai*) were designed to protect.

[3] Data on unions and union membership appear in Nōchi Seido Shiryō Shūsei Hensen Iinkai, *Nōchi seido shiryō shūsei* (Tokyo, 1969), 3:514, 524 (hereafter cited as NSSS). Data on the number of tenant households appear in annual editions of *Teikoku tōkei nenkan*.

fectures who belonged to unions were as follows: Yamanashi, 41.6 percent; Niigata, 32.0 percent; Kagawa, 29.9 percent; Tokushima, 22.0 percent; Gumma, 20.1 percent; Gifu, 18.5 percent; and Okayama, 17.1 percent.[4]

However an outside observer might evaluate these statistics, it is clear that contemporary Japanese perceived them as significant.[5] Bureaucrats in particular regarded the increase in tenant unions and union membership in late Taishō with considerable misgivings. They monitored the phenomenon carefully, keeping close track of numbers and gauging their responses accordingly. In short, the degree of unionization achieved was sufficient, in a society that was sensitive to manifestations of class consciousness, to merit definition as a social problem.

Tenant Unions: An Overview

Collective action on the part of the lower strata in rural society was by no means a new phenomenon in Japan. As Stephen Vlastos has shown, many participants in the "world renewal" (*yonaoshi*) uprisings of the Bakumatsu era were small-scale landholders, tenant farmers, or day laborers.[6] In the immediate aftermath of the Meiji land settlement, too, tenant farmers in various regions of the country acted in concert to protest rent increases or the loss of permanent tenancy rights. Indeed, in subsequent years whenever harvests were poor and the rent reductions landlords were expected to give were not deemed adequate, tenants were likely to band together to express their grievances.[7] What was unprecedented about the situation in the countryside in the 1920s, then, was not that tenant farmers were resorting to collective action as such. Rather, it was the form that their collective action took, and its thrust.

With some exceptions, to be sure, earlier protest movements in the

---

[4] NSSS, p. 524.

[5] Richard Smethurst, for example, observes that "Farmers' unions at the peak of their organizational activity enrolled only a *minuscule* segment of the nation's tenants" (emphasis added): *A Social Basis for Prewar Japanese Militarism* (Berkeley and Los Angeles: University of California Press, 1974), p. 146. I do not agree that the segment was minuscule, but in the absence of agreed-upon standards for evaluating levels of popular unrest I can only assert my opinion. I think that a more fruitful approach to evaluating Japanese tenant unions is suggested by Henry A. Landsberger in his essay on "The Role of Peasant Movements and Revolts in Development: An Analytical Framework," *I.L.R. Reprint Series*, No. 236 (Ithaca, 1968), in which emphasis is placed on the characteristics, not the quantity, of protest. I have found Landsberger's framework very helpful in my research.

[6] See Stephen Vlastos, "*Yonaoshi* in Aizu," in this volume.

[7] For a brief discussion of tenant protest before the 1920s see Ann Waswo, *Japanese Landlords: The Decline of a Rural Elite* (Berkeley and Los Angeles: University of California Press, 1977), pp. 21-23; Irwin Scheiner, "The Mindful Peasant: Sketches for a Study of Rebellion," *Journal of Asian Studies*, 32 (August 1973), 579-591.

countryside had been ad hoc in structure and relatively short-lived; the product of a particular perceived crisis, the collectivity dissolved when that crisis had passed. In contrast, the tenant unions that came into being in the Taishō era were formal organizations, with detailed rules of procedure set forth in written bylaws (*kiyaku*). Although established in many cases at a moment of crisis—for example, when heavy rains had damaged the rice crop—tenant unions were designed to function in perpetuity, or at the very least for an extended period of time.[8]

Like earlier rural protest movements, tenant unions were concerned with improving the economic and social status of their members, and they employed a number of familiar means—the drafting of petitions, for example—to achieve that end.[9] In their conception of the measures that constituted improvement and of the agency by which improvement was to be brought about, however, tenant unions differed markedly from earlier movements. To state the contrast baldly, the "world renewal" protesters of the Bakumatsu era sought to eliminate economic and social inequality in the countryside, first by destroying the homes and property of wealthy peasants, and second by obtaining the intervention of feudal authorities on their behalf. The former, in fact, was conceived of not only as a desirable end in itself but also as a means to the latter. Faced with unambiguous evidence of discontent among the peasantry, rulers would be obliged to demonstrate their benevolence (*jinsei*) by removing the causes of that discontent and restoring rural society to its natural, harmonious state.[10]

Tenant unions, on the other hand, sought to lessen economic and social inequality in the countryside by *upgrading* the status of tenant farmers. This was to be accomplished primarily by the efforts of tenant farmers themselves, by means of various forms of self-help, and by the united front they presented to others. The latter was conceived of as a crucial instrument of power. By employing it, unions attempted to manipulate their environment in constructive ways. They negotiated with landlords rather than destroying their property, and they pressured the government to provide them not with benevolent treatment but with the equity to which they felt they were entitled. Implicit in the activities of unions, and at times explicit in their public statements, was a rec-

[8] Usually bylaws made no mention of a time limit for the union's existence, although in some cases a period of ten or twenty years was specified. See Nōshōmushō, Nōmukyoku, "Honpō ni okeru nōgyō dantai ni kansuru chōsa (1924)," reprinted in NSSS, p. 31. Of the 4,650 unions in existence in 1932, 2,601 (56 percent) had been established prior to 1927 and 620 (13 percent) had been established prior to 1922; NSSS, p. 516.

[9] They also employed a variety of new means, which I will discuss at a later point. For a detailed explication of protest methods, both old and new, see Mori Kiichi, *Kosaku sōgi senjutsu* (Tokyo, 1928).

[10] See Vlastos, "*Yonaoshi* in Aizu."

ognition that the social order was both man-made and malleable. Justice lay in the future, not the past; it was to be achieved, not restored.

Both the form and the thrust of tenant unions attracted the attention of bureaucrats in the Ministry of Agriculture and received fairly extensive coverage in the reports on the tenant union movement they issued from time to time throughout the 1920s.[11] Their reports, which were based primarily on analysis of union bylaws, constitute a useful source for examining the structure and aims of tenant unions in greater detail.

In 1925, roughly 35 percent of the tenant farmers who belonged to unions were members of what the bureaucracy termed associated unions (*keitōteki kumiai*), that is, unions that were themselves members of some larger federation or alliance of tenant unions; 65 percent of the tenant farmers who belonged to unions were members of autonomous unions (*tandoku kumiai*), that is, unions that maintained no formal ties with other tenant organizations.[12] Whether associated or autonomous, however, all unions appear to have been markedly similar in structure.

Each union was organized as a voluntary association of individuals within a specified geographical area. Membership generally was open to anyone cultivating leased land within that area, that is, to pure tenant farmers who leased all the land they cultivated and to part-tenants who leased a portion of the land they cultivated and owned the rest.[13] The majority of unions encompassed a single village district (*ōaza*), equivalent in many, though not all, cases to one of the traditional hamlets of which the village was constituted. The next most common basis was the village. In 1925, for example, 63.6 percent of all unions were organ-

---

[11] The Ministry of Agriculture undertook its first general survey of tenant unions in cooperation with the Imperial Agricultural Association in 1916. In 1920 it began making its own surveys, although it relied on quantitative data on unions compiled by the Home Ministry until 1925. Until 1922 the Home Ministry was also the sole source of quantitative data on tenancy disputes. Thereafter the Ministry of Agriculture kept its own tabulations, consistently reporting substantially more disputes than did the Home Ministry, just as, after 1925, it consistently reported a slightly greater number of tenant unions. No satisfactory explanation for the discrepancies between the data reported by these two ministries has yet been uncovered. Conversation with Nishida Yoshiaki, Tokyo University. See also Nōmin Undōshi Kenkyūkai, *Nihon nōmin undōshi* (Tokyo, 1961), pp. 665, 672, 685, 883 (hereafter cited as NNUS).

[12] Calculated from data in Nōrinshō, Nōmukyoku, "Jinushi kosakunin kumiai ni kansuru chōsa (1926)," reprinted in NSSS, pp. 54, 59–63.

[13] "Honpō ni okeru nōgyō dantai," NSSS, pp. 30–31. In some cases membership was open to owner-cultivators as well, or to nonfarmers approved by the membership as a whole. Less frequently membership was restricted to individuals who tenanted at least a specified area of land (such as 2 *tan*) or to those of "good character" (*hinkō hōsei naru mono*) only (10 *tan* = 1 *chō* = 2.5 acres).

ized at the *ōaza* level; 93.8 percent of all unions were organized at the village level or below.[14]

The entire union membership was convened once or twice a year into a general assembly to hear reports on union activities and financial outlays, to decide on future undertakings, and, if necessary, to elect officers. In most cases decisions were reached by simple majority vote, although in special cases, such as a change in the union's bylaws, a two-thirds or three-quarters majority might be required. Extraordinary assemblies could be convened whenever deemed necessary by the union president or demanded by a specified percentage, usually one-fifth to one-third, of union members.[15]

Union officers included a president (usually designated *kumiaichō*, sometimes *sōdai*) whose duty it was to represent the union in dealings with others, direct the union's internal affairs, and preside at union meetings; one or two vice presidents to assist the president and substitute for him whenever he was unable to perform his duties; one or more secretaries (*kanji, riji*) to carry on the union's day-to-day operations; and a number of councilors (*hyōgiin*) to advise the president and to decide on matters delegated to them by the general membership. The union president and vice president(s) were elected by and from the membership as a whole, for terms varying in length from one to three years. Other officers were either elected by the membership or appointed by the union president. Officers generally served without salary, although in many cases their out-of-pocket expenses were reimbursed from union funds.

In most cases no qualifications for holding office were specified in union bylaws. All members were therefore eligible for election in theory. In practice, however, most union officers, the union president in particular, were men of some influence (*kuchi kiki no mono*) among local tenant farmers and in their communities as a whole.[16] What constituted that influence seems to have varied from place to place. Sometimes it was a higher than average level of education, sometimes a distinguished military record. Probably the most common requirement was a degree of affluence, based on a larger than average landholding and/or a source of nonagricultural income, which provided individuals with the economic independence and the social status to carry out official union duties.[17]

[14] NSSS, p. 520. It is possible that bureaucrats used the term *ōaza* to describe hamlets (*buraku*) that were not officially part of the administrative structure of the countryside.

[15] "Honpō ni okeru nōgyō dantai," NSSS, pp. 31-32.

[16] Ibid., p. 32.

[17] Nōshōmushō, Nōmukyoku, "Kosaku kumiai ni kansuru chōsa (1921)," reprinted in

All unions collected membership dues, although the way in which they assessed them and the amounts they charged varied considerably. Some unions required an equal sum from every member, whereas others levied dues according to the area of land individual members tenanted or the amount of rent they paid to landlords. Dues might be payable in rice (as were tenant rents in most cases) or in cash. If in cash, they might be as low as 1 *sen* per month or range upward to as much as 30 *sen* per month.[18]

In addition to articles defining organizational structure, the bylaws of all tenant unions contained articles setting forth objectives and enumerating the means that would be employed to achieve them. Although some unions cited only a single objective, most listed two or more. Bureaucrats grouped the objectives that appeared in union bylaws under six headings, which they then divided into two separate categories. In the first category were objectives they termed non-confrontational (*hitaikōteki*). These were: the promotion of harmonious relations between landlords and tenants; the promotion of friendship and mutual aid among tenants; the improvement of agriculture; and the prevention of competition for land among tenants. In the second category were a pair of confrontational (*taikōteki*) objectives: the maintenance and improvement of the terms of tenancy, and the social advancement of the tenant class.[19] Early in the Taishō period the majority of unions had concerned themselves with what bureaucrats considered non-confrontational objectives. Beginning in 1918, however, there had been a dramatic increase not only in the total number of unions, but also in the number of unions with confrontational objectives. In 1922, 88 percent of all unions cited at least one such objective in their bylaws, typically in combination with other, non-confrontational objectives. In 1926, 92 percent of all unions cited at least one confrontational objective.[20]

For each of the six objectives they identified, bureaucrats further identified a corresponding set of union activities. Their findings, although based on measures stipulated in the bylaws of individual unions, were presented in summary form with little or no attention to how frequently

---

NSSS, p. 599; Takahashi Iichirō and Shirakawa Kiyoshi, eds., *Nōchi kaikaku to jinushi sei* (Tokyo, 1955), p. 101. For examples of union leaders, see Hayashi Yūichi, "Shoki kosaku sōgi no tenkai to Taishōki nōson seiji jōkyō no ichi kōsatsu," *Rekishigaku kenkyū*, No. 442 (March 1977), pp. 1-16; Suzuki Masayuki, "Nichi-Ro sengo no nōson mondai no tenkai," *Rekishigaku kenkyū* (1974 special issue), pp. 150-161.

[18] "Kosaku kumiai ni kansuru chōsa (1921)," NSSS, p. 600.

[19] "Honpō ni okeru nōgyō dantai," NSSS, pp. 32-33.

[20] Ibid., p. 26; Nōrinshō, Nōmukyoku, *Jinushi kosakunin kumiai kiyaku jirei* (Tokyo, 1926), p. 1. The latter report contains many examples of union bylaws. For a "representative" example, incorporating all the most common features found in bylaws, see Nōshōmushō, Nōmukyoku, *Kosaku sōgi ni kansuru chōsa*, 1 (Tokyo, 1922), 211-217.

those measures were cited. No one union necessarily engaged in all the activities in any one set, nor did many unions engage in more than two or three sets of activities. What follows, then, is not a description of typical union activity, but rather a description of the entire range of union activities.[21]

The promotion of harmonious relations between landlords and tenants. Bureaucrats were able to find only a few activities relating specifically to this objective. The most common were inviting landlords to social gatherings, and offering to mediate disputes over tenanted land.

The promotion of friendship and mutual aid among tenants. Other than the holding of social gatherings for tenants and their families, all the activities bureaucrats listed related more directly to mutual aid. They were: the establishment of a fund for emergency relief to members in the event of natural disaster; the creation of flood and fire brigades; the provision of needed labor to families who had fallen behind in their work owing to the sickness or conscription of a family member; assistance to members wanting to lease additional land; the cooperative purchase of such everyday necessities as bean paste and soy sauce; and the loan of union-owned funeral goods to members.

The improvement of agriculture. Bureaucrats divided the activities relating to this objective into two categories, improvements in agricultural technology and improvements in farm management. The former included: the exchange of seeds; the standardization of seed strains; cooperation in insect control; the encouragement of deep plowing; the furnishing of materials to construct racks for drying rice; the encouragement of improved composting techniques; the construction of drainage ditches; the improvement of field paths; the joint use of farm tools; cooperative rice planting; research on possible secondary crops and by-employments; employment of a trained agricultural expert; and training courses in farming methods. The latter included: the cooperative purchase of livestock, fertilizers, and other necessities for farming; the cooperative sale of farm produce; the provision of loans for farm operations; and the encouragement of efforts to enable tenant farmers to purchase land.

The prevention of competition for land among tenants. More in the nature of agreed-upon rules of procedure than activities, the stipulations related to this objective were: that no union member would try to secure tenancy rights to additional land by offering to pay higher rents than were paid by the current tenant of that land; that decisions on whether or not to agree to higher rents demanded by landlords would be made by the

---

[21] Unless otherwise noted, the source of the following description of union activities is "Honpō ni okeru nōgyō dantai," NSSS, pp. 33-35.

union's general assembly, not by individuals; that whenever a member relinquished his cultivating rights to a plot of land he would notify the union immediately so that another member would have a chance to assume them; that no union member would agree to cultivate land currently cultivated by another member without the latter's consent; and that if a union member acquired title to land that another member tenanted he would not demand that the latter surrender the land to him until after a specified period of time had elapsed.[22]

The maintenance and improvement of the terms of tenancy. Activities related to this objective were divided by bureaucrats into three groups. First were those designed to standardize the terms of tenancy in a given locality, which included efforts to secure uniformly worded tenancy agreements and to eliminate variations in the due date for rent payments. Second were activities designed to maintain existing terms of tenancy, which usually involved resistance to landlords' demands for rent increases or the surrender of tenanted land. Third were activities designed to improve existing terms of tenancy. The latter included efforts to secure recognition of cultivating rights, temporary or permanent rent reductions, abolition of "added rice" payments and the double-baling of rent rice, and reform of the system of inspection imposed on rents.[23]

Bureaucrats observed that efforts to maintain or improve terms of tenancy often led to conflict with landlords, in which case tenant unions were likely to take one or more of the following steps: survey and prepare reports on local rent levels and crop yields; study the laws pertaining to the points at issue in the dispute; agree on a united front among union members in dealing with landlords during the dispute, with sanctions to be imposed against anyone who violated it; refuse to do farm labor or any other type of work for landlords while the dispute was in progress; provide land or monetary aid to anyone who was evicted from the land he cultivated during the course of the dispute; threaten to abandon all of the land involved in the dispute unless the union's demands were met; and make partial rent payments only.[24]

The social advancement of the tenant class. Bureaucrats noted that this

[22] Tenants who violated these stipulations generally were subject to fines or ostracism.

[23] For a discussion of rice inspection, see Waswo, *Japanese Landlords*, pp. 42-56. To compensate landlords for the loss or spoilage of rent rice during transit and storage, tenants in many parts of the country had long been required to pay an extra measure of rice (known variously as *sashimai, komimai, kanmai,* etc.) per bale of rent. In late Meiji, many landlords began requiring that tenants use double-layer bales for rent payments instead of the single-layer bales that had been employed in the past. Tenant objections to these requirements will be discussed at a later point.

[24] See also Mori, *Kosaku sōgi senjutsu,* pp. 32-56; *Jinushi kosakunin kumiai kiyaku jirei,* pp. 2-4.

was an objective found in the bylaws of recently organized unions, constituting evidence that the tenancy problem was moving into "a stage of class conflict." Most commonly tenant unions sought to achieve recognition of their right to engage in collective bargaining and, in the early 1920s, urged speedy passage of a universal manhood suffrage law. Other activities aimed at promoting the awareness (*jikaku*) and knowledge of tenant farmers included publishing union newsletters and organizing lecture meetings or training courses for union members.[25]

o

In their reports, bureaucrats placed far greater emphasis on describing tenant unions than on explaining why unions had been organized. When they did deal fleetingly with issues of causation, they attributed both the increase in number of unions after 1918 and the concurrent shift from non-confrontational to confrontational union objectives to exogenous forces. Chief among those cited were the Russian Revolution and World War I, events external to Japan. Also important were the rice riots of 1918, the industrial labor union movement, and the various democratic and socialist movements of the Taishō era, all essentially urban phenomena within Japan.[26] Other than making passing reference to the dislocating effects on tenants of the World War I economic boom and subsequent bust, bureaucrats did not discuss precisely (or even generally) how these events and developments impinged on tenants, wrought changes in their attitudes and aspirations, and resulted in tenant unions.

I will consider the policy initiatives that stemmed from this assessment of tenant unions as an "alien growth" upon the countryside in the concluding section of this paper. Here I want to examine two aspects of the descriptive material bureaucrats presented in their reports that seem to suggest another, more basic explanation: that unions were responses to endogenous changes within rural society itself and to exogenous forces that stemmed not from outside Japan or from Japanese dissidents but from the policies and procedures of the Japanese state.

As bureaucrats noted (without comment), the majority of unions were organized at the ōaza (or hamlet) level. In my view, this is a very intriguing fact. If the forces creating tenant unions came from outside rural society, how did they penetrate directly and immediately to the very core of that society, the "natural community," where traditional

[25] Unions also advocated educational reforms and the abolition of "oppressive" taxes; *Jinushi kosakunin kumiai kiyaku jirei*, p. 4.

[26] See, for example, "Honpō ni okeru nōgyō dantai," NSSS, pp. 21, 24. Bureaucrats later cited the victory of the British Labour party as a cause of increasing political acitivity by unions; "Jinushi kosakunin kumiai ni kansuru chōsa," NSSS, p. 54.

values and attitudes inimical to self-assertiveness and class consciousness supposedly remained very strong?

"Without the hamlet one cannot even get to paradise."[27] So went a rural proverb that summed up the hamlet's power over the individual and over individual households. One needed the community to obtain a proper funeral, just as one needed it in life to obtain water, firewood, recreation, or aid and comfort when disaster struck. Social cohesion and acceptance of status distinctions were necessary to survival. In theory, the poorer members of the community were most affected, and most constrained, by these imperatives. Far from identifying with others in the same situation, they competed with them for the favor of the local elite and the small but crucial benefits that favor bestowed on them.[28] Yet it was in these very communities that the poorer members abandoned competition for cooperation and organized unions.

Not every hamlet, of course, had a tenant union. What, then, might distinguish those that did from those that did not? Since, to my knowledge, bureaucrats never compiled a directory of unionized communities, one must rely on information gleaned from various case studies of tenant unions and tenancy disputes. On that admittedly imperfect basis, it appears that unionized communities differed from non-unionized communities in one or more of the following three ways.

First, unionized communities were located where agriculture had become relatively highly commercialized. Communities with unions were thus more likely to be found in the Kinki or Chubu regions of central Honshu than in the Tohoku or other economically backward regions of the country. Within the latter regions, however, communities with unions did exist in major rice-producing districts and/or in districts where sericulture was an important by-employment among local farmers. Tenant farmers in these communities were all involved in commercial farming in one way or another. Some, typically those with substantial holdings of paddy, participated directly and actively in the marketplace, selling what at times amounted to considerable quantities of rice. Those with smaller holdings often relied on wage labor, a product of commercial farming, to make ends meet. If they sold any rice at all they were likely to do so immediately after the harvest, when prices were lowest, because of their pressing need for cash. Later they might have to buy rice, at higher, early summer prices, to tide them over until their next crop was in. Whatever the size of their holdings, tenants in these communities were affected by rice (or silk) prices and were interested in maxi-

[27] Quoted in Kawamura Nozomu, "Kosaku sōgiki ni okeru sonraku taisei," *Sonraku shakai kenkyū nenpō*, No. 7 (Tokyo, 1960), p. 108.

[28] Fukutake, *Japanese Rural Society*, pp. 86, 133, 214; George M. Foster, "Interpersonal Relations in Peasant Society," *Human Organization*, 19 (1960-1961), 174-178.

mizing the amount of their harvests they could retain, that is, in reducing rent levels.[29]

Second, unionized communities tended to contain considerable amounts of reclaimed land. This meant, on the one hand, that local tenants farmed holdings that were larger and/or less fragmented than did tenants in neighboring communities, and, on the other, that they possessed, or believed they possessed, permanent tenancy rights (*eikosaku ken*) by virtue of their labor, or an ancestor's labor, in reclaiming the land they tilled.[30]

Third, unionized communities tended to be what one observer has termed "headless." That is, few if any landlords were in residence. The community consisted primarily of owner-cultivators and tenants or, in some cases, of tenants alone. Landlords might live in another hamlet of the same village, in a neighboring village, or far away in a town or city. Their absence from the community itself created both the need for self-help among remaining residents since there was no local elite to bestow favors, and the opportunity for self-help since there was no local elite to demand subordination and deference.[31]

This brings me to the second aspect of the descriptive material in official reports that bears examination: the activities of tenant unions. In my view, even the activities bureaucrats identified as non-confrontational can be construed as challenges to established norms. Mutual aid that the community was supposed to provide was provided by the union. The union also engaged in agricultural efforts that duplicated those assigned to the hamlet branch of the village agricultural association (*nō-kai*).[32] Indeed, instead of the sharp (and conveniently timed) break circa 1918 between non-confrontational and confrontational activities, one can

[29] Three excellent case studies by Nishida Yoshiaki, two concerning a district in Niigata prefecture and one in a village in Yamanashi prefecture, examine this issue in detail: "Shōnō keiei no hatten to kosaku sōgi," *Tochi seido shigaku*, No. 38 (1968), pp. 24-41; "Kosaku sōgi no tenkai," in *Meiji Taishō kyōdoshi kenkyū hō*, edited by Furushima Toshio et al. (Tokyo, 1970), pp. 346-369; and "Kosaku sōgi no tenkai to jisakunō sōsetsu iji seisaku," *Hitotsubashi ronsō*, 60 (1968), 524-546.

[30] Nishida, "Shōnō keiei," p. 25.

[31] Ushiyama Keiji, *Nōminsō bunkai no kōzō, senzenki: Niigata ken Kambara nōson no bunseki* (Tokyo, 1975), pp. 100-101. The author presents a detailed discussion of unions in "headless" communities on pp. 97-130; the problems faced by unions in communities with landlords in residence are discussed pp. 130-138. For a general discussion of absentee landlords and the effects of absenteeism on landlord-tenant relations, see Waswo, *Japanese Landlords*, pp. 81-93.

[32] Bureaucrats observed in 1924 that the involvement of unions in cooperative activities was "something to note," but they made no further comment on the subject. "Honpō ni okeru nōgyō dantai," NSSS, p. 35. As I will discuss later, I think bureaucrats were slowly becoming aware that the breakdown of other institutions designed to meet farmers' needs had contributed to the growth of tenant unions.

perceive a gradual and steady evolution. That is, tenants found it necessary or desirable to provide certain services for themselves. One of those services was not competing among themselves for land, since competition drove rent levels up; having found that they could, by cooperation, keep rent levels from rising, they began to experiment with joint action to get rents reduced; finding that lower rents did not solve all their problems, they became interested in other objectives, among them their "social advancement."[33]

That exogenous forces influenced this process is evident. Among those that bureaucrats characterized as "alien" and later Japanese scholars have viewed as "progressive" were labor union activists who returned to their native villages, typically after having been fired from their jobs for participating in strikes; university professors, writers, and intellectuals who toured the countryside giving speeches on the tenancy system, monopoly capitalism, and the proletarian movement in Japan and abroad; and books, journals, and newspapers that dealt with these and other "radical" themes.[34]

An even more powerful stimulus to new attitudes and behavior among tenants, however, was the Japanese state. It trained agricultural experts and sent them out into the countryside where, among other things, they taught tenants how to keep detailed records of their incomes and expenditures. It conscripted young tenant farmers and taught them discipline and organizational skills.[35] By means of conscription and compulsory elementary education, the state imbued tenant farmers with nationalism and with a new vocabulary of nationalistic symbols that could be and, as will be discussed later, were used to legitimate tenant grievances.

More fundamentally, the state established a system of laws and administrative procedures to organize all of Japanese society, including the countryside. Under that system tenants continued—as they had before the Meiji Restoration—to occupy an inferior status. The civil code of 1898 recognized property rights as superior to leasing rights. Until 1925

[33] Tenants in a given community did not have to experience every step of this process themselves, but could profit from the example of tenants in neighboring communities. For discussion of the ways in which tenants could and/or did discover the utility of unions on their own, see Ushiyama, *Nōminsō bunkai*, pp. 109-113; Takahashi and Shirakawa, *Nōchi kaikaku to jinushi sei*, pp. 86-89; Mori, *Kosaku sōgi senjutsu*, pp. 4-5, 54.

[34] Examples appear in George O. Totten, "Labor and Agrarian Disputes in Japan Following World War I," *Economic Development and Cultural Change*, 9, part 2 (October 1960), 204; NNUS, pp. 890-903. See also the discussion that follows on the union movement in Iwami.

[35] Ushiyama, *Nōminsō bunkai*, pp. 111-112, 120-123 n. 26; Suzuki, "Nichi-Ro sengo no nōson mondai," pp. 150-161. See also the discussion that follows on the union movement in Izumo.

only property owners were granted a voice in local and supralocal politics. But what had once been defined by custom was now, in principle, justiciable. As in the past, tenants could appeal to a higher authority for redress of their grievances, but now that authority was impartial law, not benevolent rulers. It was not coincidental that one of the measures tenant unions resorted to in conflict with landlords was "study of the laws pertaining to the points at issue in the dispute." Law had replaced bamboo spears as one of tenant farmers' major weapons, just as formal organizations, similar to those of bureaucratically controlled youth, reservists, and agricultural groups, had replaced ad hoc and transitory collectivities.

Thus far I, like the bureaucrats whose reports I have summarized above, have not discussed at all precisely how the diverse events and developments I have mentioned inpinged on tenants, wrought changes in their attitudes and aspirations, and resulted in tenant unions. To do that it is necessary to move from the general to the specific and examine tenant unions in one particular region of the country.[36]

Tenant Unions and the Tenant Movement in Izumo

Shimane prefecture lies along the Japan Sea coast of western Honshu, bordering to the east on Tottori, the south on Hiroshima, and the southwest on Yamaguchi prefectures. There were some 91 tenant unions in Shimane in 1925, with an overall membership of 5,545 (roughly 7 percent of the tenant population). These unions were not evenly distributed throughout the prefecture as a whole. Rather, they were concentrated in its eastern portion, in the region known as Izumo, one of the three *kuni*, or provinces, from which the prefecture had been constituted in the early Meiji era.

Identified in Japanese myths as the earthly place to which Susano-o was banished for such transgressions as letting piebald colts loose in the heavenly rice paddies of his sister the Sun Goddess, Izumo may have seemed to government officials in the mid-1920s to be living up to the unruly reputation of its first divine inhabitant. There were 62 tenant unions in the region in 1925, 60 of them in Nōgi and Yatsuka *gun*, its

---

[36] That the case study I am about to present is typical in any statistical sense of developments in Japan as a whole is highly unlikely. I have selected it primarily because it is well-documented, enabling one to penetrate the anonymity that surrounds the subject of tenant protest and get some sense of the issues as tenants and their leaders perceived them. For a justification of the case study method, not as a basis for generalizing about the whole of a phenomenon but as a laboratory for examining social processes that affect all constituent parts to one degree or another, see Maurice R. Stein, *The Eclipse of Community: An Interpretation of American Studies* (Princeton: Princeton University Press, 1960), pp. 94–113.

two largest administrative districts. The unions in these two *gun* had a total of 3,195 members, 57.6 percent of all the unionized tenants in the prefecture. Roughly 26 percent of all tenant farmers in Nōgi and 23 percent of all tenant farmers in Yatsuka belonged to unions, and the unions they belonged to were almost all of the sort bureaucrats recognized as confrontational, that is, unions that sought to maintain and improve the terms of tenancy and/or to bring about the social advancement of the tenant class.[37]

The confrontational stance of unions in Izumo was a fairly recent development. As late as 1920 most unions in the region were informal, clandestine organizations at the hamlet or *ōaza* level, whose leaders met under cover of darkness to discuss the state of the upcoming harvest and to decide the amount of rent reduction each tenant should request from his landlords.[38] Those unions that were formally and openly organized generally avoided use of the words "tenant farmer" or "union" in their bylaws, styling themselves "friendship societies," "cultivators' associations," or "agricultural clubs" instead.[39]

In dealing with landlords these unions generally based their appeals on expectations of benevolent treatment: once aware of their tenants' problems, landlords would, it was assumed, grant relief. Those landlords who failed to do so were subjected to various forms of ostracism, or *murahachibu*. Tenants would refuse to take part in funerals, weddings, or other occasions involving the offending landlords. Their ultimate and most explicitly economic weapon was the joint return of the land they leased; no tenant in the community would cultivate the land of any landlord who behaved improperly toward tenants.[40]

By 1925 the situation was radically different. The majority of tenant unions were formally organized as voluntary associations and openly employed the words "tenant farmer" and "union" in their bylaws. They held public meetings in the hamlet hall, local schoolhouse, or Buddhist shrine. Instead of requesting benevolence, tenants now demanded equity, and did so collectively, not individually.[41] Moreover, a consider-

[37] Compiled from data in Shimane Ken Nōrinbu, Nōchi Kaikaku Ka, *Shimane ken nōchi kaikaku shi* (Hirata, 1959), pp. 104, 106-108 (hereafter cited as SKNKS). Data on the number of tenant households are from *Shimane ken tōkeisho, 1922* (Matsue, 1923), p. 7.

[38] "Yamasaki Memo," quoted by Yoshioka Yoshinori, "Shimane ken nōmin undōshi," NNUS, p. 818.

[39] "Taishō Shōwa nōmin undō ni kansuru zadankai" (hereafter cited as "Zadankai"), in SKNKS, pp. 316-317. Tenant union leaders from Nōgi and Yatsuka *gun* took part in two separate symposia in 1956, of which this is the transcript. Bylaws of two early tenant unions in Shimane, one established in 1898 and the other in 1902, appear in SKNKS, pp. 118-120 nn. 11, 12.

[40] "Yamasaki Memo," NNUS, p. 818.

[41] Ibid., pp. 818-819.

able proportion of unions in Izumo, although still organized at the hamlet or ōaza level, now belonged to a regional body, the Tenant Federation of Nōgi and Yatsuka Districts. In place of isolated tenant unions there was now a tenant union movement.

Toward confrontation. This development of tenant unions in Izumo can be attributed to two closely related causes: the accumulation of new or newly perceived grievances among tenant farmers during late Meiji and early Taishō, and the emergence of an able group of local tenant union leaders. A contributing cause was the founding in 1922 of the Japan Farmers' Union (Nihon Nōmin Kumiai, or Nichinō), the country's first national tenant union federation, by Sugiyama Motojirō and Kagawa Toyohiko.

Since relatively few ordinary tenant farmers could or did commit their thoughts to paper, one must infer their grievances from their actions. For that purpose, reports on early tenancy disputes in Shimane constitute the best available source. In those reports one finds a number of new complaints in company with such old and familiar ones as poor harvests and the threatened loss of cultivating rights owing to the sale of tenanted land or the owner's desire to farm the land himself. The two new complaints that figured most prominently were the added burdens imposed on tenants by rice inspection, and the hardships imposed by land adjustment.

Shimane did not institute a mandatory program for inspecting all rice grown in the prefecture until the late 1920s. Beginning in late Meiji, however, various steps were taken to improve the quality and marketability of local rice. In 1906 regulations were issued to standardize the size of rice bales throughout the prefecture. At roughly the same time, a program was established for inspecting rice destined for sale outside the prefecture, and landowners were encouraged to establish procedures at the local level for improving rice quality. In response, many landlords organized fairs and awarded prizes to tenants who produced superior rice. Others established local inspection facilities and began to require rent payments in rice that met minimum standards of quality. One of the most ambitious undertakings of this sort was organized by landlords in Nōgi *gun*, a major rice-producing district in the prefecture.[42]

From the very start tenants found much to complain about in these efforts, correctly perceiving that they bore the added expenses involved while landlords reaped the profits. Among other things, tenants had, in most cases, to manufacture smaller and more durable rice bales than had been necessary in the past and spend more time in threshing and drying

[42] Nōshōmushō, Nōmukyoku, *Kosaku sōgi ni kansuru chōsa*, 2 (Tokyo, 1922), 344; SKNKS, pp. 123-125, 130-133 n. 7.

their rice before baling it. They objected, too, to continued demands from landlords for "added rice" payments, the extra quantity per bale traditionally required to compensate for leakage and spoilage, perceiving that stronger packaging and longer drying made such additional rice payments unnecessary. Protesting that soil and drainage conditions on the land they cultivated limited the quantity of high-grade rice they could produce, they opposed the imposition of quality standards on rent payments, or, if they accepted the idea of such standards, demanded that they be set as low as possible to reflect accurately local growing conditions.[43]

The land adjustment projects carried out in many parts of the prefecture in the early 1900s were designed to improve the irrigation and drainage of paddy fields, thereby solving one of the problems tenants faced in meeting quality standards for rent, and to straighten boundaries between fields, thereby making cultivation easier and more efficient. In the short run, however, land adjustment elicited far more opposition than enthusiasm among tenant farmers. They complained about the difficulties of growing crops while adjustment projects were underway, about slight but disturbing declines in the fertility of the soil in some newly adjusted fields,[44] and, most of all, about rent increases in the aftermath of adjustment. The latter, for example, was the cause of a dispute in three villages of Nōgi *gun*, where a large-scale adjustment project had been carried out in 1907. Before work commenced, landlords had agreed to hold rents at their current level for a year or two after the project was completed. Then rents might be raised in accordance with increased productivity. During 1907, however, prices for both materials and labor rose dramatically, bringing the actual cost of adjustment to almost 16 yen per *tan*, more than twice what landlords had estimated. Most landlords thereupon decided to raise rents immediately. Protesting the unfairness of such a step, tenants in the three villages banded together and refused to pay any rents at all until landlords agreed to abide by their initial promise not to raise rents for a few years.[45]

In addition to grievances such as the above, prefectural officials also cited the behavior of landlords as a source of discontent among tenants. Some landlords acted arbitrarily and arrogantly in their dealings with

[43] *Kosaku sōgi ni kansuru chōsa*, 2:344, 339; "Yamasaki Memo," NNUS, pp. 818-819. Faced with the prospect of having to pay rents in rice of at least third-class quality (or pay a penalty in rice), tenants in a village in neighboring Tottori prefecture protested that 60 percent of the rice they grew was of fourth-class quality; SKNKS, pp. 123-124. For data of a similar sort from Gifu prefecture, see NNUS, p. 651.

[44] *Kosaku sōgi ni kansuru chōsa*, 2:341, 342. Another objection was that the area of fields was now measured accurately, depriving tenants of the "slack" they had enjoyed in the past; ibid., p. 349.

[45] SKNKS, pp. 113, 121 n. 14.

tenants, like the *jitō*, or estate managers, of Japan's feudal past. Where, at the same time, landlords showed no interest in their tenants' well-being or in improving local agriculture—where, in other words, land-lords were functionally if not physically absent from their communities—a particularly volatile situation existed. This was clearly the case in Araijima, a village in Nōgi *gun*, where a dispute involving ten of the village's twelve hamlets erupted in 1921. The most militant stance in the dispute was taken by tenants in Kami-Araijima hamlet where, offi-cials noted, landlords had not supported the hamlet agricultural associ-ation or permitted the establishment of a hamlet cooperative for the purchase of tools, fertilizers, and other supplies. Instead they had estab-lished a bank and sought to make it the sole source of loans and credit in the community. Finding this state of affairs unsatisfactory, tenants organized their own association, the Kami-Araijima Tenant Farmers' Friendly Society, and began to provide for themselves many of the serv-ices—including the cooperative purchase of essential supplies—their landlords had denied them.[46]

Without these and other grievances to fuel it, the tenant movement in Izumo would have been impossible. But the existence of grievances alone was not enough. Most tenants, however upset they might be at one time or another over specific issues, lacked the verbal and concep-tual skills to link those issues into a generalized indictment of the status quo. Still dependent on landlords for access to land and on their com-munities for access to water, fuel, and other necessities, they were wary of openly defying authority and established norms of behavior. They might organize a self-help society in their own hamlet, but they re-mained unaware that tenants in other hamlets or villages faced problems similar to theirs.[47] The movement, therefore, had to be engineered. Someone had to articulate the grievances of tenant farmers, formulate a systematic statement of the problems they faced, create a program for solving those problems, and build a viable organization for achieving desired change. In Izumo this was accomplished by a small group of young, educated, and determined union leaders, chief among them Ya-masaki Toyosada.

Yamasaki was born in 1898 in Mori, a village in Nōgi *gun*. Although there were several large landlords resident in the village, none lived in Ido hamlet where his home was located. Of the fifteen families in the hamlet, fourteen owned no land at all, not even the plots on which their houses stood. Yamasaki's was the only family of means in the hamlet, owning one *chō* of paddy fields, one *tan* of upland fields, and two *chō*

---

[46] *Kosaku sōgi ni kansuru chōsa*, 2:344, 347-353.

[47] See the general discussion of these points in Landsberger, "The Role of Peasant Movements and Revolts," pp. 72-75.

of forest land. In addition they leased four or five *tan* from a village landlord and rented out one *tan* to another cultivator.[48]

Yamasaki graduated from the village elementary school in 1913 and enrolled in a nearby agricultural school. He soon quit attending classes, however. Thereafter he subscribed to a few correspondence courses offered by Nihon and Meiji universities, and in the process became interested in the philosophy of Henri Bergson, but for all practical purposes his formal education ended when he was fifteen.

One reason he quit school was his growing involvement in local politics and the tenant movement. Yamasaki's father had long served as head (*kuchō*) of Ido hamlet, and from an early age Yamasaki had assisted him in performing his duties, first running errands and later taking a more active part in hamlet business. Yamasaki appears to have enjoyed dealing with people—as he recalled years later, if there was something his father found difficult to say to someone, he would volunteer for the task—and there seems to have been a lot of dealing for him to do. Ido was, by Yamasaki's account, a tempestuous community. Adultery was not uncommon. In addition, local residents enjoyed gambling, which tended to bring them into conflict with one another over the repayment of debts, and they produced considerable quantities of "moonshine" sake, which brought them into conflict with the authorities. In late Meiji, moneylending *kō* (mutual financing clubs) were introduced into the hamlet. Many residents had difficulty repaying the loans they received, and for several years Ido was "a nest of process servers."[49]

Yamasaki seems to have regarded the trouble his neighbors got into as a product of poverty, not of moral failings on their part. He also regarded their poverty as a problem to be solved. A poor hamlet, in his view, was destined to become even poorer unless its inhabitants took measures to defend themselves. All the administrative reforms in the village during the early 1900s—the merger of shrines, consolidation of common lands, definition of water rights—had been carried out to Ido's disadvantage. Just as wealthy hamlets asserted themselves at Ido's expense, wealthy landlords took advantage of Ido's tenants, charging high rents and taking back their land—"an everyday occurrence"—if tenants fell at all behind in rent payments.

Yamasaki attributed his initial commitment to the tenant movement

---

[48] Itō Kikunosuke, ed., *Shimane ken jinmei jiten* (Matsue, 1970), p. 267; "Zadankai," SKNKS, p. 325. Yamasaki died in 1964. Portions of what follows are based on autograph letters written in the late 1950s by Yamasaki to Yoshioka Yoshinori. To distinguish between the unpublished and published portions of the letters, which I will also be referring to below, I will cite the former as "Yamasaki MS" and the latter as "Yamasaki Memo," NNUS. I owe thanks to Mr. Yoshioka for allowing me to photocopy the letters.

[49] "Yamasaki MS"; "Zadankai," SKNKS, p. 325.

to an essay he read at the age of twelve in the journal *Nihon oyobi Nihonjin*. It concerned the death of the last aboriginal Tasmanian in a Melbourne hospital and the dispatch of his bones to the British Museum. Moved to tears by the obliteration of an entire people, Yamasaki began to reflect on what had already happened in his own community. His family had once been residents of Nakatsubo hamlet, adjacent to Ido and home to thirty households. One by one the families had died out or moved away, until only his was left. No one remained to look after the graves, and finally the hamlet had been erased; the Yamasakis, as the sole survivors, were absorbed into Ido. A sinister progression of events occurred to him: the death of an individual, a family, a hamlet, and, ultimately, a people. Resolved to do something to prevent Ido from following the same sad course as Nakatsubo, Yamasaki started working to improve local conditions.

That resolve manifested itself in two ways, both of which later figured importantly in Yamasaki's career as a tenant union leader. First, he began to study law, buying for himself an inexpensive edition of the revised penal code and a copy of the civil code. He carried one or another with him wherever he went and studied the contents at every opportunity. By the age of seventeen he was known in the hamlet and in the village as something of a legal expert.[50]

Second, Yamasaki began experimenting with agricultural improvements. With several other youngsters from the local boy's association (*shōnendan*) he reclaimed some wasteland on the outskirts of his hamlet and began growing vetch.[51] As it turned out, the land in question was in the public domain and within the boundaries of another hamlet. In 1918, twenty years after the promulgation of the civil code, the government began a survey of public lands throughout the country to determine whether individual plots should revert to state ownership or be granted to their cultivators. Yamasaki and the others received a formal notice from the head of Nōgi *gun*, acting on behalf of the prefectural governor and the home minister in Tokyo, informing them that the land they cultivated was deemed state property and should be returned forthwith. On Yamasaki's advice, the group sent back a postcard stating that as far as they were concerned the land was theirs by virtue of occupancy and reclamation. Under no circumstances would they surrender it. Whenever *gun* officials appeared on the scene to confront them, the boys managed to disappear.

On August 30, the day before the deadline for resolving ownership rights, the entire group received a summons to appear at the *gun* office.

---

[50] "Yamasaki MS"; "Zadankai," SKNKS, pp. 325-326.

[51] Vetch, used as cattle fodder, a diuretic, and an antipyretic, was a major secondary crop in Izumo.

This time they agreed to go, and for several hours they were subjected to severe scolding for their recalcitrant behavior. Toward evening they were handed forms in which they renounced their claims to the land and were ordered to sign. Yamasaki nodded, and everyone signed. Then he announced that, of course, their signatures were invalid. As minors they could make no binding legal agreements without the approval of an attorney. Unfortunately it was too late in the day to arrange for that. Abruptly the boys left for home. The deadline came and went, and their right to cultivate the land in question was confirmed. The episode became something of a cause célèbre in the area, and as Yamasaki later recalled gave him confidence in his legal knowledge.[52]

In 1921, the Mori Agricultural Friendly Society, the first village-wide tenant union in Shimane, was created, and Yamasaki, then aged twenty-three, became a member. The following year he read a newspaper announcement about the planned organization of a nationwide tenant union by Sugiyama Motojirō and Kagawa Toyohiko. Interested parties were invited to attend a meeting at Kagawa's church that April. Intrigued, Yamasaki went to the meeting, finding himself one of a handful of "real farmers" among the fifty or sixty people present. Both the idea and the platform of the Japan Farmers' Union (Nichinō), the organization established at that meeting, appealed to him. In particular, he was impressed by Sugiyama's call for efforts to raise the awareness (jikaku) of tenant farmers and for "moderate, steady, rational and legal" efforts to reform the tenancy system.[53] Yamasaki returned home determined to organize a Nichinō branch in his own village and to join with tenant leaders in neighboring Tottori prefecture to form a Nichinō federation in the San'in region. In the end, he did neither, although he did become leader of a regional federation in Izumo that incorporated Nichinō's original goals.

In the first place, his proposal to affiliate with Nichinō did not appeal to the leaders of the Mori Friendly Society. "They were all old men in their fifties," Yamasaki wrote later. The head was a member of the village assembly and did only what the mayor told him to do. Several landlords served as advisors to the organization. Yamasaki therefore decided to bypass the society and form his own Nōgi-wide organization. Using Ido hamlet as his base, and with the aid of several young tenant farmers from Ido and a hamlet in a nearby village, he set to work. The young men toured Nōgi by bicycle, stopping at every hamlet with a tenant union and sounding out its leaders about their willingness to join a regional federation.[54]

[52] "Yamasaki MS"; "Zadankai," SKNKS, p. 326.
[53] Ibid., p. 317; Yoshioka, NNUS, p. 816.
[54] Ibid., p. 815; "Zadankai," SKNKS, p. 317.

At the time, Yamasaki was still interested in taking part in the planned Nichinō San'in Rengōkai, a federation of unions in Shimane and Tottori. By July of 1923, however, he had abandoned the idea. As early as its second national congress that year Nichinō had begun a "turn to the left" of which Yamasaki thoroughly disapproved. Proposals were made (unsuccessfully for the time being) to create an alliance between farmers and industrial workers and to replace the organization's original emphasis on economic reforms with an emphasis on politics. In addition, steps were taken to centralize the decision-making structure of the federation, reducing the autonomy of affiliated unions.[55] As Yamasaki recalled later, "Nichinō [leaders] began to proclaim that tenancy disputes were merely rehearsals for the revolution. That frightened farmers. I believed that it was possible for farmers to create a rational tenancy system and achieve fair rent levels all by themselves. Ultimately, they could abolish tenancy altogether, but it was necessary to proceed step by step."[56] Another factor was his dislike of what he termed the formulaic (kōshikishugi) stance of Yuihara Genzō, one of the key leaders of the tenant movement in Tottori. The man was "not a farmer" and did not pay adequate attention to actual conditions in the countryside.[57] Yamasaki therefore dissociated himself from the San'in Rengōkai and later withdrew from Nichinō itself. When Nichinō experienced its first split in 1925, Yamasaki participated in the splinter organization established by Hirano Rikizō, the All Japan Farmers' Union League (Zen Nihon Nōmin Kumiai Dōmei). Once again, however, he rapidly became disillusioned and withdrew: "I found that I'd been misled. [The league] was merely an effort to use the farmers' movement as a base for getting ahead in politics. . . . It was wrong to use unions as political tools."[58]

Instead, Yamasaki pursued an independent course, following his own ideas and instincts and building what he later described as "an organization of real farmers with their feet firmly planted on the soil."[59] In December of 1923 thirteen unions throughout Nōgi joined together to form the Nōgi Tenant Federation (Nōgi Gun Kosaku Rengōkai), with Yamasaki as its head. In 1924 a similar federation was established in neighboring Yatsuka. The two united in 1925 as the Tenant Federation of Nōgi and Yatsuka Districts (Nōgi Yatsuka Gun Kosaku Rengōkai). In July of 1926 the Shimane Prefecture Tenant Federation (Shimane Ken Kosaku Rengōkai) was formed, with over a hundred branches in the

[55] Yoshioka, NNUS, p. 816.

[56] "Yamasaki MS."

[57] "Yamasaki Memo," NNUS, p. 816.

[58] "Yamasaki MS."

[59] Yamasaki's testimony before the Kosaku Chōsakai, to be discussed later, as reported in Kosakunin, 10 October 1926, p. 3.

five *gun* of eastern Shimane. Yamasaki served as head of the federation, which controlled the tenant movement throughout Izumo.[60]

Building an organization. At its inception in 1923, the Nōgi Tenant Federation was composed of preexisting tenant unions in the district, whose leaders had responded favorably to proposals for a *gun*-wide body. Once the federation had been created, Yamasaki and his associates began to expand its scale, encouraging the formation of affiliated unions in communities where no tenant unions had existed before. The strategy they followed then and in later years consisted of four stages: the selection of appropriate communities; the identification of a local leadership cadre; the enrollment of members within the community; and the education of those members in the principles of unionism and the means of achieving rural reform.

Yamasaki was less interested in creating an extensive movement than in creating a strong one. Rather than simply moving from one community to the next, he preferred to concentrate on those communities—in most cases, hamlets—that he thought could sustain an effective local union. To him that meant communities where farming was the principal occupation of inhabitants and rice their major crop, and where few, if any, landlords resided. Landlords might live elsewhere in the village, but the farther away they lived and the larger their holdings in the community concerned, the better. Hamlets in which there were many small landlords and/or many small, part-time farmers were to be avoided.[61]

In Yamasaki's view the best choices for leaders of a new union were: adopted sons who had been born and raised in other communities; newly returned soldiers or activists in the local reservists' association (*zaigō gunjinkai*); anyone else who had left the community for a time and then returned; former landlords who had "sunk to the status of tenant farmers"; sons of owner-cultivators who were "on the verge of ruin"; men with experience as sawyers, stonemasons, or in other skilled occupations; and Buddhist priests or faith healers (*kitōshi*).[62] As indicated by this list, Yamasaki had a decided preference for "outsiders," defined either literally (individuals who came from elsewhere and had no deep roots in the community) or figuratively (individuals who had had experiences in the community or elsewhere that made them dissatisfied with the status quo). How successful he was in identifying such people in hamlets throughout Izumo is unknown. What is clear is that "outsiders" constituted the majority of the movement's top leadership. An-

[60] Yoshioka, NNUS, p. 817; SKNKS, pp. 153, 228.
[61] "Yamasaki Memo," NNUS, pp. 817-818.
[62] Ibid., p. 817.

other characteristic they had in common was youth, as the following examples suggest.

Terada Noriaki, son of a tenant farmer, was a childhood friend of Yamasaki's from Ido. He had served for two years in the army and on the basis of his past education and military record returned home in the early 1920s with a noncommissioned officer's certificate. Thereafter he helped Yamasaki organize the Nōgi federation and, as will be discussed later, took charge of the movement's publicity and publishing efforts. His union activities came to the attention of the military police who, according to Terada, prevented his promotion to corporal in the local reservists' association.

Ishiwara Toshio had been a member of the Buddhist Socialist party in Izumo before becoming interested in the federation. Although subjected to various pressures to abandon his union activities—he had to resign the headship of the fire brigade in his village, his brother was turned down for admission to military cadets' school on the grounds that a close relative was "a suspicious character," and at one point his in-laws threatened to make his wife leave him—he remained involved, specializing, like Terada, in publicity work.

Adachi Iwao became involved in federation activities at the age of seventeen, later serving as head of the youth bureau in the Shimane federation. Born in neighboring Yatsuka *gun*, he developed an interest in socialism at an early age. That proved awkward because the government had designated the community in which he lived a "model village" that embodied the best of purely Japanese virtues. Made to feel unwelcome at home, Adachi moved to Nōgi and volunteered to work with Yamasaki. The two subsequently toured Yatsuka by bicycle, organizing the *gun*-wide federaton there.[63]

Enrolling members in a new union was a relatively easy task if the first two stages of organizational strategy had been carried out properly, that is, if an appropriate community had been selected and local leaders identified. As full-time farmers, local tenants had no sources of nonagricultural income to distract their attention from the tenancy system. Producing rice as their major crop, they were aware of the burdens imposed by high rents in kind and by recently instituted standards for baling and rice quality. Subject to relatively few face-to-face contacts with landlords, they were not as constrained by traditional expectations of deferential behavior as were tenants who saw their landlords regularly. That men from their own communities were leading them (how-

[63] "Zadankai," SKNKS, pp. 320, 325. Yamasaki described the establishment of the Nōgi federation as a "revolt of youth against age." "Yamasaki MS." Another characteristic leaders had in common, which can be inferred from these examples, was an above-average level of literacy.

ever alienated or marginal those men might be) muted the defiance of norms of community solidarity that membership in a union necessarily involved.

Also helpful in attracting members were Yamasaki's growing reputation as a champion of tenant farmers in Izumo and the success of unions already affiliated with the federation in winning meaningful gains (principally, but not exclusively, rent reductions) for their members. The proclamations of Yamasaki's regional federations, which were designed to persuade ordinary tenant farmers of the legitimacy of their grievances, were another factor. Avoiding unfamiliar and therefore threatening terminology, these proclamations portrayed class action—objectively a radical departure from established norms—as a higher form of patriotism. Both to mollify fears among tenants and to forestall reprisals by officials, they invoked imperial symbols on behalf of the tenant movement. The proclamation of the Tenant Federation of Nōgi and Yatsuka Districts (1925) provides a good example:

> The majority of Japanese are farmers, and the majority of farmers are tenants. By their efforts the nation is protected, its land cultivated, and its people fed. But for many years now the evils brought about by the unimpeded power of wealthy landlords have hung like a dark cloud over the countryside, obstructing the infinite benevolence of His Imperial Majesty. Moreover, rural living standards have not kept pace with progress in the rest of the country. As a result tenant farmers have truly suffered. At this time, we tenant farmers, inspired by the fundamental principles of the Empire and by the spirit of love for humanity, stand in the forefront of rural reform. We reject all violent means, for we are convinced that championing righteousness and morality gives us greater strength.
>
> Until the light shines brightly on the countryside—We shall persevere steadily until both the fields that we love and we ourselves are favored with boundless Imperial grace. In striving to reach our goals we must resist all blandishments and be prepared to face untold persecution. Whatever voices are raised against us, we must remember that our cause is just. . . .[64]

Yamasaki was sharply criticized by contemporary leftists for "misguiding" tenant farmers with such notions as imperial benevolence and love for humanity. Later Japanese scholars of the tenant movement have also criticized him for his acceptance of "the emperor system," his use of army reservists as union leaders, and, above all, his "defection" from Nichinō. To most of these scholars, Yamasaki ranks with the leaders of

---

[64] SKNKS, p. 192 n. 2. The proclamation of the Tenant Federation of Yatsuka District, which does not refer explicitly to the emperor, appears ibid., pp. 202-203.

two other independent regional federations, Sugai Kaiten of Niigata and Yokota Hideo of Gifu, as a reactionary within the tenant movement and "traitor" to its revolutionary cause.[65] Although I tend to feel that major social and political restructuring—perhaps even a revolution—was needed in Taishō Japan, I cannot accept this negative evaluation of Yamasaki. It ignores, among other things, the success he had—greater, I think, than the more explicit and ideologically "advanced" efforts of Nichinō or its affiliates—in mobilizing tenant farmers and nurturing in them a new and implicitly revolutionary consciousness. Far from being a reactionary, he used what later came to be regarded as reactionary symbols and reactionary rhetoric with consummate skill to accomplish the crucial task of getting tenant farmers into unions and into his federation. Once that was achieved, Yamasaki and his associates began educating those tenants, instilling in them new knowledge and new ideas that enabled them both to perceive the need for change and to act to bring it about.

One of the most important facets of the fourth, educational stage of the movement's organizational strategy was publication of a newspaper, *Kosakunin* (*The Tenant Farmer*). Realizing that there were limits to what could be accomplished by personal contacts alone (*kuchi dake de wa ikenai*), Terada Noriaki suggested in 1923 that some sort of newsletter be produced to publicize the federation's activities and goals. He and a few other young men from Ido collected thirty yen, bought a mimeograph machine, and began experimenting with it.[66]

From this modest beginning evolved an increasingly polished and effective publication. In 1926 six-page issues of *Kosakunin* appeared on a regular monthly basis and were distributed to over 3,000 subscribers.[67] Professionally printed instead of mimeographed, the paper appears to have become more relevant and accessible to its intended audience than it had been initially. "You were once just a paper for literary youth," a reader wrote in 1926, presumably referring to a plethora of abstract and theoretical essays in earlier issues, "but now you have developed into something completely different."[68] That "something completely different" consisted of useful advice and inspirational messages written in

[65] "Zadankai," SKNKS, p. 324. For examples of subsequent scholarly opinion, see Hayashi, "Shoki kosaku sōgi no tenkai," especially p. 5; Yoshioka, NNUS, p. 821. Profiles of Yokota and Sugai appear ibid., pp. 1157-1162.

[66] "Zadankai," SKNKS, p. 324. For the first issue Terada composed the slogan, "Until the light shines brightly on the countryside." Beneath it appeared a crude drawing of "tenant farmers pushing the globe toward a bright future." I think the symbolism here is significant: tenant farmers were to achieve their goal by their *own* actions.

[67] "Yamasaki Memo," NNUS, p. 819. Each issue sold for 1 *sen*; a year's subscription, including postage, cost 50 *sen*. Issues for February through December, 1926 are on file at Hōsei Daigaku Ōhara Shakai Mondai Kenkyūjo, Tokyo.

[68] *Kosakunin*, 10 February 1926, p. 6.

straightforward Japanese that most tenant farmers could comprehend. *Furigana* were printed beside each Chinese character, giving its phonetic reading. Plain verb forms and a conversational style were employed.[69] Except in articles about politics, which I will discuss at a later point, the vocabulary usually was simple and concrete. On the rare occasions when a technical term or abstraction appeared, it was carefully defined.

Most of the writing for *Kosakunin* was done by Yamasaki, Terada, and other federation officers, but subscribers too were invited to submit news items, essays, poems, and reflections. The following letters from two Izumo tenant farmers give some idea of the kind of response the paper generated:

> I just received your paper. I too am a propertyless tenant farmer. I am a miserable creature who lives at the very bottom rung of capitalist society. The key to our liberation is a class newspaper like yours. By reading this kind of newspaper we get the weapons to break our chains. In that connection, please add my name to your list and lead me to the goal of liberation. I enclose stamps for a two-year subscription.

o

> When the factory where I worked was destroyed in the recent [Kanto?] earthquake, I came back to the countryside. What shocked me most about my village was the credit union. Everyone including tenant farmers contributes money, and then the landlords and wealthy people borrow that money at low interest rates and use it as capital for their investments. Poor people like us, who don't have anything to put up as collateral, can't get a loan at all. So that credit union is just a money-making tool for landlords. I think you should attack things like that all the time in your newspaper. I'll let you know if I uncover anything else about this credit union. Your paper has a lot to do in the future. Keep up the struggle. I got you thirty subscribers here. Goodbye.[70]

In addition to items on such practical topics as how to set up a cooperative to purchase farm tools,[71] *Kosakunin* devoted considerable space

[69] Polite verb forms were used in articles addressed to women; see, for example, *Kosakunin*, 10 July 1926, p. 3.

[70] *Kosakunin*, 10 February 1926, p. 6. Among other contributions from readers was a rice-planting (*taue*) song composed by the women's association of a hamlet in Araijima village entitled "Landlords' Punishment." In rough translation: "Landlords get rich and fat by squeezing tenants/Then Heaven punishes them with illness/They waste their money on fancy doctors/But that won't cure them/They should try being kind to their tenants instead"; *Kosakunin*, 10 June 1926, p. 1.

[71] *Kosakunin*, 10 June 1926, p. 3.

to legal questions of concern to tenant farmers. In the March 1926 issue, for example, an extended discussion of ordinary and permanent tenancy rights was printed. It began with the observation that one of the reasons landlords threatened lawsuits over rent arrears and other issues was to intimidate tenants; ignorant of the law and "terrified of going to court," tenants would, landlords hoped, give in to demands without a struggle. Only by knowing their rights and conquering their fear of the law could tenants protect themselves. Moreover, they could use that knowledge to improve tenancy conditions. Getting rents reduced, the article observed, was a particularly easy task: *Kosakuryō o makesasu koto mo asameshi mae no koto da.*[72] In the May issue the more specific question of how a tenant should go about protecting his rights of occupancy in the face of an eviction attempt by his landlord was discussed. Like most other articles containing useful information, this one also contained an exhortation to rely upon the union; its officers and legal advisers would do the necessary paperwork free of charge and help the tenant if he went to court.[73]

Other articles were devoted entirely to exhortation. Each issue of the paper began with an introductory essay (*kantōgen*) about some aspect of the tenancy system or the tenant movement, often taking the season as its starting point:

It is March. The plum trees are in blossom, the nightingales sing. But tenant farmers are too exhausted from . . . hard work and their miserable diet of pickled radishes to take any pleasure in the fragrance of the blossoms or the silvery voices of the birds.

All they can think about is getting some rice to eat. The crop they raised last year . . . is now completely gone. . . . [They tell themselves] the seeds they planted weren't good enough. They didn't tend their fields carefully enough. . . . This year they will use better seeds and work harder so the rice will not desert them in their time of need.

What fools tenants are to think this way! "Poverty can be overcome by diligence." That is what they've learned at school. But it's not so. No matter how hard they try, they can't solve their problems by diligence alone.[74]

Another introductory essay, this one written by Yamasaki for the June issue, invoked the experiences of farmers in early summer to attract attention:

[72] "[It] can be done before breakfast"; *Kosakunin*, 10 March 1926, p. 4.
[73] *Kosakunin*, 10 May 1926, p. 1.
[74] *Kosakunin*, 10 March 1926, p. 1.

It's that busy time of year when everyone could use some extra help in harvesting the vetch or the wheat and getting ready for planting rice. With the silkworms coming out of molt again we get hardly any sleep at night. Our joints ache from weariness . . . when we get up in the morning.

Why must we work so hard? . . . What rewards do we tenants get for our labor? Do we even get enough food to fill our bellies, or clothing to keep us warm, or decent houses to protect us from the rain?

We're not machines . . . or draft animals. We're human beings. . . . That our labor goes to make idle landlords richer . . . is enough to make me weep. Were we growing crops for the benefit of society as a whole, it wouldn't matter how hard we had to toil. If more rice or more cocoons were needed so that many people could live, we'd work for nothing if need be. . . . But we aren't going to be the means by which a few human beings can live in . . . luxury.[75]

The theme of the injustice of the status quo was dealt with in numerous other articles, among them one rather provocatively titled "Why are Tenant Unions Trying to Destroy Landlords?" Like the June introductory essay quoted above, it too made the point that tenants were not seeking change for purely selfish reasons, this time citing their dedication to the villages in which they lived:

[People ask] why have tenant farmers organized unions and set out to destroy the landlords they used to honor and obey? . . . Consider the condition of villages today. On the one hand there are tenant farmers who find it hard to make ends meet no matter how hard they work. On the other hand are landlords, who don't work at all. . . . These landlords are few in number, but the number of hard-pressed tenants has increased steadily. More and more of them have had to abandon their native villages and head for the cities. The fields of the idle landlords are no longer carefully tended and may eventually become wasteland. . . .

We feel no hatred toward landlords as individual human beings. But when we consider them as members of a community who ought to . . . be concerned about that community's future, we can only regard them as enemies. They are traitors who are destroying the villages in which they live by their own lust for riches. . . . If they would abandon their petty concerns and strive to serve the com-

---

[75] *Kosakunin*, 10 June 1926, p. 1. What I have rendered in translation as "idle landlords" was expressed in the original as *norari kurari to asonde kurashite iru* landlords, not as *kiseiteki* (parasitic) landlords. The latter, more abstract term was popular among contemporary leftists but was avoided by Yamasaki.

munity as a whole, they would benefit too. It is to get them to recognize this fact and stop charging excessive rents that we have organized tenant unions. . . . We do this out of duty and love toward our villages and toward our ancestors who settled those villages originally and brought the land under cultivation. We will go on . . . until [landlords] change their mistaken ways and vow to strive for the benefit and happiness of the entire community. We're not out to destroy landlords. We're trying to educate them.[76]

Yamasaki wrote frequently for *Kosakunin*, returning again and again to the theme that tenant farmers could improve their lives by solidarity and solidarity alone. Although aware of developments in the tenant movement in other parts of the country, he rarely referred to them. Indeed, he seems to have held both his wider knowledge of the world and his youth in check, adopting instead the homespun approach of a wise old man. Building upon what local tenant farmers knew, he sought to lead them to new perceptions. "One can't tell the value of a house when the weather is fine," he wrote on one occasion.

But in a heavy storm one knows right away if the roof is strong enough or not. . . . The same thing is true of villages. A village that has a tenant union and one that doesn't or a village with a solid union and a village with a weak union—they're all the same when things are going smoothly. . . . But in this world we don't get bumper crops every year. Landlords change too, as sons take over from their fathers. It happens sometimes that a greedy fellow becomes head of the house. . . . It's at times like that that the value of a union becomes clear. . . .

The weakest tenants are those who've formed a union under their landlord's direction. They think they're well off, but they end up paying higher rents than anybody else. Next . . . are tenants in villages with no unions at all. They get summoned one by one [to the landlord's house]. Terrified, they prostrate themselves and . . . pay whatever the landlord asks. Then come the villages with unions that don't belong to a federation. At first, just the very existence of a union in the village will scare the landlords. . . . But landlords are no fools. After a few years at most they'll start studying the law and talking with lawyers. Then the union starts having trouble. . . . Nobody is there to help. . . . The landlords sense that the union is weak and move in for the kill. . . . That's when the advantages of belonging to a federation will be clear.[77]

---

[76] *Kosakunin*, 10 March 1926, p. 3.
[77] *Kosakunin*, 10 March 1926, p. 2.

In an unusually long essay titled "The Power of Unions to Transform Dogs and Cats into Human Beings," Yamasaki cast his thoughts about unions in yet another way, this time clearly revealing his commitment to achieving dignity, as well as equity, for tenant farmers:

"Beg for three days and the taste will last three years." By relying on the benevolence of their landlords as if they were dogs or cats, tenant farmers have led a beggar's existence for a long time. . . . They and their families barely scrape by on the basis of the favors they receive—the relief, the sympathy presents, the patronage, the pity. . . . Whether they live or die, eat or starve, depends on their landlords' generosity. If tenants don't do exactly as their landlords say . . . the landlords will turn them away just as they'd turn away stray dogs. . . .

There is absolutely no reason for landlords to treat tenants like beggars, and yet they persist in doing so. . . . Recently, too, some tenant farmers have allowed themselves to be organized into landlord-tenant conciliation unions. They pride themselves on belonging to the committees that dispense bonus rice, sympathy rice when crops are poor, relief rice, and money for fertilizer or farm tools. Despite the high-sounding name and fancy organization [these conciliation associations] are nothing more than the latest means landlords have seized upon to keep tenants in their place, the latest means to keep them living like beggars. The tenants who serve on the committees think they're doing grand work, but in reality they are nothing but the landlords' cats-paws. . . .

Landlords know that they take an unfair share of the crop from tenants, and they're afraid tenants will realize it. They try to divert the tenants' attention by doling out relief rice, sympathy rice, and bonus rice. Portraying themselves as benevolent *oyakata*, they give tenants as charity what they ought to give them as their due. As a result, tenants get cheated not only out of their property, but out of their self-respect as well. . . .

The only way to change this—to free tenants from the opiate of benevolence and paternalism that oppresses them in everything they do and reduces them to groveling for favors like dogs and cats, the only way to elevate them from the demeaning status of beggars to the dignity of human beings—is by means of tenant farmer unions. Only when landlords . . . have been subjected to the pressure of a union created by tenant farmers themselves will tenant farmers become aware of their own power. Then they will begin to develop pride and self-respect. They will come to see that by relying on their own united strength they can do without favors. . . . That will be the day that dogs and cats become human beings, the day that tenants forever free themselves from humiliating dependence on landlords.[78]

The organization in action. One can divide the activities of the successive federations of tenant unions in Izumo into three general categories: those concerned with landlord-tenant relations and the tenancy system; those concerned with farm management and community life; and those concerned with politics at the local and supralocal level. Not surprisingly, given the strong views and considerable influence of Yamasaki himself, the movement continued to emphasize activities in the first category throughout its existence. Activities in the second category played in retrospect a pivotal role. On the one hand, they constituted a logical extension, which Yamasaki actively encouraged, of efforts to improve the lives and livelihoods of tenant farmers. On the other hand, they led—equally logically, it would seem—to concern with village politics and, ultimately, to concern with the policies of Shimane prefecture and the central government. Political activities, in turn, involved the movement in the rivalries of the national tenant movement, which contributed to growing dissension among the leaders of the Shimane Tenant Federation and resulted, in late 1927, in the expulsion by Yamasaki of several federation members. The tenant movement in Izumo never recovered from this rupture.

Among federation activities concerned with landlord-tenant relations and the tenancy system two figured most prominently. The first was what Yamasaki termed, not without a touch of wit, rent adjustment (*todai seiri, todai* being a local term for rent payments). If land itself could be adjusted (*kōchi seiri*) so too could tenant rents. The latter should be just as rational and efficient as the former. Instead of being determined by custom or by what Yamasaki termed "exploitation" (charging whatever the market would bear), rents should be based on the productivity of the land concerned and on an equitable sharing of risks and costs between landlord and tenant.[79]

Based partly on Yamasaki's own assessment of what was wrong with the tenancy system and partly on his reading of "A Treatise on Fair Rents" by Nasu Shiroshi, professor of agricultural economics at Tokyo University,[80] the movement's program of *todai seiri* evolved through several stages. Initially local tenant unions sought reform of the traditional system of granting rent reductions when harvests were poor. Since the Meiji era, if not earlier, it had been customary for local landlords to reduce rents in bad years so that tenants were left with a minimum of

---

[78] *Kosakunin*, 10 April 1926, p. 3.
[79] "Yamasaki Memo," NNUS, p. 819.
[80] "Kōsei naru kosakuryō," published in 1924 in the journal *Kaizō*.

four *to* of rice per *tan*. By whatever means they could devise—sometimes a petition would suffice, in other cases prolonged negotiations were required—tenants sought to raise that minimum, to six *to* at least, and to eight, ten, or twelve *to* if their bargaining position was exceptionally strong.[81]

Next, local unions began carrying out detailed surveys to determine the productivity of each plot of land within their communities and compiling equally detailed accounts of costs of production and income earned per *tan*. It is significant and by no means coincidental that both tasks were assigned to tenant farmers themselves. In Yamasaki's view, tenant farmers knew the land better than landlords or so-called agricultural "experts" from elsewhere and therefore could do a better job of surveying it.[82] That they might gain satisfaction from accomplishing the task and useful insights from keeping records of their incomes and expenditures had also, one can safely conclude, occurred to Yamasaki.

The penultimate stage of *seiri* was the calculation of fair rent levels. Yamasaki advocated and the federation appears to have adopted what he termed the 8:3:4:6 system as a guiding principle. Of the first eleven *to* of rice produced per *tan*, eight *to* would go to the tenant to cover his costs of production and three *to* would go to the landlord to cover his tax liabilities. Any remaining produce above the eleven *to* thus accounted for, which constituted only 42 percent of average yields per *tan* in Shimane for the period 1916-1920, would be divided on a 4:6 basis between landlord and tenant, respectively, compensating the former for his investment and the latter for his labor.[83]

The final stage was the presentation of proposed new rent levels to the landlords concerned. According to Yamasaki, by 1927 roughly two-thirds of all landlords in Izumo had agreed to rent adjustment, more or less along the lines described above. In some cases, the prospect of a virtually automatic determination of rents even in years of poor harvest had been enough to gain their consent. In other cases, landlords had agreed to adjustments only after tenants had shown their solidarity and determination during months or even years of disputes.[84]

The second federation activity concerned with landlord-tenant relations and tenancy conditions was conflict itself, that is, the theory and

[81] "Zadankai," SKNKS, p. 325; "Yamasaki Memo," NNUS, p. 819; 10 *to* = 1 *koku* = 5.1 bushels (U.S. dry measure).

[82] "Yamasaki Memo," NNUS, p. 819; see SKNKS, pp. 169-174 for examples of these accounts.

[83] "Zadankai," SKNKS, p. 335. Yamasaki regarded Nichinō's advocacy of 30 percent rent reductions on all tenanted land as "unrealistically mechanical"; ibid., p. 323.

[84] "Yamasaki Memo," NNUS, pp. 831-832. For a description of a difficult case, see "Zadankai," SKNKS, pp. 336-337.

practice of tenancy disputes. As promised in the pages of *Kosakunin*, the federation came to the aid of tenants or tenant unions involved in disputes, providing advice on strategy and tactics and, when necessary, free legal aid. Equally important as far as Yamasaki was concerned, the federation organized training courses and workshops throughout Izumo to inform tenant farmers about laws relating to tenancy, and in particular the tenancy conciliation law of 1924.[85]

Although Nichinō took a formal stand against the conciliation law, Yamasaki concluded after careful study of its provisions and of the proceedings of the parliamentary committee that had considered it that it had potential; if well-coached in its intricacies, tenants could use what was basically "bourgeois" legislation to their own advantage. Among other things, both sides of a dispute subject to conciliation could be made to appear personally in court. Used to delegating such tasks to their lawyers, landlords would be on unfamiliar ground.[86] While conciliation was in progress, moreover, landlords could not file suit against tenants to recover unpaid rents or to secure return of their land. Tenants therefore could use the law to gain time, negotiating privately with some of the landlords who were party to the dispute in the hope of reaching a favorable and precedent-setting settlement of outstanding differences.[87] Given the primacy accorded to private property rights in Japan, tenants could not expect a favorable decision in all cases of conciliation. But if they presented a legitimate reason for the position they took in the dispute, provided evidence to back up their claim, and observed the correct forms and terminology in all their communications with the judge, they stood a reasonable chance of success. In cases involving eviction, the only legitimate claim tenants had was possession of permanent tenancy rights. In cases involving rent arrears, their only legitimate claim was a poor harvest.[88] In addition to discussing these

---

[85] The federation retained a lawyer, but according to Yamasaki gave him more business than money; ibid., p. 327. Training courses and workshops are discussed ibid., p. 323; Yoshioka, NNUS, pp. 825, 826.

[86] "Zadankai," SKNKS, pp. 323, 329-330. Yamasaki observed that some landlords, receiving a court summons for the first time in their lives as a result of action taken by their tenants, felt that "the world had been turned upside down."

[87] Ibid., p. 332. See also Mori, *Kosaku sōgi senjutsu*, pp. 77-104.

[88] "Zadankai," SKNKS, p. 327. No tenant looked forward to crop failure, but the utility of a minor decline in yields in pressing for concessions from landlords was widely recognized enough to be proverbial: *kosaku ni wa fusaku no hō ga toku datta* (in tenancy poor harvests pay off); quoted in Takahashi and Shirakawa, *Nōchi kaikaku to jinushi sei*, p. 97. I think this attitude helps to explain why poor harvests were reported as the major cause of disputes in the 1920s. When yields declined, tenants had grounds to seek improvement in the terms of tenancy. Opportunity, not desperation, motivated their actions.

points at workshops, the federation made general guidelines and sample petitions available to all affiliated unions.[89]

Like tenants elsewhere in the country, tenants in Izumo were not interested solely in lower rents and more secure cultivating rights, important as those issues were. They also wanted improvements in farm management and community life. At the annual meeting of the Nōgi federation in 1924, for example, nine of the twenty-five proposals for action submitted to the membership by participants concerned the latter two issues. Among the specific problems identified in these proposals were the high cost of everyday necessities and farm tools, excessive demands made by the community for donated labor and monetary contributions, and lack of uniformity in the scheduling of holidays.[90]

The federation's basic response to these and other concerns was to provide information and encourage self-help by member unions. Workshops on new farming techniques and demonstrations of new tools were scheduled at annual meetings or local union gatherings, and simply written pamphlets on a variety of topics were made available below cost.[91] In December 1926, an entire page of *Kosakunin* was devoted to information about why and how local unions should establish consumer cooperatives for the purchase of salt, sugar, and other staples.[92] Earlier the same year *Kosakunin* reported in glowing terms an experiment in cooperative farming underway in Ido and Yokoyama hamlets of Mori village. Tenants in the two hamlets had pooled the land they cultivated and formed teams to carry out all farming tasks. By early June the teams had planted rice in seed beds and harvested the vetch crop. In early July they transplanted the rice seedlings into the paddy fields. Afterwards a commemorative photograph was taken, and the tenants marched triumphantly through the village.[93]

There were limits, however, to the improvements in farm management or community life that tenants could effect on their own. Even if,

---

[89] "Zadankai," SKNKS, pp. 323, 327. Yamasaki was not the only tenant leader to perceive advantages in the conciliation law. A union official in Niigata observed: "Conciliation is like [the game of] pole-pushing. The side with patience and strength in reserve wins. It's the side that can make the last strong push after a lot of feints that gets the victory"; quoted in Mori, *Kosaku sōgi senjutsu*, p. 103.

[90] SKNKS, p. 176 n. 11.

[91] *Kosakunin*, 10 June 1926, p. 3.

[92] *Kosakunin*, 10 December 1926, p. 1 of special section. Apparently many of the cooperatives that were established in 1926 went bankrupt within a few years; SKNKS, p. 222.

[93] *Kosakunin*, 10 July 1926, p. 3, and 10 June 1926, p. 3. The June article emphasized the spontaneous (*jihatsuteki*) nature of the undertaking: "It is not like other efforts at cooperative farming that only exist on paper and whose leaders devote their time to getting money from the government."

as in Ido, they constituted the entire hamlet population and therefore could decide hamlet affairs as they saw fit, they had to deal with other hamlets, and other interests, in the village if they were to realize desired changes in the allocation of water for irrigation, the scheduling of repairs on roads and bridges, or other matters that fell within the purview of the village assembly. Similarly, numerous policies of the prefectural government—concerning taxes and surtaxes, for example, or the location of agricultural experiment stations—impinged on the economic interests of tenants, just as prefectural police regulations (to be discussed later) impinged on the very existence of tenant unions and the conduct of tenancy disputes. In short, tenants were impelled toward involvement in politics.

Until 1925 that involvement was limited by property qualifications on the franchise at both the local and supralocal levels. Tenants might lobby successfully for voting rights in their own hamlets, which were not affected by government regulations on that score.[94] But only tenants who owned a fair amount of their own land could vote or run for office in village elections, and only a tiny minority of tenants owned enough land to qualify to vote in prefectural or national elections. In general, then, tenant unions relied on indirect (though not necessarily ineffectual) means to change village policies, and from time to time they petitioned *gun* or prefectural officials on issues of concern to them.

The passage of the universal manhood suffrage law in 1925 enabled tenants throughout Japan to vote and run for office at all levels, a right they exercised with some success that very year when village elections were held. Out of 9,331 villages in which elections occurred, tenants were elected to assembly seats in 3,142, acquiring a total of 9,061 seats. In 761 of those villages, tenants acquired one-third or more of the total number of seats, possessing an absolute majority of seats in 340 villages and occupying all seats in 38.[95]

As a result of village elections in Shimane, the number of tenant farmers holding assembly seats rose from 51 to 172 (out of a total of 878). Of these tenants 147 (86 percent) had "no connection" with tenant unions, a situation that prevailed throughout Japan. Eleven successful candidates were members of Nichinō-affiliated unions, located predominately in the Iwami region of western Shimane. Fourteen were members of "other unions," including an unspecified number who belonged to unions in

[94] For an example of how tenants won such voting rights, see Kawamura, "Kosaku sōgiki ni okeru sonraku taisei," pp. 119-126.

[95] Nōrinshō, Nōmukyoku, "Taishō jūyon nendo chōsonkai giin kaisen ni okeru kosakunin gawa jōsei ni kansuru chōsa," reprinted in NSSS, pp. 68, 70, and 72 (tables 1, 3, and 5). Tenants previously had occupied a total of 3,669 village assembly seats out of 42,738; ibid., pp. 71, 73 (tables 4, 6).

the Nōgi Yatsuka federation in Izumo.[96] Federation leaders may have encouraged individual tenant farmers to seek office at the village level, but no formal policy was established in that connection.

Nor was more than a modest effort made to mobilize Izumo tenants for the prefectural assembly election of 1926. Several articles about politics appeared in the February issue of *Kosakunin*. One presented a program for "the rationalization of prefectural government," which called primarily for reform of local taxes and improvement of the educational system. Another article pointed out the need for attention to prefectural politics, urged tenants to support candidates who would work on their behalf, and, significantly, called for candidates to come forward: "Anyone with common sense will do. . . . Not having money or education makes no difference at all."[97] At the time the election was less than three weeks away. No tenant candidates had yet been selected, and none would be.[98]

After February 1926 there was relatively little mention of politics in the pages of *Kosakunin*. When the subject did appear it was treated in a manner that contrasted sharply with the newspaper's general style. Both the language and the concepts employed were complex, not simple; the erudition, not the experience, of readers was being addressed. Rather than being presented as a concern of all tenant farmers, politics was dealt with as the special concern, indeed, the mission, of rural youth.

"We know well," one article began, "that all of nature is divided into predators and prey. Every living thing, be it plant or animal, must fight for its survival." The article then pointed out that youth had a vital role to play in the ongoing struggle for survival within society:

> The exploiters and the exploited are now in conflict . . . and it is our duty as members of the exploited class to join the fray. . . .
>
> History shows that all change has been carried out by youth. Is there no lesson there for us? . . . Youth must attack all systems of thought based on customs of the past. We cannot leave this task to the older generation. They've lost hope. They've lost the will to prevail. We must lead the way in building a new society.[99]

---

[96] Ibid., pp. 68-73 (tables 1, 3, 4, 5, and 6). As in Shimane, 86 percent of the tenants elected to village assemblies in 1925 had "no connection" with tenant unions; ibid., p. 70 (table 3). Why more tenant union members did not run for or succeed in obtaining village assembly seats throughout Japan is an interesting question that merits further study.

[97] *Kosakunin*, 10 February 1926, pp. 1, 2. Recommendations for tax reform included the elimination of taxes on bicycles and carts, items that many tenants possessed, and the imposition of taxes on such "luxuries" as gardens, villas, and concubines. Chief among the educational improvements called for was the creation of more lower-level agricultural continuation schools to benefit the children of tenant farmers.

[98] SKNKS, p. 220.

[99] *Kosakunin*, 10 May 1926, p. 3.

Another article in the same issue called upon young tenant farmers to use their new political rights to reform local government:

Just as a jewel, if left uncut, has no value, a human being who has never battled adversity cannot develop his full potential. . . . Lincoln, who freed hundreds of thousands of Negro slaves at the time of the American Civil War, endured great hardship [as a boy], as did Napoleon, who spent his childhood in wretched poverty. Haven't young men of the tenant class, who have fought against adversity [all their lives], developed more character than young landlords? I fervently hope these propertyless young men will soon be brandishing the sword of reform in village politics.

In every country of the world the energy of youth has played a crucial role in history. Our own Meiji Restoration, carried out by a mere handful of young men from Satsuma and Chōshū, is but one example. Like a great ball of flame their energy brought about the end of Tokugawa tyranny and the establishment of a national government. Youth easily defeated age and took command of political reform. Reflecting on their victory, it seems fit and proper that the youth of today . . . stand up against the tyranny of landlords. . . .

Fabius, a hero of ancient Rome, retreated before the overwhelming force of Hannibal's invading army rather than face him in battle. Then when Hannibal's soldiers had grown lax and dropped their guard, Fabius mobilized all his troops and launched a massive counterattack. The invading army was smashed to pieces.

Today the old guard [in the villages] has grown lax. They have no idea of the passions that stir our young blood. This is the time to act, to sound the cry for political reform spearheaded by youthful vigor. The corrupt old system will be buried, and a new village politics embodying [our] glorious aspirations will be born.[100]

While some enthusiastic young federation members wrote articles like the above, others tried to get the federation to adopt an active political program and, in particular, to cooperate with other organizations in the prefecture and the country in electoral campaigns. Initially their efforts met with a degree of success. The federation took part in a conference of proletarian groups (musansha dantai hyōgikai) in the San'in region in October 1925. In April 1926 Yamasaki attended the inaugural meeting of Hirano Rikizō's All Japan Farmers' Union League in Tokyo and agreed to become one of its directors. As mentioned earlier, however, he withdrew after a brief period, disillusioned that Hirano and others were using tenant unions to further their own political careers. Already critical of Nichinō for advocating "revolution," Yamasaki decided against for-

[100] Ibid.

mal cooperation with other tenant or proletarian organizations. The program of the Shimane Prefecture Tenant Federation, which was established in July 1926, did not foreclose the possibility of political action—as one of its goals, the organization called for passage of a law "that firmly established tenancy rights"—but it included no specific plans for getting such a law enacted. Moreover, it reiterated the movement's longstanding commitment to "moderate, rational, and legal methods" and, in what constituted a rejection of the ideological tone of recent political essays in *Kosakunin*, stated the organization's resolve to "put an end to class conflict" (*kaikyū tōsō zetsumetsu o kisu*).[101]

Rebuffed in their efforts and increasingly isolated within the movement in Izumo, a number of young federation members began to look with increasing favor on the tenant movement in western Shimane, or Iwami. Affiliated with the regional Nichino federation in Tottori prefecture, the Iwami movement had emphasized leftist politics from its inception. One of its principal leaders, Ogawa Shigetomo, was a graduate of Kansai University. Returning home to Iwami in 1924, he had first worked as an elementary schoolteacher and then had resigned to devote all his energies to organizing tenant farmers. The other leader, Toyowara Goro, had been a labor union activist in Tokyo and had been arrested for his role in a textile workers' strike in 1926. Returning to his native village in Iwami to recover from the severe case of pleurisy he had developed in prison, he became involved in the local tenant movement. In March of 1927 Ogawa and Toyowara organized their own regional federation in Iwami, the Nichino Shimane Ken Kosaku Rengōkai, with 13 branches and 572 members. Two months later they staged a May Day celebration in Iwami that resulted in numerous arrests and, in Toyowara's opinion, heightened the political consciousness of all the tenants who had taken part.[102] Another focus of interest for would-be political activists in Izumo was the Seiji Kenkyūkai (Political Study Group) in Matsue. Organized in 1923 by Fukuda Yoshisaburō, a Marxist with experience in the Tokyo labor movement, the Kenkyūkai became active after 1925 in efforts to create a Labor Farmer party organization in Shimane.[103]

Early in 1927 Nichino experienced its second split, like the first, over the issue of whether or not to support the Labor Farmer party. Sugiyama Motojirō, president of Nichino since its creation, resigned and in March organized the Zen Nihon Nōmin Kumiai (All Japan Farmers' Union, or Zennichino). Now opposed to the Labor Farmer party and

---

[101] Yoshioka, NNUS, pp. 820, 830-831.

[102] Ibid., pp. 827-829. Toyowara returned to Tokyo in June 1927. Ogawa moved to Osaka to work in Nichino headquarters at the end of that year; ibid., p. 832.

[103] Ibid., pp. 837-838.

in favor of more moderate political efforts, Sugiyama appealed to and received the support of Yamasaki. With two "defecting" unions from the Nichinō federation in Tottori, Yamasaki organized the Zen Nihon Nōmin Kumiai San'in Rengōkai (All Japan Farmers' Union Federation of the San'in Region) in April of 1927. That step precipitated a clash with pro-Nichinō and pro-Labor Farmer party members of the Izumo movement.

In July 1927, after several weeks of jockeying for position, Kimura Kamezō, a young federation member from Yatsuka *gun* who was also involved in the Seiji Kenkyūkai, issued a proclamation calling for a united front between the competing Nichinō and Zennichinō federations in Shimane "in response to historical necessity and the will of the masses." Opposed to any dealings with Nichinō and, one suspects, offended at this direct challenge to his leadership, Yamasaki expelled Kimura from the federation. Kimura then rallied his supporters in Yatsuka and succeeded in getting the *gun* tenant organization to withdraw from Zennichinō and affiliate with Nichinō. Several months later Yamasaki experienced another and more painful blow. Adachi Iwao, who had worked with him since 1923 and who was then in charge of youth affairs within the federation, issued a proclamation calling, as had Kimura, for a united front. Yamasaki responded by firing Adachi forthwith. Taking a number of supporters with him, Adachi moved to Matsue. In mid-October he, Kimura, and other Nichinō supporters in Shimane joined with the Nichinō-affiliated unions in Tottori to form the San'in Chihō Nōmin Dantai Kyōgikai (Conference of Farmers' Organizations in the San'in Region).[104]

Finally, in the spring of 1928, the breach between Nichinō and Zennichinō at the national level was healed, the result being the creation of the Zenkoku Nōmin Kumiai (National Farmers' Union, or Zennō). That June the two competing organizations in Shimane united, as well, although each wing maintained its own leadership structure "so as not to upset its members."[105] Yamasaki took part in this new Zennō federation in Shimane, but without enthusiasm. In his view, the movement was at a stalemate, caught between "landlords and bureaucrats on the one hand, and communists on the other."[106] Local organization in Izumo was "paralyzed," its older leaders "tired" from an endless stream of late-night meetings, and many of its younger leaders tending to regard the movement as a "game." Members had fallen into debt because they had spent more than they had gained in rent reductions. Lacking con-

[104] Ibid., pp. 833-836, 839-842.
[105] Ibid., pp. 842-843.
[106] "Yamasaki Memo," NNUS, p. 838.

fidence in local union leaders, they did not pay their dues.[107] In Shimane as a whole, membership in the Zennō federation had declined to 520. The most active part of the federation was its youth branch, which engaged in literary study, conducted experiments in proletarian theater, and advocated reduction of the voting age to eighteen, conscription reform, support of public libraries, and the abolition of bourgeois sports.[108]

BUREAUCRATIC RESPONSES

In early August of 1926, five tenant union leaders from throughout Japan were invited to present their views to a special committee of the Kosaku Chōsakai, a commission headed by the minister of agriculture and charged with considering proposals for new legislation concerning tenancy relations and tenant unions.[109] Yamasaki Toyosada was one of the five. After identifying himself as a "mere youth of twenty-nine," inferior in education, experience, and knowledge to the thirty or so members of the committee, he spoke for roughly an hour, describing the problems that tenant farmers in Izumo had faced in the past, the goals and methods of the union movement he led, and his views on the need for the legislation under consideration.[110]

Concerning a law to redefine tenancy relations Yamasaki expressed enthusiasm. Existing law was geared to protecting landlords' rights to collect rents. What was required, he argued, was attention to productivity, that is, to encouraging tenants to raise output. Education in farming techniques was not enough. Tenants needed to have a stake in the land they cultivated, and the way to provide that was by giving them greater security of tenure.

Yamasaki then turned his attention to tenant unions, and urged the committee to leave them alone. Although proposed legislation would indeed grant de jure recognition to unions and to their right to engage in collective bargaining, it would at the same time subject them to government regulation—and that, in his view, would do far more harm than good. "All other agricultural groups that exist today," he observed, "depend on official patronage . . . and leadership. They are weak, hothouse organizations." In no other country at no time in his-

---

[107] Ibid., p. 832.

[108] Yoshioka, NNUS, pp. 844-846.

[109] Summaries of their remarks and the remarks of six other witnesses, most of them landlords, appear in "Kosaku chōsakai tokubetsu iinkai gijiroku," in NSSS, Supplement II, 157-257.

[110] Since no complete transcript of his remarks exists, what follows is based on the summary ibid., pp. 217-220, and on his report of his testimony as published in *Kosakunin*, 10 October 1926, p. 3.

tory have such organizations ever achieved meaningful results. The only way to solve the problems villages face is to rely on "natural," not on "manufactured," organizations: "Like a pine tree that has made a place for itself on a rocky crag, tenant unions have survived despite many obstacles. . . . It is because they have grown up in the wild that they are strong, and that wild strength [*yasei no chikara*] is the only means by which the countryside can be led to a bright future."[111]

Yamasaki's positive view of "the wild strength" of tenant unions was not shared by the Japanese government. On the contrary, the very existence of "wild," unregulated organizations challenged bureaucratic conceptions of the state. At the same time, cooptation—bringing those organizations into the state's administrative structure and making them channels for the implementation of state policy—was not an acceptable response, for that would entail recognizing and legitimizing the interests, however broadly or altruistically defined, of a single social class.[112] Despite some sentiment within the Ministry of Agriculture in favor of a tenant union law, no such legislation was ever enacted. Instead the bureaucracy sought to eradicate tenant unions. To do so it employed two different approaches. The first was repression, which began with petty harassment in the early 1920s and culminated in the arrests of "radical" unionists in 1928, 1929, and 1931. The second approach was reform, first of the machinery for dealing with landlord-tenant conflict, and ultimately, albeit only partially, of the tenancy system.

Official harassment of unions and unionists took many forms. Terada Noriaki recalled that the police would drop by his house unexpectedly, asking him interminable questions and making it hard for him to meet deadlines for the reports and articles he had to write.[113] Elsewhere, officials prevented local newspapers from reporting the details of tenancy disputes. Plainclothes policemen were sent into the countryside to learn about union plans and, if possible, to discover damaging personal information about union leaders. Auditors were dispatched to investigate the account books of unions for possible misuses of union funds.[114]

Beginning in 1921 in Gifu, officials in a number of prefectures with active tenant movements issued revised police regulations (*keisatsuhan shobatsurei*) to define and establish the penalties for a wide variety of illegal acts. Making collective action by tenants difficult, if not impossible, was clearly a major purpose of these regulations. The Shimane regulations, for example, included provisions that called for the impris-

[111] "Kosaku chōsakai gijiroku," p. 220; *Kosakunin*, 10 October 1926, p. 3.

[112] See Bernard Silberman's discussion of the bureaucracy earlier in this volume.

[113] "Zadankai," SKNKS, p. 325.

[114] The above examples are from Gifu prefecture, as reported in NNUS, pp. 669-670, 689, 690-691.

onment and/or fining of those who: participated in civil or criminal suits, non-litigation cases, or any other matters in which they had no direct, personal interest, or encouraged others to make complaints or file suits unless permitted by law; engaged in violent acts or incited others to such acts during the course of a dispute (*fungi*); engaged in mass demonstrations or attempted to negotiate en masse during the course of a dispute; employed gongs, drums, conch shells, or bugles to assemble or arouse others during the course of a dispute, or who used fireworks, bonfires, pine torches, or banners for the same purpose; and incited or mobilized others not to pay taxes or public imposts.[115]

Rather than preventing collective action, however, these regulations appear on balance to have contributed to what can be termed the "modernization" of the methods unions employed. Anxious to avoid fines and imprisonment, which imposed a heavy burden both on union treasuries and on themselves, union leaders were motivated to devise new procedures for conducting disputes and for creating and sustaining solidarity among union members. Those they devised were not only legal but more effective as well. To enable them to take part in suits and other matters in which they had no direct interest, union officials were formally elected as bargaining agents by the tenants concerned and granted power of attorney, duly executed and stamped, to act on the tenants' behalf. Armed with these documents, they did not have to persuade landlords to deal with them; landlords were constrained to do so by the law itself.[116] Instead of beating drums or lighting bonfires to assemble or arouse union members, they used posters, newsletters, and lecture meetings; when they needed to notify tenant unions in other communities that their help was needed—for example, to harvest crops before they could be sold at auction—they sent out telegrams.[117] Prevented from organizing boycotts not only of local taxes but also, in some prefectures, of local schools and such traditionally communal events as funerals,[118] they concentrated on direct forms of exerting pressure on landlords and on political action (such as getting tenants or their allies elected to hamlet and village assemblies) to bring about desired changes in local policy. Instead of violence, which was hard to control and often created resentments that were difficult to overcome, they emphasized disciplined and orderly behavior at union meetings and in disputes. Far from being a drawback, that proved an asset. On the one hand, it enhanced the respectability of union membership in the eyes of local ten-

---

[115] The complete text of these regulations, revised in November of 1924, appears in SKNKS, pp. 177-178 n. 13.

[116] Mori, *Kosaku sōgi senjutsu*, pp. 44-47.

[117] For an example, see NNUS, p. 530.

[118] Ibid., pp. 663, 667, 669-670.

ant farmers and helped prevent resignations. On the other hand, it deprived landlords of an opportunity to evade the issues involved in disputes; having no grounds on which to summon local police, they had to respond to tenant demands.[119]

The final stage in the repressive approach to tenant unions began on March 15, 1928, when more than 3,000 suspected communists were arrested throughout Japan. Virtually all of the members of Nichinō's executive committee were included among those arrested, much to the relief of the current minister of agriculture, Yamamoto Tatsuo, who announced to his officials that the countryside finally was being freed from the grip of dangerous radicals.[120] Further arrests followed in April 1929 and March 1931, the latter including such local union activists as Kimura Kamezō and the leaders of the Zennō youth branch in Shimane.[121]

Not even Yamasaki escaped imprisonment. In February 1931 he was sentenced to eight months in jail for interfering with a government official in the performance of his duties (kōmu shikkō bōgai). His crime, committed in December 1926, had been to grab hold of a bailiff to prevent him from terminating an auction of standing crops that had been ordered by a local court to compensate the owners of the land in question for their tenants' refusal to pay rents. Yamasaki had mobilized nearby union members to attend the auction, and they so dominated the proceedings that the crops were being sold, to the tenants, for only a fraction of their market value. When the bailiff realized what was happening, he started to leave the scene. It was then that Yamasaki grabbed him, in effect to make him perform his duty, not to prevent him from doing so. Not even Yamasaki's legal skills, however, were adequate to mounting a successful defense in the repressive atmosphere that prevailed, although he was able to prolong the proceedings against him by means of appeals for over four years.[122]

The repressive approach to unions accorded fully with the view, discussed earlier, that unions were the product of alien forces that had penetrated rural society and contaminated tenant farmers with subversive ideas. In that sense, the arrests of union leaders represented an attempt to sanitize the countryside. Bureaucrats appear to have recognized, however, that removing leaders from the scene would only provide a palliative, not a cure. In addition to repression, they also employed reform.

In the early 1920s, at the same time that they were harassing existing

[119] Mori, Kosaku sōgi senjutsu, pp. 9, 13-18, 64.
[120] Yamamoto's remarks are quoted in Hayashi, "Shoki kosaku sōgi no tenkai," p. 15.
[121] Yoshioka, NNUS, p. 846.
[122] Ibid., p. 830; "Zadankai," SKNKS, pp. 334, 336-338.

tenant unions, bureaucrats had tried to enlist landlords in efforts to prevent new unions from being organized. Three measures had been recommended: that landlords voluntarily reduce rents in order to deprive tenants of an issue on which disputes, and hence unions, might be based; that they refer any disputes that did occur to local agricultural associations (*nōkai*) for resolution; and that they organize their tenants into conciliation associations (*kyōchō kumiai*) to promote mutual understanding and goodwill.[123] The responses these recommendations generated were far from gratifying. Few landlords lowered rents of their own volition. Rather than submitting disputes to *nōkai*, they continued trying to settle them independently or in concert with other landlords. Although some landlords organized conciliation associations, at no time before the mid-1930s did those associations rival tenant unions in either number or membership.[124] As officials in Shimane reported with a touch of exasperation, landlords remained indifferent to all warnings until after problems with their tenants had arisen, by which time it was usually too late to prevent the formation of tenant unions.[125]

The recommendations made to landlords by bureaucrats had been predicated on the assumption that landlords would rally to the cause of village and social harmony, that is, that landlords were reliable agents of state policy who would transcend private interest to work for the common good. Given evidence that landlords had a considerably less disinterested sense of vocation, bureaucrats began to realize that the countryside itself, not just external influences upon it, required their attention.

The first manifestation of this realization was the tenancy conciliation law of 1924. Instead of relying on landlords and local *nōkai*, the government established new machinery, under the direct control of the bureaucracy, to resolve tenancy disputes.[126] Next, in 1925, bureaucrats proposed and the Diet enacted regulations to promote the establishment of owner-cultivators; low-interest loans were made available to tenants to enable them to buy the land they cultivated, in what amounted to an attempt, however inadequately funded, to prevent tenants from joining

---

[123] Hayashi, "Shoki kosaku sōgi no tenkai," pp. 3, 10. Yamasaki believed that conciliation associations posed a serious threat to the tenant movement and criticized them at every opportunity.

[124] Data on the number and membership of conciliation associations appear in NSSS, pp. 540–541, 550–551. In 1929 there were 1,986 conciliation associations (less than half the number of tenant unions) with a total membership of 244,943 (77.6 percent of the membership of tenant unions). Not until 1936 were there more members of conciliation associations than there were members of tenant unions.

[125] *Kosaku sōgi ni kansuru chōsa*, 2:347.

[126] Ogura Takekazu, *Tochi rippō no shiteki kōsatsu* (Tokyo, 1951), pp. 395–425.

unions or to encourage union members to resign.[127] The industrial association law (*sangyō kumiai hō*) of 1900, which despite its name had always had a greater impact on farming than on factories, was revised to make it easier for communities to establish consumer cooperatives for the purchase of basic necessities. Finally, in 1939, as the nation mobilized for war, bureaucrats were able to overcome the objections of landed interests in the Diet and secure passage of a law to establish fair rents (*tekisei kosakuryō*); a ceiling of 1 *koku* per *tan* in rent was imposed on top-grade land, with rents on lesser grades of land to be determined accordingly. Both landlords and tenants were to participate in determining rent levels.[128]

Implicit in these measures was the acknowledgment by bureaucrats that tenant unions, although unacceptable as organizations, had served legitimate needs among tenant farmers. To eradicate unions those needs had to be met in some other way. This was as close to equity as tenants were able to get until the postwar land reform.

---

[127] For discussion of the impact of these loans, see Nishida, "Kosaku sōgi no tenkai," pp. 537-540.

[128] "Zadankai," SKNKS, pp. 334, 335-336; Ogura, *Tochi rippō*, pp. 720-732.

LIBERAL INTELLECTUALS AND SOCIAL CONFLICT IN TAISHŌ JAPAN

Peter Duus

In his superb essay on class conflict in industrial society, Ralf Dahrendorf observes that there have been two main theories of social coherence in Western political thought. One holds that "social order results from a general agreement of values . . . which outweighs all possible or actual differences of opinion and interest"; the other holds that "coherence and order are founded on force and constraint, on the domination of some and the subjection of others."[1] Dahrendorf reveals his own biases by calling the former view Utopian, and the latter Rationalist. It would stack the cards less obviously to distinguish instead between a "consensus model" or "integrative model" of society as against a "coercion model" or "conflict model."

Dahrendorf argues that each model may be appropriate for a different set of analytical problems, but that in reality consensus and coercion are intertwined. "For sociological analysis," he writes, "society is Janus-headed, and its two faces are equivalent aspects of the same reality."[2] In the history of Western social thought, however, the two models have defined alternative visions of society, and they have been regarded as mutually exclusive. The question of what held society together divided Plato from Aristotle, Hobbes from Locke, and (in more recent times) Mills from Parsons. The issue may be a universal one. It can be found as well in the pre-Han debates between Legalist and Confucian. Invar-

---

[1] Ralf Dahrendorf, *Class and Class Conflict in Industrial Society* (Stanford, 1959), p. 157.
[2] Ibid., p. 159.

iably the position one chooses on the question is critical to how one views politics and what one sees as the appropriate institutions of government. If men are naturally cohesive they require one set of institutions, but if they are not they require another.

One can hypothesize that the debate usually lies dormant in times of social peace, but surfaces in times of social disorder. In our own recent history, for example, the Parsonians dominated the placid fifties when all seemed well with America, but they were challenged by the Millsians (and neo-Marxists) in the turbulent sixties. What triggered the debate anew was domestic conflict, the explosion of the civil rights movement, followed by the antiwar agitation.

As other essays in this volume point out, the closing years of Meiji and the early years of Taishō were in some ways similar to the American sixties. Ever more visible and urgent, signs of popular unrest began with the antitreaty riots of 1905. Domestic conflict gathered momentum in the 1910s and reached full force with widespread urban strikes and rural disputes after 1918. The origins of this conflict are complex, related in part to the accelerated growth of a capitalist economy, in part to social differentiation, in part to a decline in the legitimacy of the national leadership, and in part to changes in "the general trend" (jisei) of the outside world. But whatever their origins, or whatever forms they took, violent or nonviolent, episodes of social conflict were a sign to many that Japanese society was fragmenting into a welter of competing interests, focused on narrow parochial concerns, indifferent or oblivious to the claims of the whole. To borrow Harootunian's phrase, a process of secession was at work. The purpose of this essay is to explore the reaction of the liberal intelligentsia to these symptoms of social disintegration and conflict.

Until the end of the First World War, liberal social thought in Japan was dominated by the "consensus model." Although the liberal intellectuals often talked about social conflict in the abstract, or contemplated it at long distance in Europe, America, or China, they had little opportunity to observe it firsthand at home. From the 1880s, when most Taishō intellectuals were toddlers, through the Russo-Japanese war, when they reached manhood, the whole society seemed to have its eyes fixed on an overriding common goal: creating national strength in a competitive and sometimes predatory external world. The widely felt need for unity reached even into the primary school classroom. Yoshino Sakuzō recalled a song from his childhood that began, "Comrades, 30 million strong / Let us defend and protect our Japan."[3] A generation brought up on such fare was likely to find the "consensus" model a

---

[3] *Shinjin*, 16 (November 1915), 13.

more plausible description of society than the "conflict model." Large-scale domestic social struggle was a remote possibility, and even those of an older generation who saw disorder lurking on the fringes of society were addressing themselves to a potential danger rather than a present one.[4]

Equally important, the liberal intellectuals took an optimistic view of social stratification in Japanese society. Like others of their generation they had been brought up to believe that if a man were discontent with his lot in life, he had only to work hard and study, take the top place in his classes, graduate from the university, and enter the middle-class elite. Those who failed to accept life's challenge had no legitimate claim to protest unless unfortunate circumstances had prevented them from competing with their peers. The "clerical revolution" was a fait accompli, and the mechanisms of self-improvement through education were firmly in place. There was an extensive literature on self-help, as Earl Kinmonth's recent study has shown.[5] Yoshino Sakuzō wrote his first book on how to study for examinations, and even socialists such as Katayama Sen and Kōtoku Shūsui produced an abundant corpus on "getting on" in the world. This suggests that there existed among the educated middle classes a widespread view that society was equipped with automatic self-righting mechanisms to correct dissonance between talent and achievement, between personal worth and social position. The existence of social hierarchy, which no one denied, did not necessarily lead to social conflict as long as there were open routes between statuses. Class society could exist without class conflict as long as it was an open society.

By the early 1910s, however, easy optimism about the stability (and also the justness) of Japanese society began to erode. The country was experiencing a divisiveness it had not known since the popular rights (jiyūminken) movement in the 1880s. Something was wrong, and the liberal intellectuals were concerned to understand why. For the first time, as a group, they confronted social conflict as an immediate problem.

o

The liberals approached social conflict as a problem in constitutional theory. Speculation on what caused conflict was central to the debate over democracy (minponshugi ronsō) of the 1910s. At the forefront of this debate was the question, "can constitutional representative democracy

---

[4] See Kenneth B. Pyle, "The Technology of Japanese Nationalism: The Local Improvement Movement, 1900-1918," *Journal of Asian Studies*, 33 (November 1973), 53-55.

[5] Earl Henry Kinmonth, "The Self-Made Man in Meiji Japanese Thought," Ph.D. dissertation, Wisconsin, 1974.

work in Japan?" But inextricably intertwined with it was a second one, "is our country beginning to fly apart, and if so what can be done about it?" The latter issue was perhaps more basic, and certainly more enduring. Long after the flood of articles on *minponshugi* or the definition of democracy dwindled to a trickle, the problem of social coherence or stability remained a matter of widespread intellectual concern.

The *minponshugi* debate began with an attempt to understand the popular political demonstrations of 1905-1914: the antipeace treaty movement, the first movement to protect constitutional government, the antitax movement, and the protests over the Siemens scandal. All involved public rallies and marches in downtown Tokyo, and often the speech making dissolved into popular violence against visible symbols of governmental authority.

There was no uniform reaction among the liberal intellectuals as to the desirability of the demonstrations. At one extreme was Ukita Kazutami, the editor of *Taiyō*, an old-guard Christian liberal disgusted at the blind and irrational character of the crowd, who viewed popular demonstrations with considerable distaste. Demonstrations, he grumbled, were the work of "dangerous idlers" and "rash irresponsible youths."[6] At the other extreme was Hayashi Kiroku, a Keiō professor elected to the Diet, who read the demonstrations as a sign of healthy popular vigor. When the people of a nation merely followed orders docilely, he said, then the "destruction of the state" was at hand. He even had words of praise for the Ulster insurrection against the Home Rule Bill in 1914. "The very spirit, the very courage to offer extreme resistance to the government in order to protect one's own interest and one's own freedom—herein lies the foundation of British constitutional politics."[7]

Most liberals, however, were more ambivalent about the demonstrations than either Ukita or Hayashi. They took heart in one breath, and viewed with alarm in the next. To most, the demonstrations were a temporary symptom of a painful but inevitable transition from autocratic to constitutional government. It was possible to agree with Hayashi that the demonstrations indicated a healthy new political interest among the people, heretofore largely indifferent or apathetic, but it was also possible to see them as evidence that the constitutional system was not yet fully responsive to popular opinion. As long as demonstrations were spontaneous and positive in their goals, they were to be tolerated, and even welcomed, but if led by unscrupulous and ambitious demagogues, and directed toward negative goals, they represented a clear and

---

[6] Ukita Kazutami, "Gunshū no seiryoku o riyō shite kokusei o sa'u sen to suru fūchō o ronzu," *Chūō kōron* (hereafter *CK*), 39 (April 1914), 115-118.

[7] Hayashi Kiroku, "Minshū undō o rakkan su," *CK*, 39 (April 1914), 118-122.

present danger to society.[8] While no one expected mobs to storm the Imperial Palace as they had the Bastille (even Hayashi regarded the Hibiya riots mere "child's play" compared to European demonstrations), still the socially disruptive potential of the crowd was never out of sight. The specter of the destructive, mindless mobs of the French Revolution fluttered on the edge of liberal vision.

All the liberal intellectuals agreed on one point. The demonstrations were symptomatic of a popular discontent with government. Whether this discontent was justified or not—a question some raised—it was politically significant. Demonstrations were a substitute for public debate and the formation of responsible public opinion. "The reason we see these mob explosions today," observed Ukita, "is that there is no public opinion adequate to check governmental use of its authority."[9] Nagai Ryūtarō agreed, pointing out that the demonstrations occurred because the Diet did give expression to true public opinion. Yoshino Sakuzō, though he found the demonstrations deplorable in principle, observed that they were a public judgment on "backroom politics" (anshitsu seiji), which provided no mechanism for the accommodation of public opinion. Hayashi, striking a positive note, said that the people, awakened from a state of "political numbness," took to the streets because they were no longer content to be mere spectators in politics. Their unruliness was understandable, since they had little practice or experience in "popular politics" or "group action."[10]

Popular demonstrations thus had diagnostic significance, identifying the ills of the constitutional order. Yet further questions remained: How might these ills be cured? How were recurring demonstrations to be prevented? How could popular discontent be eliminated? For most liberals the cure was to be found in minponshugi. As Yoshino Sakuzō defined it, "Minponshugi not only locates the ends of government in the welfare of the people, it also requires that the opinions of the people be weighed heavily in the final determination of policy."[11] In other words, minponshugi represented a combination of "popular participation" (usually identified with an expansion of the suffrage and the establishment of responsible cabinets) and "social policy" (more or less synonymous with the social welfare policy). Although not all the liberals used the same terminology, they were generally agreed that this combination

---

[8] Yoshino Sakuzō, "Minshūteki shii undō o ronzu," ibid., pp. 126 ff.: Nagai Ryūtarō, "In'nai no gikai to ingai no gikai," ibid., pp. 122-126.

[9] Ukita, "Gunshū no seiryoku."

[10] Hayashi, "Minshū undō o rakkan su."

[11] Yoshino Sakuzō, "Kensei no hongi o toite sono yūshū no bi o sumasu michi o ronzu," CK, 31 (January 1916), 58.

was necessary to reduce the social discontent that found expression in demonstrations.

Although the idea of popular participation had antecedents in the Meiji period, the link between "social policy" and "popular welfare" was relatively new. Before 1912, policies to promote popular welfare had usually been defined in a negative way—administrative retrenchment, reduction of heavy arms expenditures, cutting taxes—all of which lightened the burden of national development on the ordinary taxpayer. But for the liberal intellectuals of Taishō, "popular welfare" was equated with a policy of providing all members of society with "equality of opportunity." This did not mean that the government should adopt a policy of social leveling, but merely that it should guarantee everyone equal educational opportunities, a secure livelihood, and protection from the economic consequences of sickness, unemployment, accident, or old age. These ideas had been promoted by "socialists of the chair" since the 1890s, but the liberal intellectuals of the 1910s wedded them to the notion of representative democracy. The link was established by a particular conception of the state. Ukita Kazutami argued, for example, that even though the state was sovereign in form, the state and the people were the same. The prosperity of the state was the prosperity of the people, and the progress of the state was the progress of the people.[12] The two could not be separated. Given this conception of the state, it was natural to conceive of *minponshugi* as embracing both the "right to participate" and the "right to exist."

During the early years of Taishō, however, the liberals were less concerned with social policy than with political reform, for they saw the Diet as the principal integrating social mechanism. The liberals did not defend representative politics on the ground that it protected the individual's right to participate in politics; they rejected the natural rights theory so popular in the *jiyūminken* period. Instead they followed an alternate tradition, going back to the earliest arguments for desirability of constitutional government, which saw a national assembly as a mode of promoting a sense of commonweal.

The political taxonomy of the Taishō liberals posited only two alternative models for political systems (*seitai*): the autocratic state and the constitutional state. This distinction was so stark that it allowed for little subtlety of argument. In an autocratic system, the state was set against society. As Tokutomi Sohō had argued in his *Shōrai no Nihon*, "A single people (*ikko no jinmin*) does not exist in a feudal society. . . . Officials do not exist to protect the people. The people exist to serve the officials.

[12] Quoted in Sumiya Etsuji et al., *Taishō demokurashii no shisō* (Tokyo, 1966), p. 58.

In short, there is no people."[13] In a constitutional system, by contrast, the interests of state and society were identical, since representative institutions provided communications between officials (*kan*) and people (*min*). It was common for the liberal intellectuals, appropriating an earlier political vocabulary, to describe the essence of constitutional government with terms like *kanmin dōkyō, kummin dōchi, kunmin dōsei*, or *banmin dōchi*. The operative element in all these terms was jointness or commonality (*dō*), which the parliamentary mechanism provided. Constitutional government was less the apotheosis of political individualism than the pursuit of collective harmony.

Although this line of argument was not unknown in Western democratic theory, it received primary emphasis in Taishō liberal thought. As Ōyama Ikuo observed in 1917, "We believe that true national unity (*kyōkoku itchi*) emerges from an intense awareness by the people of their common interest, and this intense awareness of common interest emerges when the people have taken on a common responsibility for the operation of the state as the result of the extension of the suffrage. . . ."[14] In arguing for universal manhood suffrage, Yoshino Sakuzō suggested that granting people the right to vote would increase their willingness to make sacrifices for the state, whether by giving their lives, or simply by paying their taxes. "It is both advisable and necessary," he wrote, "to promote the material and spiritual fulfillment of all the individuals who make up the state and to act in such a way that they will work *voluntarily* for the sake of the nation"[15] Neither true solidarity nor true commitment could exist under an autocratic system that allowed no popular political participation. Representative government—*minpon-shugi* in its political aspect—offered a means of precipitating, aggregating, and solidifying social consensus, and of intensifying popular commitment to the state.

To some extent, this stress on the integrative functions of representative government may have been rhetorical. The liberal intellectuals were anxious to show that a democratic political process was neither socially divisive nor subversive of popular nationalism. But clearly there was more to it than that. Ōyama, for example, once suggested that representative democracy was more compatible with the fundamental character of man as a social being than an autocratic system was. The origin of politics, he argued, lay in the urge of men toward community. Representative government led toward community by creating a sense of

[13] Sumiya Mikio, ed., *Nihon no meicho: Tokutomi Sohō* (Tokyo, 1971), p. 163.

[14] Ōyama Ikuo, "Kokka seikatsu to kyōdō rigai kannen," in Ōta Masao, ed., *Taishō demokurashii ronsō shi* 2 (Tokyo, 1971), 11-19.

[15] Yoshino Sakuzō, "Futsū senkyo no shomondai," in *Yoshino Sakuzō-hakase minshu-shugi ronshū* 6 (Tokyo, 1948), 184-185. Emphasis added.

common interest among all members of a society, whereas an autocratic system, which sharply divided ruler from ruled, did not. Democracy, therefore, was "a return to the origin of politics."[16]

The liberal tendency to describe political life in the language of togetherness, unity, solidarity, commonality, and the like revealed an implicit assumption that the normal impulses of mankind were toward social harmony and that the proper mission of political theory was to analyze how such harmony might be achieved. Perhaps this assumption was the residue of Confucian social analysis, with its stress on mutuality, reciprocity, and equilibrium. We are accustomed to associating Confucianism with political conservatism in modern Japan, and its imprint was certainly strong on the neotraditional concept of the family state. But there are deep ambiguities in the Confucian tradition, in Japan as elsewhere, and elements in that tradition had been appropriated for liberal uses both consciously and unconsciously since the 1870s. The lack of a clear distinction between state and society in Confucianism might encourage the idea that society should be subordinated to the needs of the state, but it could also imply that those in authority had a responsibility not to rend the social fabric by despotic action. Social harmony, in other words, was not necessarily a conservative idea, especially if the burden of blame for disharmony was shifted from the ruled to the ruler, an argument behind the Mencian view that Heaven saw and heard with the eyes and ears of the people.

The liberals, of course, made a clear distinction between state and society, and they were convinced that the state existed to serve society rather than vice versa. The parliamentary mechanism provided a means of accomplishing this. But there were subtly different views on how it did so. Some saw the Diet as promoting compromise among conflicting elements, and others saw it as creating a general social consensus. The two are not quite the same thing. Nagai Ryūtarō, for example, tended to think of the Diet as an arena where competing interests (or opinions), autonomous in origin, met, clashed, and resolved their differences. He conceived parliamentary politics as a process of negotiation in which the expression of specific or partisan interest was legitimate and natural. Conflict was resolved on specific issues, and representatives were a conduit for specific opinions.[17] On the other hand, there were those who saw the Diet as an instrument to create a kind of general will. Such a position reflected less tolerance toward the legitimacy of specific interests and less confidence in the capacity of those interests to understand the needs of the whole society.

---

[16] Ōyama Ikuo zenshū (hereafter OIZ) 4 (Tokyo, 1947), 57-63.

[17] Nagai Ryūtarō, "Gikai seiji no shimei no tame ni," CK, 35 (August 1920), 56-57; see also Nagai Ryūtarō-shi daienzetsushū (Tokyo, 1924), pp. 117-118.

Both Yoshino and Ōyama tended to regard the Diet as a pulpit rather than a marketplace. They stressed the importance of representatives as opinion makers. Their theory of representation suggested a passive role for voters, essentially a plebiscitary one, in which the electorate exercised only a veto power. If representatives took positions or advanced policies that were impalatable to their constituents, then the voters might turn them out at the next election. This position did not reflect a distrust in popular wisdom, or in the ability of the public to make political judgment, so much as a narrow definition of the scope of that judgment. Yoshino was fond of resorting to the analogy of the doctor and patient to describe the relationship between a Diet member and his constituents. The patient knows he is sick, but he leaves the cure to the physician, and if the cure fails the patient can find another doctor.[18]

o

If popular discontent resulted when the Diet failed to function as an integrative mechanism, there was still a question of why the mechanism did not work properly. This required probing the causes of social conflict at a deeper level. Nearly all the liberals were agreed that one of the chief causes of the 1905-1912 demonstrations was the existence of "privileged classes" (tokken kaikyū) who monoplized political power and controlled the government in their own interests. Even the conservative Tokutomi Sohō, in an editorial responding to public furor over the Siemens affair, argued that although the Meiji era had seen "the whole people made one under a single sovereign," political power was still limited to only a small "class" made up of hanbatsu, gakubatsu, and zaibatsu.[19] Indeed, one of the chief reasons the liberals advocated electoral reform was to break the power of these privileged few in the Diet.

The liberal intellectuals clearly recognized the existence of social stratification, social inequality, and implicit social hierarchy, but they used the language of class casually, in an imprecise way, without any rigorous analytical conceptualization. Most suggested a tripartite division of society into "privileged classes" (tokken kaikyū) on top, the "middle classes" (chūsan or chūryū kaikyū) or "educated classes" (chishiki kaikyū) in the middle, and the "lower classes" (chūsan ika, chūryū ika, kasō kaikyū, gemin, etc.) below. They were by no means consistent or even very explicit in explaining why class differentiation existed, or what the cri-

[18] For an interesting discussion of the thought of both Yoshino and Ōyama, see Matsumoto Sannosuke, Kindai Nihon no seiji to ningen (Tokyo, 1966), pp. 129-198.
[19] Quoted in Kawahara Hiroshi, "Daiichiji sekai taisen to seiji shimboru no tenkan," in Hashikawa Bunzō and Matsumoto Sannosuke, eds., Kindai Nihon seiji shisōshi 2 (Tokyo, 1970), 15.

teria of differentiation were. About all that can be said with certainty is that they did not regard class differences as primarily socio-economic.

The prevailing view was that "privileged classes" existed because of historical circumstances, specifically the "failure of the Meiji Restoration," regarded by the liberal intellectuals as a liberal revolution. Nagai Ryūtarō, for example, argued that the "fundamental spirit" of the Restoration had been "equality among the four estates." The early policies of the Meiji government had been the destruction of feudal privilege and the opening of new opportunity for the common people. Privilege persisted, however, because the Restoration leaders had succeeded in destroying only the superstructure of the old order, not its ideological foundations. The "evil custom of hereditary privilege" (that is, ascriptive status) on which the feudal system had rested still remained intact. The result was that the "bureaucracy, the aristocracy, and the zaibatsu . . . in order to satisfy their own selfish desires, all brazenly ignore the demands of the people as a whole, monopolize power for themselves, and grasp honor and wealth."[20]

The idea that the differentiation of the "privileged classes" was the product of "feudal remnants" in the new society was persistent among the liberal intellectuals. They recognized, of course, that many of the privileged were persons of wealth and property, and that economic differences were involved in class differences. But the wealthy—the "big capitalists," the "big landlords," the "political merchants," the zaibatsu—were seen as a subset of the "privileged classes," and not necessarily the most important one. The significant line marking off "privileged classes" from the rest of society was political and was drawn arbitrarily.

By contrast, the distinction between "middle classes" and "lower classes" rested rather on the more legitimate criterion of achievement. When the liberal intellectuals referred to the "middle classes" they meant the "new" professional/bureaucratic middle classes, not the "old" entrepreneurial middle class. Membership in the middle class had little to do with property or the relations of production, and everything to do with educational accomplishment. The interchangeability of the terms "middle class" and "educated classes" makes this clear. Whereas privileged status was a feudal remnant, middle-class status was the result of personal merit, a rational distinction. The political implications of this position should be obvious. The "privileged classes" were a self-perpetuating closed elite, protected, for example, by tax qualifications on the right to vote. If, as most liberals suggested, the suffrage were broad-

[20] Nagai Ryūtarō, "Taishō ishin wa Meiji ishin no ronriteki kiketsu de aru," *Seinen yūben*, 5 (March 1920), 6-10.

ened to include all middle school graduates, then the way would be paved for the creation of an open elite constantly renewed by the representative mechanism. The disengagement of "privilege" and political power gave the middle class, with whom the liberal intellectuals clearly identified themselves, access to the political process. Hence the commitment to *minponshugi* flowed not simply from a particular conception of the state but also from more concrete interests.

The liberals' commitment to an open polity did not necessarily imply commitment to an egalitarian society. As we have already seen, they defined equality as "equality of opportunity" rather than complete social leveling. For example, Nagai Ryūtarō did not have social revolution in mind when he called for a Taishō Restoration "to reform the evil custom of hereditary privilege, to extend equality of opportunity to the whole people, and to achieve the idea of equality among the four estates."[21] He was simply advocating national policies to assure that every member of society would be able to "realize the true meaning of his existence"—that is, to achieve his full potential or to move as far up the social ladder as his abilities could take him. Similarly, in defending the need for a more active social policy, Horie Kiichi wrote, "in a society where those of unequal ability oppose one another and compete for existence, the weak will be oppressed by the strong, and the tendency is toward a situation where the strong devour the weak. But social policy mitigates such a tendency . . . by aiming at making every member of society display his abilities to the fullest."[22]

The liberal intellectuals thought of the social hierarchy as one in which people rose rather than fell, and their social goal was to eliminate the worst abuses of a competitive society without destroying competition itself. Even if all were given the same chance at the starting line, not all could win the race nor even finish it. A peasant's son might become a newspaper editor or a university professor, but not *all* peasants' sons could. Mobility was desirable, but it made sense only within a continuing status hierarchy. The liberals believed that social consensus was compatible with a meritocratic social hierarchy, and that social hierarchy was acceptable as long as it did not set up an impenetrable barrier between haves and have-nots. The liberal intellectuals did not want to keep the "lower classes" in their place. They merely recognized that there would always be lower classes in society, and that unless there were routes upward and out, there was likely to be an explosion of popular discontent and perhaps popular violence. Although one can agree with Dahrendorf that the "consensus" or "integrative" model of society

[21] Nagai Ryūtarō, *Kaizō no risō* (Tokyo, 1920), pp. 34-53.

[22] Horie Kiichi, "Demokurashii to keizai zaiseisaku," in Ōta, *Taishō demokurashii ronsō shi* 2:355-356.

lends itself as an "ideology of satisfaction and conservation," it does not follow that it lends itself as an "ideology of class domination," though in fact it was to be so attacked.[23]

In the theories of *minponshugi*, opportunity for self-improvement went hand in hand with broadening the political franchise. Both made the social hierarchy tolerable for those who had not reached its summit. Expanding the suffrage (and establishing responsible cabinets) gave the majority of the people control over their leaders, and social policies to guarantee "equality of opportunity" gave the majority of the society a hope of rising out of lower-status positions. Both aspects of the liberal program were conceived of as mechanisms for reducing social discontent and conflict.

As comments on the 1905-1914 demonstrations made clear, conflict was undesirable, especially if it was violent. Radical or revolutionary violence made the liberal intellectuals more nervous than did the persistence of inequality. The ills produced by inequality could be remedied through judicious reform, whereas the excesses of revolution could not. This accounts for the undercurrent of liberal ambivalence toward the idea of socialism. Socialism was acceptable as long as it meant the pursuit of a more egalitarian or more rational social order, but not when it implied the use of political violence. A 1916 editorial in the *Ōsaka asahi*, a leading liberal newspaper, illustrates this very succinctly. "Socialism has been a kind of taboo word in Japan," it began. "But after studying the matter, and observing various developments, it is clear that socialism can not be summed up simply. . . . National ownership of railroads and municipal ownership of streetcar lines have . . . been touted by the socialists. . . . Is there a civilized country in the world today that does not focus on social policy? . . . [But] among the socialists, and among some extreme advocates of radical thought, are those whose main purpose is to upset the discipline of the state or to destroy the state. Such people ought to be kept under the strictest control, like madmen, murderers, robbers."[24]

o

The *minponshugi* debate had focused primarily on the "distribution of power" (as Tokutomi called it), but by the end of World War I the concern of liberal intellectuals was shifting toward the distribution of wealth. Kawakami Haijime was probably the first to raise the issue. In his *Bimbō monogatari* he asked why, despite the advance of industry and technology, there were still so many poor people. His answer was a

---

[23] Cf. Dahrendorf, *Class and Class Conflict*, p. 284.

[24] Editorial, *Ōsaka asahi shimbun*, 4 April 1917, quoted in Sumiya Etsuji et al., *Taishō demokurashii no shisō*, p. 92.

simple one: the habit of acquisitiveness led some men to accumulate more than their share of the new wealth created by industrial progress. Such a conclusion was hardly radical, for it left the social structure of capitalism unchallenged. Kawakami argued, for example, that in order to eliminate poverty, it was more important to change men's hearts than their social organization: "if everyone in society were to change his attitude, then the problem would be solved even if social organization remained entirely as it is today."[25] It was not necessary to destroy the social hierarchy, but merely to discourage "needless extravagance," a point of view congenial to a bookish middle-class ascetic, and one shared by most advocates of *minponshugi*.

As Watanabe Tetsuzō observed, the rice riots of 1918 proved that the *Bimbō monogatari* was not mere academic theorizing.[26] The riots focused liberal attention on the problem of social coherence in a new way by linking the problem of poverty to the problem of social conflict. The mobs who broke into the storehouses of rich merchants or looted pawnshops were not incensed over exclusion from the political process. They were protesting against economic hardship and deprivation. The object of their hostility was not the political rights of the propertied classes but their property rights.

Nearly all the liberal intellectuals agreed that a popular sense of "social injustice" had prompted the riots. Ōyama Ikuo characterized them as a kind of "retaliatory confiscation" aimed at redressing a social grievance for which there was no other remedy, and Fukuda Tokuzō argued that the riots had occurred because the people had been pushed to the "point of extreme need" where their own right to survive overrode the property rights of the well-to-do.[27] Still others argued that the most general cause of the riots was popular resentment at the extremes of wealth and poverty in Japan, manifest in the extravagantly conspicuous consumption of the *narikin* (parvenu) and wartime profiteers. Such analyses, suggested that the causes of social conflict were not just historical but related to the very structure of society itself. "There are those who see the riots rather than the labor problem as the signal that marks class conflict between the propertied and the propertyless classes," editorialized the *Tōyō keizai shimpō*.[28]

To be sure, many shrank from this conclusion. It was also possible to see the rice riots as yet another constitutional crisis, revealing the

[25] Sumiya Kazuhiko, ed., *Nihon no meicho: Kawakami Hajime* (Tokyo, 1970), p. 397.

[26] Watanabe Tetsuzō, "Hachigatsu sōdō to 'Binbō monogatari' " *CK*, 33 (September 1918), 70.

[27] Quoted in Inoue Kiyoshi and Watanabe Tōru, eds., *Kome sōdō no kenkyū* (Tokyo 1962) 5:233-239.

[28] Quoted ibid., p. 240.

malfunctioning of the parliamentary system as an integrative system. Some argued that the incidents merely underlined the urgency of broadening popular participation in the constitutional process. The immediate cause of the riots, as even the official analysis of the disturbances conceded, had been the extraordinary inflation of rice prices. But why had these prices gotten out of hand? Disturbances like the rice riots occur, wrote Yoshino Sakuzō, because "governments do not bend their ear to the demands of the people." The extraordinary inflation resulted from the "insensitivity of those in power toward the livelihood problems of the ordinary man."[29] Ōyama laid blame for the riots on "bureaucratic politicians" like Terauchi, who mouthed pieties about *kyōkoku itchi* and *kanmin dōchi*, but paid them only lip service.[30] In more general terms, the *Tōyō keizai shimpō* observed, "the political process in Japan works effectively for the property-owning minority, but the propertyless classes receive hardly any security at all. In a sense, it is possible to say that the propertyless class has no government at all, and herein lies the true cause of the riots. . . ."[31] To prevent similar disturbances in the future, the government had to be made more responsive to the needs of the people, and that required electoral reform. The only new element introduced by the rice riots was a feeling that electoral reform was enlarged to mean universal manhood suffrage.

The rice riots, however, were not an isolated episode. The explosion of labor disputes in 1919-1920, the radicalization of students at imperial universities and other middle-class recruiting grounds, the return of the old socialists to public prominence, the stirrings of discontent in rural areas—all suggested that the problem of social conflict was more profound than it had been at the beginning of the Taishō period, when constitutional palliatives or social policy meliorism seemed adequate to deal with it. The consensual or integrative model of society began to lose its persuasiveness, and some liberal intellectuals defected to a more catastrophic vision of politics, which treated conflict not as a temporary or transient phenomenon but as the central dynamic of politics.

To be sure, the consensual model of society had already come under attack during the *minponshugi* debates. The most incisive critique came from Yamakawa Hitoshi, who simply denied the possibility of a consensual society. "It was long, long ago that society lost its character as a harmonious cooperative livelihood structure [*kyōdōseikatsutai*] based on common interest," he wrote in 1917. "Human society divided into two opposing class camps, and simultaneously became two livelihood struc-

---

[29] Yoshino Sakuzō, "Kome sōdō ni taisuru ichikōsatsu," *CK*, 30 (September 1918), 95-98.

[30] Ōyama Ikuo, "Kome sōdō no shakaiteki oyobi seijiteki kōsatsu," ibid., pp. 77-92.

[31] Quoted in Inoue and Watanabe, *Kome sōdō no kenkyū*, p. 240.

tures joined together by a constraining force rather than common interest. . . . To put it differently, society is a compound structure, whose cohesion is maintained by the dominant livelihood structure (class) subjugating and controlling the dominated livelihood structure (class). Under these circumstances, the sense of common interest within each class is naturally stronger, more intense, and more true than a sense of common interest among the whole."[32] It would be harder to find a more concise statement of the "conflict model" of society. Yamakawa suggested that "class division" entailed "class domination" or "class struggle" in all societies except the most primitive. Popular unruliness was not a warning to make adjustments in the integrating parliamentary mechanism, but a sign that the subjugated class, prompted by its own sense of class interest, had begun to struggle against the dominant class.

The persuasiveness of this point of view was enhanced by postwar socioeconomic dislocations. It promoted a sudden upsurge of interest in Marxist thought, and a split in the ranks of the liberal intellectuals. Men such as Ōyama Ikuo, Hasegawa Nyozekan, and Kawakami Hajime defected to the conflict-coercive view of society. They began to see struggle between interest groups or classes as the central motif of human history, and to ascribe the existence of social conflict in Japan not to transient maladjustments in the social mechanism but to deep-seated imperatives of social life. In January 1919 Kawakami founded *Shakai mondai kenkyū*, a journal devoted to exploring the ideas of Marxism, and a month later Ōyama and Hasegawa started *Warera* as a vehicle for their own new views of society.[33] Like the newly emerging generation of student radicals, they attempted to find the dynamic of history in universal laws of social conflict.

Perhaps the most original and systematic exposition of a coercion-conflict model was Ōyama's *Seiji no shakaiteki kiso*, based on a series of articles written for *Warera*. In this work, Ōyama argued that "struggle among social groups is the motor of evolution . . . and the origin of political and social inequality." Human society, he said, was made up of groups united by common interest, usually of an economic or material sort. Each group aimed at advancing its own interests and regarded every other group as an absolute enemy. Human history had to be seen as the constant and continuing struggle of each social group to dominate and subjugate the others. In its most violent form, conflict meant war, the utter destruction of weaker groups by the strong in a contest of brute force. Social domination could take other forms as well,

[32] Yamakawa Hitoshi, "Suna no ue taterareta demokurashii: Ōyama Ikuo-shi no minponshugi," in Ōta, *Taishō demokurashii ronsō shi*, 2:27.

[33] For a brief treatment of this split in the liberal ranks, see Ienaga Saburō, ed., *Kindai Nihon shisō kōza* 1 (Tokyo, 1959), 197-200; and Matsumoto Sannosuke, "Seiji to chishikijin," in Hashikawa and Matsumoto, *Kindai Nihon seiji shisōshi*, pp. 148-186.

and herein lay the origin of the state. The triumphant group subjugated the weaker by force and then enslaved it by law. In modern times, group conflict became class conflict, and the state became the means by which the dominant class exploited the weak economically. To be sure, modern society was complex, and discrete social groups were more numerous and larger in scale than in primitive societies, so social struggle became more complex. Nonetheless, ultimately the social process was no different in modern times than earlier—all groups struggled with one another for control of the state.[34]

The new model of society to which many erstwhile liberal intellectuals turned was profoundly subversive of the assumptions underlying *minponshugi*. First of all, it viewed the state as an instrument of coercion, by which social conflict was suppressed until it next exploded into overt struggle. This contrasted with the consensus model, which suggested that the state—the parliamentary state, at least—resolved conflict by remedying the specific causes that provoked it or by generating a sense of shared interest or commitment within society. In the consensus model, politics was a means of creating or maintaining community, whereas in the coercion model, it was simply a struggle for domination and power. Second, the image of the Diet was substantially altered by the conflict model. The *minponshugi* liberals, even though they complained of the temporary ascendancy of the "privileged classes," never called into question the basic neutrality of the Diet as a political institution. It was not a partisan instrument, but a place where partisan differences were resolved. The coercion model, on the other hand, denied the neutrality of the Diet, as indeed it explicitly denied the neutrality of the state, and suggested that the dominant class used it to create laws favorable to its own interests and its own continued domination. Finally, the conflict model put the social hierarchy in a rather different light. It was no longer a gently ascending slope, possible for the diligent climber to mount, but a series of heights separated by awesome, perhaps unbridgeable chasms. Social privilege was unattainable by ordinary means. It was buttressed by a social system specifically designed to perpetuate the privileges of the master class intact. "The present society is a paradise for the bourgeoisie," wrote Ōyama. "By contrast, for the proletariat [it] is like a bleak plain, severe in winter. The government does not protect the proletariat, nor does the Diet represent them, and the whole of the good life the bourgeoisie enjoy is denied to them."[35] Equality of opportunity, in other words, was an illusion.

[34] The entire text of *Seiji no shakaiteki kiso* may be found in *OIZ*, 1 (1947). The work was originally published in 1923.

[35] Ōyama Ikuo, "Minshū bunka no kisū to kyōiku," in *OIZ*, 4:333-334. For a similar observation see Horie Kiichi, "Musan kaikyū to chishiki kaikyū no sōgo dakiai," *CK*, 37 (June 1923), 170.

These views by no means captured the imagination of all liberal intellectuals. Even those who conceded that the government—including the "responsible cabinets" after 1918—was the captive of the privileged class (now more frequently defined as an economic or "propertied class") and that the laws of the country served special interests resisted the notion that conflict was an inherent feature of human social life or that social harmony was an impossible goal. In a direct response to Yamakawa's critique, for example, Yoshino commented that as an advocate of *minponshugi* he might become a socialist, but he could never become a radical.[36] What distinguished radicalism from socialism was a materialist conception of man and a belief in the inevitability of class struggle. In Yoshino's view, men had to struggle with their own consciousness, not with each other, if society were to become more just and the lower classes were to be emancipated.

Many liberals found the idea of class struggle hard to accept. In a *Chūō Kōron* symposium on "the dictatorship of the proletariat," Yoshino argued that class struggle was ultimately pointless since it did not end social injustice, but merely perpetrated it in new forms, with the workers rather than the capitalists as the master class.[37] Others expressed similar views. "I dare to think that I abhor the dictatorship of the capitalists no less than the workers do," wrote Akagi Yūhei, "but I must also say that I would object if the laborers were to entrench themselves in the citadel that had just been vacated by the capitalists."[38] In a similar vein, Horie Kiichi observed, "Of course, I find the dictatorship of the propertied classes to be wrong, just as I find the dictatorship of the propertyless classes to be wrong too." He also added, "I think that it is necessary that we abolish those elements in our country's laws and institutions that in the past have cut a gulf between the classes, . . . and that we maintain an equilibrium between classes by means of social public spiritedness."[39] Perhaps that was the sticking point for the majority of liberal intellectuals, who remained optimistic that "public spiritedness" was possible and that a balance of interests could be achieved if all members of the society modulated their parochial concerns.

o

The debate among the liberals in the immediate postwar years extended from theory to practice. The streets were filled with striking workers,

[36] Yoshino Sakuzō, "Minponshugi, shakaishugi, kagekishugi," *CK*, 36 (June 1919), 26-34.

[37] Yoshino Sakuzō, "Puroretariāto no senseiteki keikō ni taisuru chishiki kaikyū no kansō," *CK*, 36 (September 1921), 164-168.

[38] Akagi Yūhei, "Rōdō undō no bōkansha to shite," ibid., p. 148.

[39] Horie Kiichi, "Musan kaikyū ni taisuru interigenchiya no kansō," ibid., p. 128.

student agitators, and demonstrating suffragists, yet the professional politicians remained unresponsive. This raised the question of what role the intellectual should play. Should he remain detached, or should he plunge into the fray? And if he chose to join the struggle, on whose side and in what way? These were matters of continuing debate during the early 1920s.

Down to the end of the war, most middle-class intellectuals envisaged for themselves a role of moral or intellectual leadership for the less educated masses. What the intellectual had to offer society was his expert knowledge, his superior insights into social process, and above all his objectivity. Since the intellectual was able to stand above party and above class, wrote Ōyama Ikuo in 1918, he alone could provide an independent and unbiassed assessment of social events and bring the common people to a higher level of understanding. This task was essential if a true *minponshugi* were to emerge, for without the leadership of the intellectuals, democracy was likely to degenerate into mobocracy, and through mobocracy lay the path to despotism and autocracy. The "democratization" of knowledge was, he argued, requisite for an orderly "democratization" of politics. A similar position was reflected in Yoshino's conception of *tetsujin seiji* ("government by the wise") in which the popular role in politics was plebiscitary, and decision making was left to knowledgeable "men of character."

Such a conception of the intellectual as activist was entirely consonant with previous historical experience. Aside from a few professors and journalists who found their way into Diet politics, most liberal intellectuals had made the embryonic labor movement the main arena for their activism. The earliest advocates of labor unions had been middle-class intellectuals interested in "social harmony" and "self-improvement." Suzuki Bunji, the premier organizer of the Taishō unionism, was conspicuous for his advocacy of both. An adherent of the consensual model, he constantly stressed the commonality of interest between workman and employer, and his primary tactic during the early years of the Yūaikai had been to mediate disputes rather than agitate them. Less obviously, but no less importantly, he urged workers to improve their lot as individuals through study, education, and self-improvement. "Self-respect can be obtained only through the power of self-help," he wrote in 1913.[40] His early efforts to organize lecture societies and recreational clubs for workers were intended to provide ample opportunities for self-help. This philosophy of labor action was entirely consistent with liberal views on the political and social order. Working-class organiza-

[40] Stephen Large, *The Rise of Labor in Japan: The Yūaikai, 1912-1919* (Tokyo, 1972), p. 22.

tions might defend and represent worker interests, but they were not intended to raise worker consciousness as members of an economic underclass. They were to encourage the advance of workers up the social ladder through middle-class life strategies, and for this there was no better leadership than liberal middle-class intellectuals.

The changed character of postwar labor unrest called the tactics of worker uplift into question. Workers themselves were beginning to chafe under the ministration of middle-class leaders. Even before the war's end, Nishio Suehiro had split from the Yūaikai to organize his own union in part because his local Yūaikai branch president was not a working man. In 1919 Hirazawa Keishichi, who led an internal fight to purge the Yūaikai of radical intellectuals, declared quite simply, "Japan's labor movement is not a movement for the benefit of the intellectuals. It is for the benefit of the working class."[41] His complaint was prompted by sudden influx of recent university graduates, especially Shinjinkai members, into the labor movement. Matsuoka Komakichi, another working-class leader, observed that the students were lost in theory, less concerned with the practical problems of the workers than with their own elegant plans for the total reorganization of society. They saw union activity not as a legitimate end in itself but as a way to "educate" workers for social revolution.

Resentment against student radicalism extended to the older generation of liberal intellectuals. In 1923 Abe Isoo recalled an incident that neatly illustrated the situation:

> It was about five or six years ago, I think, that a certain worker organization was planning to hold a rally at the Seinenkai in Kanda. I received an invitation to appear as one of the speakers, but after I accepted there were some [in the organization] who insisted that they needed no help at all from the educated classes [*chishiki kaikyū*], . . . that [such help] would indicate they themselves were weak, and that therefore they should not invite anyone to the meeting but workers.[42]

Abe went ahead with his speech anyway, tactfully stressing that the time had come for workers to solve their own problems. The episode must have been a shock to a man who thought he had devoted his life to the cause of the downtrodden. The independence of working-class leaders, the populist activism of student radicals, and the growing persuasiveness of social conflict theory all gave special urgency to the debate on the social role of the intellectual.

The ambiguous social position of the "educated classes," a complex

[41] Ibid., p. 160.

[42] Abe Isoo, "Musan chishiki ryōkaikyū no teikyō o teisu," *CK*, 38 (June 1923), 146.

aggregate, complicated the debate. Some intellectuals were propertied. The picture of well-clothed and well-fed middle-class intellectuals mingling with working masses struck a few critics as absurd. Arishima Takeo, for example, sneered at the romantics who plunged into working-class movements, even though they had nothing in common with the workers.[43] In a satiric barb, Ubugata Toshirō wrote that if a proletarian dictatorship were established in Japan, its Lenin would wear a workman's tunic made of silk, smoke fragrant cigars, escape police spies by automobile, buy the latest labor problem books at Maruzen (to put unread on his study shelves), and fall into a funk when the public prints ceased to gossip about him.[44] For such critics, social activism by intellectuals was dilettantish dabbling.

For the most part, however, the liberals took the problem of social commitment seriously. The intellectual had a critical role to play in the conflict between worker and employer, between capitalist and proletarian. Time and again, writers referred to the "casting vote" of the intelligentsia. "The class which has the majority of the intelligentsia on its side will be strong, and the class which does not will be weak," wrote Hayashi Kimio. "This is because the intelligentsia supply the knowledge and ability which is the motor force behind social action. . . . Victory in class war will be decided by which way the intelligentsia turn."[45] Implicit in this view was a continuing conception of the intellectuals as a neuter class, with no economic interests of their own, nor any base of power except alliance with another class. Although central to the outcome of class conflict, the intellectuals were detached socially as well as intellectually. As Hayashi wistfully concluded, the intelligentsia could not themselves be victors in the social struggle but only allies of the victors.

After his conversion to the "conflict model" of society, Ōyama Ikuo argued that the position of the intellectual classes was not so different from that of the working classes. Both classes, he said, were repelled by the hypocrisy and corruption of bourgeois culture, both were dependent for their livelihood on offering their labor for pay, both as consumers lived at the mercy of market forces, both had become cogs in an inhuman economic machine, mechanically performing tasks on the orders of others without any will of their own. This bleak assessment suggested that the doctrines of self-help and self-improvement so

---

[43] Arishima Takeo, "Ryōkaikyū no kankei ni taisuru watakushi no kangae," ibid., pp. 152-154.

[44] Ubugata Toshirō, "Wasei puroretariāto nanigoto o ka nasan," CK, 36 (September 1921), 136.

[45] Hayashi Kimio, "Kaikyū tōsō no kiyasuchingu bōto," ibid., p. 126.

central to middle-class values no longer had meaning.[46] As Ōyama observed, there were fewer and fewer "empty seats at the top." The rewards of middle-class aspiration were no longer automatic, and the educated intellectual would have little to lose by casting his lot with the oppressed masses.

The path of action proposed by Ōyama was not so very different from that of the radical students who infiltrated the labor movement in 1919-1920. He was committed to the idea that a "scientific" mode of social analysis could provide a theoretical guide for social change. Indeed, he argued that social theory was useless unless applied in social practice. "Social science," he wrote, "provides knowledge about the data of group processes, and from the data assembled it reveals social laws. But a social philosophy that strives to be socially effective . . . must aim at using this knowledge to order and control group processes."[47] The intellectual was to be a social engineer, an applied social scientist, mobilizing his superior analytical skills to advance the cause of the working class in class struggle. In short, Ōyama suffered from the usual hubris of the positivist.

Yoshino, on the other hand, clung to the notion of the intellectual as a man above the partisan fray, ever mindful of the interests of the whole society. Although intellectuals might withdraw from positions of leadership in the labor movement, they still were needed to keep workers from acting solely on their own narrow interests to the neglect of the rest of society. The intellectual, in other words, could provide the "fair judgment of the outsider." At times Yoshino seemed almost condescending toward the working class, dismissing their anti-intellectual tendencies as mere petulance, like that of a child who wants to act like his parents even though he can not.[48] This was not hostile condescension, but the condescension of the professional, confident in his expertise, like a doctor when dealing with a troublesome patient.

Abe Isoo suggested a more modest role for the intellectual. "The propagation of ideas" was their proper task. The intellectuals, he said, should spread awareness of the "laws of socialism." The object of this consciousness raising was not to be the workers themselves, but the rest of society, which had to be taught sympathy for the condition of the workers. The intellectual should be publicist to the "educated classes." This was rather different from Ōyama's conception of the intellectual as social engineer. Abe did not propose to bring about social change

---

[46] Ōyama Ikuo, "Minshū bunka," CK, 35 (January 1920), 86-87.

[47] OIZ, 3:110-111.

[48] Yoshino Sakuzō, "Puroretariāto no senseiteki keikō ni taisuru chishiki kaikyū no kansō," CK, 36 (September 1921), 164-168; "Ryōsha no tadashii kankei to machigatta kankei," CK, 38 (June 1923), 181-184.

the struggle for social and economic equality (usually called "socialism"). Yoshino Sakuzō argued that even if the propertyless classes were to achieve a majority in the Diet and form a cabinet, it would be difficult to carry out reform unless there was constitutional change. The powers of the House of Peers, the Privy Council, and the *gumbatsu*—the citadels of the "privileged class"—had to be curbed or the impact of the mass electorate would be vitiated. Hirabayashi Hatsunosuke argued that until "remnants from feudal times" were swept away—by which he seems to have meant "arrogant bureaucrats" and "privileged political merchants"—the political system would be constitutional in name only. "Before the propertyless classes of Japan can develop by themselves, it is necessary that there be conditions under which they can [do so]. . . . They can develop only on a base of liberalism. . . . Therefore, the policies of Japan's proletarian parties have a dual character and a dual mission . . . of liberalism and a highly effective social policy." Rōyama Masamichi was even more explicit in his warnings. Without the firm establishment of democratic institutions it would not be possible to put socialism into effect. He criticized not only the established parties for having lost the "spirit of democracy" but the "proletarian camp" for not fully respecting it.[55]

These arguments, indeed the whole tone of the *Seiji kenkyūkai* leadership, suggest that the consensual hypothesis still governed their vision of politics. The state was not the instrument of the possessing class, to be overthrown or replaced by a new dominant class. It could respond to new social conditions and new social demands. It was fundamentally neutral, to be molded according to the will of the society at large, and under the right conditions outsiders might wrest control from the hands of an entrenched elite. Political struggle, in other words, was not conceived of as a zero-sum game, a struggle between subjugator and subjugated where all spoils went to the victor, but as a transient or temporary form of conflict, which could be resolved within the parliamentary mechanism. Apocalyptic solutions—revolution or even "revolutionary parliamentarism"—were inappropriate because they assumed that political conflict between the "propertyless masses" and their oppressors was irreconcilable. As we have seen, the notion of class struggle was set aside not only by men like Yoshino but also by soi-disant socialists like Abe, who felt that parliamentary action by the proletarian party should advance the interests of the whole people, even in small ways, rather than indulge in "class propaganda" or "class politics." What divided the "propertyless" from "propertied" was merely the possession of wealth, not exploitative or subordinating social relations. Hence the social ills

[55] Ibid., pp. 50-52, 160-162.

generated by difference in income were temporary and remediable by parliamentary action.

As Abe had feared, the *Seiji kenkyūkai* eventually fell apart, prey to the factionalism he had warned against. Disputes over the nature of the organization, over its draft platforms for reform, over its tactics, indeed over almost everything that it had been organized to discuss were exacerbated by the rapid expansion of the organization after the victory of the "protect the constitution" coalition in the 1924 election. By April 1925 it had fifty-three local branches, six prefectural councils, and over six thousand members. Expansion brought ideological diversity, and the collegial character of the original organizing group dissolved into bickering. Should the group prepare for the organization of a proletarian party or should it transform itself into a party? Should the party model itself on the English Labour party, with group membership, or should it model itself on the German Social Democrats with individual membership? Should the party cooperate with the liberal elements in the established parties or should it not? What specific policies should the party advocate? And so on. When pro-communist elements attempted to take over the organization in December 1925, a number of the original organizers withdrew, complaining that the group had begun in the "spirit of liberalism," but that the new elements who had joined after its formation did not fully understand that.

In 1927 Yamakawa Hitoshi observed that the *Seiji kenkyūkai* had not been united by common political views but only by the "vague common purpose" of promoting the establishment of a *musan seitō*.[56] The organization lacked intellectual unity and was designed to deal with a tactical problem. Middle-class intellectuals of widely varying views had been thrown together by the reluctance of the labor union leaders, especially in the Sōdōmei, to dilute their control over the organized workers. This reluctance was partly ideological and partly practical, for the labor leadership saw their own organizations as the natural foundation on which a proletarian party should rest. Though the *Seiji kenkyūkai* solved the tactical problems of the intellectuals temporarily, its members were never able to paper over the fundamental intellectual cleavages among themselves. Older liberals (over forty) saw the "proletarian party" as a vehicle for achieving the political program of *minponshugi*—though this neologism had been abandoned—whereas radical members of the younger generation (in their twenties and early thirties) wanted to launch an assault on the barricades of the bourgeois. At deeper level, the consensual model of society struggled with the conflict model, newly

[56] Yamakawa Hitoshi, "Musan seitō bunritsuki," *Shakai kagaku*, 4 (February 1927), 388-390.

clothed in the vocabulary of Marxism. It is hardly surprising that the organization became unglued so quickly.

o

Although the liberals found their way into parliamentary politics in the company of left radicals, their response to social conflict more closely resembled that of reform-minded elements in the bureaucracy. As Kenneth Pyle has suggested, a cadre of officials sensitive to the potential unruliness of Japanese society emerged in the Home Ministry after the end of the Russo-Japanese war. Armed with the "advantages of followership," and guided by the thought of the German "Historical School," they sought alternatives to the laissez-faire and socialist responses to the trauma of modernization. By integrating village institutions into the administrative structure, by creating local voluntary organizations to promote social solidarity, by shoring up the local elite, and by drafting legislation and regulations to deal with the emergent industrial labor force, they sought to contain potential conflict. By the end of World War I, there had emerged a generation of bureaucratic leaders whose thinking was rooted, as Pyle puts it, in "the ideal of a monarch and a neutral bureaucracy standing above narrow class interests, regulating economic conditions, reconciling opposing social forces, seeking to advance the interests of the whole by intervening in the economy to protect and integrate the lower classes into the nation."[57] With certain qualifications, touched upon below, the views of this bureaucratic generation were compatible with those of the liberal intellectuals, and for the most part the liberal critique of politics moved within boundaries acceptable to reform-minded bureaucrats.

In a way the liberals were bureaucrats manqué, forced into roles first as political critics, and then as activists in the proletarian party movement because the bureaucratic recruiting process made no allowances for mid-career entry into official status. The liberals were conceived in the same womb as the bureaucrats (the university); often suckled on the same milk (German social thought); and nurtured in the same environment (the meritocratic society). They also lived in the same political culture, still influenced by traditional concepts of knowledge and statecraft, which customarily put knowledge at the service of legitimate authority and made no clear distinction between the intellectual as public servant and the intellectual as private voice. Although opportunities for intellectuals to link themselves to the centers of power declined considerably after the 1890s, they retained the notion, shared by the bureau-

---

[57] Kenneth B. Pyle, "Advantages of Followership: German Economics and Japanese Bureaucrats, 1890-1925," *Journal of Japanese Studies*, 1 (Autumn 1974), 162. Also Pyle, "The Technology of Japanese Nationalism," pp. 51-65.

cracy, that knowledge brought with it social responsibility. It was also
not surprising that the liberals shared with the bureaucrats similar perspectives on the undesirability of social conflict, and that they did not
question the legitimacy of the monarchy, the appropriateness of a capitalist economic structure, or the bureaucracy's right to intervene in society.

But in certain significant ways, the tactical dispositions of the liberals
were quite different from those of the bureaucrats. First of all, the liberals, when they referred to the "people," usually excluded the rural
population—or at least did not specifically include it. Their vantage point
in politics was metropolitan, not provincial, and rarely, if ever, did they
address themselves to the problems of the countryside, as Pyle's reformist bureaucrats did. Why this was the case is difficult to explain. Perhaps
it was because the countryside represented the "Old Japan," whereas
they were aggressively interested in the "New Japan" taking shape in
the cities; or perhaps it was because they felt, as many postwar intellectuals have, that the villages were the repository of attitudes antithetical
to the cosmopolitan values they embraced. Whatever the reason, liberal
indifference to the rural sector of society gave to their analyses of Japan's
problems a thrust significantly different from that of the bureaucrats,
who saw the countryside as an important bulwark against modern social
conflict.

Second, the liberals also harbored grave doubts about whether the
administrative state, at least as it had emerged by late Meiji, could respond effectively to the problem of social conflict. They saw the administrative state as a necessary structure, but a brittle one, ready to
crack under a heavy strain despite its outwardly solid appearance. As
Bernard Silberman has argued elsewhere in this volume, some bureaucrats were bent on forcing private interests into the iron cage of bureaucratic control. They did so in the name of "national purpose," "public
interest," or "public good," all code words for administrative rationalization, or to put it more bluntly, the maximization of bureaucratic
power. The bureaucrats sought to deal with the proliferation of interests
within society through the proliferation of ministries, bureaus, and sections; they sought to control some interests through repression, regulation, or arbitration; they sought to coopt others through subsidies,
persuasion, and guidance; and their goal was a gentle tyranny, supported by fetters of red tape, not bayonets. Claiming the role of arbiter
among all interests in the name of public order and public peace, the
bureaucracy rapidly emerged as the largest and most powerful interest
group of all.

The liberal intellectuals quite rightly sensed the impossibility of the
task the bureaucrats had set for themselves. The iron cage was small

and rigid, and society a restless menagerie, too large and motley to be contained. It would have been more plausible to build an ark where the animals trooped in two by two to live in miraculous harmony. A bureaucratic structure had to be the instrument of some social force other than itself, and the liberals suggested that force had to be the Diet as an integrating institution. Social peace was not to be imposed on society for its own sake, but to be created out of the social satisfaction most likely to emerge in a parliamentary state.

We should not conclude, however, that the liberals were right and the bureaucrats were wrong. The liberal goal of a harmonious parliamentary state was no more attainable than the iron cage of the bureaucrat. Both rested on the illusion that a consensual society was possible. But as class differentiation proceeded and economic inequality became more visible, episodes of conflict, even violent conflict, were inevitable. No conceivable political structure could completely reconcile the multiplicity of emergent interests, even among the elite, let alone between elite and masses; it could only suppress, coopt, or ignore them. As Dahrendorf points out, no society can exist without consensus and conflict, and any rational political theory or strategy must accommodate both. The theory of the *minponshugi* liberals did not, and they continued to yearn for a consensual society that was at once pluralistic, interest-divided, and tolerant of inequality.

Although the ultimate fate of the liberals is beyond the scope of this essay, it is clear that the liberal impulse to define a political structure congruent with such a social vision persisted into the 1930s. Perhaps the ultimate expression may be found in the idea of "cooperativism" (*kyō-dōshugi*) so popular among the liberal-left intellectuals who participated in the *Shōwa kenyūkai*. To judge from Miki Kiyoshi's definition of the new catchword in his *Kyōdōshugi no tetsugakuteki kiso* (1939), the anti-bureaucratic impulse remained strong, as did the attachment to consensus, even though the language of the 1910s and 1920s was abandoned.

> Cooperativism, as opposed to the anarchic condition resulting from individualism or liberalism, recognizes the necessity of control from the standpoint of the whole. This control is general, rational, and planned. In contrast to totalitarian control, which easily lapses into bureaucratic control from above, cooperativism insists on voluntary cooperation (*jishuteki na kyōdō*). Cooperativism requires the achievement of total control by means of organizations from below. . . . Speaking of organization from below does not mean that cooperativism rests on abstract democracy; rather it recognizes the important significance of leaders. The leaders required by cooperativism are not authoritarian dictators nor are they separated from the people. Rather

they enter among the people, educate the people, and lead the people by taking up their demands.[58]

In short, "cooperativism" was *minponshugi* without the parliamentary mechanism, and the leaders it required were *tetsujin seijika* without an electoral constituency. It is tempting to conclude that Taishō liberalism died not with a bang in 1932, but with a whimper some years later.

[58] Furuta Hikaru, Sakuta Keiichi, and Ikimatsu Keizō, eds., *Kindai Nihon shakai shisō shi*, 2 (Tokyo, 1971), 214.

EPILOGUE: PARTS AND WHOLES

J. Victor Koschmann

Discussion that preceded final preparation of the papers composing this volume was notable not only for its intensity but for the fundamental nature of the issues confronted. Rather than being solely concerned with minor points of fact or interpretation, discussion among the authors often focused on underlying premises and assumptions. Moreover, participants criticized not only individual papers but the basic design of the project itself. Are not "history" and "synchrony" contradictory? Does not the selection of problems and events for synchronic investigation inevitably depend upon a prior, diachronic sense of what is significant and what not? Granted that a structural rather than linear approach is useful, why appeal to Lévi-Strauss or the Russian formalists rather than to the sociological accounts of structure more familiar to historians trained in the positivist tradition? Obviously, more than a week of discussion would be required to resolve such issues to anyone's satisfaction, and sometimes a tentative compromise or "agreement to disagree" was the only apparent result of such encounters. Yet that such questions were even raised and debated with so much energy provides evidence of a new sensitivity among historians of Japan to problems of theory and methodology that is not unique to this particular research project.

Aside from the considerable value of the epistemological controversy that underlay their production, the essays themselves make an important contribution to the study of modern Japan. That is true partly because each in its own right addresses a major question or event and provides fresh data and interpretation. It is true also because of the interesting ways in which, considered together, the authors' arguments diverge at some levels but converge at others.

DIVERGENCE

Consensus is by no means the salient characteristic of either group of essays included here. Rather than looking like reasonably uniform bricks in an explanatory edifice they resemble more closely the unruly components of a cubist collage. Each essay expresses its own meanings while also indicating a particular complex of associations in the historical field. When grouped together these parts form a whole, of a sort, by virtue of their placement in two encompassing compositions. Yet they adamantly resist full integration. Each continues to contest and sometimes to belie others, less in matters of fact than interpretation. We are left, therefore, with a number of "interpretations of conflict" that collectively constitute something like what Paul Ricoeur has called a "conflict of interpretations."

Perhaps the most fundamental of the various controversies that arose might at the risk of oversimplification be described as holism versus individualism. That is, certain of the authors see conflict as determined basically by structural features of society, economic relations, or knowledge. Others prefer to see it primarily as the complex, often unique result of intentional action on the part of free agents.

Sweeping examples of the former position are provided in contributions by Harootunian and Silberman. Harootunian argues that conflict in the late Tokugawa period was generated by attempts to overcome an epistemological break that occurred in the eighteenth century. A new organization of cognition and knowledge, in which things were related not primarily in terms of identity or continuity but rather by their spatial and temporal contiguity, imposed upon any participant the terms of thought and action. Indeed, in its function as ideology, knowledge virtually brought into existence as historical subjects those who would participate in discourse. Harootunian follows Louis Althusser in arguing that historical processes are "decentered": they do not respond uniquely to the intentions or actions of any particular individual or group. Historical actors, therefore, are not natural entities but rather are constituted by ideology, which functions to set individuals "in positions as subjects so as to act." It was precisely in its performance of such a function that ideology in the late Tokugawa period allowed the conflictual processes of secession that Harootunian describes.

Silberman argues that the narrowly circumscribed choices made by the Meiji government in response to problems of legitimacy and authority effectively determined the broad outlines of conflict in twentieth-century Japan. That is, the basic form of conflict was established when government leaders adopted the utilitarian premise of distribution according to wants rather than needs, and institutionalized the values of expertise and impartiality as criteria for participation in policy making. Whereas the state sought to preserve its unique authority by monopolizing those values, other groups in society also strove to gain entry to policy councils by demonstrating their own expertise and impartiality. The state proceeded to coopt groups that were successful in meeting its criteria and to exclude those that were not. The result was an inexorable process of bureaucratization and the extension of legal rationality. Of central importance to Silberman's argument, however, is the paradox that the extension of law not only increased central control over such entities as the family and local community but also reconstituted them as legal subjects with specific rights and duties and thus endowed them with a new form of autonomy. The result was an intensification of conflict.

Harootunian focuses on knowledge, Silberman on the realm of political legitimacy and authority. Other forms of holistic interpretation and explanation are employed by Hashimoto and Marshall, for whom conflict is conditioned by aspects of changing social structure, and Napier, who traces labor disputes to transformations in the labor market. Each sees conflict as following a certain "fault line" that is prescribed by trans-subjective structures. Those structures both provide individuals with the possibility of action and lay down the rules and constraints under which action must take place. In the final analysis, therefore, conflict is always at base a structural phenomenon.

Some other essays contest such holistic premises, at least in their application to particular problems under investigation. In his interpretation of the actions of bakufu leaders faced with a systemic crisis, Totman finds circumstantial factors and perceived conflicts of interest to be far more important than epistemological or economic structures. Similarly, Huber portrays activists who, regardless of their preferences for pragmatic or romantic forms of action, responded with open minds to the opportunities offered them by the political events of the time, and thus "played a direct and purposive role in bringing about the new Meiji regime." The will and actions of such individuals are not decisively determined by social, economic, or epistemological constraints. They make their own decisions and are responsible for their fate.

From essays dealing with the twentieth century, such as those by Waswo and Bartholemew, one also gains a keen sense of the particularity of the individuals and situations involved. While accepting the important role played by the Japanese state in extending legal definition and regulation to the countryside and making rights and duties justiciable, Waswo not only insists upon the important role of the "natural community" in giving rise to tenant unions and conflictual behavior but also provides a detailed case study that highlights the diversity among tenant groups. Bartholemew's study of Dr. Kitasato emphasizes the great importance of official efforts to control and coopt science and scientists. It also, however, shows that the bureaucracy did not speak with a single voice, and in fact its own disunity offered men such as Kitasato ample opportunity to set one ministerial faction against another and thereby preserve a high degree of autonomy.

Intellectuals portrayed by Duus also seem to have reacted more or less autonomously to external events. Although their positions are distinguishable in broad terms, according to whether they adhered to a consensus or a conflict model of society, they appear to have formulated their arguments in an environment that was basically undetermined. Oka, too, despite a largely holistic understanding of the emergence of "individualism" following the Russo-Japanese war, finds in the values of particular commentators like Fujii Kenjirō and Ukita Kazutami the origins of the Taishō democratic movement.

Conference participants were sometimes divided by further methodological issues, such as causal explanation versus hermeneutical understanding, universal rationality versus cultural distinctiveness, and so on. Like that between holism and individualism, however, such controversies served to enrich rather than impede intellectual production. They are issues of such magnitude that, to borrow the idiom of post-structuralist criticism, premature "closure" should be avoided. In their divergent aspects, therefore, each group of essays offers its readers not only an important portrait of conflict at a certain juncture in Japan's modern history but also an invitation to continued methodological and theoretical exploration that will contest strategies and assumptions as well as findings.

Convergence

Differences in approach need not be allowed to obscure several forms of convergence. First, it is useful to note strong thematic continuity throughout the two groups of essays that is consistent with Tetsuo Najita's identification of "bureaucratism" and "restorationism" as major alternatives for modern Japanese consciousness. In both eras, conflict led to the juxtaposition of "effective, measurable, bureaucratic performance" against "restorationist" affirmations of idealism and the "purity of the human spirit."[1] In general, treatments of the era of the Meiji Restoration give priority to the restorationist pole, whereas studies of the twentieth century emphasize bureaucratism. Nevertheless, Tot-

---

[1] See Tetsuo Najita, *Japan* (Englewood Cliffs, N.J.: Prentice-Hall, 1974; reprinted Chicago: University of Chicago Press, 1979), pp. 2 and 7.

man's essay suggests the great importance of conceptions of rational efficiency in the late Tokugawa, whereas contributions by Oka, Oka-moto, and Duus often provide poignant reminders of the potency of various forms of idealism and spiritualism in the twentieth century.

Moreover, authors have often reached similar or complementary con-clusions based on quite different realms of data and styles of analysis. An excellent example is provided by the broad agreement between Na-pier and Waswo regarding the condition of the labor market in relation to tenancy disputes. The case studies offered by Waswo, Bartholomew, and Marshall also complement Silberman's attempt to provide an over-all theory of relations between the bureaucratic state and civil society, even though as noted above they often disagree on specifics. Similarly, Harootunian provides a broad theoretical framework for interpreting the diverse and more narrowly delineated contributions of Huber, Steele, Vlastos, Totman, and Koschmann.

Beyond thematic continuity and broad agreement on facts and signif-icance, however, is evident a form of consistency that transcends Japa-nese history per se: the papers also converge in their attention to conflict as a property of social existence and discourse. That is, the essays gen-erally support what may, indeed, be a truism, that any conflict recog-nizable as such by the historian is always articulate. Conflict presup-poses protagonists, and protagonists exist only once they are defined, represented, signified, or symbolized. Hence "names" play a central role in the waging of conflict as the dichotomies and contrasts latent in language, culture, and intellectual tradition are appropriated to provide identifiable meaning to contemporary needs and interests. Conflict, it seems, is "always already" representational and therefore linguistic and symbolic. If that is the case, conflict is never isolated but inevitably enclosed at least partially in existing linguistic, symbolic, and episte-mological universes.

If conflict is always articulate, and therefore always closely bound up with constellations of meaning and representation, it cannot fully be understood without the epistemological equivalent of a wide-angle lens capable of bringing basic elements of those constellations into focus. There is, in other words, always a uniquely important place for syn-chronic, structural(ist) analysis in the study of conflict.

Events described in this volume give considerable credence to a view of conflict that links it by way of representation to encompassing wholes. It would seem to be a specific feature of social combatants in the eras of the Meiji Restoration and the early twentieth century always to refer themselves through actions as well as words to a broader, authoritative entity that serves as both a source of legitimacy and an extension in some manner of the protagonists' sense of themselves. Often at issue is precisely the power to define the "public" (ōyake), a realm that would enclose, represent, and also perhaps dominate the "private" entities that compose it.

Totman shows that in the Bakumatsu period the Tokugawa leaders began to see themselves and the bakufu in a new way. Rather than being representatives of "Japan" as a whole they were now mere "parts"— "domestic institutions among other such institutions." From that newly relative position, moreover, they finally proceeded via the mediation of European models to redefine the public realm as a "structurally unified nation." By redefining it, of course, they sought to reestablish over it their own firm control. For Mito activists the public was synonymous with kokutai, a mystical paradigm of government without politics in which order would be maintained through the sustained epiphany of Amaterasu Ōmikami. Once the contemporary scene was oriented to such a vision, acting subjects could be constituted and the shape of the world could be transformed. Nativists and leaders of new religions also acted on varying conceptions of an authoritative, public entity, authenticated by originary principles. As Harootunian observes, they sought to "unify political doctrine with religious belief . . . to overcome the perceived fragmentation of life."

For some of the radical "men of high purpose" described by Huber and for the Tokugawa loyalists of the Shōgitai examined by Steele, action itself was burdened with representational functions. The radicals acted as "Heaven's messengers," whereas the Shōgitai members sought to "restore meaning in a world that had lost coherence." For them, the principles that should inform an authoritative whole had to be present in the spirit of the act itself—loyalty, unswerving sincerity, filiality. The "public," in other words, had to manifest fully a timeless, "private" morality that could be adequately conveyed only through active demonstration.

As Vlastos, Hashimoto, and Wilson demonstrate, peasants also suggested their visions of valid authority largely through tumultuous action. Ambiguous references to "renewal" and the "world of Maitreya" were given specific content not only through pilgrimages to religious sites but in rebellious actions that often obeyed a self-imposed discipline and selected out specific targets for destruction. Through such actions peasants sought in a millenarian style both to reveal and to actualize a world of benevolence, reciprocity, and community "for all the people."

In the early twentieth century as well, conflict was accompanied by the projection of contentious images of wholeness and order. Oka demonstrates the fear embraced by many critics that received conceptions of public legitimacy and virtue had weakened. The young seemed apathetic toward national affairs, perhaps even unpatriotic. Yet accompanying their new self-centeredness and single-minded devotion to personal success was the quest for a "new morality" according to which the individual could become a "whole" unto himself and provide the foundation for new approaches to politics, international relations, and even love.

Government bureaucrats as described by Silberman envisioned a realm, controlled and defined by public law and rational decision making, in which the superior knowledge of officialdom would legitimate its privileged claim to determine the allocation of resources. Marshall and Bartholemew suggest how that vision led to conflict with academic and scientific interests and goals.

Duus's liberal intellectuals also located public authority in the central institutions where political and economic power were arbitrated, but despite their fundamental agreement with the bureaucracy's valorization of knowledge as the basis for power, they tended to focus their own energies on the political world of parties and assemblies. Conflict was often seen as a technical problem of constitutional theory, and representative assemblies as the means by which public harmony could be realized through a balance of contending forces.

For the urban rioters described by Okamoto, public authority adequate to the whole lay elsewhere. Wholeness and community were to be found not in institutions of mediation and direction but rather in a direct, intimate relationship between the emperor and his people. Rather than a political principle (or principal) as envisioned by late Tokugawa loyalists, the emperor was now to be seen as a father, sentimentally involved with popular needs and aspirations. Rather than acting in his stead, the political and bureaucratic power brokers merely succeeded in obscuring or distorting the true source of authority, which could only be the will of the emperor as manifested in the guileless actions of his people.

Bureaucratic manipulation was the target of twentieth-century peasants as well, but their sense of a meaningful whole differed. To the charisma of the imperial seat they added a new conception of the importance of class. As Waswo observes, they now sought a world in which equity (rather than benevolence) would be accessible to categories of people whose personal and legal identity owed little to traditional ideals of family relationship or even community. Similarly, Napier argues that it was as a social class rather than as individuals or communities that unskilled workers "were able to assert themselves and obtain a significant increase in both income and the ability to choose."

Thus, the "wholes" projected by social protagonists varied. In the Bakumatsu era they were often cast in an idiom of millenialism or restorationism, looking backward to a more or less hypothetical archetype or order from the past. Particular entities often claimed in the context of struggle to stand for, or represent, such an order, and as a result the Meiji Restoration appears, paradoxically, to have resulted largely from divergent attempts to stem change and reverse time. By the early twentieth century, on the other hand, change according to one or another historical agenda had become a mode of life. Competition was often considered a legitimate, indeed necessary, concommitant of social order and progress, and the elements of society were no longer severely constrained in the exercise of their will by the need to mirror a natural order.[2] Rather than identify themselves or their own aspirations with an archetype or natural whole they were often content to secure vindication of a simple claim to functional appropriateness in relation to the essentially arbitrary but legitimate form by which twentieth-century society was arranged. In both cases, however, symbolic representation remained at the very heart of conflict. Despite the widely varying degrees of explicit emphasis devoted to it, that aspect forms a thread linking the essays that comprise this volume into a conceptual whole.

[2] See Bernard S. Silberman, "Conclusion: Taishō Japan and the Crisis of Secularism" in Silberman and H. D. Harootunian, eds., *Japan in Crisis* (Princeton: Princeton University Press, 1974) for a discussion of the turn away from natural order as a legitimating concept in twentieth-century Japan.

INDEX

Abe Isoo, 430–434 *passim*
Abe Masahiro, 64–67, 83
Adachi Iwao, 389, 405
Aizawa Seishisai, 14, 42–46, 85, 89, 97
Akagi Yūhei, 428
Althusser, Louis, 28
Amakusa Shirō Tokisada, 184–185
Amano Hachirō, 131, 133–134
Amaterasu Ōmikami, 55–56, 95, 158–159
Andō Nobuyuki, 67
Anezaki Masaharu, 218
Ansei purge, 84, 109
Ansei reforms, 63–67, 68–80 *passim*
Araki Tomosaburō, 292
Arishima Takeo, 431
Asakawa Norihiko, 312
Asano Ujisuke, 72
assassination, 85, 109–110, 112–113
authority, 148, 230–256 *passim*
Azumi Gorō, 118

Bacon, Sir Francis, 295
bacteriologist, 320n
bakufu: reform of, 63–80 *passim*; prescriptions for survival of, 71–77, eviscerating the concept of, 78–80; policies of, toward Mito, 83
bakuhan system, 69–70, 76–80
Bakumatsu-Meiji period, 11
Bartholomew, James, 18, 444, 445, 447
benevolence, 150, 156–157, 163, 174–176, 380
Beyerchen, Alan, 341
Bogo imperial decree, 84–85
Boshin Imperial Edict, 217
branch families, 147–156 *passim*
Buddhism, 91, 218
Bunkyū reform, 67–71, 70–80 *passim*
bureaucracy: succession crises in, 233, 236, 256–257; promotion practices in, 238–239; effects of specialization on, 278–282; recruitment practices of, 278–280; changing tenure in, 280; ministerial conflicts within, 307–340 *passim. See also* bureaucrats; law; *specific ministries*; state

bureaucrats, 18; conceptions of education, 215–217; penetration of parties by, 240–241; ideal prescriptions for, 251; conceptions of landlords, 367n; conceptions of tenant unions, 375; conceptions of reform, 437
Bureau of Higher Education, 278–281

cartels, 247–248
center, 16
Chōshū, 71, 110, 115–116, 121–123
Christianity, 218
class conflict, 171, 173, 264–270, 344
cliques, 234
commercialization, 348–349, 376–377
commoners, 12, 74, 91–92, 165, 182–184
communitas, 100–101
community, 150–156 *passim*, 418–419
conciliation associations, 410, 410n
Condorcet, Marquis de, 295
conflict: defined, 9–10; during Meiji Restoration, 13; in Meiji-Taishō eras, 16–20; interpretations of, 26, 143, 255–256; in tenancy disputes, 398–399; as structural phenomenon, 443; "signs" of, 445
conflict model, 412–414, 426
consensus model, 412–414
contiguity, 31–32
continuity, 31–32
cooperativism, 439–440
credit, 150, 170, 172

Dahrendorf, Ralf, 412
daijōsai (Great Thanksgiving Ceremony), 96–97
Dai-Nihon shi (Great History of Japan), 82
deities, 148
department, 170
diachrony, 3
Diet, 240, 287–288, 309–310, 427
differential structure, 16, 344–345
discontinuity, 4, 6, 8, 11
dōzokudan, 149–156
Durkheim, Emile, 227
Duus, Peter, 18, 294, 444, 445, 447

Ebina Danjō, 222
ee ja nai ka, 161, 187-188
Eichenbaum, Boris, 7
Eliade, Mircea, 7, 98
Elison, George, 185
emperor, 272, 390
Engels, Frederick, 25
Enomoto Takiaki, 129, 141-142
equality, 224, 422, 427
Etō Shimpei, 137, 138
events, 5-10 passim, 15, 21
expertise, 251-253

fact, 4-6
family, 146-153
Fei, J.C.H., 348
Fisheries Institute, 327-328
Flugge, Karl, 302
Forbidden Gate, 120-123
Foucault, Michel, 30, 41
freedom, 224
Fujii Kenjirō, 223-225
Fujii Umon, 12
Fuji-kō, 54, 56
Fujimoto Tesseki, 117
Fuji Shirō, 119
Fujita Koshirō, 86
Fujita Shigeyoshi, 12
Fujita Tōko, 14, 42, 44, 83, 86
Fujita Yūkoku, 38-46 passim, 86
Fujitani Nariakira, 34, 34n
Fukuda Gen'ichirō, 129
Fukuda Tokuzō, 424
Fukuda Yoshisaburō, 404
Fukuhara Ryōjirō, 280, 333
Fukuzawa Yukichi, 295, 307, 311-312,
    317, 330, 340
Futaki Kenzō, 321

Geertz, Clifford, 8, 27
goningumi (five-house groups), 148
gōso (mass demonstrations), 155
Gotō Shimpei, 19
Gouldner, Alvin, 234
Grand Shrine of Ise, 160-161, 186
Green Dragon League, 91
gunken system, 77

Haberer, Joseph, 341
Hagstrom, Warren O., 341
Hamao Arata, 278-279, 281, 282
hamlet, 375-376

Hara Kei (Takashi), 218, 287, 291
harmony, 373, 418, 419
Harootunian, Harry, 14-15, 62, 88, 105,
    190, 277, 442, 445, 446
Hasegawa Nyozekan, 263, 426
Hasegawa Tai, 307-312 passim, 317, 327,
    340
Hasegawa Tenkei, 212
Hashimoto Mitsuru, 443, 446
Hashimoto Sanai, 58, 109
Hayashi Kimio, 431
Hayashi Kiroku, 224, 415, 416
Hayashi Shihei, 12, 14
Hibiya Riot: description of, 260-262; his-
    torical interpretations of, 262-274; par-
    ticipants in, 265-266; motives behind,
    270-274; consequences of, 274-275
Hida Otoichi, 314, 332
Hijikata Nansaemon, 115
Hirabayashi Hatsunosuke, 435
Hirai Kinzō, 206
Hirano Kuniomi, 118-119
Hirano Tomosuke, 273
Hirano Yoshitarō, 292
Hiranuma Kiichirō, 291-292
Hirata Atsutane, 47, 48, 50
Hirayama Chūeimon, 51
Hirazawa Keishichi, 430
Hirota Tsukasa, 326, 338
Hirsch, E. D., 87-88
historicity, 10
history, 3, 4-7, 97-98, 441-448 passim
Hitotsubashi Keiki. See Tokugawa Yoshi-
    nobu
holism, 442
Honda Kotarō, 339-340
Honda Toshiaki, 12, 14
Honda Toshisaburō, 130, 131
Horie Kiichi, 422, 428
Hotta Masayoshi, 67, 84
Hozumi Yatsuka, 243-244
Huber, Thomas, 69, 132, 142, 443, 446
humanistic coefficient, 6, 7
hyakushō ikki, see peasant rebellions

Ichikawa Sanzaemon, 86
Ichiki Kitokuro, 321-323
ideology, 25-30, 173-175
Ii Naosuke, 67, 84, 85, 189
Ikeda Kikunae, 339
Ikeda Nagashige, 131
Ikeda Shigemasa, 101

Ikuno incident, 118-120
impartiality, 251-253
imperial army, 141, 165-166, 172-173
imperialism, 203-204
imperial will, 233-234
Inaba Masakuni, 72-73
individuality (*kosei*), 19, 442; in Tokugawa villages, 162; after Russo-Japanese War, 197-201; effects of capitalism on, 202; prescriptions for, 208-209, 219-224
Inoue Kiyoshi, 190, 264, 270
Inoue Yasutake, 202
Institute for Aeronautical Research, 334-335
Institute for Physics and Chemistry, 335-337
Institute of Infectious Diseases, 307-337 *passim*
intellectuals, 428-433
interest groups, 230-231, 242-248, 254
inventories, 355-356
Ishiguro Tadanori, 326, 338
Ishihara Kikutarō, 321
Ishikawa Takuboku, 273
Ishikawa Tengai, 198
Ishiwara Toshio, 389
Itakura Katsukiyo, 70, 72, 78
Itakura Katsushizu, 101
itinerant laborers, 167
Iwakura Tomomi, 141
Iwakura Tomosada, 135, 140
Iwakura Tomotsune, 135, 140
Iwaya Keiichirō, 86
Izawa Takio, 328-329

Jameson, Frederic, 5
Japan Farmers' Union (Nihon Nōmin Kumiai), 381, 404-406
job mobility, 362-363

Kaieda Takeji, 137, 138
Kaiho Seiryō, 12
Kamata Eikichi, 223
Kan Masatomo, 91
Kanamori Tsūrin, 202-203
Kanasugi Eigorō, 326, 338
Kaneko Magojirō, 90
Kano Heihachirō, 9
Kasukabe Isaji, 91
Katayama Sen, 414
Katō Hiroyuki, 281, 299, 302
Katsu Kaishū, 129, 133, 135, 136

Katsura Takashige, 52-53
Katsura Tarō, 263, 318
Kawai Eijirō, 286-287
Kawakami Hajime, 290, 292, 423, 426
Kawakami Yoichi, 119
Kayabara Kazan, 215
Kazunomiya, 113
Kido Kōin, 86, 121
Kijima Matabei, 121-122
Kikuchi Dairoku, 279, 282
Kimura Kamezō, 405
Kinoshita Hiroji, 278
Kita Ikki, 272
Kitagaki Shintarō, 118-119
Kitajima Ta'ichi, 317
Kitasato Institute, 329-330
Kitasato Shibasaburō: acquires habits, 297-299; gets by, 299; takes a job, 299-300; studies abroad, 300-303; begins career, 306-312; commands authority, 312-322; resigns post, 321; reasserts authority, 329-332; enjoys significance, 337-338
Kiyama Kumajirō, 218-219
knowledge, 18-19
kōbu gattai, 68
Koch, Robert, 300-305
Koganei Yoshikiyo, 325, 338
Kohashi Kazuta, 317
kokugaku (nativism), 35-55 *passim*
kokutai (national essence), 12, 42, 446
Komai Chōon, 72
Kōmei, Emperor, 114-115
Komura Jutarō, 259
Konkōkyō, 54-58, 160, 186
Kōno Hironaka, 259-261, 337
Kosakunin (The Tenant Farmer), 391-397, 402, 404
Kōtoku Shūsui, 9, 204, 414
Kōwamondai Dōshi Rengōkai (Joint Council of Fellow Activists on the Peace Question), 259-261, 268, 270
Kracauer, Siegfried, 5-6
Kubota Seitarō, 317
Kubota Yuzuru, 282, 291, 308, 318
Kunikida Doppo, 19
Kurimoto Kon, 72
Kuroiwa Ruiko, 19, 199
Kurozumikyō, 54-58, 158-159, 160
Kurozumi Munetada, 55
Kusaka Genzui, 121-123, 191
Kyōchōkai, 246, 289
Kyoto University, 282, 292

labor unions, 244-247
landlords, 381, 382-383, 392-396 passim
land reform, 172, 382
law: political uses of, 19-20; and the state, 238, 241-242; uses of by tenant unions, 392-393, 399-400; liberals' conceptions of, 427, 428; paradoxical effects of, 443
legitimacy, 162, 174, 230-256 passim
Lévi-Strauss, Claude, 3, 4, 21, 41
Lewis, W. Arthur, 343, 344, 364
liberals: view political participation, 417-419; view constitutional system, 418; view class structure, 420-423; view economic relations, 423-428; as bureaucrats manqués, 437; and their urban bias, 438
liminality, 8, 100, 179, 183, 193
lineage, 96, 102-103
lineage relations, 146-156 passim
linearity, 21
Linz, Juan, 230
loyalist movement, 112-127 passim. See also Tengu insurrection
loyalty, 97, 130-132, 142, 234, 271-274
Loyalty to Heaven, 109-114
Lukacs, George, 38

main families (honke), 146-156 passim
Maki Izumi, 9, 115-119 passim, 122-123, 191, 215-217
Marshall, Byron, 18, 443, 445, 447
martial law, 261, 262
Maruyama Masao, 88, 103
Maruyamakyō, 54-58, 160
Marx, Karl, 25, 40
Marxism, 11, 262-270
Masamori Sonroku, 112
mass movements, 205, 224-225, 269
Masumi Junnosuke, 268
Matsudaira Katamori, 164
Matsudaira Shungaku, 67-71
Matsudaira Yorimasa, 83
Matsudaira Yorinori, 83
Matsudaira Yoritane, 83
Matsudaira Yoshinaga, 135
Matsui Naokichi, 278
Matsui Shigeru, 262
Matsumoto Buyū, 262
Matsumoto Kensaburō, 117
Matsumoto report, 262
Matsumura Kaiseki, 209
Matsuo Takayoshi, 269-270
Matsuoka Komakichi, 430

Matsuura Shinjirō, 280, 333, 337
meaning, 29-30, 87-89
Meiji, Emperor, 274-275
Meiji Restoration: historiography of, 11; as an event, 15, 20; interpretations of, 59-61, 192-194; millenarian elements in, 180-181, 192-194
Meiji-Taishō era, 11, 15-20
merit, 75, 257, 422
Merton, Robert K., 295
Metropolitan Police Board, 260-263
Midama Sampei, 115, 119
middle class, 421-422
Miki Kiyoshi, 439-440
military reforms, 64-66, 68-70, 73-74
millenarianism: of late Tokugawa Period, 160-161; definition of, 179; conceptions of time in, 180; among commoners, 182-183; goals of, 184; agents of, 184-187; values of, 191
Minami Ryōshin, 345, 346, 347, 347n, 349
Ministry of Agriculture and Commerce, 289, 319-320, 336-337
Ministry of Education, 18, 278-283, 288, 290-292, 307-340 passim
Ministry of Home Affairs, 289-292, 307-340 passim
Ministry of Justice, 288-292
Minobe Tatsukichi, 243-244
minposhugi (democracy), 414-416, 422
Miroku faith, 160
Misoguchi Shōnyo, 72
Mito domain, 81-82
Mito studies (Mitogaku), 33-55 passim
Miyabe Teizō, 115
Miyachi Masato, 267-269
Miyahiro Sadao, 51, 52
Miyajima Mikinosuke, 317
Miyake Setsurei, 199, 206
Miyata Tokuchika, 91
Miyauchi Yoshinaga, 51
Mori Arinori, 283
Mori Rintarō, 301, 302, 321, 333
Morimura Ichizaemon, 307, 330
Morito Tatsuo, 291-292
Motoori Norinaga, 47, 48, 185-186
Mount Nikkō, 95-96
Mukōyama Eigorō, 72
murahachibu (ostracism), 380
Murata Risuke, 91
Mutobe Yoshika, 49

Nagai, Ryūtarō, 416, 419, 421, 422
Nagayo Matarō, 326, 338
Nagayo Sensai, 300, 307, 311
Najita, Tetsuo, 35, 131
Nakahama Toichirō, 312
Nakahashi Tokugorō, 291
Nakane Chie, 296
Nakashima Tarōbei, 118-119
Nakayama Miki, 54-55, 159-160
Nakayama Tadamitsu, 117, 118
Napier, Ronald, 443, 445, 447
Naruse Nizō, 203
National Institute for Nutrition, 335
nationalism, 208-215, 272-274
nativism (kokugaku), 190-191
Natsume Sōseki, 9, 19
naturalist school, 200
Nezu Masashi, 269
Nishida Kitarō, 273
Nishio Suehiro, 430

Ogasawara Nagamichi, 70
Ogata Masanori, 300, 301, 307, 312
Ōgawa Genjūzō, 112
Ogawa Shigetomo, 404
Oguri Tadamasa, 72
Ogyū Noritaka, 72
Ogyū Sorai, 31-36
Ōhara Institute for the Study of Social
   Problems, 289
Ohkawa Kazushi, 346
Oka Yoshitake, 19, 444, 445, 446-447
Okada Ryōhei, 282, 337
okagemairi (pilgrimages), 98-103, 159, 185-
   186
Okamoto, Shumpei, 445, 447
Ōkubo Ichiō, 135
Ōkubo Toshimichi, 42
Okuda Gijin, 318
Ōkuma Shigenobu, 138-139, 205-206, 323
Ōkuni Takamasa, 47, 51
Okura Masayoshi, 95
Ōmori Yoshitarō, 284, 292
Ōmura Masajirō, 137, 138, 139, 141
Onozuka Kiheiji, 292
origins, 96-98, 105-106
Osatake Takeshi, 102, 104
Ōshima Masanori, 219-220
Ōshio Heihachirō, 9, 12
osso (end-run petition), 155
Ōta Yasutarō, 91
Ōtori Keisuke, 129, 141

Otsu Jun'ichirō, 337
Ōuchi Hyōei, 291-292
ōyake (public), 446
oya-ko (parent-child) relations, 153-154
Ōyama Ikuo, 418-432 passim
Ozaki Yukio, 260

Parkes, Harry, 136, 140
part/whole relationships, 32-38, 441-448
   passim
peasant militia, 92-95, 116-119, 121-122
peasant rebellions: effects of, on bakufu,
   71n; in Mito domain, 85-87, 92-95;
   funding of, 92-94; features of, 157-158,
   167-170; petitions arising from, 174-
   175; numbers of, 186, 188. See also
   Tengu insurrection; uchikowashi; yonaoshi
peasants' assemblies, 169-172 passim
Pepper, Stephen, 30
Perry, Commodore Matthew, 64
petitions, 154-156
pilgrimages, see ee ja nai ka; okagemairi;
   Tengu insurrection
plague bacillus, 314n
pluralism, 230-231, 242-248, 254
police, 262-263, 266, 267
political action: in Mito, 93-94; among samurai, 109-114, 116-123; in peasant rebellions, 169, 171; in millenarianism,
   185-188; in tenant unions, 401-406; representations of, 446
political parties, 254
political space, 42, 103-104
politics, 13
prices, 352-355
professionalism, 301-302, 338-339
proletarian parties, 433
Prussian Institute of Infectious Diseases,
   304-305
Pyle, Kenneth, 437

Rai Mikisaburō, 109
rangaku, 33
Ranis, Gustav, 348
rationality, 16, 235-236
Rawls, John, 250, 251
reciprocity, 147, 152-154
religious movements: 53-59, 158-161, 217-
   218. See also ee ja nai ka; millenarianism;
   nativism; okagemairi; yonaoshi
rent reduction, 356-358, 374, 397-398

representation, 29, 105-106
revolution, 12-13, 174-176, 256, 264-267
rice inspection, 381-382
rice riots, 424
Ricouer, Paul, 88
Rinnōji, 134, 138
Roches, Léon, 77
Rōyama Masamichi, 435
Rudé, George, 263
Russell, Bertrand, 295
Russo-Japanese War, 201-203, 268

Saigō Takamori, 137, 138, 139
Saiki Nori, 335
Saizawa Kōzō, 321, 324
Sakisaka Itsurō, 292
Sakuma Shōzan, 58
Sakurai Joji, 295-296
Sanjō Sanetomi, 115-119 passim, 137, 139-141
sankin kōtai system, 67
Sasakawa Kiyoshi, 213
Sasaki Junnosuke, 175n
Satō Sajiemon, 96
Satō Shin'en, 49
Sawa Nobuyoshi, 119
Sawayanagi Masatarō, 201, 214-215, 282
schools, 90-93
Schultze, Wilhelm, 299
secession, 40-41, 58, 413
Seiji kenkyūkai, 433-437
self-help, 373, 400, 429
Self-Help, 206-207
Seya Yoshihiko, 90-94 passim
Shakai Seisaku Gakkai, 289
Shibahara Takuji, 94
Shibata Masanaka, 72, 77
Shibuzawa Seiichirō, 131, 133-134
Shiga Kiyoshi, 314
Shijō Takaura, 115
Shimada Sakon, 112, 113
Shimane prefecture, 379
Shimazaki Tōson, 106
Shimazu Hisamitsu, 110
Shimo'oka Chūji, 324
Shindatsu uprising, 161, 162, 167n
Shintō, 55, 91, 96-98, 218
shishi (zealots, men of high purpose): 59, 85, 107-127 passim; as millenarian adherents, 180-181; revolutionary intentions of, 190-192; in Meiji era, 259
Shōgitai: origins of, 130-131; numbers in,

130, 133, 134, 136; leaders of, 131; members of, 131-132; activities of, 132-134; splits within, 133-136; assessments of, 136-138; defeat of, 139-141; post mortems for, 140-141, significance of, 142-144
Shōji Kichinosuke, 172
Shōkenkaku, 115-116, 121
Shōwa ishin, 17
significance, 29-30, 87-89
Silberman, Bernard, 16, 293, 296-297, 438, 442-447 passim
Skinner, Quentin, 99
Smelser, Neil, 20
Smethurst, Richard, 368
Smiles, Samuel, 206-207
Smith, Thomas C., 349
Social Darwinism, 18
social drama, 128-129, 142-143
social mobility, 414, 422
social stratification, 420-423
Socialism, 200, 423
solidarity, 395
Spaulding, Robert, 287-288
state: 17-18, 230-256 passim, 443; bakumatsu prelude to, 74-75; France as model for, 77-78; proper views of, 208-214; role of, in repressing tenant unions, 407-409; modernizing effects of, on tenant unions, 408; role of, in reforming tenancy conditions, 409-411; liberals' views of, 417, 427, 438-439. See also bureaucracy; bureaucrats; law; specific ministries
Steele, William, 63, 72, 446
strikes, 359-362
students, 278, 284-287
Sugai Kaiten, 391
Sunaga Denzō, 131
Suzuki Bunji, 429-430
Suzuki Shigetani, 52
synchrony, 3, 8, 21, 445

Taira, Koji, 348
Taishō democracy, 225, 254, 269
Taishō ishin, 17, 205
Takagi Tomoe, 312
Takahashi Yūsai, 263
Takano Chōei, 12
Takano Iwasaburō, 289-290
Takasugi Shinsaku, 42, 47, 59, 191
Takata Sanae, 336

Takebe Tongo, 208
Takeda Kōunsai, 87
Takekoshi Yosaburō, 12-13
Takeuchi Hyakutarō, 86
Takezaki Ritsujirō, 298n
Talmon, Yonina, 179, 191
Tamura Gyakusui, 206
Tamura Inanoemon, 86
Tanaka Giichi, 317
Tanuma Okinori, 86, 104
Tatsumi Shōjirō, 206-207
tax system, 74-76, 150
Tayasu Kamenosuke, 141
tenancy disputes, 358-359
tenant unions: numbers of, 367-368, 379-380, 387-388, 404-406; goals of, 369-370, 372-375; alliances of, 370, 403-406; materials on, 370; membership provisions of, 370-371; governance of, 371; officers of, 371; dues of, 372; features of villages with, 376-377; activities of, 377-378, 397-406; extra-village effects on, 378-379; educational programs of, 391-397; uses of law in, 399-400; role of, in electoral politics, 401-402
tenants, 349-352
tengu, 83n
Tengu insurrection: features of, 83-87; significance of, 87, 105-106; behavior in, 93-95; as originary pilgrimage, 95-103 passim; revolutionary implications of, 104-105
Tenri kyō, 54-58, 159-160, 186
Terada Noriaki, 389, 391
theory of competitive labor, 343-350 passim
theory of labor surplus, 343-350 passim
thought control, 290-292
Toda Takaakira, 83
Toennies, Ferdinand, 98
Togawa Shūkotsu, 220-222
Tokonami Takejirō, 217-218
Tokugawa house, 141. See also bakufu
Tokugawa Iemochi (Yoshitomi), 84, 112
Tokugawa Mitsukuni, 81
Tokugawa Nariaki, 44-46 passim, 82, 83
Tokugawa Yoshiatsu, 83
Tokugawa Yoshinobu, 70-73 passim, 84, 99, 129, 130, 189
Tokutomi Sohō, mentioned, 19, 198, 200, 209-211, 258, 273, 417, 420
Tokyo Imperial University: 18, 277-293

passim, 299, 307; presidents of, 281-282; faculty governance at, 282-283
Tomizu Hiroto, 282, 291
Tomokado Gorō, 131
totalization, 4, 5, 6, 21
Totman, Conrad, 87, 142, 181, 443, 445, 446
Touraine, Alain, 10
Tōyama Chinkichi, 312
Tōyama Masakazu, 279, 282
Tōyama Shigeki, 190
Tōyō keizai shinpō, 224, 424-425
Toyoda Tenkō, 42, 45
Toyowara Goro, 404
Treaty of Portsmouth, 258
Tsuchiya Seizaburō, 332, 334
Tsurumi Shunsuke, 289
Turner, Victor, 8-9, 13, 100-101, 128-129, 142-143, 179
turning point, 345, 348, 350

Ubugata Toshirō, 431
uchikowashi (smashings), 161, 168-169, 187
Ueda Mannen, 278
Ueda Masunosuke, 112
Uesugi Shinkichi, 243-244
Ugai Yoshizaemon, 84
Ukita Kazutami, 222-223, 225, 415-417
Umeno Shinkichi, 314
universal manhood suffrage, 375, 418
urban riots, 187, 265-266, 415-416. See also Hibiya Riot
utilitarianism, 249-254

village headmen, 152-173 passim
villages, 150-156 passim
Virchow, Rudolph, 305
Vlastos, Stephen, 14, 368, 446
von Behring, Emil, 303
von Mansveldt, C. G., 298
von Pettenkofer, Max, 301
von Wright, Georg Henrik, 99

wages, 345-349
Wakasugi Kisaburō, 325
Waswo, Ann, 19, 358-359, 443, 445, 447
Watanabe Kazan, 12
Watanabe Kinsaburō, 112
Watanabe Kōki, 281, 309
Watanabe Shūjirō, 66n
Watanabe Tetsuzō, 424
wealth, 154, 198, 202, 371, 383-384

White, Hayden, 6, 21
Wilson, George, 15, 446
women, 200
world renewal. See yonaoshi
World War I, 346-347
Worsley, Peter, 179-180

Yagi Itsurō, 325, 327, 335
Yamada Moritarō, 292
Yamaga Sokō, 132
Yamagata Daini, 12
Yamaguchi Naoki, 72, 77
Yamaji Aizan, 272
Yamakawa Hitoshi, 425-426, 436
Yamakawa Kenjirō, 282, 291-292, 334-335, 339
Yamakawa Kikue, 95, 100
Yamamoto Tsunetomo, 132
Yamane Masatsugu, 207-208
Yamaobe Hijōgo, 83
Yamasaki Toyosada: forms perspectives, 383-386; leads unions, 386-389; contends with national groups, 386-387, 403-406; develops organizational tactics, 388-390; attracts criticism, 390-391; offers testimony, 406-407; goes to prison, 409
Yamato incident, 116-118, 120
Yasumaru Yoshio, 188

Yersin, Alexandre, 314, 314n
Yojo'en, 330
Yokoi Shōnan, 42, 47, 58-59
Yokoi Tokio, 213-214
Yokota Hideo, 391
Yokote Chiyanosuke, 321
yonaori (world renewal), 186n
yonaoshi (world renewal): 15, 40-41, 161; general characteristics of, 157-158, 167, 175n; peasant conceptions of, 163; in Aizu, 166; definitions of, 186n, 187n. See also peasant rebellions; uchikowashi
Yoshida Shōin, 9
Yoshimura Toratarō, 117
Yoshino Sakuzō: resigns sinecure, 290
—expounds on: the masses, 225; Hibiya Riots, 263; self-help, 414; disturbances, 416; the suffrage, 418; Diet, 420; rice riots, 425; radicalism, 428; tetsujin seiji, 429; intellectuals, 432; parliamentary politics, 435
Yoshiue Shōichirō, 325
youth, 206-211, 219-224
youth groups (seinendan), 218
Yuasa Mitsutomo, 296
Yūgekitai, 121-122
Yuki Asamichi, 83

Znaniecki, Florian, 4, 5, 6

Library of Congress Cataloging in Publication Data

Main entry under title:
  Conflict in modern Japanese history.

  Based on a conference held in Monterey, Calif., July 9-14, 1978, sponsored by the Joint
Committee on Japanese Studies of the American Council of Learned Societies and the
Social Science Research Council.
  Includes index.
    1. Japan—History—Restoration, 1853-1870—Congresses.   2. Japan—History—
Meiji period, 1868-1912—Congresses.   3. Japan—History—Taishō period, 1912-1926—
Congresses. I. Najita, Tetsuo.   II. Koschmann, J. Victor.
DS881.3.C66   952.03   82-47605
ISBN 0-691-05364-2   AACR2
ISBN 0-691-10137-X (pbk.)